VIOLENCE AND EXPLOITATION AGAINST WOMEN AND GIRLS

```
HV6250.4.W65 V56764 2006
Violence and exploitation
against women and girls
39090014242172
```

ANNALS OF THE NEW YORK ACADEMY OF SCIENCES
Volume 1087

VIOLENCE AND EXPLOITATION AGAINST WOMEN AND GIRLS

Edited by Florence L. Denmark, Herbert H. Krauss, Esther Halpern, and Jeri A. Sechzer

Published by Blackwell Publishing on behalf of the New York Academy of Sciences
Boston, Massachusetts
2006

Library of Congress Cataloging-in-Publication Data

Violence and exploitation against women and girls / edited by Florence L. Denmark ... [et al.]
    p. ; cm. – (Annals of the New York Academy of Sciences, ISSN 0077-8923 ; no. 1087)
  Includes bibliographical references.
  ISBN-13: 978-1-57331-667-5 (alk. paper)
  ISBN-10: 1-57331-667-9 (alk. paper)
  1. Women–Violence against–Congresses. 2. Girls–Violence against–Congresses. 3. Women–Violence against–Prevention–Congresses. 4. Violence–Cross-cultural studies–Congresses. I. Denmark, Florence.

HV6250.4.W65V56764 2006
362.88082–dc22

2006032964

The *Annals of the New York Academy of Sciences* (ISSN: 0077-8923 [print]; ISSN: 1749-6632 [online]) is published 28 times a year on behalf of the New York Academy of Sciences by Blackwell Publishing, with offices located at 350 Main Street, Malden, Massachusetts 02148 USA, PO Box 1354, Garsington Road, Oxford OX4 2DQ UK, and PO Box 378 Carlton South, 3053 Victoria Australia.

Information for subscribers: Subscription prices for 2006 are: Premium Institutional: $3850.00 (US) and £2139.00 (Europe and Rest of World).
Customers in the UK should add VAT at 5%. Customers in the EU should also add VAT at 5% or provide a VAT registration number or evidence of entitlement to exemption. Customers in Canada should add 7% GST or provide evidence of entitlement to exemption. The Premium Institutional price also includes online access to full-text articles from 1997 to present, where available. For other pricing options or more information about online access to Blackwell Publishing journals, including access information and terms and conditions, please visit www.blackwellpublishing.com/nyas.

Membership information: Members may order copies of the *Annals* volumes directly from the Academy by visiting www.nyas.org/annals, emailing membership@nyas.org, faxing 212-298-3650, or calling 800-843-6927 (US only), or +1 212-298-8640 (International). For more information on becoming a member of the New York Academy of Sciences, please visit www.nyas.org/membership.

Journal Customer Services: For ordering information, claims, and any inquiry concerning your institutional subscription, please contact your nearest office:
UK: Email: customerservices@blackwellpublishing.com; Tel: +44 (0) 1865 778315; Fax +44 (0) 1865 471775
US: Email: customerservices@blackwellpublishing.com; Tel: +1 781 388 8599 or 1 800 835 6770 (Toll free in the USA); Fax: +1 781 388 8232
Asia: Email: customerservices@blackwellpublishing.com; Tel: +65 6511 8000; Fax: +61 3 8359 1120
Members: Claims and inquiries on member orders should be directed to the Academy at email: membership@nyas.org or Tel: +1 212 838 0230 (International) or 800-843-6927 (US only).

Printed in the USA.
Printed on acid-free paper.

Mailing: The *Annals of the New York Academy of Sciences* are mailed Standard Rate. **Postmaster:** Send all address changes to *Annals of the New York Academy of Sciences*, Blackwell Publishing, Inc., Journals Subscription Department, 350 Main Street, Malden, MA 01248-5020. Mailing to rest of world by DHL Smart and Global Mail.

Copyright and Photocopying
© 2006 The New York Academy of Sciences. All rights reserved. No part of this publication may be reproduced, stored, or transmitted in any form or by any means without the prior permission in writing from the copyright holder. Authorization to photocopy items for internal and personal use is granted by the copyright holder for libraries and other users registered with their local Reproduction Rights Organization (RRO), e.g. Copyright Clearance Center (CCC), 222 Rosewood Drive, Danvers, MA 01923, USA (www.copyright.com), provided the appropriate fee is paid directly to the RRO. This consent does not extend to other kinds of copying such as copying for general distribution, for advertising or promotional purposes, for creating new collective works, or for resale. Special requests should be addressed to Blackwell Publishing at journalsrights@oxon.blackwellpublishing.com.

Disclaimer: The Publisher, the New York Academy of Sciences, and the Editors cannot be held responsible for errors or any consequences arising from the use of information contained in this publication; the views and opinions expressed do not necessarily reflect those of the Publisher, the New York Academy of Sciences, or the Editors.

Annals are available to subscribers online at the New York Academy of Sciences and also at Blackwell Synergy. Visit www.annalsnyas.org or www.blackwell-synergy.com to search the articles and register for table of contents e-mail alerts. Access to full text and PDF downloads of *Annals* articles are available to nonmembers and subscribers on a pay-per-view basis at www.annalsnyas.org.

The paper used in this publication meets the minimum requirements of the National Standard for Information Sciences Permanence of Paper for Printed Library Materials, ANSI Z39.48-1984.

ISSN: 0077-8923 (print); 1749-6632 (online)
ISBN-10: 1-57331-667-9 (paper); ISBN-13: 978-1-57331-667-5 (paper)

A catalogue record for this title is available from the British Library.

Digitization of the *Annals of the New York Academy of Sciences*

An agreement has recently been reached between Blackwell Publishing and the New York Academy of Sciences to digitize the entire run of the *Annals of the New York Academy of Sciences* back to volume one.

The back files, which have been defined as all of those issues published before 1997, will be sold to libraries as part of Blackwell Publishing's Legacy Sales Program and hosted on the Blackwell Synergy website.

Copyright of all material will remain with the rights holder. Contributors: Please contact Blackwell Publishing if you do not wish an article or picture from the *Annals of the New York Academy of Sciences* to be included in this digitization project.

ANNALS OF THE NEW YORK ACADEMY OF SCIENCES

Volume 1087
November 2006

VIOLENCE AND EXPLOITATION AGAINST WOMEN AND GIRLS

Editors
FLORENCE L. DENMARK, HERBERT H. KRAUSS,
ESTHER HALPERN, AND JERI A. SECHZER

This volume is the result of a Psychology Section meeting at the New York Academy of Sciences, held on November 18, 2005, in New York City, and sponsored by the New York Academy of Sciences. The conference was cosponsored by the Pace University psychology department, in New York City; the International Organization for the Study of Group Tensions; the Academic Division of the New York State Psychological Department; and Division of Women's Issues of the New York State Psychological Association.

CONTENTS

Preface. *By* JOY K. RICE xi

Part I. Conceptualizing Violence and Exploitation against Females

Introduction. *By* FLORENCE L. DENMARK, HERBERT H. KRAUSS,
 ESTHER HALPERN, AND JERI A. SECHZER 1
Perspectives on Violence. *By* HERBERT H. KRAUSS 4
A Protoscientific Master Metaphor for Framing Violence. *By*
 HERBERT H. KRAUSS 22

Part II. Violence against Girls, Adolescents, and Young Women

Sexual Aggression toward Women: Reducing the Prevalence. *By*
 GWENDOLYN L. GERBER AND LINDSAY CHERNESKI 35
Adolescent Girls Speak about Violence in Their Community. *By*
 ROSEANNE L. FLORES 47

Who Wins in the Status Games? Violence, Sexual Violence, and an
  Emerging Single Standard among Adolescent Women. *By*
  BEATRICE J. KRAUSS, JOANNE O'DAY, CHRISTOPHER GODFREY, KEVIN RENTE,
  ELIZABETH FREIDIN, ERICA BRATT, NADIA MINIAN, KRAIG KNIBB,
  CHRISTY WELCH, ROBERT KAPLAN, GAURI SAXENA, SHAWN MCGINNISS,
  JACQUELINE GILROY, PETER NWAKEZE, AND SAUNDRA CURTAIN 56
Cyberspace Violence against Girls and Adolescent Females. *By*
  JUNE F. CHISHOLM 74
Early Violence Prevention Programs: Implications for Violence Prevention
  Against Girls and Women. *By* MICHELLE GUTTMAN,
  BARBARA MOWDER, AND ANASTASIA YASIK 90
International Perspectives on Sexual Harassment of College Students: The
  Sounds of Silence. *By* MICHELE PALUDI, RUDY NYDEGGER,
  EROS DESOUZA, LIESL NYDEGGER, AND KELSEY ALLEN DICKER 103

Part III. Violence against Women

Intimate Partner Violence: New Directions. *By* MAUREEN C. MCHUGH AND
  IRENE HANSON FRIEZE 121
Battered Woman Syndrome: Empirical Findings. *By* LENORE E.A. WALKER ... 142
Factors That Influence Abusive Interactions between Aging Women and
  Their Caregivers. *By* MARGOT B. NADIEN 158
Violence and Exploitation against Women and Girls with Disability. *By*
  DANIEL B. ROSEN 170
Gender-Based Violence: Concepts, Methods, and Findings. *By*
  NANCY FELIPE RUSSO AND ANGELA PIRLOTT 178
Restoring Rape Survivors: Justice, Advocacy, and a Call to Action. *By*
  MARY P. KOSS 206
Violence against Women as a Public Health Issue. *By* JOAN C. CHRISLER AND
  SHEILA FERGUSON 235

Part IV. Cultural and International Perspectives on Violence against Women

Cultural Beliefs and Domestic Violence. *By* MADELINE FERNÁNDEZ 250
Violence against Women in Mexico: Conceptualization and Program
  Application. *By* SUSAN PICK, CARMEN CONTRERAS, AND ALICIA
  BARKER-AGUILAR 261
Domestic Violence in the Chinese and South Asian Immigrant Communities. *By*
  ELIZABETH MIDLARSKY, ANITHA VENKATARAMANI-KOTHARI, AND
  MAURA PLANTE 279
Domestic Violence in Israel: Changing Attitudes. *By* VARDA MUHLBAUER 301
Lack of Mutual Respect in Relationship: The Endangered Partner. *By*
  AMOS A. ALAO 311
Violence against Pregnant Women in Northwestern Ontario. *By*
  JOSEPHINE C. H. TAN AND KATHRYN V. GREGOR 320

An Exploration of Female Genital Mutilation. *By* ERIKA M. BARON AND
FLORENCE L. DENMARK 339
International Sexual Harassment. *By* JANET SIGAL 356
United Nations Measures to Stop Violence against Women. *By*
EVA E. SANDIS 370

Part V. Conclusion

Summary and Conclusion. *By* FLORENCE L. DENMARK, HERBERT H. KRAUSS,
ESTHER HALPERN, AND JERI A. SECHZER 384
Epilogue. *By* VITA C. RABINOWITZ 387

Index of Contributors 391

The New York Academy of Sciences believes it has a responsibility to provide an open forum for discussion of scientific questions. The positions taken by the participants in the reported conferences are their own and not necessarily those of the Academy. The Academy has no intent to influence legislation by providing such forums.

Preface

The topic of this Annals, *Violence and Exploitation against Women and Girls* could not be more timely or pertinent to key issues affecting the health and welfare of women. The many distinguished contributions offer us an important international review of cross-national and cross-cultural research on the prevalence and prevention of violence against women and girls. The tremendous social, economic, and psychological costs of violence and abuse against women and girls are documented with examples from female genital mutilation, to domestic violence, to abuse of particularly vulnerable populations, such as disabled women and pregnant women. Articles on adolescent violence present cutting-edge research on so-called "sexual scoring," where very young women are coerced by peers and older male adolescents to participate in group sexual activities and "cyberbullying" practices that involve at-risk online activities for young girls. Violence against women knows no age barriers, and other contributions to this volume document that even elderly women can be abused by their caretakers.

Modes of treatment and prevention are also key themes that are discussed across the various articles. Preventative efforts to decrease the incidence of violence against women and girls may include early education, changing sex role–stereotyped attitudes and behaviors, and working to achieve gender equality in terms of power differentials between men and women in relationships. Addressing how social institutions, such as popular media, film, and music, help to perpetuate sexual violence and harassment is still another key area of concern. Certainly efforts at the international level call for multifaceted interventions and legislation that would raise awareness in societies that still condone cultural practices that are destructive of women and exploit them. Thus other informative articles in the volume discuss United Nations (UN) measures to stop violence against women as well as the approach of the World Health Organization (WHO) in attempting to create a uniform database for reporting violence, defining violence, and devising a topology of violent acts.

Another theme that cuts across the articles in this volume is the important issue of cultural influence on domestic violence and the adoption of a culturally sensitive framework for the development of effective interventions aimed at decreasing domestic violence against women. We are also presented with the provocative question of whether is it always women who are the victims, as some research finds that women are increasingly likely to inflict violence as well as to be victims of violence. Thus we are called upon to develop new concepts of intimate partner violence that account for these findings.

The various articles in this volume offer the reader a heart-rendering picture of how women suffer violence, exploitation, and abuse in countries as diverse as Botswana and Israel. Today, it is increasingly recognized that violence against women is a global health and social problem, and in the last two decades many countries have undertaken large-scale, national, qualitative research to assess the frequency and level of violence against women. Often under pressure from women's NGOs within the UN, government bodies have attempted to expose and analyze what is now perceived to be an enormous worldwide social issue. One important goal of this research is to educate the public and policy makers about the need to develop measures to address a reality that until now has remained behind closed doors, although violence against women is, in fact, a public issue for every country in the world. Irrespective of the methods of collection, the sample, or the country in which the sample was collected, the global statistics give us high rates of violence perpetrated against women, from more than 50% of women in a Portuguese sample, to 68% in a Belgian study, to 51% in a Canadian study. Nearly one-third of all visits to emergency rooms by women in the United States occur because of violence or abuse. Even in the socially progressive Nordic countries, women experience high levels of violence; a Finnish study reports 52% of adult women had been the victims of violence, and statistics collected by women's shelters in Sweden indicate that a Swedish woman is battered every 20 minutes. Acts of violence are committed against women among all economic and educational strata. Domestic violence cuts across social, racial, ethnic, and economic groups. In Italy, for example, 45% of perpetrators of violence toward their partner had university degrees. In the few minutes it takes you to read this preface, a woman in every country of the world will be raped, beaten, or sexually exploited.

The high incidence of violence against women worldwide has many serious repercussions for women's physical, emotional, and economic well-being. Although a higher education or income does not necessarily decrease the chances of violence and abuse for women, certainly low-income women and women on public assistance are at particular risk for experiencing the catastrophic effects of repeated abuse and partner violence, in large part because they have far fewer resources and support for escape or to change their circumstances. Poor women are very likely to be the victims of prior or current abuse and violence. In the United States, more than half of all women trying to leave welfare face the devastating barrier of violence from intimate partners. Americans have long been concerned with the high rates of violence in their society, and since the recent change in their welfare laws, a number of studies have begun to explicate the high rates of violence and abuse among women in poverty and women on welfare. An ethnically diverse population of women and women living in poverty are at especially high risk for all types of violence inside and outside of the home, particularly for life-threatening and severe assaults. In many cities, poor women live in neighborhoods where the level of assault in all types of relationships is very high and the availability of protective or preventive services unusually low. The few studies focusing on the reports of poor women document much higher rates of frequent, uncontrollable, and life-threatening events than in the general population, and survey research consistently and dramatically documents the pervasiveness of violence in the lives of women on public assistance with reports of severe physical violence experienced by 30% to 75% of women across the United States. Violence interferes with work, job training, and education and thus undermines women's attempts at economic independence. Domestic violence is also strongly correlated with homelessness, and when a woman leaves an abusive relationship she often has nowhere to go.

Despite the prevalence of violence in the lives of women living in poverty, research on low-income women, and the ways in which poverty and social policies contribute to and maintain the prevalence of violence in their lives, is in the early stages. There are many methodological problems, including the difficulties in comparison of diverse samples, the reluctance of many women to report violence, which is frequently tied to cultural norms, and the changing definition of what constitutes "violence." For example, in Latino culture, maintaining patriarchal control through physical threats and hitting of wives is frequently considered necessary and normative. Cultural factors and values may also suppress help seeking by ethnically diverse women, such as among Asian women, where the cultural shame of exposing any conflict or abuse is very high. Minority status within a multicultural society may also present special problems. Immigrant status, little knowledge of the English language, and no family support are critical factors in the responses of some minority women to the dangers they face in an abusive relationship.

We know that women who have suffered abuse are more likely to suffer posttraumatic stress disorder (PTSD), depression, and somatization than those who have never experienced abuse; the more extensive the abuse, the greater the risk of PTSD. However, another methodological and conceptual difficulty appears here in the use of a diagnosis that may be gender biased. Despite the greater prevalence and chronicity of PTSD among females, the construct was based on data from male combat veteran experiences, resulting in measurement bias that may affect both research and practice.

Trauma and violence prevention is an important area to consider for research because (1) girls and women as a group are exposed to more traumatic stressors than boys and men; (2) the mental health of women and girls may be severely affected, resulting not only in immediate psychological symptoms, but also lifetime risk for self-destructive or suicidal behavior, anxiety and panic attacks, eating disorders, substance abuse, somatization disorder, and sexual adjustment disorders; and (3) psychologists are not regularly trained to work specifically with trauma survivors, which can reduce the effectiveness of the treatment survivors receive. Thus the American Psychological Association recently recommended that psychologists who practice in these areas receive specialized training to better understand and meet the special needs of women involved in partner violence.

A range of supportive psychological, social, medical, and legal services are necessary to help women successfully remove themselves from abusive situations and to become economically self-sufficient. Pervasive violence may leave women with physical injuries and psychological consequences that make daily functioning difficult. Abuse can have long-term physical effects on women, sometime damaging their hearing or eyesight or leaving them with chronic pain that interferes with their ability to work or to get training. Sufferers may feel helpless and terrified, experiencing flashbacks of the original trauma in recurrent and intrusive thoughts or dreams, have trouble sleeping, and be unable to concentrate. The more extensive the abuse, the greater the risk of PTSD. One hopeful sign is that these effects may not be permanent; in some studies women whose abuse was not current showed lower rates of symptoms and higher scores on self-esteem and mastery measures.

Psychological and economic control by the batterer, coupled with a lack of skills and resources and the demands of parenting, and the situation of living in a dangerous neighborhood, isolate many low-income abused women. Women who are fleeing violent men may be too afraid to seek work if they have to entrust young children to the care of strangers. Jealous abusers often will do everything they can to prevent their women partners from attending classes or their jobs, including violent threats, beatings, harassing calls at work, preventing sleep, and reneging on promises of child care or transportation. Abuse is cited by 25% to 30% of battered women as the reason they lost their jobs. It is not surprising, then, that other studies have found that women who had experienced physical violence by a partner were more likely to remain on public assistance for longer periods, and that a lifetime history of violent victimization was a strong determinant of welfare "cycling" (more than one episode of public assistance). Even when these women manage to find jobs, they are likely to be low wage, unskilled, and part time. The experience of violence is also a factor. Poor women whose partners had threatened them or used a knife or gun against them have been found to be employed in significantly lower status, lower paying jobs than women who have not experienced these severe threats and assaults with a weapon.

Each battered woman faces different risks and therefore has different needs for restoring safety, self-sufficiency, and self-esteem. Because each battered woman's risks are different, determining specific needs must be done on a case-by-case basis. There is no formula for safety or self-sufficiency. Options that may work for one woman will increase the danger for another. For example, leaving a relationship can increase risks for some battered women and their children and diminish them for others. A question frequently asked about abused women is, "Why do they stay?" This question does not reflect the real issues and considerations a woman must face, such as "Should I stay and risk the violence?" "If I leave will the violence be worse?" "Should I leave and place my children and myself in greater poverty?" "Will it be worse to be homeless?" and "Should I risk losing my children in a custody battle?"

Battered women use complex and creative safety plans to reduce the risks that they and their children face. Like any person making a significant life decision, abused women must consider the consequences of pursuing certain options. In some cases, determining what a particular battered woman needs will be as simple as asking her, and some women will know exactly what they need to be safe and self-sufficient. Like all people, abused women in violent relationships have basic needs for housing, food, mental and physical health care, safety, and the basics of human dignity—privacy, opportunity, and self-determination. Other women may need advocacy to explore their risks and options. Working with battered women to help them on all fronts may be complex. It is work best done by trained advocates and therapists who can provide these women with confidential opportunities to explore their risks and plans.

In sum, battered and abused women need a wide range of responses, flexible services, and supportive policies to enhance their safety and self-sufficiency and to restore their self-esteem and welfare. These might include mental and physical health evaluation and referral; relocation services; confidential advocacy, shelter, and other domestic violence support services; educational and vocational training; legal representation concerning divorce, custody, visitation, and protective orders; evaluation of immigration status and ethnic or cultural issues; and the effective enforcement of criminal laws and court orders to help free them from their partners' control and to keep them and their children safe.

Much of the data and many of the women's stories presented in these articles are difficult to read without being moved, shocked, or upset. I hope that all readers come away from this information with renewed conviction that the problem that once was behind closed doors and had no name, has been named and that solutions must be aggressively and consistently pursued with all the intelligence, motivation, and effort we can muster. The task at hand is a very complex one that involves ending violence in environments that are inextricably linked—family microsystems within macronational systems and the global macrosystem in which all nations are embedded. A social problem of such magnitude and importance, one that ultimately affects not only half of humanity, but all people, will need to be addressed at all systemic levels—individual to institutional, familial to societal, and local to global.

JOY K. RICE
University of Wisconsin
Madison, Wisconsin

Introduction

FLORENCE L. DENMARK,[a] HERBERT H. KRAUSS,[a]
ESTHER HALPERN,[b] AND JERI A. SECHZER[a]

[a]*Pace University, New York, New York 10038, USA*
[b]*Tel Aviv University, Tel Aviv, Israel*

As far back in time as can be traced, well before they wrote, humans practiced violence against each other. In so far as is known, no time or system was free of it (Walker, 2001). To be sure, its incidence and prevalence waxed and waned, yet violence has always been with us, and never so more than in the last 100 years or so (Summerfield, 1997).

Recognizing that acts of violence produced many harmful effects beyond direct injury and suffering and that a "dramatic worldwide increase in the incidence of intentional injuries affecting people of all ages and both sexes, but especially women and children..." has occurred; resolution WHA49.25 of the forty-ninth World Health Assembly declared violence a "leading worldwide public health problem" (WHO, 1996) and requested its director general to take a number of steps designed to reduce both violence and its deleterious consequences. Among these were to be a series of initiatives intended to produce a better understanding of violence's cause and the circumstances that facilitated and sustained its expression.

A report summarizing the director general's preliminary efforts to fulfill the requests of resolution WHA49.25 was issued as the "World Report on Violence and Health" (Krug, Dahlberg, Mercy, Zwi, & Lozano, 2002). Therein may be found an attempt to formulate an acceptable and meaningful definition of violence, a useful typology of violent acts, and a model for conceptualizing violence from the public health framework. It also included a compilation of demographic information about various forms of violence and their occurrence.

Though the "World Report on Violence and Health" succeeds in drawing attention to the ubiquity of violence and the damage violence inflicts upon the individual, the community, and the polity, that report also makes it clear that a cross-cultural and cross-societal perspective on violence must be adopted if it is to be understood and its noisome consequences are to be reduced. The report is less successful in providing an acceptable definition of violence and consequently a useful typology of violent acts. Nor is it obvious that its public health model is indeed the best-suited paradigm for diagnosing and treating violence and its sequelae (Krauss, 2005).

While considerable headway can be made against violence without a complete understanding of its cause, nature, and manifestations, clearly having such an accurate conceptualization ought to provide a guide to its reduction. Surely one does not have to understand fully, for example, why men rape, to reduce rape's incidence and prevalence; one only needs to prohibit it and punish it severely when it occurs. But just as self evident is that knowing the circumstances (e.g., when one is not in control of their cognitive facilities or during ethnic conflict) when rape is most likely to happen and eliminating the possibility would also likely prove useful.

That something must be done immediately to halt violence against women and girls is obvious; for as Garcia-Moreno, Heise, Jansen, Ellsberg, and Watts (2005) have deduced, violence against women and girls is rampant. Their review of the epidemiological literature suggests that one in three women or girls across the globe have been victimized in childhood, adolescence, or adulthood. In some societies that rate is greatly exceeded. The "WHO Study on Women's Health and Domestic Violence Against Women"(Garcia-Moreno, Jansen, Ellsberg, Heise, and Watts, 2005) found, after conducting 24,000 interviews with 15- to 49-year old women at 15 sites in 10 countries (Bangladesh, Brazil, Ethiopia, Japan, Peru, Namibia, Samoa, Serbia, and Montenegro, Thailand, and Tanzania), that between 35% and 76% of those surveyed had been physically or sexually assaulted. Even more concerning was the extent it found violence against women and girls to be culturally institutionalized. In about half of the sites, of the women studied, between 50% and 90% of the women agreed, depending on the question asked, that it was acceptable for a husband to beat his wife if she disobeyed him, refused his sexual overtures, did not complete her housework on time, or questioned whether her husband might be guilty of infidelity.

As part of the effort to inform all interested parties about what is known about violence against women, how its occurrence might be reduced, and the techniques through which its consequences might be ameliorated, two of the editors of this volume, Florence L. Denmark and Herbert H. Krauss of Pace University, brought together a group of experts to present a workshop on this topic at the New York Academy of Sciences to concerned academics and practitioners. This workshop was hosted by the Academy and cosponsored by Pace University and the International Organization for the Study of Group Tensions. The success that greeted the workshop stimulated our interest in producing a book that would address the subject more comprehensively and with greater attention to detail. Prior to the workshop held at the Academy, another one of the editors, Esther Halpern of Tel Aviv University, organized a program on violence against women that was held in London, England. Jeri Sechzer, of Pace University, is another editor who has also explored violence against women and is committed to work in this area.

The book that you are about to peruse is organized into sections flowing from general information regarding violence against women to specific descriptions of it in the United States and in countries worldwide. Its four sections include a conceptualization of violence against females; an exploration of violence against girls, adolescents, and young women; an examination of cultural and international perspectives on violence against women; and a summary article.

REFERENCES

GARCIA-MORENO, C., HEISE, L., JANSEN, H.A.F.M., ELLSBERG, M. & WATTS, C. (2005). Violence against women. *Science, 310*, 1282–1283.

GARCIA-MORENO, C., JANSEN, H.A.F.M., ELLSBERG, L. HEISE, L. & WATTS, C. (2005). *WHO multi-country study on women's health and domestic violence against women: Initial results on prevalence, health outcomes and women's responses.* Geneva: World Health Organization.

KRAUSS, H.H. (2005). Conceptualizing violence. In F. Denmark, H.H. Krauss, R.W. Wesner, E. Midlarsky & U.P. Gielen (Eds.), *Violence in the schools: Cross-national and cross-cultural perspectives* (pp. 11–35). New York: Springer.

KRUG, E.G., DAHLBERG, L.L., MERCY, J.A., ZWI, A.B. & LOZANO, R. (2002). *World report on violence and health.* Geneva: World Health Organization.

SUMMERFIELD, D. (1997). *The social, cultural and political dimensions of contemporary war. The American heritage dictionary (2nd college ed.).* Boston: Houghton Mifflin.

WALKER, P.L. (2001). A bio-archaeological perspective on the history of violence. *Annual Review of Anthropology, 30*, 573–599.

WHO GLOBAL CONSULTATION ON VIOLENCE AND HEALTH. (1996). *Violence: A public health priority.* Geneva: World Health Organization. (document WHO/EHA/SPL.POA. 2).

Perspectives on Violence

HERBERT H. KRAUSS

Pace University, New York, New York, USA

> ABSTRACT: The worldwide rise in violence, especially that directed against females of all ages, led the World Health Organization (WHO) to undertake steps to deal with that problem. To do so, WHO adopted a public health approach. This entailed (1) developing a definition of violence, (2) devising a typology of violent acts, (3) creating a uniform database for reporting violence, and (4) promulgating a model for understanding violence and its attendant phenomena. This essay reviews, analyzes, and critiques those efforts.
>
> KEYWORDS: bioarchaeological; sexual violence; violence

INTRODUCTION

If it is melodramatic to assert that human history is written with a mixture of blood and misery drawn from the victims of human violence, it is not overstated to say that Clio has frequently dipped her pen in that ink. In fact, as Krauss (2005, p. 11) has pointed out, "Before humans learned to objectify their experiences, concretize them symbolically, and transmit them in ideograph they had mastered the ability to prey on one another." An irenic Garden of Eden existed only in myth.

PREHISTORY OF VIOLENCE

Recent discoveries and improvements in bioarchaeological research technology have opened a window on how humans lived before recorded history—not pacifically (Walker, 2001). Well before the advent of modern humans between 200,000 and 120,000 years ago (Gibbons, 2003), cut marks found on excavated human skeletal fragments suggest that some Neanderthals engaged in cannibalism, and correspondences between the state of human remains and animal food refuse at a New Stone Age site in France (La Baume Fonlebregoua) indicated that Neanderthals were not the only cannibalistic hominids. By the

---

Address for correspondence: Herbert H. Krauss, Pace University, 41 Park Row, Rm 1313, New York, New York 10038. Voice: 212-346-1434; fax: 212-346-1618.
e-mail: hkrauss@pace.edu

Mesolithic era, the increased incidence of small points found embedded in human bone demonstrates that homicide not only occurred then, but was not rare. The first clear evidence of mass murder comes from a collection of 38 skulls from a 7720-year-old site in Bavaria. Homicide was not just an Old World prerogative. Points embedded in human bones and crushed human skulls found in excavations at a number of the earliest Native American sites argue that similar patterns of violence were imported and established themselves in the New World (Walker, 2001).

Five conclusions may be drawn from Walker's review of bioarchaelogical investigations of prehistoric people:

1. "Everywhere we probe into the history of our species we find evidence of a similar pattern of behavior . . . All the evidence suggests that peaceful periods have always been punctuated by episodes of warfare and violence." (p. 590)
2. "As far as we know, there are no forms of social organization, modes of production, or environmental settings that remain free from personal violence for long." (p. 590)
3. Two trends in the development of weapons have grown—their lethality and their ability to injure at a distance.
4. Not all modern patterns of violence can be found in the prehistoric bioarchaeological record. One that cannot is the "battered child syndrome." "Such abusive behavior leaves clear skeletal stigmata that my colleagues and I have looked for in vain in many large prehistoric skeletal series . . . It seems likely that treating children in this way was simply impossible in earlier societies." (p. 591)
5. "One sobering pattern that emerges from a survey of past violence is the close relationship seen between large-scale outbreaks of violence and climatic uncertainty." (p. 591)

HISTORY OF VIOLENCE

If prehistory was marked by predations against fellow humans, what can be said of historical times? It can be stated fairly that matters grew worse. Consider that the Old Testament, New Testament, and Koran, each averred to be, by their adherents, God's revealed truth, and, then and now, foremost among man's sources of moral instruction, often portray human violence as necessary exercises of power to attain the greater good. These words of God, if they did not precipitate it, were used to justify enormous carnage by those who worship the God of Peace. The wars springing up around the so-called "Protestant Reformation"—the wars of Religion (CE 1562 to 1598) and the Thirty Years' War (1618 to 1648)—are examples of this. In the latter, a third of Germany's population perished. Illustrative too are the various "Inquisitions" and other savageries with which heresy and witchcraft were pursued for the moral education of the masses. What more need one to be convinced that human history is also a history of human violence than a consideration of the human destruction that naturally accompanies city-state, state, and empire building, or that always seems to follow upon mass ethnic migrations, or attends life's all-too-typical brutal interactions between the oppressor and the oppressed. To say this, however, is not to say all humans are vicious, incorrigible beasts, incapable of taking the right lessons from their historical experience. "The laws of religion in Europe, which pitted Protestants against Catholics and led to enormous devastation, eventually produced a new idea, that of tolerance—"Tolerance, and the associated idea of the separation of church and state," as Lewis (1998, p. 19) points out. Within the span of 100 years, the notion that those who did not share the majority's practices in worshipping the Christian God ought be tolerated was extended to the idea that they ought also be granted political rights—"[N]either Pagan nor Mahometan, nor Jew ought to be excluded from the civil rights of the commonwealth because of his religion" (John Locke, 1689, *Letter Concerning Toleration*, cited in Lewis, 1998, p. 20). Then came a call for coexistence with mutual respect, as exemplified in President George Washington's letter to a Jewish community leader in Newport, Rhode Island,

> The citizens of the United States of America ... all possess alike liberty of conscience and immunities of citizenship. It is now no more that toleration is spoken of, as if it was by the indulgence of one class of people that another enjoyed the exercise of their inherent rights. For happily the government of the United States, which gives to bigotry no sanction to persecution no assistance, requires only that they who live under its protections, should demean themselves as good citizens, in giving it on all occasions their effectual support. (cited in Lewis, 1998, p. 20)

Thomas Jefferson's reasoned embrace of religious diversity (again a citation from Lewis, p. 20), followed: "the maxim of civil government should be reversed and we should rather say 'divided we stand, united, we fall.'"

No, not all humans are brutes, and humans can indeed profit from history. But their learning curve seems too slow to keep pace with their capacity for expressing aggression. Why wisdom about how to live in harmony is so dearly bought can only be conjectured. Perhaps history is too often too local, human experience too particular to lead to easy generalization (for example, see Lewis, 1998 on tolerance of other religions in Islam). Perhaps people insufficiently preserve and transmit to future generations lessons painfully learned. Perhaps they take the wrong meaning from experience and pass that on all too well.

MODERN TIMES

Unfortunately, rather than diminish over time, human mayhem reached crescendo in the 20th century of the common era. Rummel (1994) estimated that 191 million lost their lives in the top 25 incidents of collective violence in that century. There were World War I and World War II as well as the depravity, depredation, and destruction wrought by Hitler and his henchmen and Stalin and his comrades. Leaving aside incidents in which governments succeeded in intentionally starving to death enemies of the revolution or enrolled them in lethal re-education programs or the massacre of one ethnic group by another, to say nothing of the calculated rape of its women, between 1945 and 1997, Summerfield (1997) identified 160 wars or armed conflicts that had taken place or were in progress. As Nelson Mandela accurately and aptly stated:

> The twentieth century will be remembered as a century marked by violence. It burdens us with its legacy of mass destruction, or violence inflicted on a scale never seen and never possible before in human history. But this legacy— the result of new technology in the service of ideologies of hate is not the only one we carry, nor that we must face up to.
>
> Less visible, but even more widespread, is the legacy of day-to-day, individual suffering. It is the pain of children who are abused by people who should protect them, women injured or humiliated by violent partners, elderly persons maltreated by their caregivers, youths who are bullied by other youths, and people of all ages who inflict violence on themselves. This suffering—and there are many more examples that I could give—is a legacy that reproduces itself as new generations learn from the violence of generations past, as victims learn from victimizers, and as the social conditions that nurture violence are allowed to continue... In many societies, violence is so dominant that it thwarts hope of economic and social development. We cannot let that continue. (Mandela in Krug, Dahlberg, Mercy, Zwi, & Lozano, 2002, Forward)

Unless effective measures are taken to stem the red tide of violence, one can only expect more of the same. For instance, in 2000, 520,000 were murdered, 815,000 committed suicide, and 310,000 died in war-related circumstances ("WHO's Global Burden of Disease Project for 2000, Version 1" cited in Krug *et al.*, 2002, p. 10).

VIOLENCE AGAINST WOMEN

Although sexual violence against women is underreported for obvious reasons (e.g., stigmatization) and, in most countries, there is little research into its incidence; it is widespread. "Available evidence suggests that in some countries nearly one in four women may experience sexual violence by an intimate partner... and up to one-third of adolescent girls report their first sexual experience as being forced" (Krug *et al.*, 2002). WHO's recent investigation of women's health and domestic violence (Garcia-Moreno, Jansen, Ellsburg, Heise, & Watts, 2005) continues the trend of disquieting news about physical and sexual assault on women. Garcia-Moreno *et al.* found on the basis of 24,000 interviews conducted with 15- to 49-year-old women in 10 countries

(Bangladesh, Brazil, Ethiopia, Japan, Peru, Namibia, Samoa, Serbia Montenegro Thailand, and Tanzania) that 35% to 76% of those surveyed had been physically or sexually assaulted. Of those women who had ever had an intimate partner, 15% to 71% had been assaulted by him. Of these, 21% to 66% indicated that they had told no one of the assault. This is not surprising because at about half of the interview sites 50% to 90% of women queried indicated that it was acceptable for a man to beat his wife if she disobeyed him, refused him sex, did not complete her housework, was unfaithful or was suspected of being unfaithful, or asked him about his involvement with other women. What was shocking was that of the women interviewed who had been pregnant, depending on the interview site, from 1% to 28%, admitted they had been beaten when pregnant by the child's father. If the victims of nonlethal assaults, those injured in war, children who are abused or neglected, and so on, are added to the victims of sexual assault and homicide, the toll of violence is truly staggering.

THE WORLD HEALTH ORGANIZATION RESPONDS TO VIOLENCE

"Noting with considerable concern the dramatic worldwide increase in the incidence of intentional injuries affecting people of all ages and both sexes, but especially women and children," (resolution WHA49.25 cited in World Health Organization, 2002, p. 2), the Forty-ninth World Health Assembly (Geneva, 1996) ratified resolution WHA49.25. The Assembly's implicit intent was to draw the attention of an international audience to the need to take action to reduce violence and to better treat violence's consequences. The resolution also ordered that a number of actions, both strategic and tactical, be taken to combat violence, particularly violence against females. It declared violence to be a public health problem. It urged its member states to take all appropriate measures to reduce violence within their borders. And it requested that the director general of the World Health Organization (WHO) accomplish the following: (1) Produce a nosology of violence; estimate the rate at which each type of violence occurs; determine each type's etiology; and assess each type's noxious sequelae; and do these things taking gender into account. (2) Identify programs, especially community-based programs, which effectively prevent violence or, if it occurs, effectively reduce violence's deleterious effects.

The resolution further requested WHO's director general to promote public health research on violence, develop an international epidemiological database on the occurrence of violence and its consequences, disseminate all relevant information developed about violence, and collaborate with all appropriate organizations attempting to reduce violence or mitigate violence's consequences. Lastly, it requested the director general to inform the World Health Assembly's Executive Board at its 99th session of the success achieved to date in fulfilling the charge of resolution WHA49.25 and "to present a plan of action for progress toward a science-based public health approach to violence prevention." (resolution WHA49.25 cited in World Health Organization, 2002, p. 3)

As with all major initiatives of the World Health Assembly, resolution WHA49.25 did not spring full grown from the head of Zeus as did Athena. Its progenitors were the findings of a series of international conferences—the World Summit for Social Development, the International Conference on Population and Development (Cairo, 1994), the Fourth World Conference on Women (Beijing, 1995), and the Third International Conference on Injury Prevention and Control (Melbourne, 1996), to name a few. Each conference of the set had a focus other than violence, but each came to recognize that violence's malignant influence needed to be diminished before its primary aim could be achieved.

In sum, in the 1990s an international consensus emerged about the pressing need to reduce violence and its toxic consequences. Especially salient was the concern of the international community to safeguard women and children, populations disproportionately targeted for violence and vulnerable to it.

WHO'S PUBLIC HEALTH MODEL FOR VIOLENCE AND ITS REDUCTION

Because the typical response of any society to violence and its aftermath is poorly conceived, poorly coordinated, and rarely persistent, WHO proposed a science-based public health model of violence prevention that is multidisciplinary, focuses on the health of communities and populations, concentrates its efforts on those at greatest risk, and aims at preventing harm from occurring or reoccurring. Its implementation, required

"—defining and monitoring the extent of the problem;

—identifying the cause of the problem;

—formulating and testing ways of dealing with the problem;

—applying widely the measures that are found to work." (WHO, 2002)

While other sections in this volume will attend to each of these, this essay focuses upon the first two.

Defining Violence

At its simplest, a definition needs to tell us what something is and what it is not, and how to recognize when it is present and when it is not. Without definition, communal, comprehensible discourse about violence cannot proceed. It is no wonder, therefore, that adequately defining *violence* is key to

WHO's coming to grips with it. To a degree, every definition must be seen as a complex social construction. Centuries have passed before the meaning of "physical constants" such as "second" or "meter" became fixed. For more culturally and value-laden constructs such as violence, arriving at a workable, useful, and consensually agreed upon definition is likely to prove even more difficult. There are many reasons why reaching consensus will be difficult. One is what Walker (2001) labels *cultural contingency*. The meaning of violence varies from culture to culture and sometimes within the same culture (e.g., Barton, 1969; Cohen & Vandello, 1998; Gelles, 1990; Harris, 2001; Krohn-Hansen, 1994; Miller, 1993) as the following example illustrates:

> It was a typical husband-wife argument. She wanted to visit her parents. He wanted her to stay at home. So they settled it in what some here say is an all-too-typical fashion, Rosalynn Isimento-Osibuamhe recalled of the incident in December 2001. Her husband Emmanuel, followed her out the door. Then he beat her unconscious, she says, and left her lying in the street near their apartment.
>
> Mrs. Isimento-Osibuamhe, then 31 and in the fifth year of her marriage, had broken an unwritten rule in this part of the world; she had defied her husband. Surveys throughout sub-Saharan Africa show that many men and women, too—consider such disobedience ample justification for a beating.
>
> In Zambia, nearly half of women surveyed said a male partner had beaten them, according to a 2004 survey financed by the United States—the highest percentage of nine developing nations surveyed on three continents. (LaFraniere, 2005, August 11, pp. A1, A10).

Another is that even when a "standard" definition of violence exists, that definition may be more honored in the breach than the observance, thereby, vitiating it. For example, even though the official federal definition of child abuse given in United States' Child Abuse Prevention and Treatment Act of 1974 (PL93-237) was ostensibly clear,

> ...the physical or mental injury, negligent treatment, or maltreatment of a child under the age of eighteen by a person who is responsible for the child's welfare under circumstances which would indicate the child's health or welfare is harmed or threatened thereby (cited in Gelles, 1990, pp. 51–52)

and most investigations into child abuse have been "influenced" by that federal definition, Gelles (1990, p. 52) was forced to conclude that it is mistaken, "to assume there is uniformity in how child abuse is nominally defined by researchers. In point of fact, most studies of child abuse cannot be compared because of wide disparity of definitions in use." To cite another example:

> The turmoil began a year ago with the Amnesty International report which took Sweden to task for failing to adequately curb violence against women

and help them cope with their situations. The organization also cited spotty prosecutions, vague statistics, old fashioned judges and unresponsive local governments.

> The report praised Sweden's laws as 'unambiguous,' but warned that 'strongly worded legislation is not a sufficient instrument to insure women's right to a life without violence.' (Alvarez, 2005, p. A4)

Yet a third obstacle to arriving at an acceptable meaning of violence is posed by influential pressure groups wishing to modify the temporarily in-place definition to suit their sectarian interests. In the United States, as Moynihan points out most characteristically, "Liberals traditionally have been alert for upward redefining that does injustice to individuals. Conservatives have been correspondingly sensitive to downward redefining that weakens societal standards" (Moynihan, 1993, p. 30). It should, therefore, not shock that some members of the Religious Right believe abortion ought to be classed as murder and some liberals believe that spanking children ought be classed as child abuse.

WHO's Definition of Violence

By Moynihan's standard, WHO's definition of *violence* is liberal, as it takes pains to preserve and expand protections offered to society's weakest members. It defines violence as:

> The intentional use of physical force or power, threatened or actual, against oneself, another person, or against a group or community, that either results in or has a high likelihood of resulting in injury, death, psychological harm, maldevelopment or deprivation. (WHO Global Consultation on Violence and Health, 1996)

If the test of its adequacy be the extent to which it can provide a standard for meaningfully and clearly delimiting whether an act is violent, then WHO's definition of *violence* has notable defects; it is, at once, too abstract, too broad, and too complex.

As elaborated by WHO, not only is the intentional use of physical force producing harm considered violence, but so too is the malintentioned threat to apply the power to coerce that inheres in all unequal intimate, social, cultural, and institutional power relationships—those between, for example, intimates, parent and child, teacher and pupil, doctor and patient, employer and employee, peace officer and citizen. Furthermore, WHO also defines as violence the malintentioned failure to take action when appropriate action would prevent or ameliorate injury. According to Krug *et al.* (2002, p. 5):

> The inclusion of the word 'power,' in addition to the phrase 'use of physical force,' broadens the nature of a violent act and expands the conventional understanding of violence to include those acts that result from a power relationship, including threats and intimidation. The 'use of power' also serves

to include neglect or acts of omission, in addition to the more obvious violent acts of commission, thus, 'the use of physical force or power' should be understood to include neglect and all types of physical, sexual and psychological abuse, as well as suicide and other self-abusive acts. This definition covers a broad range of outcomes – including psychological harm, deprivation and maldevelopment . . .

If practicable, differentiating between an accident and a premeditated action intended to promote or cause harm is clearly desirable, especially if one wishes to advance a psychology of responsible agency; however, it is not clear if doing so is essential to a depiction of violent action. Instead, one might simply map the relationships between circumstance and outcome, the relationship, for example, between the presence of firearms and the likelihood that someone will be shot, or between family income and the number of children with physical trauma admitted to emergency rooms. To say that the incorporation of a notion of intention into a definition of violence adds complexity is an understatement. When one adds intention to a definition, questions such as "Who is to determine it?" and "On what basis can a determination of it be made?" arise. Characteristically, WHO arrogated to itself the determination of intention. WHO's justification: Its belief that if the worldwide prevalence of violence was to be reduced, an international, enlightened public health paradigm need be substituted for local standards.

> Violence, according to Walters and Parke . . . , is culturally determined. Some people mean to harm others but based upon their cultural backgrounds and beliefs, do not perceive their acts as violent. The definition used by the World Health Organization, however, defines violence as it relates to health or well-being of individuals. Certain behaviors—such as hitting a spouse—may be regarded by some people as acceptable cultural practices, but are considered violent acts with important health implications for the individual. (Krug et al., 2002, p. 5)

Given the acknowledged difficulties interested parties have had in reaching consensus defining violence, it seems reasonable to ask whether WHO's depiction of violence improves on past attempts. By what criteria might such a judgment be made? Perhaps by those proved valuable in evaluating the unified validity of an assessment tool (Messick, 1993). Were the uniform validity approach to evaluating WHO's definition of violence to be employed, information pertinent to a number of issues would need be collected and considered. Following Messick, one would want evidentiary assurance that the definition could be applied with similar results by different, trained users working in different contexts. One would also wish a demonstration that the definition covered all that it was necessary to fully represent what was intended when one speaks of violence and yet was not overinclusive. There would also have to be evidence that the definition possessed incremental utility; that is, that it was more useful than its rivals. And, one would also need to know the nature and frequency of adverse events associated with the definition's implementation;

for example, does a reduction in the disciplinary prerogatives of husbands lead to an increase in divorces? Issues such as these would have to be satisfactorily dealt with before WHO's definition of violence or any other ought to be considered sound. Therefore, by any rigorous standard WHO's definition of violence is, at best, a work in progress. This said, it nevertheless possesses significant virtues, although in truth, these are more a function of WHO's unique status than the care with which its definition of violence was drawn. One of the definition's virtues is that it permits compiling statistics (e.g., incidence) based upon a consistent definition of violence to begin, both within and across societies. And it makes possible, within the limits of the reliability and validity of those estimates, meaningful cross-societal and cross-subcultural analyses of violence, which may contribute to and deepen our understanding of the etiology of violence and how it might be prevented. A second is that it legitimates the belief that violence is not just a local matter but one of international concern. Yet a third is that, if it gains international acceptance, WHO's definition of violence could potentially extend to the world's most vulnerable populations—women, children, the infirm, the elderly, the poverty stricken, refugees— a measure of protection from coercive power. In identifying them as victims and those who trespass against them as aggressors, WHO opens the door to the possibility that these vulnerable populations might come to be protected.

WHO's Typology of Violence

WHO's typology of violence (Krug *et al*., 2002) is rational and categorical rather than empirical. It divides violence into three major categories—self-directed, interpersonal, and collective—based upon the circumstances in which the violent act took place. Each of these categories is further subdivided. The focus of self-directed violence is self-evident. It has two subcategories: suicidal behavior and self-abuse (e.g., self-mutilation). Violence inflicted by another individual or a small group of individuals is interpersonal violence. Such violence is further divided into family, intimate partner, and community violence. Of the three, only community violence requires elaboration. Youth violence, rape or sexual assault by strangers, and violence perpetrated in institutional settings fall into it. Collective violence is "the instrumental use of violence by people who identify themselves as members of a group against another group or a set of individuals, in order to achieve political, economic, or social objectives" (WHO, 2002, p. 5). It includes armed conflicts, genocide, terrorism, human rights abuses, and organized violent crime. The collective violence category has three major subdivisions. The subdivision into which it falls depends upon whether the violent act is directed toward achieving social, political, or economic ends. It should be noted that further subclassification along the circumstance or context dimension is possible and potentially useful.

For example, each of its current subdivisions might be further parsed as a function of who the victim of violence was—a child, an adolescent, adult, or elder, for instance.

Crossed with context in WHO's schema is a nature of violence dimension. This has four major categories: physical violence, sexual violence, psychological violence, and deprivation or neglect. This allows, if only major or primary categories are considered, a three (self-directed, interpersonal, collective) by four (physical, sexual, psychological, deprivation or neglect) matrix with twelve cells (e.g., sexual aggression against a stranger).

Any summary judgment of the value of WHO's typology of violence must necessarily resemble that reached for its definition of violence—defective but useful. Because its definition of violence lies at its heart, the WHO's typology is difficult to operationalize. This is especially true of its psychological violence and deprivation and neglect cells. Undoubtedly, for the near future, the best data will be located in the cross-section defined on the one hand by the categories of physical and sexual violence and on the other by self-directed, interpersonal, and collective violence; but, even there, until the exact details for classifying incidents of violence are spelled out and promulgated, tested (for reliability and validity), adopted, and adhered to, even the data in those cells will be suspect.

UNDERSTANDING VIOLENCE

To date, no acceptable, comprehensive understanding of violence holds the field (Krauss, 2005). Nor is there likely to be one shortly, even assuming that such a feat is possible. One impediment to early success in theory development will be the breadth and high level of abstraction of WHO's definition of violence. On the surface, at least, it is unlikely that such seemingly disparate phenomena as rape, wife-beating, child neglect, unprotected sex by those who know they are HIV positive, school yard bullying, war, ethnic and religious conflict, murder, forced prostitution, elder abuse, suicide, and so on are likely to be nontrivially accounted for by the same set of variables or constraints. Nor is the admitted dearth of reliable and valid data about the incidence of violence's manifold acts and the circumstances in which they occur likely to be remediated soon. Without such data, it is difficult to see around what, besides ideology or emotion, any putative grand explanation of violence might coalesce. What is clear is that with respect to some forms of violence, suicide, for one, that enough is known about its complex causes that a plan for its reduction cannot be well formulated until the contributions made by interacting variables or dynamics, biological as well as societal, which produce it are delineated, estimated, and prioritized. To enable us to see violence from a perspective wide enough to encompass it and yet sharp enough to discern its constituents, WHO has proposed the adoption of an Ecological Model of Violence.

WHO's Ecological Model of Violence

WHO's Ecological Model of Violence (Krug *et al.*, 2002; WHO, 2002) differentiates among four overlapping levels of factors that influence being victimizer or victim. The individual level focuses upon personal biological (e.g., brain injury) and historical factors (education); the relationship level, upon close interpersonal relationships (e.g., family structure, friendship nets); the community level, upon characteristics of local settings (e.g., schools, workplaces, neighborhoods); and the societal level or social or cultural norms, or institutional practices (e.g., a woman's place is in the home). WHO designed this model to serve as a framework for summarizing knowledge about violence much the same way as it envisioned its typology as delineating its varieties. The model is intended to compile and organize information about the person-level, relationship-level, community-level, and societal-level factors that contribute to one type of violent act to determine whether or not the same mix also produces other violent acts.

WHO's Ecological Model is superior to its current alternatives in many respects. One advantage that it possesses is that while it supports focal disciplinary research (such as Raine's, 1993) investigation of frontal lobe functioning in murders or Kojima's modeling of the economics of infanticide), it clearly stipulates that a proper and useful understanding of human behavior in general, and violence in particular, requires a multilevel, multivariable approach. In doing so, it affirms the important role emergence (e.g., Van Gulick, 2001) and downward causation (Campbell, 1974) play in systems that influence human action and recognizes the forces that "realities" other than that of physical reality can exert on human lives. Those of Popper's (1979) World II and World III, for example,

> [T]he world consists of at least three ontologically distinct sub-worlds; or, as I shall say, there are three worlds: the first is the physical world or the world of physical states; the second is the mental world or the world of mental states; and the third is the world of intelligibles, or of *ideas in the objective* sense; it is the world of possible objects of thought: the world of theories in themselves, and their logical relations; of arguments in themselves; and of problem situations in themselves. The three worlds are so related that the first two can interact, and the last two can interact. The first world and the third world cannot interact, save through the intervention of the second world, the world of subjective or personal experiences. (pp. 154–155)

From the Popperian perspective, the stereotypic belief held by Classical Era Greek men that women were rageful and dangerous (Harris, 2001) can be as "real" a contributor to a husband's striking his wife as her slapping his face. Certainly, it is not convincing to argue *Mein Kampf's* depiction of Jews did not influence the actions of Nazi-era Germans against them. A depiction of the Holocaust solely in terms of rival ethnic groups competing for scant resources, while it might have been appealing to Hitler, is obviously speciously incomplete, just as is Wilson's (1998) socio-biological explanation of the murderous violence which, in 1994, once again spilled over in Rwanda when units of Rwanda's army, mostly Hutus, killed more than half a million Tutsis and moderate Hutus. Two million of the remaining Hutus fled Rwanda where thousands subsequently perished of starvation and disease. Granting, "On the surface it would seem, and so was reported by the media, that the Rwandan catastrophe was ethnic rivalry run amok," Wilson (1998, p. 288), posited "a deeper cause, rooted in environment and demography,"—Rwanda's population exceeded its carrying capacity. Its production of food was

> overbalanced by population growth. The average farm size dwindled, as plots were divided from one generation to the next. Per capita grain production fell by half from 1960 to the early 1990s. Water was so overdrawn that the hydrologists declared Rwanda one of the world's twenty-seven water-scarce countries. The teenage soldiers of the Hutu and Tutsi then set out to solve the population problem in the most direct way. (Wilson, 1998, p. 288)

Wilson's explanation of Rwanda's tragedy is not defective because he hypothesized that competition over scarce resources could have played a role in the eruption of violence; it may have. His explanation ought to be discarded for two good reasons. First, he averred a conclusion with insufficient proof; he transformed "what if" into "as if" with insufficient evidence. Second, because if one restricts oneself to a consideration only of a person's interaction with Popper's World I, the physical world, as does Wilson, then "one cannot build a plausible explanation of human action given the potentially non-singular set of possible cognitively and historically contrived life worlds actualizable at any given time" (Krauss, 2005, p. 22).

The view that World III is "real" and influential is not confined to "social scientists." Read (2005, p. 111) uses it to explain the transition from primate to hominid forms of social organization:

> Under the scenario proposed here, evolution of forms of social organization has shifted from change in frequency of individual traits driven by individual fitness to evolution driven by coherency of conceptual systems for the social organization of society. As a consequence the '[cultural] system has become independent from biology in such a way that the constraints acting for stabilization or for changes in a given culture are internal' (Ripoll & Vauclair, 2001, p. 355) ... and fitness arises from the impact the conceptual system has on parameters for group competition. Group fitness in this scenario is related to the cognitive ability to formulate a conceptual system of relations with an underlying structure that enables transmittal of a complex system of organization at the behavioral level by shifting transmission from individual phenotypic transmission to transmission of group properties via a coherent system of relations.

More directly pertinent to violence is C. R. Harris's (2004) account of jealousy. Jealousy is typically ranked among the top three motives for homicide in cases where motive has been established (rage arising from a quarrel and murder during the commission of a crime are the other two). During the 1990s individuals (e.g., Buss, 1995; Buunk, Anglietner, Oubard, & Buss, 1996) describing themselves as evolutionary psychologists began applying Darwin's theory to a number of issues of psychological concern—jealousy being but one of them. Common to their approach were five assumptions (Pervin, 2002): (1) Humans have a common nature; (2) Inherent to it are evolved psychological mechanisms adapted for reproductive success; (3) These mechanisms were designed to solve past problems rather than those that have arisen recently; (4) These mechanisms were directed toward successfully dealing with specific delineated challenges rather than general problems—"In other words, many aspects of our cognitive and emotional functioning are hard-wired into us rather than being products of our unique experiences." (p. 139); (5) It is more productive to ask how evolved human nature creates culture than how human culture creates human action.

Jealousy, evolutionary psychologists aver, Harris (2004) submits, arose because it gave those with it a fitness advantage; on the whole, jealous individuals had greater reproductive success. Furthermore, jealousy, as did other emotions associated with mating, took on a different character in men than women. The hard-wired jealousy module in women came to be activated by their mates' *emotional* infidelity; the hard-wired circuitry in men by their mates' *sexual* infidelity. This occurred because men expend resources on women they love, and women, because their offspring lose resources if their mates' affection is stolen. Their mate's just having sex with others does not directly threaten that affection. On the other hand, from the man's point of view, expending resources to ensure the reproductive success of offspring not his own was a poor evolutionary bargain, hence his concern about infidelity. Harris's (2004) review of the extant research, however, suggested a contrary interpretation: that robust sex differences in jealousy did not exist, that both men and women are alert to flirtatious behavior, and that natural selection "shaped fairly general jealousy mechanisms designed to operate across a variety of interpersonal contexts" (p. 71). Her conclusion—"Jealousy could certainly be an innate and adaptive emotion, but its form may be better explained by social-cognitive approaches, as well as developmental theory, than by theories based on proposed sex differences in our ancestors' mating strategies" (p. 62).

A multilevel focus is one advantage of WHO's Ecological Model; its pragmatism is a second. At its heart, pragmatism is an attitude as well as a method. As an attitude it stands in opposition "to the absolute separation of thought from action, pure from applied science, of intuition or revelation from experience or experimental verification, of private interest from public concern..." (Weiner, 1973, p. 551). As a method it acts as if truth is simply "the fittest thing to believe in" (Rorty cited by Delacampagne, 1999, p. 263). "[I]n other words," Delacampagne offers, truth is "the set of statements that have been shown most useful for making sense of reality, and for living better lives" (p. 263). If consilience in science is taking place, it is not of the type envisioned by Wilson (1998). Instead of the hegemony of the Culture of Science over the Culture of the Humanities or, to use the terms that embed the issue in its historical context, the *Naturwissenschaften* over the *Geisteswissenschaften* (Berlin, 1974) what is increasingly being seen is an ascendancy of the pragmatic and the hermeneutic. Central to this movement is the growing belief that dichotomies as *Naturwissenschaften* and *Geisteswissenschaften* are largely "straw men" and that "true practitioners in either field pursue aims and methods that are in principle identical or at any rate cognate to each other." (Berlin, 1974, p. 9). In Popper's (1979) view:

> Science, after all, is a branch of literature; and working in science is a human activity like building a cathedral.
>
> Labouring the difference between science and the humanities has been a fashion, and has become a bore. The method of problem solving, the method of conjecture, and refutation is practiced by both. It is practiced in reconstructing a damaged text as well as in constructing a theory of radioactivity. (p. 185)

The figure Popper uses, that of reconstructing a damaged text, is no accident. It is intended to invoke the practice of hermeneutics. Hermeneutics arose out of philology and Homeric and Biblical studies (Campbell, 1988; Gadamer, 1976, 2001). As observation is the key to the natural sciences (Feynman, 1998), *verstehen* or empathy is central to the humanities (Berlin, 1998).

> A scholar is deciphering an archaic text. On first reading he gets fragmentary hunches, which he forces into a guess at the overall direction of the message. Using this, he goes over it again, decoding a bit more, deciding on plausible translation of a few words he has never encountered before. He repeats this hermeneutic cycle or spiral again and again, revising part guesses and making new ones for previously unattempted sections. If he is being successful and has extensive enough texts to properly prove his translation hypothesis, he arrives at such a remarkable confidence that he can in places decide that the ancient scribe made a clerical error, and that he, the modern, knows better what that ancient intended than what the ancient's written text records... (Campbell, 1988, p. 478)

That scholar can decipher that text because he can project into it, imagine the person who wrote it, empathize with that person's intent. In effect, the scholar enters into a conversation with that text and through that the person who wrote it (Gadamer, 1976, 2001).

The most profound and optimistic proponent of hermeneutics in science was Donald T. Campbell. He rejected the position that validity of interpretation could not be achieved and saw "validity-seeking hermeneutics" as bridging the artificial schism between the natural sciences and the humanities (Campbell, 1988). His turn to "validity-seeking hermeneutics" came because he believed the collapse of logical positivism required a reconceptualization of science and its methods and that a unified human science could only emerge from an evolving combination of post-positivist natural science and hermeneutic epistemology.

Although it does offer a useful lattice upon which data about violence can grow, WHO's Ecological Model provides no information-organizing and data-generating master metaphor with which to conceptualize violence. As one-sided as it is, the trope of biological evolution has proven useful for framing answerable questions about nature's contributions to violent behavior. Were the conjectures it stimulated supported, then progress toward a coherent model of jealousy-precipitated violence, for example, would have been achieved.

REFERENCES

American Psychological Association. (1993). *Violence and youth: Psychological response*. Washington, DC: Author.

AVAREZ, L. (2005, April 6). Sweden boldly exposes a secret side of women's lives. *The New York Times*, p. A4.

BARTON, R.F. (1969). *Ifugao law*. Berkeley, CA: University of California.

BERLIN, I. (1974). The divorce between the sciences and the humanities. *Salmagundi*, 24, 9–39.

BERLIN, I. (1998). *The proper study of mankind*. NY: Farrar, Straus, Giroux.

BUSS, D.M. (1995). Evolutionary psychology: A new paradigm for psychological science. *Psychological Inquiry*, 6, 1–30.

BUUNK, B.P., ANGLEITNER, A., OUBAID, V., & BUSS, D.M. (1996). Sex differences in jealous in evolutionary and cultural perspective. *Psychological Science*, 7, 359–363.

CAMPBELL, D.T. (1974). 'Downward causation' in hierarchically organized systems. In F.Y. Ayala & T. Dobzhansky (Eds.), *Studies in the philosophy of biology* (pp. 179–186). New York: Macmillan.

CAMPBELL, D.T. (1988). *Methodology and epistemology for social sciences: Selected papers*. E. S. Overman (Ed.). Chicago: University of Chicago Press.

COHEN, D. & VANDELLO, J. (1998). Meanings of violence. *Journal of Legal Studies*, 27, 567–584.

DELACAMPAGNE, C. (1999). *A history of philosophy in the twentieth century*. M.B. DeBevoise (Trans.) Baltimore, MD: Johns Hopkins University Press.

FEYNMAN, R.P. (1998). *The meaning of it all*. Reading, MA: Perseus Books.

GADAMER, H.G. (1976). *Philosophical hermeneutics,* trans. D.E. Linge. Berkeley, CA: University of California Press.

GADAMER, H.G. (2001). In Palmer, R.E. (Ed.), *Gadamer in conversation: Reflections and commentary*. New Haven: Yale.

GARCIA-MORENO, C., HEISE, L., JANSEN, H.R.M.F., ELLSBERG, M. & WATTS, C. (2005). Violence against women. *Science*, 310, 1282–1283.

GARCIA-MORENO, C., JANSEN, H.A.F.M., ELLSBERG, L., HEISE, L. & WATTS, C. (2005). *WHO multi-country study on women's health and domestic violence against women: Initial results on prevalence, health outcomes and women's responses*. Geneva: World Health Organization.

GELLES, R.J. (1990). Methodological issues in the study of family violence. In G.R. Patterson (Ed.), *Depression and aggression in family interaction* (pp. 49–74). Hillsdale, NJ: Laurence Erlbaum Associates.

GIBBONS, A. (2003). Oldest members of *Homo sapiens* discovered in Africa. *Science, 300,* 1641.

GOULD, S.J. (2003). *The hedgehog, the fox, and the magister's pox; Mending the gap between science and the humanities.* NY: Harmony.

HARRIS, C.R. (2004). The evolution of jealousy. *American Scientist, 92(1),* 62–71.

HARRIS, W.V. (2001). *Restraining rage.* Cambridge: Harvard University Press.

KRAUSS, H.H. (2005). Conceptualizing violence. In Denmark, F., Krauss, H.H., Wesner, R.W., Midlarsky, E. & Gielen, U.P. (Eds.), *Violence in the schools: Cross-national and cross-cultural perspectives* (pp. 11–35). New York: Springer.

KROHN-HANSEN, C. (1994). The anthropology of violent interaction. *Journal of Anthropological Research, 50,* 367–381.

KRUG, E.G., DAHLBERG, L.L., MERCY, J.A., ZWI, A.B., & LOZANO, R. (2002). *World report on violence and health.* Geneva: World Health Organization.

LA FRENIERE, S. (2005, August 11). Entrenched epidemic: Wife-beatings in Africa. *The New York Times,* p. A1.

LEWIS, B. (1998). The historical roots of racism. *American Scholar, 67,* 17–25.

MANDALA, U. (2002). [Forward]. In World Health Organization, *World report on violence and health: summary.* Geneva: Author.

MATTAINI, M.A., TWYMAN, J.S., CHIN, W. & LEE, K.N. (1996). Youth violence. In M.A. Mattaini & B.A. Thyer (Eds.), *Finding solutions to social problems* (pp. 75–111). Washington, DC: American Psychological Association Press.

MERCY, J.A., ROSENBERG, M.L., POWELL, K.E., BROOME, C.V., & ROPER, W.L. (1993). Public health policy for preventing violence. *Health Affairs, 12,* 7–29.

MESSICK, S. (1993). *Foundations of validity: Meaning and consequences in psychological assessment.* (Research Report). Princeton, NJ: Educational Testing Service.

MILLER, W.I. (1993). *Humiliation.* Ithaca, NY: Cornell University.

MORSON, G.S. (1991). Bahktin and the present moment. *American scholar, 60,* 201–222.

MOYNIHAN, D.P. (1993). Defining deviancy down. *American Scholar, 62,* 17–30.

PERVIN, L.A. (2002). *Current controversies and issues in personality,* (3rd ed). Hoboken, NJ: John Wiley & Sons.

POPPER, K.R. (Rev. Ed.). (1979). *Objective knowledge: An evolutionary approach.* New York: Oxford University Press.

RAINE, A. (1993). *The psychopathology of crime.* New York: Academic Press.

READ, D.W. (2005). Change in the form of evolution: transition from primate to hominid forms of social organization. *Journal of Mathematical Sociology, 29,* 91–114.

RIPOLL, T. & VAUCLAIR, J. (2001). Can culture be inferred only from the absence of genetic and environmental factors. *Behavioral and Brain Sciences, 24(2),* 309–382.

RUMMEL, R.J. (1994). *Death by government: genocide and mass murder since 1900.* New Brunswick, NJ: Transaction Publications.

SUMMERFIELD, D. (1997). The social, cultural and political dimensions of contemporary war. The American heritage dictionary (2nd college ed.) (1982). Boston: Houghton Mifflin.

VAN GULICK, R. (2001). Reduction, emergence and other recent options on the mind/body problem. In A. Freeman (Ed.) *The emergence of consciousness* (pp. 1–34). Charlottesville, VA: Imprint Academic.

WALIA, A. (2005). Female foeticide in Punjab: Exploring the socio-economic and cultural dimensions. *Idea, 10.* Retrieved July 27, 2006, from http://www.ideajournal.com/articles.php?id=37.

WALKER, P.L. (2001). A bio-archaeological perspective on the history of violence. *Annual Review of Anthropology, 30,* 573–599.

WEINER, P.P. (1973). Pragmatism. In P.P. Weiner Editor-In-Chief, *Dictionary of the history of ideas, Vol. III.* (pp. 551–570) New York: Scribner's.

WORLD HEALTH ORGANIZATION. (2002). *World report on violence and health: Summary.* Geneva: Author.

WHO Global Consultation on Violence and Health. (1996). *Violence: a public health priority.* Geneva: WORLD HEALTH ORGANIZATION (document WHO/EHA/SPL.POA. 2).

WILSON, E. (1998). *Consilience.* New York: Knopf.

A Protoscientific Master Metaphor for Framing Violence

HERBERT H. KRAUSS

Pace University, New York, New York, USA

ABSTRACT: Every new field of investigation requires a guiding scheme or frame. Its purpose is to provide a heuristic for discovery and a structure for organizing information. Neither the World Health Organization's public health nor a biosocial model of violence are adequate for providing a protoscientific frame for conceptualizing violent acts. This essay suggests a master metaphor—Burke's Dramatism—through which to deepen and expand our knowledge of violence and what must be done to reduce its toll. An illustrative example is presented.

INTRODUCTION

As detailed in the previous article "Prespectives on Violence," the World Health Organization (WHO) (Krug *et al.*, 2002), recognizing the noxious influence violence exerted globally, decided to curtail the worldwide prevalence of violence and to ameliorate violence's deleterious consequences. To accomplish this, WHO took a number of actions. Among them were the following: (1) it generated a definition of violence; (2) it produced a typology of violence; and (3) it presented a pragmatic, multilevel framework upon which research about violence and its consequences might be arrayed. What WHO refrained from doing, apart from arguing strongly that a scientific public health model was the paradigm most suitable for understanding violence's etiology and treatment, was to offer an encompassing figure through which this understanding might be achieved and appropriate remediation be informed. Whether the proposed public health model is indeed the ideal backbone for developing and structuring knowledge about violence is, to be sure, disputable. So ingrained is violence, especially violence against women and girls, into the very fabric of most cultures that it is fair to question whether some other schema, political, economic, moral, or religious, for conceptualizing and dealing with it might prove better (Krauss, 2005). Such argument, however, falls beyond the scope of this essay save in one respect.

Address for correspondence: Herbert H. Krauss, Pace University, 41 Park Row, Rm 1313, New York, New York 10038. Voice: 212-346-1434; fax: 212-346-1618.
 e-mail: hkrauss@pace.edu

Ann. N.Y. Acad. Sci. 1087: 22–34 (2006). © 2006 New York Academy of Sciences.
doi: 10.1196/annals.1385.021

Diesing (1991) following Kuhn (1970) asserts convincingly that each new field of study, if it is to develop, needs an organizing conceptual scheme. Without one, the endeavor is apt to end in a chaos of fact gathering yielding no coherent pattern. To be sure, the scheme or frame chosen must be corrigible. Just as important, it must also prove to be a suitably stimulating heuristic for "... reasoning is not a process of formal logical deduction. It is a heuristic process of search, or discovery, in which theories (frames) provide the questions and expected answers and data provide material for actual answers ..." (Diesing, 1991, p. 267). To be sure, the initial frame selected is not likely to be the last retained as the field moves from a preparadigmatic to paradigmatic state. But having a frame is indeed essential. One needs

> ... a search routing, a series of questions about the situation one is in, a heuristic of discovery... The frame or scenario constitutes the setting ... and the process ... through which we move. In research the theory or exemplar we are following tells us the steps to take, the data to uncover, where to find the data, the data processing needed. That is, the slots in the frame determine what questions to ask and what kind of questions to ask and what kinds of answers would be appropriate; the frame constitutes our expectations or preunderstanding (Diesing, 1991, p. 258).

The question is how best to choose a frame, or, if one has been selected and proven deficient, what to substitute in its place.

> Frame theory tells us that search is guided by a frame, which structures an area and provides questions to ask. When the field is new and no frame exists, an analogy or metaphor suggests a frame. In the case of the Prisoner's Dilemma, the name itself is an analogy: in early cognitive experiments the behaviorist *S-O-R* or *S-H-R* scheme was the analogy. The analogy provides the initial questions, questions that guide research: how does the "prisoner" solve the dilemma; if perception is a response to stimulus, what cognitive variables intervene; if a dream is a "message" from the unconscious, how can we decode the message?
>
> At this stage, no testing occurs at all, even though the experimenters may well have expectations and misstate hypotheses in their published reports. The task is to produce data that answer the question (Diesing, 1991, pp. 308–309).

If Krauss (2006, this volume) is correct in concluding that each model is useful in its own limited way, the public health and biosocial models are both deficient as master metaphors for violence—the first because culturally sanctioned violence is best not viewed as a disease or occupational injury, the latter because it gives too short shrift to culturally sanctioned and institutionalized violence while overemphasizing the contribution made by biology. What might be a model, one that is potentially capable of giving appropriate voice to the contribution made by the multiplex of interacting variables whose confluence produces violent acts? Before offering a nomination, however, a few words should be devoted to what is meant by "culture" and why depicting its influence is so important.

"By *culture*," White (1959, p. 3) indicates, "we mean an extrasomatic temporal continuum of things and events dependent upon symboling. Specifically and concretely, culture consists of tools, implements, utensils, clothing, ornaments, customs, institutions, beliefs, rituals, games, works of art, languages, etc." All peoples possess a culture and each individual acquires one.

> He [a baby] acquires his culture from the world outside himself, from his human, cultured associates ... If the baby is born into one cultural setting, he will acquire a certain language, certain patterns of behavior ... and so on. If born into another and different kind of setting, he will acquire another set of cultural equipment ... Cultural forces impinge upon them from the outside, as Durkheim once put it, just as cosmic forces do (White, 1959, pp. 12–13).

In part, as Casson (1994, p. 63) points out, a "culture is an idealized cognitive system ... that exists in the minds of individual members of a society ... ," but it is, as White suggested, also more than that. It is a living template by which the individuals' world, beliefs, and actions are ordered and given meaning.

> A *society* is one aspect of the behavior of living material bodies; it is a form of behavior assumed by them. The nature of societies is to be seen in the fact that they are forms of behavior in which the living character of the component material bodies is maintained. In short, social organization is merely the interorganismal of the nutritive, protective, and reproductive behavior ... Social organization is not merely a means of maintaining life; it is *a form* of life, of the life process itself (White, 1959, p. 208).

While it may not prescribe all action or comprise all of an individual's let alone everyone's cognitive world (Bock, 1994; Casson, 1994; Diesing, 1991), clearly an individual's particular biology, experiences, location, and history must be taken into account as must the comprehensiveness and thoroughness with which the society governs thought and action. When a core cultural value is involved, considerable force is employed to ensure appropriate conformity. Whether she be Viking or Indian or a member of an African tribe that has adopted the practice of seeing that a man is accompanied to the hereafter by a woman, there is no viable alternative for her as his chosen companion to be but at his side when he dies. If she chooses to flee, she will be restrained. If she escapes, no one will offer her succor. Whether she wishes to share his fate or not, whither he goes, so too must she. Geertz (1973, pp. 50–51) puts the central position that culture holds in forming, motivating, and directing human action this way:

> Our ideas, our values, our acts, even our emotions, are like our nervous system itself, cultural products—products manufactured, indeed, out of tendencies, capacities, and dispositions with which we were born, but manufactured nonetheless. Chartres is made of stone and glass. But it is not just stone

and glass; it is a cathedral, and not only a cathedral, but a particular cathedral built at a particular time by certain members of a particular society. To understand what it means, to perceive it for what it is, you need to know rather more than the genetic properties of stone and glass and rather more than what is common to all cathedrals. You need to understand also—and, in my opinion, most critically the specific concepts of the relations among God, man, and architecture that, since they have governed its creation, it consequently embodies. It is no different with men: they, too, every last one of them, are cultural artifacts.

Having argued that any guiding master metaphor or master analogy for framing an understanding of human violence that is cross-societal must give appropriate weight to culture as well as biology, individual as well as communal history, there remains the need to select just such a candidate. I believe that Dramatism fills the bill as an initial master metaphor.

DRAMATISM: A MASTER METAPHOR

From Shakespeare's "All the world's a stage and all the men and women merely players," (As You Like It, Act II, 7) to modern social science (e.g., Geertz, 1973; Goffman, 1959; Kelly, 1955; Sarbin, 1954) the stage has been used by creative artists to portray the human condition and by those in human sciences as a metaphor by which to understand it. When the theater is formally used by scientists as a guiding frame to depict the human condition, the technique is called "dramaturgical analysis." Dramaturgical analysis as a perspective for understanding human action "is characterized by assumptions that the meaning of both the event and the self is constructed by actors through social interaction, and that the unit of analysis is not the individual but interacting persons" (Hare & Blumberg, 1988). From this perspective, substituting the word "play" for "text,"

> [A] culturally prescribed action is like a text in that it expresses or means something to or about those who move through it. Like a text, the steps in the sequence contribute to the meaning and to the movement toward completion. Also, as with a text, the actors can provide verbal interpretations of these actions during the process or afterwards, that is they can explain what they are intending to do or what they mean to express. These running interpretations can also serve to patch up breakdowns of coordination among the actors and can supplement the nonverbal cues that normally coordinate the action (Diesing, 1991, p. 124).

The most comprehensive contemporary formulation of "the plays the thing" is the Dramatism of Burke (e.g., 1966, 1969a, 1969b). Burke opens the description of his system with a definition:

> Man is the symbol-using (symbol-making, symbol-misusing animal) inventor of the negative (or moralized by the negative) separated from his natural

conditions by instruments of his own making goaded by the spirit of the hierarchy (or moved by the sense of order) and rotten with perfection. (Burke 1966, p. 16)

That is, people, though at root animals, excel the others in cognitive competency. Once humans have ideas they try to actualize them, to live within them and by them. The most significant of humankind's cognitive creations is the concept of the negative or "not" of an action, thing, or idea. Because of this humans can think "I shalt not." Being able to do this, Burke believes, makes choice and "morality" possible. And, in Burke's system, choice and morality are essential to character and character is essential to the human personality. Their cognitive aptitude and their need and ability to actualize their cognitive schemata necessarily estrange humans from Nature. Nature alone does not determine human actions nor fully circumscribe human behavior; culture is their managing director. Even the expression of necessary biological processes such as eating and elimination, defending and copulating, are channeled, modified, and regulated by culture; hence anorexia and martyrdom. Once an idea has been conceived or a culture has been produced, humans are driven to perfect it. Consequently, human cultures and the moralities that characterize them trend toward greater and greater conceptual cohesion and order, greater and greater differentiation and ramification, and greater and greater intrusion into and control over the lives of individuals.

Having described the human condition, Burke (especially in 1969a) moves on to the "five key terms of dramatism" (p. xv): *act, scene, agent, agency, and purpose*. For Burke (1969a, p. xv), "any complete statement of motives will offer *some kind* of answer to these five questions: what was done (act), when or where it was done (scene), who did it (agent), how he did it (agency), and why (purpose)." At first glance, this model seems to be simplicity itself. It can be. But it also makes possible pragmatic, intricate, deep, and dynamic interpretations of human behavior.

> Our term, 'Agent,' for instance, is a general heading that might, in a given case, require further subdivision, as an agent might have his act modified (hence partly motivated) by friends (co-agents) or enemies (counter-agents). Again, under 'Agent' one could place any personal properties that are assigned a motivational value, such as 'ideas,' 'the will,' 'fear,' 'malice,' 'intuition,' the 'creative imagination.' ... Machines are obviously instruments (that is, 'Agencies'); yet in their vast accumulation they constitute the industrial scene, with its own peculiar set of motivational properties. War may be treated as an Agency, insofar as it is a means to an end; as a collective Act, subdivisible into many individual acts; as a Purpose, in schemes proclaiming a cult of war. For the man inducted into the army, war is a Scene, a situation that motivates the nature of his training; and in mythologies war is an Agent, or perhaps better a super-agent, in the figure of the war god ... (Burke, 1969a, pp. xix–xx)

Furthermore, if warranted, the compass of dramatism may be extended. One may inquire about other factors that affect either the play's production or reception. What is its genre?—Theater of the Absurd? a Morality Play? Classical Greek Tragedy? or Comedy? If Comedy, is it Farce? or Slapstick? Is it tightly scripted? Is it well directed? How is it cast? Are the actors classically trained or products of the Method? Is there a play within the play? Is it good theater? Is it convincing? If originally written elsewhere, does it translate well? For what audience is it written? Was the audience moved? And so forth.

While no one yet seems to be intentionally compiling "A Compendium of Plays of Violence, Volume I" or writing its companion volume "How to Stage and Promote Plays of Violence," having such reference works available would undoubtedly add to our understanding of violence and its prevention. To illustrate that point, what follows is a synopsis of a play that might be included in such a compendium.

Death in Philadelphia: A Play of Violence

The author of *Death in Philadelphia* intends that the meaning taken of his play by the audience differ from the meaning ascribed to it by the cast. In fact, the playwright expects that each of the affinity groups which the audience comprises will take a different message from the theater, although all should know that they are watching a Morality Play. In these ideologically charged times, the author wishes those on the Right to believe the play warns that more effective police control is necessary to keep the animals at bay and those on the Left will view the tragic destruction of two people by an uncaring, ethnic and gender-biased, capitalist, socio-political-economic system. Should there be any communists in the audience, the author desires that they perceive the play as a call to revolution. He expects no true reactionaries will attend a Broadway show. The actors, non-professionals all, recruited by ads broadcast on a rap station, will immediately know when their lines are read to them that the play's theme is Honor, its style, naturalism. Since the author has written a play of action, one action driving another, he spends little effort on either character development or dialogue. He does spend considerable time setting each scene but offers few stage directions. Instead, the actors are told to feel into what is happening and be themselves. Nonetheless, the play's structure is not free-form; its progress seems quite coherent and well paced. This is because the play's sets change frequently, and the play's action sequences are determined largely by the setting in which they occur. To the audience, the actors' behavior appears spontaneous, not robotic at all. The actors, when they are made aware of their actions, report that they are just behaving. They do not feel in the least scripted.

The play is set in an area of North Philadelphia where once resided enclaves of various working-class ethnic groups, Irish, Italian, Polish, and Jewish. Each has long since left for the greener suburbs. After their exodus, it became home first to those of the vast northward urban migration from the South, later to those unable to move on. In the 1960s the *Philadelphia Daily News* renamed the area "The Jungle."

It is a place of two-bedroom, one-bath row houses. Never grand, though once well kept, most of these houses have been condemned as unsafe, many are abandoned. The houses and sidewalks are covered with graffiti; trash is everywhere. At the end of each block, where there were once small grocery or candy stores, now stand a variety of establishments—a Pentecostal church, a crackhouse, an all-purpose store that cashes checks. Each has bars across its windows and either a steel door or a security gate.

Within the immediate neighborhood are two schools, an elementary school and a junior high. To enter students must pass through metal detectors. While there is considerable bullying in the elementary school, compared to the neighborhood it is a safe haven. These children have been exposed to violence early on. A recent survey found 30% of current 1st and 2nd graders (Mattaini, Twyman, Chin, & Lee, 1996) have witnessed shootings; 90% of those in grades 1 to 6 have seen violent acts and in 70% of those episodes a weapon was present. While attending the junior high school is not exactly dangerous, it is not threat-free either. Organized gangs abound (Lober & Hay, 1997). Being adolescents, conflict over gender relations is omnipresent and potentially lethal (Lober & Hay, 1997). The academic performance of students at both schools is dismal. Successful students are among the most bullied, scorned, and envied. By the time many of the poorer students reach the 9th grade, the transition to high school, they no longer find reason to attend and leave for the excitement of the streets. Better that than clogging up the halls or causing problems is the dominant administrative attitude about these departures. Expectedly, teachers "turn over" at a high rate. Many leave the profession. Others stick it out until they can arrange transfers to other schools where they erroneously presume that instead of keeping order they will be able to teach.

The neighborhood is almost exclusively African American. There is little legitimate, on-the-books work in it. There is a considerable amount of hustling going on, however; women, drugs, guns, and theft-recycled-goods are for sale and readily available. The Jungle is bounded by a number of transitional neighborhoods. Those interested in "chump change" find low-skill work there or elsewhere in the city, low skill as few have marketable skills because of educational and other deficiencies. Women are more employable than men since they appear less threatening and better socialized. At one time, city officials saw the civil service as the employer of last resort, so a larger number of residents than might be expected work in city agencies.

For those living in the Jungle, direct intimate, human contact with those outside its perimeter is limited. The further outside of it, whether measured in physical or socioeconomic distance, the less likely one is to interact with them in other than formal ways. This same relationship, of course, holds for all Americans, but for others, even if they are not Caucasian, the borders are more permeable. Although their personal contact with others outside of it is limited, the zone's residents have easy access to mass culture. Everyone there seems tuned in. I-Pods, cell phones, CD players seem hard-wired into heads. Through these transmitters stream ceaseless depictions of violent acts (e.g., American Psychological Association, 1993) and themes of misogyny, alienation, and injustice. The dominant messages conveyed are "trust no one," "might makes right," and "get it when you can." If conscious majoritarian mores be considered the standard, the ethos of the Jungle is antimonian. A devotee of Jung might point out that those in the zone have been infected in various degrees by the Shadow projected by the dominant culture (e.g., Jung, 1971). This is not to say that those within the Jungle do not experience a "positive" culture. Most do, especially its adolescents and young men. For want of a better descriptor it may be called a culture of Honor (Cohen & Vandello, 1998; Weber, 1999). Here the playwright quotes Weber (1999)

> This honor—in the sense that lasted for many centuries—is power, and the glory that comes from power, and the *fama* . . . that reflects a reputation for power. Infamy is the loss of public esteem that goes with losing power and reputation; and with infamy goes ignominy, literally losing your name . . . (p. 81)

> Status . . . 'is achieved in part through the deference and appreciation others show a person about his fighting skills.'. . . '[T]he hard invincible young black male who has no chinks in his armor, who is always ready for battle, grandly refusing most forms of emotional vulnerability, is an asset in today's urban zones.' The world of honor is comparative, hence competitive, as each champion, whether Achilles, Roland or a gang member in the hood, strives to outdo the others. Gang history, like ancient and less ancient history, is a litany of competitive aggression that challenges, confirms, or alters authority and status . . . (p. 83)

The play's *dramatis personae* include Tyronne, the protagonist, Jannissa, Jesse, Tyronne's current woman, and Samson. Only the first two are sketched in any detail. All we know of Samson is that he is in his early twenties and a group leader of the York Avenue Posse. Tyronne is about eighteen. An almost ebony color, he is very well muscled. He stands about 6 feet 3 inches and weighs about 190 pounds. He has cold eyes, a perpetual scowl, and saunters with a rhythmic swagger conveying an air of spring-taut menace. He seems always in entourage. Almost all accompanying him are late adolescent males with perhaps one or two females and one or two preteens in orbit. None of the males match his physique. Closest to him always seems to be Jesse. Jesse, about eighteen, is lighter in hue and has a fluent, quick rap. He seems to steer the group, but subtly; he clearly defers to Tyronne.

Tyronne's biological mother was 16 when she had him. She had no prenatal care. At birth Tyronne was diagnosed as having "Infant Alcohol Syndrome." Most likely his mother was getting high or down using a variety of chemical substances at the time. His father could have been any of a number of males with whom she regularly partied (Rohner, 1975). For the first few years of his life, Tyronne lived with her (she left her mother's house when her pregnancy began to show) and the male who was seeing her and could tolerate his irritability. Discipline was erratic and brutal (e.g., Evans, Gonnella, Marcynyszyn, Gentile, & Salpekar, 2005; Patterson, 1997; Reiss, 2005) as it had been for his mother. By five, he was a terror—calm one moment, explosive the next, aggressive, seemingly without provocation (Mark & Ervin, 1970). When he entered school, he was placed in special education, his tested IQ score was 60. Shortly thereafter, he was removed from his mother's custody. He spent the next 10 years in one foster home placement or another. By 16, his behavior, both at school and in foster care, was easier to ignore than deal with. He dropped out of both.

The Newkirk Crew recruited him at 12 because of his fearless rages that could at times be directed against gang enemies. He became a feared enforcer at 17. He began holding drugs for dealers rather late, at 14, because higher-ups did not trust his judgment earlier. He enjoyed getting wired.

He began carrying a box cutter in 2nd grade, "to defend myself," and a gun in 8th grade. Picked up a number of times by the police—he was never caught armed—he gained considerable experience with the juvenile justice system. Never convicted of a crime, he did spend a number of days behind bars, but never for a prolonged period. Although he enjoyed the streets more, he was not intimidated by jail. No one or nothing frightens him.

His general attitude toward others, especially women, is one of superiority; women are nothing but 'hos. He trusts no one and is sensitive to any slight. Because he is slow to understand what is happening in complex situations, he looks to others, especially Jesse, to guide his actions. In spite of his strength, he feels vulnerable; he senses he is living in harm's way. At times he feels helpless. Helplessness is intolerable. His antidote is ensuring the cooperation of others by threat and action (Henrich, 2006).

Jannissa at 15 is physically mature and a "knockout." She lives with three younger sisters, her mother, and grandmother. Her father left her mother for another when Jannissa was 12. He lives out of state and aside from sending a card or a present at what seem like random intervals, neither his children nor his wife have contact with him. Jannissa's grandfather died last year. His passing was very painful to her as they were quite close.

Jannissa's mother works for the postal service and is exhausted when she arrives home, especially now. Her mother, who oversaw the house and the children, seems to have grown old overnight. Perhaps it is her "lupus" or diabetes that has sapped her strength, perhaps it is depression, perhaps a bit of everything. In any event, her burdens have doubled, and she has become much more severe in her attitude toward the children and much more irritable.

As the eldest, Jannissa has assumed more responsibility for caring for her sisters. Dealing with them is no fun. While they have been taught to be respectful to adults, they are constantly fussing among themselves. Their parents had trained them to stand up for themselves with peers, physically, if necessary, and they do not automatically defer to Jannissa (Saarnii, 1990). Making matters worse is 10th grade. Jannissa, usually an above-average student, is not adjusting well to her first year in high school. Because it draws from a wider area than the zone, it is filled with new faces and classes are more difficult. Never good at math, she finds geometry a horror. Making things worse, she has less time to study and less help with her classwork with both her mother and grandmother preoccupied. In all, she feels as if she had fallen into a pit. Her peers date and party. She is Cinderella.

THE PLAY IS IN THREE ACTS

Act I: The Seduction

Scene 1 is set in the school's lunchroom. Jannissa is noticed by Jesse. He moves on her. She likes attention. He is good looking, older, and respected by the other students, or perhaps he is feared. He invites her to party. She says she cannot. He tells her he will come for her when everyone in the house is asleep as the party won't jump until after midnight.

Scene 2 is set in the gang's clubhouse. Jesse and Jannissa arrive. Music is blaring. People are dancing. Her arrival is noted. She relishes the attention. People drink and smoke reefer. A few do lines. The action is intense and contagious. Tyronne notices the new girl. She joins the scene, Jesse at her side. Shortly, she is led into a side room and repeatedly raped by Tyronne. Jesse takes her to her home sobbing. He warns her not to betray the gang and turns her loose.

Scene 3 takes place at Jannissa's house. Her mother awakens and comes downstairs. She takes in Jannissa and berates her. She calls her a bitch in heat and a whore and orders her out of her sight. Jannissa, already wounded, feels destroyed. Zombie-like she goes to her room.

Act II: Compliance

Scene 1 is played between Tyronne and Jesse at the clubhouse. Tyronne demands primary use of Jannissa from Jesse. Jesse then reluctantly agrees.

Scene 2 is at a party in the clubhouse. Jesse tells Jannissa that she is now Tyronne's. She sobs. Tyronne slaps her. She sobs; he slaps her repeatedly.

Scene 3 opens on a local street. Jannissa is now part of Tyronne's entourage. When the sauntering entourage encounters a member of the crew, there is much hand slapping and "high fiving." Jannissa does not participate in the ritual. During the stroll, the group encounters Jannissa's mother and sister who ignore the entourage.

Act III: Death

Scene 1 is set in Tyronne's apartment. It is late afternoon. Tyronne arrives with a woman. He asks Jannissa what she made for dinner. Jannissa does not reply quickly enough; he slaps her. Tyronne and the other woman leave for a restaurant. When they return Jannissa is gone. Tyronne is silently furious. He and the woman party.

Scene 2, the next day. Jesse comes to Tyronne's apartment to discuss the week's receipts. Tyronne is irritable. He is hungover. Casually, Jesse asks where Jannissa is. Tyronne indicates no interest. Jesse then tells him he just saw her with Samson. Tyronne glares and then they all leave for the street.

Scene 3 opens in a restaurant. Jannissa is sipping coffee at the counter. Next to her is Samson. She pays him no mind. He talks softly to her at first, then becomes angry. She leaves; he follows. Just then Tyronne, the woman, and Jesse arrive. This is too much for Jannissa. She screams at the other woman, then at Tyronne. Tyronne smilingly slaps her. The other woman taunts Jannissa. Samson tells Tyronne to take his trash off the street. Shots ring out. Tyronne and Jesse run.

If well done, a sense of propulsive inevitability attends a play. For those absorbed in it, players and audience alike, all happens as it must. But, if there is any lesson the social sciences and humanities can teach, it is that the perception that events must necessarily happen as they have is illusion. The only inevitability is people's absorption into the plot line and either their reflexive or practiced adherence to it. While plays are completed in their performance, humans retain what Baktin (Morson, 1991, p. 208) terms *unfinalizability*—"their capacity to outgrow, as it were from within and to render *untrue* any externalizing and finalizing definition of them"—until they utter their last word or author their last action. Until then, the play, our roles, and ourselves can be rewritten.

To believe otherwise is to be in what Sartre (1988) calls "bad faith." For it is indeed obvious that interventions in or alterations to the play by any or all of the following—a playwright, director, actors, characters, stagehands, audience, or some other agent or agency—before or during the play's run could alter its outcome. What if Tyronne's nervous system was not compromised by his mother's drug use and he was not so physiologically prone to explosive action? In that circumstance would Jannissa have been shot? What if Jannissa's mother had not thrown her out of the house? What if she did and Jannissa found a city- or privately run safe haven? What if guns were not available? What if Tyronne lived in the suburbs and his parents were well off? What if there was a job with a living wage available to Tyronne? What if the United States did not glorify violence but instead reinforced nonviolent conflict resolution? What if no one came to the play; would the playwright craft another similar work? What if Tyronne decided he did not wish to harm Jannissa? The "what ifs," of course, could continue forever. This play's outcome, it should be obvious, was only inevitable because it occurred. Alternative conclusions, indeed alternative plays, could, and indeed ought, have been written, plays of higher moral and aesthetic taste, certainly plays with less violent themes.

One last observation. There is little doubt that dramatism provides a useful master metaphor for analyzing violent acts. If one is to use it successfully one must take care that the play perceived in the mind is indeed the play performed. Before concluding that it is, the observer ought to bring all the truth-seeking processes available to the critical mind to bear on the issue and critically weigh the generated evidence, especially that which makes the plot implausible. To paraphrase McHugh (1995), the narrative power of a play can blind everyone to other explanations of what is indeed occurring. Those who try to work without the play forgo a vital way of appreciating the ways of violence. If, however, the plays conceived to account for acts of violence are written too hurriedly and with excess license they will hinder the development of effective steps to reduce their prevalence and diminish their sequelae.

REFERENCES

American Psychological Association. (1993). *Violence and youth: Psychological response*. Washington, DC: Author.

BOCK, P.K. (1994). *Psychological anthropology* (pp. 61–96). Westport, CT: Praeger.

BURKE, K. (1966). *Language as symbolic action*. Berkeley: University of California Press.

BURKE, K. (1969a). *A grammar of motives*. Berkeley: University of California Press.

BURKE, K. (1969b). *A rhetoric of motives*. Berkeley: University of California Press.

BURKE, K. (1966). *Language as symbolic action*. Berkeley: University of California Press.

CASSON, R.W. (1994). Cognitive anthropology. In P.K. Bock (Ed.) *Psychological anthropology* (pp. 61–96). Westport, CT: Praeger.

COHEN, D., & VANDELLO, J. (1998). Meanings of violence. *Journal of Legal Studies 27*, 567–584.

DAWKINS, R. (1976). *The selfish gene*. Oxford: Oxford University Press.

DIESING, P. (1991). *How does social science work?* Pittsburgh, PA: University of Pittsburgh Press.

EVANS, G. W., GONNELLA, C., MARCYNYSZYN, L. A., GENTILE, L., & SALPEKAR, N. (2005). The role of chaos in poverty and children's socioemotional adjustment. *Psychological Science, 16*, 560–565.

GEERTZ, C. (1973). *The interpretation of cultures*. New York: Basic Books.

GOFFMAN, E. (1959). *The presentation of self in everyday life*. Garden City, NY: Doubleday.

HARE, P.A., & BLUMBERG, H.H. (1988). *Dramaturgical analysis of social interaction*. New York: Praeger.

HENRICH, J. (2006). Cooperation, punishment, and the evolution of human institutions. *Science, 312*, 60–61.

JUNG, C.G. (1971). Psychological types. In (R.F.C. HallRev. trans.) *The collected works of C. G. Jung* (Vol. 6). Princeton, NJ: Princeton University Press. (Original work published 1921)

KELLY, G.A. (1955). *The psychology of personal constructs*. New York: Norton.
KRUG, E.G., DAHLBERG, L.L., MERCY, J.A., ZWI, A.B. & LOZANO, R. (2002). *World report on violence and health*. Geneva: World Health Organization.
KUHN, T. (1970 [orig. publ. 1962]). *The structure of scientific revolutions*. 2nd ed. Encyclopedia of Unified Science, Vol. 2., No. 2. Chicago: University of Chicago Press.
LOBER, R. & HAY, D. (1997). Key issues in the development of aggression and violence from childhood to early adulthood. *Annual Review of Psychology*, *48*, 371–410.
MARK, V.H. & ERVIN, F.R. (1970) *Violence and the brain*. New York: Harper & Row.
MCHUGH, P.R. (1995). What's the story? *American Scholar*, *64*, 191–203.
PATTERSON, G.R. & YOERGER, K. (1997). A developmental model for late onset delinquency. In D.W. Osgood (Ed.), *Motivation and delinquency* (pp. 119–177). Nebraska Symposium on Motivation. Lincoln, NE: University of Nebraska Press.
REISS, D. (2005). The interplay between genotypes and family relationships: reframing concepts of development and prevention. *Current Directions in Psychological Science*, *14*, 139–143.
ROHNER, R. (1975). *They love me, they love me not*. New Haven, CT: HRAF Press.
SAARNI, C. (1990). Emotional competence: How emotions and relationships become integrated. In R.A. Thompson (Ed.), *Socioemotional development* (pp. 115–182). Lincoln, NE: University of Nebraska Press.
SARTRE, J.P. (1988). *Essays in existentialism*. New York: Citadel.
WEBER, E. (1999). The ups and downs of honor. *American Scholar*, *68*, 79–91.
WHITE, L.A. (1959). *The evolution of culture*. W. Baskin (Ed.). New York: McGraw Hill.

Sexual Aggression toward Women

Reducing the Prevalence

GWENDOLYN L. GERBER AND LINDSAY CHERNESKI

John Jay College of Criminal Justice, The City University of New York, New York, USA

ABSTRACT: Date rape or acquaintance rape is far more common than rape by strangers and can lead to serious health and adjustment problems for girls and women. Research has found women and men to be similar in many of their views about sexual assault. However, studies on attribution of blame have highlighted differences in the ways in which men and women attribute blame in sexual assault. Men attribute less blame to perpetrators of sexual assault than do women, regardless of whether the perpetrator is female or male. This suggests that men identify with the power associated with the role of perpetrator. Ways of reducing the prevalence of men's sexual aggressiveness toward women are addressed.

KEYWORDS: rape; date rape; violence; health; women; male privilege; power

INTRODUCTION

The sexual assault of women by men in dating situations is a significant problem in our society. A common belief is that most rapists are strangers (Muehlenhard & Kimes, 1999). However, it has become increasingly clear that acquaintance rape is far more common than rape by strangers. Date rape or acquaintance rape is defined as "unlawful sexual intercourse accomplished by force or fear with a person known to the victim who is not related by blood or marriage" (Wallace, 1999).

Statistics have shown that 50% to 88% of rape victims know their perpetrators (Rabkin, 1979; Russell, 1984). Further, research indicates that as many as 15% to 30% of women will experience date rape at some point in their lives (White & Kowalski, 1998). These estimates may be low because many women who have been victimized fail to report rapes and are unwilling to indicate on self-report measures that they have been a victim of sexual assault (Koss, 1992).

Address for correspondence: Gwendolyn L. Gerber, Psychology Department, John Jay College of Criminal Justice, The City University of New York, 445 W. 59th St., New York, New York 10019 USA. Voice: 212-673-4512; fax: 212-237-8742.
 e-mail: ggerber@jjay.cuny.edu

This is an especially serious problem within the United States because it has the highest overall rate of rape of any industrialized country (Allison & Wrightsman, 1993). In addition, the United States has a high rate of acquaintance rape in which the victim and perpetrator are acquainted with one another. One study (Koss & Oros, 1982) found that 20% to 30% of college students had engaged in, or been the victim of, sexual coercion. Another study, this time with college males, found that 28% of them had admitted to having engaged in sexual coercion (Rapaport & Burkhart, 1984). Further, approximately one-third of college males reported that there was some likelihood that they would rape a woman if it were guaranteed that they would not be caught.

In a large study of students from colleges and universities across the country, 12% of the women reported that they had been victims of rape or attempted rape; an additional 15% had experienced assault that met the legal definition of rape, even though they did not label their experience as rape (Koss, Gidcycz, & Wisniewski, 1987). Other research confirms these high rates of rape among college women, particularly those involving acquaintance rape (Calhoun, Bernat, Clum, & Frame, 1997; DeKeseredy, 1997). Koss, Dinero, Seibel, and Cox (1988) found that 15% of female college students reported that they had been raped, and of these women, 85% had been victimized by an acquaintance. The high rates of date rape found among college students extend to students attending high school and may be related to a male sense of entitlement. A survey of high school students found that 43% of boys and 32% of girls thought it was acceptable for a boy to force sex upon a girl if they had been dating for a long period of time (Muehlenhard & Linton, 1987). These results seemed to indicate that males felt they had a greater sense of entitlement with respect to having sex within the context of a long-term relationship, for boys rated date rape as more acceptable than did girls (Muehlenhard & Linton, 1987). Other research has supported the notion of a sense of male entitlement, for male raters perceived aggressors as having more of a right to have sex with the victim when they were involved in a love relationship (Sheldon-Keller, Lloyd-McGarvey, West & Canterbury, 1994).

Women who have been sexually assaulted generally encounter more severe health and adjustment problems following the experience (McCahill, Meyer, & Fischman, 1979). When compared to nonvictimized women, victims of rape generally perceive themselves as less healthy and are twice as likely to formally complain of physical health problems (Koss, 1993). Women who have been raped or are victims of attempted rape also manifest higher levels of suicidal thoughts, attempted suicide, and "nervous breakdowns" compared to victims of other types of criminal assault (Kilpatrick *et al.*, 1985). Victims of acquaintance rape, in particular, suffer from heightened feelings of self-blame and betrayal, which further impede their recovery (Browne, 1991; Roth, Wayland, & Woolsey, 1990). When examining the long-term effects of rape, Foa (1998) found that 32% of rape victims met the criteria for posttraumatic stress disorder (PTSD) following the incident; furthermore, at a year follow-up, 12% of those women still exhibited symptoms of PTSD.

As evident from these findings, the sexual assault of women by men is a serious problem with both immediate and long-term effects on the victim. To help ameliorate this problem, it is crucial that we gain greater understanding of the factors that contribute to the perception by some men that sexual assault can be acceptable. Such understanding can enable us to develop workshops and other modalities that will be effective in reducing the prevalence of sexual assault, particularly on college campuses.

Many of the myths about rape help to perpetuate this type of violence against women. Rape myths are defined as "attitudes and beliefs that are generally false but are widely and persistently held, and that serve to deny and justify male sexual aggression against women" (Lonsway & Fitzgerald, 1994); for example, the myth that all women want to be raped, that no woman can be raped if she does not want it, and that when a woman says, "No," she really means, "Yes" (Yoder, 2003). Rape myths are more accepted by men than women, individuals who adhere to traditional gender role attitudes, and those who tolerate violence against women (Anderson, Cooper, & Okaura, 1997; Caron & Carter, 1997). Rape myths are also more prevalent among older individuals and those who are less educated (Anderson, Beattie, & Spencer, 2001). However, research indicates that, for both males and females, the most potent predictor of rape myth acceptance is adherence to traditional gender roles and stereotypes (Caron & Carter, 1997).

Power and control issues seem to play a critical role in the crime of rape. Men often have a tendency to misperceive women's behavior as being seductive (Abbey, McAuslan, & Ross, 1998). Sexually aggressive men, in particular, are more likely to misinterpret neutral behavior as sexual (Anderson, Simpson-Taylor, & Herman, 2002). When such misperceptions occur, these men often respond that they have been "led on" by the woman. Placing the responsibility for their behavior on the woman serves as a defense for their sexual aggression because some people believe that leading a man on can justify rape (Goodchilds & Zellman, 1984).

Power issues also play a role in dating relationships. One reason date rape may be so prevalent among college students is because of the culture's dating practices in which men are given the more powerful position in relation to women (White *et al.*, 1998). According to (Lloyd 1991), dating for males is all about "staying in control," while dating for females is about "dependence on the relationship." Research has suggested that when a male pays for the date, he is placed in a position of power and may feel more entitled to have forced sex with his date (Muehlenhard & Linton, 1987). Further, a survey of high school students revealed that 39% of boys and 12% of girls found it acceptable for a boy to force a girl to have sex if he spent a lot of money on her (Giarrusso, Johnson, Goodchilds, & Zellman, 1979). Many college students also believe that if a woman allows a man to pay for the entire date, not only is she interested in having sex, but it is also more acceptable for the man to force her to have sex (Muehlenhard, Friedman, & Thomas, 1985).

Other factors relating to victim blame have been identified in the literature. Research has shown that there is a relationship between the amount of victim blame and the level of force that occurred during the victimization. The more force that was described, the less the victim was blamed (Krulewtiz & Payne, 1978; Shotland & Goodstein, 1983; Tieger, 1981). The degree of resistance exercised by the victim also has an impact on blame. The victim is blamed more when she resists her attacker later in the incident, rather than sooner, because it is believed that later resistance would indicate that she was initially consenting to the encounter (Kopper, 1996). Victims of rape are also believed to be more responsible for the attack when they have had prior sexual experiences; this belief reflects stereotypes about promiscuous women who "ask to be raped" (L'Armand & Pepitone, 1982). Finally, research has found that victims of acquaintance rape are blamed more than victims of stranger rape (Bell, Kuriloff, & Lottes, 1994).

Alcohol consumption within a date rape situation is associated with more blame placed on the victim. Muehlenhard and Linton (1987) point out that alcohol is a major risk factor in dating situations because it lowers men's inhibitions against sexual violence, making it more likely they will think that date rape is acceptable. In surveys of incarcerated rapists and college students, both believed that if the rapist was intoxicated, he was less responsible. On the other hand, if the woman was intoxicated, she was regarded by both groups as *more* responsible for the rape (Muehlenhard & Linton, 1987). Research also indicates that some men believe that because a woman is imbibing alcohol, she is more interested in having sex, and both female and male college students assume that when a woman and man are seen drinking alcohol together, they will later engage in consensual sex (Abbey, Philip, Zawacki, & Saen, 2003).

There is some evidence that viewing pornography can have an effect on the perception of a rape. Scott (2000) found that after women viewed coercive sex scenes from a movie, they were more likely to endorse rape myths. Further, repeated viewing of pornography by men led to an increase in acceptance of rape myths, desensitization toward violence against women, and, most importantly, an increased motivation to act aggressively toward women (Scott, 2000).

Some evidence indicates that women as well as men focus on the victim's behavior instead of the perpetrator's behavior in assessing blame. Female college students viewed a sexual harassment scenario depicting a professor trying to kiss his female student (Fine, Genovese, Ingersoll, Macpherson, & Roberts, 1996). A series of 84 questions were then asked about the woman/victim and also about the male/harasser. Seventy-five percent of the responses directed toward the woman/victim focused on her behavior, whereas only 47% of the responses directed toward the male/harasser focused on his behavior. The researchers suggested that subjects placed more blame on the victim because they focused on her behavior and not on the deviant behavior of the harasser.

Furthermore, subjects seemed to be looking for some outside explanation that would explain the harasser's behavior (Fine *et al.*, 1996).

Males and females are also similar in the number of rape myths they endorse (Buddie & Miller, 2001). When examining the personal beliefs about rape victims among college students, both males and females listed the same number of rape myths. Interestingly, when asked to list cultural stereotypes about rape victims, the females in the study listed more rape myths than did males, indicating that females were more aware of the rape myths that are held by society at large (Buddie & Miller, 2001).

Although research has found women and men to be similar in many of their views about sexual assault, studies on attribution of blame have highlighted differences in the ways in which women and men attribute blame in sexual assault. Men generally blame the perpetrators of sexual assault less than do women; they also blame the victims more (Bell *et al.*, 1994; Calhoun, Selby, & Waring, 1976; Deitz, Littman, & Bentley, 1984). Research has found that the more males identified with the rapist, the more they blamed the victim (Bell *et al.*, 1994). These findings are consistent with Shaver's (1970) defensive attribution theory, which postulates that individuals tend to blame victims more when they see themselves as dissimilar to the victim.

This raises the question of why men place less blame on perpetrators as compared to women. One explanation for this sex difference involves the "just world" hypothesis. Individuals who believe in a just world hold that the world is a fair place and whatever rewards or consequences befall us are well deserved. This view helps individuals feel in control of their environment because they believe that "bad" things only happen to "bad" people (Anderson *et al.*, 2001).

Most commonly, research on attributions of blame has used a scenario with a male rapist and a female victim. According to Shaver's (1970) defensive attribution theory, people are more likely to blame those whose personal characteristics are dissimilar to their own. This serves a self-protective function because people can reassure themselves that they are not responsible for negative events. According to the theory, when attributing blame in a rape situation, men see themselves as being more similar to the male rapist, because he is male, than to the female victim. By contrast, women, who identify with the female victim, are hesitant to stigmatize themselves by holding the victim responsible. Consequently, they are less likely to blame the victim compared with men; they also attribute more responsibility to the rapist.

Thus, when individuals attribute blame in rape situation, it often has been assumed that similarity is based on gender. Men identify more with the male rapist because he is male, and women identify more with the female victim because she is female. The problem with this assumption is that in rape situations, gender is confounded with the roles of perpetrator and victim because the rapist is generally male and the victim is generally female.

A study conducted by Gerber, Cronin, and Steigman (2004) addressed the problem of the confounding of gender with the roles of perpetrator and victim.

This study raised serious questions about the assumption that men are more lenient toward the perpetrators of sexual assault because they identify more with other males. The Gerber *et al.* (2004) study differed from most research in this area, which generally has used a rape scenario involving a male perpetrator and a female victim. Instead, this study used different sexual assault scenarios, which varied with the gender of both the perpetrator of the assault and the victim. All possible gender combinations were included in the study: a male perpetrator with a female victim and a female perpetrator with a male victim, in addition to scenarios in which the perpetrator and victim were either both males or both females.

As in most of this research, college students read a description of a sexual assault that took place between two college students who were acquainted with one another. Subjects then rated the extent to which they blamed the perpetrator and the extent to which they blamed the victim. Results showed that men attributed less blame than women to the perpetrators of the sexual assault, regardless of whether the perpetrator was female or male. Thus, men's identification appeared to be with the role of perpetrator, which is an aggressive and powerful role, even when the perpetrator was female.

These results challenge the assumption that men attribute less blame to perpetrators because they identify with another male. Instead, men appear to identify with some aspect of the role of perpetrator of a sexual assault. This explanation is consistent with society's condoning of sexual aggression by men and the finding that men are almost always the perpetrators of rape. By the same token, women, who are most frequently the targets of sexual assault, would identify more with the role of the victim, thereby placing more blame on the perpetrator.

However, the question of why men identify more with the role of sexual aggressor cannot be explained by the frequency with which men are perpetrators, because most men are not perpetrators, or potential perpetrators, of sexual assault. Instead, men's identification with the role of sexual aggressor may rest on a more fundamental level, namely, issues of male and female identity. When examining gender and power in a larger context, societal beliefs equate masculinity with power and dominance (Stewart & McDermott, 2004). By contrast, femininity is linked with powerlessness and, because of this, the role of victim is more often associated with women (White, Donat, & Bondurant, 2001).

Beliefs about gender are taught, directly or indirectly, to children of both sexes at a very early age. For instance, aggression is tolerated among boys, but not among girls. Boys come to learn that aggression is a means of power over others and most importantly over women, while girls learn it is appropriate for them to behave in a more submissive manner (White *et al.*, 1998). These stereotypes continue to place women in the low power position and at a heightened risk for sexual victimization.

The personality traits that define male identity, like assertiveness, are called the *instrumental* traits (Spence, Helmreich, & Holahan, 1979), and previous research has shown that these traits are associated with a role that is powerful, not with gender (Gerber, 1988, 1991). Powerful individuals of both sexes are perceived as having many socially desirable instrumental traits. By the same token, the personality traits that define female identity such as warmth and accommodation toward others are called the *expressive* traits and result from roles that reflect absence of power. Persons of both sexes who have little power in a relationship are perceived as having many of these socially desirable expressive traits.

Research on *physical* violence, which is a form of exercising power, suggests that perpetrators of sexual assault may not be perceived solely in negative ways (Gerber, 1991). Instead, they may be perceived as having the socially desirable instrumental personality traits, which are associated with power. A study of physical violence in hypothetical marital relationships (Gerber, 1991) found that, regardless of sex, the more powerful physically abusive person was perceived as having more traditionally masculine-typed instrumental and dominating personality traits; the less powerful victim was ascribed with more traditionally feminine-typed expressive and submissive traits. This indicates that violent persons of both sexes were perceived as having many socially desirable instrumental or assertive personality traits in addition to dictatorial and egotistical traits, which are viewed as *undesirable*. Thus, the personality traits that are associated with power, even coercive, violent power, include the socially *desirable* traits that are also linked with masculinity.

To be considered masculine, society forces men to reject everything feminine; if men fail to do so, they risk being criticized for their lack of masculinity (Kahn, 1984). Thus, when given a choice between identifying with the role of perpetrator or the role of victim, men likely would identify with the more powerful role even when the perpetrator is female because the personality traits associated with this role are ones that are also linked with masculinity. The unacceptable alternative for men would be to identify with the powerless role of victim, which is associated with personality traits that are stereotyped as feminine. Because the traits associated with a powerless victim role are those that also are used to define femininity, women would be more likely to feel similar to the victim of a sexual assault, even when the victim is male.

Many college males struggle with issues relating to their identity as men. In some cases, they find that acts of aggression, including sexual aggression, can give them a sense that they possess the high-status, more powerful, instrumental, or assertive personality traits that our culture uses to define male identity. If so, then one way of making sexual assault less acceptable would be to develop methods for changing the stereotypes about perpetrators of sexual assault to bring them more in accordance with reality. For, in actuality, perpetrators of sexual assault often feel they are inadequate as men and have few socially desirable instrumental personality traits (Kaplan, 1999).

Most important, the tendency of men to blame perpetrators less in comparison to women has implication for the leniency with which perpetrators of sexual assault are perceived and treated, particularly in settings that are dominated by men. In male-dominated settings such as sports, perpetrators of sexual assault frequently can receive lenient treatment. For example, in one case a sports commentator was fired and then reinstated by a major television network after being convicted of a sexual assault in which he bit a woman hard enough to break the skin (Kaplan, 1999). The sports commentator was Marv Albert and when he was reinstated, the *New York Post* celebrated the occasion with a story that was headlined, "He scores! Marv gets return gig with NBC"(Kaplan, 1999). The question that arises is how leniently such perpetrators would be treated in settings comprised primarily of women.

The traditional male-female relationship in our society is one in which the man has more power than the woman and, as part of this role, takes the initiative in sexual interactions. Encouraging the formation of more egalitarian relationship between women and men would help reduce this power differential and mitigate the problem of rape (Caron & Carter, 1997; Gerber, 1989). Other efforts to reduce the prevalence of rape need to address the root problem involving the tolerance of sexual aggressiveness by men. More efforts need to be directed toward young males in our society with an emphasis on rape not being a "viable sexual outlet" (Caron & Carter, 1997).

Increased education about rape is needed, starting at the junior high school level. Programs should emphasize that men can control their sexual urges and that under no circumstances are women to be blamed for rape (Matlin, 2004). Since women college students are at increased risk to experience sexual assault, it is recommended that mandatory programs be established for *all* freshman college students, both female and male (Fouts & Knapp, 2001). In addition, men's groups such as fraternities and athletic teams, should become involved with rape prevention programs on college campuses to help change attitudes and behaviors that contribute to the prevalence of sexual assault (Binder, 2001).

Finally, societal attitudes that glorify aggression, including sexual aggression toward women, need to be changed. This can only be done by examining and questioning the cultural attitudes and beliefs that underlie the sexual assault of women by men, and disseminating these findings, thereby enabling people to rethink their assumptions about the problem of sexual assault and sexual aggressiveness by men.

ACKNOWLEDGMENTS

The preparation of this paper was supported in part by a grant from the City University of New York PSC-CUNY Research Award Program.

REFERENCES

ABBEY, A., P. MCAUSLAN & L.T. ROSS. 1998. Sexual assault perpetration by college men: the role of alcohol, misperception of sexual intent, and sexual beliefs and experiences. Journal of Social and Clinical Psychology *17*, 167–195.

ABBEY, A., B.O. PHILIP, T. ZAWACKI & C. SAEN. 2003. Alcohol's effects on perceptions of a potential date rape. Journal of Studies on Alcohol *64*, 669–677.

ALLISON, J.A. & L.S. WRIGHTSMAN. 1993. Rape: the misunderstood crime. Sage. Newbury Park, CA.

ANDERSON, I., G. BEATTIE & C. SPENCER. 2001. Can blaming victims of rape be logical? Attribution theory and discourse analytic perspectives. Human Relations *54*, 445–467.

ANDERSON, K.B., H. COOPER & I. OKAURA. 1997. Individual differences and attitudes toward rape: a meta-analytic review. Personality and Social Psychology Bulletin *23*, 295–315.

ANDERSON, V., D. SIMPSON-TAYLOR & D. HERMAN. 2002. Rules about rape. Unpublished manuscript, Indiana State University, Terre Haute.

BELL, S.T., P.J. KURILOFF & I. LOTTES. 1994. Understanding attributions of blame in stranger rape and date rape situations: an examination of gender, race, identification, and students' social perceptions of rape victims. Journal of Applied Social Psychology *24*, 1719–1734.

BINDER, R. 2001. Changing a culture: sexual assault prevention in the fraternity and sorority community. *In* Sexual Violence on Campus: Policies, Programs, and Perspectives. A.J. Ottens & K. Hotelling, Eds.: 120–140. Springer. New York.

BROWNE, A. 1991. The victim's experience: pathways to disclosure. Psychotherapy *28*, 150–156.

BUDDIE, A.M. & A.G. MILLER. 2001. Beyond rape myths: a more complex view of perceptions of rape victims. Sex Roles *45*, 139–160.

CALHOUN, K.S., J.S. BERNAT, G.A. CLUM & C.L. FRAME. 1997. Sexual coercion and attraction to sexual aggression in a community sample of young men. Journal of Interpersonal Violence *12*, 392–406.

CALHOUN, L.G., J.W. SELBY & L.J. WARRING. 1976. Social perception of the victim's causal role in rape: an exploratory examination of four factors. Human Relations *29*, 517–526.

CARON, S.L. & B.D. CARTER. 1997. The relationships among sex role orientation, egalitarianism, attitudes toward sexuality, and attitudes toward violence against women. Journal of Social Psychology *137*, 568–587.

DEKESEREDY, W.S. 1997. Measuring sexual abuse in Canadian university/college dating relationships: the contribution of a national representative survey. *In* Researching Sexual Violence Against Women: Methodological and Personal Perspectives. M.D. Schwartz, Ed.: 43–53. Sage. Thousand Oaks, CA.

DEITZ, S.R., M. LITTMAN & B.J. BENTLEY. 1984. Attribution of responsibility for rape: the influence of observer empathy, victim resistance, and victim attractiveness. Sex Roles *10*, 261–280.

FINE, M., GENOVESE, T., S. INGERSOLL, *et al.* 1996. Insisting on innocence: accounts of accountability by abusive men. *In* Myths about the Powerless. B. Lykes, A. Banuzizi, R. Liem & M. Morris, Eds.: 128–158. Temple University Press. Philadelphia.

FOA, E.B. 1998. Rape and posttraumatic stress disorder. *In* Behavioral Medicine and Women: A Comprehensive Handbook. K.A. Blechman & K.D. Brownwell, Eds.: 742–746. Guilford. New York.

FOUTS, B. & J. KNAPP. 2001. A sexual assault education and risk reduction workshop for college freshmen. *In* Sexual Violence on Campus: Policies, Programs, and Perspectives. A.J. Ottens & K. Hotelling, Eds.: 98–119. Springer. New York.

GERBER, G.L. 1988. Leadership roles and the gender stereotype traits. Sex Roles *18*, 649–668.

GERBER, G.L. 1989. Gender stereotypes: a new egalitarian couple emerges. *In* Gender in Transition: A New Frontier. J. Offerman-Zuckerberg, Ed., 47–66. Plenum Medical Book. New York.

GERBER, G.L. 1991. Gender stereotypes and power: perceptions of the roles in violent marriages. Sex Roles *24*, 439–458.

GERBER, G.L., J.M. CRONIN & H.J. STEIGMAN. 2004. Attributions of blame in sexual assault to perpetrators and victims of both genders. Journal of Applied Social Psychology *34*, 2149–2165.

GIARRUSSO, R., P. JOHNSON, J. GOODCHILDS & G. ZELLMAN. 1979. Adolescents' cues and signals: sex and assault. Acquaintance Rape and Adolescent Sexuality. Symposium conducted at the meeting of the Western Psychological Association. San Diego, CA.

GOODCHILDS, J.D. & G.L. ZELLMAN. 1984. Sexual signaling and sexual aggression in adolescent relationships. Pornography and Sexual Aggression. Academic Press. Orlando, FL. 233–243.

KAHN, A. 1984. The Power War: Male Response to Power Loss Under Equality. Psychology of Women Quarterly *8*, 234–247.

KAPLAN, D. 1999. He scores! Marv gets return gig with NBC. New York Post: 3, June 30.

KILPATRICK, D.G., C.L. BEST, I.J. VERONON, *et al.* 1985. Mental health correlates of criminal victimization: a random community survey. Journal of Consulting and Clinical Psychology *53*, 866–873.

KOPPER, B.A. 1996. Gender, gender identity, rape myth acceptance, and time of initial resistance on the perception of acquaintance rape blame and avoidability. Sex Roles *34*, 81–93.

KOSS, M.P. 1992. The under-detection of rape: methodological choices influence incidence estimates. Journal of Social Issues *48*, 61–75.

KOSS, M.P. 1993. Rape: scope, impact, interventions, and public policy responses. American Psychologist *48*, 1062–1069.

KOSS, M.P., T.E. DINERO, C.A. SEIBEL & S.L. COX. 1988. Stranger and acquaintance rape: are there differences in the victim's experience? Psychology of Women Quarterly *9*, 1–24.

KOSS, M.P., C.J. GIDCYCZ & N. WISNIEWSKI. 1987. The scope or rape: sexual aggression and victimization in a national sample of students in higher education. Journal of Consulting and Clinical Psychology *55*, 162–170.

KOSS, M.P. & C.J. OROS. 1982. Sexual Experiences Survey: a research instrument investigating sexual aggression and victimization. Journal of Consulting and Clinical Psychology *50*, 455–457.

KRULEWITZ, J.E. & E. J., PAYNE. 1978. Attributions about rape: effects of rapist force, observer sex and sex role attitudes. Journal of Applied Social Psychology *8*, 291–305.

L'ARMAND, K. & A. PEPITONE. 1982. Judgments of rape: a study of victim-rapist relationship and victim sexual history. Personality and Social Psychology Bulletin *8*, 134–139.

LONSWAY, K.A. & L.F. FITZGERALD. 1994. Rape myths: in review. Psychology of Women Quarterly *18*, 704–711.

LLOYD, S.A. 1991. The dark side of courtship. Family Relations *40*, 14–20.

MATLIN, M.W. 2004. The Psychology of Women. Thomson/Wadsworth. United States.

MCCAHILL, T.W., L.C. MEYER & A.M. FISCHMAN. 1979. The Aftermath of Rape. Lexington Books. Lexington, MA.

MUEHLENHARD, C.L., D.E. FRIEDMAN & C.M. THOMAS. 1985. Is date rape justifiable? The effects of dating activity, who initiated, who paid, and men's attitudes toward women. Psychology of Women Quarterly *9*, 297–309.

MUEHLENHARD, C.L. & L.A. KIMES. 1999. The social construction of violence: the case of sexual and domestic violence. Personality and Social Psychology Review *3*, 234–245.

MUEHLENHARD, C.L. & M.A. LINTON. 1987. Date rape and sexual aggression in dating situations: incidence and risk factors. Journal of Counseling Psychology *34*, 581–592.

RABKIN, J.G. 1979. The epidemiology of forcible rape. American Journal of Orthopsychiatry *8*, 634–647.

RAPAPORT, K. & B.R. BURKHART. 1984. Personality and attitudinal characteristics of sexually coercive college males. Journal of Abnormal Psychology *93*, 216–222.

ROTH, S., K. WAYLAND & M. WOOLSEY. 1990. Victimization history and victim-assailant relationship as factors in recovery from sexual assault. Journal of Traumatic Stress *3*, 169–180.

RUSSELL, D.E.H. 1984. Sexual Exploitations: Rape, Child Sexual Abuse and Workplace Harassment. Sage. Beverly Hills, CA.

SCOTT, B.A. 2000. Women and pornography: what we won't know can hurt us. *In* Lectures on the Psychology of Women. J.C. Chrisler, C. Golden & P.D. Rozee, Eds.: 271–287. McGraw-Hill. Boston.

SHAVER, K.G. 1970. Defensive attribution: effects of severity and relevance on the responsibility assigned for an accident. Journal of Personality and Social Psychology *14*, 101–113.

SHELDON-KELLER, A., E. MCGARVEY-LLOYD, M. WEST & R.J. CANTERBURY. 1994. Attachment and assessment of blame in date rape scenarios. Social Behavior and Personality *22*, 313–318.

SHOTLAND, R.L. & L. GOODSTEIN. 1983. Just because she doesn't want to doesn't mean its rape: an experimentally based causal model of the perception of rape in a dating situation. Social Psychology Quarterly *46*, 220–232.

SPENCE, J.T., R.L. HELMREICH & C.K. HOLAHAN. 1979. Negative and positive components of psychological masculinity and femininity and their relationships to self-reports of neurotic and acting out behaviors. Journal of Personality and Social Psychology *37*, 1673–1682.

STEWART, A.J. & C. MCDERMOTT. 2004. Gender in Psychology. Annual Review of Psychology *55*, 519–545.

TIEGER, T. 1981. Self-rated likelihood of raping and social perception of rape. Journal of Research in Personality *15*, 147–158.

WALLACE, H. 1999. Family violence: legal, medical, and social perspectives. Second edition. Allyn & Bacon. Boston.

WHITE, J.W., P.L.N. DONAT & B. BONDURANT. 2001. A developmental examination of violence against girls and women. *In* Handbook of the Psychology of Women and Gender. R.K. Unger, Ed.: 343–357. John Wiley & Sons. Hoboken, NJ.

WHITE, J.W. & R.M. KOWALSKI. 1998. Male violence toward women: an integrated perspective. *In* Human Aggression: Theories, Research, and Implications for Social Policy. R.G. Geen & E. Donnerstein, Eds.: 203–228. Academic Press. San Diego.

YODER, J.D. 2003. Woman and Gender: Transforming Psychology. Prentice Hall. Upper Saddle River, NJ.

Adolescent Girls Speak about Violence in Their Community

ROSEANNE L. FLORES

Hunter College of The City University of New York, New York, USA

ABSTRACT: Adolescent girls growing up in urban environments have been placed at increased risk for being exposed to violence in their communities. Yet few studies have examined their perceptions of the risk factors, violence, and the pressures they face on a daily basis. The present research describes two adolescent girls' perspectives concerning the challenges, fears, hopes, risks, and pressures they have experienced growing up in their community. The results have implications for violence intervention and prevention programs with adolescent girls living in urban environments.

KEYWORDS: adolescent; girls; violence; urban; intervention; Latina

ADOLESCENT GIRLS SPEAK ABOUT VIOLENCE IN THEIR COMMUNITY

Community violence hurts children and continues to be a problem in the United States. Many children living in urban communities witness family violence, drug trafficking, shootings, school violence, stabbings, beatings, and verbal abuse on a regular basis (Dulmus & Hilarski, 2002). Not only are children living in violent communities the victims of violence, but also at times they are the perpetrators of violence.

Although all children are victims of violence the literature has demonstrated that there is a tendency for adolescent girls to be exposed to more violent acts than boys, and to be susceptible to more intense emotional and physical reactions than boys (DiNapoli, 2003).

Moreover, it has been found that girls witness a large number of violent acts either in the media or in their day-to-day lives (DiNapoli, 2003).

Some of the consequences of exposure to violence are physical harm such as broken bones and fractures, physiological damage such as changes in the child's heart rate due to trauma (Buka, Stichick, Birdthistle, & Earls, 2001),

Address for correspondence: Roseanne L. Flores, Hunter College of The City University of New York, 695 Park Avenue, New York, NY 10021, USA. Voice: 212-650-3537; fax: 212-772-5628.
e-mail: rflores@hunter.cuny.edu

and in some cases death. Children and adolescents exposed to violence also may experience trauma and emotional harm such as depression, behavioral problems, fear and uncertainty, relationship problems, and in some cases posttraumatic stress disorder (Buka *et al.*, 2001; Baily & Whittle, 2004).

Prior to September 11, 2001, although children had been exposed to chronic levels of violence in their communities, children in the United States were not thought to suffer from posttraumatic stress disorder and the ravages of violence and war. More recently, however, as children have become exposed to more increasingly dangerous and persistent forms of violence in their communities, they have begun to use coping mechanisms that have altered their personalities and patterns of behavior symptomatic of posttraumatic stress disorder (Garbarino, 1999; Buka *et al.*, 2001).

Although violence is prevalent in some urban communities, it has been found that certain interventions can help to minimize the impact of the violence. For example, for children suffering from the psychological distress of violence such as posttraumatic stress disorder, counseling or therapy may be in order to teach children to cope with the uncertainty in their environment (Horowitz, Mckay, & Marshall, 2005). The support of family and friends has also been found to help children cope with violence in their communities (DiNapoli, 2003). Within the community itself children have benefited from support from adult mentors, after-school programs, and community outreach programs (Reese, Vera, Thompson, & Reyes, 2001). Children have also benefited from schools teaching strategies for conflict resolution and for functioning as a safe, secure, and stable haven (Howard, Kaljee, & Jackson, 2002).

In addition, having a strong social network can provide children with a way to insulate themselves against the violence in their communities. Garbarino (1999) argues that if children exposed to community violence are surrounded by a strong social network, they will be able to weather the challenges presented by the community better than their peers who do not have such a network. Thus it is necessary to know whether children and adolescents perceive that they have the availability of such a social network in their everyday lives.

While previous research has examined the effect of community violence on youth in general, very few studies to date have addressed adolescents' perspectives of violence in their communities (Reese *et al.*, 2001; Horowitz *et al.*, 2005) and their perceptions of a social network. Moreover, few studies have examined what girls specifically say about violence in their communities. If we are to construct adequate intervention and prevention programs that will empower adolescent girls and their families living in high violence urban communities to thrive and grow, then it is important to hear their voices.

The purpose of the present research was to expand upon the previous studies that examined the risk factors identified by adolescents living in urban environments. The goal of this research was to describe the risks, challenges, and pressures that adolescent girls face growing up in urban communities to create meaningful intervention and prevention programs.

METHOD

The research reported in this article was part of a larger study that examined urban adolescent girls' and boys' perceptions of violence in their community. This article will focus on the interviews with two Latina adolescent girls.

Participants

The participants for this study were two Latina adolescent girls ages 13 and 14 years enrolled in a public school in Spanish Harlem. Both girls were in the 8th grade at the time of the study.

Procedure

The girls were invited to participate in a study in which they would describe their experience of growing up as a girl in their community. Both girls received informed parental consent and gave verbal assent prior to their participation in the study. The interview lasted for approximately 45 min. The interview was audiotaped and transcribed verbatim.

Interview Questions

The interview questions are listed below:
Hopes, Dreams, Challenges, and Fears

(1) What do you like best about being a girl?
(2) What are the challenges you face as a girl living in the city?
(3) What do you hope to achieve as a young girl in middle school, high school, and after high school?
(4) What do you think it will take to achieve these goals?
(5) When I think about my family life, I feel I have most control over?
(6) When I think about my family life, I feel I have no control over?
(7) When I think about myself as a student, I feel I have most control over?
(8) When I think about myself as a student I have no control over?

Challenges in the Community

(1) Currently, the greatest pressure on girls my age is?
(2) When you hear the word "violence," what thoughts come to mind? Please describe.
(3) When I think about my personal safety, I feel I have the most control over...? Because...

(4) When I think about my personal safety, I feel I have **no control** over...?
Because...
(5) What do you do to stay safe?
(6) Could you describe a situation when someone your age felt pressured to use violence? Did they?
(7) When you hear the word "gang" what thoughts come to mind? Please describe.
(8) Do you know anyone in a gang?
(9) What are some reasons a girl joins a gang?

Support Systems

(1) If you are worried about something, whom do you talk to?
(2) What is it about this person/people that makes you feel comfortable talking to them when you are worried about something?
(3) If you could develop a program for girls your age what do you think the program could do to make you feel safer? What do you think *you* could do?

RESULTS AND DISCUSSION

The following section describes the girls' responses in each of the three categories: *Hopes, dreams, challenges, and fears; challenges in the communities; and support systems in the community.* The results are presented as answers to each of the interview questions. The names of the individuals presented in this article have been changed.

Hopes, Dreams, Challenges, and Fears

On Being a Girl

The girls expressed that what they liked best about being a girl was that they could get dressed up, do their nails, and get their hair done, while at the same time participate in sports.

Challenges Faced by Girls in New York City

When asked this question there was an initial silence and then one of the girls said "gangs, violence." When asked to explain herself a little more, she said "there are a lot of them!" The girls did not appear to be afraid of the gangs, but acknowledged that they existed. The girls were also asked about the benefits of living in New York City. Both stressed that they could do lots of things, they could have fun by going to the movies and parties, and for one girl the basketball court.

Achievement of Girls in Middle School and High School and Beyond

Both girls said they wanted to graduate and go to high school, with one of the girls expressing a desire to receive awards at her graduation. When asked about the type of award she wanted to receive she said "just one for sports." The other girl, a little more shy, after some prompting from her friend said she wanted to receive awards in English and Social Studies. After finishing high school both girls said they wanted to attend college. Upon completion of college, one of the girls said she wanted to join the Women's National Basketball Association (WNBA), and the other had hopes of going into the fashion industry, or becoming a cosmetologist, or backup singer in a music group.

Attaining Achievement of Goals

When asked how they would go about reaching their goals both said, "by working hard," doing well in school, studying hard, and "acting good in classes." When probed concerning what that meant, one girl stated by not having a bad attitude and by doing your homework and classroom projects.

Control over Aspects of Family Life

When asked about what they felt they had control over at home one of the girls said her chores, the other one said not getting in trouble. One of the girls volunteered that she had been adopted and felt she had no control over her mother.

On Being a Student

When asked what they had control over in school, both girls suggested they had control over their teachers, their own behavior, and doing their own homework. When asked about what they felt they had no control over in school they said the principal, what other people say, and the security guards. Both girls expressed fear of the security guards in their school and described a very violent event that had occurred between a student and a security guard that made them feel sad, frightened, and unsafe. The following is their perception of what occurred:

They want to bust a kids lip open. ... He was supposed to go to (EHT) the principal told him, but he said no and he just sat there so ummm Mrs. R. called security, and they came upstairs and started ... And then, yeah but then they were about to let him go, the security guard was about to leave, but then Mrs. R. called him back in. Mrs. R. was standing by the door, the security guard was standing next to Mark and he choked him and got him up out of his seat and took him by the sink. Then Mark was like let me go, let me go, then Mark took off his jacket because the guy was grabbing him by his jacket because he had his jacket on, and then he had his book bag under his jacket so he had ... (said something unclear), and the security guard took his jacket, he got out of his jacket. Then he went over to the corner of the other sink, and then the security guard had pushed him against the book shelf and Mark ran towards the window, and the security guard went over and started hitting him, and decked him in the lip and busted his lip open. Then Mark was trying to hit back because the security guard got him mad, and the security guard kept on hitting him, threw him into the table, the security guard threw Mark into the table. Mark might leave school now, I mean not leave school now, yeah he left.

After describing the above situation the girls were asked to describe how they felt about security, one girl stated rather sharply "Nothing!"

Challenges in the Community

Pressures Faced by Adolescent Girls

When asked about the pressures girls their age face, both girls said that some girls their age feel pressured to smoke, drink, and date. One girl expressed that the type of clothing girls wore could cause them to feel pressured. In addition, both girls indicated that family problems caused them to worry.

Violence in the Community

When asked what they thought about when they heard the word "violence" the girls said "murder, fighting, cursing, getting shot, and gangs." One of the girls described her encounters with dead people in her community. She said:

> Yes, the first time was a body in a black bag, the second time was just a dead guy sitting on the bench they dropped him off out of a van and sat him there with a book in his hand like he was reading and he was dead. (girl chuckles) Everybody went over there. There were a lot of reporters and cops they wouldn't let us pass though, but we saw the guys face.

Personal Safety and Use of Violence

After describing the above event the girls were asked what they thought about their personal safety and what they felt they had most control over. They were also asked about what they thought they could do to stay safe. Both girls felt that they could talk to someone, call the police, stay around people they knew, or stay in their homes.

When asked if they felt pressured to use violence the girls said that they felt pressured to use violence more with other girls than with boys.

> One reason given was "because boys could badly injure you, . . . but girls they cat fight. Yeah they're soft, you could just knock them out. And the easiest thing to do when you fight a girl is to pull their hair out. It depends if they have any hair. Put them on the floor and start pulling and kicking them. Yeah, pull their hair, and break their bones."

Gangs

When asked to describe what thoughts came to mind when they heard the word "gang" the girls said "weapons, drugs, and killings. One girl replied it depends if it's a bad gang. Like the bad gangs have guns and knives. . . . good gangs . . . they hang out. . . Like some people say that they are in a gang when they always hang out with each other. They have a group name. When asked to give some reasons why they thought people joined gangs the girls said "to fit in . . . to feel safe because you know some people are bullies . . . they will help you, to be a bodyguard or something . . .

When asked if they knew anyone in a gang one of the girls responded that her brother belonged to a gang, but that he "is not in a serious gang like the bloods where you cut people, he is just in a gang with his friends and everything."

Support Systems

Social Support

In response to the questions concerning social support the girls responded that they talked to their family members. They talked to their mothers, aunts, cousins, and one girl to her sister-in-law. When asked why they chose these relatives one girl said she did not choose males because she felt more comfortable with women. When asked what about developing a program that would make people feel safer the girls said they would want a program where "they could trust people and talk about anything . . . yeah and keep it confidential." One girl expressed a desire for a youth empowerment group. However, both girls were not sure what they could do to get such a group started.

The results from this study suggest that even though these girls are surrounded daily by violence, because of the social network of family and friends they have learned to insolate themselves from some of the fallout. In addition, they have learned how to protect themselves from violent incidents by "minding their own business," befriending people in gangs to stay safe, and by talking with family and friends. These findings support previous research that examined urban African American youths' perceptions of community violence. (Howard et al., 2002).

However, although they have been insulated from some of the violence in their community, these girls have also at times become the perpetrators of violent acts either by fighting with other girls or participating in gang activities. Thus, because their social network consists of violent and nonviolent members of their community, the network has been infiltrated with people who will not only shelter them from violence, but also at times inflict it upon others themselves and therefore the benefits of the support system have diminished.

IMPLICATIONS FOR INTERVENTION PROGRAMS

Understanding how adolescent girls perceive the risks, challenges, and pressures they are surrounded by in their everyday lives is essential for developing intervention programs that will empower these girls to thrive and development in their communities. The interview data from this study suggest that although high violence communities pose great dangers for adolescent girls, if there are social support networks in place girls will be able to grow and develop in positive ways. For example, although the girls articulated quite graphic descriptions of the types of violence they experienced, that is, viewing a dead body on a park bench, they were able to remain positive and focus on events that would allow them to succeed in the future. For one of the girls, getting good grades in school would allow her to pursue her dream to design clothes, and for the other getting good grades and playing sports might eventually get her into the WNBA. Moreover, both girls reported having family and friends to speak with when things became difficult.

Yet, even though these girls have a social support system, it is somewhat fragile. For example, schools are usually thought to provide a safe haven for children and in general, children view security guards in schools as people who are there to protect them and keep them safe. The findings of this study, however, demonstrate just the opposite. The girls in this study felt betrayed by adults in their school, and had lost a sense of respect and trust for the adults who were supposed to protect them. In this case, the social network that would have provided them hope, failed them. According to previous research, having a strong social support network all around is crucial to protecting children from the effects of violence in their communities (Horowitz, et al. 2005). Thus when the system breaks down the benefits of the system cease to exist.

So what can be done to help empower girls to grow and continue to develop positively in their communities without resorting to the use of violence? While previous research using interviews and focus groups have addressed the negative issues surrounding violence in the community, the present study not only addressed the negative aspects of community violence, but focused on the positive aspects of girls' lives with the hope of using this information to create experiences and programs that will allow them to thrive. The findings from this study suggest that girls have positive life events that they are proud of. Using this information, programs could be created in which girls could work with mentors and peers to create programs that would focus on positive and healthy ways of being a girl. As was expressed by one of the girls, she wanted to begin an "empowerment group," but did not know where to start. If these types of programs could be started in which girls felt that their voice would be heard and their suggestions would be taken seriously, then the girls would feel they had more control over themselves and their environments. The skills acquired through such mentoring would also provide them with skills that would allow them to succeed in other areas of their lives. In addition, this information could be shared with parents, schools, and the rest of the community.

While we will probably never rid communities of all types of violence, providing girls and boys with the skills and social networks that can help to temperate the violence in their communities is a start. It is hoped that the knowledge obtained from this in-depth interview is a beginning step in providing information that will lead to the construction of prevention and intervention programs based on the adolescents' feelings and experiences of violence in their communities.

REFERENCES

BAILY, S. & N. WHITTLE. 2004. Young people: victims of violence. Curr. Opin. Psychiatry *17*, 263–268.

BUKA, S.L., T.L. STICHICK, S.M. BIRDTHISTLE & M.D. Earls. 2001. Youth exposure to violence: prevalence, risks, and consequences. Am. J. Orthopsychiatry *71*, 298–310.

DINAPOLI, P.P. 2003. Guns and dolls: an explosion of violent behavior in girls. Adv. Nurs. Sci. *26*, 140–148.

DULMUS, C. & C. HILARSKU. 2002. Children and Adolescents Exposed to Community Violence. *In* Handbook of Violence. L.A. Rapp-Paglicci, A.R. Roberts & J.S. Wodarski, Eds.: 129–147. John Wiley & Sons. New York, NY.

GARBARION, J. 1999. The Effects of Community Violence on Children. *In* Child Psychology: A Handbook of Contemporary Issues. L. Balter & C.S. Tamis-LeMonda, Eds.: 412–428. Taylor and Francis. Philadelphia, PA.

HOROWITZ, K., M. MCKAY & R. Marshall. 2005. Community violence and urban families: experiences, effects, and directions for intervention. Am. J. Orthopsychiatry *753*, 356–368.

HOWARD, D.E., L. KALJEE & L. JACKSON. 2002. Urban African American adolescents' perceptions of community violence. Am. J. Health Behav. *26*, 56–67.

REESE, L.E., E.M. VERA, E.M.K. THOMPSON & R. REYES. 2001. A qualitative investigation of perceptions of violence risk factors in low-income African American children. J. Clin. Child Psychol. *30*, 161–171.

Who Wins in the Status Games? Violence, Sexual Violence, and an Emerging Single Standard among Adolescent Women

BEATRICE J. KRAUSS, JOANNE O'DAY, CHRISTOPHER GODFREY, KEVIN RENTE, ELIZABETH FREIDIN, ERICA BRATT, NADIA MINIAN, KRAIG KNIBB, CHRISTY WELCH, ROBERT KAPLAN, GAURI SAXENA, SHAWN McGINNISS, JACQUELINE GILROY, PETER NWAKEZE, AND SAUNDRA CURTAIN

The Hunter College Center for Community and Urban Health, New York, New York, USA

ABSTRACT: Throughout U.S. history, women have changed their sexual behaviors in response to, or as actors affecting, economic, political, and legal imperatives; to preserve health; to promote new relationship, identity or career paths; to assert a set of values; as a result of new reproductive technologies; or to gain status. In adjusting to pressures or goals, women have not always acted, or been able to act, in the interests of their own health, identity, or status. As this article will demonstrate, women, in the short or long run, may attempt to preserve status at the cost of other values such as health. This may occur through conscious and critical choice or through less conscious processes in reaction to relatively larger forces whose impact has not been critically analyzed. With the awareness in the 1980s in the United States of an emergent and incurable sexually transmissible infection, HIV, it would have been anticipated that a new sexual caution may have appeared. Yet, across several research projects in the late 1990s and into the 21st century, as our research team interviewed youth in a high HIV seroprevalence neighborhood in New York City about HIV prevention, we began to hear that a substantial minority of young women and men were participating in social settings for sexual behavior that (1) put youth at risk for HIV; (2) appeared to be motivated by acquisition of status ("props," "points"); and (3) offered few ways for women to win in these status games. We estimate from one random dwelling unit sample that about one in eight youth have been present in these settings and half of them have participated in risky sexual behavior in such settings. The settings are often characterized by men's publicly offhand attitudes toward sexual encounters, are organized around men's status maintenance, and evidence peer

Address for correspondence: Beatrice J. Krauss, Hunter College, Center for Community and Urban Health, 425 E. 25th Street, New York, NY 10010. Voice: 212-481-4283; fax: 212-481-5015.
e-mail: bkrauss@hunter.cuny.edu

pressures that are poorly understood by both young men and women participants. To regain status, some women participants have adopted attitudes more characteristic of men.

Keywords: adolescents; women; sexual risk; status; HIV; violence

INTRODUCTION

Throughout U.S. history, women have changed their sexual behaviors in response to, or as actors affecting, economic, political, and legal imperatives; to preserve health; to promote new relationship, identity or career paths; to assert a set of values; as a result of new reproductive technologies; or to gain status (e.g., Cott, 2002; Grewal & Kaplan, 2001; Rouse, 2002; Woloch, 1999). However, in adjusting to these pressures or goals, women have not always acted, or been able to act, in the interests of their own health, identity, or reputation. As this article will demonstrate, women, in the short or long run, may attempt to preserve status, which represents standing in a culture or subculture and is linked to constructions of identity by others, at the cost of other values such as health. Attempts at status preservation may occur through conscious and critical choice, on the part of individual women or the culture around them, or through less conscious processes in reaction to relatively larger forces. Furthermore, women's sexual behaviors may be central to the identity and status labels women apply to themselves or that others apply to them. These labels may mediate how women are treated, or allow themselves to be treated, by others, even in situations that are not, or are not overtly, sexual.

In fact, since the 19th century, three turning points in women's sexual and reproductive norms, often cited by women's studies historians (e.g., Cott, 2002; Davidson, 1988; Grewal & Kaplan, 2001; Rouse, 2002; Woloch, 1999), illustrate the complex factors that may influence women's identity and status. The first was the mid-19th century Industrial Revolution, which accelerated the emergence of urban areas and the concomitant rural to urban population shift, which had begun earlier in that century, especially in the northern states and especially among white populations. It was accompanied by economic pressures for smaller families, thus promoting fertility control; potential isolation of nuclear from extended families, thus emphasizing social control of relationships within the nuclear family; and overcrowding and loss of privacy, thus increasing partner choices and the regulation of fidelity. It also underscored a male breadwinner/dependent female construction of family, relationships, and labor among middle-class families, thus reducing women's potential economic independence; and promoted separation of work and home among all classes, including a growing number of single men and single women laborers, thus potentially reordering the spheres in which women could gain status, and, in some factory settings, increasing chaperoning and surveillance of such "unattached" women.

The second—during the period at the end of World War I—saw the passage of the 19th Amendment giving women the right to vote and other evidence of a new equality between men and women. It was accompanied by the emergence of various kinds of "New Women," (e.g., the college-educated "coed") who, in contrast to Victorian women, saw themselves as deserving the economic, political, social, and relational rights of men.

With the advent of penicillin in the 1940s, and its curative powers over syphilis, the stage was set for a third key turning point that occurred in the late 1960s at the height of the Civil Rights movement and other social and political movements, with the introduction to the market of The Pill. The birth control pill reliably freed women from another biological hazard of heterosexual sex, the burden of unintended pregnancy; it also promised to change a woman's relationship to the labor market as well as to her male sexual partners.

While it may be tempting to read this history as, in part, an evolution toward economically and emotionally egalitarian relationships between men and women in the case of heterosexual relationships, each era manifested a variety of reactions and counter-reactions to its major trends, often captured in new gender-specific labels for women that frequently contained central assumptions about sexual and relationship behavior—e.g., the "flapper" in contrast to the "coed" of the 1920s.

> She smoked, drank, danced, and voted. She cut her hair, wore make-up, and went to petting parties. She was giddy and took risks. She was a flapper.(http://history1900s.about.com/od/1920s/a/flappers.htm, accessed June, 2006)

Indeed, there even were presumptions about the motivations for relationship behavior of the more conservative "coed"; she was said to be seeking status and economic stability by finding a wealthy and well-educated marriage partner in college, to attain her "Mrs." degree. But both were adjusting to major trends in emancipation and work in their era.

A NEW HEALTH CHALLENGE

The 1980s, however, brought a new sexual health challenge to the United States. With the awareness in the 1980s in the United States of an emergent and incurable sexually transmissible infection, HIV, it would have been anticipated that a new sexual caution may have appeared, one that could hearken back to prepenicillin days with its suggested, presumed, and not always achieved, health protections through virginity prior to marriage, early marriage, fidelity within monogamous marital relationships, and lifetime monogamy (e.g., the themes of Henrik Ibsen's late 19th century "problem plays," *Ghosts* and *Hedda Gabler,* concern intrafamilial transmission of syphilis and marital fidelity).

In fact, national surveys (Abma & Sonenstein, 2001; Althaus, 2001) of youth risk behavior do suggest that the proportion of never-married U.S. teenagers who have had intercourse dropped for the first time since the initiation of the surveys in the 1970s, from 56% in 1988 to 52% in 1995. The drop, however, was almost wholly attributable to reports of intercourse by males (60% to 55%). Women's reports remained virtually unchanged (51% to 49%) and the proportion of women who had sex before age 15 years actually increased (11% to 19%), almost reaching parity with the stable figure for male early intercourse (21%). Additional figures regarding risk are complex—number of lifetime partners, condom use at first and subsequent intercourse, concurrent condom and hormonal contraceptive use (excluding the pill)—but indicate substantial risk for young women for both sexually transmitted infections (STIs) and unintended pregnancy. For example, in 1995, 63% of 15–19-year-old never-married sexually active women reported more than one lifetime partner, only 38% reported that their partner used a condom at last intercourse, and just 8% reported joint use of a condom and hormonal contraception at last intercourse.

The 1995 report (Abma & Sonenstein, 2001) also called attention to the age differential between young women and their sexual partners. Overall, 34% of 15–19-year-old women indicated that their most recent sexual partner was 4 or more years older; these data highlighted concerns already present in the literature about power differentials and exploitation of young women by older men (Darroch, Landry, & Oslak, 1999; Marshall, 2003; Reid & Bailey, 1992). In the context of the HIV epidemic, such exploitation takes on special importance. Young women are more biologically vulnerable to heterosexual transmission of HIV than are young men (efficiency of male-to-female transmission is 2.3 times greater than the efficiency of female-to-male transmission; Nicolosi, Correa-Leite, Musicco, Arrici, Gavazzeni, *et al.*, 1994), through immaturity of their cervixes (Chaisson, 1995; Hitchcock, 1996; Lifson, 1992), and young women may experience additional risk attendant on disruption of the vaginal mucosal barrier posed by STIs, trauma, defloration, or bleeding (Darroch & Frost, 1999).

If these facts were well known and widespread, and cultures or subcultures had a central focus on women's health, one would expect the emergence of norms designed to be protective of women's health in a way cognizant of the cultures within which women live.

However, across several research projects in the late 1990s and into the 21st century, as our research team interviewed youth in a high HIV seroprevalence (10%) neighborhood in New York City (NYC) about HIV prevention, we began to hear that a substantial minority of young women and men were participating in social settings for sexual behavior that (1) put youth at risk for HIV; (2) appeared to be motivated by acquisition of status ("props," "points"); and (3) offered few ways for women to win in these status games. This phenomenon was corroborated by other reports in NYC, New York State (NY), and across the United States. We came to call it "sex in group settings (SIGS)," and defined the settings as those in which at least one couple is having sex while others present are aware of the sexual activity. We chose this descriptive phrase carefully, because SIGS takes a variety of forms (e.g., planned or unplanned; regularly scheduled or unscheduled; different couples in different rooms, all couples in the same room, or serial intercourse with the same young women each in a different room; all participants invited to SIGS or drop-ins allowed) and has differing effects on bystanders (naïve or with educated expectations) as well as on participants. We wished to discriminate SIGS from some representations in the popular press of "sex parties" (Lewin, 2005), an overly general characterization, which represent only a small proportion of SIGS, many of which are unplanned, and for many of which the sex itself is also unplanned.

In the remainder of this article, we present the first case that energized our concerns about health risks, a brief summary of the subsequent research and literature review that solidified our unease, a summary of our first look at data in an ongoing project that assisted us in understanding the meaning of what was happening, an emerging framework for potentially understanding the phenomena, some insights about context, discussion, and our planned next steps. Central to this article is an outline of the adjustments young women have made to SIGS, which appear to be one arena for male and female status "games" (Dash, 1996) where maintenance of an identity or status becomes more important than maintenance of health.

THE FIRST CASE

From 1995 to the present, we have been conducting an NIMH-funded longitudinal randomized clinical trial (Parent/Preadolescent Training for HIV Prevention [PATH]), with randomized dwelling unit sampling for 375 families in a high HIV seroprevalence neighborhood, to test the efficacy of parent training in preventing HIV in preadolescent youth (Krauss, Godfrey, Yee, Goldsant, Tiffany, *et al.*, 2000). SIGS came to our attention during a PATH post-baseline interview with a 12-year-old boy who reported that he had felt "pressured" to have his first sexual intercourse at a group party because others assumed that he was not a virgin. The boys were having sex by "going one at a time" into one of several rooms, each with a girl inside. In fact, when he entered a room, he found a girl whom he had considered, until this moment, to be "a buddy." His reluctance to have sex with her was overcome by his fear of being outed as a virgin. He reported that he had sex and that he and the girl "never spoke to each other again." His account confirmed that this incident was not connected to gang activity—the usual context in which one hears about group sex (e.g., initiation of young women into gangs through sex with several gang members)—but that similar events occurred in various forms throughout the neighborhood (Krauss, Krauss, O'Day, & Rente, 2005). We were immediately concerned, because of the evident health and mental health risks involved, and the extent to which this was not an isolated incident.

We therefore found five neighborhood youth informants, both male and female, three from reviewing our records on sexually active youth, and two nominated by PATH's youth advisory board as knowledgeable about the neighborhood. They told us of other instances of SIGS; indeed four of the youth themselves had been present at SIGS.

CONFIRMATION FROM OTHER RESPONDENTS

Because of these accounts, we applied for an NIH Office of AIDS Research supplement (OAR supplement) to interview 76 neighborhood 10–24-year-olds to explore this phenomenon in more depth. We received this award in 1999. We also added new questions at PATH's 3-year follow-up to see if youth reported their first, most recent, or any other sexual experiences in the last 30 days in the context of these gatherings. Of the first 150 PATH respondents, about 21% were sexually active. More than a third of them reported at least one sexual experience in SIGS; for the majority of SIGS participants this included their first sexual experience. SIGS participants in the PATH sample averaged 15.8 years of age, with the first SIGS experience occurring at a mean age of 13.8 years. They had a mean of 10.7 lifetime sexual partners; in contrast, sexually active youth who were not SIGS participants had a mean of three lifetime sexual partners.

More than 60% of the OAR supplement study youth, representing a broader age range than PATH youth, had heard of SIGS, 34% had attended SIGS, and half of attendees reported risk behavior in SIGS. Those who engaged in sexual risk behaviors in SIGS usually began at the age of 13 years. The majority had their first sexual experience in SIGS. Half reported multiple partners; 50% of their anal and vaginal sex acts were described as unprotected, as were most oral/penile or oral/vaginal sex acts. The majority attended more than one event, some attending almost weekly for more than two or three years. Attendees gave detailed descriptions of 130 selected, specific events where they were present.

Content analysis of these events reported from OAR supplement participants' early recollections until 1999 (when the OAR supplement interviews were conducted) indicated that the prototypic SIGS was organized by boys (although girls organized some and some were unplanned but evolved from mixed sex groups) with plans made for recruitment of participants and acquisition of drugs. The locale was usually an unsupervised apartment. The typical SIGS had 8–15 participants, lasted 5–8 hours, began with sharing of marijuana and alcohol, and included multiple couples having sex in one room or boys going from room to room to have sex with the girl in each room. The reported age range was from 12 to 27 years, with age mixing (e.g., at least a 5-year age range) and ethnic diversity. Generally, boys gained status ("props") with neighborhood male peers from participation, and even denigration by girls (being called "a dog") may have led to status gain among some, but not all, males.

However, while girls considered it flattering to be invited, especially to events organized by older boys, unless a girl was an organizer who did not participate in sex, she was likely to experience a status decrement from both male and female peers after participation. Some girls handled this by going to out-of-neighborhood events, or by developing a personal agenda (e.g., becoming pregnant after sex with multiple partners so that no one but the girl would have claims on the baby, having sex with a popular partner otherwise inaccessible, obtaining gifts in advance of participation). One SIGS was said to be preemptively organized by a girl who thought it would happen anyway so she should "at least choose the boys." Some male and female recruits were initially naïve as to likely activities within SIGS; one was organized by girls to ensure a young adolescent long-term survivor with perinatally acquired HIV lost her virginity "on time."

Despite these disclosures, most young women, in contrast to young men, were reluctant to discuss SIGS, possibly because of the pervasive status decrements for female participation. Thus we applied for and received NIMH funding to do an additional qualitative/quantitative study, performing a series of three in-depth interviews with 30 young women and 30 young men, ages 13–22 years, street-recruited through random geographic sampling, half of whom were SIGS participants and half of whom were not, to be followed by a quantitative study with 300 similarly recruited youth. We briefly discuss qualitative findings here.

SIGS NOW

The phenomenon of SIGS seems to have changed as we have examined it. In contrast to our 1999 respondents, our qualitative respondents, interviewed from 2002 to 2006, report smaller and largely unplanned SIGS encounters. SIGS seems to be less often described as separate organized events, "parties" if you will, but may have been integrated into the general scheme of cross-gender relationships, with multiple sexual encounters evolving from mixed sex groups just "hanging out," and through normalization of sex with age peers, "friends with benefits," divorced from prior notions of romantic, intimate, committed attachment.

Yet, while specific forms of SIGS and nomenclature about SIGS may have changed, what has not changed is the perjorative nature of the terms applied to women who are available for multiple partnerships in SIGS or, for that matter, elsewhere. Among the terms we heard used in interviews by males were: "walkable" (a young woman good-looking enough to be seen with as you walked her to the subway after having sex with her), "douser" (a young woman who would do anything you asked her to), "jump off" (a casual secondary partner who may be involved with SIGS) and many more (e.g., "ho"). The young women who were described in this manner were not candidates to become a "wifey," a steady or main partner in a committed relationship (Knibb & Krauss, 2004). And, as with other youth nomenclature, specific terms may have different meanings in different contexts: the ubiquitous verb "hook-up" may mean a third party promoting a couple getting together, having sex, making an emotional connection, or even finding each other in a crowd. In some sense, however, the sexually tinged terms applied to women tended to paint their entire character. While a male can be a "Player" and a "dog," Dietrich (1998) captures the compartmentalization of women in the subtitle of her book: "Bitches, 'ho's and schoolgirls." Women are one or the other.

Furthermore, SIGS, throughout each of the studies, especially in the descriptions provided by men, were characterized by an emotional flatness and avoidance of intimacy. In one scene described to us, men were "playing spades and doing our homework" while waiting their turn for a sexual encounter. At least one man spoke disparagingly of women "hugging up," trying to please a partner emotionally to engender a commitment without having sex, and other men reported they "talked on the low" about an emotionally intimate relationship to preserve identity as a "player." Young women sometimes described their discovery of the lack of intimacy. One young woman, brought by her sister to SIGS as part of trading sex for drugs, thought she had developed a relationship with one of the dealers over time. When she confessed her feelings, he hit her and said, "do you love me now?"

CONFIRMATION IN THE LITERATURE

We conducted a literature review and queries of other researchers to understand the extent to which SIGS occurred elsewhere and was not an isolated set of events in one neighborhood at one time. In the process, we discovered SIGS has been associated with at least four documented clusters of STI and HIV cases in youth across the United States:

(1) Rothenberg, Sterk, Toomey, Potterat, Johnson, *et al*. (1998) used a social network approach to identify a core transmission group for a syphilis outbreak in a predominantly white, middle-class, suburban community in Georgia. Their investigation determined that this core group consisted of 19 white girls (most under 16 years of age) who arranged sex parties with groups of boys (80 boys in total), divided between networks of older white suburban males and inner-city age-peer minority males. These parties took place at girls' homes while their parents were out for the evening. They included sequential/simultaneous sex partners and a wide range of high-risk sexual activities. Drugs and alcohol use were often involved.

(2) The gonorrhea rate among 15–19-year-old adolescents in Syracuse, NY, was almost twice the national rate. Focus groups were conducted among

adolescents and young adults in the eight inner-city, high-minority census tracts where the majority of the infections were reported. Some of the young women reported "running a lab," having sex with multiple partners in abandoned houses, or "running a train," a female engaging in serial intercourse with several males. Participants often described sexual activity occurring in conjunction with drug use ("hang out, use drugs, then sex happens") (Welych, Laws, Fioroto, Durham, Cibula *et al.*, 1998).

(3) and (4) The Centers for Disease Control and Prevention (CDC) reported two HIV clusters (CDC, 1999, 2000) one in a rural county in upstate New York and the other in a small town in rural Mississippi. Neither article reported SIGS, but additional inquiries indicated that SIGS were among the risks in the former case (Holmberg, personal communication, November 2000) while "motel parties" of younger girls with older men were directly associated with the HIV cluster in the latter case (St. Lawrence, CDC, personal communication, October 2000).

Other published reports of SIGS can be found in journalistic, anthropological, and elicitation research accounts. The *New York Times* (Jarrell, 2000) reported that NYC 12–13-year-olds engaged in unprotected oral sex at dance clubs or parties before parents returned home from work. Young women at these events reported performing oral sex with young men because of the perceived lower HIV risk associated with the activity (compared to vaginal or anal intercourse), and because oral sex provided a means of satisfying curiosity about sex. Franks (2000) described interviews with middle-class urban male and female adolescents who reported experimenting with sexual activity with their friends in group settings, often to alleviate boredom or stress. These accounts document how, and to a much lesser extent why, both male and female adolescents willingly participate in, and often orchestrate, SIGS.

However, some accounts reveal considerable exploitation of participants during these events, usually of girls by older boys. Sales (1997) interviewed adolescents in NYC private schools and found that participation in SIGS often left girls susceptible to considerable denigration and stigmatization from male and female peers, despite the girls' initial beliefs that such sexual experimentation and experience would provide the girls with enhanced social status. She found that boys gain "fame" or "props" for their participation, whereas girls became known as "bitches," "whores," or "chickenheads." These encounters have also been reported in journalistic and anthropological accounts from Washington, DC and metropolitan areas in California (Dash, 1996; Dietrich, 1998), and from survey, formative, or elicitation research in Brooklyn (Bolyard, Friedman, Maslow, Sandoval, Krauss, *et al.*, 2005), Washington Heights (O'Sullivan, Meyer-Bahlburgh, & Watkins, 2000) and the South Bronx (Freudenberg, Roberts, Richie, Taylor, McGillicuddy, *et al.*, 1999) in NYC, and in Chicago (Paikoff, University of Illinois, at Chicago, personal communication, 1999). In the Freudenberg study (1999), which specifically mentioned hooky parties (skipping school to attend social events), young women said they did not disclose incidents to adults, some of which involved coercion of sex, because it also meant disclosing that they had skipped school.

Finally, any computer search can quickly lead the reader to a chat room site where the dynamics discussed here—central sexually suggestive meeting room discourse for multiple couples, with separate rooms for more explicit sexual encounters—are mimicked. Other media (e.g., videos, music) outline SIGS as well; such media may have a facilitating effect on promoting risky sexual behavior (Brown, L'Engle, Pardun, Guang, Kenneavy, *et al.*, 2006).

MEANING

In the PATH project, we had collected baseline data from 10–13-year-old boys ($n = 199$) and girls ($n = 176$) on their expected feelings about their first sexual encounter, and on their expected gains and losses from having sex in general. From these data, we obtained some insight on the pressures and values internalized early about sexual behavior that may guide later sexual behavior.

Taken together, data indicate that young men anticipate more status ("feel adult" [42.3% of men vs. 4.9% of women, $p < .0001$]; "get respect" [34.6% vs. 7.8%, $p < .0001$]; "feel independent" [33.1% vs. 2.9%, $p < .0001$]), pressure to be sexual in relationships ("keep boyfriend/girlfriend") [41.5% vs. 7.8%, $p < .0001$]; "feel wanted" [27.7% vs. 8.8%, $p < .0001$]; "afraid of losing the other" [27.3% vs. 5.7%, $p < .0001$]; "do what the person wants" [17.4% vs. 2.9%, $p < .0001$;], curiosity ("find out what's good about it") [54.8% vs. 41.2%, $p = .042$]; "be curious" [37.1% vs. 19.0%, $p = .002$]), and pleasure ("feel pleasure") [30.0% vs. 10.8%, $p < .0001$]; "excited and turned on" [18.9% vs. 9.5%, $p = .042$]) attendant on becoming sexually experienced than do young women. The results are interesting in that such statements as "afraid of losing the other" are often associated with young women's desires to keep partners, but here are more often endorsed by young men in what appears to be the context of young men's feelings that others expect them to be sexual and, if they are not, they will be rejected by their peers. Youth advisors confirmed this interpretation. Young women, on the other hand, expect more losses ("lose self respect" [30.3% vs. 42.1%, $p = .019$]; "lose virginity"[29.5% vs. 45.2%, $p = .013$) than do young men (only "catch STDs" is endorsed more often by young men, 74.2% vs. 55.8%, $p = .03$). The last finding regarding sexually transmitted infections is troubling in that young women are actually more biologically vulnerable to STIs than young men (Darroch & Frost, 1999), even though the young men perceive themselves as being more vulnerable.

AN EMERGING FRAMEWORK

SIGS may indicate a significant shift among adolescents in the prevalence of protections against sexual risk, which were formerly present in group activities as noted theorist John Bancroft suggests: "in earlier models of adolescent sexuality, keeping together in groups was a way of delaying the specific pairing process, and although such groups may have involved some petting, sitting on laps, etc., so that there would be an erotic component, the group would have ensured that certain limits were maintained" (personal communication, Indiana University, July 2001; see also Bancroft, 2000). In response to a description of SIGS, he asks, "Are we seeing a similar group process, in terms of avoiding specific pairings, but a change of the sexual boundaries? It seems to imply that sexual activity per se is OK as long as it's not part of a relationship. If so, that is important to understand."

The group process seems to be organized around status with peers—most often resulting in status increases for men and decreases for women rather than control of specific pairings or of "going too far." Even youth who have not participated sexually at these events report "bystander" effects; that is, consequences (e.g., labeling, psychological reactions) of just having been there.

Peer modeling and peer pressure for risk seems heightened in SIGS, but are present to a lesser degree in other settings where youth meet and have romantic or erotic relationships (Kinsman, Romer, Furstenberg, & Schwartz, 1998). Generally, however, youth social settings and the pressures for risk are poorly understood—even, it seems, by the youth themselves. Most of our youth's narratives about SIGS or other "sexual possibility situations" clearly indicate peer pressure is present, yet participants have difficulty in labeling any social strategy that is likely to increase risky sex as peer pressure. In contrast, they have no difficulty in identifying peer pressure tactics to encourage substance use—even when these are similar behaviors. In fact, we had to learn to ask our questions about peer pressure for sex differently. We asked open-ended questions about how events unfolded and probed for specific details, e.g., how did you happen to find yourself at the gathering (probes: where were you when attending was suggested, were you with anyone, who, how did they react, who was asking, were they with anyone, how did they ask). Youth may have difficulty resisting social pressures they do not recognize or may be resistant to recognizing social pressures in the sexual arena for reasons that we do not yet understand.

At this point in our understanding of SIGS, our theoretically informed description of SIGS (borrowing from Sullivan's [1996] treatment of persistent and temporary delinquency) moves from the contextual to the individual back to the social consequences of actions that may have been influenced by peer pressure. Elements (see FIG. 1) include: the local opportunity structure for risk ("It is easy to hold hooky parties because our school only takes attendance in the first period and most of our parents are in the WEP [welfare to work] program so no one is home"); techniques for recruitment into affiliation groups or settings that promote risk ("We told them we're only inviting the good-looking girls"); psychological factors such as the emotions and values accompanying

| Perceived sexual/relational norms | Perceived social contexts for sexual/relational interaction |

| Social controls/pressures facilitating/inhibiting context entry |

| Social pressures within social contexts |
| Incident risk |
| Social labeling and other consequences |
| Status and relationship management |
| Continued risk |

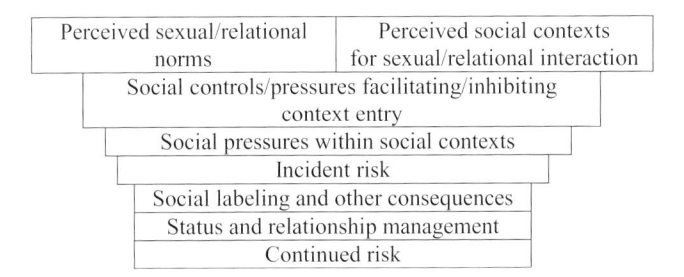

FIGURE 1. Individual, social, and neighborhood/contextual processes operate as a funnel that step by step limits the options for relational/sexual risk behavior of the young women and men who enter SIGS.

recruitment and risk participation ("We're drinking and smoking blunts and weed. We get all woozy. We're dancing and we start touching. We see what other people are doing. Things just happen."); immediate or delayed consequences for participation in risk ("Everyone got what they wanted," "One girl got pregnant and kept the baby, a couple of others had abortions, a miscarriage"); labeling processes by self (private) ("I think those parties are a Junior High [immature] thing") and others (public) after participation ("The one who gets the most is the Man"); evocation of differential social interaction based on those labels ("Of course, a girl who went to one of these could never be your girlfriend"); and management and control by neighborhood, peer, adult, or institutional socializing agents, which can mitigate, avoid, or worsen labeling effects ("Some of these guys they talk about the girls 'Oh, I hit this.' They sound stupid telling everyone their business"). Although the participants do not recognize these elements, they often appear in our participants' narratives as these quotes illustrate (Krauss, O'Day, Godfrey, & Rente, 2003).

Some young women appear to have made an adjustment to the largely negative labeling effects by becoming organizers of the SIGS, informal and formal, a tactic that gives women power and control over who attends and what happens, but does not necessarily signal sexual participation with its attendant negative labels. This control has also been evident in one-to-one relationships, particularly regarding men who young women do not particularly care about. Others have adopted the male standard of these settings—"Playette"—to become someone whose status is similar to the Player. And some women have taken the role of exploiting other women, providing women friends and relatives, most often younger than themselves, for participation in SIGS. During the last two years, we have heard in a health education program our center runs for women in juvenile detention that more young women in this role refer to themselves as "pimps," eschewing female-gendered labels.

Women, however, are often more generous than young men in the characterization of female participants, especially when they recognize the power differentials and exploitive behavior in the situation. One woman, a bystander, expresses her assessment of the exploitation of younger women and her feelings about it:

> Yep they do everything to them girls and those girls don't do nothing.
>
> Especially the fourteen year olds and fifteen year olds. It is really sad....
>
> These guys are like twenty-four, twenty-five. They are older.... It be like, it be like twenty guys in one apartment. Twenty guys and it will be like three or four girls. Three or four girls and they will all go from girl to girl to girl....
>
> They will meet different girls like in different boroughs and bring them over and stuff like that but if they don't find no girls they will get the same girls that live in the neighborhood.... I mean it's nothing good. It's nothing good but I feel that if they [the girls] are letting it happen more than once then they must enjoy what is going on. They must like it but honestly I think too it's the environment thing. Like their household or stuff like that.... I think if like if some of them is adopted, some of them is adopted, some of them live in shelters and some of them are just in their house [where] their mom will smoke. They will do drugs and they will do what they want, too. They will follow their mom's footsteps basically.... They [the guys] consider the girls that let them do anything with them 'scuzzes.'"

Why then do not older women intervene on behalf of younger, less experienced women? We hypothesize that in some cases, by making a positive comparison of herself to the younger woman, the more experienced woman is able to credit herself with a higher status. Lack of protective behavior may feed into status maintenance. Yet other peers increase their status by taking on a protective and parenting role, e.g., providing guidance about school, college, careers, and prosocial life paths (Welch, Rente, O'Day, Godfrey, Krauss, *et al.*, 2004).

CONTEXT

When asked to indicate their neighborhood's most serious problems, until the World Trade Center disaster of 9/11/01, young men and women from this neighborhood ranked them, most serious to least serious, as: drug sales, drug use, welfare reform, HIV/AIDS, unemployment, teen pregnancy, STIs, crime, concerns about preparation of youth for adulthood, and violence (Krauss, Franchi, O'Day, Pride, Lozada, *et al.*, 2003). After 9/11, threats of terrorism and bioterrorism were added to, and remain on, this list. Thus, youth are becoming sexual adults against a generalized backdrop of social, economic, and community violence. In one small study, we found over a quarter of youth have been threatened with a knife, gun, or weapon. Additionally, substantial percentages have experienced losses from multiple sources: about 25% know an average of 4–5 persons killed in the World Trade Center disaster; about half know an average of 4 persons harmed by community violence; and our PATH study shows nearly half of 10–13-year-olds know two to three people with HIV, one-third of whom have died (Krauss, Godfrey, O'Day, & Freidin, 2006). Furthermore, many men in this neighborhood experience incarceration, leading to an expectation that their presence may only be intermittent; men may become a scarce commodity with women having lowered expectations of continuous long-term relationships (e.g., Adimora & Schoenbach, 2005).

DISCUSSION

At least one researcher (McGill, 2000) has indicated neighborhood violence as a predictor of early intercourse, while others have hypothesized that careers of risk and pleasure occur in conjunction with fatalism about closed future options (e.g., Carrera, 1995; Jessor, 1998; Lammers, Ireland, Resmick, & Bloom, 2000). With other paths closed, some youth "win" and find successful careers in the status games. Some women, as figures cited previously indicate, are engaging in sexual intercourse in the United States at an increasingly earlier age, attaining parity with young men for age of sexual debut; some of this behavior may reflect attempts at early status gains, but some may indicate predatory behavior of older men toward younger women (Gupta, 2000; Marshall, 2003).

From PATH, with its random dwelling unit sampling, we estimate about one in eight youth are participating in SIGS, and about half have performed risky sexual behavior at SIGS. Young women may be engaging in behavior in SIGS (e.g., sex with older men, with multiple partners who confer "sexual experience") that they think will increase their status with other young men and women, but which results most often in status decrements and exposure to health risks. The young women may be hoping to attain what is called "ascribed" status (status conferred by association with someone of higher status), but are achieving neither that nor "achieved" status (status earned on the basis of behavior, expertise, or other resources) (Kornblum, 1997).

Gupta (2000) suggests that the special vulnerability of women to sexual risk occurs because of women's preemptively ascribed low power and status within cultures or subcultures worldwide (see also Amaro, 1995; Pulerwitz, Amaro, DeJong, Gortmaker, & Rudd, 2002.), a status deficit from which some women may attempt to recover by whatever means are at hand and from which some women cannot recover because of real power differentials— e.g., a 14-year-old girl attending a party at which 20 older men are present. Gupta, however, also suggests that the pervasive "double standard" that not only confers, but expects, more sexual freedom from men has been detrimental to men's as well as to women's health. It is her thesis that no one is winning under norms promoting and maintaining gender-based status and power inequalities.

SIGS, then, as a phenomenon, raises multiple questions: (1) Why do vulnerable young women (e.g., younger women) fail to perceive the negative status effects of participating in SIGS, which would be apparent by observing what happens to others? (2) Why do older young women, who know firsthand how negative status effects are achieved, not do more to prevent the younger women from participating in SIGS? (3) Why is expected status more important than health for these women and under what conditions can these values be reversed or brought into harmony? (4) Who do young women believe will confer enhanced status and is this exploited by the recruitment techniques of young men or young women? (5) How can young men and women be enlisted in preserving women's (and men's) health? (6) What does SIGS provide those women who participate that other community options do not? (7) Does SIGS qualitatively differ from social forms such as the club scene, fraternity/sorority makeout rooms, sexual mixing games (e.g., spin the bottle, seven minutes in heaven) and other romantic/erotic venues that vary across ages, cultures, economic groups, and sexual subcultures?

Finally, in conducting our studies, we found youth singularly ignorant about the concept, and definition, of sexual assault and about pertinent NY law. We therefore authored a brief guide on that topic, with the assistance of health, youth, and legal advisors, which we have given to youth who have participated in our studies and which we plan to distribute more widely. We have also amended, wherever we have found it, advice to teens that presumes socializing in groups is "safer" and infers more protections against risks than socializing in twos or threes (e.g., our draft of the NYC Public Schools K-12 HIV curriculum, http://www.nycenet.edu/Offices/TeachLearn/OfficeCurriculumProfessional Development/HealthEducation/Resources/HIVAIDSCurric, accessed June 2006).

PLANNED NEXT STEPS

As our quantitative data are collected, we intend to describe and quantify the types of life plans and peer pressures that are associated with some young men and women never attending SIGS, others attending and leaving, others participating in risk behaviors at SIGS, and others avoiding risk at SIGS. We wish to use this knowledge to design culturally appropriate health-preserving interventions for young women and men.

ACKNOWLEDGMENTS

Beatrice J. Krauss, Ph.D., is Executive Director of the Hunter College Center for Community and Urban Health and a Professor of Urban Public Health at Hunter College, City University of New York. The co-authors were staff members, interns, or Fellows at the Center for Community and Urban Health performing work on projects supported by grants from the National Institute of Mental Health, MH53834, MH62975, and MH66631.

We gratefully acknowledge the generous and continuing contributions of the parents and children of the Lower East Side.

REFERENCES

ABMA, J.C. & F.L. SONENSTEIN. 2001. Sexual activity and contraceptive practices among teenagers in the United States, 1988 and 1995. Vital and Health Statistics 23, 1–79.

ADIMORA, A.A. & V.J. SCHOENBACH. 2005. Social context, sexual networks, and racial disparities in rates of sexually transmitted infections. Journal of Infectious Diseases 191(Suppl 1), S115–S122.

ALTHAUS, F. 2001. Levels of sexual experience among U.S. teenagers have declined for the first time in three decades. Family Planning Perspectives 33, 180–181.

AMARO, H. 1995. Love, sex, and power. Considering women's realities in HIV prevention. American Psychologist 50, 437–447.

BANCROFT, J. (Ed.). 2000. The Role of Theory in Sex Research. Indiana University Press. Bloomington, IN.

BOLYARD, M., S. FRIEDMAN, C. MASLOW, M. SANDOVAL, B. KRAUSS & P. MATEU-GELABERT. 2005. A Study of High-Risk Group Sex Events. Paper presented at AIDS Impact Conference, Capetown, South Africa.

BROWN, J.D., K.L. L'ENGLE, C.J. PARDUN, G. GUANG, K. KENNEAVY & C. JACKSON. 2006. Sexy media matter: exposure to sexual content in music, movies, television, and magazines predicts Black and White adolescents' sexual behavior. Pediatrics 117, 1018–1027.

CARRERA, M.A. 1995. Preventing adolescent pregnancy: in hot pursuit. SIECUS Report 23, 16–19.

CENTERS FOR DISEASE CONTROL AND PREVENTION. 1999. Cluster of HIV-positive young women—New York, 1997–1998. Morbidity and Mortality Weekly Report 48, 413–416.

CENTERS FOR DISEASE CONTROL AND PREVENTION. 2000. Cluster of HIV-infected adolescents and young adults—Mississippi, 1999. Morbidity and Mortality Weekly Report 29, 861–864.

CHAISSON, M. 1995. Women and HIV. Presented at the monthly Institute for AIDS Research Seminar, National Development and Research Institutes, Inc., New York, NY.

COTT, N. 2002. Public Vows: A History of Marriage and the Nation. Harvard University Press. Boston, MA.

DARROCH, J.E. & J.J. FROST. 1999. Women's interest in vaginal microbicides. Family Planning Perspectives 31, 17–23.

DARROCH, J.E., D.J. LANDRY & S. OSLAK. 1999. Age differences between sexual partners in the United States. Family Planning Perspectives 31, 161–167.

DAVIDSON, C.N. 1988. No more separate spheres! American Literature 70, 443–463.

DASH, L. 1996. When Children want Children: The Urban Crisis of Teenage Childbearing. William Morrow and Company. New York, NY.

DIETRICH, L.C. 1998. Chicana Adolescents: Bitches, 'Ho's, and Schoolgirls. Praeger. Westport, CT.

FRANKS, L. 2000. The sex lives of your children. Talk Magazine 2, 102–107, 157.

FREUDENBERG, N., L. ROBERTS, B.E. RICHIE, R.T. TAYLOR, K. MCGILLICUDDY & M.B. GREEN. 1999. Coming up in the Boogie Down: lives of adolescents in the South Bronx. Health Education and Behavior *26*, 788–805.

GREWAL, I. & C. KAPLAN. 2001. An Introduction to Women's Studies: Gender in a Transnational World. McGraw Hill. Boston, MA.

GUPTA, G.R. 2000. Gender, Sexuality and HIV. Presented in a plenary session at the International AIDS Conference, Durban, South Africa.

HITCHCOCK, P.J. 1996. Screening and treatment of sexually transmitted diseases: an important strategy for reducing the risk of HIV transmission. AIDS Patient Care and STDs *10*, 10–15.

JARRELL, A. 2000. The face of teenage sex grows younger. New York Times, April 2, Section 9, pp. 1, 8.

JESSOR, R. (Ed.). 1998. New Perspectives on Adolescent Risk Behavior. Cambridge University Press. Cambridge, UK.

KINSMAN, S.B., D. ROMER, F.F. FURSTENBERG & D.F. SCHWARZ. 1998. Early sexual initiation: the role of peer norms. Pediatrics *102*, 1185–1192.

KNIBB, K. & B. KRAUSS. 2004. Relationships and Urban Adolescent Vernacular: Who are You and What are You to Me; Implications for HIV Risk Reduction. Poster presented at the National Institute of Mental Health AIDS Research Training Meeting, Washington, DC.

KORNBLUM, W. 1997. Sociology in a Changing World. Holt, Rinehart and Winston, Inc. New York, NY.

KRAUSS, B.J., D. FRANCHI, J. O'DAY, J. PRIDE, L. LOZADA, N. ALEDORT *et al.* 2003. Two shadows of the Twin Towers: missing safe spaces and foreclosed opportunities. Families in Society *84*, 523–529.

KRAUSS, B., C.C. GODFREY, J. O'DAY & E. FREIDIN. 2006. Hugging my uncle: the impact of a parent training on children's comfort interacting with persons with HIV. The Journal of Pediatric Psychology *31*, 891–904.

KRAUSS, B.J., C. GODFREY, D.S. YEE, L. GOLDSAMT, J. TIFFANY, L. ALMEYDA. 2000. Saving Our Children From a Silent Epidemic: the PATH Program for Parents and Pre-adolescents. *In* Working with Families in the Era of HIV/AIDS. W. Pequegnat & J. Szapocznik, Eds.: 89–112. Sage. Thousand Oaks, CA.

KRAUSS, B., H. KRAUSS, O'J. DAY & K. RENTE. 2005. Sexual Violence in the Schools. *In* Violence in the Schools: Cross-national and Cross-cultural Perspectives. F. Denmark, H. H. Krauss, R.W. Wesner, E. Midlarsky & U.P. Gielen, Eds.: 101–117. Springer. New York, NY.

KRAUSS, B.J., J. O'DAY, C. GODFREY & K. RENTE. 2003. Peer Pressure is Like the Weather: People talk About Peer Pressure but Rarely do They Operationalize It. Presented in Poster Session at the NIMH Conference on Role of Families in Preventing and Adapting to HIV/AIDS, Washington, DC.

LAMMERS, C., M. IRELAND, M. RESNICK & R. BLUM. 2000. Influences on adolescents' decision to postpone onset of sexual intercourse: a survival analysis of virginity among youths aged 13 to 18 years. Journal of Adolescent Health *26*, 42–48.

LEWIN, T. 2005. Are these parties for real? New York Times, June 30, E, pp. 1, 6.

LIFSON, A. 1992. Transmission of the Human Immunodeficiency Virus. *In* AIDS: Etiology, Diagnosis, Treatment and Prevention. V.T. DeVita, S. Hellman & S. Rosenberg, Eds.: 111–122. Lippincott. Philadelphia, PA.

MARSHALL, A. (Ed.). 2003. State of the World Population 2003: Making One Billion Count Investing in Adolescents' Health and Rights. United Nations Publications. New York, NY.

McGill, D.A. 2000. Factors that predict a pregnancy risk profile in adolescents: Risk behaviors, perceptions and neighborhood context. Doctoral dissertation, Loma Linda University. Dissertation Abstracts International: Section B: The Sciences and Engineering *60*(9-B), 4559.

Nicolosi, A., M.L. Correa-Leite, M. Musicco, C. Arici, G. Gavazzeni & A. Lazzarin. 1994. The efficiency of male-to-female and female-to-male sexual transmission of the Human Immunodeficiency Virus: a study of 730 stable couples. Epidemiology *5*, 570–575.

O'Sullivan, L.F., H.F.L. Meyer-Bahlburg & B.X. Watkins. 2000. The influence of peer norms and social contexts on the development of sexual behavior in urban, low-income, African-American and Latina families. Manuscript submitted for publication.

Pulerwitz, J., H. Amaro, W. De Jong, S.L. Gortmaker & R. Rudd. 2002. Relationship power, condom use and HIV risk among women in the USA. AIDS Care *14*, 789–800.

Reid, E. & M. Bailey. 1992. Young woman: Silence, Susceptibility and the HIV epidemic, AIDS in Society Infold (Oct./Nov.).

Rothenberg, R.B., C. Sterk, K.E. Toomey, J.J. Potterat, D. Johnson, M. Schrader. 1998. Using social network and ethnographic tools to evaluate syphilis transmission. Sexually Transmitted Diseases *25*, 154–160.

Rouse, L.P. 2002. Marital and sexual lifestyles in the United States: attitudes, behaviors, and relationships in social context. Haworth Clinical Practice Press, Binghamton, NY.

Sales, N.J. 1997. The sex trap. New York Magazine 30, 27–33.

Sullivan, M.L. 1996. Developmental transitions in Poor Youth: Delinquency and Crime. *In* Transitions Through Adolescence: Interpersonal Domains and Context. J.A. Graber, J. Brooks-Gunn & A.C. Petersen, Eds.: 141–164. Lawrence Erlbaum. Mahwah, NJ.

Welch, C., K. Rente, J. O'Day, C. Godfrey, B. Kravss, N. Minian, *et al.* 2004. The role of friends and family in providing life direction and preventing HIV. Poster presented at the NIMH Conference on the Role of Families in Preventing and Adapting to HIV/AIDS, Atlanta, GA.

Welych, L.R., B. Laws, A.F. Fiorito, T.H. Durham, D.A. Cibula, & S.D. Lane. 1998. Formative research for interventions among adolescents at high risk for gonorrhea and other STDs. Journal of Public Health Management and Practice *4*, 54–61.

Woloch, N. 1999. Women and the American Experience. McGraw Hill. Boston, MA.

Cyberspace Violence against Girls and Adolescent Females

JUNE F. CHISHOLM

Pace University, New York, New York, USA

ABSTRACT: Children and adolescents today are the first generation raised in a society in which technological literacy is essential for effective citizenship in the 21st century. With many more youth using digital technologies for educational and recreational purposes, there has been an increase in social problems in cyberspace, exposing them to different forms of cyberviolence. This article gives an overview of the developments in cyberspace, describes different types of cyberviolence, and focuses on cyberbullying among girls and adolescent females as both victims and perpetrators of cyberbullying. At-risk online activities among girls and adolescent females as well as strategies to promote cybersafety are presented. Current research and future directions for research are reviewed.

KEYWORDS: cyberviolence; cyberbullying; ICTs

Although no voice has yet been given to the experience of children [and adolescents] enticed by the new opportunities for violent activity in cyberspace or lured into an exploitative online encounter, anecdotal evidence has suggested that virtual interactions have resulted in subsequent repercussions for young people's physical and social well being. (Berson *et al.*, 2002)

INTRODUCTION

The use of digital technology, including computers, cell phones, multiplayer video games, and so on, in the home and, most recently, on-the-go (e.g., blackberries, mobile phones) for recreational purposes, has increased among our youth over the past 15 years. Children and teens between the ages of 8 to 18 years spend an average of 8 hours per day using Information and Communication Technologies (ICTs) (ISG, 2001). A recent survey conducted by *Seventeen* magazine of girls aged 12 to 18 years showed that 74% of adolescent girls spend the majority of the time online in chat rooms or sending IMs (instant messages) and e-mails (Berson *et al.*, 2002).

Address for correspondence: June F Chisholm, Pace University, Department of Psychology, 41 Park Row, New York, NY 10038.
e-mail: jchisholm@pace.edu

More recently, schools have implemented computer technology for educational purposes, the tremendous benefits of which are evident. The National Center for Education Statistics (2001) reports that 99% of public schools in the United States have access to the Internet. ICTs are used to access a broad range of information from a variety of Internet sources (e.g., blogs, journals, newspapers, etc.) for learning and building skills in the following areas: critical thinking, communication, knowledge acquisition, creativity, and collaborative problem solving. Indeed, children and adolescents today are growing up in a society in which technological literacy is essential for effective citizenship in the 21st century (Berson & Berson, 2003; Gurak, 2001; Kubey, 2002).

These technologies have created a new frontier, commonly known as "cyberspace." The term "cyberspace" first appeared in *Neuromancer*, a science fiction novel, by William Gibson (1984) who referred to it as a consensual hallucination (Berson, 2003). It describes an intangible, nonmaterial location or dimension created by computer systems to which people gain access, allowing them to communicate with one another via e-mail, engage in research, "surf the net," and so on. In cyberspace, files, mail messages, and graphics are the "objects" and, in this medium, different modes of transportation and delivery move the objects around. The movement involved in this type of activity requires pressing keys on a keyboard, moving a mouse, or voice commands. Some computer programs consist of games that are designed to give the user an experience that resembles physical reality; in virtual reality, for instance, the user is presented with feedback affecting the sensory systems such that occurrences in cyberspace feel real.

Unfortunately, with the increased use of ICTs among children and adolescents, we are witnessing the emergence of social problems in cyberspace involving a range of activities by some youth and adults that misuse and/or abuse these technologies, endangering the well being of children, adolescents, and adults alike. Thus, for some, entering cyberspace is more of a trek through a cyber wilderness, reminiscent of the wild, wild West in the United States in the 1800s (e.g., the history of the expansion of the United States into the "new frontier" during this period reveals a time of achievements, rapid growth, and development as well as a sense of lawlessness and danger). In 2005 a private high school in New Jersey banned blogs and MySpace.com accounts in an effort to protect students from exposure to or engagement in inappropriate and/or illegal activities online (e.g., sexual exploitation by predators, harassment, etc.). This action caused controversy; those opposed to the banning questioned the legality of the decision as well as the wisdom in banning the online sites rather than educating students about the inherent dangers in using these sites (Bruno, 2005). In view of the recent announcement in the media about the merger of Google.com (a major search engine) with MySpace.com (a major social network for youth) and the anticipated economic bonanza for the business world, banning MySpace.com use seems futile. Other avenues to curtail inappropriate online behavior among teenagers need to be explored and implemented.

One out of every 17 youth reported being threatened or harassed while using the Internet (US Department of Justice, 2001). A survey of 1,500 students in the United States, grades 4 to 8, found that 42% had been victims of online bullying and 21% had received mean-spirited or menacing emails/IMs (instant messages) (ISAFE, 2003). In another survey of 1,500 children between the ages of 10 and 17 years, 25% reported being exposed to unwanted sexual material while online; approximately 19% of these young people were propositioned while online (Mitchell, Finkelhor & Wolak, 2001, 2003).

The social problems occurring in cyberspace are not limited to the United States. The scope of this phenomenon is international, involving many countries (Australia, Canada, Japan, United Kingdom, Russia, and New Zealand to name a few), affecting people all around the world from all walks of life (e.g., adults and children, men and women, rich and poor, privileged and disenfranchised). Liau et al. (2005) explored risky Internet behavior among adolescent Internet users in Singapore and found that those adolescents who were frequent users of the Internet (e.g., daily online activity) participated in chat rooms and online games, and disclosed personal information online and had face-to-face meetings with someone first encountered online. In Scotland and New Zealand, social problems have emerged with the increased use of cell phones, especially text messaging, to such an extent that some schools have banned mobile phones (Smith & Williams, 2004). The following text message, "When you are feeling down... bash a Christian or Catholic to lift up" was found on the cell phone of one of the perpetrators of a gang rape in Sydney, Australia (Wockner, 2002, p. 3).

THE PSYCHOLOGICAL CHARACTERISTICS OF CYBERSPACE

The anonymity involved in creating a screen name encourages the acting out of fantasies lending a "masquerade" quality to online activity. A normally withdrawn person can act out aggressions online that she or he would never express in public. Inexperienced, immature young men and women seeking companionship may tend to act inappropriately online. Berson et al. (2002) discuss the "culture of deception" and anonymity prevalent in online communication as serious concerns because they lead to disinhibition. Adolescent youth, especially females who spend the majority of their time online in chat rooms, and sending e-mails and IMs, are vulnerable and at risk. The anonymous, often provocative online exchanges that, for some, represent innocent, though misguided efforts to establish intimate and positive online relationships create varying degrees of risk or safety in online social encounters. Many young people who have had a negative online experience that caused discomfort do not report the incident or seek help to cope with their reaction (Beran & Li, 2005; Mitchell *et al.*, 2005).

Zizek (2004) argues that the social function of cyberspace in our society today is to bridge the gap between an individual's public symbolic identity and that identity's fantasmatic background. Ideas, fantasies, beliefs, all part of the inner world, are more readily and immediately projected into the public symbolic space. The technological phenomenon of the "screen," and the mechanics of its functioning, create a logic that impacts other spheres of psychological/social functioning of the user, especially for youth (Wallace, 1999).

Suler's (2005) discussion of the characteristics of cyberspace, which affect psychological functioning and may predispose vulnerable youth to act out online and/or be targeted for abuse, supports Zizek's perspective. The reader is referred to Suler's (2005) text, *The Psychology of Cyberspace* (available online at http://www.rider.edu/suler/psycyber/psycyber.html) for a comprehensive discussion of these characteristics: reduced sensation, texting, identity flexibility, altered perception, equalized status, transcended space, temporal flexibility, social multiplicity, and media disruption.

The following brief discussion of texting, identity flexibility, and online disinhibition (which occurs as a function of the interplay of the characteristics) highlights the "Janus-like" quality of cyberspace as a gateway into activities that can be simultaneously good and bad, depending upon one's perspective. "Texting" involves typing ideas/thoughts and reading those of others seen in e-mail, chat rooms, IMs, SMS, and blogs; it constitutes the most common form of social interaction with its own unique language, a text-based form of communication that helps to forge an identity of membership in a group and/or community. The following text message illustrates this: "lmao ur funny ill c u latr iight" translates into, "Laugh my ass off you are funny I'll see you later, alright?" Users thus have a sense of belonging and are sensitive to signs of being included or excluded, valued or criticized, and so on. "Identity flexibility" is a consequence of texting because of the lack of face-to-face cues and the sense of anonymity that one has options with how they present themselves; i.e., texting as a written form of communication permits opportunities to experiment with self expression (e.g., being younger or older, male or female, changing ethnicity, etc.) in a variety of cyberspace environments. Online "disinhibition" refers to the loosening of psychological barriers that serve to block the release of innermost, private thoughts, feelings, and needs. In short, online social interactions can and often do change the way in which an individual generally self discloses and self creates. Parks and Floyd (1996) noted that children tended not to think about the risks involved in disclosing personal information online to strangers. Once again, the effect of disinhibition may be benign or "toxic" (e.g., taking the risk to explore aspects of one's self in a safe environment vs. exploring the "dark side" of the Internet in unsafe ways, misbehaving, etc.).

PSYCHOLOGICAL VULNERABILITIES OF ADOLESCENTS AND CYBERSPACE

The needs and motivations of adolescents have been well researched and presented in the psychological literature. Adolescents are learning who they are, what is important to them, what they value, how to relate to others, making friends and maintaining friendships, what their goals for the future are, and developing skills and competencies to become productive citizens to name a few of their concerns. In short, they are focused on identity, intimacy, self-esteem, wanting to belong, becoming more autonomous and separating from family, establishing and maintaining a more mature way of managing and regulating emotions, and preparing for a career/occupation. Cyberspace offers all sorts of opportunities for adolescents to satisfy that need to express, explore, and experiment with their identity and learn about the world. Indeed, this generation of adolescents has been described in the literature as being "always on," that is, continually connected to ICTs in this, the information age.

According to Gross (2004), communication is the most important use of the Internet for today's adolescents. While teens continue to learn critical thinking skills, they are not automatically inclined to apply these skills in their face-to-face social interactions as they strive for healthy emotional adjustment. Nor are they inclined, or indeed, cognitively and emotionally capable of applying these skills in their online activities. Moreover, their increasing independence from adult scrutiny and their inclination to solve their problems without parental/adult assistance complicate efforts to develop effective prevention/intervention programs to minimize online victimization.

GENDER DIFFERENCES IN ONLINE BEHAVIOR

Initially, the Internet was viewed primarily as a "male domain" because, up until recently, more men than women were using computers and going online. Efforts to improve computer involvement of girls in schools and the advent of cell phones have increased the number of females using this technology (AAUW, 2000; Smith & Williams, 2004). As female participation has increased, sex-related differences in online behavior have emerged. Herring (2004) notes differences in online communication styles based on gender. Females use more supportive language, express appreciation more directly, and foster community building. Males use adversarial language (e.g., sarcasm), self-promotion more than community building, and "flaming" (antagonistic, confrontational speech). Inexperienced, immature, young men and women seeking companionship may tend to act inappropriately online. Subrahmanyam *et al.* (2006) found gender differences in identity presentation and sexual exploration in monitored and unmonitored online teen chat rooms. Specifically, youth who self-identified as younger and female were more likely to participate in a protected environment of monitored chat than were those youth who self-identified as older and male. The latter were more likely to participate in unmonitored chat rooms. Also, females were more likely to produce implicit sexual communication (e.g., "eminem is hot"), whereas males tended to produce more explicit sexual communication (e.g., "whats up horny guys IM me..." (p. 399). Hence, the potential danger in cyberspace is in part due to the desires and needs of those who use Internet online services for social communication.

The literature on gender differences in the expression of aggression finds that girls tend to engage in a passive, relational style of aggression that extends into their online behavior (e.g., spreading rumors, the threat of withdrawing affection, excluding someone from a social network, and/or important social function) (Crick *et al.*, 2002). For example, a teen who has not been "IMed" (instant messaged) about the color scheme for the clothes to be worn the next day at school will be tomorrow's social outcast among her peers; wearing the wrong colors announces to all that she had been excluded from the previous evening's online discussion. There is also evidence suggesting that individuals who do not receive text messages when they expect to feel left out and dejected (Taylor & Harper, 2003). With respect to online bullying, "Mean Girls" is one kind of bullying done in a group for "fun" at the expense of the feelings of the target (STAR-W, 2005). As the name suggests, this type of bullying is distinctive and typically seen among females, reflecting another gender-based difference in online activity (Star-W, 2005).

Berson *et al.* (2003) found that 92% of 10,800 girls aged 12 to 18 years who participated in an online survey use a home computer as their primary access site. When online, 58% of the girls spend their time sending instant messages or e-mails to friends, 20% surf for new things on the Web, and 16% spend most of their time in chatrooms. Only 1% indicated that the majority of time online was spent working on building a web site, reading discussion boards, interacting at game sites, or engaging in homework and research.

I asked students in my undergraduate course on the Psychology of Women about any online experiences that caused discomfort for them or others. Many, unfortunately, had stories to share. One student wrote,

> As of May 2004 I graduated from ... High School, a small Catholic school in California. When I was in school the Internet was merely a tool used for research for upcoming research papers, but in the 2004–2005 school year this changed drastically. During my spring semester of college at Pace I became aware of an Internet service called "MySpace." It is a free web site in which members join, and then create their own web pages. On their pages people put pictures of themselves, schools they have attended, bulletins and other voluntary information about themselves. The biggest attraction of "MySpace" is something called a "wall"; each personal page has one. A person's wall consists of comments about them made by fellow "MySpace" friends (friends can only become friends by request and acceptance).

> By May of 2005 I joined MySpace after a friend told me about all the people from her past that she was able to reconnect with. When I joined MySpace I was also able to get in touch with people I had not seen in years, I was able to talk to them and see how they were doing, I loved the experience. As I spent more time on the actual site I became aware that there were people using the site in a negative manner. While I was surfing pages one day I came upon many pages from the kids that were in the grade below me in high school. They were now seniors and seemed to be out of control. Most of the pages I came across chronicled tales of people's drug abuse and underage drinking, and many of the girls' pages were laden with personal tales of their own sexual exploits. I was shocked to see these things because in my mind these kids were still the innocent juniors I once knew. When I thought I couldn't be any more shocked I read a bulletin (a mass message sent to all of one's MySpace friends) calling a girl a slut and listing her actual phone number "for a good time."
>
> I went home for the summer and decided to ask one of my friend's younger sisters who was still at my high school about the MySpace usage. She told me of even more occurrences like the one above. She even told me about students starting sexual rumors about a teacher. The rumors got back to the school of course and the teacher was constantly harassed. After this, the school was forced to step in. The first step the school made was to attempt to ban My Space usage. This was of course impossible because it violated freedom rights of students; so they did the next best thing, held many conferences about it and eventually banned MySpace from all school computers. Today the exact same things are going on because students can of course go online at home and do whatever they want. There are a small but powerful group of people who are using this web site negatively and it is impacting the reputation of the school and girls everywhere." (M.H., 2005)

This student's account of her experience illustrates several issues. She is an adolescent who observes that her response and participation in cyberspace differs from younger adolescents. The difference reflects not only maturational processes of adolescence but also the time frame in which digital technology has become a significant influence in our society and in the social functioning of youth. Her initial response mirrors how an entire generation, prior to the explosion of this technology, used computers. It is therefore important to include cohort variables when conducting research in this area. Second, what motivated her to explore this Internet site has been discussed in the literature on gender in which needs for social affiliation and communication are important for females. Third, the nature of the abuse she witnessed online has been discussed in the literature on belongingness theory (Baumeister & Leary, 1995); research on ostracism has demonstrated that simply being ignored and excluded is enough to produce depressive symptoms and lower self-reported satisfaction levels of self-esteem (Smith & Williams, 2004; Williams, 2001; Ybarra *et al.*, 2004). Lastly, this student's commentary on the harmful effect of the behavior of a minority of users on themselves and the rest of the community of users underscores the need for appropriate adult supervision of this online activity to curb "out of control" behavior and promote safe online environments (Aftab, 2000).

CYBERSPACE VIOLENCE

Cyberviolence consists of different types of inappropriate and/or potentially harmful online behavior including: cybercrimes (e.g., exposure to hate, violence, misinformation, consumer exploitation), cybersexploitation, cyberstalking, and cyberbullying. Cyberbullying involves children and adolescents as both victims and perpetrators of dangerous, threatening, and/or violent activity in cyberspace. The limited psychological research generated to date indicates that this kind of inappropriate online activity occurs in part because of the nature of the Internet as discussed previously and the characteristics of the users (Berson & Berson, 2002).

CYBERBULLYING

Cyberbullying, unlike bullying in which the bully confronts his/her target face-to-face in, at best, a few settings, intensifies the targeted person's experience of harm by virtue of the nature of cyberspace. In cyberspace, the bully is able to hide behind a screen name, hence act anonymously with little to no fear of punishment, before a much larger audience, also anonymous and unimaginably huge, spanning continents, cultures, and nationalities as well as time. The consequences of this abuse can shift from the psychological to the physical, from cyberspace to a real physical location. In Japan, an 11-year-old girl fatally stabbed a classmate in the school yard after an intense online argument the night before (Nakamura, 2004).

Cyberbullying occurs in chat rooms, online bulletin boards, e-mail, instant messaging, web sites, cell phones, and online multiplayer video games (e.g., Halo 2, EverQuest, Star Wars Galaxies), and entails one or more of the following socially inappropriate online behaviors: harassing, humiliating, intimidating, sending derogatory insults or threats in messages, teasing, and using inappropriate language. Harassment, for instance, consists of a range of activities including impersonating others online, posting defamatory or embarrassing personal information about others, physical and emotional abuse, stalking people online, and threatening violence (Mitchell *et al.*, 2005).

It has been suggested that there are different types of cyberbullies determined by their motivation and what they do online (Star-W, 2005). The "Vengeful Angel" views him/herself as defending a friend who is being or has been bullied in school by shifting the bullying online. The "Power-Hungry" cyberbully resembles more closely the playground bully who uses coercion and intimidation to assert their power and control over others; when this bully has technical knowledge and uses the Internet as a tool for bullying, the term "Revenge of the Nerds" is used. This type of cyberbully can damage someone's computer. The "Inadvertent Cyberbully" is one whose online reactions stem from misunderstandings online. Lastly, "Mean Girls", consists of a group of females targeting a victim.

The technology allows for the effects of bullying to spread quickly throughout the online community greatly intensifying the pressure and experience of harm, humiliation, and/or exploitation. The rapid, extensive circulation and proliferation of threatening information or pictures to the targeted individual and simultaneously to a multitude of strangers online, the practice of online "slamming" in which "bystanders" participate in the online harassment, "flaming" (an antagonistic, "in your face" argumentative style of online communication used primarily, but not exclusively by males), and, as seen in online games, cheating, forming roving gangs, and blocking entryways are examples of how cyberbullying differs from what is usually deemed to be bullying behavior (Beran & Li, 2005; ECPAT International, 2005; Espelage & Swearer, 2003; Fekkes *et al.*, 2005; Herring, 1994).

Without doubt, this generation of young people is increasingly communicating in ways unfamiliar to adults in venues only dimly grasped by them. While parents may be doing an admirable job of supervising and guiding their children and teens in "offline" activities, youth today are less likely to be adequately supervised *while in cyberspace* by caring, knowledgeable adults (Aftab, 2000). The irony is that parents, sitting right next to their child who is in a dangerous situation online, may be totally clueless about the present danger because they and their child are in the comfort and safety of home. The parents, as a result, perceive no danger and therefore fail to protect their child. Consequently, our youth are at risk for short-term/transitory harm as well as long-term psychological/physical damage, particularly when social interactions initiated online with someone impersonating a peer shift to real physical encounters with adult predators (Berson, 2003; Butterfield, 2002).

RESEARCH ON AT-RISK ONLINE BEHAVIORS

As with any technology, the knowledge required to navigate the Internet and other digital technologies (e.g., cell phones, palmtops) involves both expertise and skills in the mechanical use of the equipment as well as knowledge and skills about using the Internet for the purpose of communication, social networking, education, research, business enterprises, and so on. Many youth today are seemingly whiz kids about *how* to use these devices, but deficient in comprehending the ramifications of some of the uses to which these technologies are applied.

The ability of youth to distinguish between online behaviors that pose little or no risk of harm to self and/or others is contingent upon an interplay of factors including, but not limited to, the amount of time spent online engaged in certain social interactive activities; their cognitive/emotional development and level of functioning; and the extent of parental/adult monitoring/supervision of online activity (Liau et al., 2005; Mitchell et al., 2001). At-risk online behaviors include the following: giving out personal information online, agreeing to meet with someone in person met online, receiving and sending photos, receiving and sending suggestive or threatening e-mail, and participating in chatrooms where the content results in discomfort (Berson & Berson, 2002; Hashima et al., 1999). Research suggests that troubled youth and youth who tend to have high rates of Internet use, use chatrooms, talk with strangers online, and use the Internet in households other than their own tend to be at risk for online victimization (Mitchell et al., 2001).

Another potential risk factor deals with the ease with which our young can access global information and make use of information obtained through digital technologies. On the one hand, this access has the potential to expand their awareness and exposure to diverse cultural and social worldviews. However, material obtained online may be illegal, inappropriate, age-restricted, or simply inaccurate/specious. Exposure to and acting on misinformation and/or inappropriate material online may be harmful to the cognitive/emotional or physical well being of youth.

CURRENT RESEARCH

The popular literature is informing the general public about the dangers for the growing number of youth for whom the Internet has become an integral part of their daily lives (Bergner, 2005; Bruno, 2005; Picker, 2006; Swartz, 2005). Articles in magazines and newspapers are appearing more frequently than just 1 year ago. The response from the scientific community, in the United States at least, has seemingly been slower (New Zealand and Canada, for example, have been in the forefront with identifying cyberviolence and launching initiatives to prevent it). There is now a journal devoted to issues involving cyberspace, *CyberPsychology & Behavior*. However, a lag continues in the dissemination of information from research based on representative samples of youth examining the impact of online experiences to the cognitive and psychosocial functioning of youth and identifying the characteristics of youth at risk for online victimization (Finkelhor et al., 2003, Chap. 21; Mitchell et al., 2003; Ybarra et al., 2004).

PREVENTION

Preventing cyberviolence, especially cyberbullying, involves complex interventions informed by knowledge in which coordinated efforts across communities and domains, including education, health, justice, and the workplace, combat the social forces/norms that give rise to this form of online behavior.

The Children's Online Privacy Act (COPA) enhances monitoring online activities of youngsters. It went into effect in the United States in 2000 and requires that web site operators and Internet service providers obtain verifiable parental consent when personal information is collected online from children under the age of 13 years (COPA, 2006). Additional preventative activities/strategies include

- Development of awareness programs for teachers, parents, and youth
- Legislation designed to criminalize certain inappropriate online activity (e.g., the Electronic Antistalking Act of 1995)
- Hotlines where people can report illegal content on Internet sites
- Age-appropriate supervision and monitoring of online activity
- Discussion with parent(s) about online safety
- Instruction by teachers about cybersafety
- Technological developments that help to limit the amount of unwanted/harmful content

Several initiatives in the United States, within other countries, and internationally have launched projects to accomplish these objectives. ECPAT International (End Child Prostitution, Child Pornography and Trafficking of Children for Sexual Purposes), I-SAFE America, and the Internet Safety Group (ISG) from New Zealand are three such organizations with this mission.

ECPAT International is a network of organizations and individuals working around the world to protect children from all forms of sexual exploitation and violence (www.ecpat.net). As part of the United Nations study in 2005 on violence against children, ECPAT generated a report that contained a section on cyberbullying to contribute to the international effort to protect youth from violence (Muir, 2005).

I-SAFE America is a nonprofit educational foundation established in 1998 to provide students with the awareness and knowledge they need to recognize and avoid dangerous, harmful online behavior. This objective is accomplished through two major activities: providing the I-SAFE school education curriculum to schools nationwide and community outreach, which includes events for the community-at-large and school-based assemblies for the student population at which Internet safety issues are discussed (I-SAFE America, 2003).

ISG is an independent organization whose members include educators at all levels of the school system (elementary grades through college) government groups, representatives of law enforcement agencies, the judiciary, community groups, businesses, libraries, and individuals. In 2000 the Internet Safety Kit for schools, the NetSafe web site, and their toll-free NETSAFE Hotline were launched (www.netsafe.org.nz). What is stressed in these programs and projects is that education (e.g., curricula) designed for specific groups (e.g., youth, parents, teachers, school administrators, law enforcement, legislators, etc.) is crucial to reducing and/or eliminating at-risk online behavior. Empowering parents with knowledge about existing unsafe activities and teaching them skills to adequately monitor/supervise online activities are deemed important components of many intervention strategies. It is noteworthy, however, that parental supervision techniques have not been too effective in lowering adolescent risky online activity. This may be due in part to the attitudes of teens who do not disclose information about their online activities to their parents. Moreover, studies measuring parental monitoring are in fact assessing the level of parental knowledge rather than parents' efforts in tracking and surveillance (Kerr & Statin, 2000; Liau *et al*. 2005).

For youth and adult users, the literature encourages "netiquette," that is, online manners encouraging acceptable conduct when engaged in an interchange with people in cyberspace (Berson, 2000; Cole, 2001; Willard, 2002). Clearly articulated rules assist youth in behaving courteously and respectfully to others, facilitating positive social interactions with others. Application of the rules enables young people to apply critical thinking skills to online activity, thereby promoting healthy, productive social discourse and participation (Kubey, 2002).

Some of the rules of "netiquette" include the following advice to young online users:

- Never give out your password to anyone other than a parent/guardian
- Don't share secrets, photos, or anything online that might be embarrassing if someone (an entire school) found out
- Don't send messages when you're angry to avoid saying something you'll regret later
- Be a good cyberfriend—don't send e-mails or IMs written by a friend to anyone else without that friend's permission
- Be as nice online as you are offline
- Know that if you act like a cyberbully, there will be consequences/punishment

HOW TO REPORT CYBERVIOLENCE

Incidents of cyberviolence can be reported in several ways:

- CyberTipline   Unsolicited, obscene materials and/or threats can be reported to http://www.missingkids.com/cybertip/ or by calling 1-800-843-5678
- ISP   Report harassment to the offender's Internet service provider and request that the abuser's account be suspended or blocked
- Local police   There may be laws in place that prohibit cyberbullying. If the harasser threatens violence or abduction, contact the police immediately

- School — Many schools now include online bullying in their antiharassment policies
- Supportive Adult — Enlisting the aid of an adult may facilitate taking appropriate action to stop the bullying

DIRECTIONS FOR FUTURE RESEARCH

The discussion on cyberspace and cyberbullying reflect the emergence of a new field of inquiry on how the Internet influences the lives of children and adolescents. Psychological theories and research are in the early stages; the studies to date have relied on a few select studies that have used questionnaires/surveys for the methodology, conducted online and offline. The focus has mainly been on identifying types of online activities and the frequency of use among young people. Mitchell *et al.* (2005) suggest that

> the implementation of population-based studies about Internet use and problematic Internet experiences should help in the development of norms in this area, which, in turn, is an important component in the development of public policy, prevention, and intervention in this field. More research is also needed concerning the mental health impact of various problematic Internet experiences. Internet problems may be adding some unique dynamics to the field of mental health that require special understanding, new responses, and interventions in some cases... For example, are persons with impulse control problems drawn to certain aspects of the Internet, such as pornography and gaming, which could further exacerbate their symptoms? Does Internet exposure exacerbate preexisting mental health difficulties? (p. 507).

Greenfield and Yan (2006), surveying the empirical literature on the impact of virtual reality on psychosocial functioning of children and adolescents, ask the following: "How should we think of the Internet from a developmental perspective? What are the uses to which the Internet is put and what do children and adolescents get from it?" (p. 392). They suggest another possible direction for future research, which involves looking at the Internet as a "new object of cognition" (p. 393), that is, the interplay of Internet involvement and cognitive/emotional development of children, adolescents, and adults. Researchers interested in this line of inquiry will have to tackle the complex challenges unique to the Internet because, unlike other media/electronic devices (e.g., TV), Internet users participate in and co-construct the virtual social and physical world of this phenomenon. An offshoot of this line of inquiry may explore developmental trends of bullying across age groups and domains. For example, are the school yard bullies of 15 years ago the office online bullies of today in the workplace?

Cyberbullying requires much more empirical study to further our understanding of this phenomenon. Results from existing studies need to be replicated and validated. Future research needs to develop additional measures to determine how to reduce the risk of being victimized, identifying and assisting those who have been subjected to cyberbullying, and determining how to prevent it.

It is important for researchers, clinicians, and other professionals who work with youth to better understand the diversity among the victims of cyberbullying as well as the diversity among cyberbullies. Current research indicates that considering the age, gender, social class, access to ICTs, and individual preferences regarding online activities of children and adolescents is crucial to understanding the interplay of the online activity and the user's experience of being bullied and bullying.

Existing support services need to become sensitized to the needs of children and adolescents who have suffered abuse and/or are abusing others in this venue to appropriately address their vulnerability and victimization. As discussed in the literature, many youth never report their experience of cyberbullying and cope with the negative feelings/experience on their own. Therefore, additional training for mental health and other professionals is necessary to enable them to recognize the signs of cyberbullying that contribute to psychological distress and interpersonal difficulties, and interfere with the normal developmental tasks of childhood and adolescence.

REFERENCES

AFTAB, P. (2000). *The parent's guide to protecting your children in cyberspace.* New York, NY: McGraw-Hill.

AAUW (2000). Tech Savvy: Educating Girls in the New Computer Age. Washington, DC: AAUW Educational Foundation Research.

BAUMEISTER, R.F., & LEARY, M.R. (1995). The need to belong: desire for interpersonal attachments as a fundamental human motivation. *Psychological Bulletin, 117,* 497–529.

BERAN, T., & LI , Q. (2005). Cyber-harassment: a study of a new method for an old behavior. *Journal of Educational Computing Research, 32*(3), 265–277.

BERGNER, D. (2005, January 23). The mind of a cybermolester. The New York Times Magazine: The New York Times, 26–61.

BERSON, M.J. (2000). *Rethinking research and pedagogy in the social studies: the creation of caring connections through technology and advocacy.* Theory & Research in Social Education, 28, 121–131.

BERSON, I. (2003). Grooming cybervictims: the psychosocial effects of online exploitation for youth. *Journal of School Violence, 2*(1), 5–18.

BERSON, I. & BERSON, M. (2002). Evolving a Community Initiative to Protect Children in Cyberspace. Florida Mental Health Institute, University of South Florida.

BERSON, I., & BERSON, M. (2003). Digital literacy for effective citizenship. *Social Education., 67*(3), 164–167.

BERSON, I., BERSON, M. & FERRON, J. (2002). Emerging risks of violence in the digital age: lessons for educators from an online study of adolescent girls in the United States. [electronic version]. *Meridian: A Middle School Computer Technologies Journal, 5*(2), retrieved September 28, 2005 from http://www.ncsu.edu/meridian/sum2002/cyberviolence/index.html.

BRUNO, L. (2004, October 24). Blogging ban provokes debate over cyberspace. *Daily Record*, p. 1–6.
BUTTERFIELD, L. (2002). NetSafe: The New Zealand model for Internet (ICT) safety education. Netalert, Growing Australia Online.
COLE, J.I. *et al.* (2001) UCLA Internet Report 2001: Surveying the Digital Future Year Two. Los Angeles, CA: UCLA Center for Communication Policy. Available at www.ccp.ucla.edu.
COPA (2006). http://www.ftc.gov/bcp/conline/pubs/buspubs/coppa.htm. Accessed August 8, 2006.
CRICK, N.R., CASA, J.F. & NELSON, D.A. (2002). Toward a more comprehensive understanding of peer maltreatment: studies of relationship victimization. *Current Directions in Psychological Science, 11*, 96–101.
ESPELAGE, D.L. & SWEARER, S.M. (2003). Research on school bullying and victimization: What have we learned and where do we go from here? *School Psychology Review, 32*(3), 365–383.
FEKKES, M., PIJPERS, F.I.M. & VERLOOVE-VANHORICK, S.P. (2005). Bullying: Who does what, when and where? Involvement of children, teachers and parents in bullying behavior. *Health Education Research, 20*(1), 81–91.
FINKELHOR, D., MITCHELL, K. & WOLAK, J. (2003). The exposure of youth to unwanted sexual material on the Internet: a national survey of risk, impact and prevention. *Youth & Society, 34*(3), 330–358.
GREENFIELD, P.M. & SUBRAHMANYAM, K. (2003). Online discourse in a teen chat room: new codes and new modes of coherence in a visual medium. *Journal of Applied Developmental Psychology, 24*, 713–738.
GREENFIELD, P.M. & YAN, Z. (2006). Children, adolescents and the Internet: a new field of inquiry in developmental psychology. *Developmental Psychology, 42*(3), 391–394.
GROSS, E.F. (2004). Adolescent Internet use: what we expect, what teens report. *Journal of Applied Developmental Psychology, 25*, 633–649.
GURAK, L.J. (2001). *Cyberliteracy: Navigating the Internet with awareness*. New Haven, CT: Yale University Press.
HASHIMA, P. & FINKELHOR, D. (1999). Violent victimization of youth versus adults in The National Crime Victimization Survey. *Journal of Interpersonal Violence, 14*, 799–819.
HERRING, S. (1994). Gender differences in computer-mediated communication: Bringing familiar baggage to the new frontier.
ISG. (2001). Girls on the Net—the survey of adolescent girls' use of the Internet in New Zealand. Auckland: The New Zealand Internet Safety Group. Retrieved on Sept. 19, 2005, from http://www.netsafe.orgnz/research/research_girls.aspx I-SAFE America, retrieved August 8, 2006, from http://www.ncjrs.gov/pdffiles1/nij/ISAFE.pdf.
KUBEY, R. (2002). How media education promotes critical thinking, democracy, health, and aesthetic appreciation. In: *Thinking critically about media: Schools and families in partnership*. Cable in the Classroom, (1–6). Alexandria, VA. www.ciconline.org. http://www.cnn.com/2006/TECH/Internet/02/21/myspace.dangers.ap/index.html. Teens at risk on social Web sites.
KERR, M. & STATIN, H. (2000). What parents know, how they know it, and several forms of adolescent adjustment: further support for a reinterpretation of monitoring. *Developmental Psychology, 36*, 366–380.

LIAU, A.K. KHOO, A. & ANG, P.H. (2005). Factors influencing adolescents' engagement in risky Internet behavior. *CyberPsychology & Behavior*, 8(6), 513–520.
MITCHELL, K.J., BECKER-BLEASE, K.A. & FINKELHOR, D. (2005). Inventory of problematic Internet experiences encountered in clinical practice. *Professional Psychology: Research and Practice*, 36(5), 498–309.
MITCHELL, K., FINKELHOR, D. & WOLAK, J. (2001). Risk factors for and impact of online sexual solicitation of youth. *Journal of the American Medical Association 285*(23), 3011–3014.
MITCHELL, K., FINKELHOR, D. & WOLAK, J. (2003). The exposure of youth to unwanted sexual material on the Internet: a national survey of risk, impact, & prevention. *Youth & Society 34*(3), 330–358.
MUIR, D. (2005). *Violence against children in cyberspace*. ECPAT International. Retrieved from ECPAT_cyberspace_2005_ENG
NAKAMURA, A. (2004, June 5). Killing stokes fears over impact of net. *The Japan News*. Retrieved from http://202.221.217.59/print/news/nn06-2004/mn20040605a5.htm
PARKS, M.R. & FLOYD, K. (1996). Making friends in cyberspace. *Journal of Computer-Mediated Communication. 46*, 80–97.
PICKER, L. (March, 2006). The new danger online. *Good Housekeeping*, 112–116. Statistics from: Finkelhor, D., Mitchell, K., & Wolak, J. (March, 2001). Highlights of the youth internet safety survey. *U.S. Department of Justice*. OJJDP Fact Sheet #04.
SMITH, A. & WILLIAMS, K. (2004). R U there? Ostracism by cell phone text messages. *Group Dynamics: Theory, Research and Practice*, 8(4), 291–301.
STAR-W (Students Using Technology to Achieve Reading and Writing) (2005). Retrieved September 19, 2005, from http://www.starw.org/b2b/4TypesofCybullies.htm.
SUBRAHMANYAM, K., GREENFIELD, P. & SMAHEL, D. (2006). Connecting developmental constructions to the Internet: Identity presentation and sexual exploration in online teen chat rooms. *Developmental Psychology*, 42(3), 395–406.
SWARTZ, J. (2005). Schoolyard bullies get nastier online. *USA Today* retrieved from www.uastoday.com/tech/news/2005-03-06-2005-cover-cyberbullies_x.htm.
TAYLOR, A.S. & HARPER, R. (2003). The gift of the gab: A design oriented sociology of young people's use of mobiles. *Journal of Computer Supported Cooperative Work (CSCW)*, 12, 267–296.
WALLACE, P. (1999). *The psychology of the Internet*. Cambridge: Cambridge University Press.
WILLARD, N. (2002). Computer ethics, etiquette & safety for the 21st century student Eugene, Ore.: International Society for Technology in Education (ISTE).
WILLIAMS, K.A. (2001). *Ostracism: The power of silence*. New York: Guilford Press.
WOCKER, C. (2002). Bash a Christian: Rapists' hi-tech message of hate. *The Daily Telegraph*, p. 3.
YBARRA, M., LEAF, P. & DIENER-WEST, M. (2004). Sex differences in youth-reported depressive symptomatology and unwanted Internet sexual solicitation. *Journal of Medical Internet Research*, 6(1), e5. Retrieved Sept. 28, 2005. http://www.jmir.org/2004/1/e5/.
ZIZEK, S. (2004). What can psychoanalysis tell us about cyberspace? *Psychoanalytic Review*, 91(6), 801–830.

Early Violence Prevention Programs

Implications for Violence Prevention Against Girls and Women

MICHELLE GUTTMAN, BARBARA MOWDER, AND ANASTASIA YASIK

Psychology Department, Pace University, New York, NY 10038, USA

ABSTRACT: This chapter considers violence prevention programs in light of aggression and violence directed toward girls and women. More specifically, current violence prevention programs, directed toward young children and/or their caregivers, are discussed with a special consideration for the Adults and Children Together (ACT) Against Violence Training Program developed by the American Psychological Association (APA) and the National Association of Education of Young Children (NAEYC). Data supporting ACT is presented, with implications for further program development and evaluation. Finally, parent education, theory and research, and professional services related to violence prevention are discussed.

KEYWORDS: violence prevention; females; aggression; youth; training programs

INTRODUCTION

Watching the news, reading the newspaper, looking at video games, viewing children's television, and observing children in school each provide evidence of the presence of aggression and violence in children's lives (Guttman & Mowder, 2005). Much of that aggression and violence is directed toward girls and women. For instance, the vast majority of domestic violence cases involve male aggression and power assertion toward women. And, video games frequently portray women as objects or targets for violent behavior.

The literature on children's exposure to media violence (e.g., television, movies, video games) strongly suggests that viewing violence is a contributing factor to the development of aggression. Recently, Huesmann *et al.* (2003) conducted a follow-up study of their 1977 longitudinal study of 557 children regarding children's television habits and subsequent aggressive behavior. Results indicate that television viewing between ages 6 and 9, children's identification with aggressive same-sex television characters, and the perception that television violence is realistic are significantly correlated with adult aggression for both men and women. In fact, the stronger the beliefs the more adult aggression, regardless of how aggressive the individuals behaved as children. They found that when exposed to high levels of media violence in early childhood, men as well as women are at increased risk for developing aggressive and violent behavior.

Furthermore, Anderson *et al.* (2003) looked at the research pertaining to violent films, music, television, and video games, consistently finding evidence that media violence increases the likelihood of aggressive and violent behavior in both immediate and long-term contexts. More specifically, short-term exposure increases the likelihood of physical as well as verbally aggressive behavior, thoughts, and emotions. Media violence also produces long-term effects by providing aggressive scripts and supporting beliefs about social behavior.

Early childhood is an especially important period for learning many skills such as those in the interpersonal and problem-solving realm. This developmental time period lays the foundation for much of socioemotional development, including the formation of interpersonal relations through relating to others (Bornstein & Lamb, 1999). Early childhood is also the time when children develop their views of roles and relationships, including gender roles. The developing views of gender roles include expectations of behavior toward girls and women. During this period of development, aggression and violence enters into young children's lives in a variety of ways such as through experiences within the family, at school, in the community, and through multiple media sources. Taken as a whole, these experiences significantly influence how the female gender is perceived and treated in everyday situations.

Certainly, domestic violence is a major issue regarding aggression and violence toward girls, and especially women. Edelson (1999) reviewed the literature focusing on the behavioral, emotional, and cognitive problems of child witnesses of domestic violence. Studies using the Child Behavior Checklist reveal that these children exhibit aggressive and antisocial behaviors as well as fearful and inhibited behaviors (i.e., both externalizing and internalizing). Specifically, children who witness domestic violence show more anxiety, depression, trauma symptoms and temperament problems compared to those who do not have such experiences (Edelson, 1999). In a related study, examining 118 studies on the psychosocial outcomes of children exposed to interparental violence, Kitzmann *et al.* (2003) found that violence-exposed children exhibit physical and verbal aggression in response to conflict. Not surprisingly, these children also tend to exhibit negative cognitions as well as affect.

As a result of exposure to aggressive models, what children see during their early period of development shapes how they react in other situations or conflicts that might arise (Guttman & Mowder, 2005). Such an outcome is not surprising given that Bandura's (1973) social learning theory postulates children learn aggressive behavior the same way they learn other kinds of behavior, through observation and imitation. In other words, children internalize the behavior they frequently witness in role models (e.g., media characters, parents), incorporating their actions into their own behavioral repertoire. Furthermore, Bandura (1973) maintains that children acquire entire repertoires of novel aggressive behavior from observing aggressive models, retaining response patterns over extended periods of time. An important aspect of the entire process is the consequence following the aggressive behavior. If rewarded, children's likelihood of imitating the behavior, and related beliefs that this action is favorable, increases. According to this well-accepted theory, observing violence leads to imitation of aggressive behavior as well as the incorporation of aggressive attitudes and beliefs.

Huesmann (1988, 1998) added an information-processing perspective to social learning theory, leading to a social-cognitive observational learning theory. From this perspective, three cognitive structures are relevant: schemas about a hostile world, scripts for social problem solving that rely on aggression, and normative beliefs that aggression is acceptable. Therefore, through repeated observations of violence (e.g., people in their families, media), children develop biased world schemas by attributing hostility to the world and others around them (Huesmann, 1988). Hostile attributions increase children's likelihood of behaving aggressively. In addition, observing violence provides aggressive social scripts, easily retrieved from memory, which can become well established in children's behavioral repertoires. Therefore, on the basis of exposure to aggression and violence, children develop normative beliefs regarding the acceptability of aggression, increasing their likelihood of using aggressive behavior to solve interpersonal conflicts. Huesmann (1998) argues that, ultimately, children repeatedly exposed to violence habituate to aggression, do not experience violence as aversive, and accept violence as an appropriate response in diverse situations and settings.

The negative impact of exposure to violence begins early in children's lives (Guttman & Mowder, 2005). For example, Cirillo et al. (1998) indicate that violence significantly affects the psychological and physical abilities of young children to thrive, resulting in devastating effects on children's functioning. Functioning affected includes activities in the home, school, and in peer relationships. The potential for adverse effects especially on girls and women is clear. Given the prevalence of violence in children's lives as well as the detrimental effects violence exposure may have on women's development and treatment by others, violence prevention programs targeting young children and those who influence their lives (e.g., parents, teachers) are clearly needed. Building positive relationships between children and those in their lives (e.g., teachers) has the potential to offset the accumulation of violent media and other associated negative role models and, instead, potentially sets a more affirmative foundation for later development.

VIOLENCE PREVENTION PROGRAMS

A number of early violence prevention programs have been evaluated with regard to their success at reducing the effects of violence on young children (Guttman & Mowder, 2005), including Childreach, Second Step: A Violence Prevention Curriculum, Resolving Conflict Creatively Program (RCCP), PeaceBuilders, The Incredible Years, and The RETHINK Parenting and Anger Management Program. Each of the programs takes a different point of view in addressing the issue of violence prevention.

Childreach (Goodwin, Pacey & Grace, 2003) is an early identification, short-term intervention program for children under the age of 6 years, designed to address aggression as well as other young children's behavioral issues. This program provides a variety of services, including consultation, intervention for the child and family, staff training, parent training, and referral liaison services. To assess possible behavioral improvements, Goodwin *et al*. (2003) used a pre- and postmethod of assessment with a teacher-rated measure of adjustment. The evaluation revealed significant improvements in most areas of behavior (e.g., hostility, peer relations, withdrawal, and productivity) examined, with the exception of dependency. Preschool teachers and childcare staff reported high levels of satisfaction with the Childreach program. In general, research demonstrates that Childreach is an effective secondary prevention program for decreasing preschoolers' aggressive behavior.

Second Step: A Violence Prevention Curriculum (Grossman *et al*., 1997) is a social and emotional skills curriculum that teaches children attitude and behavior changes related to aggression and violence. In this program, teachers develop children's emotional understanding, empathy, impulse control, problem solving, and anger management skills through 30 specific lessons. There is also a companion program that teaches parents to practice and reinforce prosocial behaviors at home. Grossman *et al*. (1997) evaluated Second Step and found that physical aggression decreased and prosocial behavior increased among participating students.

RCCP is another prevention program; this approach teaches students choices for dealing with conflict (Aber *et al*., 1998). RCCP also focuses on helping students develop skills needed to make those choices. The program targets teachers, parents, school administrators, and others working with children in grades K–12 by providing teacher training and coaching, classroom instruction, administrator training, parent training, and peer mediation (i.e., training selected students as peer mediators). Aber *et al*. (1998) evaluated the impact of RCCP on 5,053 children from grades 2–6. Results from this study reveal a significant positive impact on children who receive a substantial amount of instruction in the RCCP curriculum as opposed to those with less instruction in RCCP. There were increases in prosocial behavior, problem solving, and academic success, and decreases in aggressive and destructive behaviors (Aber et al., 1998).

PeaceBuilders is a schoolwide, elementary school-based, violence prevention program designed to change the school climate. The program instructs parents, staff, and students on rules and activities to improve children's social competence and reduce aggression (Flannery et al., 2003). PeaceBuilders, as a program, is purposely woven into the school's everyday routine rather than scheduled in a specific time slot or subject-limited process. In a study conducted by Flannery et al. (2003), more than 4,000 students from 8 matched schools were randomly assigned to either the immediate postbaseline intervention group or to a delayed intervention group. In this study, the delayed intervention group received the PeaceBuilders program 1 year after the immediate intervention group, which continued to receive the program in the second year. Flannery et al. found that the PeaceBuilders program improved students' social competence. In addition, declines in teacher-reported aggressive behavior were found, especially for children in the program for 2 years. Beyond asserting the importance of intervention, Flannery et al. (2003) also stress the importance of early preventive interventions, especially strategies focusing on increasing positive skills as well as those targeting a reduction of aggressive behavior in young children. These results highlight the importance of intervening early in children's lives to help put them on a positive developmental course that can be maintained over time.

The Incredible Years is a research-based curricula for reducing children's aggression and behavior problems, and increasing their social and emotional competence at home and at school (Taylor et al., 1998). There are separate programs for childcare providers, children ages 3–8 years, parents, and teachers. In the parent training component, for example, there is an emphasis on nonviolent discipline strategies and teaching children problem-solving skills, anger management, and social skills. With teachers, there is training on the importance of praise, decreasing inappropriate behavior in the classroom, and strategies to promote children's social and emotional competence in school. For children, there is empathy training, learning rules, problem solving, anger management, how to make friends, and being successful in school. In six randomized studies by Taylor et al. (1998), home, laboratory, and classroom observations show that The Incredible Years' child, parent, and teacher programs effectively reduce aggressive behaviors in children; these results are sustained in 2- and 3-year follow-up studies.

Last, the RETHINK Parenting and Anger Management Program is a research-based, preventive educational workshop for educators, parents, and other professionals working with young children. The RETHINK program provides materials for teaching parents how to manage their anger as well as teach anger management skills to their children. Fetsch *et al.* (1999) evaluated the RETHINK program with 75 parents using a one-group, pretest-posttest design. Participants received a 6-week series of skill-enhancing workshops (i.e., a full-day workshop for parent educators, a 6-week program for parents). This preliminary evaluation indicates that the RETHINK Parenting and Anger Management Program reduces family conflict, and domestic, physical, and verbal aggression as well as results in positive changes in parenting and anger management skills (Fetsch *et al.*, 1999). In addition, all participants reported that their knowledge about parenting and anger management increased as a direct result of participating in RETHINK. These results suggest that the RETHINK program effectively assists parents with anger management. Despite the promising results, Fetsch *et al.* report that one limitation of their study is their failure to obtain a no-treatment comparison group.

The results of these evaluation studies (Goodwin *et al.*, 2003; Grossman *et al.*, 1997; Aber *et al.*, 1998; Flannery *et al.*, 2003; Taylor *et al.*, 1998; Fetsch *et al.*, 1999) provide evidence for the effectiveness of early intervention programs in breaking the potentially dangerous chain of events leading to violence and aggression in children. Thus, early prevention and intervention efforts can lessen aggression in elementary school-aged children (Leff *et al.*, 2001; Scheckner *et al.*, 2002). Another recently developed program is the Adults and Children Together (ACT) Against Violence Prevention Program, recently evaluated by Guttman *et al.* (2006).

THE ACT AGAINST VIOLENCE TRAINING PROGRAM

The ACT Against Violence Prevention Program, developed in 2000, is a national antiviolence initiative developed by the American Psychological Association (APA) in collaboration with the National Association for the Education of Young Children (NAEYC). The ACT program is based on research demonstrating that the early years (i.e., ages 0–8 years) constitute a critical time when children are learning basic skills that have a long-lasting impact on their lives. The goal of the ACT program is to disseminate research-based knowledge on violence prevention to those who work with young children (DaSilva, Sterne, & Anderson, 2000).

Unlike many violence prevention programs, ACT focuses exclusively on adults, helping them model and teach positive ways for young children to deal with anger and resolve conflicts. The ACT training program is considered a social-cognitive intervention, based on the assumption that children learn by observing and imitating adults in their lives (Bandura, 1973; DaSilva *et al.*, 2000)., The ACT training program further assumes that violence results in part from individuals' lack of problem-solving and social skills to deal with conflicts (DaSilva *et al.*, 2000). The program disseminates information targeting four areas of violence prevention to adults who either raise or work with children and families. Specifically, the program consists of four modules, one set tailored for parents and the other parallel program for early childhood professionals, on important skills for early violence prevention: Anger Management, Social Problem Solving, Discipline, and Media Violence.

The Anger Management module recognizes that children who have high levels of anger and do not possess the skills necessary to regulate these negative emotions (Denham *et al.*, 2002) are prone to behavioral problems and peer difficulties. The objective of the Anger Management module is for those working with young children to learn skills to help children express anger appropriately and channel their angry feelings in more constructive ways (DaSilva *et al.*, 2000)., To accomplish this, the Anger Management module focuses on topics such as helping children manage anger effectively, helping adults express and channel their anger, and anger management as a violence prevention asset.

On the basis of research showing the importance of social skills in children's lives (Mayeux & Cillessen, 2003; Schwartz & Proctor, 2000), the ACT training program also includes a Social Problem Solving module that identifies strategies to teach social problem-solving skills to young children (DaSilva *et al.*, 2000). This portion of ACT covers topics such as the importance of teaching social problem-solving skills, a developmental view of when children learn social skills, and the role of families and others working with young children in teaching these skills.

Due to extensive research showing the harmful effects of harsh disciplinary behavior on children (Patterson & Dishion, 1985; Weiss *et al.*, 1992), the ACT training program includes discipline as a module. The objective of the Discipline module is to teach strategies for responding to young children's challenging behavior, helping adults in children's lives create plans for preventing and managing those behaviors (DaSilva *et al.*, 2000). A number of topics are discussed in the Discipline module, including the relationship between discipline and violence prevention, child development issues, and the distinction between discipline and punishment.

Finally, On the basis of extensive research demonstrating the negative effects of media violence on young children (Anderson *et al.*, 2003; Huesmann *et al.*, 2003; Huesmann & Miller, 1994; Wood, Wong & Chachere, 1991), the ACT training program includes this topic as one of the four modules. The objective of the Media Violence module is to teach about the relationship between exposure to media violence and aggressive behavior (DaSilva *et al.*, 2000). The topics covered in this module include the impact of media violence on young children's lives, child development issues on how children view television differently by age, and strategies to reduce the impact of media violence on young children.

EVALUATION OF THE ACT TRAINING PROGRAM

Building upon prior violence prevention evaluation research (Fetsch *et al.*, 1999; Flannery *et al.*, 2003; Goodwin *et al.*, 2003; Grossman *et al.*, 1997), Guttman *et al.* (2006) examined the effectiveness of the ACT training program among psychologists and others working with young children. Specifically, the impact of the ACT Training Program on participants' knowledge levels as well as their perception of knowledge gained was evaluated. Also, the perceived usefulness of the modules was examined to determine if psychologists would be likely to utilize this prevention program in their own practice.

Participants were obtained from ACT training workshops offered at conferences for early childhood organizations (e.g., Association of Early Childhood and Infant Psychologists), school district in-service presentations, and university/college workshops. A sample of early childhood professionals working in preschool settings, elementary schools and mental health settings in the New York area as well as doctoral level students in a combined school-clinical child psychology program were recruited for this project. A total of 226 participants (85% female, 15% male) received the ACT training program. A comparison sample of 51 participants (80% female, 20% male) was obtained through graduate training programs and did not receive the ACT training until completion of the study. In general, the sample was predominantly Caucasian between the ages of 20–39 years and had at a minimum some graduate training.

The participants received four ACT knowledge questionnaires at pre- and posttraining, one for each of the modules in the ACT training program (i.e., Anger Management, Social Problem Solving, Discipline, Media Violence). Participants also completed four perception questionnaires, one for each ACT module. After the ACT training, participants in the treatment group were also asked about their view of the usefulness of the information presented in the modules. Participants responded to this question on a 7-point Likert-type scale with responses ranging from 1 (*not useful*) to 7 (*extremely useful*). Training sessions typically occurred over 3–4 hours and included an introduction to the ACT training program, presentation of the four modules, interactive activities, and time for discussion and/or questions. For the comparison group, which did not receive the training, the knowledge questionnaires were completed once and then after approximately 3–4 hours the knowledge questionnaires were completed a second time. At the completion of the posttest, each participant in the comparison group was provided with some materials from the ACT training program.

Guttman *et al.*'s (2006) results revealed that there was a significant difference between treatment and comparison groups for mean knowledge gains from pretest to posttest on the anger management, social problem-solving, discipline, and media violence questionnaires. As predicted, for each ACT module the treatment group had a significantly greater mean gain in knowledge from pretest to posttest, whereas the comparison group did not. With regard to perceived knowledge gained, significant increases in the treatment groups' perception of knowledge from pretest to posttest was evident for all four ACT training modules. Although all four modules were reported as useful (mean rating above 5 on a 7-point Likert scale), the participants did differentiate on the usefulness of the modules. Specifically, the media violence module was found to be statistically significantly more useful than the anger management, social problem-solving and discipline modules. Finally, it was reported that 94.7% of participants indicated that the ACT training program made a difference to them.

DISCUSSION

There currently exist a number of programs aimed at reducing violence exposure and negative consequences associated with such exposure among children and adolescents. Each of these programs has demonstrated some success in helping these populations handle the adverse effects of exposure to and/or witnessing violence and preventing further negative consequences (Guttman & Mowder, 2005). However, there has not been any research evaluating the effectiveness and utility of antiviolence training programs targeting the adults in young children's lives. Guttman *et al.* (2006) sought to add to the literature concerning violence prevention programs by evaluating the effectiveness of a relatively new program, the ACT training program, which focuses on the adults who have an impact in the lives of children from birth to 8 years of age.

According to the results of Guttman *et al.* (2006), the ACT training program does have a positive impact on early childhood professionals' knowledge of violence prevention. This finding is of particular importance for the consideration of ACT as a viable early childhood violence prevention program that works with the adults in children's lives. According to Bandura's (1973) social learning theory, children's aggressive behavior is predominantly learned through observation and modeling. One prominent origin for children's aggressive behavior is aggression that is modeled and reinforced by family members. Studies of familial determinants of aggression show that parents who favor aggressive solutions to problems have children who tend to use similar aggressive tactics in dealing with others (Bandura, 1973; Huesmann, 1988; Patterson, Reid, & Dishion, 1992). Therefore, the ACT training program's ability to increase early childhood professionals' knowledge of violence prevention for young children is of great importance because this information can then be taught to parents/caregivers. As a result, ACT-trained professionals potentially assist families in improving their own coping and emotion regulation capacities, resulting in appropriate role models for children.

Those trained in the ACT program also had significant increases in their perception of knowledge gained from pretest to posttest. This finding reveals that those who received the ACT training program believed that they learned information about early childhood violence prevention they did not have before the presentation of this program. This result also is important because for the ACT training program to be successful, the program not only has to increase participants' knowledge but recipients also need to believe they have gained valuable information. The combination of increased knowledge and knowledge perception tend to make ACT-trained professionals likely to utilize the violence prevention strategies in their own work with children as well as to help others who have an influence in children's development.

IMPLICATIONS OF ACT TRAINING PROGRAM FOR VIOLENCE PREVENTION AND AWARENESS

Awareness of the impact of violence on young children, particularly regarding girls and women, is important for professionals, teachers, and parents. Because the ACT training program provides developmentally based psychoeducation to participants, there is potential for children's reactions to violence in the community, home, and media to not be overlooked. The Guttman *et al.* (2006) study provides some evidence that violence prevention information can inform knowledge about and perceptions of competence in four research-based areas related to violence prevention. With the knowledge gained, parents and early childhood professionals can employ a host of behavioral strategies with young children regarding managing emotions, appropriate behavior, problem solving, and treatment of others, especially girls and women.

The ACT training program also has many specific beneficial aspects for administrators, school psychologists, teachers, and other school staff. For example, with knowledge gained from this program, teachers could expand upon their existing classroom management strategies. That is, the ACT training program's anger management and social problem-solving modules provide information regarding peer conflict resolution from a developmentally appropriate perspective. Furthermore, these modules address how adults can manage their own feelings during conflict situations. Once these strategies are in place, teachers can devote attention to their main responsibility in the classroom, teaching, instead of spending time dealing with behavior problems. The ACT training program may also aid school psychologists in providing children with age-appropriate techniques to effectively handle conflicts with peers as well as assist families regarding appropriate interactions with and management of their children at home. Overall, the results of this study have important implications in that they address the initial success of one of the first early childhood violence prevention programs that focuses on those most influential in young children's lives at a time when violence is becoming increasingly prevalent in their lives.

With regard to violence toward girls and women, specifically, the ACT training program may provide techniques to adults who, in turn, provide role models for such issues as anger regulation toward girls as well as boys. The demonstration of appropriate emotion regulation gives young children positive role models regardless of gender issues. Furthermore, positive social problem solving may offer children various avenues to resolve their gender-based as well as other conflicts. Essentially, the ACT training program, although not designed specifically for gender-related violence prevention issues, may have potential in this regard by providing research-based violence prevention techniques. Further research is indicated, however, to determine if the ACT training program, or other violence prevention programs as well, are specifically effective in reducing violence against girls, and ultimately women, in our society.

CONCLUSION

Unfortunately, young children are exposed to or witness violence at a high level, consistent with violence prevalence in today's society. Furthermore, violence toward girls and women is indisputable. Unfortunately, too, violence in relationships and the accessibility of violence for problem solving is learned early. To address the prevalence of violence toward girls and women, violence prevention programs targeting young children is appropriate and necessary (before perceptions become solidified and behavioral repertoires established).

Despite societal concerns, there are not many violence programs that focus on young children in general, and fewer yet specifically directed toward adults in young children's lives. The results of the Guttman *et al.* (2006) study fill a gap in the research literature by providing preliminary evidence for the ACT training program as a successful early childhood violence prevention program. Early childhood professionals, community leaders, parents, family members, and caregivers need to take the lead in reducing the violence that children experience, hear about, and see in the media and in their environments. This effort could become possible with appropriate antiviolence programs that provide useful information for professionals and families on how to accomplish the goal of reducing violence as well as the impact of violence in the lives of children. This study provides one of the first steps for viewing the ACT training program as a program that can assist in making this goal a reality.

REFERENCES

ABER, J.L., S.M. JONES, J.L. BROWN, *et al.* 1998. Resolving conflict creatively: evaluating the developmental effects of a school-based violence prevention program in neighborhood and classroom context. Development and Psychopathology *10*, 187–213.

ANDERSON, C.A., L. BERKOWITZ, E. DONNERSTEIN, *et al.* 2003. The influence of media violence on youth. Psychological Science in the Public Interest *4*, 81–110.

BANDURA, A. 1973. Aggression: a social learning analysis. Prentice-Hall, Englewood Cliffs, NJ.

BORNSTEIN, M.H. & M.E. LAMB. 1999. Developmental psychology: an advanced textbook (4th edition). Lawrence Erlbaum, Inc, Englewood Cliffs, NJ.

CIRILLO, K.J., B.E. PRUITT, B. COLWELL, *et al.* 1998. School violence: prevalence and intervention strategies for at-risk adolescents. Adolescence *33*, 319–330.

DASILVA, J., M.L. STERNE & M.P. ANDERSON. 2000. ACT Against Violence training program manual. American Psychological Association and National Association for the Education of Young Children.Washington, D.C.

DENHAM, S.A., K. BLAIR, M. SCHMIDT & E. DEMULDER. 2002. Compromised emotional competence: seeds of violence sown early?

EDELSON, J.L. 1999. Children's witnessing of adult domestic violence. Journal of Interpersonal Violence *14*, 839–870.

FETSCH R., C. SCHULTZ & J. WAHLER. 1999. A preliminary evaluation of the Colorado RETHINK Parenting and Anger Management Program. Child Abuse and Neglect *23*, 353–360.

FLANNERY, D.J., A.T. VAZSONYI, A.K. LIAU, *et al.* 2003. Initial behavior outcomes for the PeaceBuilders universal school-based violence prevention program. Developmental Psychology *39*, 292–308.

GOODWIN, T., K. PACEY & M. GRACE. 2003. Childreach: violence prevention in preschool settings. Journal of Child and Adolescent Psychiatric Nursing *16*, 52–60.

GROSSMAN, D.C., H.J. NECKERMAN, T.D. KOEPSELL, *et al.* 1997. Effectiveness of a violence prevention curriculum among children in elementary school. Journal of the American Medical Association *277*, 1605–1611.

GUTTMAN, M. & B.A. MOWDER. 2005. The ACT Training Program: the future of violence prevention aimed at young children and their caregivers. Journal of Early Childhood and Infant Psychology *1*, 25–36.

GUTTMAN, M., B.A. MOWDER & A. YASIK. 2006. The ACT Against Violence Training Program: a preliminary investigation of knowledge gained by early childhood professionals. Professional Psychology: Research and Practice.

HUESMANN, L.R. 1988. An information processing model for the development of aggression. Aggressive Behavior *14*, 13–24.

HUESMANN, L.R. 1998. The role of social information processing and cognitive schema in the acquisition and maintenance of habitual aggressive behavior. *In* Human aggression: Theories, research, and implications for policy. R.E. Geen & E. Donnerstein (Eds.): 73–109. Academic Press. New York, New York.

HUESMANN, L.R. & L.S. MILLER. 1994. Long-term effects of repeated exposure to media violence in childhood. *In* Aggressive behavior: current perspectives. L.R. Huesmann Ed.: 153–186). Plenum Press. New York, NY.

HUESMANN, L.R., J. MOISE-TITUS, C. PODOLSKI & L.D. ERON. 2003. Longitudinal relations between children's exposure to TV violence and their aggressive and violent behavior in young adulthood: 1977–1992. Developmental Psychology *39*, 201–221.

KITZMANN, K.M., N.K. GAYLORD, A.R. HOLT & E.D. KENNY. 2003. Child witnesses to domestic violence: a meta-analytic review. Journal of Consulting and Clinical Psychology *71*, 339–352.

LEFF, S.S., T.J. POWER, P.H. MANZ, *et al.* 2001. School-based aggression prevention programs for young children: current status and implications for violence prevention. School Psychology Review *30*, 344–362.

MAYEUX, L. & A.H. CILLESSEN. 2003. Development of social problem solving in early childhood: stability, change and associations with social competence. Journal of Genetic Psychology *164*, 153–173.

PATTERSON, G.R. & T.J. DISHION. 1985. Contributions of families and peers to delinquency. Criminology *23*, 63–79.

PATTERSON, G.R., J.B. REID & T.J. DISHION. 1992. Antisocial boys: a social interactional approach (Vol. 4), Castalia. Eugene, OR.

SCHECKNER, S., S.A. ROLLIN, C. KAISER-ULREY & R. WAGNER. 2002. School violence in children and adolescents: a meta-analysis of the effectiveness of current interventions. Journal of School Violence *1*, 5–33.

SCHWARTZ, D. & L.J. PROCTOR. 2000. Community violence exposure and children's Social adjustment in the school peer group: the mediating roles of emotion Regulation and social cognition. Journal of Consulting and Clinical Psychology *68*, 670–683.

TAYLOR, T.K., F. SCHMIDT, D. PEPLER & H. HODGINS. 1998. A comparison of eclectic treatment with Webster-Stratton's Parents and Children Series in a Children's Mental Health Center: a randomized controlled trial. Behavior Therapy *29*, 221–240.

WEISS, B., K.A. DODGE, J.E. BATES & G.S. PETTIT. 1992. Some consequences of early harsh discipline: child aggression and a maladaptive social information processing style. Child Development *63*, 1321–1335.

WOOD, W., F.Y. WONG & J.G. CHACHERE. 1991. Effects of media violence on viewers' aggression in unconstrained social interaction. Psychological Bulletin *109*, 371–383.

International Perspectives on Sexual Harassment of College Students

The Sounds of Silence

MICHELE PALUDI,[a] RUDY NYDEGGER,[a] EROS DESOUZA,[b] LIESL NYDEGGER,[a] AND KELSEY ALLEN DICKER[c]

[a]*School of Management, Union Graduate College, Lamont House, Schenectady, NY*

[b]*Department of Psychology, Illinois State University, Normal, IL*

[c]*Department of Psychology, Union College, Schenectady, NY*

ABSTRACT: The incidence, psychological dimensions, reporting, and impact of sexual harassment of college students throughout the world are reviewed. Special attention is paid to methodological constraints in conducting cross-cultural research in sexual harassment, including difficulty in securing research participants, different methodologies to collect incidence data, use of retrospective data, and varying, definitions of sexual harassment. Recommendations for implementing intervention programs are offered. The strategies suggested deal with the social causes that maintain the harassment, including renegotiating the balance of power between men and women.

KEYWORDS: sexual harassment; college; cross-cultural; research; intervention

INTRODUCTION

"Our lives begin to end the day we become silent about things that matter."

—Martin Luther King, Jr.

Silence surrounds sexual harassment on college campuses throughout the world. In 1978 the Project on the Status and Education of Women of the Association of American College referred to sexual harassment as a "hidden issue." This term was coined to highlight the silence that surrounded sexual harassment on an individual and organizational level. Frequently, victims were afraid to come forth with complaints for fear of retaliation or they did not

---

Address for correspondence: Michele Paludi, School of Management, Union Graduate College, Lamont House, Schenectady, NY, 12308. Voice: 518-377-5091; fax: 518-377-5091. email: MPaludi@aol.com

Ann. N.Y. Acad. Sci. 1087: 103–120 (2006). © 2006 New York Academy of Sciences.
doi: 10.1196/annals.1385.012

know about their campus' policy prohibiting sexual harassment. In addition, campus administrators did not promptly investigate complaints brought to their attention. A similar silence has also occurred in earlier grades as well as in the workplace. For example, the AAUW Educational Foundation's "The AAUW Report: How Schools Shortchange Girls" (1992) labeled sexual harassment as part of the "evaded curriculum" to connote the silence that exists around this topic by administrators and teachers.

Internationally, most countries do not have the term sexual harassment or laws protecting students from sexual harassment, contributing to individuals remaining silent about their experiences and hence not filing complaints with their universities (or workplaces) (e.g., Barak, 1997; DeSouza & Solberg, 2003; Echikson & Trinephi, 1998; Husbands, 1992). Furthermore, college students may not even know what behaviors actually constitute sexual harassment if they have not been trained on this form of victimization. Pryor *et al.* (1997) reported that college student definitions of sexual harassment in Germany, Australia, Brazil, and North America vary. For example, they found that the most frequent definitional response for North Americans, Australians, and Germans connoted unwanted verbal or physical sexual overtures. The most common response for Brazilian college students was "to seduce someone, to be more intimate (sexually), to procure a romance" (p. 524). In addition, they found that Australians, Germans, and North Americans defined sexual harassment as an abuse of power, gender discrimination, and harmful sexual behavior. Brazilians defined sexual harassment as innocuous seductive behaviors.

In addition, Tang *et al.* (1995) reported that the majority of college students in their sample (80%) did not perceive unwanted pressure for dates and joking about students' sex (i.e., male; female) as sexual harassment. Similarly, Mayekiso and Bhana (1997) found that South African college students only included unwelcome touching or fondling in their definition of sexual harassment. Denga and Denga (2004, pp. 2–3) reported that many of the behaviors labeled as sexual harassment in the western part of the world are not classified as such by Nigerian University students in their sample (see TABLE 1).

Further, Denga and Denga (2004) reported that "The Nigerian students' view differs from the Western view simply in terms of strictness and cultural

TABLE 1. Western versus Nigerian view of sexual harassment

Western view	Nigerian view
Subtle pressure for sexual activity	Too mild to constitute sexual harassment
Leering or ogling of a woman's body	This is regarded as foolishness, not sexual harassment
Constant brushing against a woman's body	This constitutes sexual harassment
Stalking a woman	This is superfluous affection

mores which make Nigerian regard behaviours like subtle pressure and sexist remarks about a woman's clothing or body irrelevant to sexual harassment" (p. 3). We will return to this issue about cultural values later in this article. These definitional issues along with the failure of college campuses to deal effectively with as well as prevent sexual harassment contribute to the "hidden nature" of sexual harassment.

Significant attempts have been made since the late 1970s in the United States and in the 1990s for some countries to develop policies and investigatory procedures to ease victims' fears of coming forth with their complaints of sexual harassment and to assist administrators in developing an educational program on sexual harassment prevention for their campus community (Paludi & Paludi, 2003). However, close to 30 years after the Project on the Status of Education of Women's coining of the term "hidden issue," sexual harassment is threatened to become silenced again, being foreshadowed by substantial attention being paid to other issues. This backlash against sexual harassment has resulted in colleges focusing on bullying, alcohol, or hazing prevention (Stein, 2004). Furthermore, colleges that have subsumed their sexual harassment policy under an antidiscrimination policy keep this topic as well as victims silenced.

In this article, we will focus on legal definitions of sexual harassment across cultures, the incidence rates of sexual harassment of college students noting methodological constraints on collecting international data, and the impact of sexual harassment on students' emotional and physical health, interpersonal relationships, and career development. We also offer recommendations for campuses to prevent and deal with sexual harassment, making it central to their mission rather than marginal and part of the evaded curriculum.

INCIDENCE OF SEXUAL HARASSMENT AMONG COLLEGE STUDENTS

"There are times when silence has the loudest voice."

—Leroy Brownlow

In her review of sexual harassment across 29 cultures, Barak (1997) concluded that "it is not the phenomenon of sexual harassment that is different among countries, but rather the way it is being behaviorally manifested, which is probably due to different behavioral standards related to different cultures" (p. 268). Thus, sexual harassment is universal; the behavioral expression of sexual harassment varies by culture (Donovan & Drasgow, 1997; Gelfand *et al.*, 2002).

For example, Hill and Silva (2005) reported findings from their nationally representative survey of 2,036 undergraduate students (1,096 women; 940 men) commissioned by the American Association of University Women Educational Foundation. Their research found that sexual harassment is experienced by the majority of college students. Approximately one-third of the students reported physical harassment, including being touched, grabbed, or forced to do something sexual. Hill and Silva (2005) also reported that men and women are equally likely to experience sexual harassment, although in different ways. For example, women were more likely to report experiencing sexual comments and gestures while men reported experiencing homophobic comments. Furthermore, Hill and Silva (2005) found that men are more likely than women to harass. This gender difference has been noted since the initial research studies in sexual harassment.

DeSouza and Solberg (2003) reviewed incidence rates of sexual harassment of college students in the following countries: Australia, Brazil, China, Italy, Israel, Pakistan, Puerto Rico, Sweden, and Turkey. Their review indicated that the incidence rates of sexual harassment are relatively high in all countries surveyed. In Australia, Gardner and Felicity (1996) reported that among 126 undergraduate women, 53.2% experienced it from instructors and 88.1% from peers. Fitzgerald and Gelfand (1994) reported that undergraduate women in the United States and Brazil reported similar amounts of gender harassment and sexual coercion but differed in experiences of unwanted sexual attention: Brazilian college women reported higher rates of this form of sexual harassment than American college women.

For certain student groups the incidence of sexual harassment appears to be higher than others (Barickman *et al.*, 1992; DeFour, 1996; Dziech, 2003). For example:

Women of Color, especially those with "token" status.

Students in small colleges or small academic departments where the number of faculty available to students is quite small.

Women students in male populated fields, e.g., engineering.

Students who are economically disadvantaged and work part time or full time while attending classes.

Lesbian women who may be harassed as part of homophobia.

Physically or emotionally disabled students.

Women students who work in dormitories as resident assistants.

Women who have been sexually abused.

Inexperienced, unassertive, socially isolated women who may appear more vulnerable and appealing to those who would intimidate or coerce them into an exploitive relationship.

Ethnic women and women of color are especially vulnerable to sexual harassment from their professors; they are subject to stereotypes about sex, are viewed as sexually mysterious and inviting, and are less sure of themselves in their careers. They also frequently experience an interface between racism and sexual harassment (Chan *et al.*, 1999; DeFour *et al.*, 2003; DeSouza & Solberg, 2003). For example, Lombardo *et al.* (1996) found that 48.2% of women students in Italy reported having experienced comments about their bodies, 29.3% seductive behavior, 3.4% bribery (e.g., being offered a reward for engaging in sexual activity), 4.5% coercion (e.g., coercing someone by threat of punishment), and 25.8% sexual assault. Gardner and Felicity (1996) found that among Australian women students, 91.3% indicated that they had experienced at least once a sexually harassing behavior from professors or peers. Mecca and Rubin (1999) reported that African American women college students indicated they experienced a high degree of sexual touching. Uhari and colleagues (1994), in their study of sexual harassment among medical students in Finland, reported that most incidents of sexual harassment were of a sex discrimination nature: women students were denied career opportunities because of their sex.

Peer sexual harassment is common among college students in the United States as well as the world (Hill & Slava, 2005; Sandler & Shoop, 1997). The main verbal form of peer sexual harassment experienced by women students involves "lewd" comments or sexual comments. Tang *et al.* (1996) reported that peer sexual harassment of Chinese women and men college students occurred twice as frequently as faculty-student sexual harassment. Gardner and Felicity (1996) reported that 88.1% of Australian women college students indicated that they had experienced at least once a sexually harassing behavior from peers.

Fitzgerald and Omerod (1993) concluded that:

> "...it seems reasonable (if not conservative) to estimate that one out of every two women will be harassed at some point during her academic or working life, thus indicating that sexual harassment is the most widespread of all forms of sexual victimization studied to date" (p. 559).

This estimate has been supported by countless numbers of empirical research studies using different methodologies to collect incidence data in different parts of the world (e.g., Barak, 1997; Buchanan, 2005; DeFour, 1996; DeFour *et al.*, 2003; Dziech, 2003; DeSouza, 2005; DeSouza & Solberg, 2003; Gruber, 1997; Sigal *et al.*, 2001). For a review of intercultural and intracultural research, see DeSouza and Solberg (2003) and DeFour *et al.* (2003).

METHODOLOGICAL CONCERNS

We note that differences in incidence rates may be due to methodological variations among research studies both within the United States and in comparing cross-cultural incidence rates (Paludi, 2000; Sigal & Jacobsen, 1999). These methodological issues make a comparative analysis of sexual harassment difficult (Pryor & McKinney, 1995). For example, some researchers have used retrospective data in collecting incidence rates, e.g., asking senior college students about their experiences being sexually harassed in their first year in college. Other researchers have asked college students about their more immediate experiences with sexual harassment. Students have also been asked to focus on the most severe incident of sexual harassment. Asking students to remember and focus on their worst incident may yield distorted data regarding the severity of sexual harassment they frequently experienced.

In addition, direct questions about sexual harassment may elicit unreliable incidence rates since individuals do not typically understand what constitutes sexual harassment (Fitzgerald *et al.*, 1988). Thus, both random and systematic errors are introduced into the methodology. Furthermore, several measurement instruments used to collect incidence data have not been submitted to psychometric analyses, including reliability and validity. Some research studies have used the Sexual Experiences Questionnaire (Fitzgerald *et al.*, 1988); others have used surveys designed only for their study (e.g., Denga & Denga, 2004). Thus, comparing incidence rates with studies that have not used the identical measuring instrument also poses a methodological problem (DeSouza & Solberg, 2003). Kamal and Tariq (1997) reported that they experienced difficulty in obtaining volunteers for their research despite the fact confidentiality was guaranteed, thus making it hard to obtain accurate incidence data.

Finally, cross-cultural studies may not be using the same definition of sexual harassment as do researchers in the United States. As DeSouza and Solberg (2003) stated: "The use of different methodologies, including survey methods, instructions, wording of survey items, timeframes, and sampling techniques, makes cross-cultural comparisons problematic if not impossible" (p. 16). One notable exception is Sigal *et al.* (2005), who ensured the methodology used in their research, which included a scenario, was comparable in all cultures.

We need to recognize that there is a great deal of variation among students, due to ethnicity, age, class, stage in their relationship, sexual orientation, stage in career development, and other cultural and social circumstances. Thus, focusing on differences between and among cultures ignores within-group variability. Furthermore, the overemphasis on differences provides confirmation of the stereotype that the United States and other countries are "opposite" and that the United States is normative and other countries are a deviation from the norm.

REPORTING SEXUAL HARASSMENT

"Saying nothing sometimes says the most."

—Emily Dickinson

Research with college students (and employees) across the globe indicates that despite the fact they report experiencing behaviors that fit the legal definition of sexual harassment, they do not label their experiences as such (Jaschik & Fretz, 1991; Jaschik-Herman & Fisk, 1995; Magley *et al.*, 1999). For example, Ramos (2000) found that among women college students in Puerto Rico, 60% experienced gender harassment, 28.4% experienced unwanted sexual attention, and 2% sexual coercion. In addition, 48.6% reported experiencing unwanted sexual attention and gender harassment. However, a mere 8.5% of the women students labeled these experiences as sexual harassment.

Tang et al. (1996) reported that Chinese students reported a lower rate of sexual harassment incidents than students in the United States. Tang et al. interpreted this finding as reflecting the secretive nature of the issue of sexual harassment in China. They also hypothesized that the incidence of sexual harassment in China may in fact be actually lower because of the strong values of maintaining social harmony and mutual respect in this culture that does not typically exist in the United States. Marin and Marin (1991) recognized that Latino cultures are cultures of honor as well and Latinas may take offense at unwanted sex-related behavior because of the norms of respeto and dignidad. Cultures of honor, unlike the individualist culture of the United States, are defined by the interconnection between male honor and female chastity (L'Armand et al., 1981; Magnarella, 1974). In addition, sexual harassment, like other forms of sexual victimization, is more common in cultures that are characterized by male dominance and by a high degree of violence in general.

Geyer et al. (1997) found that unlike the American participants in their research, German participants exhibited significantly more positive attitudes toward women and a corresponding low tolerance for sexual harassment. Research has suggested Dutch and German individuals are characterized as being more egalitarian in their gender role attitudes (e.g., DeLeon, 1993; Van Yperen & Buunk, 1991). They may therefore hold egalitarian beliefs about women and men in the workplace and academia, which includes no tolerance of sexual harassment.

Reilly et al. (1986) found that 61% of American women college students victimized by sexual harassment ignored the behavior or did nothing in response and 16% asked or told the faculty member to stop. In addition, students' initial attempts to manage the initiator are rarely direct. Furthermore, the first or first several incidents of sexual harassment are often ignored by students, and especially when the behavior is subtle (Fitzgerald et al., 1990). Hill and Silva (2005) noted that 35% of the students in their sample told no one about their experiences with sexual harassment. Approximately half of the students confided in a friend and only 7% reported the incidents to a college employee.

Marin and Guadagno (1999) hypothesized that victims are reluctant to label their experiences as sexual harassment as well as to report the victimization because they fear negative evaluation from peers. Furthermore, Dziech and Weiner (1984) and Garlick (1994) reported that the discrepancy between experience and labeling is a consequence of the ambiguous nature of sexual harassment. Sexual harassment of an implicit nature occurs more frequently on college campuses than explicit demands for sex (in return for a higher grade, letter of recommendation).

Malovich and Stake (1990) reported that women students who were high in performance self-esteem and who held egalitarian gender role attitudes were more likely to report incidents of sexual harassment than women who were low in self-esteem and held traditional gender role attitudes. Similar results were obtained by Brooks and Perot (1991) who noted that self-defined feminist students reported incidents of sexual harassment more than non-feminists. Sigal and Jacobsen (1999) found support for this relationship with their samples in The Netherlands and Germany. Tang *et al.* (1996) noted that women victims of sexual harassment they studied in Hong Kong may not report their experiences out of shame and embarrassment. Collectivism and filial piety apparently contribute to Hong Kong women students under-reporting sexual harassment.

Thus, there is not a one-to-one correspondence between incidence and reporting of sexual harassment by students (see DeSouza & Solberg, 2004 for a distinction between legal and psychological responses in this regard). However, as Magley *et al.* (1999) noted, "whether or not a woman considers her experience to constitute sexual harassment, she experiences similar negative psychological, work and health consequences" (p. 399). We now address the impact of sexual harassment on students' health, career goals, and interpersonal relationships.

IMPACT OF SEXUAL HARASSMENT ON COLLEGE STUDENTS

I decided it is better to scream. . . ..Silence is the real crime against humanity.

—Nadezhda Mandelstam

Research with college students in several countries has documented the high cost of sexual harassment to individuals (e.g., Danksy & Kilpatrick, 1997; Hill & Silva, 2005; Lundberg-Love & Faulkner, 2005; Lundberg-Love & Marmion, 2003; Quina, 1996; Sigal, *et al.*, 2005). This research indicates that there are career-related, psychological, and physiological outcomes of being sexually harassed. For example, women students have reported decreased morale, decreased satisfaction with their career goals, and lowered grades. Furthermore, women students have reported feelings of helplessness and powerlessness over their academic career, strong fear reactions, and decreased motivation. Women college students have also reported headaches, sleep disturbances, eating disorders, and gastrointestinal disorders as common physical responses to sexual harassment (Lundberg-Love & Marmion, 2003; Thacker & Gohmann, 1996; Wasti *et al.*, 2000).

Lombardo *et al.* (1996), for example, found that among women nursing college students, a significant negative impact on women's health occurred as a consequence of sexual harassment. Danksy & Kilpatrick (1997) noted that responses to sexual harassment are influenced by disappointment and self-blame in the way others react and the stress of sexual harassment induced life changes such as loss of teaching or research fellowships, loss of student loans, and disrupted educational career path. Schneider's (1987) research indicated that 29% of women reported a loss of academic or professional opportunities and 13% reported lowered grades or financial support because of sexual harassment.

Ramos (2000) reported that Spanish college women attending the University of Puerto Rico found that sexual harassment had a negative impact on health, academic success, and psychological well being. Women who had been sexually harassed reported more physical symptoms, poorer mental health, greater academic withdrawal, lower self-esteem, and lower life satisfaction than women who had not been sexually harassed. Dansky and Kilpatrick (1997) and Quina (1996) noted that symptoms are exacerbated by experiencing repeated sexual harassment and sexual harassment in front of peers. In addition, symptoms become more pronounced the longer the student has to endure the sexual harassment.

When sexual harassment occurs on campuses the individual who is rightly the focus of institutional response is the victim. This is a positive factor because it means that whatever help or support that is available will be targeted to the victim who is certainly most deserving of the assistance. What is often overlooked, however, is how pervasive and destructive sexual harassment is to the whole campus and the people in it—including others who were not even involved or perhaps even aware of the harassment. When these types of problems are not dealt with they tend to erode or corrupt the campus culture in such a way as to create other problems as well. What is even worse is when the victim becomes the focus of *negative* attention from the campus in the form of blame or reprisals. This will not only create further harm to the victim, but also the campus and other people will be negatively impacted by this additional problem.

How people cope with the reality of sexual harassment depends on many factors including their own personality, their history and family background, previous experiences as a victim of harassment, the campus and its culture, and many other factors. According to Knapp *et al.* (1997), coping with sexual harassment falls into four categories:

- Advocacy seeking (finding people to intervene and to help)
- Social coping (seeking help and support from colleagues)
- Avoidance/denial (simply ignoring what has happened and withdrawing socially)
- Confrontation/negotiation (trying to deal directly with the perpetrator of the harassment)

Helping victims deal with harassment in a positive and healthy manner is the responsibility of an educational institution that is in the business of training and teaching.

DEALING WITH AND PREVENTING SEXUAL HARASSMENT

Laws and Policies Prohibiting Sexual Harassment

"Sticks and stones are hard on bones. Aimed with angry act, words can sting like anything. But silence breaks the heart."

—Phyllis McGinley

Husbands (1992) reviewed sexual harassment policies in 23 countries and reported that only the following 9 countries had specific statutes against this form of sexual victimization: Australia, Belgium, Canada, France, Germany, New Zealand, Spain, Sweden, and the United States. These statutes were influenced by cultural differences and legal systems (Sigal & Jacobsen, 1999). For example, sexual harassment is not illegal in Pakistan (Kamal & Tariq, 1997); in South Africa, sexual harassment and other forms of harassment are prohibited in its Labor Relations Act (1998); in Germany, sexual harassment is defined as touching the body and making sexual remarks in addition to displaying objectionable pornographic pictures publicly (Protection of Employees Act, 1994). Aeberhard-Hodges (1996) reviewed the European Commission's Council Resolution defining sexual harassment for their member states. This resolution defined sexual harassment, similar to the United States definition, as unwelcome, unreasonable, and offensive conduct. Subsequent to Husbands's (1992) review, Echikson & Trinephi (1998) reported that except for Greece and Portugal, the remainder of the 15 European Union members have an antisexual harassment statute.

In addition to differences in outlining the behaviors that comprise sexual harassment, countries differ as to whether they define sexual harassment civilly or criminally. For example, in France sexual harassment is a crime (Aeberhard-Hodges, 1996). These statutes allow individuals to file sexual harassment complaints in court or within their workplaces. Certainly one measure of how sexual harassment is perceived in countries is the presence or absence of sexual harassment policies.

The United Nations passed a complaint procedure for women victims of discrimination, permitting them to file their complaint with the United Nations if their home country is unwilling to resolve the complaint. (Lederer, 2000). In Brazil, sexual harassment from a superior to a subordinate is defined as a crime punishable by 1–2 years in prison (Assedio, 2001). In the United States sexual harassment is a civil offense. Sexual harassment is legally defined as "unwelcome sexual advances, requests for sexual favors, and other verbal or physical conduct of a sexual nature" when any one of the following criteria is met:

- Submission to such conduct is made either explicitly or implicitly a term or condition of the individual's employment or academic standing;

- Submission to or rejection of such conduct by an individual is used as the basis for employment or academic decisions affecting the individual;
- Such conduct has the purpose or effect of unreasonably interfering with an individual's work or learning performance or creating an intimidating, hostile or offensive work or learning environment.

There are two types of sexual harassment situations that are described by this legal definition: quid pro quo sexual harassment and hostile environment sexual harassment.

Quid pro quo sexual harassment involves an individual with organizational power who either expressly or implicitly ties an academic or employment decision or action to the response of an individual to unwelcome sexual advances. Thus, a teacher may promise a reward to a student for complying with sexual requests (e.g., a better grade, letter of recommendation for college or a job) or threaten a student for failing to comply with the sexual requests (e.g., threatening to not give the student the grade earned).

Hostile environment sexual harassment involves a situation where an atmosphere or climate is created by a professor, staff, or other students in the classroom, or other area on campus that makes it difficult, if not impossible, for a student to study and learn because the atmosphere is perceived by the student to be intimidating, offensive, and hostile.

Sexual harassment includes, but is not limited to the following:

- Unwelcome sexual advances;
- Sexual innuendos, comments, and sexual remarks;
- Suggestive, obscene or insulting sounds;
- Implied or expressed threat of reprisal for refusal to comply with a sexual request;
- Patting, pinching, brushing up against another's body;
- Sexually suggestive objects, books, magazines, poster, photographs, cartoons, e-mail, or pictures displayed in the school/work area;
- Actual denial of an academic-related benefit for refusal to comply with sexual requests.

Thus, in the United States, sexual harassment can be physical, verbal, visual, or written. These behaviors are often committed by individuals who are in supervisory positions or by peers. And these behaviors also constitute sexual harassment if they occur between individuals of the same sex or between individuals of the opposite sex.

According to Title IX of the 1972 Education Amendments:

No person in the United States shall, on the basis of sex, be excluded from participation in, or denied the benefits of, or be subjected to discrimination under any educational program or activity receiving federal assistance.

Title IX is an antidiscrimination statute that prohibits discrimination on the basis of sex in any educational program or activity receiving federal financial assistance. Title IX is at the heart of efforts to create gender equitable colleges. Title IX requires educational institutions to maintain policies, procedures, and programs that do not discriminate against anyone based on sex. Title IX extends to recruitment, admissions, educational activities and programs, course offerings, counseling, financial aid, health and insurance benefits, scholarships, and athletics.

EDUCATION

Never be bullied into silence. Never allow yourself to be made a victim. Accept no one's definition of your life, but define yourself.

—Harvey Fierstein

In determining how an organization can best respond to sexual harassment, it may be helpful to look at how victims actually cope when it happens. As mentioned earlier in this article, victims may use a variety of different types of coping strategies to deal with harassment. Typically, sexually harassed women engage in trial-and-error approaches to coping with the harassment. They will learn over time what types of responses work and which do not. Harassed women, regardless of culture or class, tend to use a variety of coping responses other than formal advocacy seeking. The few women who do respond officially usually do so after the harassment gets so bad that harm has already been caused (Cortina *et al.*, 2005).

In dealing with sexual harassment, colleges need to be sensitive to the needs, backgrounds, and experiences of students who have been victimized by others in this way. Understanding how to deal effectively with sexual harassment in any college means that the organization must deal with an increasingly global and diverse student body. Some of the things that must be considered in crafting organizational responses to sexual harassment include such things as:

- Look at novel intervention strategies that are accessible across cultural groups.
- Officials who deal with diverse groups need to be trained to understand and appreciate the differences and how best to protect and deal with these differences.
- Counselors who deal with victims of harassment must be appropriately trained to do so, but must also be trained in dealing with a diverse population of clients.

Most campuses that have developed programs for managing the problem of sexual harassment typically rely on several approaches to the problem. First, they will usually try to educate people by making them aware of the problem and its impact, and what people's responsibilities are with respect to these problems. Second, they usually have some disciplinary guidelines indicating the possible consequences for those found to be guilty of sexually harassing another member of the organization. There has been some research of the effectiveness of these types of programs, and Perry *et al.* (1998) report that training programs intended to prevent sexual harassment are more effective when done in face-to-face settings rather than by using video training. Another group (Bingham & Scherer, 2001) developed a training program that used handouts, oral presentations by mixed-sex dyads, and a five-min discussion to answer questions. Although they found that some attitude change occurred regarding sexual harassment, the training was not totally effective in changing all attitudes that people had about this problem area. Kearney *et al.* (2004) found that an interactive workshop with peer-facilitated discussion on sexual harassment was very helpful to most students. However, they also started off with an assumption that perhaps different types of people might respond better to different types of training. Thus, they used gender-role conflict as a mediating variable for the male subjects. The assumption was that men students who reported more gender-role conflict would not have the same response to training as other men. They operationally defined gender-role conflict as having a narrowly defined sense of what masculinity represents and more likely to subscribe to very traditional and even stereotypical ideas of masculinity. Kearney *et al.* (2004) reported that their training led to better recognition of sexual harassment when it was presented, but the training did not change many attitudes regarding the tolerance of sexual harassment. Further, as expected, men with more gender-role conflict were less affected by the training. Thus, they conclude that the men most in need of help in this area were also the ones least likely to benefit from the training.

We believe that Kearney *et al.*'s (2004) assumption is correct—there is no reason to believe that one form of training or treatment will be equally effective for all people. The clear message here, it seems, is that schools must have a variety of programs that are culturally sensitive and accessible to a diverse group of students and other members of the campus community. Further, programs must be multi-modal, multi-faceted, interesting, relevant, and appropriate for the groups they are attempting to reach.

One group that is often neglected when putting programs together is the perpetrators. Certainly, schools should and need to deal with the needs of the victims first and foremost, and then deal with prevention in a vigorous, public, and serious way. However, by not dealing with the perpetrators, harm may also be done to the organization and to the perpetrators themselves. Many perpetrators do not even imagine the harm that they cause to others, but sometimes, and often too late, they do recognize the harm that comes to them. Sbraga & O'Donohue (2000) pointed out some of the negative results that occur to the perpetrators of sexual harassment, and as can be seen, many of the negative results also vary substantially and adversely impact the organization as well. Some of the negative consequences for perpetrators of sexual harassment include: professional and personal reprisals, strained relations with coworkers, lowered productivity, demotions, loss of jobs, potentially less employable, and often they are shocked or embarrassed by their own behaviors. It is also the case that campuses should be interested in making the organization the best place it can be for all members of its community.

It also seems likely that of the people who commit sexual harassment, there are some who would truly want to change after seeing the impact of their behavior on others, and it seems very important to make sure that these people are reached and given the training and opportunity to change. For those perpetrators who see nothing wrong with their behavior and continue to blame the victims and society, the training should also point out the negative consequences that await those who will continue to abuse others without regard to the negative effect of their behavior.

In summary, when designing organizational programs to deal with sexual harassment care should be taken to make these programs as effective as they can be and to reach the broadest audience possible. Programs must be sensitive to the rights of victims and potential victims, and make sure that this group is protected and provided the help and support that they need. Further, these programs must look at the culture of the campus and how this culture must reflect the values that protect the individuals from any form of abuse or harassment. Programs must also respect cultural differences and diversity, but must insist on protecting the rights of all members of the organization so that they may be free of abuse, harassment, or aggression in any form. Finally, programs should reach out to all members of the community and address their different and varied needs and perspectives including perpetrators who, as a group, may also need help and motivation to change.

As DeSouza and Solberg (2003) concluded: "... just erecting laws or guidelines to prevent sexual harassment is insufficient unless they are carried out. In countries where women have been and are viewed as unequal to men, new laws or procedures designed to prevent harassment may conflict with hundreds of years of culture ... Education of what sexual harassment is ... and preventive training at schools and work settings ... may be more effective than popular short-term solutions" (p. 25).

We recommend intervention programs similar in scope to that designed by Fawcett *et al*. (1999) for dealing with intimate partner violence in Iztacalco, Mexico and in Japan, Chile, Russia, Greece, Mexico, Nicaragua, and Argentina (Walker, 1999). The goal of these programs is to assist women in recognizing and disclosing the battering and to encourage fewer victim-blaming attitudes among family members and friends of the victims. Fawcett *et al*. (1999) reported that women were unaware of what levels of violence were acceptable and thus of when to intervene. Their intervention program involved peer and community outreach using posters and other media and a 12-session workshop to train women as agents of community change. An intervention program similar to this one can be designed and implemented with women across the world. Topics to discuss in an intervention program on sexual harassment include:

- Sexual harassment as an organizational and community problem;
- Legislation;
- Forms of sexual harassment;
- Gender role expectations and sexual harassment;
- Socialization of women and violence against women;
- Socialization of men and sexual harassment;
- Personal and campus consequences of sexual harassment of women;
- Crisis-intervention skills;
- Community intervention.

The strategies used to deal with sexual harassment will deal with the social causes that maintain the harassment, including renegotiating the balance of power between men and women.

REFERENCES

AAUW Educational Foundation. 1992. *The AAUW Report: How schools shortchange girls*. The American Association of University Women Educational Foundation. Washington, DC.

AEBERHARD-HODGES, J. 1996. Sexual harassment in employment: recent judicial and arbitral trends. Int. Labor Rev. *135*, 499–533.

Assedio sexual no local de trabalho agora e crime [Sexual harassment at the workplace is now a crime]. 2001. Folha de Sao Paulo, Sao Paulo, Brazil.

BARAK, A. 1997. Cross-cultural perspectives on sexual harassment. *In* Sexual Harassment: Theory, Research, and Treatment. W. O'Donohue, Ed.: 263–300. Allyn & Bacon. Needham Heights, MA.

BARICKMAN, R., M. PALUDI & V. RABINOWITZ. 1992. Sexual harassment of students: victims of the college experience. *In* Victimization: An International Perspective. E. Viano, Ed.:153–165. Springer. New York, NY.

BINGHAM, S. & L. SCHERER. 2001. The unexpected effects of a sexual harassment education program. J. Appl. Behav. Sci. *37*, 125–153.

BROOKS, L. & A. PEROT. 1991. Reporting sexual harassment: exploring a predictive model. Psychol. Women Q. *15*, 31–47.

BUCHANAN, N. 2005. Incorporating race and gender in sexual harassment research: the racialized sexual harassment scale. Paper presented at the Conference of the International Coalition Against Sexual Harassment, Philadelphia, PA.

CHAN, D., C. TANG & W. CHAN. 1999. Sexual harassment: a preliminary analysis of its effects on Hong Kong Chinese women in the workplace and academia. Psychol. Women Q. *23*, 661–672.

CORTINA, L. & S. LIM. 2005. Interpersonal mistreatment in the workplace: the interface and impact of general incivility and sexual harassment. J. Appl. Psychol. *90*, 483–496.

DANSKY, B. & D. KILPATRICK. 1997. Effects of sexual harassment. *In* Sexual harassment: theory, research, and practice. W. O'Donohue, Ed.:152–174 Allyn & Bacon. Boston, MA.

DeFour, D.C. 1996. Racism and sexual harassment. *In* Sexual Harassment on College Campuses: Abusing the Ivory Power. M. Paludi, Ed.: 49–55 State University of New York Press. Albany, NY.

DeFour, D.C., G. David, F. Diaz & S. Thompkins. 2003. The interface of race, sex, sexual orientation and ethnicity in understanding sexual harassment. *In* Academic and Workplace Sexual Harassment: A Handbook of Cultural, Social Science, Management, and Legal Perspectives. M. Paludi & C. Paludi, Eds.: 31–45. Praeger. Westport, CT.

DeLeon, B. 1993. Sex role identity among college students: a cross-cultural analysis. Hisp. J. Behav. Sci. *15*, 476–489.

Denga, D. & H. Denga. 2004. Sexual harassment: a student's view from a Nigerian University. The African Symposium, *4, March*.

DeSouza, E. 2005. Issues related to same-sex harassment in the United States and the world. Paper presented at the Conference of the International Coalition Against Sexual Harassment, Philadelphia, PA.

DeSouza, E. & J. Solberg. 2003. Incidence and dimensions of sexual harassment across cultures. *In* Academic and Workplace Sexual Harassment: A Handbook of Cultural, Social Science, Management, and Legal Perspectives. M. Paludi & C. Paludi, Eds.: 4–30. Praeger. Westport, CT.

Donovan, M. & F. Drasgow. 1997. Establishing the measurement equivalence of a measure of sexual harassment across five samples: a multiple comparison of differential item functioning. Paper presented at the annual meeting of the Society for Industrial-Organizational Psychology, St. Louis, MO.

Dziech, B. 2003. Sexual harassment on college campuses. *In* Academic and Workplace Sexual Harassment: A Handbook of Cultural, Social Science, Management, and Legal Perspectives. M. Paludi & C. Paludi, Eds.: 147–171. Praeger. Westport, CT.

Dziech, B. & L. Weiner. 1984. The Lecherous Professor. Beacon Press. Boston, MA

Echikson, W. & M. Trinephi. 1998. Is this harassment, or "Le Flirt?" Business Week, *3566*, 110J.

Fawcett, G., L. Heise, L. Isita-Espejel & S. Pick. 1999. Changing community responses to wife abuse: a research and demonstration project in Iztacalco, Mexico. Am. Psychol. *54*, 41–49.

Fitzgerald, L. & A. Omerod. 1993. Sexual harassment in academia and the workplace. *In* Psychology of Women: A Handbook of Issues and Theories. F. Denmark & M. Paludi, Eds.: 553–581. Greenwood. Westport, CT.

Fitzgerald, L. & M. Gelfand. 1994. Sexual harassment in Latin America: prevalence and perceptions in Brazil. Paper presented at the annual convention of the American Psychological Association, Los Angeles, CA.

Fitzgerald, L., S. Shullman, N. Bailey, *et al.* 1988. The incidence and dimensions of sexual harassment in academia and the workplace. J. Vocat. Behav. *32*, 152–175.

Fitzgerald, L., Y. Gold, & Y. Brock. 1990. Responses to victimization: validation of an objective policy. Journal of College Student Personnel *27*, 34–39.

Garlick, R. 1994. Male and female responses to ambiguous instructor behaviors. Sex Roles *30*, 135–158.

Gardner, J. & A. Felicity. 1996. Sexual and gender harassment at university: experiences and perceptions of Australian women. Aust. Psychol. *31*, 210–216.

Gelfand, M., L. Fitzgerald, & F. Drasgow. 2002. The structure of sexual harassment: a confirmatory analysis across cultures and settings. J. Vocat. Behav. *47*, 164–177.

Geyer, B., J. Sigal, M. Gibbs, *et al.* 1997. Cross-cultural reactions to academic sexual harassment: a German-American comparison. Poster session presented at the annual meeting of the Eastern Psychological Association, Washington, DC.

Gruber, J. 1997. An epidemiology of sexual harassment: Evidence from North America and Europe. *In* Sexual harassment: Theory, Research and Treatment. W. O'Donohue, Ed.: 84–9867h. Allyn and Bacon. Needham Heights, MA.

Hill, C. & E. Silva. 2005. Drawing the line: Sexual harassment on campus. American Association of University Women Educational Foundation. Washington, DC.

Husbands, R. 1992. Sexual harassment law in employment: an international perspective. Int. Labor Rev. *131*, 535–559.

Jaschik, M. & B. Fretz. 1991. Women's perceptions and labeling of sexual harassment. Sex Roles *25*, 19–23.

Jaschik-Herman, M. & A. Fisk. 1995. Women's perceptions and labeling of sexual harassment in academia before and after the Hill-Thomas hearings. Sex Roles *33*, 439–446.

Kamal, A. & N. Tariq. 1997. Sexual harassment Experience Questionnaire for workplaces of Pakistan: development and validation. Pakistan J. Psychol. Res. *12*, 1–20.

Kearney, L.K., A.B. Rochlen & E.B. King. 2004. Male gender role conflict, sexual harassment tolerance, and the efficacy of a psychoeducative training program. Psychology of Men and Masculinity *5*, 72–82.

Knapp, D., R. Faley, S. Ekeberg & C. Dubois. 1997. Determinants of target responses to sexual harassment: a conceptual framework. Acad. Manage. Rev. *22*, 687–729.

L'Armand, K., A. Pepitone & T. Shanmugam. 1981. Attitudes toward rape: a comparison of the role of chastity in India and the United States. J. Cross Cult. Psychol. *12*, 284–303.

Lederer, E. 2000. New complaints procedure for discrimination against women takes effect. Associated Press World Stream, CX20000358U6181.

Lombardo, L., L. Pedrabissi & M. Santinello. 1996. La diffusione delle molestie sessuali in un contesto lavorativo (The diffusion of sexual harassment in the workplace). Bolletino di Psicologi Applicata. *218*, 25–34.

Lundberg-Love, P. & D. Faulkner. 2005. The emotional sequelae of sexual harassment. Paper presented at the Conference of the International Coalition Against Sexual Harassment, Philadelphia, PA.

Lundberg-Love, P. & S. Marmion. 2003. Sexual harassment in the private sector. *In* Academic and workplace sexual harassment: A Handbook of Cultural, Social Science, Management and Legal Perspectives. M. Paludi & C. Paludi, Eds.: 77–101. Praeger. Westport, CT.

Magley, V., C. Hulin, L. Fitzgerald & M. DeNardo. 1999. Outcomes of self-labeling sexual harassment. J. Appl. Psychol. *84*, 390–402.

Magnarella, P. 1974. Tradition and Change in a Turkish Town. Wiley. New York, NY.

Malovich, N. & J. Stake. 1990. Sexual harassment of women on campus: individual differences in attitude and belief. Psychol. Women Q. *14*, 63–81.

Marin, A. & R. Guadagno. 1999. Perceptions of sexual harassment victims as a function of labeling and reporting. Sex Roles *41*, 921–940.

Marin, G. & B. Marin. 1991. Research with Hispanic Populations. Sage. Newbury Park, CA.

Mayekiso, T. & K. Bhana. 1997. Sexual harassment: perceptions and experiences of students at the University of Transkei. S Afr. J. Psychol. *27*, 230–235.

MECCA, S. & L. RUBIN. 1999. Definitional research on African American students and sexual harassment. Psychol. Women Q. *23*, 813–817.

PALUDI, M. 2000. Contributions from the discipline of psychology to the understanding and prevention of sexual harassment in education and the workplace. Part of panel presentation: Sexual harassment: Evolution of an issue, B. Dziech, chair. Presented at the International Coalition Against Sexual Harassment, Washington, DC.

PALUDI, M. & C. Paludi, (Eds.). 2003. Academic and Workplace Sexual Harassment: A Handbook of Cultural, Social Science, Management and Legal Perspectives. Praeger. Westport, CT.

PERRY, E., C. KULIK & J. SCHMIDKE. 1998. Individual differences in the effectiveness of sexual harassment training. J. Appl. Soc. Psychol. *28*, 698–723.

Project on the Status and Education of Women. 1978. Sexual harassment: a hidden issue. Association of American Colleges.Washington, DC.

Protection of Employees Act. 1994. Second Act on Equality for Men and Women (Germany), Section 10.

PRYOR, J. & K. MCKINNEY. 1995. Research on sexual harassment: lingering issues and future directions. Basic Appl. Soc. Psych. *17*, 605–611.

PRYOR, J., E. DESOUZA, J. FITNESS, *et al.* 1977. Gender differences in the interpretation of social/sexual behavior: a cross-cultural perspective on sexual harassment. J. Cross Cult. Psychol. *28*, 509–534.

QUINA, K. 1996. Sexual harassment and rape: a continuum of exploitation. *In* Sexual harassment on college campuses: Abusing the ivory power. M. Paludi, Ed.: 183–197. State University of New York Press. Albany.

RAMOS, A. 2000. Sexual harassment at the University of Puerto Rico. DAI *60*, 5839.

REILLY, M., B. LOTT. & S. GALLOGY. 1986. Sexual harassment of university students. Paper presented to the convention of the Association for Women in Psychology, Oakland, CA.

SANDLER, B. & R. SHOOP. 1997. Sexual Harassment on Campus: A Guide for Administrators, Faculty and Students. Allyn and Bacon. Boston, MA.

SBRAGA, T. & W. O'DONOHUE. 2000. Sexual harassment. Annu. Rev. Sex Res. *11*, 258–285.

SCHNEIDER, B. 1987. Graduate women, sexual harassment and university policy. J. Higher Educ. *58*, 46–65.

SIGAL, J. & H. JACOBSEN. 1999. A cross-cultural exploration of factors affecting reactions to sexual harassment. Psychol. Public Policy Law *5*, 760–785.

SIGAL, J., T. RASHID, A. ANJUM, *et al.* 2001. Cross-cultural and gender differences in response to academic sexual harassment: a comparison of Pakistan and American college students. Paper presented at the meeting of the Eastern Psychological Association, Washington, DC.

SIGAL, J., M. GIBBS, C. GOODRICH, *et al.* 2005. Cross-cultural reactions to academic sexual harassment: effects of individualist vs. collectivist culture and gender of participants. Sex Roles *52*, 201–215.

STEIN, N. 2004. Gender violence and gender safety in US schools. Paper presented at the First International Conference on Gender Equity Education in Asia-Pacific Region, Taiwan.

TANG, C., M. YIK, F. Cheung, *et al.* 1995. How do Chinese college students define sexual harassment? J. Interpers. Violence *10*, 503–515.

TANG, C., M. YIK, F. CHEUNG, *et al.* 1996. Sexual harassment of Chinese college students. Arch. Sex. Behav. *25*, 201–215.

Intimate Partner Violence

New Directions

MAUREEN C. McHUGH[a] AND IRENE HANSON FRIEZE[b]

[a]*Department of Psychology, Indiana University of Pennsylvania, Indiana, Pennsylvania, USA*

[b]*University of Pittsburgh, Pittsburgh, Pennsylvania, USA*

> ABSTRACT: This review examines multiple forms of intimate partner violence, including women's use of violence, and argues for development of more complex conceptualizations of intimate partner violence. As new victims are identified, partner violence has been reconceptualized. Research findings indicate that women are both victims and perpetrators in intimate partner violence, challenging previous conceptualizations and explanations. The authors argue that how researchers conceptualize intimate partner violence influences how they study and measure it. The authors call for researchers to develop more complex constructions of gender, and to distinguish between distinct forms of intimate partner violence.
>
> KEYWORDS: domestic violence; women; batterer

INTRODUCTION

Overview

Since the 1970s when feminists called attention to the problem of husbands beating their wives, widespread changes have occurred in our consciousness concerning this phenomenon. Over the past 35 years, approaches to domestic violence have evolved from viewing the problem as limited to a very few problematic marriages, and disbelieving and blaming battered women, to recognizing the prevalence of serious levels of physical violence and psychological abuse in many intimate relationships. Within the research on partner violence, some topics like the prevalence of violence against women and the characteristics and reactions of the victim have received extensive attention. Generally, there has been less attention on the batterer and other topics such

---

Address for correspondence: Maureen C. McHugh, Department of Psychology, Indiana University of Pennsylvania, Indiana, PA 15705, USA. Voice: 724-357-2448; fax: 724-357-2214.
 e-mail: MCMCHUGH@IUP.edu

as the degree to which women use violence with their intimate partners has only more recently become the focus of study. The explosion of research on intimate violence makes a review or an overview a difficult job. The following review examines the multiple forms of intimate abuse, including women's use of violence, and argues for viewing intimate violence in a sociocultural context.

Naming the Violence

What we name a phenomenon both reflects and determines how we conceptualize it. Without a name, we have difficulty discussing our experience. As our conception of the problem develops or changes, so does our vocabulary. Early researchers used terms like *wife abuse* and *domestic violence*; this reflected the initial focus on the physical violence experienced by married, heterosexual women. Once the silence about battering was broken, additional victims were identified (including lesbians and gay men, unmarried cohabituating couples, dating couples, and women in the process of separation and divorce). Terms such as *wife abuse* and *wife battering* are not inclusive enough to cover all these experiences. Many women are battered by intimates in nonmarital relationships.

Today researchers do not agree on what to call this phenomena; this reflects differences in their conceptualization of partner violence. Debates about definitions and labels are struggles about conceptualization and ideology (McHugh, Livingston, & Ford, 2005). For example, some researchers continue to use the terms *"domestic violence," "family violence,"* and *"spouse abuse."* These individuals generally view violence as gender symmetrical that is equally likely to be perpetrated by men and women. Feminist researchers prefer terms such as *women battering* and contend that generic terms such as *domestic violence* and *spouse abuse* do not distinguish between battering and mutually combative relationships, ignore the nature and consequences of violence, and obscure the dimensions of gender and power that are fundamental to understanding the abuse of women (Breines & Gorden, 1983; Schecter, 1982).

The emergence of new terms such as *dating violence* and *lesbian battering* reflects our realization that women other than wives experience violence in their relationships. While it is important to include such relationships in our analysis, giving each form of violence experienced by women in their intimate relationships a different name or term may obscure the persistent and pervasive nature of such violence and may prevent us from examining such violence for underlying causes. Assigning different labels to different women for their experienced violence may divide and isolate them. In our review, we use the term *intimate partner violence* to refer to physical injury to one's partner in the context of intimate (romantic/sexual) relationships; *intimate partner abuse* refers to physical, psychological, and/or sexual coercion perpetrated in the context of an intimate relationship.

Estimated Prevalence

Estimates are that more than one-fourth of intimate relationships involve at least one incident of physical assault. Koss (1990) reports that 25–33% of married individuals engage in some form of domestic violence at some point in their relationship. Straus, Gelles, and Steinmetz (1980) report 28% in their national survey of more than 2,000 homes. Russell (1982) reports 21% for her San Francisco sample of currently or previously married women. Frieze and her colleagues found that 34% of a general community group of ever-married women reported being attacked at least once by a male partner (Frieze, Knoble, Washburn, & Zomnir, 1980). Others indicate lifetime prevalence rates of being a victim of domestic violence at between 18% and 30% of women, with yearly rates of husband-to-wife violence at 10–12% (Hotaling & Sugarman, 1986; Schulman, 1979; Smith, 1987). A Canadian national population survey of 12,300 women conducted in 1993 indicated that 29% of ever-married women have been assaulted by a spouse, and 16% of women had been assaulted by a date or boyfriend (Johnson, 1998).

In the past decade we have come to realize that violence is as prevalent among cohabituating and dating couples as it is among married couples. Prevalence rates for violence among nonmarried heterosexual couples are consistently about 25% (Cate, Henton, Koval, Christopher, & Lloyd, 1982; Makepeace, 1983), but some research suggests an even higher rate. For example, Deal and Wampler (1986) report that 47% of their college sample has some experience with violence in dating relationships.

Rates of intimate abuse have been found to differ among various cultural and ethnic groups. African American women experience intimate violence at a higher rate than European Americans (Cazenave & Straus, 1979) and are more likely to be killed by a partner or former partner (O'Carroll & Mercy, 1986). Latina women also have a greater risk of partner abuse than Anglo women, but less risk than African American women (Neff, Holaman, & Schluter, 1995). Latina women are likely to experience violence for a longer duration and may feel cultural pressure to remain in a violent relationship (Gondolf, Fisher, & McFerron, 1991). Native Americans in urban areas have been found to have histories of family violence as high as 80% (Chester, Robin, Koss, Lopez, & Goldman 1994). While Asian women may have lower rates of intimate abuse than other ethnic groups (Koss, Goodman, Browne Fitzgerald, Keita, & Russo, 1994), some Asian women such as military wives and mail order brides may be particularly vulnerable to abuse (Jang, 1994).

Violence is also prevalent in gay male and lesbian relationships. In a study of 90 lesbian couples, Coleman (1991) found that 46% used repeated acts of physical abuse. Research has indicated that violence occurs in lesbian relationships at the rate of 25% (Brand & Kidd, 1986) to 48% (Gardner, 1989), which are comparable to the rates established for heterosexual relationships. Gardner (1989) explicitly compared the rates of violence reported by individuals in heterosexual (28%), gay male (38%), and lesbian couples (48%). Like the violence in heterosexual couples, violence in lesbian couples increases in frequency and severity over time (Renzetti, 1988)

A substantial amount of research effort has focused on the prevalence of woman battering, and this question continues to be a central and controversial issue. Early estimates of both incidence and prevalence were based on reports from intact couples, and were applied only to abuse occurring within current marital relationships. Later, community (urban) samples yielded higher estimates when women respondents were asked if they had ever been assaulted. Incidence rates are further increased if we include women who are battered in the context of nonmarital relationships.

By providing statistical evidence of the extent of wife abuse, researchers have played a critical role in making this a social issue. Estimates of intimate abuse are necessary for obtaining resources to address the issue on a local or societal level such as funding for shelters and additional research. Incidence and prevalence rates can be used to document increases and decreases in the phenomena over time. Incidence rates also have important etiological and intervention implications. The perspective that abuse of women by their partners is the result of individual pathology is less convincing as an explanation for a phenomenon that occurs in approximately one-fourth of relationships. High incidence rates are typically interpreted as indicating the existence of structural or societal causes such as societal support of male aggression and relationship scripts that include violence. McHugh and her colleagues (McHugh & Bartoszek, 2000; McHugh et al., 2005) argue that existing theoretical explanations are not adequate to explain the varied and extensive forms of intimate partner violence.

Measuring Intimate Violence

While many validated and standardized scales to measure partner mistreatment have been published (Gondolf, 1998), most of the research has relied on the use of the Conflicts Tactics Scale (CTS) designed by Straus (1979) and used extensively by Straus, Gelles, and their colleagues (e.g., Straus, 1979; Straus & Gelles, 1986; Straus et al., 1980). Continued use of this scale allows for comparability of results, but also perpetuates inadequacies in the literature. The scale asks one of the members of a couple about a list of specific things he or she did during a conflict or disagreement with the other. This person also reports on what the other member of the couple did during their disagreements. There are three categories of behaviors: rational discussion, expressions of anger, and physical violence. The specific behaviors listed range from trying to discuss the issue calmly; to argued heatedly, but short of yelling; to various violent actions such as throwing something at the partner, pushing, grabbing or shoving the partner, or hitting the partner. Violent actions and threats of such actions are included. Individuals are generally given a score depending on how many of the violent actions or threats of violent actions they have done.

In most cases, couples are classified as "violent" if they have *ever done any* of the violent behaviors. Researchers may also count up the number of violent incidents to get an overall measure of the level of violence. This means that slapping or pushing someone once results in the label "violent" being applied to this person and to the relationship.

The use of the CTS has been criticized by many researchers (see Frieze, 2005 or McHugh, 2005 for a fuller discussion of these issues). The scale neither differentiates initiated violence from acts of self-defense nor does the CTS assess the seriousness of the injuries inflicted. The CTS does not allow for consideration of the victims' ability to repel or restrain offenders, or to retaliate against them.

Furthermore, by endorsing any violence on the CTS, the person is labeled as an "abuser" or as a "batterer" by the researcher, and the targets of the acts are classified as "victims" or as "battered." Such labels may not reflect how the person sees him or herself. This discrepancy between the labels applied by the researchers and by the individuals involved in the situation can be seen in a study of female employees at a large southeastern university. Women in this study were asked if they had experienced any of a list of violent actions (a procedure similar to the CTS). Then, for each of the events they experienced, they were asked if this was an instance of physical abuse and if they thought of themselves as a "victim of violence." They were also asked if they thought of themselves as a "battered woman." More than one-third of the women did not accept any of these three types of labels for the acts they had experienced. Others accepted one or more of the labels, but not all of them (Hamby & Gray-Little, 2000).

Another problem with the CTS measure of couple violence is that the focus of this measure is on violent behaviors, but not necessarily on the meanings of those actions or the effects of these behaviors (Brush, 1990). Thus, a large strong man might slap a woman and injure her severely. A small woman might slap a larger man and he would hardly notice it, with no real injury at all. With the CTS, both actions would be weighted equally. Because of this criticism, Straus has revised his measure, calling it the CTS2 (1996). Both the CTS and the CTS2 assume that couple violence is associated with disagreement and conflict. The CTS2 includes questions about violent actions, like the original CTS. In addition, there are questions about how serious one's injuries are. Another criticism of the CTS is that it includes only a small number of possible violent behaviors (Marshall, 1994). CTS severe violence items ask about kicking, biting, or hitting with a fist, hitting with an object, beating someone up, and using a knife or gun. Three items assess "minor" violence: throwing something, pushing, grabbing or shoving, and slapping. Because of this limitation, many researchers create new items when they use the CTS or a modified version.

Partly as a result of reliance on the CTS, little research has been conducted on the effects of psychological and sexual abuse within intimate relationships.

Psychological abuse has primarily been studied as an aspect of a physically abusive relationship (e.g., Tolman, 1992; Walker, 1979). There is increasingly an understanding of both the prevalence and the seriousness of psychological abuse (Chang, 1996; Tolman, 1992). More than one-half of women reported emotional abuse as the reason for divorce (Cleek & Pearson, 1985), and 27% of college women characterized at least one of their dating relationships as abusive (Raymond & Brushi, 1989).

Alternative measures have been developed. For example, the Spouse Abuse Index (ISA) developed by Hudson and McIntosh (1981) is recommended by Gondolf (1998). The 30 items of the ISA addresses psychological as well as physical abuse. Instruments like the ISA may be administered as a follow-up to screening questions about violence. However, these scales are less likely to be used. Reliance on a single scale, the CTS, has limited our understanding of intimate partner violence (McHugh *et al.*, 2005).

The self-reports that are relied on in the CTS and in other measures of interpersonal violence are affected by people not wanting to make themselves look bad and perhaps not wanting their partners to look bad (Hui, 2001). They may also be inaccurate because they depend on the person having a good memory of the events being measured. Such limitations are a problem any time we rely on self-reports of behavior to know what people are actually doing. But, the limitations of self-reports are a special problem in studying violence and aggression (see Yllo & Bograd, 1988).

Some forms of violence may not be recognized as something memorable and are simply forgotten. Thus, if a friend pushes us at a party and laughs about it, we may not take this seriously and will forget about it. But, such pushing would be labeled as "violent" by researchers. This type of situation of unrecognized acts of physical aggression probably occurs for much low-level violence among acquaintances and partners—it is not extreme, no one is injured, and everyone laughs when it happens. There is no reason we would tend to remember this happening and we would never consider reporting this on a crime victimization survey or to the police or to researchers asking about "violence" directly.

FOCUS ON THE WOMAN AS VICTIM

Early research focused on the characteristics of women who were battered. Initially battered women were seen as causing their own suffering. Subsequently feminist research challenged misconceptions about the identity of battered women. Research documented that abuse can occur across regional, occupational, ethnic, racial, and class groups. A review of the first 15 years of research indicated that the characteristics of the battered woman did not predict the violence (Hotaling & Sugarman, 1986; Sugarman & Hotaling, 1989).

"*Why does she stay?*" is probably the most often asked question about woman abuse. In class discussions, public forums, and research literature, people continue to voice this question first and foremost. This question reveals a basic premise about woman battering—if the woman would leave, she would not get beaten. Often the intervention strategy is focused on the victim; the solution is to physically and psychologically relocate the woman. This perspective may be both victim blaming and counterproductive. The batterer may continue to stalk or terrorize her after leaving, or he may go on to batter someone else.

Early research focused on the logistical reasons why some women did not leave an abusive husband. For example, the woman may have stayed due to a lack of money, transportation, or a safe place to go (Bowker, 1983; Browne & Williams, 1989). Others have suggested that social factors such as loss of social status, disapproval of family and friends, and feelings of failure or guilt for abandoning the relationship limit her options for leaving (Dobash & Dobash, 1979; Frieze, 1979; Walker, 1979). Abused women's perceptions of alternatives may be influenced by societal expectations related to gender and role relationships that encourage women to be self-sacrificing and adaptive, and to care for and protect those close to them regardless of the cost (Browne, 1987; Walker & Browne, 1985). Researchers have also emphasized psychological factors underlying women's decisions not to leave. Walker's work suggested that battered women have learned helplessness (Walker, 1979, 1983, 1984). In this model, women have developed motivational, cognitive, and behavioral deficits as a result of the battering. Chandler's (1986) phenomenological analysis of battered women's experiences suggests that overriding fear and a loss of a sense of self characterize the severely battered woman. Other research perspectives emphasize the emotional bonds that battered women form with their abusers (Browne, 1987; Dutton & Painter, 1981; Walker, 1983).

Some researchers have challenged this view of battered women as helpless and resigned to being battered. Some research emphasizes the help seeking, coping mechanisms, and survival skills of battered women. For example, Gondolf and Fisher (1988) critique the learned helplessness model of wife abuse, and examine the ways in which battered women in their Texas sample acted assertively and logically in response to the abuse. The women in their sample, like the women studied by Bowker (1983), persistently sought help from a wide range of sources. The more intensified and prolonged the abuse, the greater the variety and the extent of their help seeking. These studies suggest that individuals and agencies have failed to adequately respond to battered women's requests for help. Many women return to or remain with their abusers because they lack access to community resources (Gondolf, 1988; Sullivan, Basta, Tan, & Davidson, 1992).

The fact that women stay in relationships because they fear retaliation from the violent partners has been obscured by our attention to economic, social, and psychological factors. Some battered women fear that their violent husbands will retaliate against them and their children if they try to leave (Ridington, 1978). Threats of kidnapping and custody battles are common tactics used by abusive partners to keep women in violent relationships (Stahly, 1996). This fear is a realistic one. Women who have left an abusive partner have been followed and harassed for months or even years, and some have been killed (Browne, 1987; Jones, 1981; Pagelow, 1981). Evidence suggests that in many cases the man's violence escalates in response to a separation (Fields, 1978; Fiora-Gormally, 1978; Pagelow, 1981). Stahly (1996) reports the National Crime Survey of the Department of Justice documenting that 70% of domestic violence crime does not occur until after the relationship has ended. Walker (1995) reports that women are at increased risk for severe violence and homicide after leaving the batterer.

As a result of research documenting the prevelance and seriousness of intimate partner violence against women, a national network of shelters have been established. Over the years these agencies have sheltered millions of women from violence. Yet, the shelters cannot accommodate all battered women and may have inadvertently limited our attempts to intervene in intimate partner violence. Shelters have led researchers to focus on women as victims and at the same time hold women responsible for solving intimate partner violence. Krenek (1998) addresses the inadequacy of shelters as THE solution to partner violence. She points out that now police and prosecutors may expect the battered woman to go to the shelter, and to leave the abuser and the domicile. She suggests that in some localities police punish women who do not leave by arresting them. Krenek (1998) and Stahly (1996) both ask the same question: *Why should a woman and her children have to leave home to feel safe?*

FOCUS ON THE MAN AS BATTERER

Who are these men that batter their intimate female partners? One of the most consistent findings with regard to batterers is that they are more likely to have a history of violence in their family of origin (Hotaling & Sugarman, 1986). Men who have witnessed parental violence and men who have been abused as children or adolescents are more likely to become batterers than those who have not (Caesar, 1988; Coleman, Weinman, & His, 1980; Fitch & Papantonio, 1983; Hastings & Hamberger, 1988; MacEwen & Barling, 1988; Rosenbaum & O'Leary, 1981; Sugarman & Hotaling, 1989; Telch & Lindquist, 1984). Witnessing parental violence has been found to be more predictive than experiencing abuse as a child (Tolman & Bennett, 1990). As many as three-quarters of men seeking counseling for battering witnessed abuse between their parents, whereas half were abused as children (Fitch & Papantonio, 1983).

Drug and alcohol use has been found to be a consistent risk marker for use of violence toward a female partner (Coleman *et al.*, 1980; Hotaling & Sugarman, 1986; Telch & Lindquist, 1984). There is, however, no direct relationship between the amount of alcohol consumed and battering (Leonard, Bromet, Parkinson, Day, & Ryan, 1985; VanHasselt, Morrison, & Bellack, 1985), and the violence/battering occurs independently of alcohol and drug abuse. Chronic alcohol abuse is more predictive of battering than acute intoxication, although both are predictive (Tolman & Bennett, 1990). Binge drinkers have the highest rates of battering (Gelles, Lackner, & Wolfnersss, 1994).

While researchers have been unable to identify a unitary batterer personality profile (Hastings & Hamberger, 1988), higher rates of certain psychiatric conditions have been found among batterers (Rosenbaum *et al.* 1997). Personality disorders and characteristics such as antisocial, borderline, and narcissistic occur at higher rates among batterers (Hamberger & Hastings, 1991; Hart *et al.* 1993; Hastings & Hamberger, 1988).

Generally, men who batter are more likely than nonviolent partners to be violent or aggressive in other ways and with other people. They are more likely to have a criminal history (Roberts, 1987; Bland & Orn, 1986; White & Straus, 1981) and to have used violence outside of the home (Graff, 1979; Hotaling & Sugarman, 1986; Rouse, 1984; Shields, McCall, & Hanneke, 1988). White and Straus (1981) report that batterers are twice as likely as nonviolent husbands to have an arrest record for a serious crime, and Gayford (1975) reports that 50% of his sample of male batterers had spent time in prison. Somewhere between one-third (Flynn, 1977) and 46% of batterers (Fagen, Stewart, & Hansen, 1983) have been arrested for other violence. Batterers have consistently higher rates of committing child abuse than men who are not violent with their partners (Hotaling & Sugarman, 1986). Thus, the violence and aggression used by at least some batterers is not confined to their partner.

The clearest conclusion one can draw from the available literature, however, is that batterers are a heterogeneous group, and there is a great deal of inconsistency in the literature. It makes sense that not all batterers are alike. There may be various types of batterers with different etiological and abuse patterns and with implications for diverse interventions (Dutton, 1988; Gondolf, 1988; Saunders, 1992). Furthermore, the results of a particular study may depend on how the sample was recruited. Batterers who have been reprimanded by the courts to batterer groups may differ significantly from men in a community survey who admit to use of violence toward their partner.

PATTERN OF VIOLENCE

Battering has been constructed as a pattern of domination, intimidation and coercive control (Dutton & Goodman, 2005; Pence & Paymar, 1993; Dasgupta, 2002). Research on women who have experienced serious physical violence has resulted in the identification of some patterns of battering within intimate relationships. One pattern is that the physically abusive partner often physically and socially isolates his victim, perhaps even prior to the use of any physical violence. Women are often discouraged from daily calls home or other interactions with immediate family. They report that their partner criticized their friends and limited their social interactions. Sometimes the partner provided transportation to and from classes or work thus limiting socializing afterward.

Browne (1987) and Walker (1984) note that abused women report that their partners were extremely attentive and affectionate early in the relationship. They showed great interest in the women's whereabouts, a desire to be with them all the time, intense expressions of affection and jealousy, and wanted an early commitment to a long-term relationship. Over time these behaviors that were initially seen as evidence of love became intrusive, controlling, and triggers to assault. The women have become emotionally and geographically isolated, making them vulnerable to abuse. The abuser's concern for the wife's whereabouts becomes a form of surveillance, and the batterers are often described as evidencing severe and delusional jealousy (Frieze *et al.*, 1980; Hotaling & Sugarman, 1986).

Similarly, psychological abuse often precedes physical violence. Continuing criticism, correcting, and humiliation undermine the woman's confidence. Increasingly she sees herself as someone who is not competent or capable enough to live independently. She is encouraged to view the world as hostile and to see others as not interested in her.

Partner violence often escalates in severity and frequency over time (Pagelow, 1981, 1997). Intimate violence may end in death. Approximately 4,000 women are killed by their spouses or lovers each year (U.S. Department of Justice, Bureau of Statistics, 1994, as cited in Stahly, 1996). This is one pattern of intimate violence that is recognized based on extensive interviews with battered women, often in a shelter situation. Some researchers have begun to identify this as the pattern of violence, suggesting that a single episode of violence is an indication that the violence will escalate and is likely to be accompanied by psychological abuse. Recent research suggests that this may not be the only or the most likely pattern of violence in intimate relationships.

WOMEN'S USE OF VIOLENCE

Recent evidence suggests that women's participation in and even initiation of violence is higher than we originally thought. When we review the empirical data, using the CTS or other similar methods, a large number of studies have reported that both sexes admit to using violence against their intimate partners (Frieze, 2005; McHugh, 2005). Straus and his colleagues (e.g., Straus *et al.*, 1980) presented some of the first indications that not all relationship violence was perpetrated by men to women, and that some women were violent toward their husbands. Using the CTS in a nationally representative sample, Straus and his colleagues (Straus & Gelles, 1986; Straus *et al.*, 1980) report that women initiate both minor and severe forms of physical violence with the same frequency as men. Saunders (1986) indicates that as many as 75% of battered women report using minor forms of violence as measured by the CTS.

Partly as a result of measurement inadequacies, use of the CTS has led to confusion over the mutuality of domestic violence. Strauss (1979) and Steinmetz

(1978) have interpreted symmetry in incidences reported by males and females as indicative of mutual violence. Others (Browne, 1989; Browne & Dutton, 1990; Dobash, Dobash, Cavanagh, & Lewis, 1998) have challenged this conclusion. The interpretation that men and women are equally combative ignores the physical and economic power disparities between men and women, and fails to consider the motive for or consequences of aggressive acts (Johnson, 1998). The CTS does not distinguish between use of violence and initiation of violence. Women defending themselves against hostile or even deadly attacks would be classified as engaging in mutual domestic violence in this research. Furthermore, for example, a woman pushing or slapping her partner may be viewed as the primary aggressor. However, our label and interpretation may be different when we know that she has been battered on a regular basis for 16 years and has just recently begun to retaliate or to defend herself.

In a study of women arrested for domestic violence, Hamberger (1997) found that about two-thirds of the women were battered and used violence to protect themselves or to retaliate. Although many of the women acknowledged initiating violence, they generally did so in the context of a relationship in which the male partner initiated violence more often and was likely to have initiated the overall pattern of violence. Studies have found that women are more likely to use violence in self-defense or retaliation and are significantly more likely to sustain injuries (Makepeace, 1986). Men, however, are more likely to use violence for intimidation and forced sex and use more severe forms of violence (Bookwala *et al*., 1992; Makepeace, 1986). Frieze and McHugh (1992) document the impact that male violence has on the power dynamics within marriage. Abusive husbands, by their own admission, use force to get what they want (Bograd, 1998), whereas women report using violence in self-defense (Saunders, 1986). Hamberger (1997) argues that asking who initiated the violence is too simplistic. He argues that it is necessary to understand partner violence as having occurred in a context. The history of the violence, the development and patterns of the violence, and the personal definitions of the individuals involved are part of this context (Hamberger, 1997).

Given these perspectives, we must still acknowledge the existence of female-initiated violence. In his study of women arrested for domestic violence, Hamberger (1997) found that 25% of the women reported starting the violence 100% of the time and that one-third of the sample could not be classified as battered women. Similarly, Pagelow (1985) acknowledges the existence of violent women who "create an atmosphere of fear for their husbands" (p. 274).

Over time there has been more and more research and clinical evidence that women are sometimes violent toward their intimate partners. Some of this evidence came from continuing studies of married couples. For example, in a recent analysis of a national representative sample, Anderson (2002) found that 10% of all couples reported some type of violence to each other in the last year. Looking at the patterns of violence in more detail, it was noted that in 7% of the couples both were violent. For 2% of the couples, only the woman was violent, and for 1%, only the man was violent. This study shows the same general pattern of more women reporting engaging in violent acts toward their partner than men seen in results reported by Straus and his colleagues (1980). Other studies of couples living together show similar patterns (see a meta-analysis by Archer, 2000).

Williams and Frieze (2005) found similar data, again using a nationally representative sample of 3,505 men and women in stable couple relationships. Overall, 18% of the sample reported some violence in their relationship. To address questions raised about whether the violence was mutual and who was the more violent, the man or the women, the violence group was divided into mutual and one-sided violence relationships. About 4% of the sample reported that both they and their partners used severe violence and 5% reported mutual low-level violence. More men than women reported being the targets of one-sided violence, and more women than men reported being the violent one in the couple. Recently, other researchers have similarly documented multiple patterns of mutual violence in heterosexual couples (Milan, Lewis, Ethier, Kershw, & Ickovocs, 2005; Weston, Temple, & Marshall, 2005).

These data indicating female "violence" toward intimate partners cannot and should not be ignored (McHugh, 2005). The question is how these data should be interpreted. Feminists contend that gender and unequal distribution of power between men and women are important explanatory factors in intimate violence (e.g., Dobash & Dobash, 1979). Others have consistently argued that intimate violence is a human issue, and that women are as likely as men, or even more prone than men, to use physical violence in intimate relations (McNeely & Mann, 1990). Bograd (1990) argues that the importance of gender in understanding violence is not contingent on data establishing men as the (only) batterers. Acknowledging that women are (increasingly) violent has profound implications for both individuals and social movements (Hamberger, 1997). Even while rejecting the conclusion that women's violence is equivalent to men's, we may need to rethink our conceptions of gender issues in partner violence. Three recent special issues of professional psychological journals have focused on the questions raised by research documenting women's use of violence in intimate relations and the gender issues raised by this research (Frieze & McHugh, 2005; McHugh & Frieze, 2005).

TOWARD NEW CONCEPTUALIZATIONS AND EXPLANATIONS

Recent research that challenges our conceptions of who is a victim and who is a perpetrator also argues for new conceptualizations of intimate violence. As Richardson (2005) points out, we have been slow to recognize or acknowledge that some women use physical aggression against others. The idea that women use violence is resisted in part because women violence disputes our representation of interpersonal violence; demonstrates methodological and measurement shortcomings in our research; questions the adequacy of our explanatory theories of violence; challenges our notions about men and women; and contests our conceptions of gender (McHugh, 2005). McHugh and her colleagues (McHugh *et al.*, 2005) argue against the conceptualization of intimate violence as a single truth or as a debate between polarized positions, and reject either/or dichotomies as simplistic and not helpful, and have encouraged researchers to recognize how research methods, questions, and measures may impact our conclusions about the mutuality of violence versus battering (McHugh & Bartoszek, 2000; McHugh *et al.*, 2005; McHugh, 1993, 2005). In samples drawn from samples of women in battered women's shelters, we are most likely to find a high percentage of severely abused women. Probably very few of these women, if any, are intimate abusers or mutual combatants. However, in samples of women from the community or in samples drawn from college populations, we may be more likely to see a range of intimate abuse situations that include women who abuse their partners and mutually violent couples. Even within a small clinic sample, Vivian and Langhinrichsen-Rohling (1994) identified three subgroups of spouses: a large number of couples who reported mutual but low-level violence; a small subgroup of battered men (by female partners); and a substantial number of couples identified as battered wives and male batterers. Furthermore, age or cohort effects might account for some of the differences in findings. Female initiated and mutual violence may be more common among younger women. One interpretation is that postfeminist young women see violence as a gender-neutral behavior.

One of the difficulties in understanding inconsistencies in data relates to the ways in which "intimate partner violence" is measured. As mentioned earlier, any acts of physical aggression, no matter how minor, are labeled by researchers as "violence." Much of this "violence" is not severe and does not lead to injury. The label of "violence" for such situations is misleading and has led to the mistaken idea that the findings of empirical research identifying female violence indicate that women, more than men, are severely injuring their partners. This is not the case. Most of the female aggression is low level as is the case for men. There are a few very violent women and probably a larger number of very violent men, but the large majority of couple "violence" is not what one would generally associate with the label of "violent." For example, research indicates that women who report having hit their partners do not necessarily see themselves as using violence and men having been hit or pushed by their women partners may not view themselves as victims of violence. Is hitting violence regardless of the experience and meaning it has for the participants? Alternatively, women, whose clothes have been trashed, may see this as more violent than a slap; yet this act is not counted as violence in research because it is not recorded by the scales used to measure partner violence. How many times did he slap you? may not be the most important question we need to ask about intimate conflict. McHugh and her colleagues (McHugh *et al.*, 2005) argue that different conceptualizations of violence and abuse can contribute to a pluralistic, complex, and multilayered conception of intimate partner abuse. Reliance on a single measure that oversimplifies, reduces, or reifies our construction of violence would be viewed as problematic.

Who we study as victims or perpetrators turns out to be critical to our construction of interpersonal violence. Studying wives as victims leads to the construction of wife abuse, the idea that helpless women are victimized by abusive male partners, whereas studying lesbian partners engaged in mutual violence leads to alternative conceptualizations. Others (Hamby, 2005; Johnson, 1995; Saunders, 2000) have argued that sample differences between family conflict and violent crime studies, and between shelter and clinical samples and community samples can at least partly explain finding unilateral "battering" versus retaliatory or mutual abuse (e.g., Johnson & Ferraro, 2000; Swan & Snow, 2003). The identification and documentation of varied types and patterns of intimate partner violence (e.g., Johnson & Leone, 2005; Weston, Temple, & Marshall, 2005; Williams & Frieze, 2005) has been suggested as a way to reconcile inconsistencies in the findings. Who we study turns out to determine our conceptualization of intimate violence. Thus, we need to carefully consider which populations of people are neglected by our research and why. One sample characteristic we have not attended to carefully in this issue is age. Much of the existing research on relationship violence over-represents young adults. There are reasons to believe that interpersonal violence is influenced by age and life span development (Frieze, 2005). Seniors are one example of a neglected population. Senior couples were found to be less violent (Bookwala *et al.*, 2005). There is also evidence for cultural and ethnic variations in patterns of intimate violence, too complex to be reviewed here (McHugh & Frieze, 2005).

The patterns of violence may be affected not only by the composition of the research sample, but also by the larger sociohistorical context of the research. The respondents live in a particular time and place. Young people differ from older individuals, not only by age, but also in the sociohistorical context in which they were socialized. For example, young men and women in the United States today were raised in an era of television viewing and video games that were not a part of the childhoods of people over 50 years of age. Research has documented that exposure to media violence impacts the acceptability and use of violence, and yet this understanding is rarely raised as a factor in the literature on relationship violence. We often fail to connect intimate violence with other forms of violence, even though the studies reported here indicate that as our experience of violence increases, so does the likelihood of our using violence (Fagan & Wexler, 1987; Sullivan, Meese, Swan, Mazure, & Snow, 2005; Tifft, 1993). Social norms about violence and particularly about gender and violence change over time, and may differ by region and culture.

One approach to IPV is the construction of theoretically or empirically based patterns to classify violent couple relationships (e.g., Frieze, 2005; Johnson, 1995; Johnson & Leone, 2005; Williams & Frieze, 2005; Weston *et al.*, in press). Men and women may perform different patterns of violence, or they may experience violence victimization differently even when the violent actions are the same For example, Johnson (1995) posits a typology of common couple violence and patriarchal terrorism to explain conflicting data on intimate abuse. The more gender-balanced violence found in community samples may fit into the pattern of common-couple violence which is typically mild in nature. The more severe and commonly male-perpetrated violence epitomized by the "battered woman" and evidenced in clinical samples may fit the patriarchal terrorism pattern. Johnson's patterns emphasize the importance of distinguishing between overlapping, but divergent phenomena. Similarly, using community samples, Williams and Frieze (2005) and Weston and her colleagues (2005) have identified several patterns or types of couple violence based on frequency and severity of the violence. Weston and her colleagues (Weston *et al.*, 2005) demonstrate that among women who were involved in mutual violence, the most commonly reported pattern was for their male partners to be the primary perpetrator based on frequency and severity descriptions.

CONCLUSIONS

Implicitly or explicitly the research we conduct on intimate violence and our intervention efforts reflect underlying ideological perspectives. The focus of our research, the terms and measures we use, and the intervention strategies we employ both inform and are directed by our theories of intimate violence. An initial focus on wife beating led to theories of marital dynamics and deficiencies in the wives who were beaten, and intervention efforts entailed sheltering and counseling the abused wife. Research that employs the terms and measures of the domestic violence perspective emphasizes the mutuality and interactive aspects of intimate violence and supports interventions directed toward dyadic or family conflict resolution. Feminist research has directed our attention toward the (male) batterer and has coined terms that embody the gendered aspects of intimate violence. Heterosexist biases rendered violence in gay and lesbian relationships invisible.

The research documenting the prevalence of violence across all forms of intimate relationships and research increasingly indicating that women can be perpetrators calls for new theoretical perspectives. Research demonstrating gender similarities in use of violence in intimate relationships (as reviewed by Archer, 2000 and Frieze, 2005) challenges our stereotypic understanding of relationship violence as unilateral and requires us to explore the complexities of interpersonal violence. Along with Anderson (2005), we call for researchers and theorists to develop more complex constructions of gender as one path to understanding violence in interpersonal relationships. Both Anderson (2005) and Brush (2005) point out that feminist and sociological conceptions of gender have progressed to become more complex and interaction oriented, but on the research on intimate violence, gender continues to be treated as a dichotomous categorization equivalent to sex and to be seen as an inherent characteristic of individuals.

The incidence of intimate violence indicates the futility of intervening at the individual level. Intimate partner violence neither exists in a vacuum nor limits itself to easy definitions and simplistic categories. Current research attests to the importance of considering the context of intimate violence, including the type of relationship in which violence occurs, the relevant gender roles and norms, and other aspects of the sociohistorical context. To find ways to reduce the levels of violence experienced in our lives and in our intimate relationships, we must adopt complex models of intimate partner violence and use multiple methods, measures, and perspectives in our research.

REFERENCES

ARCHER, J. 2000. Sex differences in aggression between heterosexual partners: a meta-analytic review. Psychol. Bull. *126*, 651–680.

ANDERSON, K.L. 2002. Perpetrator or victim?: relationships between intimate partner violence and well-being. J. Marriage Fam. *64*, 851–863.

ANDERSON, K.L. 2005. Theorizing gender in intimate partner violence research. Sex Roles *52*, 853–856.

BLAND, R. & H. ORN. 1986. Family violence and psychiatric disorder. Can. J. Psychiatry *31*, 129–137.

BOGRAD, M. 1998. Feminist perspectives on wife abuse: an introduction. *In* Feminist Perspectives On Wife Abuse. K. Yllo & M. Bograd, Eds.: 1–27. Sage. Beverly Hills, CA.

BOGRAD, M. 1990. Why we need gender to understand human violence. J. Interpers. Violence *5*, 132–135.

BOOKWALA, J., I.H. FRIEZE, C. SMITH & K. RYAN. 1992. Predictors of dating violence: a multivariate analysis. Violence Vict. *7*, 297–311.

BOOKWALA, J., J. SOBIN & B. ZDANIUK. 2005. Gender and aggression in marital relationships: a life-span perspective. Sex Roles. *52*, 797–806.

BOWKER, L.H. 1983. Beating Wife Beating. Lexington Books. Lexington, MA.

BRAND, P.A. & A.H. KIDD. 1986. Frequency of physical aggression in heterosexual and female homosexual dyads. Psychol. Rep. *59*, 1307–1313.

BREINES, W. & L. GORDEN. 1983. The new scholarship on family violence. Signs: A J. Women in Cultural and Society *8*, 490–531.

BROWNE, A. 1987. Are women as violent as men? Commentary at the meeting of the American Society of Criminology. Reno, NV.

BROWNE, A. & D.G. DUTTON. 1990. Escape from violence: risks and alternatives for abused women. *In* Family Violence: Perspectives in Research and Practice. R. Roesch, D.G. Dutton & V.F. Sacco, Eds.: 67–91. Simon Fraser University Press. Burnaby, BC.

BROWNE, A. & K.R. WILLIAMS. 1989. Exploring the effect of resource availability and the likelihood of female-perpetrated homicides. Law and Society Review. *23*, 75–94.

BROWNE, A. 1987. When battered women kill. Macmillan. New York, NY.

BRUSH, L.D. 1990. Violent acts and injurious outcomes in married couples: methodological issues in the National Survey of Families and Households. Gend. Soc. *4*, 56–67.

BRUSH, L.D. 2005. Philosophical and political issues in research on women's violence and aggression. Sex Roles *52*, 867–873.
CAESAR, P.L. 1988. Exposure to violence in the families of origin among wife-abusers and martially nonviolent men. Violence Vict. *3*, 49–63.
CATE, R.M., J.M. HENTON, J. KOVAL, K.S. CHRISTOPHER & S. LLOYD. 1982. Premarital abuse: a social psychological perspective. J. Fam.Issues *3*, 79–91.
CAZENAVE, N. & M. STRAUS. 1979. Race, class network embeddedness and family violence: a search for potent support systems. J. Comp. Fam. Stud. *10*, 281–299.
CHANDLER, S. 1986. The Psychology of Battered Women. Unpublished doctoral dissertation. Department of Education, University of California, Berkeley.
CHANG, V.N. 1996. I Just Lost Myself: Psychological abuse of Women in Marriage. Praeger. Westport, CT.
CHESTER, B., R. ROBIN, M. KOSS, *et al*. 1994. Grandmother dishonored: violence against women by male partners in Indian communities. Violence Vict. *9*, 259–274.
CLEEK, M.G. & T.A. PEARSON. 1985. Perceived causes of divorce: an analysis of interrelationships. J. Marriage Fam. *47*, 179–183.
COLEMAN, K.H., M.L. WEINMAN & B.P. HIS. 1980. Factors affecting conjugal violence. J. Psychol. *105*, 197–202.
COLEMAN, V.E. 1991. Violence in Lesbian Couples: a Between Groups Comparison. Doctoral dissertation, California School of Professional Psychology, Los Angeles, 1990. Dissertation Abstracts International *51*, 5634B.
DASGUPTA, S.D. 2002. A framework for understanding women's use of nonlethal violence in intimate heterosexual relationships. Violence Against Women *8*, 1364–1389.
DEAL, J.E. & K.S. WAMPLER. 1986. Dating violence: the primacy of previous experience. J. Soc. Pers. Relat. *3*, 457–471.
DOBASH, R.E. & R.P. DOBASH. 1979. Violence Against Wives. The Free Press. New York, NY.
DOBASH, R.P., R.E., DOBASH, K. CAVANAGH & R. LEWIS. 1998. Separate and intersecting realities: A comparison of men's and women's accounts of violence against women. *Violence Against Women 4*, 382–414.
DUTTON, D.G. 1988. Profiling of wife assaulters: preliminary evidence for a trimodal analysis. Violence Vict. *3*, 5–29.
DUTTON, D.G. & S.L. PAINTER. 1981. Traumatic bonding: the development of emotional attachments in battered women and other relationships of intermittent abuse. Victimology *6*, 139–155.
DUTTON, M.A. & L.A. GOODMAN. 2005. Coercion in intimate partner violence: Toward a new conceptualization. *Sex Roles 52*, 743–756.
FAGAN, J.A., D.K. STEWART & K.V. HANSEN. 1983. Violent men or violent husbands? Background factors and situational correlates. *In* The Dark Side of Families: Current Family Violence Research. D. Finkelhor, R. Gelles, G. Hotaling & M.A. Straus, Eds.: Sage. Beverly Hills, CA.
FAGAN, J.A. & S. WEXLER. 1987. Crime at home and in the streets: the relationship between family and stranger violence. Violence Vict. *2*, 5–23.
FIELDS, M.D. 1978. Does this vow include wife beating? Human Rights *7*, 40–45.
FIORA-GORMALLY, N. 1978. Battered women who kill: double standard out of court, single standard in? Law Hum. Behav. *2*, 133–165.
FITCH, F.J. & A. PAPANTONIO. 1983. Men who batter: some pertinent characteristics. J. Nerv. Ment. Dis. *171*, 190–192.
FLYNN, J.P. 1977. Recent findings related to wife abuse. Soc. Casework *58*, 13–20.

FRIEZE, I.H. 2005. Hurting the One You Love: Violence in Relationships. Thomson Wadsworth. Belmont, CA.

FRIEZE, I.H. 1979. Perception of battered wives. In New Approaches to Social Problems: Applications of Attribution Theory. I.H. Frieze, D. Bar-Tal & J.S. Carroll, Eds.: 79–108. Jossey Bass. San Francisco.

FRIEZE, I.H., J. KNOBLE, C. WASHBURN & G. ZOMNIR. 1980. Types Of Battered Women. Paper presented at the Association for Women in Psychology. Santa Monica, CA.

FRIEZE, I.H. & M.C. MCHUGH. 1992. Power strategies of wives in violent and nonviolent marriages. Psychol. Women Q. *16*, 449–465.

GARDNER, R.A. 1989. The Parental Alienation Syndrome and the Differention between Fabricated and Genuine Child Sex Abuse. Creative Therapeutics. Cresskill, NJ.

GAYFORD, J.J. 1975. Wife battering: a preliminary study of 100 cases. Br. Med. J. *1*, 194–197.

GELLES, R.J., R. LACKNER & G.D. WOLFNER. 1994. Men who batter: the risk markers. Violence Up Date, *4*, 1, 2, 4, 10.

GONDOLF, E. & E.R. FISHER. 1988. Battered Women as Survivors: An Alternative to Treating Learned Helplessness. Lexington Books. Lexington, MA.

GONDOLF, E.W., E.R. FISHER & R. MCFERRON. 1991. Racial differences among shelter residents: a comparison of Anglo, Black and Hispanic battered women. *In* Black Family Violence: Current Research and Theory. R. Hampton, Ed.: 39–51. Sage. Newberry Park, CA.

GONDOLF, E.W. 1998. Assessing Woman Battering In Women's Health Services. Sage. Thousand Oaks, CA.

GRAFF, T.T. 1979. Personality Characteristics Of Battered Women. Unpublished doctoral dissertation, Brigham Young University, UT.

HAMBERGER, L.K. 1997. Female offenders in domestic violence: a look at actions in their context. *In* Violence and Sexual Abuse at Home: Current Issues in Spousal Battering and Child Maltreatment. R. Geffner, S.B. Sorenson & P.K. Lundberg-Love, Eds.: 117–130. Haworth Press. New York, NY.

HAMBERGER, L.K. & J.E. HASTINGS. 1991. Personality correlates of men who batter and nonviolent men: some continuities and discontinuities. J. Fam. Violence *6*, 131–147.

HAMBY, S.L. & B. GRAY-LITTLE. 2000. Labeling partner violence: when do victims differentiate among acts? Violence Vict. *15*, 173–186.

HAMBY, S.L. 2005. Measuring gender differences in partner violence: implications from research on other forms of violent and socially undesirable behavior. Sex Roles *52*, 725–742.

HART, S.D., D.G. DUTTON & T. NEWLOVE. 1993. The prevalence of personality disorders among wife assaulters. J. Personal. Disord. *7*, 329–341.

HASTINGS, J.E. & L.K. HAMBERGER. 1988. Personality characteristics of spouse abusers: a controlled comparison. Violence Vict. *3*, 31–47.

HOTALING, G.T. & D.B. SUGARMAN. 1986. An analysis of risk markers in husband to wife violence: the current state of knowledge. Violence Vict. *1*, 101–124.

HUDSON, W. & S. MCINTOSH. 1981. The assessment of spouse abuse: two quantifiable dimensions. J. Marriage Fam. *43*, 873–885.

HUI, C.H. 2001. Double rating as a method to encourage candid responses to self-report instruments. J. Appl. Soc. Psychol. *31*, 21–30.

JANG, D. 1994. Caught in a web: immigrant women and domestic violence. Nat. Clearinghouse Leg. Serv. Rev. *Special Issue*, 379–405.

JOHNSON, H. 1998. Rethinking survey research on violence against women. *In* Rethinking Violence Against Women. R.E. Dobash & R.P. Dobash, Eds.: 23–52. Sage. Thousand Oaks, CA.

JOHNSON, M.P. 1995. Patriarchal terrorism and common couple violence: two forms of violence against women. J. Marriage Fam. *57*, 283–294.

JOHNSON, M.P. & FERRARO, K.J. 2000. Research on domestic violence in the 1990s: making distinctions. J. Marriage Fam. *62*, 948–963.

JOHNSON, M.P. & J.M. LEONE. 2005. The differential effects of intimate terrorism and situational couple violence: findings from the National Violence Against Women Survey. J. Fam. Issues *26*, 322–349.

JONES, A. 1981. Women Who Kill. Holt, Rinehart & Winston. New York, NY.

KOSS, M.P. 1990. The women's mental health research agenda: violence against women. Am. Psychol. *45*, 374–380.

KOSS, M.P., L.A. GOODMAN, A. BROWNE, L. FITZGERALD, G.P. KEITA & N.F. RUSSO. 1994. No safe haven: violence against women at home, at work, and in the community. American Psychological Association. Washington, DC.

KRENEK, K. 1998. Keynote Address. Annual Conference of the PASSHE Women's Consortium and Mid-Atlantic Nation Women's Studies Association. Shippensburg University, PA.

LEONARD, K.E., E.J. BROMET, D.K. PARKINSON, N.L. DAY & C.M RYAN. 1985. Patterns of alcohol use and physically aggressive behavior in men. J. Stud. Alcohol *46*, 279–282.

MACEWEN, K.E. & J. BARLING. 1988. Multiple stressors, violence in the family of origin, and marital aggression: a longitudinal investigation. J. Fam. Violence *3*, 73–87.

MAKEPEACE, J.M. 1983. Life events, stress, and courtship violence. Fam. Relat. *32*, 101–109.

MAKEPEACE, J.M. 1986. Gender differences in courtship violence victimization. Fam. Relat. *35*, 383–388.

MARSHALL, L.L. 1994. Physical and psychological abuse. *In* The Dark Side of Interpersonal Communication. W.R. Cupach & B.H. Spitzberg, Eds.: 281–311. Erlbaum. Hillsdale, NJ, England: Lawrence Erlbaum.

MCNEELY, R.L. & C.R. MANN. 1990. Domestic violence is a human issue. J. Interpers. Violence *5*, 129–132.

MCHUGH, M.C. 1993. Studying battered women and batterers: feminist perspectives on methodology. *In* Battering and Family Therapy: a Feminist Perspective. M. Hansen & M. Harway, Eds.: 54–68. Sage. Newbury Park, CA.

MCHUGH, M.C. 2005. Understanding Gender and Intimate Partner Abuse. Sex Roles *52*, 717–724.

MCHUGH, M.C. & T.A. BARTOSZEK. 2000. Intimate Violence. *In* Issues in the Psychology of Women. M. Biaggio & M. Hersen, Eds.: 115–144. Plenum. New York, NY.

MCHUGH, M.C., N.A. LIVINGSTON & A. FORD. 2005. A postmodern approach to women's use of violence: developing multiple and complex conceptualizations. Psychol. Women Q. *29*, 323–336.

MILAN, S., J. LEWIS, K. ETHIER, T. KERSHAW, J.R. ICKONOCS. 2005. Relationship violence among adolescent mothers: frequency dyadic nature, and implications for relationship dissolution and mental health. Psychol. Women Q. *29*, 302–312.

NEFF, J., B. HOLAMAN & T.D. SCHLUTER. 1995. Spousal violence among Anglos, Blacks, and Mexican Americans: the role of demographic variables, psychosocial, predictors, and alcohol consumption. J. Fam. Violence *10*, 1–21.

O'CARROLL, P. & J. MERCY. 1986. Patterns and recent trends in black homicide. *In* Homicide among Black Americans. D. Hawkins, Ed.: 44–62. University Press of America. Lanham, MD.

PAGELOW, M. 1981. Woman-Battering. Sage. Beverly Hills, CA.

PAGELOW, M.D. 1985. The battered husband syndrome: social problem or much ado about little? *In* Marital Violence. I.N. Johnson, Ed.:Routledge and Kegan. London.

PAGELOW, M.D. 1997. Battered women: a historical research review and some common myths. *In* Violence and Sexual Abuse at Home: Current Issues in Spousal Battering and Child Maltreatment. R. Geffner, S.B. Sorrenson & P.K. Lundberg-Love, Eds.: 97–116. Haworth Press. New York, NY.

PENCE, E. & M. PAYMAR. 1993. Education Groups For Men Who Batter: The Duluth Model. Springer. New York, NY.

RAYMOND, B. & I.G. BRUSCHI. 1989. Psychological abuse among college women in dating relationships. Percept. Mot. Skills *69*, 1283–1297.

RENZETTI, C.M. 1988. Violence in lesbian relationships: a preliminary analysis of causal factors. J. Interpers. Violence *3*, 381–399.

RIDINGTON, J. 1978. The transition process: a feminist environment as reconstructive milieu. Victimology *3*, 563–575.

RICHARDSON, D.S. 2005. The myth of female passivity: thirty years of relationship. J. Marriage Fam. *60*, 70–78.

ROBERTS, A.R. 1987. Psychosocial characteristics of batterers: a study of 234 men charged with domestic violence offenses. J. Fam. Violence *2*, 81–93.

ROSENBAUM, A. & K.D. O'LEARY. 1981. Marital violence: characteristics of abusive couples. J. Consult. Clin. Psychol. *49*, 63–71.

ROUSE, L.P. 1984. Models of self-esteem, and locus of control as factors contributing to spouse abuse. Victimol. Int. J. *9*, 130–141.

RUSSELL, D.E.H. 1982. Rape In Marriage. Macmillan. New York, NY.

SAUNDERS, D.G. 1986. When battered women use violence: husband abuse or self-defense? Violence Vict. *1*, 47–60.

SAUNDERS, D.G. 1992. A typology of men who batter: three types derived from cluster analysis. Am. J. Orthopsychiatry *62*, 264–275.

SAUNDERS, D. 2000. Are physical assaults by wives and girlfriends a major social problem? A review of the literature. Violence Against Women *8*, 1424–1448.

SCHECHTER, S. 1982. Women and Male Violence: The Visions and Struggles of the Battered Women's Movement. South End Press. Boston, MA.

SCHULMAN, M. 1979. A Survey of Spousal Violence Against Women in Kentucky. Study No. 792701 for the Kentucky Commission on Women. U.S. Department of Justice-LEAR. Washington, DC.

SHIELDS, N.M., G.J. MCCALL & C.R. HANNEKE. 1988. Patterns of family and nonfamily violence: violent husbands and violent men. Violence Vict. *3*, 83–97.

SMITH, M.D. 1987. The incidence and prevalence of woman abuse in Toronto. Violence Vict. *2*, 173–187.

STAHLY, G.B. 1996. Battered women: why don't they just leave? *In* Lectures on the Psychology of Women. J.C. Chrisler, C. Golden & P.D. Rozee, Eds.: 289–308. McGraw-Hill. New York, NY.

STEINMETZ, S. 1977. The battered husband syndrome. Victimology *2*, 499–509.

STRAUS, M.A. 1979. Measuring intrafamily conflict and violence: the Conflict Tactics Scales. J. Marriage Fam. *41*, 75–88.

STRAUS, M. & R. GELLES. 1986. Societal change and change in family violence from 1975–1985 as revealed by two national surveys. J. Marriage Fam. *48*, 465–479.

STRAUS, M.A., R.S. GELLES & J.K. STEINMETZ. 1980. Behind Closed Doors: Violence in the American Family. Anchor/Doubleday. Garden City, NJ.

SUGARMAN, D.B. & G.T. HOTALING. 1989. Violent men in intimate relationships: an analysis or risk markers. J. Appl. Soc. Psychol. *19*, 1034–1048.

SULLIVAN, C.M., J. BASTA, C. TAN & W.S. DAVIDSON, II. 1992. After the crisis: a needs assessment of women leaving a domestic violence shelter. Violence Vict. *7*, 267–275.

SULLIVAN, T.P., K.J. MEESE, S.C. SWAN, C.M. MAZURE, & D.L. SNOW. 2005. Precursors and correlates of women's violence: child abuse traumatization, victimization of women, avoidance coping, and psychological symptoms. Psychology of Women Quarterly *29*(3), 290–301.

SWAN, S.C. & D.L. SNOW. 2003. Behavioral and psychological differences among abused women who use violence in intimate relationships. Violence Against Women *9*, 75–109.

TELCH, C.F. & C.U. LINDQUIST. 1984. Violent vs. nonviolent couples: a comparison of patterns. Psychotherapy *21*, 242–248.

TIFFT, L.L. 1993. Battering of Women: The Failure of Intervention and the Case for Prevention. Westview Press. Boulder, CO.

TOLMAN, R.M. 1992. Psychological abuse of women. *In* Assessment of Family Violence: a Clinical and Legal Sourcebook. R.T. Ammerman & M. Hersen, Eds.: 291–310. John Wiley & Sons. New York, NY.

TOLMAN, R.M. & L.W. BENNETT. 1990. A review of quantitative research on men who batter. J. Interpers. Violence *5*, 87–118.

VAN HASSELT, V.B., R.L. MORRISON & A.S. BELLACK. 1985. Alcohol use in wife abusers and their spouses. Addict. Behav. *10*, 127–135.

VIVIAN, D. & J. LANGHINRICHSEN-ROHLING. 1994. Are bi-directionally violent couples mutually victimized: a gender-sensitive comparison. Violence Vict. *9*, 107–124.

WALKER, L.E. 1979. The Battered Woman. Harper & Row. New York, NY.

WALKER, L.E.A. 1983. The battered woman syndrome study. *In* The Dark Side of Families: Current Family Violence Research. D. Finkelhor, R.J. Gelles, G.T. Hotalling & M.A. Straus, Eds.: 31–47. Sage. Beverly Hills, CA.

WALKER, L. 1984. The Battered Woman Syndrome. Springer. New York, NY.

WALKER, L.E.A. 1995. Foreword. *In* Violence and the Prevention of Violence. L.L. Adler & F.K. Denmark, Eds.: ix–xiii. Praeger Publishers. Westport, CT.

WALKER, L.E. & A. BROWNE. 1985. Gender and victimization by intimates. Journal of Personality. *53*(2), 179–195.

WESTON, R., J.R. TEMPLE & L.L. MARSHALL. 2005. Gender symmetry and asymmetry in violent relationships: patterns of mutuality among racially diverse women. Sex Roles *53*, 553–571.

WHITE, S.O. & M.A. STRAUS. 1981. The implications of family violence for rehabilitation strategies. *In* New directions in the Rehabilitation of Criminal Offenders. S.E. Martin, L.E. Sechrest & R. Redner, Eds.: 103–129. National Academy of Sciences. Washington, DC.

WILLIAMS, S.L. & I.H. FRIEZE. 2005. Patterns of violent relationships, psychological distress, and marital satisfaction in a national sample of men and women. Sex Roles *52*, 771–784.

YLLO, K. & BOGRAD, M. (Eds.) 1988. Feminist Perspective On Wife Abuse. Sage. Newberry Park, CA.

Battered Woman Syndrome
Empirical Findings

LENORE E.A. WALKER

Nova Southeastern University, Center for Psychological Studies, Ft. Lauderdale, Florida, USA

ABSTRACT: The construct of Battered Woman Syndrome (BWS) has been conceptualized as a subcategory of posttraumatic stress disorder (PTSD). It is composed of the following symptoms: (*a*) re-experiencing the battering as if it were reoccurring even when it is not, (*b*) attempts to avoid the psychological impact of battering by avoiding activities, people, and emotions, (*c*) hyperarousal or hypervigilance, (*d*) disrupted interpersonal relationships, (*e*) body image distortion or other somatic concerns, and (*f*) sexuality and intimacy issues. This article presents empirical data derived from administering the Battered Woman Syndrome Questionnaire (BWSQ) to women of four countries—United States, Spain, Greece, and Russia. The data support a theory of BWS.

KEYWORDS: Battered Woman Syndrome (BWS); posttraumatic stress disorder (PTSD); hyperarousal

INTRODUCTION

During the 1970s there was a revival of the interest in the psychological influence on women's well-being of various forms of men's violence against women. The time urgency felt by advocates and public officials in attempting to solve this age-old problem permitted public policies to become developed based more on the testimonies of victims and advocates largely from the United States and other countries of the Western world, than on empirical research. The various hearings before the U.S. Commission on Civil Rights in 1979, Attorney General's Task Force on Criminalization of Violence Against Women and Children in 1983, Surgeon General's Report on Violence Against Women and Children in 1985 as well as hearings before different committees of the U.S. Congress in the 1980s and 1990s (Walker, 1999) were examples of this.

Address for correspondence: Prof. Lenore E.A. Walker, Ed.D., Nova Southeastern University, Center for Psychological Studies, 3301 College Avenue, Ft. Lauderdale, FL 33314. Voice: 954-322-0348; fax: 954-322-0397.

e-mail: drlewalker@aol.com

Statistics on the incidence and prevalence of domestic violence (DV) were gathered in many countries around the world and reported in the various documents published by the United Nations (Malley-Morrison, 2004). In 1978, this author was granted the funds to conduct one of the first large scale empirical studies of violence against women from the U.S. National Institute of Mental Health (Walker, 1984/2000). It was the results of this study that named the psychological impact from DV as Battered Woman Syndrome (BWS). However, over the years, the use of the term BWS has been challenged, usually by nonclinical psychologists and battered women advocates without psychological training. Its meaning was also altered depending upon the discipline and philosophy of the particular group that was using it (Allard, 2005; Dutton, 2004; Mechanic, 2004).

Initially those with the greatest interest in DV and its aftermath were women themselves, most of whom were loosely organized in what was first known as the "Women's Liberation Movement" and then the "Feminist Movement." The major goal of this political movement was to empower women so that they could be treated as equals with men in the world (Chesler, 2005). What became known as the "Battered Women's Movement," made up of both advocates and professionals, supported this goal by focusing on the abuse of power by men to keep control of women (Schechter, 1982). Feminist theories focused on men's unequal use of violence and its devastating psychological impact on women and children. Sociological theories were proposed (Straus & Gelles, 1990; Gelles, 1993) and most supported the findings that men used violence as a tool to keep women subjugated. From time to time, there appeared in the literature a study that found women used violence at similar rates to men but these were discounted because these studies rarely differentiated between those instances in which a woman used physical means to defend herself or was the primary aggressor. Indeed, these arguments continue today.

In time, advocates, became disenchanted with the use of BWS as a term to describe the psychological impact from DV and began to use the term, "intimate partner violence" (IPV) to describe what had formerly been called DV (Dutton, 2004). In fact, there is an entire lexicon of language that is considered politically correct by feminist advocates, which sometimes sets them apart from academics that prefer more operationally defined terms when conducting research (Walker, 1999). The APA Presidential Task Force on Violence and the Family (APA, 1996), which this author chaired, recommended that the various disciplines that contribute to our understanding of violence and the family develop and adopt a uniform set of term terms and definitions so that the research can be compared. Until that occurs, it is necessary to define terms and theories explicitly. In this article, DV and IVP will be used interchangeably and where there are other definitions that are known to be different, the one used in this research will be made explicit.

Psychological Theories to Explain Impact from DV or IVP

The three main psychological theories that are used to explain the psychological impact from DV today are (*a*) BWS as a subcategory of posttraumatic stress disorder (PTSD), (*b*) ecological theory that incorporates both trauma and other situational factors including a patriarchal societal structure that tolerates if not actually facilitates men's violence against women, and (*c*) a system's approach to psychological interactions casting blame on both men and women for their contribution to the violence in a relationship. The third approach, using system's theory, which has some similarity to the original psychiatric theories of masochism, has not been empirically studied and has been rejected by feminist psychologists and advocates, who find it harms battered women or at least does not help them heal from the abuse they have experienced nor does it empower women to stay safe from further violence. It will not be discussed here.

Ecological theory, whose proponents are led by feminist advocates, lacks empirical data to support its differentiation from the trauma theories of PTSD and BWS, which both account for the abuse of power and control in the motivation of the abuser. Some argue that the ongoing nature of abuse that many of the victims[1] experience make the term, *post* trauma, not applicable and even suggest that IPV is a continuous and unrelenting form of serial abuse (Mechanic, 2004). This argument does not take into account the continuous reinforcement of the periods of loving or at least nonviolent behavior that the women describe occurs as the cycle theory of violence describes below. Furthermore, the Diagnostic and Statistical of Mental Disorders-Fourth Edition, Text Revision (DSM-IV-TR) (APA, 2000) makes it clear that the trauma that triggers the PTSD response may occur one or more times as long as it causes psychological distress or fear in the victim. The ecological theory also does not account for the changes in the autonomic nervous system that have been found in studies of those who have experienced trauma as described below.

This article will focus on the empirical data that has been gathered to date to support the first theory, BWS. This theory, which asserts BWS is a subcategory of PTSD, incorporates feminist, trauma, and biopsychosocial models. The *feminist model* emphasizes that being a girl or woman places one in the highest risk category for becoming a victim of a man's violence, victimization together with inequality in society can cause mental health distress, and that social validation, support, and empowerment can protect women and girls from, or even reverse, these effects. The *trauma model* emphasizes that exposure to trauma can cause psychological problems in both healthy and clinical populations. Verbal psychotherapy with or without medication may ameliorate some

---

[1] "Victim" is not a term typically used by advocates who prefer the term "survivor." However, psychologists may prefer using "survivor" to apply to those former victims who make some changes to protect themselves.

or all of the problems, although it may be expected that some residual effects, including some loss of resilience, may be experienced. The *biopsychosocial model* emphasizes the response of the autonomic nervous system in dealing with traumatic stressors. Neurotransmitters and other biochemicals released into the nervous system help people cope with and adapt to perception of danger from trauma. Continued dysregulation of these biochemical substances can negatively impact on the person's ability to function and cause the anxiety, depression, avoidance, and other symptoms that are part of mental illness diagnoses.

While not explicitly a part of the BWS theory itself, BWS's association with the dynamics of battering relationships helps to understand the interpersonal context within which the woman experiences violence. As discussed earlier, most psychological theories today accept that IPV is a disorder of power and control; the abuser uses these for the purpose of controlling the victim (Dutton, Keltman, Goodman, Weinfurt, & Vankos, 2005). The areas where the abuse is most clearly acknowledged is when there is physical or sexual abuse to force the woman into compliance with the batterer's demands. Psychological coercion is acknowledged as part of the power dynamic and often is the glue that holds these relationships together. Applying aversive psychological tactics in a random and variable manner together with some periods of withdrawal of the aversive stimuli and substitution of pleasurable or loving behavior is known to create psychological dependency, learned helplessness, or other deleterious conditions for victims.

The theory of learned helplessness was first introduced in the literature when Seligman (1975) and his colleagues, searching for an understanding of exogenous depression, attempted to create depression in the laboratory, first in animals (mostly dogs) and then in human subjects (mostly college students). They applied aversive stimulation to the subjects (electrical stimulation for the dogs and loud noises for the students) that they could not control in a random and variable manner. They found changes in the arousal patterns of those subjects who underwent the noxious regimen. The cognitive, emotional, and behavioral actions of the students were also demonstrated to be adversely affected. Although Seligman theorized that he created a type of depression in the laboratory, a careful reading of his results today suggest he really elicited a PTSD response from his subjects. The original research on BWS hypothesized that the battered woman's perception that she received random and variable aversive stimuli from the abuser, interspersed with some loving behavior, also caused her to develop a PTSD response (Walker, 1984/2000). In fact, the original findings were consistent with PTSD, although it was not used in the study as it had not yet appeared as a diagnosis in 1977 when the study was designed.

Analysis of the data from four battering incidents from each of 400 subjects (1,600 battering incidents) indicated that the pattern of violence was consistent with the cycle of violence theory that was hypothesized. The pattern consisted of the initial courtship period followed by three phases that repeated themselves in a cycle. The first phase was named the *tension-building* phase where the perception of danger from the batterer kept escalating at different rates for different people. The battered woman tried to please the man during this period and her behavior could slow down or speed up movement into the second phase, or the *acute battering incident*. The second is the shortest part of the cycle but has the highest risk for physical or sexual damage. The third phase was called the period of *loving-contrition*. During it, the batterer apologized and engaged in loving behavior. In some relationships, there was no loving behavior that could be recognized but the third phase was characterized only by a decrease or temporary cessation in the violence.

METHODOLOGY

1978 Study

BWS as a subcategory of PTSD was first identified after studying more than 400 battered women in a stratified convenience sample who met the criteria set forth in the research protocol. The first incident that was remembered, the second incident that could be remembered, the worst or one of the worst, and the final incident prior to the research interview were detailed with both forced-choice and open-ended questions. More than 5,000 variables were analyzed in that research using three specific theories around which the data were organized: learned helplessness, cycle of violence, and signs and symptoms of psychological distress that constitute BWS (Walker, 1984/2000). The BWS was created from analyzing the data from symptoms noted on the Battered Woman Syndrome Questionnaire (BWSQ) and the accompanying assessment instruments. The BWSQ that was originally constructed to measure for BWS in 1978 is compared to its recent revision in TABLE 1.

2002 Study

In the latter study, the BWSQ that had been revised several times over the intervening years was again revised to try to shorten it to under 3 hours, and a pilot version was administered to volunteers recruited from a battered woman shelter, counseling groups, and a convenience sample of women drawn from the South Florida area (Richmond et al., 2005). The definition of BWS was operationalized and can be found in TABLE 2.

Several new assessment instruments standardized to measure PTSD were added to the BWSQ battery. Scaling techniques were used to create scales to assess for areas that did not previously have standardized assessment instruments that could be utilized easily with this population (Duros, Barry, Passeri,

TABLE 1. Construct of the Battered Woman Syndrome Questionnaire comparing the 1978 and 2002 versions

Construct of BWSQ
- BWSQ #1
  - 100 pages More than 4,000 variables
  - 6 h to administer
  - LH, Cycle, and MH Q
  - 400 sample
  - 200 women own control with Q on nonbat relationship
  - Trained interviewers
  - 6 states in the United States to stratify sample using NORC data
  - NIMH funding
  - Looking for theories
- BWSQ #2
  - 50 pages Fewer variables that appear to discriminate
  - 3 h to administer
  - LH, Cycle, MH Q, Scales
  - 30–50 women in each sample
  - Standardized tests provide controls
  - Trained interviewers
  - Multisite, multilingual, multicountry data
  - NSU Presidential Scholar funding (minimal)
  - Validating and expanding BWS theory

& Walker, 2006). This included assessment of power and control variables using indices of isolation, over possessiveness, jealousy, and intrusiveness created from responses to items of the BWSQ, an assessment of psychological abuse using the Amnesty International Definition of Psychological Torture, an assessment of the cycle of violence, and indices of physical violence and sexual abuse. Instruments that measure attachment and for feelings of betrayal in adult relationships were also added as was one designed to measure sexual satisfaction. Briere's (1998) Trauma Symptom Inventory (TSI) and the Detailed Assessment of Posttraumatic Stress (DAPS) were two standardized instruments added to the BWSQ battery (Briere & Elliott, 1997). Others that were used in the 1978 administration were deleted in the current study to keep the battery within the shorter time frame.

The English version of the BWSQ and accompanying assessment instruments have been translated into different languages including Spanish (both for Latin American countries and Spain), Greek, Russian, Italian, Haitian Creole, and French) at this time. Obviously, the standardized sample cannot be utilized to make statistical comparisons but trends will be noted.

TABLE 2. 2002 Battered woman syndrome definition

Battered Woman Syndrome
- PTSD criteria:
  – Re-experiencing the event
  – Numbing of responsiveness
  – Hyperarousal
- For BWS, Three additional effects:
  – Disrupted interpersonal relationships
  – Difficulties with body image/somatic concerns
  – Sexual and intimacy problems

Sample

The sample used in the 2002 BWSQ study was comprised of women volunteers who met the same inclusive criteria as participants did in the earlier study and who come from several different countries as well as the South Florida region of the United States. It is also planned to utilize women who have emigrated to the United States from their countries of origin and compare their responses with those women of similar demographics from those countries of origin. To date, data collection from the latter sample has just begun. Data have been collected from Russian battered women in prison, women in Spain who attend outpatient psychotherapy groups for battered women, women from a battered woman's shelter in Greece, and in the United States. There is ongoing data collection in Spain, Italy, Colombia, Peru, Haiti, and in a local detention center and a mental health center in South Florida. In addition, advertisements have been placed in a large number of community organizations in sites in the United States to which graduate psychology students have access. Volunteers are accepted if they have experienced at least two physical, sexual, and psychological battering incidents.

Analysis of Data

Data are entered into an Statistical Package for the Social Sciences (SPSS) program and are just starting to be analyzed. The data presented in this article were in part presented at symposia at the American Psychological Association meetings. These data are part of a separate but companion research program where some of the women participants in this research are offered a 12 session manualized group psychotherapy program called, *Survivor Therapy*. Other measures of mental health functioning have been administered to these participants but have not yet been analyzed. It is hoped to determine the efficacy of this form of treatment that is based on a feminist and trauma model.

RESULTS

The results of the first 76 women analyzed for BWS using the definition of PTSD plus additional BWS criteria can be found in FIGURE 1.

The internal consistency of the items selected for the analysis indicated the PTSD variables in the BWSQ have an Alpha at 0.68, the items selected for Body Image Distortion have an Alpha at 0.68, the items assessing for Sexuality Satisfaction have an Alpha at 0.46, and the items assessing the victims perception of the abuser's Power & Control have an Alpha of 0.60 and 0.47, respectively. The results for PTSD alone can be found in FIGURE 2 (Duros *et al.*, 2006).

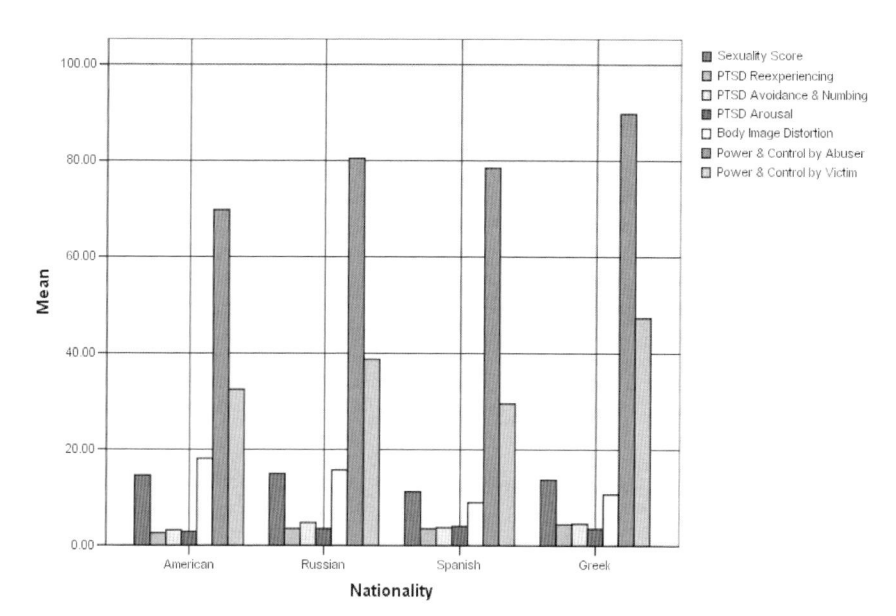

FIGURE 1. Cross-national comparison of PTSD and BWS criteria.

The preliminary results in FIGURES 1 and 2 indicate that there is a high presentation of symptoms that are considered to make up PTSD and BWS in women across the four national groups studied. As can be observed in FIGURE 1, the Greek women studied report themselves more under the power and control of their abusers than all others sampled but the Russian women. Body distortion appeared to be most prominent in the U.S. women and least prominent for the Spanish women. The U.S. women state they experience the fewest PTSD symptoms as is shown in FIGURE 2. Nonetheless, all four groups meet the DSM-IV (APA, 2000) criteria for PTSD. All of the women say they have more avoidance symptoms than anxiety and hyperarousal. Of course, these differences may change when the entire sample is analyzed and compared to the additional assessment measures.

To determine if the construct of BWS as a subcategory of PTSD was accurately being measured by the BWSQ, we used two recently developed tests of the impact of interpersonal trauma standardized on a U.S. population. These tests, the TSI and the DAPS, were analyzed for the first sample of battered women in the 2006 sample. Preliminary results for the TSI and the BWSQ are presented in TABLE 3. As can be seen from the graphs, the sample is approaching the significant TSI score of 65 on the 10 clinical scales that are said to make up the clinical PTSD syndrome experienced by victims of interpersonal trauma on whom the test was standardized. It is believed that as more data are added to the sample, these results will be more robust (Duros & Walker, 2006).

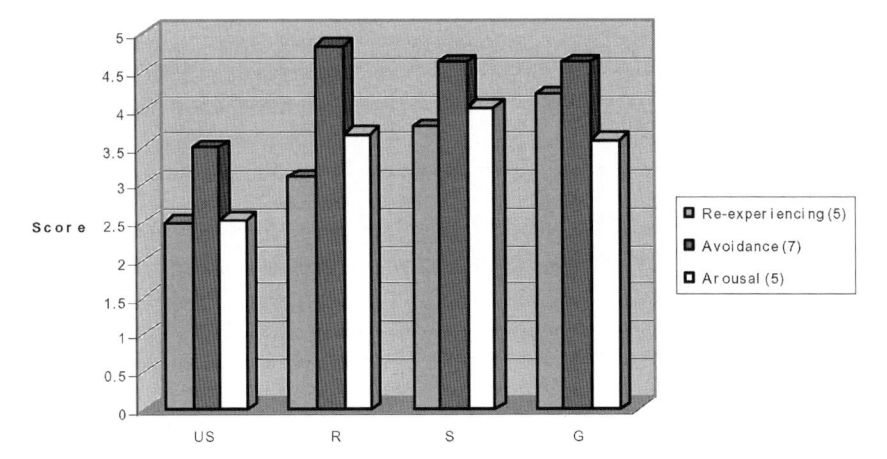

FIGURE 2. Cross-national comparison of PTSD symptoms in battered woman.

DISCUSSION AND IMPLICATIONS

The initial results indicate that PTSD does exist in battered women. BWS has been empirically shown to be a subcategory of PTSD. This indicates the importance of PTSD and BWS as categories from which diagnoses, treatment plans, and forensic evaluations must be considered. Many of the additional criteria used in the BWSQ are suggested in the proposed diagnosis of PTSD Not Otherwise Specified as is discussed further below. These findings do not rule out other diagnoses that individual battered women may also have developed but it does suggest that these diagnoses should not be eliminated in favor of no real diagnosis or others not yet as carefully studied.

Limitations

Obviously, because data collection is incomplete and drawn from convenience samples, one must be cautious about the conclusions made from preliminary analyses. Larger number of subjects and better sampling procedures will permit more definitive comparisons to be made in addition to the criteria for PTSD and BWS that this preliminary analysis utilized. It is also intended to compare women who still live in their country of origin with immigrants to the United States to assess for the impact of isolation and immigration, another important issue raised. The U.S. Violence Against Women Act passed and renewed by Congress for the past 10 years gives special status to immigrant women who obtain their ability to apply for U.S. citizenship through husbands who become abusive.

TABLE 3. Trauma symptoms as reported on Walker's BWSQ

	Re-experiencing	Avoidance/Numbing	Hyperarousal
OVERALL	M = 3.04, SD = 1.41	M = 4.21, SD = 2.90	M = 3.23, SD = 1.32
United States	M = 3.00, SD = 1.48	M = 3.87, SD = 2.08	M = 3.03, SD = 1.52
Colombia	M = 3.00, SD = 1.87	M = 3.00, SD = 2.00	M = 3.20, SD = 1.30
Russia	M = 3.10, SD = 1.25	M = 5.05, SD = 1.19	M = 3.55, SD = 1.32
Caucasian	M = 2.60, SD = 1.35	M = 3.60, SD = 2.14	M = 2.60, SD = 1.43
Hispanic	M = 2.50, SD = 2.07	M = 2.50, SD = 2.17	M = 2.83, SD = 1.47
African American	M = 4.50, SD = 0.58	M = 3.75, SD = 0.96	M = 4.25, SD = 0.96
Asian ($n = 1$)	M = 4.00	M = 7.00	M = 5.00
Other ethnicity	M = 3.24, SD = 1.23	M = 5.08, SD = 1.15	M = 3.23, SD = 1.32
Outpatient ($n = 1$)	M = 4.00	M = 4.00	M = 3.00
Mental health facility	M = 2.22, SD = 1.86	M = 2.33, SD = 2.00	M = 2.33, SD = 1.50
Prison	M = 3.37, SD = 1.30	M = 5.03, SD = 1.43	M = 3.73, SD = 0.98
Advertisement	M = 2.83, SD = 1.03	M = 3.67, SD = 1.83	M = 2.75, SD = 1.42
Other	M = 2.75, SD = 1.89	M = 4.00, SD = 2.16	M = 3.00, SD = 1.83

Other limitations are associated with the nature of self-report historical data. Memories may be altered by repeated trauma events. Comparisons of data from past memories with more current objective test data can assist in understanding this issue. Translations of the BWSQ to Haitian, Creole, Spanish, French, and Italian have not been checked by professional translators, although it has been done by doctoral psychology students or psychologists who speak those languages fluently. The Greek and Russian translations were done by professional translators.

Advocates are concerned that once a battered woman is given a diagnosis, she will be labeled and stigmatized as mentally ill. This is an important concern because it has happened prior to the newer understanding of IPV and is still occurring in child endangerment and child custody cases. Some mental health professionals erroneously conclude battered women are unfit to parent their children because they somehow permitted themselves to be abused. These concerns are often applied to poor women from minority groups who do not have adequate resources to obtain good legal counsel. Nonscientific labels such as Parental Alienation Syndrome (PAS) (Walker, Brantley, & Rigsbee, 2004) may also be given to battered women who fight for sole custody to protect themselves and their children no matter what their socioeconomic status.

Benefits of PTSD and BWS Theory

A conceptual theory that covers the issues needed to provide good psychotherapy interventions by mental health professionals is a worthy goal if only to offer those battered women who have psychological issues appropriate treatment. Despite its shortcomings, the *DSM* system and the International Classification of Diseases (ICD) gives health professionals a common language that helps obtain reliable and valid diagnoses across all classes and societies (APA, 2000). The ability to utilize the multi-axial system of the *DSM* permits more than one diagnosis along with estimates of the strength of the stressors and the woman's ability to function at the time of diagnosis. If properly used, this system can capture the context and impact from the environment that is important in understanding the battered woman. Such diagnoses point the path to effective interventions and have important forensic psychology implications.

Of course, not all battered women develop BWS and of those who do, not all need professional intervention. Studies have shown that battered women with good support systems and access to these resources may heal and move on to live violence free lives. However, in the United States and other countries, both advocates and mental health workers are concerned about how to treat those battered women who do seek assistance, especially if they have experienced multiple traumas or have multiple diagnoses. For example, women who have been abused or maltreated as children and then are abused by their intimate partner may have developed a major affective disorder, such as depression or even bipolar disorder, and need professional care. Others may have a serious long-term mental illness and then become involved with an abusive partner. It is common for battered women to use prescription drugs or even alcohol and other street drugs to manage their psychological pain. They may need treatment for both the impact from abuse and their dependence upon these substances. Utilizing PTSD with a subcategory of BWS may call attention to the multiple issues raised by a dual diagnosis for the clinician (e.g., Walker, 1994).

Implications for Treatment

Very few treatment approaches designed for use with abused women have been subjected to empirically based efficacy studies. Survivor Therapy is currently being studied as an important treatment approach that deals with the empowerment and safety issues of victims of violence as well as the clinical symptoms that may be present whether they came before or after the abuse experience. Theoretically based in cognitive-behavioral, trauma, and feminist theories, this therapy can be used with individuals or groups. It is difficult to know how much of an individual's problem in a particular area is due to a symptom of mental illness or because of the experience of abuse. Therefore, the length of the intervention may be variable depending on the individual woman.

TABLE 4. Survivor therapy program

12 Units
   1. Labeling and validation of abuse and safety planning
   2. Cognitive restructuring
   3. Recognizing danger and building strengths
   4. Reducing stress and PTSD symptoms
   5. Cycle of violence
   6. PTSD
   7. Impact on children
   8. Grieving relationships and letting go
   9. Emotional reregulation
   10. Rebuilding new relationships
   11. Pleasing behaviors and compliance issues
   12. Termination

Survivor Therapy

Survivor therapy has been manualized. It is divided into 12 units, with each unit consisting of psychoeducational materials, skill-building, clinical processing, and homework to practice and reinforce new skills learned. It is a strength-based approach focusing on reinforcing the areas in which the women function well rather than focusing on what they do that is "wrong." Clinical issues are not directly addressed until one-third through the program so as to give time for the women to be validated and supported for their experiences, gain cognitive clarity, and rebuild trust in relationships. Relaxation training, cognitive restructuring, and other approaches to controlling anxiety and intrusive experiences are introduced, and, once mastered, emotional re-regulation techniques are developed. Women may spend a minimum of 3 months to 1 or more years dealing with the issues raised in this treatment approach. A 12-week group version is currently being studied with women also in individual therapy in an outpatient clinic and those who volunteered to be on a special DV unit in jail while awaiting trial on a variety of charges. The titles of the 12 sessions can be found in TABLE 4. Although the evidence-based treatment program is based on a weekly group, this program has been used in individual and group treatment for the past 10 years.

Forensic Implications

Perhaps the greatest controversy about the use of BWS and PTSD diagnoses is associated with experts testifying in the forensic arena (Feder & Henning, 2005). It is rare that a battered woman does not have some contact with the legal system whether it is for a divorce, child custody and visitation determination, removal to another state, obtaining a civil or criminal injunction or restraining order, juvenile issues around children, drug court, or other civil or criminal proceedings. Given the counterintuitive and often unusual or even bizarre experiences of battered women, they are often sent to mental health professionals to help their attorneys or judges figure out how to best deal with their issues (Kaser-Boyd, 2004). Advocates for battered women fear using a diagnosis in the court proceedings will cause battered women to be mislabeled as mentally disabled and be revictimized by the court decisions. In fact, that does occur in family law cases where women attempt to protect their children from abusive fathers. It is less stigmatizing in the criminal court system where special new laws have been designed to help protect battered women and children.

Criminal Court

Laws have been changed in the United States and other countries to make it easier for battered women to obtain criminal (and civil) restraining orders or orders of protection upon their testimony that they have been abused and fear it will happen again. Usually a temporary restraining order (TRO) is granted, and the affected abuser is given a chance to come to court to challenge it within a certain amount of time, usually 3–4 weeks. While the TRO is pending, the battered woman is usually granted exclusive use of the marital home and temporary custody of the children. The alleged batterer may be required to contribute money for maintenance and child support, if there are children, and is ordered to stay away from the woman. If the batterer violates this order, a warrant may be issued for his arrest and incarceration. If he abuses her while the order is in effect, he is subject to more serious penalties. At the hearing to make the TRO more permanent (usually it is granted for 1 year subject to renewal) the batterer may present evidence to show that he did not abuse the woman and, therefore, ask that the order be vacated. Expert witness testimony that the woman has developed BWS and PTSD may be provided to the judge at these hearings. Most importantly, for further legal proceedings, if the judge makes what is called "a finding of fact" that DV has occurred, then the family court judge must take it into account when awarding access to children.

Family Court

Family Court is usually different from criminal or juvenile court. In Family Court, the judge must decide if a marriage is "irretrievably broken" and if so, then the marital property is divided according to whether it is an "equitable distribution" or "community property" state. Equitable distribution means that marital property gets divided fairly, as a function, in part, of what each party contributed coming into the marriage. Community property states simply divide property equally. If the couple signed a valid prenuptial or postnuptial agreement specifying how property was to be allocated, then that agreement may determine how the marital assets are divided. In some states, such as Colorado, people may be considered "defacto" married whether or not they have had a formal marriage ceremony. Many battered women claim that they were coerced into signing a prenuptial agreement and ask the court to overturn it. Expert witnesses may provide testimony about PTSD and BWS at such hearings.

Child Custody, Visitation, and Removal to Another State

The most contentious child custody disputes often have allegations of DV or child abuse, usually made by the mother against the father. The father may counter with allegations of "Parental Alienation Syndrome" accusing the mother of turning the children against him. In some cases, mental health diagnoses such as Munchausen-by-Proxy may also be alleged as a counterclaim, and each side might use expert witness testimony to try to prove their claims. PTSD and BWS may be used by the mother to counter claims of other mental illnesses, but this is rarely successful in family court. Unfortunately, this leaves the children unprotected especially when the father continues to assert abusive power and control against the mother and children.

Civil Personal Injury Cases

In civil personal injury cases, called torts, expert witness testimony about BWS and PTSD may be offered to prove psychological damages from DV or sexual abuse. Although it may be difficult to determine if the PTSD came before or after a particular trauma (called the nexus), such diagnoses may be offered since the law often requires the last party to injure someone to take full responsibility. Even in jurisdictions where "comparative negligence" or sharing responsibility is the rule, it may be important to testify that a battered woman who does not leave her abusive partner has psychological reasons for not doing so including fears that she may be more seriously harmed or killed.

CONCLUSIONS

The theory that the psychological impact from DV or IPV can be conceptualized using PTSD and BWS has been empirically tested by revalidating the BWSQ across several nations. Although the research study is not yet complete, the preliminary analysis of the data indicate that many battered women do develop BWS. It is suggested that viewing BWS as a subcategory of PTSD may be helpful in the assessment of the psychological impact of IPV, the development of treatment plans in those with psychological problems arising from abuse, and in focusing expert witness testimony in forensic cases in spite of its acknowledge limitations.

REFERENCES

ALLARD, A.S. 2005. Rethinking battered woman syndrome: a black feminist perspective. *In* Domestic Violence at the Margins: Readings on Race, Class, Gender, and Culture. N.J. Sokoloff & C. Pratt Eds.: 194–205. Rutgers University Press. New Brunswick, NJ.

AMERICAN PSYCHIATRIC ASSOCIATION. 2000. Diagnostic and Statistical Manual of Mental Disorders. Fourth Edition, Text Revision (DSM-IV-TR). Author. Washington, DC.

AMERICAN PSYCHOLOGICAL ASSOCIATION. 1996. Report from the Presidential Task Force on Violence and the Family. Author. Washington, DC.

BRIERE, J. & D.M. ELLIOTT. 1997. Psychological assessment of interpersonal victimization effects in adults and children. Psychotherapy *34*, 352–364.

CHESLER, P. 2005. The Death of Feminism: What's Next in the Struggle for Women's Freedom. Palgrave Macmillian. New York, NY.

DUROS, R., H. BARRY, C. PASSERI & L.E.A. WALKER. 2006. Battered Woman Syndrome: a cross-national comparison in the U.S., Russia, Greece & Spain. Presentation in Symposium at the American Psychology-Law Society, St. Petersburg, FL, March.

DUROS, R. & L.E.A. WALKER. 2006. Battered Woman Syndrome, PTSD, and implications for treatment recommendations. *In* Presentation in Symposium on Forensic Psychology for the Independent Practitioner, Eds.: L.E.A. Walker & D.L. Shapiro Chairs, American Psychological Association Annual Meeting, New Orleans, LA, August.

DUTTON, M.A. 2004. Complexity of women's response to violence, a response to Briere and Jordan [Electronic version]. Journal of Interpersonal Violence *19*, 1277–1282.

DUTTON, M.A., S. KALTMAN, L.A. GOODMAN, K. WEINFURT & N. VANKOS. 2005. Patterns of intimate partner violence: correlates and outcomes. Violence and Victims *20*, 483–497.

FEDER, L. & K. HENNING. 2005. A comparison of male and female dually arrested domestic violence offenders. Violence and Victims *20*, 153–171.

GELLES, R.J. 1993. Through a sociological lens: social structure and family violence. *In* Current controversies in family violence. R.J. Gelles & D.R. Loeske, Eds.: 182–196. Sage. Newbury Park, CA.

KASER-BOYD, N. 2004. Battered woman syndrome: Clinical features, evaluation, and expert testimony. *In* Sexualized Violence Against Women and Children: A Psychology and Law Perspective. B.J. Cling, Ed.: 41–70. Guilford Press. New York, NY.

MALLEY-MORRISON, K. (Ed.) 2004. International Perspectives on Family Violence and Abuse. Lawrence Erlbaum Associates. Mahwah, NJ.

MECHANIC, M.B. 2004. Beyond PTSD: mental health consequences of violence against women, a response to Briere and Jordan. Journal of Interpersonal Violence *19*, 1283–1289.

SCHECHTER, S. 1982. Women and Male Violence: The Visions and Struggles of the Battered Women's Movement. South End Press. Boston, MA.

SELIGMAN, M.E.P. 1975. Helplessness: On Depression, Development, and Death. W.H. Freeman. San Francisco, CA.

STRAUS, M.A. & R.J. GELLES (Ed.) 1990. Physical Violence in American Families. Transaction. New Brunswick, NJ.

RICHMOND, K., K. DAVID, J. JOHNSON, A. LYDA, P. VILLAVICENCIO & L.E.A. WALKER. 2005. BWS Research from a Feminist and International Perspective. Presentation at American Psychological Association Annual Meeting. Washington, DC, August.

WALKER, L.E.A. 2001. Politics, psychology and battered women. Journal of Trauma Practice *1*, 81–102.

WALKER, L.E.A. 1984/2000. The Battered Woman Syndrome, Second Edition. Springer. New York, NY.

WALKER, L.E.A. 1999. Psychology and domestic violence around the world. American Psychologist *54*, 21–29.

WALKER, L.E.A. 1994. Abused women and survivor therapy: a practical guide for the psychotherapist. American Psychological Association. Washington, DC.

WALKER, L.E.A., K.L. BRANTLEY & J.A. RIGSBEE. 2004. A critical analysis of Parental Alienation Syndrome and its admissibility in family court. Journal of Child Custody *1(2)*, 47–74.

Factors That Influence Abusive Interactions between Aging Women and Their Caregivers

MARGOT B. NADIEN

Fordham University, New York, New York, USA

ABSTRACT: Research findings suggest that one or more factors—personality and/or drug or financial dependency, cognitive and personality impairments, contextual factors, or severe stress—render elders vulnerable to caregiver maltreatment (i.e., either abuse or neglect), but may also make them more prone to abusing their caregivers. However, it is often the interaction between elders and caregivers that determines whether maltreatment will actually occur. Maltreatment of elders is less likely when caregivers (1) are free of mental impairments and of drug and personality dependency, (2) are trained to cope with the stress of caregiving and of highly provocative and/or abusive elders, (3) and are adequately reimbursed and socially supported.

KEYWORDS: elder abuse; caregiver–elder interactions; stress; dependency; mental impairments

INTRODUCTION

Violence against old-agers, often referred to as elder maltreatment or mistreatment, may be directed against older males as well as females. Both males and females may be the perpetrators or the immediate cause of maltreatment, and both may be the victims or outcomes of maltreatment (Johnson, 1991). Yet, since gender differences in genes and lifestyle have resulted in more than 70% of persons over the age of 65 years being female, and since, in virtually all cultures, the proportion of female to male elders rises as people move through their 70s and 80s (Bogue, 1985; Giordano & Giordano, 1983; Kosberg, 1988; Quinn & Tomita, 1986; Wolf, Strugnell, & Godkin, 1982), elder violence is mainly a female issue (Albert & Cattell, 1994; Nadien, 1995).

Before exploring various features of violence against aging women, let us first review the general meanings of maltreatment and some of its forms. Maltreatment differs according to *type*. Thus violence may be physical (both sexual

TABLE 1. Forms of elder maltreatment: physical, psychological, and material (legal or financial) sources

Types of Suffering	Forms of Maltreatment	
	Abuse	Neglect
Physical	Physical assault; sexual assault; being grabbed, pushed, or shoved; substance abuse among self-abusers; self-inflicted pain	Deprivation of conditions required for survival (e.g., denial of food, medicine, protection against the elements); elder's disregard of survival needs (e.g., self-starvation, non-protection against needs for medicine and protection against the elements)
Psychological	Verbal threats, insults, or aggression; coercion; confinement; abandonment	Deprivation of social stimulation or social acceptance or social support
Material (legal or financial)	Deprivation of civil rights or personal property; misinformation about entitlements	Failure to provide needed information, legal counsel, or representation

NOTE. This table represents an adaptation of material taken from Margot B. Nadien (1996). Aging women: Issues of mental health and maltreatment. *In* Women and mental health. vol. 789. J. A. Sechzer, S. M. Pfafflin, F. L. Denmark, A. Griffin, & S. J. Blumenthal, Eds.: 129–145. Annals of the New York Academy of Sciences. New York.

and nonsexual), psychological, or material (legal or financial). As indicated in TABLE 1, when maltreatment is *physical*, *abuse* entails physical assault, sexual molestation, slapping, grabbing, pushing, or restraining. But when violence involves *neglect*, it usually entails a caregiver's refusal or failure to fulfill an obligation, and is associated with the denial of food, medicine, shelter, needed assistance, or other items required for well-being or survival.

When suffering is *psychological*, *abuse* involves mental anguish that may derive from verbal aggression, coercion, ridicule, confinement, abandonment, or threats of aggression, either sexual or nonsexual in nature. By contrast, psychological *neglect* stems from isolation and the denial of social acceptance and stimulation. And when suffering is *material*, *legal*, or *financial*, then *abuse* occurs when illegal or improper exploitation occurs, as when people are robbed of financial or other personal property. However, *neglect* is held to be material or legal when needed information or legal help is withheld (Block & Sinnott, 1979; Cassell, 1989; Duke, 1991; Hall, 1989; Johnson, 1991; Nadien, 1995, 1996; Pillemer & Finkelhor, 1988; Sengstock & Hwalek, 1987).

The violence of maltreatment differs as to whether it is self-imposed or imposed by others. For example, the elderly maltreat themselves by abusing drugs or alcohol, or by choosing homelessness and in so doing, exposing themselves to weather extremes and the acts of predators. And when suffering from illness or accidents, the elderly neglect themselves through self-starvation and failing to seek needed shelter or assistance. At the psychological level, the old harm themselves by unwarranted self-reproach or self-imposed isolation. And at the material or legal level, elders abuse themselves by giving away essential personal items and neglect themselves by refusing needed help or legal advice (Duke, 1991; Sengstock & Hwalek, 1987; Sengstock & Liang, 1982).

In domestic situations, a caregiver is often a family member—a spouse, an adult child (usually a daughter or daughter-in-law), or a more distant relative. However, some caregivers are home healthcare workers.

The Extent of Abuse against Old Persons

Elder abuse is largely unknown in developing countries and even in most developed nations. When limited to maltreatment in domestic settings (and thus excluding the many abuse cases in long-term institutions), the earliest reports were in 1988 of 140,000 cases throughout the United States, with individual state systems producing detailed compilations of all cases of elder abuse, neglect, and exploitation only by 1990 (Tatara, 1990). However, aside from a number of individual state reports of elder violence, only two nationwide studies have yielded data (Fisher & Regan, 2006). One is the National Elder Abuse Incidence Study, which indicated that more than 76% of surveyed women over the age of 60 years had suffered emotional/psychological abuse, and more than 71% had suffered physical abuse (National Center on Elder Abuse, 1998). A second study, the National Crime Victimization Survey, estimated that intimate-partner victimizations among women aged 55 years and over had occurred among 118,000 intimate partners during the nine-year period of 1993–2001 (Rennison & Rand, 2003).

An evaluation of differing state reports suggests that neglect is the most common form of maltreatment, followed by physical abuse (which includes sexual abuse), and then neglect (Albert & Cattell, 1964; Roberto, Tester, & Duke, 2004). Sexual abuse has been defined by the National Center on Elder Abuse as *nonconsensual sexual contact of any kind with an elderly person* (Lingler, 2004).

Although there are seemingly clear-cut distinctions between abuse and neglect, some ambiguity surrounds these two forms of maltreatment. One factor is that the frequency, duration, and severity of an act and consequences determine whether it is viewed as abuse or as neglect. Another reason for ambiguity is that the terms "neglect" or "abuse" may apply either to the *victim's condition* or to the *responsible person's intention*. Yet another difficulty is that individual states vary in their definitions of abuse and neglect (Daly & Jogerst, 2001). And a further complication is that some researchers question a given state's definitions, arguing that the crucial factor in identifying a behavior as maltreatment is a person's *perception* of that behavior (Wolf, 1996).

Indications of Elder Abuse and Neglect

Despite inconsistencies in the way a given behavior is defined, several signs warn of possible elder abuse and neglect. As noted by Wolf (1996), physical abuse can be inferred from bruises, cigarette burns, fractures, sprains, lacerations, abrasions, and multiple injuries, and deliberate overmedication is suggested by an elder being disoriented or in a stupor. Victims of physical and/or sexual abuse might also reveal agitation, hesitancy in speaking openly, eating disturbances, sleeping disorders, fears, phobias, or being upset when touched physically. Signs of neglect include skin disorders, untreated bedsores, and other injuries; hunger, malnutrition, or dehydration; lack of clean clothing or bedding; the absence of prescribed medication, required dentures, hearing aids or eyeglasses; and frequent visits to an emergency room with vague complaints.

Caregivers appear to be emotionally abusing elders when they harass, intimidate, or infantilize them; when they threaten punishment; or when they force elders to leave their home or enter a care facility. Caregivers show neglect when they leave an elder alone for extensive time periods; withhold affection; fail to provide needed assistance; or deny to elders the right of privacy or of autonomous decision making. Also indicative of caregiver maltreatment are suspicious explanations of physical abuse such as "the victim fell," and questionable justifications of financial abuse such as "the money was owed to me," or "it was a gift," or "I just borrowed it" (Wolf, 1996).

This article will examine issues relating to the perpetrators of elder maltreatment and their elderly victims. The focus will be mainly on aging women as targets of maltreatment. However, for purposes of comparison, occasional references will be made to men as perpetrators or as victims.

SOME GENERAL CHARACTERISTICS OF ABUSERS AND THEIR VICTIMS

What makes people vulnerable to maltreatment? When people are *less powerful* and *more dependent* than others, they may become subject to the control of others. Both the very young and the very old are at risk of control by others. Among the very young, dependency stems from not yet having the physical and psychological growth to protect themselves against the maltreatment by stronger others. In the case of the very old, however, dependency stems from a *loss* of self-reliance owing to physical or mental impairments. These impairments among elders lead to their need for help with the activities of everyday life (ADLs) such as bathing, dressing, feeding, and toileting, or to their need for assistance with the instrumental activities of daily life (IADL's) such as grocery shopping, cooking, maintenance of the home, and the handling of personal finances.

That many elders require aid with ADLs and IADLs and/or the management of their everyday lives relates to the fact that in most developed countries, approximately 85% of persons over the age of 70 years must cope with one or more chronic and somewhat debilitating disorders such as arthritis, chronic obstructive pulmonary disorder, diabetes, Parkinson's disease, and various heart disorders. Additionally, almost 50% of persons over the age of 85 years (the fastest growing age segment within the U.S. population) need assistance because of a loss of vision or hearing as well as mental impairments associated with Alzheimer's disease, strokes, or other forms of dementia. While some impaired elders remain in their community with the aid of caregivers, approximately 25% of this oldest group requires periodic nursing-home care (Vitality for Life, 1993).

Perpetrator–victim differences in violent behavior distinguish females and males, the topic to which we now turn.

Gender Differences

A few differences are found among women and men in their roles as perpetrators or victims of maltreatment. When gripped by uncontrollable anger or frustration, men use physical abuse more often than women to vent their emotions, whereas women rely more often than men on verbal abuse.

What accounts for differing forms of violence favored by men and women? Are the underlying influences biological or cultural? As to biological makeup, might a man's strong musculature and large reserves of testosterone predispose him to use physical abuse, and might a women's more frail skeleton and predominance of estrogen over testosterone account for her reliance on verbal abuse?

Gerber (1995) offers an alternative explanation by suggesting that men and women are greatly influenced by cultural expectations. She holds that social stereotypes of appropriate masculinity lead men to display "mastery, subjugation and even destruction of others" (p. 149), whereas stereotyped female traits of interpersonal sensitivity and caringness lead women to eschew physical violence as unfeminine and to rely instead on a more hidden and less censurable behavior—that of verbal abuse.

Interestingly, in gender conflicts, a man's act of physical abuse is often blamed on having initiated the conflict. Yet, sometimes it is a woman who starts a cycle of violence by taunting, complaining, deriding, or in other ways verbally abusing the man. In such cases a man's hitting, pushing, or other aggressive acts represent his *reaction* to the woman's verbal abuse (Cirillo, 1995).

Gender Factors and Alcoholism

Alcoholism is present in a large percentage of cases (Wolf, 1966). A review of the literature shows that substance abuse in a man is often linked to his acts of physical violence, whereas substance abuse in a woman may arouse physical or sexual abuse (Testa, 2004).

Abusers and Victims

In domestic situations, elder abuse is usually committed by family members. Spousal abuse often occurs when the caregiver is verbally or physically assaulted by a demented care recipient, but spousal abuse or neglect may occur when the caregiver is suffering from stress arising from the caretaking role or from the elder's ill health.

Abuse by an adult child occurs most often when the adult child is mentally ill or alcoholic, is dependent on the parent for housing or money, or is motivated by simple greed (Bengtson, Rosenthal, & Burton, 1996). As will become apparent in the discussion below, elders are vulnerable to abuse or neglect when they are dependent, mentally or physically ill, or lonely.

MALTREATMENT: A PERPETRATOR–VICTIM INTERACTION

As noted earlier, it is the need for help with daily-life activities that renders elders vulnerable to abuse or neglect. So let us now examine those personality traits and situational factors that predispose people to becoming either the perpetrators of maltreatment or its victims—or both.

As indicated in the extreme left-hand column of TABLE 2, four broad variables may be implicated in elder violence. One entails dependency and power imbalances between elders and their caregivers. Another involves personality or cognitive difficulties found not only among dependent elders, but often among their caregivers. A third factor relates to the context within which elders and their caregivers lead their lives. And a fourth variable concerns some sources of stress that may contribute to suffering.

One or more of these four variables may apply to potential elderly *victims* of maltreatment (i.e., those whose characteristics are noted in the middle column of TABLE 2), yet the same variables may also pertain to those caregivers who become *perpetrators* of maltreatment (those whose characteristics are noted in the right-hand column).

As noted in TABLE 2, *dependency* is a pervasive feature of both the victims and the perpetrators of maltreatment. Physically based dependency of elders who need part-time or full-time home care may trace to such organic and irreversible conditions as heart disease, strokes, osteoporosis, rheumatoid arthritis, osteoarthritis, or Alzheimer's disease (Siegler & Costa, 1985); but physical impairments may also derive from potentially reversible conditions such as the temporary effects of infections or of *pseudodementia*, a severe depression that may result from deteriorated health, vision, hearing, or motor control, or from a loss of autonomy, loved ones, and valued activities. Physical dependencies may be outgrowths not only of physical disabilities, but also of cognitive disorders associated with some form of dementia.

TABLE 2. Factors contributing to the vulnerability of elders to maltreatment by caregivers

Variables	Factors relating to elderly victims and their situation	Factors relating to the perpetrators and their situation
Dependency	Cognitive deterioration; dependent personality disorder; economic dependence on the caregiver	Cognitive impairment; substance abuse; economic dependence on the elder
Possible effects: A power imbalance	Dependency on the caregiver renders elders susceptible to maltreatment	Caregivers have power over elders except when elders have economic dominance over them
Cognitive and/or personality impairments	Dementia; behavior that is violent or provocative (ingratitude, making unceasing demands, or complaints)	Weak ego and poor tolerance of frustration or stress; violence or coerciveness; antisocial personality
Contextual Factors: Shared home	Lack of privacy	Lack of privacy and of relief from elder's demands
Isolation (social and geographical)	Loneliness; maltreatment goes undetected	Loneliness; maltreatment goes untreated; lack of respite care
Ageism	Expect and accept victimization	View elders as mentally and physically incompetent, and may feel entitled to maltreat them
Sources of stress and suffering	Loss of valued persons and activities; loss of autonomy and self-respect	Actual or perceived loss of privacy, independence and leisure; lack of social support and of respite care

NOTE. This table represents an adaptation of material taken from Margot B. Nadien (1996). Aging women: Issues of mental health and maltreatment. *In* Women and mental health. vol. 789. J. A. Sechzer, S. M. Pfafflin, F. L. Denmark, A. Griffin, & S. J. Blumenthal, Eds.: 129–145. Annals of the New York Academy of Sciences. New York.

While caregivers in nursing homes or hospital settings tend to be independent, caregivers in the home, whether they be family members or home-care workers, are more prone to dependency. However, unlike elders, the dependency of caregivers is not physical, but results from economic reliance on their caretaking role, especially, if they suffer from drug dependency, limited skills, or cognitive deficits that limit their eligibility for more lucrative work. When economically dependent, some caregivers may financially maltreat elders by stealing their money or other personal property. Other caregivers, if resentful of their role, may project anger onto their elderly charges and then maltreat them, either physically or psychologically.

Personality or cognitive difficulties are a second general variable. That some elders need caregiving because of cognitive and personality difficulties is suggested by data showing that in developed nations, 20% of elders over age 79 suffer from Alzheimer's disease, and 48% of those over the age of 85 years show progressive cognitive and behavioral deficits. When suffering from impaired short-term memory, reasoning, or ego controls, some elders repeatedly ask the same questions, raise endless complaints, or show unrelenting hostility (Godkin, Wolf, & Pillemer, 1989; Johnson, 1991; Vitality for Life, 1993).

How caregivers respond to elders' physical or mental ailments will differ depending on the caregiver's own mental state. Some caregivers find caregiving rewarding because of its financial returns or because they enjoy fulfilling an aging person's needs. These caregivers are usually able to tolerate the stress of long and lonely hours of coping with elders who may be demanding, complaining, forgetful, incontinent, depressed, and even abusive. But devotion to elders is rarely found among caregivers if they resent their role. Reluctant caregivers may be family members who dislike the elder or dislike caretaking. Or they may be low-paid workers who settle for elder care because of being unable to find more desirable or lucrative work. When such caregivers are substance abusers or mental retardates, or when they are immature, egocentric, depressed, or antisocial, they may deal with elders' provocative behavior with anger, abuse, or intentional neglect (Fulmer & O'Malley, 1987; Hwalek & Sengstock, 1986; Kosberg, 1980; Quinn & Tomita, 1986).

In some respects, relationships between elders and their caregivers are interactive. Thus elders who are dependent or mentally ill may provoke maltreatment, especially in caregivers who are themselves dependent or mentally impaired. Caregiver abuse, in turn, may lead elders to retaliate.

Contextual and *inner stressors* are also sources of elder maltreatment. They tend to be interactive on those occasions when they trigger a vicious cycle of *elder provocation*, *caregiver retaliation*, and then *elder counter-retaliation*. As noted in TABLE 2, contextual sources of tension include the sharing of a home, which infringes on the privacy of both the elder and the caregiver. There is also the loneliness of being socially and perhaps geographically isolated from other people. And there are the pernicious effects of *ageism,* the negative stereotypes of the old as mentally incompetent and foolish—stereotypes that, when internalized, may cause elders to feel undeserving of respect and may lead caregivers to feel entitled to be abusive or neglectful (Coyne, 1991).

TABLE 2 shows that maltreatment may also arise from anger or depression kindled by *inner stressors*. For elders, inner stressors include the lowered sense of autonomy and self-esteem that so often accompany a decline in physical or mental abilities, or that arise in consequence of some form of loss—the loss of health or of meaningful activities, the loss of the spouse or other significant persons, or the loss of a customary way of life. As for caregivers, stress stems from too little independence, leisure, and privacy because of the caregiving situation, and too few sources of recreation, respite care, and meaningful social relationships with contemporaries (Fulmer & O'Malley, 1987; Godkin, Wolf, & Pillemer, 1989; Johnson, 1991; Kosberg, 1980; Pillemer & Finkelhor, 1989; Quinn & Tomita, 1986).

Let us now consider the future likelihood of reducing elder maltreatment.

POSSIBLE WAYS OF REDUCING ELDER MALTREATMENT

Accelerating advances in medical care may reduce many of the problems of aging, but they are unlikely to obliterate all need for caregiving. The urgency of reducing elder maltreatment stems from the fact that within developed nations, persons aged 85 years and over represent the fastest growing age segment, with maltreatment estimated to range from 4% to 10% of those persons who are most vulnerable to dependency and thus most needful of caregiving. But what steps can be taken?

One step would be to sensitize the lay public to conditions that relate to elder maltreatment and to encourage various institutions—the government, educational and religious organizations, the arts, and the media—to disseminate information about elder abuse and neglect, and about ways to curb them. A second step would be to try to reduce *ageism* by training people from childhood onward to recognize and cope with their frustration and anger, not by maltreating others, but by searching for realistic and non-harmful ways of reducing their own tension. Additionally, because of the many stresses associated with the care of elders, especially mentally impaired elders, caregivers need special training to deal with dependent elders and, at the same time, require more social support and respite care.

CONCLUSION

Because this picture painted of elder maltreatment may seem a bit grim, let me depict elder maltreatment within a broader context. First, we need to recognize that known cases of elder abuse or neglect are limited mainly to those elders who require assistance with the *activities of daily life*. This means that extensive help from caregivers is required not by all elders, but only by those who are dependent on personal care by others. Moreover, the expected rise in scientific and medical innovations and the improved methods of health care may reduce the incidence of elder physical and mental illness—and, in so doing, may reduce the numbers of elders dependent on caregivers.

A second issue inheres in the way we conceptualize the manifestations of psychological maltreatment which, as noted in TABLE 1, include verbal insults, confinement, rejection, and lack of social acceptance or social support. Is not this definition of psychological maltreatment so broad that it could pertain to almost all people of *all* ages? Have many of us not been subject to psychological abuse or neglect at different stages of our lives? As infants and young children, might we have sometimes felt that we suffered *psychological neglect* at the hands of parents or nannies who had to divide their attention and energies between us and other members of our family? As schoolchildren, were there not occasions when we experienced as *psychological abuse* the taunting by other children or our exclusion from cliques or gangs to which other children belonged? And all through childhood, adolescence, and adulthood, did not some of us experience as psychological maltreatment the indifference, criticism, or outright rejection of significant others—a peer or spouse or child or colleague or employer? In essence, then, might the current conceptions of abuse and neglect, at least those that are psychological, be so broad as to lead many of us to label ourselves as having been "abused" or "neglected" as a child, spouse, parent, friend, or colleague? And might this not imply that to be human means to be liable to being a victim and also liable to becoming an unwitting perpetrator of maltreatment?

In this connection, let me consider one final point. If elder abuse and neglect are typical of the maltreatment that may be directed against people at various ages across the life span, why should special attention be directed toward the maltreatment of elders? One answer is that in contrast to most other age groups, frail or ill elders, like the very young, are unable to defend themselves against the brutalizing effects of neglect or abuse.

REFERENCES

ALBERT, S.M. & CATTELL, M.G. (1994). *Old age in global perspective: Cross-cultural and cross-national views*. New York: G. K. Hall & Co., an imprint of Macmillan Publishing Co.

BENGTSON, V., ROSENTHAL, C., & BURTON, L. (1996). Paradoxes of families and aging. In R.H. Binstock & L.K. George (Eds.), *Handbook of aging and the social sciences* (pp. 253–282). San Diego, CA: Academic Press.

BLOCK, M.R. & SINNOTT, J.D. (Eds.). (1979). *The battered elder syndrome*. College Park, MD: University of Maryland Center on Aging–University of Maryland Press.

BOGUE, D.J. (1985). *The population of the United States: Historical trends and future projections*. New York: Free Press.

CASSELL, E.J. (1989). Abuse of the elderly: Misuses of power. *New York State Journal of Medicine (New York Hospital-Cornell Medical Center) 89*, 159–162.

CIRILLO, J. (1995). Prevention of family violence for the female alcoholic. In L.L. Adler & F.L. Denmark (Eds.), *Violence and the prevention of violence* (pp. 169–175). Westport, CT: Praeger.

COYNE, A.C. (1991). The relationship between cognitive impairment and elder abuse. In T. Tatara & M.M. Rittman (Eds.), *Findings of five elder abuse studies* (pp. 3–20). Washington, DC: National Aging Resource Center on Elder Abuse.

DALY, J.M. & JOGERST, G. Statute definitions of elder abuse. *Journal of Elder Abuse and Neglect 13*, 39 (47)–57.

DUKE, J. (1991) A national study of self-neglecting adult protective services clients. In T. Tatara & M. M. Rittman (Eds.), *Findings of five elder abuse studies* (pp. 23–50). Washington, DC: National Aging Resource Center on Elder Abuse.

FISHER, B.S. & REGAN, S.L. (2006). The extent and frequency of abuse in the lives of older women and their relationship with health outcomes. *The Gerontologist. 46 (27)*, 200–209.

FULMER, T.T. & O'MALLEY, T.A. (1987). *Inadequate care of the elderly: A health care perspective on abuse and neglect*. New York: Springer.

GELLES, R.J. (1983). An exchange/social control theory. In D. Finkelhor, R.J. Gelles, G.T. Hotaling & M.A. Straus (Eds.), *The dark side of families: Current family violence research* (pp. 151–165). Beverly Hills, CA: Sage.

GERBER, G.L. (1995). Gender stereotypes and the problem of marital violence. In L.L. Adler & F.L. Denmark (Eds.), *Violence and the Prevention of Violence* (pp. 145–155). Westport, CT: Praeger.

GODKIN, M.A., WOLF R.S. & PILLEMER, K.A. (1989). A case comparison analysis of elder abuse and neglect. *International Journal of Aging and Human Development. 28*(3), 207–225.

GIORDANO, N.H. & GIORDANO, J.A. (1983). *Family and individual characteristics of five types of elder abuse: Profiles and predictors.* Paper presented at the meeting of the Gerontological Society of America, Chicago, IL.

HALL, P.A. (1989). Elder maltreatment items, subgroups, and types: Policy and practice implications. *International Journal of Aging and Human Development. 28*(3), 191–205.

HWALEK, M.A. & SENGSTOCK, M.C. (1986). Assessing the probability of abuse of the elderly: Toward development of a clinical screening instrument. *Journal of Applied Gerontology. 5*(2), 153–173.

JOHNSON, T.F. (1991). *Elder mistreatment: Deciding who is at risk.* Westport, CT: Greenwood Press.

KOSBERG, J.I. (1988). Preventing elder abuse: Identification of high risk factors prior to placement decisions. *The Gerontologist. 28*(1), 43–50.

KOSBERG, J.I. (1980). Family maltreatment: Explanations and interventions. Paper presented at the meeting of the Gerontological Society of America. San Diego, CA.

LINGLER, J.H. (2004). Ethical issues in distinguishing sexual activity from sexual maltreatment among women with dementia. *Journal of Elder Abuse and Neglect. 15*(2), 85–102,

MOODY, H.R. (1994). *Aging: concepts and controversy.* Thousand Oaks, CA: Pine Forge Press.

NADIEN, M.B. (1995). Elder violence (maltreatment) in domestic settings. In L.L. Adler & F.L. Denmark (Eds.), *Violence and the prevention of violence* (pp. 177–190). Westport, CT: Praeger.

NADIEN, M.B. (1996). Aging women: Issues of mental health and maltreatment. *Annals of the New York Academy of Sciences 789* (pp. 129–145). New York: New York Academy of Sciences.

NADIEN, M.B. (2000). Gender, health, and behavior among aging North Americans. In A.L. Comunian & U.P. Gielen (Eds.), *International perspectives on human development* (pp. 601–613). Lengerich, Germany: Pabst.

NADIEN, M.B. & DENMARK, F.L. (2000). Aging women: Stability or change in perceptions of personal control. In M.B. Nadien & F.L. Denmark (Eds.), *Females and autonomy: A life-span perspective* (pp. 130–154). Boston, MA: Allyn & Bacon.

RENNISON, C. & RAND, M. (2003). Non-lethal intimate partner violence: Women age 55 or older. *Violence Against Women. 12*, 1417–1428.

PILLEMER, K.A. & FINKELHOR, D. (1988). The prevalence of elder abuse: A random sample survey. *Gerontologist. 28*, 51–57.

PILLEMER, K.A. & FINKELHOR, D. (1989). Causes of elder abuse: Caregiver stress versus problem relatives. *American Journal of Orthopsychiatry. 59*(2), 179–187.

QUINN, M.J. & TOMITA, S.K. (1986). *Elder abuse and neglect: Causes, diagnostics and intervention strategies.* New York: Springer.

QUINN, M.J. & TOMITA, S.K. (1993). Vitality for life: Psychological research for productive aging. *Observer.* Human Capital Initiative, Report 2. Washington, DC.

ROBERTO, K.A., TEASTER, P.B. & DUKE, J.O. (2004). Older women who experience mistreatment: Circumstancs and outcomes. *Journal of Women and Aging. 16*(1/2), 3–16.

SECHZER, J. A., PFAFFLIN, S. M., DENMARK, F. L., GRIFFIN, A. (Eds.) (1996). *Women and Mental Health*. New York Annals of the New York Academy of Sciences.

SENGSTOCK, M.C. & HWALEK, M. (1985). *Comprehensive index of elder abuse*. Detroit, MI: Wayne State University.

SENGSTOCK, M.C. & HWALEK, M. (1987). A review and analysis of measures for the identification of elder abuse. *Journal of Gerontological Social Work*. *10*(3/4), 21–35.

SENGSTOCK, M.C. & LIANG, J. (1982). *Identifying and characterizing elder abuse*. Final report submitted to NRTA-AARP Andrus Foundation. Detroit, MI: Institute of Gerontology, Wayne State University.

SIEGLER, I.C. & COSTA, P.T. Jr., (1985). Health-behavior relationships. In J.E. Birren & K.W. Schaie (Eds.), *Handbook of the psychology of aging* (*Vol. 2*, pp. 144–166) New York: Van Nostrand Reinhold.

TESTA, M. (2004). The role of substance use in male-to-female physical and sexual violence: A brief review and recommendations for future research. *Journal of Interpersonal Violence*. *19*(12), 1494–1505.

Vitality for Life (1993). Psychological research for productive aging. *Observer* (pp. 7–24). Washington, DC: American Psychological Society.

WOLF, R.S. (1996). Understanding elder abuse and neglect. *Aging*. *367*, 4–13.

WOLF, R.S., GODKIN, M.A. & PILLEMER, K.A. (1984). *Elder abuse and neglect: Final report from three model projects*. Worcester, MA: University of Massachusetts Medical Center–University Center on Aging.

WOLF, R.S., STRUGNELL, C.P. & GODKIN, M.A. (1982). *Preliminary findings from three model projects on elderly abuse*. Worcester, MA: University of Massachusetts Medical Center on Aging.

Violence and Exploitation against Women and Girls with Disability

DANIEL B. ROSEN

D. Rosen Associates

ABSTRACT: This article seeks to explore issues concerning women and girls with disability who have experienced violence and exploitation. Owing to different methodologies of data collection, it is difficult to precisely determine the exact number of women and girls who are affected. The literature suggests that violence and exploitation against women and girls with disability occur at a rate 50% higher than in the rest of society. It also points out a number of additional critical issues: professionals are uneducated nd insensitive to the needs of these populations; increasing numbers of women and girls living with disability exacerbate the problem; women and girls with disability are uneducated about their rights and responsibilities; and action must be taken to halt this epidemic.

KEYWORDS: violence; exploitation; women; girls; disability

INTRODUCTION AND BACKGROUND INFORMATION

The purpose of this article is to analyze the literature concerning violence and exploitation against women and girls with disability in the hope of discovering the extent of the problem and possible solutions. One of the first impressions of the reader must be the relative dearth of literature that exists on this subject. That which exists are primarily case studies or small group studies as well as anecdotal reports. Almost universally, authors believe and studies support two premises: (1) that women and girls with disability are the victims of violence and exploitation to a higher degree than is commonly assumed; (2) that collection of data on women and girls with disabilities who are subject to violence and exploitation is nearly impossible owing to systemic roadblocks to collection.

According to the U.S. Census of 2000, 19.1% of females over the age of 5 years (approximately 25,306,717) had some type of disability. In addition, 5.3% of the female population over the age of 65 years (approximately 1 million) lives in nursing homes. Together these two groups represent a population

Address for correspondence: Daniel B. Rosen, Ph. D., President, D. Rosen Associates, 207 E. 30th St., Suite 2-B, New York, NY 10016-8277. Voice: 646-269-2800; fax: 212-889-0514.
e-mail: DRosenAssociates@aol.com

Ann. N.Y. Acad. Sci. 1087: 170–177 (2006). © 2006 New York Academy of Sciences.
doi: 10.1196/annals.1385.002

of more than 26 million or 24.4% of females in the United States. Excluded from this analysis are girls under the age of 5 years, women in the military, and women in congregate living situations other than nursing homes. It is not unreasonable then to perceive that somewhere close to 33% of all women and girls in the United States have a disability. One-third of these women are actively parenting children under the age of 18 years.

Slightly more women than men have a disability. Women of color have three times the rate of disability compared to other ethnic groups. Native American and African American women have the highest rates found in the United States.

We also know that about 33% of women with disability who work, and 40% of women with severe disability who work, live in poverty. As a group in the United States, men and women of working age with disability have an unemployment or under-employment rate approaching 60%. This is higher then any other sector of the population, including men and teens of color, who many consider to have the highest rates of unemployment.

WHY ARE THE STATISTICS SO INEXACT?

In trying to assess the extent of disability in children in the United States, Sullivan (2006) states that "estimates vary according to how disability status is defined, the severity of the disability, the age range employed in defining the disability status, and the need for disability-related services as a function of meeting the defined disability criteria" (p. 214). She further indicates that prevalence data are determined by a variety of factors including "eligibility determinations for receiving health, education, and income services and/or supplements from the federal government" (p. 215). More simply, every entity counts according to its own criteria, and there is no governmental (state or federal) requirement of a singular, consistently applied methodology of counting.

TERMS

For clarity in this article, we will utilize the following operational definitions:

1. *Disability* is defined as chronic physical, affective, and/or cognitive condition(s) that, to a significant extent, preclude normal activities of daily functioning. Disability can affect individuals of all ages. Examples range from common conditions such as arthritis to rare conditions such as Wolman disease. Other examples include blindness and decreased vision, brain injury, cardiac disease, deafness and hearing loss, depression, diabetes, eating disorders, emphysema, fibromyalgia, HIV/AIDS, learning disability, loss of or lost use of a limb, mental retardation, morbid obesity, muteness, post-polio complications, schizophrenia, stroke, and both alcohol and drug abuse.

2. *Stigma* is defined as "rejection of individuals because those individuals have an attribute that compromises their identity in the eyes of others." More importantly, stigma often results in some form of depersonalization or discrimination that can result in violence or victimization, as demonstrated by Goffman (1961).
3. *Violence* is force (physical or psychological) that is used to abuse, demean, physically harm, or injure an individual.

WHY DOES VIOLENCE AND EXPLOITATION AGAINST WOMEN AND GIRLS WITH DISABILITY OCCUR?

The *Disability Digest*, an Australian web site, provides insight into some of the reasons why women with disability experience violence:

1. *Social myths*—people with disabilities are often dismissed as passive, helpless, child-like, nonsexual, and burdensome. These prejudices tend to make people with disabilities less visible to society, and suggest that [because they are not seen] abuse, especially sexual abuse, is unlikely.
2. *Learned helplessness*—people with disabilities, particularly people with cognitive disabilities or those who have been living in institutions for a long time, are encouraged to be compliant and cooperative. This life history can make it harder for a woman to defend herself against abuse.
3. *Lack of sex education*—there is a tendency to deny sex education to people with intellectual disabilities. If a woman with no knowledge of sex is sexually abused, it is harder for her to seek help because she may not understand exactly what is happening to her.
4. *Dependence*—the woman may be dependent on her abuser for care because her disability limits her economic and environmental independence.
5. *Misdiagnosis*—authorities may misinterpret a cry for help; for example, a woman's behavior might be diagnosed as anxiety rather than signs of abuse. In other situations, workers may not be aware that domestic violence also includes financial or emotional abuse, or may not be sensitive to the signs.
6. *The abuser takes control*—if the woman seeks help, follow-up may be difficult because the abuser isolates her and prevents her from using the phone or leaving the house. (*Disability Digest* website, second page)

WHAT DOES THE LITERATURE TELL US?

Kvam (2004) conducted a retrospective study of adults in Norway who were deaf and had attended special schools. His results: "Deaf children are at greater risk of sexual abuse than hearing children. The special schools for the deaf represent an extra risk of abuse, regardless of whether the deaf pupils live at home or in board schools" (p. 250).

Hines and Malley–Morrison (2005) report that with the exception of children with autism, maltreatment of those with disabling conditions significantly exceeded the rates of those who were not disabled in the United States. They also report that Brown, Cohen, Johnson, and Salzinger (1998) in their study of children with disability in New York found that children where the mother's pregnancy or where the child's birth was difficult were the most likely to be physically abused. They also found that children with intellectual disability were most likely to be neglected. And children with a physical disability were most often the victims of sexual abuse.

In a study done in Canada, Sobsey and Doe (1991) found that 82% of the cases at a university handled by its disability and sexual abuse project involved sexual abuse of women. Over 95% of the women knew their attacker and 44% of the abusers were identified as care attendants.

In September 1998 the U.S. Department of Justice's *Office for Victims of Crimes Bulletin* indicated that "68% to 83% of women with disabilities will be sexually assaulted during their lifetime, this represents a 50% higher rate than the rest of the population." (Brouner, 2001)

The National Center for Injury Prevention and Control further compounds the power of the figures above when it indicates, "Only 19% to 23% of all sexual violence cases (perpetrated against people with disabilities) were limited to one episode" (Brouner, 2001).

In 2003 Milberger *et al.* recruited 177 women with disability through a variety of sources. Within this cohort 100 women (56%) reported having been abused. They also found that of the group, those who were disabled by hearing impairment and those disabled with multiple forms of disability had significantly higher levels of abuse than those with these disabilities who were not abused.

A study by Welbourne, Lipschitz, Selvin, and Green (1983) found that 50% of the women who were blind from birth had been sexually assaulted. The authors concluded that abusers more readily abused others when they believed that they could not be identified.

In 1997 Chenoweth, building on the work of Welbourne *et al.* (1983), pointed out that violence perpetrated on women with disability was generally neither "voiced nor heard."

Also in 1997 Young *et al.* looked at the characteristics of the abusers of women with disability. Emotional abuse by husbands was reported by 26% of the women; 18% of the women reported their husbands as physically abusing them. Interestingly, when it came to sexual assault the women most often reported the abuser to be a stranger (12% of the cases).

This last study may explain a recommendation by Monahan and Lurie (2003), who suggested that both girls and women with disability might require treatment for childhood sex abuse.

In 2003 Haworth Press simultaneously published both as a double edition of the journal *Women & Therapy*, 26 (1/2), and as a book entitled *Women with Visible and Invisible Disabilities: Multiple Intersections, Multiple Issues, Multiple Therapies*, the only journal/book exclusively dedicated to all aspects of disability experienced in the lives of women and girls. Topics included increased risk factors experienced by women and girls with disability, health/wellness issues, social relationships and roles, sexuality, spirituality, identity, employment, and violence. The outcomes of these studies provide the reader with a better understanding of disability as an integral aspect of identity, the need to develop cultural competence related to disability, and a better understanding how disability intertwines with other aspects of identity. This journal/book supports all of the research presented in this article.

WHAT HAPPENS AFTER VIOLENCE AND EXPLOITATION OCCUR AGAINST WOMEN AND GIRLS WITH DISABILITY?

The literature has clearly indicated that violence and exploitation of women and girls with disability is rampant and understudied. I will answer the question by using several studies that asked victims themselves about their postviolence experience.

Milberger *et al*. (2003) discovered that many women and girls with disabling conditions did not seek help or report that they did not receive adequate help. Questioned further about their actions, the following answers were elicited: able to handle things themselves; preferring to use their own sources of support; not knowing where to seek assistance; embarrassment; feeling guilt about being a burden to others; feeling that the incident was their fault; fear of retributive action by the perpetrator; fear of not being believed; and concern that, if they had a physical disability, the service provider would lack accessible accommodations.

Nosek *et al*. (2001) recommended the development and testing of interventions to assist women and girls with disability to recognize abuse, protect themselves in abusive situations, and remove themselves from abusive relationships and situations.

In Great Britain, Hendey and Pascall (1998) studied 42 young adults with severe disability. Young women reported fears about vulnerability, and some who had left home and later returned reported that they experienced highly restricted social lives caused by anxiety owing to a fear of community violence.

A study of women with disability who experienced domestic violence was done in North Carolina. It was a cross-sectional survey of domestic violence programs in the state. The response rate by community providers of the questionnaires sent out was 85%. The following challenges to serving women with disability were raised: lack of funding; lack of training; and for those with physical disability, structural limitations at service locales. (Chang *et al.* 2003).

WHAT DO WE NEED TO DO TO END VIOLENCE AND EXPLOITATION OF WOMEN AND GIRLS WITH DISABILITY?

What has become painfully clear is that women and girls with disability have been and will continue to be the victims of abuse and exploitation until those interested in eradicating this problem change the status quo. The literature, and my own experiences in the field, leads me to the following suggestions:

1. We must educate women and girls with disability that they are entitled to a life free of violence and exploitation. We need to provide them with training, appropriate to their level, in a proactive fashion and from a young age.
2. We must train all citizens that women and girls with disability are entitled to a life without violence and exploitation, as are all other citizens. We must provide stricter enforcement of laws that protect women and girls with disability.
3. We must assist women and girls with disability to understand what resources are available to them, and, as a society we must ensure that all necessary resources are created.
4. We must educate all professionals: emergency medical technicians, firefighters, nurses, police, physicians, psychologists, social workers, and teachers about the systemic issues and their responsibility to actively protect and defend women and girls with disabling conditions.
5. We must create a singular system to completely and accurately keep track of the incidence levels of violence and exploitation against women and girls with disability to allow a better understanding of the breadth of this problem and to create appropriate punishments for abusers and exploiters.
6. We must continue to research this issue to ensure a fuller and more complete understanding of the problem and to be able to create solutions.

Even if all of these suggestions are implemented to the fullest extent possible, history has taught us that violence and exploitation will not end. However, we can be assured that any affirmative action as a society will change the lives of women and girls with disability who are the victims of the most violence and exploitation.

REFERENCES

Banks, M.E. & Kaschak, Eds. 2003. Women and Therapy, 26(1/2).
Banks, M.E. & Kaschak, Eds. 2003. Women with visible and invisible disabilities: Multiple intersections, multiple issues, multiple therapies. Haworth Press. New York.
Barnett, O., C.L. Miller-Perrin & R.D. Perrin. 2005. Family violence across the lifespan. Sage Publications. Thousand Oaks, CA.
Brady, S.M. 2001. Sterilization of girls and women with intellectual disabilities: Past and present justification. Violence Against Women 7, 432–461.

BROUNER, J. 2001. Look again: domestic violence and disability. Retrieved March 3, 2006 from www.cara-seattle.org/w_look.html.

BROWN, J., P. COHEN, J.G. JOHNSON & S. SALZINGER. 1998. A longitudinal analysis of risk factors for child mistreatment: Findings of a 17-year prospective study of officially recorded and self-reported child abuse and neglect. Child Abuse and Neglect *22*, 1065–1078.

CHANG, J.C., S.L. MARTIN, K.E. MORACCO, *et al*. 2003. Helping women with disabilities and domestic violence: Strategies, limitations, and challenges of domestic violence programs and services. Journal of Women's Health *27*, 699–708.

CHENOWETH, L. 1997. Violence and women with disabilities: Silence and paradox. *In* Women's encounters with violence: Australian experiences. S. Cook & J. Bessant Eds.: 21–39. Sage Publications. Thousand Oakes, CA.

CORRIGAN, P., F.E. MARKOWITZ, A. WATSON, *et al*. 2003. An attribution model of public discrimination towards persons with mental illness. Journal of Health Social Behaviour *44*, 162–179.

DISABILITY DIGEST. 2004. Domestic violence and women with disabilities. Retrieved March 3, 2006 from http://www.disability.vic.gov.au/.../pages/Domestic_violence_and_women_with_disabilities.

EL-BASSE, N., L. GILBERT, E. WU, *et al*. 2005. Social Science and Medicine *61*, 171–183.

FEERICK, M.M. & G.B. SILVERMAN. 2006. Children exposed to violence. Paul H. Brookes Publishing. Baltimore, MD.

GOFFMAN, E. 1961. Asylums. Anchor Books. Garden City, NY.

HENDY, N. & G. PASCALL. 1998. Independent living: gender, violence and the threat of violence. Disability and Society *13*, 415–4127.

HINES, D. & K. MALLEY-MORRISON. 2005. Family violence in the United States. Sage Publications. Thousand Oaks, CA.

JANS & STODDARD. 1999. Chartbook on women and disability in the U.S.: An InfoUse report. U.S. Department of Education, National Institute on Disability and Rehabilitation Research. Washington, D.C.

KVAM, M.H. 2004. Sexual abuse of deaf children. Child Abuse Neglect *28*, 241–251.

LI, L., J.A. FORD & D. MOORE. 2000. An exploratory study of violence, substance abuse, disability and gender. Social Behavior and Personality *28*, 61–71.

MANSTEAD, A.S.R. & M. HEWSTONE, Eds.1996. The Blackwell Encyclopedia of Social Psychology. Blackwell Publishing. Malden, MA.

MILBERGER, S., N. ISRAEL, B. LEROY, *et al*. 2003. Violence against women with physical disabilities. Violence and Victims *18*, 581–590.

MONAHAN, K. & A. LURIE. 2003. Disabled women sexually abused in childhood: Treatment consideration. Clinical Social Work Journal *31*, 407–418.

MORINGTON, M. 2001. Domestic violence-domestic terrorism. *In* Good practice with vulnerable adults. J. Pritchard, Ed.: pp. 185–203. Jessica Kingsley Publishers, Ltd., Philadelphia.

MORRIS, R.L. 2005. Abuse of women with disabilities. Dissertation Abstracts International *65*, 3580-A.

NOSEK, M.A., C.C. FOLEY, R.B. HUGHES & C.A. HOWLAND. 2001. Vulnerabilities for abuse among women with disabilities. Sexuality and Disability *19*, 177–189.

SAXTON, M., M.A. CURRY, L.E. POWERS, *et al*. 2001. "Bring me my scooter so I can leave you": a study of disabled women handling abuse of personal care providers. Violence Against Women *7*, 393–417.

SOBSEY, D. & T. DOE. 1991. Patterns of sexual abuse and assault. Sexuality and Disability *9*, 243–260.
STILES, B.L., S. HALIM & H. KAPLAN. 2003. Individuals with physical limitations. Criminal Justice Review *28*, 232–253.
SULLIVAN, P.M. 2006. Children with disabilities exposed to violence. *In* Children exposed to Violence. M.M. Feerick & G.B. Silverman, Eds.: 213–237. Sage Publications. Thousand Oaks, CA.
WELBOURNE, A., D.S. LIPSCHITZ, H. SELVIN & R. GREEN. 1983. A comparison of the sexual learning experiences of visually impaired and sighted women. Journal of Visual Impairment and Blindness *77*, 256–259.
YOUNG, M.E., M.A. NOSEK, C.A. HOWLAND, *et al.* 1997. Prevalence of abuse of women with physical disabilities. Archives of Physical Medicine and Rehabilitation *78*, S34–S38.

Gender-Based Violence

Concepts, Methods, and Findings

NANCY FELIPE RUSSO AND ANGELA PIRLOTT

Department of Psychology, Arizona State University, Arizona, USA

ABSTRACT: The United Nations has identified gender-based violence against women as a global health and development issue, and a host of policies, public education, and action programs aimed at reducing gender-based violence have been undertaken around the world. This article highlights new conceptualizations, methodological issues, and selected research findings that can inform such activities. In addition to describing recent research findings that document relationships between gender, power, sexuality, and intimate violence cross-nationally, it identifies cultural factors, including linkages between sex and violence through media images that may increase women's risk for violence, and profiles a host of negative physical, mental, and behavioral health outcomes associated with victimization including unwanted pregnancy and abortion. More research is needed to identify the causes, dynamics, and outcomes of gender-based violence, including media effects, and to articulate how different forms of such violence vary in outcomes depending on cultural context.

KEYWORDS: gender-based violence; gender; intimate partner violence; domestic violence; reproduction; media effects

INTRODUCTION

Women in Asia and the Middle East are killed in the name of honor. Girls in West Africa undergo genital mutilation in the name of custom. Migrant and refugee women in Western Europe are attacked for not accepting the social mores of their host community. Young girls in southern Africa are raped and infected with HIV/AIDs because the perpetrators believe that sex with virgins will cure them of their disease. And in the richest, most developed countries of the world, women are battered to death by their partners (Amnesty International, 2004, p. iii-iv).

The United Nations has identified gender-based violence against women as a global health and development issue, and a host of policies and public

Address for correspondence: Nancy Felipe Russo, Department of Psychology, Box 871104, ASU, Tempe, AZ 85287-1104. Voice: 480-965-0380; fax: 480-965-8544.
e-mail: Nancy.russo@asu.edu

education programs have been undertaken around the world that aim at reducing such gender-based violence (United Nations, 1989). This article highlights new conceptualizations, methodological issues, and research findings that can inform such activities, particularly with regard to intimate partner violence.

Our focus on gender-based violence against women is not to imply that women are never violent against men. The rates and forms of violence, including intimate partner violence, vary widely across cultures (Kishor & Johnson, 2004). In the United States, recent studies have reported that women and men commonly commit violent acts such as shoving, hitting, or throwing objects against each other, and have found little difference in prevalence rates for such acts by gender (Archer, 2000, 2002; Brush, 1990, 2005; Frieze, 2005; Frieze & Mettugh, 2005; Frieze & McHugh, 2005).

Gender shapes the meaning of violent acts differently for women and men, however, and that meaning varies widely depending on the situational and cultural context. For example, severity of specific physical acts will be rated differently depending on whether or not the perpetrator of the act is male or female (Marshall, 1992a, 1992b). A full understanding of gender-based violence requires going beyond a focus on sex differences in rates and ratings of specific acts to examine how various aspects of gender shape the predictors, dynamics, and outcomes of violence for both women and men.

Interdisciplinary research will make critical contributions to this examination for it must take place on multiple levels. Psychological meaning of acts and experiences for the perpetrator, victim, and outside observer will reflect the situational, structural, and cultural context. In particular, the cultural discourse that justifies gender differences in social and economic status, objectifies women, and sexualizes violence needs to be incorporated in the analysis of the dynamics of gender-based violence. We highlight some of the elements of gender-based violence that can differ for women and men, with our goal to encourage more complex, multilevel approaches in the study of how such violence is experienced in the lives of women and men.

Our focus here on gender-based violence against women should be taken as a reflection of the need to limit our scope and not as a dismissal of the importance of understanding how gender affects violence by and toward *both* women and men. Indeed, violence is an interpersonal behavior and both a stimulus as well as a consequence of interaction. A full understanding of gender's impact on violence against women requires considering women's behaviors toward their partners as well, including their violent behaviors.

THEORIZING GENDER AND ITS RELATION TO INTIMATE VIOLENCE

Research that has examined gender differences in violence against women all too often equates gender with the categories of male and female. Gender thus is treated as a personal attribute of the individual (e.g., Archer, 2003). However, theoretical conceptions of gender have evolved far beyond traditional "sex difference" models. Research findings based on such models have some usefulness but are not very informative with regard to understanding the dynamics of gender as currently conceptualized.

Today gender is theorized as a complex, multilevel cultural construct that determines the meanings of being female or male in a particular situational context (Anderson, 2005; Deaux & Major, 1987; Frable, 1997; Hamilton & Russo, 2006; Ridgeway & Smith-Lovin, 1999). In Western society, gender is typically organized around the social categories of male versus female and assigned at birth based on biological sex (which may be defined anatomically or genetically, depending on the situation). The cultural package that constitutes the meaning of one's gender assignment to a category should not be confused with the category itself.

Gender can be thought of as a package of many interconnected elements—including gendered traits, emotions, values, expectations, norms, roles, environments, and institutions—that change and evolve within and across cultures and over time. Gender is also a "master" (or a meta-) status that determines social position in society, one that typically accords women with less power, privilege, and resources than men (Bourne & Russo, 1998).

Gender defines the appropriateness of behavioral, psychological, and social characteristics of males and females over the life cycle, and shapes the way we construe ourselves (Cross & Madsen, 1997). When doing so it interacts with other dimensions of social difference, and the dynamics of the various elements of gender may differ depending on one's specific mix of social identities and roles. For example, in some contexts, being a good mother who devotes herself to her children is the role expectation for being a wife, and the roles are highly compatible. In contrast, in another context being a good wife may mean serving as a trophy for your husband's success and sending children off to boarding school so that you can make your husband's needs the priority in your life.

The need to appreciate the complex dynamics of social identity and difference led Russo and Vaz (2001) to argue that researchers need to develop a "diversity mindfulness" that appreciates the complex interplay of the intersections of gender and other dimensions of difference (p. 280). Age, ethnicity, race, sexual orientation, class, physical ability, and size are among the social dimensions associated with stigmatized identities that may elicit prejudice and discrimination, confer differential access to power and privilege, and converge with gender to magnify or diminish risk for experiencing violence.

Gender's "rules" (i.e., expected behaviors, rewards, and sanctions for violating those expectations) change over the life cycle. Sometimes there is abrupt change as a result of discrete life events such as losing one's virginity, getting married, having one's first child, or starting a new job. Gender organizes women's roles at home and work in ways that place extraordinary burdens on women while at the same time limiting their access to coping resources. The dramatic changes in women's workforce status and participation that have occurred over the last five decades have not been accompanied by a concomitant sharing of responsibilities in the family (Coltrane, 2000; Steil, 1997; Tichenor, 2005). Gendered inequalities at home and at work create gender differences in perceived entitlements and give different meanings to the resources women and men bring to their relationships. Although such inequalities are associated with risk and outcomes for experiencing violence, the relationship is complex (Steil, 1997; Tichenor, 2005).

Reducing gender-based violence will require new theories that articulate how various aspects of gender mediate and moderate the effects of social, psychological, and biological factors over the life cycle and influence the risk, experience, and outcomes of interpersonal violence between women and men. One thing that can be concluded at present, however, is that the predictors, meanings, and outcomes of gender-based violence are multifaceted and differ for women and men—as perpetrators and as victims.

GENDER-BASED VIOLENCE AGAINST WOMEN

Gender-based violence against women has been defined as "any act that results in, or is likely to result in physical, sexual, or psychological harm or suffering to women, including threats of such acts, coercion or arbitrary deprivation of liberty, whether occurring in public or private life" (United Nations, 1995, Platform for Action D.112). This definition, which emerged from the 1995 United Nations Conference on Women in Beijing, represents an international consensus on how to conceptualize the dynamics of gender-based violence and encompasses child sexual abuse, coercive sex, rape, stalking, and intimate partner violence.

The term "gender-based" is used because such violence is shaped by gender roles and status in society. Gender-based violence against women does not encompass every violent act a woman may happen to experience (being threatened by a weapon during a robbery, for example). A complex mix of gender-related cultural values, beliefs, norms, and social institutions implicitly and even explicitly have supported intimate partner violence and provided little recourse for its victims (Koss, Bailet, & Yuan, Herrera, & Lichter, 2003; Koss, Goodman, Browne, Fitzgerald, Keita, & Russo, 1994; Russo, 2006). In particular, gender roles and expectations, male entitlement, sexual objectification, and discrepancies in power and status have legitimized, rendered invisible, sexualized, and helped to perpetuate violence against women.

RECOGNIZING GENDER-BASED VIOLENCE AS A PROBLEM

One of the ways that gender has differentially shaped the meaning of violent acts by women and men is by differentially conferring legitimacy on male violence against women. With legitimacy has come invisibility for the victims (Keller, 1996; Stark, Flitcraft & Frazier, 1979). Marriage as social institution has come under particular scrutiny for providing men an entitlement to batter and rape their wives and providing legitimacy for their actions (Finklehor & Yllö, 1985; Russell, 1990; Stets & Strauss, 1992; Straus, Gelles, & Steinmetz, 1980). Ironically, it was not until the late 1980s that intimate violence became identified as the leading public health risk to adult women by the surgeon general of the United States (Koop, 1985). The invisibility of male violence against women is truly remarkable given its pervasiveness and profound health, social, and economic consequences.

With the rise of what has become a global women's movement, the legitimacy and invisibility of such violence became challenged. Today, male gender-based violence against women is globally recognized as a health, economic development, and human rights concern (Amnesty International, 2004; Herrera, Koss, Bailey, Yuan, & Lichter, 2006; Koss, Heise, & Russo, 1994; Krahé, Bieneck, & Möller, 2005; Russo, Koss, & Goodman, 1995; National Center for Injury Prevention and Control [NCIPC], 2003; United Nations General Assembly, 1993; World Health Organization, 2001). Yet, in many parts of the world, such violence continues to be viewed as a private matter and is implicitly—indeed, sometimes, explicitly—condoned.

Around the world, girls and women continue to experience gender-based violence over the life cycle in homes, schools, churches, workplaces, the streets and even therapeutic settings (Heise, Ellsberg, & Gottemoeller, 1999; Koss, Goodman, & Browne, 1994; Russo *et al.* 1995; Krahé *et al.* 2005; Shane & Ellsberg, 2002). A recent transnational review of population-based survey data found the lifetime proportion of women experiencing physical assault by an intimate partner to range from 10% to 69% (Krug, Dahlberg, Mercy, Zwi, & Lozano, 2002).

In the United States, the National Violence Against Women Survey estimated one out of five (22.1%) women to be physically assaulted in their lifetime, and one in 13 (7.7%) to be raped by an intimate partner. An estimated 1.3 million women experienced physical assault and more than 201,394 women had experienced rape at the hands of an intimate partner in the previous year (Tjaden & Thoennes, 2000). Intimate partner violence has been the most common source of injury to women in the ages of 15 to 44 years, more frequent than muggings, auto accidents, and cancer deaths combined (Dwyer, Smokowski, Bricout, & Wodarski, 1995). Physical assault against both married and unmarried women has been a widespread problem, crossing racial, sexual orientation, age, and socioeconomic lines (Koss, 1988; Stark & Flitcraft, 1988, 1996).

NEW CONCEPTUALIZATIONS

Today researchers are discovering new ways to conceptualize, study, intervene, and prevent gender-based violence against women. The search for new conceptualizations has identified an array of methodological issues that have led to new challenges for researchers who seek to increase our understanding of this complex phenomenon (Brush, Dutton, Green, Kaltman, Roesch et al., 2006).

Feminist perspectives have qualitatively changed the way that researchers conceptualize, operationally define, and study multifaceted forms of gendered violence over the life cycle (Edwards, 1991; Marin & Russo, 1999). In particular, such perspectives have broadened the focus for research beyond the psychological characteristics of the individual perpetrator and/or victim, or on an investigation of family relationships (Yllö, 1988) and begun to reconceptualize rape and other forms of male violence as forms of power and control (Brownmiller, 1975; Dobash & Dobash, 1977; Medea & Thompson, 1974; Russell, 1975). Although recognizing physical differences may contribute to the dynamics of gender-based violence, in general this theorizing has emphasized the social construction of male violence, not the biology or pathology of the individual (Kelly, 1988; Koss et al., 1994; McHugh, Frieze, & Browne, 1993).

There has been a shift from viewing different forms of male violence against women as separate entities toward viewing violence as a unitary phenomenon with diverse manifestations that vary depending on context (Koss et al., 1994). Gender-based entitlements, power, objectification, and status are now recognized as playing critical roles in the dynamics of gender-based violence. Major institutions (including criminal justice, health, academic, scientific, military, athletic, and religious institutions) are seen as reinforcing patriarchal values that encourage and maintain those entitlements, foster gender-based violence, and encourage stigmatization of voices that challenge the status quo (Koss et al., 1994; Marin & Russo, 1999).

While gender, power, and structural dimensions of violence are recognized as potent forces in the dynamics of gender-based violence, the emerging picture is recognized as increasingly complex (Frieze, 2005; Marin & Russo, 1999; McHugh & Frieze, 2005; McHugh, 2005). Theorizing about the relations of gender, power, and violence has gone far beyond a simplistic focus on direct effects of patriarchal values or sex role beliefs on rates of specific acts perpetrated by women and men. As theory has progressed, research, treatment, intervention, and public policy responses to theoretical advances have lagged behind (Dutton and Corvo [2006] critique approaches based on this simplistic focus; although their vision of feminist perspectives is limited of a particular radical perspective, their call for complex approaches is timely). New knowledge based on new, integrative methods that encompass interdisciplinary, biobehavioral perspectives is needed (e.g., Dutton, Green, Kaltman, Roesch et al., 2006).

METHODOLOGICAL ISSUES

Androcentric (i.e., male-centered) bias affects what becomes figure and what becomes ground in our perception, influences how we interpret what we perceive and remember, and shapes our conceptions of what is normal versus unusual. As Edwards (1991) has observed, "There is no area where androcentric bias is more visible and systematic than male violence against women" (p. 14).

We focus here on gender-based intimate partner violence (IPV), which encompasses acts performed by an intimate partner that include physical, sexual, and emotional abuse, including physical assault, verbal abuse, forced intercourse, and other forms of sexual coercion as well as a variety of controlling behaviors aimed at restricting freedom of action (e.g., isolation from family and friends).

A variety of methodologies have been applied in the study of violence, both qualitative and quantitative, and there are a number of data sources that include national surveys that are used for research on gender-based violence (Hamby, 2005). The Conflict Tactics Scales (Straus, Hamby, & Warren, 2003) or variations thereof are arguably the most widely used of the behavioral checklists in surveys to assess incidence, prevalence, and nature of interpersonal violence. Hamby (2005) articulates the strengths and limitations of various data sources including those of behavioral checklists, which include underreporting, false-negative and false-positive problems, difficulties with referent periods, reporting load and respondent fatigue, overly brief or poorly worded questions, effects of social norms on reporting, and the distortions that can occur in the retrospective recall of events. The extent to which disclosure issues that differ for men and women affect reporting of various violent acts is unknown, but the possibility raises validity issues with regard to self-report checklists. Hamby suggests that with regard to sensitive material, audio computer-assisted self-interviews (audio-CASI) are "likely to be one avenue to progressing toward a gold standard of assessment" (Hamby, 2005, p. 739). She also identifies a number of methodologies that have been underutilized in research on gender-based violence but have documented effectiveness in research on other forms of relationship distress and stigmatized behavior including weekly calendar methods and electronic diary data collected through the internet or palm-sized computers.

In keeping with advances in cognitive science and the now recognized moderating role of appraisals in determining the relationship between stressors and mental health outcomes (Folkman & Moskowitz, 2004), it is important to go beyond simply focusing on the occurrence of acts and consider their meaning and context (DeKeseredy & Schwartz, 1998; Dutton, Burghardt, Perrin, Chrestman, & Halle, 1994). Violent acts may play a role in creating the meaning for other, apparently more benign behaviors that become threatening in a context of coercive control. New conceptualizations of the dynamic of violence and the role of coercive control in gender-based violence are other new frontiers for research (Dutton & Goodman, 2005).

Postmodern perspectives, which emphasize socially constructed meanings, are a source of new concepts and methods as well. McHugh, Livingston, and Ford (2005), suggest that such perspectives encourage "multiple, varied, and even inconsistent views" of intimate violence (p. 332). Their analysis challenges researchers to recognize that there is a sociohistorical context for all research with potential to influence the research process in all its stages from selection of topic to interpretation and dissemination of results.

Challenges to researchers who seek to study IPV arise from methodological and ethical as well as conceptual issues (Desai & Saltzman, 2001; Ellsberg, Heise, Pena, Agurto, & Winkvist, 2001; Schwartz, 2000; White, Smith, Koss, & Figueredo, 2000). Confidentiality and safety of research participants must be preserved and referral information that identifies places to go for help made available to them. Interviewers require special training and sensitivity if they are to conduct interviews in the nonjudgmental and empathic way needed to obtain disclosure of violent events (Garcia-Moreno, Watts, Jansen, Ellsberg, & Heise, 2003; Kishor & Johnson, 2004; WHO, 2001, 2004).

Community-based survey research is being used to document the worldwide prevalence of violence against women (Kishor & Johnson, 2004). Not all dimensions of gender-based violence are typically measured in cross-national surveys, which share the problems of self-report surveys identified above (Hamby, 2005), and further must consider variations in cultural relevance and meaning of the specific behaviors studied. Qualitative research will be needed to illuminate the meanings of violence and coercive acts in the cultural contexts in which women experience them (WHO, 2001).

Researchers have begun to focus on ethnic populations to redress the lack of research on violence in the lives of ethnic minority women, which must overcome silencing around intimate violence issues found in ethnic communities (Sanchez-Hucles & Dutton, 1999; Sorenson, 1996; West, 1998). Researchers have investigated male-perpetrated violence in African American (Brice-Baker, 1994; Marsh, 1993; Russo, Denious, Keita, & Koss, 1997), Native American (Chester, Robin, Koss, & Goodman, 1994; Gutierres, Russo, & Urbanski, 1994; Norton & Manson, 1995), Hispanic American (Perilla, Bakerman, & Norris, 1994; Sorensen & Telles, 1991; Ramos, Koss, & Russo, 1991), and Asian American populations (Song, 1996; see also Sanchez-Hucles & Dutton, 1999).

GENDER-BASED VIOLENCE, ENTITLEMENTS, AND SOCIAL CONTROL

Researchers are beginning to study how IPV reflects assumptions of male entitlement and privilege and functions as a form of social control that maintains a subordinate social and political status for women (Koss, Goodman, et al., 1994; Marin & Russo, 1999). Men who connect masculinity with being able to control and dominate their partners are more likely to be abusive

(Goodrum, Umberson, & Anderson, 2001). Gender-based violence may reflect the discrepancy between men's belief that they should be more powerful than their partners and the reality of their power. Men who perceive they are not as powerful as they "should be" may seek to redress the situation through use of physical dominance (Dutton, 1988). Research suggests that dissatisfaction with the level of power in dating relationships is correlated with violence for both women and men, but the predictors of using violence differ depending on the perpetrator's gender (Kaura & Allen, 2004).

The link between male intimate partner violence and a variety of socially controlling behaviors has been found cross-culturally. Kishor and Johnson (2004) found a strong link between intimate partner violence and husbands' controlling behaviors, specifically (1) becoming jealous or angry if the wife talks with another man, (2) frequently accusing her of being unfaithful, (3) not permitting her to meet girlfriends, (4) limiting her contact with her family, (5) insisting on knowing where she is all the time, and (6) not trusting her with money. The risk for violence directly increased with the number of controlling behaviors on the part of the husband across the diverse cultures studied (Kishor & Johnson, 2004). More needs to be known about the meanings of violence or threat of violence as it is used to control women in specific contexts.

Stigma and the associated emotion of shame combine to become a powerful form of social control. Gender-based violence is experienced as both stigmatizing and shameful (Buchbinder & Eisikovits, 2003; Eisikovits & Enosh, 1997). Shame has also been identified as a factor in inhibiting women from disclosing their experiences of violence to others and from seeking help (Giles-Sims, 1998). Shame may also moderate outcomes of violence. One study found that shame was a key predictor for the relation between psychological violence and PTSD (Street & Arias, 2001).

Although the relationship of stigma to psychological and interpersonal relationships has burgeoned in recent years, the dynamics of stigmatization, shame, power, and gender-based violence continues to be a neglected area of research. As Link and Phelan (2001) have emphasized, stigma depends on power—social, political, and economic—but even power dynamics *per se* is all too often overlooked in analyses of stigma. As they point out, "there is a tendency to focus on the attributes associated with those [stigmatizing] conditions rather than on power differences between people who have them and people who do not" (p. 375).

In particular, the relationship of gender role transgressions to various forms of stigma and its associated sanctions, which include rejection and social exclusion, need to be more fully understood. That knowledge can provide a foundation for building women's resistance to stigmatizing cultural messages. Research on the relationship of stigma to self-esteem suggests that the causal dynamics are complex. For example, there is a relationship between greater exposure to sexism, threat appraisals, and reductions in self-esteem among pessimistic women that is not found among optimistic women (Kaiser, Major, & McCoy, 2004).

At the same time, research on how to foster social change that could reduce stigmatization as a force for the enforcement of gender role norms that support gender-based violence is needed. As Link and Phelan (2001) point out, intervening in the stigma process either requires (1) producing fundamental changes in beliefs and attitudes or (2) changing the power relations that enable dominate groups to act on those stigmatizing beliefs and attitudes. The potential for success of either approach will depend on knowledge of the interrelationships among entitlements, power, stigma, and gender-based violence.

LINKS AMONG GENDER, POWER, AND SEXUALITY

Social structures themselves often reflect inequitable gender relationships that serve to maintain the legitimacy of male violence. Relationships between female workers and male employers, wives and husbands, female patients and male doctors, female athletes and male coaches, for example, share common structural and ideological features that place women in positions of subordination to men.

These inequities reinforce a patriarchal worldview in which women's subordination is normal, natural, and expected, and where powerful and competent women are stigmatized and disliked (Rudman, 1998; Rudman & Glick, 1999, 2001). Further, some studies in the United States have found that for some men (in particular men who are likely to sexually harass women), power and sexuality are linked such that women's subordination is associated with sexual attractiveness (Bargh, Raymond, Strack, & Pryor 1995; Pryor 1987; Pryor & Stoller, 1994). Although the dynamics of the linkages have yet to be fully understood, experimental research by Bargh et al. (1995) in which either power or sex was primed in male participants high in likelihood to sexually harass, suggests that priming power encourages thoughts of sexuality and not *vice versa*.

There has been a great deal of theoretical, methodological, and substantive work that has found sexual objectification to be a powerful influence on women's thoughts, feelings, and behaviors in Western culture (Frederickson & Roberts, 1997; McKinley, 1996; McKinley & Hyde, 1996; Tiggemann & Kuring, 2004). Although more knowledge is needed, some research suggests that sexualization of violence and objectification of women contribute to exposure to abusive experiences. Research examining the link between women's objectification experiences (OE), daily hassles, coercive sexual experiences, and depressive symptoms in college women found that the most important contributors to the effect of OE frequency were being called degrading, gender-stereotyped names, and being the target of offensive (sexualized) gestures

(Burnett, 1995). However, the tendency to rely on the opinions and evaluations of others moderated this relationship.

In developed societies in particular, the media are powerful cultural forces that model interactions between men and women. Insofar as the media provide models that perpetuate gendered inequalities, reinforce and perpetuate ideologies of male dominance (physical and sexual), sexualize violence, and objectify women, they provide mechanisms for gender to influence violence against women. Understanding the dynamics of gender-based violence can be informed by examining through a cultural lens how the media socializes, normalizes, and advocates such ideologies, leading to links between sex and power that operate beyond conscious awareness.

MEDIA INFLUENCES

Mass media influence our perceptions, cognitions, and behaviors related to gender as well as violence through many channels including radio, television, movies, magazines, and the Internet. The impact of media exposure to sexual and violent content including pornographic content (Caputi, 2003; Jensen, 1995; Russell, 1980, 1988; Silbert & Pines, 1984; Sommers & Check, 1987) thus becomes of central concern for researchers who seek to understand the determinants of gender-based violence against women in technologically developed societies. Teenagers spend about half of their waking hours engaged in some form of media: an estimated 3 hours of watching television, 1.5 hours listening to music, less than 1 hour watching movies, three-fourths of an hour reading, and one-half hour on the computer per day (Brown, Steele, & Walsh-Childers, 2002). Researchers predict that by the time a 7-year old reaches 70 years, they will have spent 7–10 years of his or her life in front of a television (Roberts, 2000). By the age of 14 years, it is estimated that the average American child has viewed more then 8,000 murders and 100,000 other acts of violence on television alone (Huston, Donnerstein, Fairchild, Feshbach, Katz, Murray, Rubinstein, Wilcox, & Zuckerman, 1992). Although findings from correlational designs are problematic with regard to causality, effects of exposure to violence against and sexual degradation of women have been documented in experimental studies as well (Linz, Donnerstein, & Penrod, 1984; 1988; Mulac, Jansma, & Linz, 2002).

Media have been found to perpetuate rape myths by portraying sexual violence against women in television and movies congruent with such beliefs (Brinson, 1992). Rape myths include belief that: (a) the victim is promiscuous; (b) it is the victim's fault; (c) the victim wanted to be raped; (d) the victim lies about the rape (Burt, 1980); or (e) the rapist is psychologically or biologically unable to resist his sexual impulses (Groth, 1979). Television and movies tell the tale of rape such that "it is acceptable to rape and be raped in certain circumstances, especially when the victims and offenders fail to fit mythical profiles"

(Bufkin & Eschholz, 2000, p. 1338). Some evidence suggests that exposure to violent pornography in particular cannot only affect men (Demaré, Briere, & Lips, 1988; Donnerstein, 1980)-–it can affect women's attitudes and fantasies about rape as well (Corne, Briere & Esses, 1992).

Media provide social learning tools for children and teens in developing their ideas about appropriate norms in different behaviors (Bryant & Zillman, 1994) including those related to sex and aggression. For example, 61% of teens aged 13–15 years have been found to depend on television and movies for sources of information about sex, STDs, drugs, alcohol, and violence (Kaiser Family Foundation, 1999); more than half report learning about pregnancy and birth control from television; and more than half of girls report learning about sex from magazines (Princeton Survey Research Associates, 1996). Communications researchers critique the media for failing to provide an accurate portrait of reality on these important matters (e.g., Huston, Wartella, & Donnerstein, 1998; Lowry & Shidler, 1993). Although it is recognized that media can play a powerful role in communicating values, setting norms, and establishing expectations for behavior, the full impact of media influences on gender-based violence has yet to be documented.

MUSIC—A NEW FRONTIER FOR RESEARCH IN UNDERSTANDING LINKS BETWEEN GENDER AND SEXUALIZED VIOLENCE AGAINST WOMEN

The impact of new technology that substantially increases both audio and visual exposure to popular music in particular has yet to be fully felt, but even the current levels of such exposure have raised concerns due to the violent and sexual nature of its content. In a recent content analysis of six types of media, Pardun, L'Engle, and Brown (2005) found that music contained substantially more sexual content (40%) than movies (12%), television (11%), magazines (8%), Internet web sites (6%), or newspapers (1%). Furthermore, music was more likely to focus on sexual innuendos, sexual intercourse, divorce, and deteriorating relationships as compared to other forms of media.

Music reflects its larger social and political context, and mysogynism in popular music is not new—derogatory views of women have been expressed in many genres including rock, country, and the blues. In particular, rap music emerged in the 1970s as a vehicle for expressing ideas and emotions related to the experience of blacks in the United States. The dominance of misogynistic themes in rap did not emerge until the late 1980s but is now a constant theme with many popular artists including Ice T., N.W.A., and 2 Live Crew (Adams & Fuller, 2006).

Hip hop, rap, and heavy metal have been the target of most discussion due to their extremely violent and sexual nature (Greeson & Williams, 1986; Perry, 2003; St. Lawrence & Joyner, 1991). Violent themes are common with research reporting from 15% to 50% of rap music videos as containing violent imagery (Gow, 1990; Greeson & Williams, 1986; Sherman & Dominick, 1986). In addition to normalizing antisocial behavior in general, rap lyrics promulgate themes of rape, torture, abuse, and other forms of degradation of women. Zimmerman (1992) found that in particular gangster rap music, which is becoming more "mainstream" in popular culture, portrays women as sex objects and victims of sexual violence. Similar concerns have been voiced about the content of heavy metal rock music (St. Lawrence & Joyner, 1991).

Research has documented the negative impact of sexual and violent music on attitudes toward women. Wester, Crown, Quatman, and Heesacker (1997) found that even brief exposure to sexually violent rap music in participants unfamiliar with the genre increased belief in adversarial sexual relationships. Heavy metal music has also been known to increase men's sex-role stereotyping and perceived entitlements including the view that "a woman should never contradict her husband in public," and negative attitudes regarding vocational, education, and intellectual roles of women (St. Lawrence & Joyner, 1991). Research by Barongan and Hall (1996) found that participants exposed to misogynous music were significantly more likely to act aggressively toward female confederates and to misperceive their reactions, concluding that "misogynous music facilitates sexually aggressive behavior and supports the relationship between cognitive distortions and sexual aggression" (p.195). Other research suggests that exposure to such music increases hostile and aggressive thoughts (Anderson, Carnagey, & Eubanks, 2003), and that long-term exposure to violent music can lead to more permanent hostility toward women (Anderson & Bushman, 2002).

The combination of visual imagery with lyrical messages makes music videos an especially potent source of information about social roles, consumerism, and culture (Sun & Lull, 1986). Music videos predominantly rely on themes of implicit sexuality, objectification, dominance, and implicit aggression (Vincent, Davis, & Boruszkowski, 1987). Males display dominant and aggressive behaviors while women behave in subservient and implicitly sexual ways. Women are also the recipients of implicit, explicit, and aggressive advances, and are portrayed as enjoying aggressive sex (Sommers-Flanagan, Sommers-Flanagan, & Davis, 1993).

Evidence suggests that the storylines shown in music videos shape consumer attitudes and schemas, particularly gender-role schemas. Frequent music video exposure is associated with holding more stereotypical sexual and gender role attitudes as well as stronger acceptance of women as sex objects and support of dating as a game (Ward, 2002; Ward, Hansbrough, & Walker, 2005). In addition, exposure to traditional imagery in music videos is associated with adversarial sexual beliefs (Kalof, 1999). Furthermore, research suggests that greater exposure to violent rap music videos is associated with greater acceptance of violence: participants viewing violent music videos were found more likely to accept the use of violence, report a higher likelihood to use violence, and accept violence against women (Johnson, Jackson, & Gatto 1995).

As Adams and Fuller (2006) point out, the roots and impact of mysogynism in rap music must be understood in the history and context of racism in the United States, which includes racialized misogyny. Fully understanding the meanings and impact of exposure to such themes on women and men of diverse class and ethnicity will require consideration of this historical and situational context and multilevel approaches. Media influences have been found to shape perceptions, beliefs, attitudes, and behaviors that link power, sexuality, and violence against women. Given the rapid spread of new technology, opportunity for exposure to music containing messages of explicit sexualized violence against women will continue to increase dramatically. The concomitant need for more sophisticated understandings of how gender, race, and class intersect to mediate and moderate the meanings and outcomes of such exposure makes prevention activities in this area an urgent priority.

Mass media can be used to promote sexualized views of women, foster links between sexuality and subordination, and reinforce behaviors and practices that undermine gender-based violence. But it can also be used as a means to educate the public about the pervasiveness, multiple manifestations, causes, and consequences of such violence. There is now a growing body of interdisciplinary research on gender-based violence that is being applied in public education programs, reflected in criminal justice and health care systems, and influencing new laws and policies cross-nationally that provide models for designed evidence-based culturally-sensitive prevention and intervention programs (Heise et al. 1999; Jasinski & Williams, 1998; Koss et al., 2003; Koss, et al., 1994; Renzetti, Edleson, & Bergen, 2001; Russo, Koss, & Ramos, 2000; World Health Organization [WHO], 2002, 2004).

OUTCOMES OF VIOLENCE

The destructive effects of male violence extend beyond the woman to her family and society. The negative physical and mental health effects have concomitant social and economic costs. In the United States alone, the costs of intimate violence are estimated to exceed $5.8 billion each year. More than two-thirds of that cost ($ 4.1 billion) goes for direct medical and mental health care service delivery (NCIPC, 2003).

Women who have been victimized suffer both immediate and long-range consequences to their physical and mental well-being, and these consequences are similar for multiple forms of victimization (Browne, 1997; Coker, Smith, King, & McKeown, 2000; Goodman, Koss & Russo., 1993; Heise et al., 1999; Herrera, et al., 2006; Koss & Heslet, 1992; Koss, et al., 2003; Krug et al., 2002; Resnick, Acierno, & Kilpatrick, 1997). Although many effects are immediately apparent following the violent episode(s), other effects may surface as intermittent problems or may last for years (Goodman et al., 1993; Koss & Heslet, 1992; Koss et al. 1991). Depression and anxiety increase with ongoing violence (Sutherland, Bybee, & Sullivan, 1998) and decrease as violence diminishes or stops (Campbell & Sullivan, 1994). Revictimization complicates the understanding of outcomes (Beitchman et al., 1992). Women who experience child sexual abuse have higher risk for experiencing rape and other forms of victimization in adulthood (Resnick, Acierno, & Kilpatrick, 1997; Russo & Denious, 2001; Wyatt, Guthrie, & Notgrass, 1992; Koss, et al., 2003).

Indirect effects of partner violence can be far reaching. One of the major indirect consequences of gender-based violence is the effect on children who may witness or be involved in the abuse (for reviews, see Geffner, Jaffe, & Suderman, 2000; Holden, Geffner, & Jouriles, 1998; Koss et al., 2003). Violence against women and against children is highly correlated—if one is being abused, it is likely that the other is as well. Even when children are not abused themselves, witnessing partner violence may have far-reaching consequences. Male children who have witnessed a father batter a mother are more likely to use violence in their own adult lives than those from nonabusive homes (Straus, Gelles, & Steinmetz, 1980). In addition, partner violence in the home is predictive of children's general psychopathology (McCloskey *et al.*, 1995). Even sibling and parental warmth fail to buffer the negative effects of partner violence on children's mental health.

That violence has multiple biological, neurological, physiological, biological, behavioral, social, and economic consequences for women and their families is no longer in doubt. The focus now is on identifying the pathways between the various forms of IPV and its multiple outcomes that so complicate the development of effective prevention and treatment (Babcock, Green, & Robie, 2004). New integrative and interdisciplinary theoretical perspectives as well as multilevel methods that encompass biobehavioral and sociocultural perspectives are needed (e.g., Dutton *et al.*, 2006).

VIOLENCE AND REPRODUCTIVE ISSUES

Reproductive consequences of intimate violence including childhood sexual abuse, rape, and partner violence, include high-risk sexual behavior and sexually transmitted diseases (Koss et al., 1991; Sturm, Carr, Luxenberg, Swoyer, & Cicero, 1990).

In particular, IPV and unwanted pregnancy would be expected to be linked for a variety of reasons (see Russo & Denious, 1998). Violent partners are more likely to demand unprotected sex and refuse to use a condom (Russo & Denious, 2001). Having a child also increases a women's dependency on her partner and, for him, it becomes an additional point of leverage to exercise control via threats to harm the child (Ptacek, 1997).

Indeed, unwanted pregnancy is highly correlated with exposure to intimate violence including childhood physical and sexual abuse, rape, and partner violence (Dietz, Spitz, Anda, Williamson, McMahon et al., 2000; Russo & Denious, 2001; Wyatt, Guthrie, & Notgrass, 1992). In the United States, among new mothers who reported that their husband or partner had "physically hurt" them during the 12 months before delivery, 70% also reported their pregnancy was unintended (Gazmararian et al. 1995). The positive association is strongest among unmarried women, reminding us that national surveys that focus solely on married women underestimate the prevalence of intimate partner violence in women's lives (Gazmararian et al., 1995).

Cross-culturally, Kishor and Johnson (2004) found that in eight of nine countries studied, experiencing partner violence was linked with a higher likelihood of having an unwanted birth. The extent to which forced pregnancy might be used as a tactic to keep women from leaving a violent relationship is unknown. Also unknown is the level of contribution forced pregnancy may make to the persistence of high rates of unintended pregnancy around the globe (Russo, 2006).

A focus on pregnancy intendedness or wantedness among children born does not encompass what are arguably the most unwanted pregnancies, that is, those terminated by abortion. Differential access to abortion may contribute to differences in rates of unwanted pregnancies ending in births across countries, making cross-cultural comparisons problematic. Research on violence in the lives of women who have abortions confirms a strong link between violence and unintended and unwanted pregnancy. Women who report having an abortion are more likely to report experiencing childhood physical and/or sexual abuse, being a victim of rape (by someone other than the intimate partner), having a violent partner, and having a partner who refused to wear a condom (Russo & Denious, 2001).

Analyses of data from the National Comorbidity Survey comparing women who had an abortion versus delivery on their first pregnancy found a similar pattern of results with regard to experience of rape, molestation, child physical abuse, being held captive/kidnapped/threatened with a weapon, or being physically attacked: 39% of women in the abortion group experienced some type of violence compared to 26.8% of women in the birth group. In particular, women in the abortion group had significantly higher rates of rape (15.1% vs. 7.5%) and molestation (18.3% vs. 11.6%), respectively. Women who reported multiple abortions (an indicator of repeat unwanted pregnancy) were significantly more likely to be physically attacked (21.5%) than women who reported none (6.7%) or one (7.9%) abortion; 41% of women who had two or more abortions experienced some form of violence (Steinberg & Russo, 2007).

These findings have important implications for policy and practice in the context of the current sociopolitical context in which some researchers are seeking to prove that abortion has damaging health consequences to justify public policies restricting abortion access (Russo & Denious, 2005). Insofar as such efforts encourage women who have histories of victimization or currently live in violent contexts to attribute their mental health problems to their abortion experience, such efforts may set back the progress that has been made in helping women focus on and deal with the consequences of experiencing such violence. It has even been suggested that a history of abortion may serve as a marker for identifying patients at risk for mental health problems (e.g., Cougle, Reardon, & Coleman, 2004).

But when experience of violence and other covariates are properly controlled, having an abortion is not found to have a significant effect on mental health outcomes, whether generalized anxiety disorder, social anxiety, or PTSD are measured. However, being raped, physically attacked, and held captive/threatened with a weapon continue to be independent predictors of mental health outcomes when pregnancy outcome and relevant covariates are controlled. These findings are congruent with the results of numerous studies, including longitudinal research, that support a causative role for victimization in the development of negative mental health outcomes as well as risk for unwanted pregnancy (e.g., Dietz, Spitz, & Anda, 2000).

Thus, emphasizing abortion as a marker or screening factor is inappropriate insofar as focusing on abortion distracts attention from factors that actually do increase risk for mental health problems. It is the violence in women's lives that is associated with unwanted pregnancy—violence that occurs and puts women at higher risk for mental health problems regardless of pregnancy outcome. It is important that clinicians explore the effects of violence in women's lives to avoid misattribution of the negative mental health outcomes of victimization to having an abortion (Rubin & Russo, 2004). To do otherwise may be to impede full understanding of the origins of women's mental health problems and prolong their psychological distress.

CONCLUSION

Gender-based violence is a complex, multifaceted phenomenon that is experienced differently by women and men. As such, sophisticated approaches in theory and method are needed to conceptualize and study the factors that mediate and moderate the relation of gender to the experience of intimate violence. Such violence takes multiple forms, is rooted in patriarchal social structures and cultural roles of women and men, and is reinforced by media images. The psychological, social, and behavioral effects of such violence on women, men, families, and society are widespread and long lasting, Understanding, predicting, and preventing gender-based violence will require a complex and comprehensive approach that intervenes at individual, interpersonal, and structural levels and that is responsive to cultural difference.

REFERENCES

Amnesty International (2004). *It's in our hands: Stop violence against women*. Osney Mead, Oxford, United Kingdom: Alden Press.

Adams, T. M. & Fuller, D B. (2006). The words have changed but the ideology remains the same: Misogynistic lyrics in rap music. *Journal of Black Studies, 36*, 938–957.

Anderson, C.A. & Bushman, B.J. (2002). Human aggression. *Annual Review of Psychology, 53*, 2377–2378.

Anderson, C.A., Carnagey, N.L. & Eubanks, J. (2003). Exposure to violent media: The effects of songs with violent lyrics on aggressive thoughts and feelings. *Journal of Personality and Social Psychology, 84*, 960–971.

Anderson, K.L. (2005). Theorizing gender in intimate partner violence research. *Sex Roles, 52*, 853–865.

Anderson, K.L. & Umberson, D. (2001) Gendering violence: Masculinity and power in men's accounts of domestic violence. *Gender & Society, 15*, 358–380.

Archer, J. (2000). Sex differences in aggression between heterosexual partners: A meta-analytic review. *Psychological Bulletin, 126*, 651–680.

Archer, J. (2002). Sex differences in physically aggressive acts between heterosexual partners: A meta- analytic review. *Aggressive and Violent Behavior, 7*, 313–351.

Babcock, J.C., Green, C.E. & Robie C. (2004). Does batterers' treatment work? A meta-analytic review of domestic violence treatment. *Clinical Psychology Review, 23*, 1023–1053.

Bair-Merritt, M.H., Blackstone, M. & Feudtner, C. (2006) Physical health outcomes of childhood exposure to intimate partner violence: A systematic review. *Pediatrics, 117*, 278–290.

Bargh, J.A., Raymond, P., Pryor, J.B. & Strack, F. (1995). Attractiveness of the underling: An automatic power → sex association and its consequences for sexual harassment and aggression. *Journal of Personality and Social Psychology, 68*, 768–781.

Barongan, C. & Hall, G. (1996). The influence of misogynous rap music on sexual aggression against women. *Psychology of Women Quarterly, 19*, 195–207.

Beitchman, J.H., Zucker, K.J., Hood, J.E., DaCosta, G.A., Akman, D. & Cassavia, E. (1992). A review of the long-term effects of child sexual abuse. *Child Abuse and Neglect, 16*, 101–118.

Berns, N. (2001). Degendering the problem and gendering the blame: Political discourse on violence against women. *Gender & Society, 15*, 262–281.

Bourne, L.E. Jr. & Russo, N.F. (1998). *Psychology: Behavior in Context*. New York, NY: W.W. Norton.

Brice-Baker, J.R. (1994). Domestic Violence in African-American and African-Caribbean families. Special Issue: Multicultural views on domestic violence. *Journal of Social Distress and the Homeless, 3*, 23–38.

Brinson, S. (1992). The use and opposition of rape myths in prime-time television dramas. *Sex Roles, 27*, 359–375.

Brown, J.D., Steele, J.R. & Walsh-Childers, K. (Ed.) (2002). *Sexual teens, sexual media: Investigating media's influence on adolescent sexuality*. Hillsdale, NJ: Lawrence Erlbaum.

Browne, A. (1997). Violence in marriage: Until death do us part? In A.P. Cardarelli (Ed). *Violence between intimate partners: Patterns, causes, and effects* (pp. 48–69). Needham Heights, MA: Allyn & Bacon.

BROWNMILLER, S. (1975). *Against our will: Men, women and rape*. New York, NY: Simon and Schuster.
BRUSH, L. (1990). Violent acts and injurious outcomes in married couples: Methodological issues in the National Survey of Families and Households. *Gender & Society*, 4, 56–67.
BRUSH, L. (2005). Philosophical and political issues in research on women's violence and aggression. *Sex Roles*, 52, 867–874.
BRYANT, J. & ZILLMAN, D. (Eds.) Media effects: Advances in theory and research (pp. 17–41). Hillsdale, NJ: Lawrence Erlbaum.
BUCHBINDER, E. & EISIKOVITS, Z. (2003). Battered women's entrapment in shame: A phenomenological study. *American Journal of Orthopsychiatry*, 73, 355–366.
BURNETT, R. (1995). *Gendered objectification experiences: Construct validity, implications for depression and phenomenology*. Dissertation. Duke University. (Summary available at www.JeanHamiltonMD.com).
BUFKIN, J. & ESCHHOLZ, S. (2000). Images of sex and rape: A content analysis of popular film. *Violence Against Women*, 6, 1317–1344.
BURT, M. (1980). Cultural myths and support for rape. *Journal of Personality and Social Psychology*, 38, 217–230.
CAMPBELL, J.C. (2002). Health consequences of intimate partner violence. *Lancet*, 359, 1331–1336.
CAMPBELL, J.C. & LEWANDOWSKI, L.A. (1997). Mental and physical health effects of intimate partner violence on women and children. *Psychiatric Clinics of North America*, 20(2), 353–374.
CAPUTI, J. (2003). Everyday pornography. In G. Dines & J. Humez (Eds.) *Race, Gender, and Class in Media* (pp. 434–450). Thousand Oaks: Sage Publications.
CHESTER, B., ROBIN, R., KOSS, M. & GOODMAN, D. (1994). Grandmother dishonored: Violence against women by male partners in American Indian communities. Special Issue: Violence against women of color. *Violence and Victims*, 9, 249–258.
COKER, A.L., DAVIS, K.E., ARIAS, I., DESAI, S., SANDERSON, M., BRANDT, H.M. & SMITH, P.H. (2002). Physical and mental health effects of intimate partner violence for men and women, *American Journal of Preventive Medicine*, 23, 260–268.
COKER, A.L., SMITH, P.H., BETHEA, L., KING, M. & MCKEOWN, R.E. (2000). Physical health consequences of physical and psychological intimate partner violence. *Archives of Family Medicine*, 9, 451–457.
COLTRANE, S. (2000). Research on household labor: Modeling and measuring the social embeddedness of routine family work. *Journal of Marriage and the Family*, 62, 1208–1233.
CORNE, S., BRIERE, J. & ESSES, L.M. (1992). Women's attitudes and fantasies about rape as a function of early exposure to pornography. *Journal of Interpersonal Violence*, 7, 454–461.
COUGLE J.R., REARDON D.C. & COLEMAN, P. K. (2004). Generalized anxiety following unintended pregnancies resolved through childbirth and abortion: a cohort study of the 1995 National Survey of Family Growth. *Journal of Anxiety Disorders*, 19, 137–146.
DEAUX, K. & MAJOR, B. (1987). Putting gender into context: An interactive model of gender-related behavior. *Psychological Review*, 94(3), 369–389.
DEMARÉ, D., BRIERE, J. & LIPS, H.M. (1988). Violent pornography and self-reported likelihood of sexual aggression. *Journal of Research in Personality*, 22, 140–153.

DeKeseredy, W.S. & Schwartz, M.D. (1998). Measuring the extent of woman abuse in intimate heterosexual relationships: A critique of the Conflict Tactics Scales. U.S. Department of Justice, Violence Against Women Online Resources. Available at http://www.vaw.uma.edu/documents/vawnet/ctscritique/ctscritique.html.

Desai, S. & Saltzman, L.E. (2001). Measurement issues for violence against women. In C. M. Renzetti, J. L. Edleson & R. K. Bergen (Eds.) *Sourcebook on violence against women* (pp. 35–52). Thousand Oaks, CA: Sage.

Dietz, P., Spitz, A.M., Anda, R.F., Williamson, D.G., McMahon, P.M., Santelli, J.S., Nordenberg, D.F., Filetti, V.J. & Kendrick, J. S. (2000). Unintended pregnancy among adult women exposed to abuse or household dysfunction during their childhood, *Journal of the American Medical Association*, *282*, 1259–1364.

Dobash, R.P. & Dobash, R.E. (1977). *Violence against wives: A case against patriarchy*. New York, NY: The Free Press.

Donnerstein, E. (1980). Aggressive erotica and violence against women. *Journal of Personality and Social Psychology*, *39*, 269–277.

Dutton, D.G. (1988). *The abusive personality: Violence and control in intimate relationships*. New York, NY: Guilford Press.

Dutton, M.A., Burghardt, K.J., Perrin, S.G., Chrestman, K.R. & Haile, P.M. (1994). Battered women's cognitive schemata. *Journal of Traumatic Stress*, *7*, 237–255.

Dutton, M.A. & Goodman, L. (2005). Coercive control and intimate partner violence: toward a new conceptualization. *Sex Roles*, *52*, 743–756.

Dutton, M.A., Goodman, L.A. & Bennet, L. (1999). Court-involved battered women's responses to violence: The role of psychological, physical, and sexual abuse. *Violence and Victims*, *14*, 89–104.

Dutton, M.A., Green, B., Kaltman, S. I., Roesch, D.M., Zeffiro, T.A., Krause, E.D. (2006). Intimate partner violence, PTSD, and adverse health outcomes. *Journal of Interpersonal Violence*, *21*, 955–968.

Dwyer, D.C., Smokowski, P.R., Bricout, J.C. & Wodarski, J.S. (1995). Domestic violence research: Theoretical and practical implications for social work. *Clinical Social Work Journal*, *23*, 185–198.

Edwards, A. (1991). Male violence in feminist theory: An analysis of the changing conceptions of sex/gender violence and male dominance. In J. Hamner & M. Maynard (Eds.), *Women, violence, and social control* (pp. 13–29). Atlantic Highands, NJ: Humanities Press International.

Eisikovits, Z.C. & Enosh, G. (1997). Awareness of guilt and shame in intimate violence. *Violence and Victims*, *12*, 307–322.

Ellsberg, M.C.L., Heise, L., Pena, R., Agurto, S. & Winkvist, A. (2001). Researching domestic violence against women: Methodological and ethical considerations. *Studies in Family Planning*, *32*, 1–16.

Finkelhor, D. & Yllö, K. (1985). *License to rape: Sexual abuse of wives*. New York: Holt, Reinhardt, and Winston.

Fischer, A.R. & Good, G.E. (1998). New directions for the study of gender role attitudes: A cluster analytic investigation of masculinity ideologies. *Psychology of Women Quarterly*, *22*, 371–384.

Folkman, S. & Moskowitz, J.T. (2004). Coping: Pitfalls and promise. *Annual Review of Psychology*, *55*, 745–774.

Follingstad, D.R., Bradley, R.G., Laughlin, J.E. & Burke, L. (1999). Risks factor and correlates of dating violence: The relevance of examining frequency and severity levels in a college sample. *Violence and Victims, 14,* 365–380.

FRABLE, D.E.S. (1997). Gender, Racial, Ethnic, Sexual, and Class Identities. *Annual Review of Psychology 48,* 139–62.

FREDRICKSON, B. & ROBERTS, T-A. (1997). Objectification theory: Towards an understanding of women's lived experiences. *Psychology of Women Quarterly, 21,* 173–206.

FRIEZE, I.H. (2000). Violence in close relationships—development of a research area: Comment on Archer (2000). *Psychological Bulletin, 126,* 681–684.

FRIEZE, I.H. (2005). Female violence against intimate partners: An introduction. *Psychology of Women Quarterly, 29,* 229–237.

FRIEZE, I.H. & DAVIS, K. (2002). Perspectives on stalking research. In K.E. Davis, I.H. Frieze & R.D. Mariuro (Eds.), *Stalking: Perspectives on victims and their perpetrators* (pp. 1–5). New York, NY: Springer.

FRIEZE, I.H. & MCHUGH, M.(Eds.) (2005). Female violence against intimate partners. *Psychology of Women Quarterly, 29,* Whole No. 3.

GARCIA-MORENO, C., WATTS, C., JANSEN, H., ELLSBERG, M. & HEISE, L. (2003). Responding to violence against women: WHO's multicountry study on women's health and domestic violence. *Health and Human Rights,* 6(2), 113–127. Available from http://www.who.int/gender/documents/en/vawhealthandhumanrights.pdf.

GAZMARARIAN, J.A., , M.M., SALTZMAN, L.E., JOHNSON, C.H., BRUCE, F.C., MARKS, J.S. & ZAHNISER, S.C. (1995). The relationship between pregnancy intendedness and physical violence in mothers of newborns. *Obstetrics & Gynecology, 85,* 1031–1038.

GEFFNER, R., JAFFE, P.G. & SUDERMANN, M. (2000). *Children exposed to domestic violence: Current research, interventions, prevention, & policy development.* New York, NY: Haworth Press.

GILES-SIMS, J. (1998). The aftermath of partner violence. In J.L. Jasinski & L.M. Williams (Eds.), *Partner violence: A comprehensive review of 20 years of research* (pp. 44–72). Thousand Oaks, CA: Sage.

GOODMAN, L.A., KOSS, M.P. & RUSSO, N.F. (1993). Violence against women: Physical and mental health effects. Part I: Research findings. *Applied & Preventive Psychology: Current Scientific Perspectives, 2,* 79–89.

GOODRUM, S., UMBERSON, D. & ANDERSON, K.L. (2001). The batterer's view of the self and others in domestic violence. *Sociological Inquiry, 71,* 221–241.

GOW, J. (1990). The relationship between violent and sexual images and the popularity of music videos. *Popular Music and Society,* 14(4), 1–10.

GREESON, L.E. & WILLIAMS, R.A. (1986). Social implications of music videos for youth. *Youth and Society, 18,* 177–189.

GROTH, A. (1979). *Men who rape: The psychology of the offender.* New York, NY: Plenum.

GUTIERRES, S.E., RUSSO, N.F., URBANSKI, L. (1994). Sociocultural and psychological factors in American Indian drug use: Implications for treatment. *International Journal of the Addictions, 29,* 1761–1786.

HAMBY, S. (2005). Measuring gender differences in partner violence: Implications from research on other forms of violent and socially undesirable behavior. *Sex Roles,* 52(11), 725–742.

HAMILTON, J.A. & RUSSO, N.F. (2006). Women and depression: Research theory and social policy. *In* C.L.M. keyes & S.H. Goodman (Eds.), Women and Depression:

A handbook for the social, behavorial, and biomedical sciences (pp. 479–522). New York, NY: Cambridge University Press.

HARNED, M.S. (2001). Abused women or abused men? An examination of the context and outcomes of dating violence. *Violence and Victims, 16*, 269–285.

HARRISON, L.A. & ABRISHAMI, G. (2004). Dating violence attributes: Do they differ for in-group and out-group members who have a history of dating violence? *Sex Roles, 51*, 543–550.

HEISE, L.L. (1998). Violence against women: An integrated, ecological framework. *Violence Against Women, 4*(3), 262–290.

HEISE, L.L., ELLSBERG, M. & GOTTEMOELLER, M. (1999, December). Ending violence against women. Population reports, Series L, No.11. (pp. 1–45). Baltimore, MD: Johns Hopkins University School of Public Health, Population Information Program.

HEISE, L.L., PITANGUY, J. & GERMAIN A. (1994). Violence against women: The hidden health burden. World Bank Discussion Paper #225. Washington, D.C.: The World Bank.

HERRERA, V.M., KOSS, M.P., BAILEY, J., YUAN, N.P. & LICHTER, E.I. (2006). Survivors of male violence: Research and training initiatives to facilitate recovery from depression and posttraumatic stress disorder. In J. Worell & C.D. Goodheart (Eds.). *Handbook of Girls' and Women's Psychological Health* (pp. 455–466). New York, NY: Oxford University Press.

HOLDEN, G., GEFFNER, R. & JOURILES, E. (Eds.). (1998). *Children exposed to marital violence: Theory, research, and applied issues.* Washington, DC: American Psychological Association.

HUSTON, A.C., WARTELLA, E. & DONNERSTEIN, E. (1998). *Measuring the effects of sexual content in the media.* Menlo Park, CA: Kaiser Family Foundation.

HUSTON, A.C, DONNERSTEIN, E., FAIRCHILD, H.H, FESHBACH, N.D, KATZ, P.A, MURRAY, J.P, RUBINSTEIN, E.A, WILCOX, B.L & ZUCKERMAN, D. (1992). *Big world, small screen: The role of television in American society.* Lincoln, NE: University of Nebraska Press.

JASINSKI, J.L. (2001). Physical violence among Anglo, African American, and Hispanic couples: Ethnic differences in persistence and cessation. *Violence and Victims, 16*, 479–490.

JASINSKI, J.L. & WILLIAMS, L.M. (Eds.) (1998). Partner violence: A comprehensive review of 20 years of research. Thousand Oaks, CA: Sage Publications, Inc.

JENKINS, S.S. & AUBÉ, J. (2002). Gender differences and gender-related constructs in dating aggression. *Personality and Social Psychology Bulletin, 28*, 1106–1118.

JENSEN, R. (1995). Pornographic lives. *Violence Against Women, 1*, 32–54.

JOHNSON, J., JACKSON, L. & GATTO, L. (1995). Violent attitudes and deferred academic aspirations: Deleterious effects of exposure to rap music. *Basic and Applied Social Psychology, 16*, 27–41.

JOHNSON, M.P., (1995). Patriarchal terrorism and common couple violence: Two forms of violence against women. *Journal of Marriage and the Family, 75*, 283–294.

JOHNSON, M.P. & FERRARO K.J. (2000). Research on domestic violence in the 1990s: Making distinctions. *Journal of Marriage and Family, 62*, 948–963.

KAISER FAMILY FOUNDATION. (1999, March 1). *Kids ready to talk about today's tough issues before their parents are: Sex, AIDS, violence, and drugs/alcohol.* Press release.

KALOF, L. (1999). The effects of gender and music video imagery on sexual attitudes. *The Journal of Social Psychology, 139*, 378–385.

KAURA, S.A. & ALLEN, C.M. (2004). Dissatisfaction with relationship power and dating violence perpetration by men and women. *Journal of Interpersonal Violence, 19,* 576–588.

KELLER, E.L. (1996). Invisible victims: Battered women in psychiatric and medical emergency rooms. *Bulletin of the Menninger Clinic, 60,* 1–21.

KELLY, L. (1988). *Surviving sexual violence.* Minneapolis, MN: University of Minnesota Press.

KENNEDY, A.C., (2006). Urban adolescent mothers exposed to community, family, and partner violence: Prevalence, outcomes, and welfare policy implications. *American Journal of Orthopsychiatry, 76,* 44–54.

KILPATRICK, D.G. (1990). Violence as a precursor of women's substance abuse: The rest of the drugs-violence story. Presented in the symposium *Critical Issue—Substance Abuse and Violence: Drugs and Violent Crime.* American Psychological Association Convention, Boston MA.

KIMMEL, M.S. (2002). "Gender symmetry" in domestic violence: A substantive and methodological research review. *Violence Against Women, 8,* 1332–1363.

KISHOR, S. & JOHNSON, K. (2004). *Profiling domestic violence: A multi–country study.* Calverton, MD: ORC Macro.

KOOP, C.E. (1985). *The surgeon general's workshop on violence and the public health.* Washington, DC: US Government Printing Office.

KOSS, M.P. (1988). Women's mental health research agenda: Violence against women. *Women's Mental Health Occasional Paper Series.* Washington, DC: National Institute of Mental Health.

KOSS, M.P. & HESLET, L. (1992). Somatic consequences of violence against women. *Archives of Family Medicine, 1,* 53–59.

KOSS, M.P., BAILEY, J.A., YUAN, N.P., HERRERA, V. M. & LICHTER, E.L. (2003). Depression and PTSD in survivors of male violence: Research and training initiatives to facilitate recovery. *Psychology of Women Quarterly, 27,* 130–142.

KOSS, M.P., GOODMAN, L.A., BROWNE, A., FITZGERALD, L., KEITA, G.P. & RUSSO, N.F. (1994) *No safe haven: Male violence against women at home, at work, and in the community.* Washington, DC: American Psychological Association.

KOSS, M.P., HEISE, L. & RUSSO, N.F. (1994). The global health burden of rape. *Psychology of Women Quarterly, 18,* 509–530.

KOSS, M.P., KOSS, P.G. & WOODRUFF, W.J. (1991). Deleterious effects of criminal victimization on women's health and medical utilization. *Archives of Internal Medicine, 151,* 342–357.

KRAHÉ, B., BIENECK, S. & MÖLLER, I. (2005). Understanding gender and intimate partner violence from an international perspective. *Sex Roles, 52,* 807–827.

KRUG, E.G., DAHLBERG, L.L., MERCY, J.A., ZWI, A.B. & LOZANO, R. (2002). *World report on violence and health.* Geneva, Switzerland: World Health Organization.

LINZ, D.G., DONNERSTEIN, E. & PENROD, S. (1984). The effects of multiple exposures to filmed violence against women. *Journal of Communication, 34,* 130–147.

LINZ, D.G., DONNERSTEIN, E. & PENROD, S. (1988). Effects of long-term exposure to violent and sexual degrading depictions of women. *Journal of Personality and Social Psychology, 55,* 758–768.

LOWRY, D.T. & SHIDLER, J.A. (1993). Primetime TV portrayals of sex, "safe sex," and AIDS: A longitudinal analysis. *Journalism Quarterly, 70,* 628–637.

MADRIZ, E. (1997). Images of criminals and victims: A study on women's fear and social control. *Gender & Society, 11,* 342–356.

Malamuth, N.M. & Ceniti, J. (1986). Repeated exposure to violent and nonviolent pornography: Likelihood of raping ratings and laboratory aggression against women. *Aggressive Behavior*, *12*, 129–137.

Malamuth, N.M., Check, J.V.P. & Briere, J. (1986). Sexual arousal in response to aggression: Ideological, aggressive, and sexual correlates. *Journal of Personality and Social Psychology*, *50*, 330–340.

Marin, A.J. & Russo, N.F., (1999). Feminist perspectives on male violence against women: Critiquing O'Neil and Harway's model. In J.M. O'Neil & M. Harway (Eds.). *New Perspectives on Violence Against Women* (pp. 18–35). Thousand Oaks, CA: Sage Publications.

Marsh, C. (1993). Sexual assault and domestic violence in the African American community. *Western Journal of Black Studies*, *17*, 149–155.

Marshall, L.L. (1992a). Development of the severity of violence against women scales. *Journal of Family Violence*, *7*, 103–121.

Marshall, L.L. (1992b). The severity of violence against men scales. *Journal of Family Violence*, *7*, 189–203.

McCloskey, L.A., Figueredo, A.J., Koss, M.P. (1995). The effects of systemic family violence on children's mental health. *Child Development*, *66*, 1239–1261.

McHugh, M.C. (2005). Understanding gender and intimate partner abuse. *Sex Roles*, *52*, 717–724.

McHugh, M.C. & Frieze, I.H. (Eds.) (2005). Understanding gender and intimate partner violence: Theoretical and empirical approaches. *Sex Roles*, *52*, Whole No. 11/12.

McHugh, M., Frieze, I.H. & Brown, A. (1993). Research on battered women and their assailants. In F.L. Denmark & M.A. Paludi (Eds.). *Psychology of women: Handbook of issues and theories* (pp. 513–552). Westport, CN: Greenwood Press.

McHugh, M., Livingston, N.A. & Ford, A. (2005). A postmodern approach to women's use of violence: Developing multiple and complex conceptualizations, *Psychology of Women Quarterly*, *29*, 323–336.

McKinley, N.M. (1995). Objectified body consciousness scale. In J.K. Thompson (Ed.). *Exacting beauty: Theory, assessment, and treatment of body image disturbance* (pp. 233–234). Washington, DC: American Psychological Association.

McKinley, N.M. & Hyde, J.S. (1996). The objectified body consciousness scale: Development and validation. *Psychology of Women Quarterly*, *20*, 181–215.

Medea, A. & Thompson, K. (1974). *Against rape*. New York, NY: Farrar, Straus and Giroux.

Meyers, M. (1997). *News coverage of violence against women: Engendering blame*. Newbury Park, CA: Sage.

Mulac, A., Jansma, L.L. & Linz, D.G. (2002). Men's behavior toward women after viewing sexually-explicit films: Degradation makes a difference. *Communication Monographs*, *69*, 311–328.

National Center for Injury Prevention and Control (2003). *Costs of intimate partner violence against women in the United States*. Atlanta, GA: Centers for Disease Control and Prevention.

Norton, I. & Manson, S. (1995). A silent minority: Battered American Indian women. *Journal of Family Violence*, *10*, 307–318.

Pardun, C.J., L'Engle, K.L. & Brown, J.D. (2005). Linking exposure to outcomes: Early adolescents' consumption of sexual content in six media. *Mass Communication & Society*, *8*, 75–91.

PERILLA, J., BAKERMAN, R., NORRIS, F. (1994). Culture and domestic violence: The ecology of abused Latinas. *Violence and Victims, 9*, 325–339.

PERRY, I. (2003). Who(se) am I? The identity and image of women in hip hop. In G. Dines & J. Humez (Eds.), *Gender, Race, and Class in Media* (pp. 136–148). Thousand Oaks, CA: Sage Publications.

PRINCETON SURVEY RESEARCH ASSOCIATES. (1996). *The Kaiser Family Foundation survey on teens and sex: What they say teens need to know and who they listen to*. Menlo Park, CA: Kaiser Family Foundation.

PRYOR, J.B. (1987). Sexual harassment proclivities in men. *Sex Roles, 17*, 269–290.

PRYOR, J.B., LAVITE, C.M. & STOLLER, L.M. (1993). A social psychological analysis of sexual harassment: The person/situation interaction. *Journal of Vocational Behavior, 42*, 68–83.

PRYOR, J.B. & STOLLER, L.M. (1994). Sexual cognition processes in men high in the likelihood to sexually harass. *Personality and Social Psychology Bulletin, 20*, 163–169.

PTACEK, J. (1997). The tactics and strategies of men who batter: Testimony from women seeking extreme orders. In A.P. Cardarelli (Ed), *Violence between intimate partners: Patterns, causes, and effects* (pp. 104–123). Needham Heights, MA: Allyn & Bacon.

RAMOS, L., KOSS, M.P. & RUSSO, N.F. (1999). Mexican-American women's definitions of rape and sexual abuse. *Hispanic Journal of Behavioral Sciences, 21*(3), 236–265.

RANDO, R.A., ROGERS, J.R. & BRITTAN-POWELL, C.S. (1998). Gender role conflict and college men's sexually aggressive attitudes and behavior. *Journal of Mental Health Counseling, 20*, 359–369.

RENZETTI, C.M., EDLESON, J.L. & BERGEN, R.K. (Eds.) (2001). *Sourcebook on violence against women*. Thousand Oaks, CA, Sage Publications, Inc.

RESNICK, H.S., ACIERNO, R. & KILPATRICK, D.G. (1997). Health impact of interpersonal violence. 2: Medical and mental health outcomes. *Behavioural Medicine, 23*, 65–78.

RICHARDSON, D.S. (2005), The myth of the female passivity: thirty years of revelations about female aggression. *Psychology of Women Quarterly, 29*, 313–322.

RIDGEWAY, C.L. & SMITH-LOVIN, L. (1999). The Gender system and interaction. *Annual Review of Sociology, 25*, 191–216.

ROBERTS, D.F. (2000). Media and youth: Access, exposure, and privatization. *Journal of Adolescent Health, 27*, 8–14.

RUBIN, L. & RUSSO, N.F. (2004). Abortion and mental health: What therapists need to know. *Women & Therapy, 27* (3/4), 69–90.

RUDMAN, L.A. (1998). Self-promotion as a risk factor for women: The costs and benefits of counter-stereotypical impression management. *Journal of Personality and Social Psychology, 74*, 629–645.

RUDMAN, L.A. & GLICK, P. (1999). Feminized management and backlash toward agentic women: The hidden costs to women of a kinder, gentler image of middle-managers. *Journal of Personality and Social Psychology, 77*, 1004–1010.

RUDMAN, L.A. & GLICK, P. (2001). Prescriptive gender stereotypes and backlash toward agentic women. *Journal of Social Issues, 4*, 743–762.

RUSSELL, D. (1975). *Rape: The victim's perspective*. New York, NY: Stein and Day.

RUSSELL, D.E.H. (1990). *Rape in marriage*. Bloomington, IN: Indiana University Press.

Russell, D.E.H. (1980). Pornography and violence: What does the new research say? In L. Lederer (Ed.), *Take back the night: Women on pornography* (pp. 218–238). New York, NY: William Morrow.

Russell, D.E.H. (1988). Pornography and rape: A causal model. *Political Psychology, 9*, 41–73.

Russo, N.F. & Denious, J. (1998). Understanding the relationship of violence against women to unwanted pregnancy and its resolution. In L.J. Beckman & S.M. Harvey (Eds.), *The new civil war: The psychology, culture, and politics of abortion* (pp. 211–234). Washington, DC: American Psychological Association.

Russo, N.F. & Denious, J.E. (2001). Violence in the lives of women having abortions: Implications for public policy and practice. *Professional Psychology: Research and Practice, 32*, 142–150.

Russo, N.F. (2006). Violence against women: A global health issue. *Proceedings of the 28th International Congress of Psychology, Bejing, 2004.* New York, NY: Psychology Press (Taylor & Francis Group).

Russo, N.F., Denious, J., Keita, G.P. & Koss, M.P. (1997). Intimate violence and black women's health. *Women's Health: Research on Gender, Behavior, and Public Policy, 3*(3&4), 315–348.

Russo, N.F., Koss, M.P. & Goodman, L. (1995). Male violence against women: A global health and development issue. In Adler, L.L. & Denmark, F.L. *Violence and the prevention of violence* (121–127). Westport, CT: Praeger.

Russo, N.F., Koss, M.P. & Ramos, L. (2000). Rape: A global health issue. In J. Ussher (Ed.), *Women's health: Contemporary international perspectives* (pp. 129–142). London, UK: British Psychological Society.

Sanchez-Hucles, J. & Dutton, M.. (1999). The interaction between societal violence and domestic violence: Racial and cultural factors. In M. Harway & J.M. O'Neil (Eds.), *What causes men's violence against women?* Thousand Oaks, CA: Sage Publications.

Schwartz, M.S. (2000). Methodological issues in the use of survey data for measuring and characterizing violence against women. *Violence Against Women, 6*, 815–838.

Scott-Giliba, E., Minne, C., Mezey, G.C. (1995). The psychological, behavioural and emotional impact of surviving an abusive relationship. *Journal of Forensic Psychiatry, 6*, 343–358.

Shane, B. & Ellsberg, M. (2002). Violence against women: effects on reproductive health. *Outlook, 20*(1), 1–8.

Sherman, B.L. & Dominick, J.R. (1986). Violence and sex in music: TV and rock 'n' roll. *Journal of Communication, 36*, 79–93.

Silbert, M.H. & Pines, A.M. (1984). Pornography and sexual abuse of women. *Sex Roles, 10*, 857–869.

Silverman, J.G., Raj, A., Mucci, L.A. & Hathaway, J.E. (2001). Dating violence against adolescent girls and associated substance use, unhealthy weight control, sexual risk behavior, pregnancy, and suicidality. *Journal of American Medical Association, 286*, 572–579.

Sommers, E.K. & Check, J.V. (1987). An empirical investigation of the role of pornography in the verbal and physical abuse of women. *Violence and Victims, 2*, 189–209.

Sommers-Flanagan, R., Sommers-Flanagan, J. & Davis, B. (1993). What's happening on music television? A gender-role content analysis. *Sex Roles, 28*, 745–753.

SONG, Y.I. (1996). *Battered women in Korean immigrant families: The silent scream.* New York, NY: Garland.
SORENSON, S.B. (1996). Violence against women: examining ethnic differences and commonalities. *Evaluation Review, 20,* 123–145.
SORENSON, S.B. & TAYLOR, C.A. (2005). Females' aggression toward intimate male partners: An examination of social norms in a community-based sample. *Psychology of Women Quarterly, 29*(1), 78–96.
SORENSON, S.B. & TELLES, C.A. (1991). Self-reports of spousal violence in a Mexican-American and non-Hispanic White population. *Violence and Victims, 6,* 3–15.
ST. LAWRENCE, J.S. & JOYNER, D.J. (1991). The effects of sexually violent rock music on males' acceptance of violence against women. *Psychology of Women Quarterly, 15,* 49–63.
STARK, E. & FLITCRAFT, A. (1988). Violence among intimates: An epidemiological review. In V.B. Van Haselt, R.L. Morrison, A.S. Bellack & M. Herson (Eds.), *Handbook of Family Violence,* (pp. 213–293). New York, NY: Plenum Press.
STARK, E. & FLITCRAFT, A. (1996). *Women at risk.* Thousand Oaks, CA: Sage Publications.
STARK, E., FLITCRAFT, A. & FRAZIER, W. (1979). Medicine and patriarchal violence: The social construction of a "private" event. *International Journal of Health Services, 9,* 461–493.
STEINBERG, J.R. & RUSSO, N.F. (2006). Abortion and anxiety disorder: What's the relationship? Unpublished manuscript.
STETS, J. & STRAUS, M.A. (1992). The marriage license as a hitting license. *Physical violence in American families.* New Brunswick, NJ: Transaction Publishers.
STRAUS, M.A., HAMBY, S.L. & WARREN, W.L. (2003). *The conflict tactic scales handbook.* Los Angeles, CA: Western Psychological Services.
STRAUS, M.A. & GELLES, R.J. & STEINMETZ, S. (1980). *Behind closed doors: Violence in the American family.* Garden City, NY: Anchor Press.
STURM, J.T., CARR, M.E., LUXENBERG, M.G., SWOYER, J.K., CICERO, J.J. (1990). The prevalence of Neisseria Gonorrhoea and Chlamydia trichomatous in victims of sexual assault. *Annals of Emergency Medicine, 19,* 142–144.
SULLIVAN, T.P., MEESE, K.J., SWAN, S.C., MAZURE, C.M. & SNOW, D.L. (2005). Precursors and correlates of women's violence: Child abuse traumatization, victimization of women, avoidance coping, and psychological symptoms. *Psychology of Women Quarterly, 29,* 290–301.
SUN, S.W. & LULL, J. (1986). The adolescent audience for music videos and why they watch. *Journal of Communication, 36,* 115–125.
TICHENOR, V. (2005) Maintaining men's dominance: Negotiating identity and power when she earns more, *Sex Roles, 53,* 191–206.
TIGGEMANN, M. & KURING, J.K. (2004). The role of body objectification in disordered eating and depressed mood. *British Journal of Clinical Psychology, 43,* 299–311.
TJADEN, P. & THOENNES, P. (2000). *Full report of the prevalence, incidence, and consequences of violence against women: Findings from the National Violence Against Women Survey.* Washington DC: National Institute of Justice/Centers for Disease Control and Prevention. Available at: http://www.ojp.usdoj.gov/nij.
TOLMAN, R.M., EDLESON, J.L. & FRENDRICH, M. (1996). The applicability of the theory of planned behavior to abusive men's cessation of violent behavior. *Violence and Victims, 11,* 341–345.

UNITED NATIONS (1989). *Violence against women in the family.* New York, NY: United Nations.
UNITED NATIONS (1995). *Report of the Fourth World Conference on Women, Beijing 4-15 September 1995.* New York, NY: United Nations.
UNITED NATIONS GENERAL ASSEMBLY (1993, December 20). *Declaration on the elimination of violence against women.* Proceedings of the 85th Plenary Meeting, Geneva, Switzerland.
VAN ANDERS, S.M. (2004). Why the academic pipeline leaks: Fewer men than women perceive barriers to becoming professors. *Sex Roles, 51,* 511–522.
VINCENT, R.C., DAVIS, D.K. & BORUSZKOWSKI, L.A. (1987). Sexism on MTV: The portrayal of women in rock videos. *Journalism Quarterly, 64,* 750–755, 941.
WARD, L.M. (2002). Does television exposure affect emerging adults' attitudes and assumptions about sexual relationships? Correlational and experimentational confirmation. *Journal of Youth and Adolescence, 31,* 1–15.
WARD, L.M., HANSBROUGH, E. & WALKER, E. (2005). Contributions of music video exposure to Black adolescents' gender and sexual schemas. *Journal of Adolescent Research, 20,* 143–166.
WEST, C.M. (1998). Lifting the "political gag order": Breaking the silence around partner violence in ethnic minority families. In J.L. Jasinski, L.M. Williams *et al.* (Eds.), *Partner violence: A comprehensive review of 20 years of research* (pp. 184–209). Newbury Park, CA.: Sage Publications.
WESTER, S., CROWN, C., QUATMAN, G. & HEESACKER, M. (1997). The influence of sexually violent rap music on attitudes of men with little prior exposure. *Psychology of Women Quarterly, 21,* 497–508.
WESTER, S., CROWN, C., QUATMAN, G. & HEESACKER, M. (1997). The influence of sexually violent rap music on attitudes of men with little prior exposure. *Psychology of Women Quarterly, 21*(4), 497–508.
WHITE, J.W., SMITH, P.H., KOSS, M.P. & FIGUEREDO, A.J. (2000). Intimate partner aggression—what have we learned? Comment on Archer (2000). *Psychological Bulletin, 126,* 690–696.
WORLD HEALTH ORGANIZATION (2001). *Putting women first: Ethical and safety recommendations for research on domestic violence against women.* Geneva, Switzerland: Department of Gender and Women's Health.
WORLD HEALTH ORGANIZATION (2002). *World report on violence and health.*
WORLD HEALTH ORGANIZATION (2004). *Gender-based violence.* Web-site: http://www.who.int/gender/violence.
WYATT, G. (1994). Sociocultural and epidemiological issues in the assessment of domestic violence. *Journal of Social Distress and the Homeless, 3,* 7–21.
WYATT, G.E., GUTHRIE, D. & NOTGRASS, C.M. (1992). Differential effects of women's child sexual abuse and subsequent sexual revictimization. *Journal of Consulting & Clinical Psychology, 60,* 167–173.
YLLÖ, K. (1988). Political and methodological debates in wife abuse research. In K. Yllö and M. Bograd (Eds.), *Feminist perspectives on wife abuse.* Sage Publications: Newbury Park, CA.
ZIMMERMAN, K. (1992, March 16). Censure for censor bills. *Variety,* 72–74.

Restoring Rape Survivors

Justice, Advocacy, and a Call to Action

MARY P. KOSS

University of Arizona, Tucson, Arizona

ABSTRACT: Rape results in mental and physical health, social, and legal consequences. For the latter, restorative justice-based programs might augment community response, but they generate controversy among advocates and policy makers. This article identifies survivors' needs and existing community responses to them. Survivors feel their legal needs are most poorly met due to justice system problems that can be summarized as attrition, retraumatization, and disparate treatment across gender, class, and ethnic lines. Empirical data support each problem and the conclusion that present justice options are inadequate. The article concludes by identifying common ground in advocacy and restorative justice goals and calls for a holistic approach to the needs of rape survivors that includes advocating for expanded justice alternatives. A call to action is issued to implement restorative alternatives to expand survivor choice and offender accountability. Conventional and restorative justice are often viewed as mutually exclusive whereas the author argues they are complementary.

KEYWORDS: date rape; acquaintance rape; sexual assault; restorative justice

RESTORING RAPE SURVIVORS: JUSTICE, ADVOCACY, AND A CALL TO ACTION

Date and acquaintance rape and nonpenetration offenses are many women's only direct experience of violence. Rape affects 18% of American women in their lifetimes according to a recent national survey (Tjaden & Thoennes, 1998). Eight of 10 women were raped by a man they knew. Nonpenetration sexual offenses are even more common. In a recent survey, 49% of female respondents had been victimized by indecent exposure in their lifetime; more than one-third experienced two or more separate crimes (Riordan, 1999). Among college women 5% had someone expose their sexual organs to them *within the past 7 months*, and another 3% were observed naked (Fisher, Cullen & Turner,

2000). A Canadian survey found that 83% of women had received obscene or threatening telephone calls in their *adult lifetime*. (Smith & Morra, 1994). In the United Kingdom 19% of women received obscene phone calls in the *prior year* (Buck, Chatterton & Pease, 1995).

Sexual assault has well-documented deleterious psychological and physical health consequences (e.g., Golding, 1999a; 1999b; Yuan, Koss & Stone, 2006). In addition to these effects, many social and economic problems may present themselves and exacerbate distress such as employment, educational, and immigration status issues (Frederick & Lizdas, 2003; Seidman & Vickers, 2005). These effects create what could be termed *survival needs* that can be ameliorated through informal social support or through formal community agencies and systems. Sex crimes, like any other intentional harm done to one human being by another, cause a sense of transgression that triggers needs for acknowledgment of wrongdoing and repair of the damage caused (Koss, 2000). These are justice *needs*. Formal justice institutions including police, prosecutors, judges, prisons, probation/parole services, and criminal and civil procedures are tasked with responding to these needs. However, in recent years, there have been increasingly insistent critiques of existing response to gender-based crimes and calls for expanded justice options for rape (Braithwaite & Daly, 1998; Bublick, 2006; Daly, 2005; Daly & Curtis-Fawley, 2006; Clay-Warner & Burt, 2005; Koss, 2000; Koss, Bachar & Hopkins, 2003; Koss, Bachar, Hopkins & Carlson, 2004a; 2004b; Seidman & Vickers; 2005; Sherman & Strang, 2004; Strang & Braithwaite, 2002; Strang, 2002, 2004). These discussions have raised considerable questions and even overt resistance among some criminologists, jurists, antirape advocates, and policy makers including critiques from a gendered as well as class and ethnicity perspective (e.g., Cunneen, 2004; Daly, 2005; Daly & Stubbs, 2005; LaFree, 1980; 1981; 1989; Smith, 2005). Often the critics focused on intimate partner physical violence, which differs in important ways from sexual assault, and on specific models of alternative justice that are now discredited for application to crimes against women (Hopkins, Koss & Bachar, 2004). Many sexual assaults are discrete events and the major justice hurdle is the state's ability to prove the case and the impact of the justice process (Curtis-Fawley & Daly, 2005). In contrast, the most pressing concern with domestic violence is ensuring safety.

This article covers five topics including: (*a*) enumerating the survival and justice needs created by sexual assault; (*b*) identifying the range of community service providers who contribute to restoring survivors; (*c*) evaluating the efficacy of existing criminal and civil options to satisfy justice needs equably across gender, ethnic, and class lines; (*d*) mapping the convergence of restorative justice (RJ) values and the goals and priorities of the antirape movement; and (*e*) issuing a call to action to those working to end sexual assault that is holistic, involves efforts to change community norms, enlarge survivor services, improve survivor satisfaction of justice needs, and increase offender accountability. Progress on the agenda would strengthen existing legal avenues and expand them through promotion of thoughtfully designed nonadversarial, restorative justice-based options. These goals are often seen as a zero-sum game where any development of restorative justice options must come at the expense of continued efforts to strengthen conventional justice. The author argues that these efforts are complementary.

This article focuses on sex crimes *outside* the context of longstanding relationships. Thus, marital rape is explicitly excluded. Admittedly this is an arbitrary distinction that oversimplifies women's real experiences, yet it is consistent with how sexual assault and domestic violence are addressed within state criminal statutes. The acronym *SV* to represent survivor/victim is used in this article. This term is an attempt to blend the language practices characteristic of the justice system with that of the services and advocacy community. It is most definitely not done to dehumanize or reduce the sense of intentional harm conveyed by the word "victim." The word *offender* is used to refer to the person responsible for perpetrating an illegal sexual act. *Rape* is defined as unwanted oral, anal, or vaginal penetration against consent through force, threat of force, or when incapacitated. The term *sexual assault* signals reference to a broader range of sexual crimes ranging from indecency through rape. The term *restorative justice program* is used in the article to refer to community conferencing, which is just one approach among many that claim to be restorative. It is a process whereby parties affected by a specific crime "collectively resolve how to deal with the aftermath of the offense and the implications for the future" (Marshall, 1999, p. 5).

Due to space limitations, topics that are mentioned briefly but not examined in depth include: the history of restorative justice (see Strang, and Braithwaite, 2002; Poulson, 2003; Von Hirsch, Roberts, Bottoms, Roach & Schiff, 2003; Weitekamp, 1999), the spectrum of approaches considered to be restorative justice (see Zehr & Toews, 2004), outcome evaluation of the various forms of restorative justice (see Bazemore, O'Brien & Carey, 2005; Sherman, Strang, Angel, Woods, Barnes, Bennet & Inkpen, 2005), sexual assault forensic evidence (DuMont & Parnis, 2006), and legal issues and standards that must be addressed by restorative justice (e.g., Reimund, 2005; Skelton & Frank, 2004; Van Ness, 2003). A particularly unfortunate consequence of space constraints is inability to avoid homogenizing SVs, whereas the author clearly recognizes that they are not "ageless, colorless, genderless, and classless individuals," (Young, 2002, p. 146, cited in Dignan, 2005, p 167). Scholars that have examined these status variables and addressed indigenous issues in the implementation of restorative justice programs include Amstutz (2004), Cunneen (2004), Daly (2005), Daly & Stubbs (2005, 2006), Goel (2000), Haiaha (2004), Jasso (2005), Jenkins (2000), Herman (2004), Roche (2003), Raye (2004), Smith (2005), and Zehr & Torres (2004).

A number of authors have discussed and empirically examined the needs of those who experience sex crimes. *Survival needs* include physical health, mental health, economic issues such as housing and employment, educational opportunities or retraining, and immigration problems (Seidman & Vickers, 2005). These needs are generally unrelated to the offender or anything he/she can do (Achilles, 2004), nor is the criminal justice system generally capable of addressing them (Herman, 2004).

Existing alongside of survival needs are *justice needs*. Victimization by intentional harm elicits what are now considered to be instinctual needs to restore the balance of social obligation of one person to another. Qualitative research with SVs on three continents revealed that they desire to tell their story, be heard, have input into how to resolve the violation, receive answers to questions, observe offender remorse, and experience a justice process that counteracts isolation in the aftermath of crime (Herman, 2004; Strang, 2004).

Four observations flow from the conceptualization of SV needs into survival and justice categories. First, there is no single entity offering services to SVs that can assert ownership of the response to sexual assault, nor is it feasible for one institution to offer an all-encompassing approach to healing across the spectrum of needs. Second, a wide variety of community agencies and service providers are already involved in the business of "restoring" SVs (Achilles, 2004). Community-based services that restore SVs include medical care, forensic examinations, mental health treatment, counseling, social services, and spiritual support (Herman, 2004). Third, interdependencies exist; Daly (2005) reported that success in reducing recidivism among juvenile sex offenders through a restorative justice program in South Australia was tied to participation in a community-based sex offender treatment program. Finally, the rationale for expanded justice options rests on how well conventional criminal and civil processes are currently meeting SVs' justice needs. The following material extensively examines empirical evaluations of justice system response to sexual assault.

EMPIRICAL EVALUATION OF JUSTICE SYSTEM PROCESS

The largest single impediment to meeting SVs justice needs through existing mechanisms is the small numbers who are able to access legal processes. Lack of access has alternatively been referred to as attrition, which occurs at each of the multiple layers of the justice system.

Reporting

Just 16% of rapes are reported to the police according to the *Rape in America Study* (Kilpatrick, Edmunds & Seymour, 1992). In Canada, 1 in 3 women disclosed rape victimization in a survey conducted by Statistics Canada, but only 6% of them said they informed authorities (Walby & Maybell, 2001). Felson and Paré (2005) performed a secondary analysis on data from the National Violence Against Women Survey (Tjaden & Thonnes, 1998). Findings showed that SVs of rape were far less likely to report their victimization to police (22%) compared to victims of physical assault including both intimate and nonintimate physical violence (78%). SVs underreported rape in spite of viewing it as more serious than physical assault. The web site for the National Crime Victimization Survey lists the reporting rate for rape and sexual assault as 36% and the rate for rape including attempts as 47% (accessed at http://www.ojp.usdoj.gov/bjs/pub/pdf/cvus/current/cv0491.pdf). Women were much less likely to report (15%) than men (85%) as reported by Felson and Paré (2003). Reporting was significantly less common if victim and offender knew each other in any way or were drinking, even when the sexual assault was observed by a third party. Rape among college women is particularly unlikely to be reported; estimates have been at 5% from national surveys reported in 1988 and most recently in 2000 (Fisher, Cullen & Turner, 2000; Koss, 1988). Acquaintance rape SVs were particularly likely to say they were too embarrassed, feared they would not be believed, questioned whether the police could or would do anything, or considered the offense too minor to report compared to those victimized by unknown offenders. There was no evidence suggesting that SVs in the United States feared reprisals from male partners (Felson & Paré, 2003). And, contrary to conventional wisdom, there was also no gender bias in reporting identified in this study; both male and female SVs were equally unlikely to report. A statewide assessment of SVs receiving care at 19 sexual assault centers in Maryland showed that more than half (56%) waited years before disclosing and 70% of respondents indicated they would not disclose to police (Monroe *et al.*, (2005).

If an SV decides to report and a police complaint is filed, the next step is identifying a suspect. The proportion of rape cases where a suspect arrested was 34% in Hawaii and 36% in Indianapolis (Chandles & Torney, 1981; LaFree, 1981; 1989). Spohn & Horney (1992) examined the effects of rape law reforms on reporting of rape (and other justice accountability indicators) in six cities; the first three were in states with strong sexual assault law reform; the last three were governed by weak reforms. Reforms had no positive effects on reporting except in Detroit (Michigan had strong reforms) and in Houston (Texas had weak reforms). The investigators concluded that the changes in reporting were related not to the substantive content of the law but to publicity surrounding the reforms that informed victims of new laws (for similar data and a comprehensive review of rape law reform see Clay-Warner & Burt, 2005).

Police are tasked with obtaining information that is relevant to determining case merit; in other words, they must provide answers to questions that they know prosecutors will ask them. Studies in Australia, New Zealand, and the United States have reported high levels of police disbelief of rape complainants, with officers' estimates of false reporting ranging from 10% to 70% (Campbell & Johnson, 1997; Jordan, 2004). A content analysis of police officers' definitions of rape revealed that 19% of officers had definitions consistent with reformed rape statutes, 31% focused their definitions primarily on penetration and consent, and 51% had mixed definitions based on old laws and victim blaming views (Campbell & Johnson, 1997; Campbell, 1998). In Ethiopia police typically defined rape as breaking the hymen (Human Rights Watch, 1999). Without medical proof of virginity prior to violation, police refused to register a rape complaint. In a police file examination in Auckland, New Zealand, Jordan (2004) found that police judged 33% of rape complaints as false and decided to stop investigating. No investigation of the complaint was conducted in three of four cases where the victims were drunk and eight of ten cases where the victim and offender were intimates or even slightly acquainted. Other reasons recorded for considering the rape reports to lack merit included comments that the victim was drunk or stoned, delayed reporting, had previous consensual sex with accused, was psychiatrically disturbed or intellectually impaired, perceived as immoral, or had a history of previous rape or abuse. Of course, none of these factors has any bearing on whether a rape actually occurred. Surveys of US rape crisis centers revealed 17 states where adult rape complainants had been required to take a polygraph exam before their charges would be accepted and 11 states where children were polygraphed (Sloan, 1995).

Many SVs faced with these unsupportive early indicators of how adversarial justice operates withdrew their charges, which is often documented by police as "uncooperative victim," "false rape allegations," or "recantations" (Kanin, 1994). DuMont and Parnis (2006) indicated that rulings by police that there was no crime (unfounding) ranged from 6% in Toronto to 60% in Chicago. The cases that proceeded and those that were filtered out depended on (see Campbell & Johnson, 1997): (1) community resources allocated to address sexual assault and the coordination of the services (Fairstein, 1993; US Department of Justice, 1992); (2) type of rape—stranger rapes are investigated more thoroughly and are more likely to be charged than nonstranger rapes (Fairstein, 1993; Kerstetter, 1990; Madigan & Gamble, 1991); (3) assaults involving weapons and injuries (LaFree, 1981; Kerstetter, 1990; Rose & Randall, 1982); and (4) victim characteristics thought to undermine their credibility (Rose & Randall, 1989).

Prosecution

In the United States, some misdemeanor sexual assaults are resolved by field arrest, which is an equivalent process to receiving a traffic ticket. Those cases that police investigate and deem worthy of further consideration are presented to prosecutors. These personnel are district or county attorneys in the United States. Other British-based legal systems use police prosecutors for the initial determination of case merit in many sexual assaults. In either approach, prosecutors have the option to indict or decline to issue charges. In Japan the rate of indictment for rape was dramatically lower than for any other crime including manslaughter and murder (Yoshida, 2003 referencing the Japanese Institute of the Ministry of Justice, 1999). Among rape cases, 40% failed indictment compared to less than 3% for bodily injury cases, 2% of traffic offenses resulting in bodily injury, and 4% of blackmail cases. Among reported rapes approximately half to less than 15% are rejected for charging by prosecutors depending on the study (Frohmann, 1991; 1997; 1998; Frazier & Haney, 1996; Harris & Grace, 1999). For example, in a sample of 567 rapes reported in Hennepin County, Minnesota, only 70 (12%) were indicted. A total of 31 studies internationally were located by DuMont and Parnis (2006), which identified legal outcomes for reported cases. The proportion of charges issued among the total number of rapes reported was 16% in the two US jurisdictions with the global average being 28% (see DuMont & Parnis, 2006 for citations of individual studies). These authors furthermore reported that there was no relationship between the victim's emotional state or the presence of semen and the progression of cases through the legal system. Moderate-to-severe documented physical injuries including injuries to the head, neck, or face, attempted strangulation, and fractures were the strongest predictors of positive prosecutorial outcomes.

Many studies have shown that prosecutors' determination of case merit is affected by extra-legal factors including race, age, and occupation of the offender and SV, their relationship, the severity of the violence, and SV risk-taking behavior, drug use, reputation, or moral character (for a metaanalysis see Whately, 1996). From the prosecution perspective, the ideal SV is one who has little-to-no relationship to the offender, is virtuous and going about legitimate business, was above reproach in behavior prior to the rape, reports a single occurrence, was raped by an unambiguously bad offender, has demographic characteristics that signal power, influence, or sympathy, shows visible, appropriate expressions of trauma, and are open to help (Dignan, 2005).

A large number of empirical studies support that the SVs least likely to see an offender convicted are older, poorer, of negative reputation including being deemed promiscuous or a prostitute, with a psychiatric history, drug abuse problem, or criminal record, who could be perceived as engaging in "risk-taking" behavior, and neither overtly resisted the assailant nor reported to police soon after the incident (see Du Mont & Parnis for individual citations). Estrich (1987) observed that prosecution virtually never occurred if the SV and offender were intimates, even if their level of acquaintance was not romantic (e.g., worked together) or they had just met that evening. The only exceptions were cases of medico-forensically documented serious injury and the availability of an expert witness (also see Estrich, 1985).

Often an SV's report is discredited if her/his behavior conflicts with prosecutors' *perceptions* of the typical citizen's *assumptions* about the characteristics of rape and the behavior of victims (Frohmann, 1991; 1997; 1998). Although prosecutors may intellectually reject the appropriateness basing case merit on these grounds, they feel themselves positioned downstream of jurors, obligating them to take into account what they believe are the myths and stereotypes held by the general public. In the minority of cases that are being seriously examined for potential indictment, prosecutors must take an inventory of negative facts about the SV and identify any holes in her/his story (Seidman & Vickers, 2005). Information uncovered that could be viewed as exculpatory must be shared with the defense. Prosecutors may use victims' living circumstances, relationship with the suspect, and behavior to construct a hypothetical scenario that could create reasonable doubt in jurors' minds including reframing the incident as consensual sex or imputing motives for false allegations such as to cover up infidelity, pregnancy, or sexual disease. If victims reside in racially mixed, lower-class neighborhoods, prosecutors often conclude that misinterpretation of them by a white middle class jury will lead to a not guilty verdict (Frohmann, 1997). Both women of color and victims of acquaintance rape were less likely to have their cases pursued by criminal justice (Campbell, 1998; Razack, 1998). If allowed to proceed, survivors of color contended with tension between their needs for justice and felt obligations to buffer racism in the criminal justice system (CJS). African American men constitute 35% of the rapists currently incarcerated and 48% of the total prisoners in the United States (Greenfield *et al.*, 1998). These practices are supported by the defense's continuing ability to establish an SV's motive to lie by litigating the character, conduct, and mental health and the continuing beliefs that there is a certain fixed set of behaviors that are consistent with rape trauma including hysteria, torn clothes, and other indicators of resistance, even though these are not statutory elements of rape law (Bublick, 2006).

Trials and Verdicts

Although the foregoing data establish that indictment rarely occurs, empirical studies have examined those cases that proceeded to trial. Frazier and Haney (1996) determined that 9% of reported rapes were closed by plea agreement and just 3% eventually were tried in a courtroom (Frazier & Haney, 1996). The Home Office in England indicated that in 1999, 7% of adjudicated rapes resulted in a guilty verdict (Kelly, 2001). Rape was the least likely to be proved of any sexual offense among juvenile trials in Australia (Daly & Crutis-Fawley, 2006; Daly, Curtis-Fawley & Bonhours, 2003). The conviction rate for rape has declined steadily in virtually every country over the past 30 years (Kelly, 2001). Nine studies internationally reported conviction rates for rape. The global average was 15%; the only two US cities included reported that 12% of rape cases tried resulted in conviction (for citations of individual studies, see Du Mont & Parnis, 2006).

The contribution of medico-forensic evidence to conviction rates has also been explored. These studies are of particular interest because the establishment of a trained corps of sexual assault examiners has been a high priority for

SV advocates. Herbert and Wiebe (1989) studied 130 rape cases with forensic documentation taken by trained examiners. Charges were issued in 19%, proceedings were stayed in 6%, 13% had proceeded to trial and the conviction rate in the presence of forensic evidence, and expert testimony was 8%. Even among cases documenting the presence of ano-genital injury or biological evidence such as semen matching the accused, less than one-third were retained in the system to proceed to trial (see Du Mont & Parnis, 2006). Just 10% of the cases involved introduction of the medical forensic exam into evidence. The remainder appeared to serve no legal purpose at trial. Feldberg (1997) examined additional Canadian data and concluded, "Medical evidence [did] not contribute significantly to a guilty verdict..." (p. 98).

The US courts often respond differently to rape cases depending on whether the victim and offenders were strangers to each other or were acquainted even though this distinction is not statutory (Campbell, 1998; Ferraro & Boychuk, 1992; Razack, 1998). This observation holds internationally (see Du Mont & Parnis, 2006). When judges and juries were independently polled about the guilt or innocence of the defendant, juries were equally likely to convict compared to judges in stranger rapes. In contrast, juries were much less likely to weigh the evidence in favor of the SV compared to judges when the parties were acquainted. The term *jury leniency* refers to instances when judges, who are deemed better equipped to evaluate the evidence on the basis of their training and experience, indicated that they would have found the defendant guilty, whereas the jury decided for acquittal. In contrast, the juries are less lenient for stranger rape than for virtually any other crime (Bryden & Lengnick, 1997). The only data that disaggregated conviction rates for intimate and nonintimate rape demonstrated that only 25% of rape cases involving acquaintances resulted in convictions (Weninger, 1978). In Washington, D.C., only 9% of defendants who were ex-spouses, boyfriends, or cohabiting partners of the victim were convicted (Williams, 1981). Frazier and Haney (1996) found no difference in conviction rates, but when convicted, acquaintance rape perpetrators received shorter sentences and were more likely to serve time in a workhouse as opposed to prison. Madigan and Gamble (1991) identified three clusters of rape cases according to their likelihood of proceeding through the criminal justice system: Cases that proceeded through the justice process were cluster 1 (89% were changed, 39% were ended in a plea bargain, and 28% were convicted at trial). This cluster consisted of women raped by strangers with weapons and who were injured in the assault. These outcomes were also associated with communities that had more resources for victimized women and more coordination to streamline service delivery. Cluster 2 cases were dropped early in the process with only 8% being charged. They involved SVs raped by a stranger without the use of a weapon, women raped by someone they knew without a weapon, SVs who were drinking and intraracial (same race) rapes. Cluster 3 were cases that fell apart, despite continual intervention by advocates; in 6 of 10 cases the outcome was inconsistent with SVs' expressed wishes. Women raped by nonstrangers without use of a weapon and interracial rapes were more likely to be in this cluster—women of color raped by white men.

Kelly (2001) reviewed studies on attrition in the UK criminal justice system. She reported that depending on the data source, case loss was 36–67% at the police stage, 30–64% at the prosecution stage, and 20–33% at the court stage (reviewed in Kelly, 2001; see Bryden, 2000 and Bryden & Lengnick, 1997 for reviews of the smaller number of studies that have examined the US data). Data from the National Violence Against Women Survey are particularly instructive to summarize the attrition problem because it begins with the numbers of sexual assaults disclosed to interviews rather than commencing at the police report stage (Tjaden & Thonnes, 1998). The investigators identified 2,594 separate rape incidents among the 8,000 female respondents. The numbers of rapes that were reported, prosecuted, convicted, and jailed were 441, 33, 13, and 9, respectively. As a proportion of the 2,594 incidents disclosed to survey interviewers, just 0.03% resulted in incarceration (Tjaden & Thonnes, 1998). It has been concluded that rape is the "least reported, least indicted and least convicted non-property felony in America" (Seidman & Vickers, 2005, p. 472, citing Hart & Rennison, 2000).

Civil Tort Options

The US Department of Justice estimated that the out-of-pocket expenses of rape are $7.5 billion per year (Miller, 1996). When pain, suffering, and lost quality of life had a monetary value attached to them, the estimate reached $127 billion (also see Post, Mezey, Maxwell & Wilbert, 2002; Waters, Hyder, Rajkotia, Basu, Rehwinkel & Butchart, 2004). To seek compensation for these damages, SVs have the option to sue under civil tort law using a variety of grounds such as intentional infliction of emotional harm. Unfortunately, the resources of the offender are often too small or there is no "deep pockets" third party such as a university or shopping mall with the resources to pay damages sufficient to interest an attorney in pursuing the case unless the SV is willing to pay all costs for the action. Bublick (2006) examined state appellate decisions for all rape cases nationally from January 1, 2000 to December 31, 2004. The total number of cases was 100. Of course, cases that are appealed do not represent all civil tort actions filed because 95% of them are settled before trial and not all lower court judgments are pursued to higher courts. Due to sealed documents, it may be impossible to precisely estimate the number of civil rape torts filed. However, examination of the judgments that were appealed showed that most involved third-party defendants such as a university named for negligence related to date or acquaintance rape. Virtually none of the appeals were against the first party (offender) and the small number that were consisted of stepfathers and other loosely related relatives. The appellate decisions were discouraging as many favored the defendant such as opinions that homeowners insurance is not obligated to compensate an SV raped in an unsupervised parental home or that malpractice insurance does not apply to sex assaults perpetrated by health care providers. Because settlements are private, tort actions in the case of rape fail to achieve not only the aims of public justice, but also the prevention and community norm change goals of the antisexual assault advocacy community. Private justice fails to validate the SV among her family, friends, and community as a legitimate victim and does not express public condemnation of wrongful conduct. Additionally, private justice does not contribute to individual and general deterrence of future offenders by imposing sanctions that may outweigh any perceived benefits of criminal sexual conduct.

Nontort Civil Actions

SVs clearly differentiate between what they consider "offensive" and "defensive" legal actions (Seidman & Vickers, 2005). Nontort civil litigation, or the assistance of an attorney to advocate for SV rights through institutional processes, may include the following issues discussed by Seidman and Vickers (2005): (a) privacy protection for medical, psychiatric, and rape crisis center records; (b) immigration status and petitions for change in status; (c) access to medical and counseling benefits through various employer benefit plans such as disability and unemployment compensation; (d) lease termination and assistance in emergency transfer or admission rights to public housing; (e) access to protective orders, which unfortunately require a degree of relationship such as marriage, substantial dating, or blood to make orders available; (f) educational interventions including privacy protections, promotion of educational stability, on-campus housing actions, class or exam schedules, employment or work-study maintenance, tuition-loss prevention, and financial aid loss; (g) maintenance of employment, using sexual harassment law if the rape occurred in the workplace, response to wrongful termination, and access to protected leave under the federal family and medical leave act or state laws; and (h) victim compensation denial for medical expenses or lost wages, with the caveat that the SV must participate in the justice system to be eligible. Clearly, when these issues arise, they are critical to restoring victims and contribute to prevention of a negative financial and emotional spiral. Sadly, Seidman and Vickers (2005) note that the legal workforce willing to accept these cases for no fee is miniscule. Without access to counsel, it is unreasonable for SVs to be aware of their legal rights or to have the perseverance and resiliency to pursue them unsupported in the immediate post-assault period.

Impact of Legal Reforms

Surveys of rape crisis centers reveal that 95% or more offered police and court advocacy and 70% engaged in public lobbying to reform rape laws

(Campbell, Baker & Mazurek, 1998). The movement has achieved spectacular success by the standards of social change. Statutory changes have been achieved across all 50 states and at the federal level including removing the spousal exclusion, expanding the definition of rape, eliminating the corroboration requirement, instituting the rape shield against sexual history as evidence, establishing specialized police and prosecution sex crime units, opening avenues for tort civil action, and increasing punitive responses for sexual assault (longer sentences, sex offender registration, community notification, and civil commitment). Antiviolence advocates have also achieved reforms in victims' rights legislation and have pressured the conventional justice system to become more responsive to SVs through potentially restorative practices such as implementing impact statements, establishing compensation schemes, and broadening civil options.

There are several important considerations in evaluating the impact of these reforms. First, there are SVs for whom the current justice options have performed admirably, although the evidence suggests that their numbers are small both literally and proportionately. Second, those for whom the system works well are not representative of all SVs because outcomes depend on both the type of rape and the kind of victim. Third, hard-won broader definitions of sexual assault and stiffer sanctions come into play only when cases proceed through sentencing, which has been demonstrated to be a small fraction of the crimes that occur. Fourth, the number of persons on sex offender registries may be large but examination of them will reveal that they inadequately represent the most prevalent forms of sexual assault against adult SVs. Finally, due weight must be given to the empirical evidence and opinions of jurists and criminologists. In 1990 almost 20 years after the initiation of legal reforms, no improvement was found in six major urban jurisdictions for rates of investigation, charging, and findings of guilt (Horney & Spohn, 1990). A subsequent replication showed very slight improvement in prosecution rates, but only for stranger rapes and only in two jurisdictions (New York City and Washington, DC; Spohn & Horney, 1992; also see Clay-Warner & Burt, 2005; Schulhofer, 1998). Legal scholars have not minced words:

- "A growing body of social-scientific evidence indicates that, contrary to reformers' expectations, the much-heralded evidentiary reforms have had little impact on reporting, processing, and conviction rates in sex crimes cases" (Bryden, 2000, p. 217).
- "...Many of these statutory reforms, which focused primarily on rape victims' existence within the criminal justice system, have been a profound disappointment" (Seidman & Vickers, 2005, p. 467).
- "The potential for sexual assault victims to use tort actions as an alternative to criminal law is not supported by current usage" (Bublick, 2006).

Victim advocates say that if they were raped, knowing what they know, they would not go to court or even try to pursue their justice needs (Curtis-Fawley &

Daly, 2005). Yet, the actual activities of the movement against sexual assault have been characterized as an overreliance on the criminal law to control men's violence against women (Martin, 1998, Snider, 1998). Estrich (1986) observed that many feminists' overriding goal is to "write the perfect statute" (pp. 1092–1093). Legal scholars have challenged feminist uses of 'punitive criminalization strategies,' which they conclude rest on naïve beliefs that criminal law has the capacity to bring about social change and that deterrence promotes safety (Martin, 1998; Estrich, 1986). Initiatives focused on criminal statute change and promotion of tort actions sometimes clash with other values of advocates and they may not see the issues the same as SVs, especially along race, gender, and class lines (also see Snider, 1998, pp. 5–6).

RE-TRAUMATIZATION BY THE JUSTICE SYSTEM

Referring to the justice system, McBarnet (1988) said, "If victims feel that nobody cares about their suffering, it is in part because institutionally nobody does..." (p. 300). Most SVs perceive that sex crimes are trivialized by the criminal justice system, although even "minor" sexual assaults have been demonstrated to be traumatic to women (Cox, 1988; Smith & Morra, 1994; Riordan, 1999). For example, one recent textbook demeaned nonrape sex crimes by referring to them under the chapter title "nuisance sex behaviors" (Holmes & Holmes, 2002). The term *critogenic harms* has been coined to denote the traumatization of litigants caused by the justice process (Gutheil, Bursztajn, Brodsky & Strasburger, 2000).

Pretrial

The potential for retraumatization by the justice system begins at the level of police officers' response and investigation. Case facts and clarifying information may be obtained humanely, without framing questions as placing responsibility for the crime on the SV or scaring her/him about how defense attorneys might hypothetically treat them at trial. However, SV survey responses show that 46% of SVs were dissatisfied with police interviews (Monroe *et al.*, 2005). Later, prosecutors must prepare their witnesses for trial, which includes what legal professionals may view as toughening up to prepare for cross-examination, but SVs may perceive differently (Konradi, 1997). SVs often believed that they are the client of the justice system are shocked that they have little control over critical decisions including whether or not their case is pursued. They may be dismayed to learn that their identify is a matter of public record (e.g., Sefl, *et al.*, 1999; Des Rosiers, Feldhusen & Hankivsky, 1998; Frazier & Haney, 1996; Herman, 2004). Data collected from doctors, nurses, and police officers found significant agreement in recall between SVs and system personnel regarding services that were provided and statements made or actions taken (Campbell, 2005; also see Campbell & Bybee, 1997). However, both groups of service providers significantly underestimated their effect on SVs, who reported much more distress than providers thought.

Trial

SVs who participate in a civil or criminal trial learn that their role is to serve as "evidentiary cannon fodder" for the defense attorney (Braithwaite & Daly, 1998, p. 154). SVs are expected to testify about graphic details of sexual assault in open court, and even rape shield laws fail to guarantee their protection from questions about their social and sexual history when these issues are ruled relevant to determining consent. And, in the era of DNA, consent is the primary defense that is used in all rape cases. SVs may experience revictimization by the environment of formality, attorney questioning that exacerbates self-blame, and perpetrator's who under advice of counsel maintain innocence (Holmstrom & Burgess, 1975, 1978; Konradi, 1999; Madigan & Gamble, 1989; Martin & Powell, 1994; Matoesian, 1993; McCahill *et al.*, 1979; Sanday, 1996). Self-blame has been demonstrated to be a primary predictor of the amount of distress experienced by SVs and the length of their recovery (Koss & Figueredo, 2004a, 2004b). Thus, exacerbation of it is detrimental both to SVs' sense of justice and to their mental and physical health survival needs.

Finally, SVs discover that they are not viewed as individuals who have unique needs and preferences about what consequences the offender should face (Hopkins, Koss & Bachar, 2004). Instead, statutes present standard sentencing guidelines that allow a narrow range of sentencing options. And, although SVs have been accorded the right to submit an impact statement in the sentencing phase, their requests such as reparation or treatment for the offender are at the discretion of the judge, orders that are obtained are often not enforced, and any monetary award to victims comes second to the offender's obligation to pay fines to the court (see Harrsion, 2006). British-based legal systems (e.g., the United States [except Louisiana], Canada, New Zealand, and Australia), as opposed to Napoleonic law-based systems (e.g., France, Mexico), operate on the assumption of innocence until proven guilty. Under this standard, legal counsel advises offenders to maintain innocence until a favorable plea agreement is reached, or in trials, throughout the proceedings and even afterward to preserve appeal rights. SVs are particularly traumatized when offenders continue to deny the SVs' assertions and maintain that the act was consensual sex and not a crime (Holmstrom & Burgess, 1975, 1978; Madigan & Gamble, 1989; Martin & Powell, 1994; Matosian, 1993; Sanday, 1996). SVs feel ignored, excluded, and profoundly disrespected, alienated, and unsatisfied with their experiences in the criminal justice system (Herman, 2005).

Data from 16 criminal trials before juries in the United States revealed that most victims believed rapists had more rights, the system was unfair, victims' rights were not protected, and they were not given enough information or control over handling their case (Frazier & Haney, 1996). Some of the other sources of dissatisfaction stem from inherent features of adversarial justice that implement the numerous protections accorded offenders under the US Constitution. The ratings of a mixed group of victims (35% sexual assault, 43% physical assault, 22% other) whose cases were tried in German courts before a panel of judges showed that even without jury trials for rape, victims perceived the procedures as unfair, viewed testifying as moderately stressful, and found that enduring the delay before trial was very stressful (Orth & Maercker, 2004). SVs' overall ratings of their experience were negative and they experienced little moral satisfaction (Orth & Maercker, 2004). Australian juvenile sex crimes that were adjudicated in criminal court took 6.6 months compared to 3.2 months for alternative justice. Lack of communication about court dates and plea agreements represent failures of the justice system to observe victim rights legislation. Among the methods that advocates have used to lessen traumatization has been to provide courtroom accompaniment services. But because so many features of the trial are immutable, accompaniment has been described as handholding on a walk through hell (Weisz, 1999).

Civil tort actions have been promoted as less traumatizing to victims. Because SVs retain the attorney, they are more in control of decision making and better informed of case progress. Despite some advantages over criminal processing, tort procedures introduce problems and additional antivictim biases unique to civil proceedings (Bublick, 1999). Procedural differences in civil law that are favorable to SVs include a lower standard of proof than criminal proceedings (preponderance of evidence as opposed to beyond a reasonable doubt) and depending on the grounds for the action, it may not be necessary to prove rape. However, there are disadvantages as well. Civil trials are also adversarial and many states have adopted comparative fault doctrines that may be used in civil but not in criminal actions. Comparative fault establishes the portion of blame for the harm that is attributed to the SV. Illustrative cases cited by Bublick (1999) include the case of *Morris v. Yogi Bear's Jellystone Park Camp Resort* involving the gang rape of a 13-year old by three 17-year old youths with whom she was drinking on camp property. The three defendants were found 78% responsible, the park 10%, and the victim 12%. Another rape victim was held 30% negligent for being in streets that "were dangerous for a young lady at 3:00 AM" (quote on p. 1460). A woman raped by a man with whom she had gone to a bar was 51% responsible for being raped. SV conduct to which comparative fault has been assigned include: going outside alone at night to hail a cab, walking to a car in a hotel parking lot, taking 5 steps inside the door before closing it, and failing to double-check door or window locks. Commenting on these rulings, Bublick (1999) noted that in contrast many states do not allow failure to wear a seatbelt to be considered comparative fault in civil torts involving vehicular injury. A further negative experience for the SV is having a retaliatory lawsuit against them filed by the plaintiff, which happened to all five SVs who pursued civil tort actions among a nonrepresentative series of volunteers interviewed by Herman (2005). In another study, interviews with SVs who pursued civil tort actions revealed that they did not obtain the justice satisfaction that they sought. Often their prime motivation was to be heard and validated for the wrong that they suffered, yet the settlements, if received, were monetary and virtually universally excluded any acknowledgement of wrongdoing by the first- or third-party defendant (Des Rosiers, Feldthusen & Hankivsky, 1998).

Behavioral Outcomes

Some but not all studies reveal that trial participation predicts negative victim outcomes. Insensitive attempts to obtain the testimony of Bosnian rape survivors was shown to result in feelings of shame, lack of trust, fear of reliving bad memories, fear of reprisals, and suicide attempts (Allen, 1996). SVs whose cases were prosecuted in the US courts scored higher on measures of distress than those whose cases were not prosecuted (Cluss, Broughton, Frank, Stewart & West, 1983). The prevalence rate for PTSD in SVs of rape ranges from 35% to 70% depending on the study (Orth, Montada & Maercker, 2006). Testifying was one of four significant predictors of PTSD symptoms among adult SVs of child rape (Epstein, Saunders & Kilpatrick, 1997; for contradictory findings with adult SVs in Germany see Orth & Maercker, 2004). Increased nightmares, decreased social activities, more dissatisfaction with heterosexual relationships, loss of appetite, recurrence of phobias, and greater psychological distress have been documented among victims whose cases went to trial (Holmstrom & Burgess, 1975). Australian SVs who were randomly assigned to restorative justice conferences had lower levels of PTSD than those who did not (Sherman & Strang, 2004). The coping responses used by SVs to reduce their subjective feelings of injustice included minimizing the harm of rape and excusing or justifying the offender's behavior (Orth & Maercker, 2004).

Sex offending is reinforced by low prosecution and conviction rates combined with SV self-protective minimizing and justifying coping mechanisms. Social psychological research has shown that not-guilty rape verdicts increase both men's and women's rape myth acceptance, which are one of the best predictors of juror's refusal to convict of rape. Not-guilty rape verdicts create a self-perpetuating, downward negative spiral in public response to date and acquaintance rape because prosecutors fail to charge when they think juries will not convict (Frohman, 1996; 1997; 1998). Even when reforms have put strong laws in place prohibiting sexual offenses, they cannot successfully compete with a citizenry that condones sexual violence (Koss, 2000).

VICTIM-CENTERED OPTIONS

Various sources including the National Organization for Victim Assistance as well as jurists have written that a more victim-centered justice option for crimes such as sexual assault would include processes that (*a*) pursue cases where there is evidence supporting probable cause that a sexual assault occurred; (*b*) respond to SVs' concerns regarding having input, choice, being treated as autonomous individuals, and voicing the emotional impact of their experience; (*c*) shorten the time between crime and consequence to reduce SV stress; (*d*) offer a less formal environment; (*e*) give SVs input into the consequences and plan of activities for the offender; (*f*) allow a process for victims to seek reparations and moral justice satisfaction; (*g*) provide for some form of censure by the community and validation of the SV; (*h*) and offer a process to ensure completion of offender obligations and his/her pledge not to reoffend (see Des Rosiers *et al.*, 1998; Koss *et al.*, 2004; Strang, 2004; Zehr & Toews, 2004).

Restorative Justice

A growing literature encourages consideration of restorative justice for crimes against women including sexual assault (see Strang & Braithwaite, 2002; Bazemore & Earle, 2002; Coker, 1999; Daly, 2002; Dignan & Cavadino, 1996, Hudson, 1998, Koss, 2000; Koss, *et al.*, 2004a, 2004b; Peled, Eiskovitz, Enosh & Winstok, 2000; and Snider, 1998). Restorative justice philosophy, which focuses on empowerment of SVs, acceptance of responsibility by offenders, repair of harm, and strengthening the social support, is hard to disagree with and very congruent with the values of the antiviolence movement (e.g., Hudson, 2002; Johnstone, 2004). There are many practices that claim to be restorative justice so care is needed to clarify whether discussion is directed to restorative justice philosophy in general or to a specific approach. In many sectors the term restorative justice has been erroneously used as synonymous with mediation and points made by Astor (1991) have become written in concrete in advocacy and academic lore thus complicating the growth of better models. Mediation is thoroughly discredited for gender-based violence. The vocabulary and theoretical foundation of mediation identifies a conflict that two parties will negotiate assisted by a third party. Sex crimes are crimes, they are not conflicts; neither do they involve "parties." There are SV(s) and offender(s). Restorative justice recognizes crimes and offenders, there is no push to reconcile, nor is victimization erased (Daly & Stubbs, 2006). Furthermore, a theoretical model such as mediation that ignores patriarchal power may be seemingly neutral while nevertheless disadvantaging women's ability to speak and be heard, or even silence them. Often, mediation has been court ordered or otherwise coerced. This is not empowering nor does it expand SV choice.

Finally, requiring SVs to "negotiate" on their own behalf negates some of the central functions of a justice system, which are to enforce social codes and hold violators accountable.

Many people believe that community conferencing is the most evolved restorative justice model. Conferencing typically occurs instead of a conventional trial, although interventions could occur at multiple points in the justice process including precharging and postconviction phases such as sentencing, in prison, prerelease, or postrelease. Conferencing involves SVs and their family and friends directly speaking about the impact they experienced to the offender and creating the set of activities and actions that the offender will undertake to demonstrate acceptance of responsibility, repair the harm caused, and resolve root causes of offending. However, unique features of sexual violence argue against taking a conferencing model off the shelf and implementing it. First, sexual victimization involves intense shame, stigma, and high levels of emotional distress. Scientific literature has established that even after taking into account personal history and social characteristics that could explain symptom severity, sexual assault still provokes more serious psychological distress than other crimes. Second, sexual assault SVs, including those who experience noncontact crimes that did not result in a direct threat to their physical integrity, fear for their safety. Third, sexual violence is a severe violation of personal trust. It is not appropriate to expect that a rapist who apologizes (whether required or voluntary), compared to a burglar, will or should be believed or that forgiveness could or should occur. Fourth, without monitoring plan fulfillment, SVs may experience repetition of trust violation and be placed at safety risk. Finally, rape supportive myths and attitudes in the general community are well documented. Without careful planning and preparation, community validation of sexual assault cannot be assumed. The material that follows attempts to gather purported positive features and hypothesized concerns about restorative justice conferencing as applied to gender-based violence.

Many merits of restorative justice conferencing have been advanced. It condemns violence in meaningful and consequential ways, permits telling stories, encourages admissions of offending, validates SVs' experiences and reassures them that they are not to blame, provides more options for those who do not want formal prosecution, and provides space for airing upsetting aspects of the incident that may not formally qualify as crimes and therefore would be excluded by any other legal process. Conferencing is premised on offenders taking responsibility for their acts and provides a flexible and nonadversarial setting to address the crime. It follows an agenda that ensures that all participants are guided to speak and to listen, and that opportunities to speak and be heard are balanced. Other advantages are directly involving family and friends in the support of the SV and potentially in disrupting the offenders' networks of reinforcement of violence-promoting beliefs. The ability to marshal material resources and direct them to SV needs is another advantage. Coker (2004) observes that restorative justice conferencing must operate with explicit antiviolence engendered egalitarian norms. The author suggests that restorative justice is a transformative justice model that can address the ways in which racism and economic subordination as well as childhood experiences of abuse relate to an offender's use of violence in intimate relationships while stressing personal responsibility for the decision to use violence. Empirical studies have demonstrated that the satisfaction of SVs is higher for juvenile sex crimes with conferencing compared to court (empirical papers are available online, see www.daly.griffith.au.edu). In short, conferencing promotes an individualized and more holistic response to SVs' justice needs. (Coker, 2004; Curtis-Fawly & Daly, 2005; Daly & Stubs, 2006).

Nevertheless, concerns have been expressed including that restorative justice is revictimizing, retreats to soft justice, reprivatizes response to gender violence, coerces SVs to participate, assumes sufficient community opposition to gendered violence, and emphasizes healing over punishment (Curtis-Fawley & Daly, 2005), unstudied outcomes on offenders, and safety concerns (Daly & Stubbs, 2006; Koss *et al.*, 2004a). For an extensive discussion of these concerns and specific suggestions for a program model that attempts to allay them, see Koss *et al.* 2004b. A study of advocates in Australia is illuminating because it demonstrates that the dialogue about advantages and limitations has been productive. Several advocates believed that restorative justice may be most effective is a parallel process to establish criminal proceedings. Nancarrow's (2006) interviews with advocates about their attitudes toward restorative justice revealed that they would be in favor of conferencing if it were in the context of sentencing but not as an alternative to going to court. The informality of restorative justice was seen as beneficial for some victims. Advocates noted the importance of the SV voice and the opportunity to speak about her/his experience. They noted the ability of restorative justice to address power imbalances. Advocates also believed that restorative justice could serve offenders because it lowers the stakes for acknowledging their criminal behavior. Advocates observed that victims of gender violence often bear guilt and self blame that is reinforced by criminal processes about their behavior and relationship choices. Advocates viewed restorative justice for adults with more trepidation, but their greatest concerns were about domestic violence, not sex crimes.

CALL TO ACTION

Feminist writers and activists have made numerous arguments against alternatives to conventional adversarial justice that appear compelling until they are mapped onto scientific evidence of actual justice system functioning. These arguments contrast with the expressed wishes of many SVs and fail to adequately address the degree of traumatization that is entailed in SVs' efforts to meet their justice needs through existing choices. Advocates and feminist scholars have identified the criminal justice system as one of the institutions that contributes to the continued subordination of women, an idea that dates to Brownmiller (1979). "A feminist politics cannot vacate the field of reforming law and justice, and there must be engagement with the state and allied political entities; but at the same time, we should expect modest gains and seek additional paths to social change" (Daly and Stubbs, 2005, p. 18). "The movement's alliances with the CJS, which are so critical to the evolution of CJS practices, have taken on such importance in some programs that other, potentially more effective and liberating approaches may have been given short shrift; ...advocates must avoid relying too heavily on the criminal justice system for women's protection, recognizing that it is not an option for many women, and must supplement their CJS reform work with a more holistic approach..." (Frederick & Lizdas, 2003, p. 3). At present it is vitally important to shift community norms away from tolerance and support of violence, a goal that has always been important, and is one that individual woman cannot accomplish (Frederick & Lizdas, 2003). Advocates and RJ proponents share the value of addressing criminal incidents in their social context including class, gender, and ethnicity considerations and in transferring resources to victims (Coker, 2004). The movements share principles, yet diverge in application. It is hard to disagree that crime causes harm, must be repaired, and involves multiple persons who should be served well and whose needs should not come at the expense of another if justice is to be done. Study of advocates in Queensland, Australia demonstrated that 80% were generally positive or cautiously positive about offering choice in justice options.

"State control over criminal justice principles and images is relatively easy to maintain if one is considering solely the traditional criminal justice system with its hierarchy of agencies, headed by the courts. Control is much more difficult to maintain when local government, health, education, voluntary sector groups, the private sector, and the public are involved. And as those groups become involved, so they may increasingly question the legitimacy of the traditional model of delivery of criminal justice" (Shapland, 2003, p. 214). Yet, scholars of the movement against sexual assault have provided voluminous data that although a coordinated community response has been a high value, it has occurred in a context of deradicalization (Campbell, et al., 1998, p. 477; Martin, 2005). Shapland (2003) quotes Laura Nadar's remarks before the California Alumni Association that "America's been flattened. We've been flattened by what I describe as 'harmony ideology'—you mustn't be contentious, you mustn't raise issues; and by fear..." (p. 39). A survey of rape crisis center directors found that few described current efforts directed at developing new prevention programs. One director observed that they "alter the curriculum a bit here and there to touch on more current topics, but it's pretty well-established" (Campbell et al., 1998, p. 473; for a metaanalysis of prevention program outcomes, see Hanson & Broom, 2005).

The dialogue will be more fruitful if conventional and restorative justice are viewed as capable of coexistence. (Curtis-Fawley & Daly, 2005). It is ironic that the lack of data to confirm or mollify critics of restorative conferencing stems from feminists and survivor groups' failure to advocate for its application to gender-based violence, or even actively opposing it. Across multiple world jurisdictions restorative justice for sexual assault is forbidden all states of Australia except South Australia and Queensland (and here only for juvenile sex crimes). Although New Zealand is the most advanced country in applying restorative justice conferencing to adult crimes, sexual assault is excluded (Curtis-Fawley & Daly, 2005). Programs that bring SVs and offenders together are forbidden by policy in the United States and are barred from applying for grants funded through the Violence Against Women Act. Justice alternatives are excluded as a form of prevention funded by the Centers for Disease Control and Prevention. Funding for victimization research from the National Institute of Justice is generally reserved for implementations of random assignment experimental designs, yet in doing so, the very element of choice is removed from SVs. Curtis-Fawley and Daly conclude that the result of advocacy for blocking restorative choices has been "... a dearth of evidence on how restorative justice might work in practice rather than in the theoretically best or worst case scenarios" (2005, p. 609).

Nevertheless, "pockets of retribution-weary community members" are piloting alternative programs (Frederick & Lizdas, 2003). In the field of adult sexual assault, there is only one operational program internationally as this article is being written (www.restoreprogram.publichealth.arizona.edu of which the author is the Principal Investigator); the funding for the other model (Phaphamani Rape Crisis Centre, Uitenhage, South Africa) has expired. The establishment of these programs face massive obstacles including virtual exclusion from funding, community attitudes, criminal justice system lethargy, poor morale, and frequent staff rotation or turnover, political ideology, continuing traumatizing interactions of justice personnel with SVs, and constant concerns about program sustainability.

The dialogue has just begun between restorative justice and victim service providers and its continuance is vital (Amstutz, 2004). These groups share common ground because both emphasize restoring victims, promoting the role of community in responding to crime, addressing the social context in which crime is committed, changing community norms, and prevention of sexual violence (Frederick & Lizdas, 2003). SV survival and justice needs should be paramount and resources should be adequately directed to them before thinking about justice as it relates to the offender (Achilles, 2004). This author provides a useful chart that is aimed at helping victim advocates and restorative justice advocates work holistically and strategically. She suggests the need to work on each other's boards to become familiar with both types of services directed at survival needs and justice needs, participate in volunteer training, etc. Proponents of restorative justice must avoid problematic words including forgiveness, reconciliation, and mediation, and claims that go beyond what any form of justice can deliver to promote SV healing across both their survival and justice needs.

Hopefully, this article has attempted to provide the motivating background for a call to action by SV advocates and policy makers. A renewed conversation about the antisexual violence policy agenda is urgently needed. Any movement can benefit from creating energizing new visions on behalf of SVs that expand the ways in which we fight for change and advocate for more and better-resourced services. We all know only too well that these sorts of system changes do not happen without hard work by many people to create the prerequisite political and collaborative climate, to advocate for funding to nurture new programs, and to achieve attitudinal and behavioral changes at multiple levels. Thankfully, the antisexual violence movement has never been deterred by challenge.

ACKNOWLEDGMENT

The production of this publication was supported by Grant Number CCR921709 from the Centers for Disease Control and Prevention, National Center for Injury Control and Prevention.

REFERENCES

ACHILLES, M. (2004). Will restorative justice live up to its promise to victims? In H. Zehr & B. Toews (Eds.), *Critical issues in restorative justice* (pp. 65–74). Monsey, NY: Criminal Justice Press and Cullompton, Devon, UK: William Publishing.

ALLEN, B. (1996). *Rape/war. The hidden genocide in Bosnia-Herzegovina and Croatia*. Minneapolis, MN: University of Minnesota Press.

AMSUTZ, L.S. (2004). What is the relationship between victim service organizations and restorative justice? In H. Zehr & B. Toews (Eds.), *Critical issues in restorative justice* (pp. 85–94). Monsey, NY: Criminal Justice Press and Cullompton, Devon, UK: William Publishing.

ASTOR, H. (1991). Swimming against the tide: Keeping violent men out of mediation. In J. Stubbs (Ed.), *Women, male violence, and the law* (pp. 147–173). Sydney, Australia: Institute of Criminology.

BAZEMORE G. & EARLE, T. H. (2002). Balance in the response to family violence: Changing restorative principles. In H. Strang & J. Barithwaite (Eds.), *Restorative justice and family violence* (pp. 153–177). Melbourne, Australia: Cambridge University Press.

BAZEMORE, G., O'BRIEN, S. & CAREY, M. (2005). Energy and substance of organizational and community change in response to crime and conflict: The emergence and potential of restorative justice. *Public Organization Review: A Global Journal*, 5, 287–314.

BRAITHWAITE, J. & DALY, K. (1998). Masculinities, violence and communitarian control. In S.L. Miller (Ed.), *Crime control and women: Feminist implication in criminal justice policy* (pp. 151–180). London, UK: Sage Publications.
BROWNMILLER, S. (1975). *Against our will: Men, women and rape.* New York, NY: Simon & Schuster.
BRYDEN, D.P. & LENGNICK, S. (1997). Rape in the criminal justice system. *Journal of Criminal Law & Criminology, 87*, 1194–1384.
BRYDEN, D.P. (2000). Redefining rape. *Buffalo Criminal Law Review, 3*, 317–512.
BUBLICK, E.M. (1999). Citizen no-duty rules: rape victims and comparative fault. *The Columbia Law Review, 99*, 1413–1490.
BUBLICK, E.M. (2006). Tort suits filed by rape and sexual assault victims in civil courts: Lessons for courts, classrooms and constituencies. *Southern Methodist University Law Review, 59*, 55–122.
BUCK, W., CHATTERTON, M. & PEASE, K. (1995). *Obscene, threatening and other troublesome telephone calls to women in England and Wales, 1982–1992.* London, England: Home Office.
CAMPBELL, R. (1998). The community response to rape: victim's experiences with the legal, medical, and mental health systems. *American Journal of Community Psychology, 26*, 355–380.
CAMPBELL, R. (2005). What really happened? A validation study of rape survivors' help-seeking experiences with the legal and medical systems. *Violence and Victims, 20*, 55–68.
CAMPBELL, R. & JOHNSON, C.R. (1997). Police officers' perceptions of rape: Is there consistency between state law and individual beliefs? *Journal of Interpersonal Violence, 12*, 255-269.
CAMPBELL, R., BAKER, C. K. & MAZUREK, T.L. (1998). Remaining radical? Organizational predictors of rape crisis centers' social change initiatives. *American Journal of Community Psychology, 26*, 457–483.
CAMPBELL, R., SEFL, T., BARNES, H.E., AHRENS, C., WASCO, S.M. & ZARAGOZA-DIESFELD, Y. (1999). Community services for rape survivors: Enhancing psychological well-being or increasing trauma? *Journal of Consulting and Clinical Psychology, 67*, 847–858.
CHANDLER, S.M. & TORNEY, M. (1981). The decisions and the processing of rape victims through the criminal justice system. *California Sociologist, 4*, 155–169.
CLAY-WARNER, J. & BURT, C.H. (2005). Rape reporting after reforms: Have times really changed? *Violence Against Women, 11*, 150–176.
CLUSS, P.A., BOUGHTON, J., FRANK, E., STEWART, B.D. & WEST, D. (1983). The rape victim: Psychological correlates of participation in the legal process. *Criminal Justice and Behavior, 10*, 342–357.
COKER, D. (1999). Enhancing autonomy for battered women: Lessons from Navajo peacemaking. *University of California Law Review, 47*, 1–99.
COKER, D. (2004). Race, poverty, and the crime-centered response to domestic violence: A comment on Linda Mill's insult to injury: Rethinking our responses to intimate abuse. *Violence Against Women, 10*, 1331–1353.
COX, D.J. (1988). Incidence and nature of male genital exposure behavior as reported by college women. *The Journal of Sex Research, 24*, 227–234.
CUNEEN, C. (2004). What are the implications of restorative justice's use of indigenous traditions? In H. Zehr & B. Toews (Eds.), *Critical issues in restorative justice* (pp. 345–354). Monsey, NY: Criminal Justice Press and Cullompton, Devon, UK: William Publishing.

CURTIS-FAWLEY, S. & DALY, K. (2005). Gendered violence and restorative justice: The views of victim advocates. *Violence Against Women*, *11*, 603–638.

DALY, K. (2005). *Seeking justice in the 21st century: The contested politics of race and gender*. Brisbane, Australia: School of Criminology and Criminal Justice, Griffith University.

DALY, K., CURTIS-FAWLEY, S. & BOUHOURS, B. (2003a) Sexual offence cases finalized in court, by conference, and by formal caution in South Australia for young offenders, 1995–2001. Brisbane Australia: School of Criminology and Criminal Justice, Griffith University.

DALY, K. & STUBBS, J. (2005). Feminist theory, feminist and anti-racist politics, and restorative justice. In G. Johnstone & D. van Ness (Eds.), *Handbook of Restorative Justice*. Cullompton Devon, UK: William Publishing.

DALY, K. & STUBBS, J. (2006). Feminist engagement with restorative justice. *Theoretical Criminology Special Issue on Gender, Race, and Restorative Justice*, *10*, 9–28.

DES ROSIERS, N., FELDTHUSEN, B. & HANKIVSKY, O.A.R. (1998). Legal compensation for sexual violence: Therapeutic consequences and consequences for the judicial system. *Psychology, Public Policy, & Law*, *4*, 433–451.

DIGNAN, J. (2005). *Understanding victims and restorative justice*. Berkshire, England: Open University Press.

DIGNAN, J. & CAVADINO, M. (1996). Towards a framework for conceptualizing and evaluating models of criminal justice from a victim's perspective. *International Review of Victimology*, *4*, 153–182.

DU MONT, J. & PARNIS, D. (2006). *The uses and impacts of medico-legal evidence in sexual assault cases: A global review*. Unpublished document prepared for the Gender Health Unit, World Health Organization, Geneva, Switzerland.

EPSTEIN, J.N., SAUNDERS, B.E. & KILPATRICK, D. G. (1997). Predicting PTSD in women with a history of childhood rape. *Journal of Traumatic Stress*, *10*, 573–588.

ESTRICH, S. (1986). Rape. *Yale Law Journal*, *95*, 1087–1184.

ESTRICH, S. (1987). *Real rape*. Cambridge, MA: Harvard University Press.

ESTRICH, S. (1995). "Is it rape?" In P. Searles and R. Berger (Eds.), *Rape and society: Readings on the problem of sexual assault* (pp. 183–193). Boston: Westview Press.

FAIRSTEIN, L. (1993). *Sexual violence: Our war against rape*. New York, NY: William Morrow.

FELDBERG, G. (1997). Defining the facts of rape: The uses of medical evidence in sexual assault trials. *Canadian Journal of Women and the Law*, *9*, 89–114.

FELSON, R.B. & PARÉ, P. (2005). The reporting of domestic violence and sexual assault by non-strangers to the police. *Journal of Marriage and Family*, *67*, 597–610.

FERRARO, K.J. & BOYCHUCK, T. (1992). The court's response to interpersonal violence: a comparison of intimate and nonintimate assault. (pp. 209–225). In E.S. Buzawa & C.G. Buzawa (Eds.), *Domestic Violence: The changing criminal justice response* (pp. 209–225). Westport, CT: Auburn House.

FISHER, B.S., CULLEN, F.T., and TURNER, M.G. (2000). The sexual victimization of college women. Washington, DC: US Department of Justice, Office of Justice Programs. (NCJ 182369).

FRAZIER, P.A. & HANEY, B. (1996). Sexual assault cases in the legal system: Police, prosecutor, and victim perspectives. *Law and Human Behavior*, *20*, 607–628.

FREDERICK, L. & LIZDAS, K.C. (2003). The role of restorative justice in the battered women's movement. Battered Women's JUSTICE Project (BWJP).

Accessed October 30, 2006 at http://data.ipharos.com/bwjp/documents/restroative_justice.pdf

FROHMANN, L. (1991). Discrediting victims' allegations of sexual assault: Prosecutorial accounts of case rejections. *Social Problems, 38*, 213–226.

FROHMANN, L. (1997). Convictability and discordant locales: Reproducing race, class, and gender ideologies in prosecutorial decision making. *Law & Society Review, 31*, 531–555.

FROHMANN, L. (1998). Constituting power in sexual assault cases: Prosecutorial strategies for victim management. *Social Problems, 45*, 393–407.

GOEL, R. (2005). Stia's trousseau: Restorative justice, domestic violence, and South Asian culture. *Violence Against Women, 11*, 639–665.

GOLDING, J.M. (1999). Intimate partner violence as a risk factor for mental disorders: A Meta-Analysis. *Journal of Family Violence, 14*, 99–132.

GOLDING, J.M. (1999). Sexual assault history and medical care seeking: The roles of symptom prevalence and illness behavior. *Psychology & Health, 14*, 949–957.

GUTHEIL, T.G., BURSZTAJN, H., BRODSKY, B., STRASBURGER, L.H. (2000). Preventing "critogenic" harms: minimizing emotional injury from civil litigation. *Journal of Psychiatry and Law, 28*, 5–19.

GREENFIELD, L.A., RAND, M.R., CRAVEN, D., FLAUS, P.A., PERKINS, C.A., RINGEL, WARCHOL, C., MASTON, C. & FOX, J.A. (1998). Violence by intimates: Analysis of data on crimes by current or former spouses, boyfriends, and girlfriends. (NCJ-167237). Washington, DC: US Department of Justice, Bureau of Justice Statistics.

HAKIAHA, M. (2004). What is the state's role in indigenous justice? In H. Zehr & B. Toews (Eds.), *Critical issues in restorative justice* (pp. 635–364). Monsey, NY: Criminal Justice Press and Cullompton, Devon, UK: William Publishing.

HANSON, R.K. & BROOM, I. (2005). The utility of cumulative meta-analysis: Application to programs for reducing sexual violence. *Sexual Abuse: A Journal of Research and Treatment, 17*, 357–374.

HARRIS, J. & GRACE, S. (1999). A Question of evidence? Investigating and prosecuting rape in the 1990s (Rep. No. 196). Room 201, Home Office, 50 Queen Anne's Gate, London, Great Britain: Research, Development & Statistics Directorate, Information and Publications Group.

HARRISON, K. (2006). Community punishment or community rehabilitation: Which is the highest in the sentencing tariff? *The Howard Journal of Criminal Justice, 45*, 141–158.

HERBERT, C.P., WIEBE, E.R. (1989). That notwithstanding clause again. *Canadian Medical Association Journal, 141*, 97–98.

HERMAN, J.L. (2005). Justice from the victim's perspective. *Violence Against Women, 11*, 571–602.

HERMAN, S. (2004). Is restorative justice possible without a parallel system for victims? In H. Zehr & B. Toews (Eds.), *Critical issues in restorative justice* (pp. 75–84). Monsey, NY: Criminal Justice Press and Cullompton, Devon, UK: William Publishing.

HOLMES, R.M. & HOLMES, S.T. (2002). *Current perspectives on sex crimes*. Thousand Oaks, CA: Sage.

HOLMSTROM, L.L. & BURGESS, A.W. (1975). Rape: The victim and the criminal justice system. *International Journal of Criminology & Penology, 3*, 101–110.

HOLMSTROM, L.L. & BURGESS, A.W. (1978). *The victim of rape: Institutional reactions*. New York, NY: Wiley.

HOPKINS, C.Q., KOSS, M.P. & BACHAR, K.J. (2004). Applying restorative justice to ongoing intimate violence: Problems and possibilities. *St.Louis University Public Law Review*, *23*, 289–312.

HOPKINS, C.Q., KOSS, M.P. & BACHAR, K. (2004). Incorporating feminist theory and insights into a restorative justice response to sex offenses. *Violence Against Women*, *11*, 693–723.

HORNEY, J. & SPOHN, C. (1990). Rape law reform and instrumental change in six urban jurisdictions. *Law & Society Review*, *25(1)*, 117–153.

HUDSON, B. (1998). Restorative justice: The challenge of sexual and racial violence. *Journal of Law & Society*, *25*, 237–256.

HUDSON, B. (2002). Restorative justice and gendered violence: Diversion or effective justice? *British Journal of Criminology*, *42*, 616–634.

HUMAN RIGHTS WATCH. (1999). *Crime or custom? Violence against women in Pakistan*. New York, NY: Human Rights Watch.

JASSO, G. (2005). Culture and the sense of justice: A comprehensive framework for analysis. *Journal of Cross-Cultural Psychology*, *36*, 14–47.

JENKINS, R. (2000). Identity, social process and epistemology. *Current Sociology*, *48*, 7–25.

JOHNSTONE, G. (2004, October 11) The idea of restorative justice, Inaugural Lecture, University of Hull.

JORDAN, J. (2004). Beyond belief? Police, rape and women's credibility. *Criminal Justice*, *4*, 25–59.

KANIN, E.J. (1994). False rape allegations. *Archives of Sexual Behavior*, *23*, 81–91.

KELLY, L. (2001). Routes to (in)justice: A research review on the reporting, investigation and prosecution of rape cases. University of North London: Child and Woman Abuse Studies Unit.

KERTSETTER, W.A. (1990). Justice pursued: The legal and moral basis of disposition in sexual assault cases. American Bar Foundation Working Paper Series, No. 9129.

KILPATRICK, D.G. & EDWARDS, C.N. & SEYMOUR, A.E. (April 23, 1992). *Rape in America: A report to the nation*. Arlington, VA: National Crime Victims Center.

KONRADI, A. (1997). Too little too late: Prosecutors pre-court preparation of rape survivors. *Law and Social Inquiry*, *22*, 1101–1154.

KONRADI, A. (1999). 'I don't have to be afraid of you': Rape survivors' emotion management in court. *Symbolic Interaction*, *22*, 45–77.

KOSS, M.P. (1988). Hidden rape: Sexual aggression and victimization in a national sample of students in higher education. In A.W. Burgess (Ed.), *Rape and Sexual Assault II* (pp. 3–25). New York, NY: Garland Publishing, Inc.

KOSS, M.P. (2000). Blame, shame and community: justice responses to violence against women. *American Psychologist*, *55*, 1332–1343.

KOSS, M.P., BACHAR, K.J. & HOPKINS, C.Q. (2003). An innovative application of restorative justice to the adjudication of selected sexual offenses. In H. Kury & J. Obergfell-Fuchs (Eds.), *Crime Prevention: New Approaches* (pp. 321–333). Mainz: Germany: Weisser Ring.

KOSS, M.P., BACHAR, K.J., HOPKINS, C.Q. & CARLSON, C. (2004). Expanding a community's justice response to sex crimes through advocacy, prosecutorial, and public health collaboration. *Journal of Interpersonal Violence*, *19*, 1435–1463.

KOSS, M.P., BACHAR, K.J., HOPKINS, C.Q. & CARLSON, C. (2004b). Justice responses to sexual assault: Lessons learned and new directions. In M. Eliasson (Ed.),

Undoing harm: International perspectives on interventions for men who use violence against women (pp. 37–60). Uppsala, Sweden: Uppsala Women's Studies: Uppsala University.

Koss, M. & Figuerado, A.J. (2004a). Cognitive mediation of rape's mental health impact: constructive replication of a cross-sectional model in longitudinal data. *Psychology of Women Quarterly, 28,* 273–286.

Koss, M. & Figuerado, A.J. (2004b). Change in cognitive mediators of rape's impact on psychosocial health across 2 years of recovery. *Journal of Consulting and Clinical Psychology, 72,* 1063–1072.

LaFree, G.D. (1980). The effect of sexual stratification by race on official reactions to rape. *American Sociological Review, 45,* 842–854.

LaFree, G.D. (1981). Official reactions to social problems: Police decisions in sexual assault cases. *Social Problems, 28,* 582–594.

LaFree, G.D. (1989). *Rape and criminal justice: The social construction of sexual assault.* Belmont, CA: Wadsworth.

Madigan, L. & Gamble, N.C. (1991). *The second rape: Society's continued betrayal of the victim.* London, UK: MacMillan.

Marshall, T. (1999). *Restorative justice: An overview.* London, UK: Home Office Research, Development and Statistics Directorate.

Martin, P.Y. & Powell, R.M. (1994). Accounting for the second assault: Legal organizations' framing of rape victims. *Law & Social Inquiry, 19,* 853–890.

Martin, D.L. (1998). Retribution revisited: A reconsideration of feminist criminal law reform strategies. *Osgoode Hall Law Journal, 36,* 151.

Martin, P.Y. (2005). *Rape work: Victims, gender, and emotions in organization and community context.* New York, NY: Routledge, Taylor & Francis Group.

Matoesian, G. (1993). *Reproducing rape: Domination through talk in the courtroom.* Chicago, IL: University of Chicago Press.

McBarnet, D. (1988). Law, policy, and legal avoidance: Can law effectively implement egalitarian policies? *Journal of Law and Society, 15,* 113–121.

McCahill, T.W., Meyer, L.C., Fischman, A.M. (1979). The aftermath of rape. Lexington, MA: Lexington Books.

Miller, T.R., et al. (1996). Victim costs and consequences: a new look. Washington, DC: The US Department of Justice.

Monroe, L.M., Kinney, L., Weist, M.D., Spriggs-Dafeamekpor, D., Dantzler, J. & Reynolds, M.W. (2005). The experience of sexual assault. *The Journal of Interpersonal Violence, 20,* 767–776.

Nancarrow, H. (2006). In search of justice for domestic violence and family violence: Indigenous and non-indigenous women's perspectives in Australia. *Theoretical Criminology, 10,* 87–106.

Orth, U. & Maercker, A. (2004). Do trials of perpetrators retraumatize crime victims? *Journal of Interpersonal Violence, 19,* 212–227.

Orth, U., Montada, L. & Maercker, A. (2006). Feelings of revenge, retaliation motive, and posttraumatic stress reactions in crime victims. *Journal of Interpersonal Violence, 21,* 229–243.

Post, L.A., Mezey, N. J., Maxwell, C. & Wibert, W. N. (2002). The rape tax: Tangible and intangible costs of sexual violence. *Journal of Interpersonal Violence, 17,* 773–782.

Peled, E., Eiskovitz, Z., Enosh, G. & Winstok, Z. (2000). Choice and empowerment for battered women who stay: Toward a constructivist model. *Social Work, 45,* 9–21.

POULSON, B. (2003). A third voice: A review of empirical research on the psychological outcomes of restorative justice. *Utah Law Review, 167*, 167–203.

POWELL, L.A. (2005). Justice judgments as complex psychocultural constructions: An equity-based heuristic for mapping two and three dimensional fairness representations in perceptual space. *Journal of Cross-Cultural Psychology, 36*, 48–73.

RAYE, B. (2004). *How do culture, class and gender affect the practice of restorative justice? Critical issues in restorative justice.* Monsey, NY: Criminal Justice Press and Cullompton, Devon, UK: William Publishing.

RAZACK, S.H. (1998). Looking white people in the eye: Gender, race, and culture in courtrooms and classrooms. In K. Daly & J. Maher (Eds.), *Criminology at the crossroads: Feminist readings in crime and justice* (pp. 225–245). New York, NY: Oxford.

REIMUND, M.E. (2005). Law and restorative justice: friend or foe? A systemic look at the legal issues in restorative justice. *Drake Law Review, 53*, Rev. 667.

RIORDAN, S. (1999). Indecent exposure: the impact upon the victim's fear of sexual crime. *Journal of Forensic Psychiatry, 10*, 309–346.

ROCHE, D. (2003). Accountability in restorative justice. Clarendon Studies in Criminology. Oxford, UK: Oxford University Press.

ROSE, V.M. & RANDALL, S.C. (1982). The impact of investigator perceptions of victim legitimacy on the processing of rape/sexual assault cases. *Symbolic Interaction, 5*, 23–36.

SANDAY, P.R. (1996). *A woman scorned: Acquaintance rape on trial.* New York, NY: Doubleday.

SCHULHOFER, S.J. (1998). *Unwanted sex: The culture of intimidation and the failure of law.* Cambridge, MA: Harvard University Press.

SEIDMAN, I. & VICKERS, S. (2005). The second wave: an agenda for the next thirty years of rape law reform. *Suffolk University Law review, XXXVIII*, 457–490.

SHAPLAND, J. (2003). Restorative justice and criminal justice. Just responses to crime. In A. von Hirsch, J. Roberts, A.E. Bottoms, K. Roach & M. Schiff (Eds). *Restorative justice & criminal justice: competing or reconcilable paradigms?* (pp. 195–218). Hart Publishing, Oxford and Portland, Oregon.

SHERMAN, L.W. & STRANG H. (2004). Restorative justice: what we know and how we know it. Working paper #1. Philadelphia: University of Pennsylvania Jerry Lee Center of Criminology.

SHERMAN, L.W., STRANG, H., ANGEL, C., WOODS, D., BARNES, G.C., BENNETT, S. & INKPEN, N. (2005). Effects of face-to-face restorative justice on victims of crime in four randomized, controlled trials. *Journal of Experimental Criminology*, 367–395.

SLOAN, L.M. (1995). Revictimization by polygraph: The practice of polygraphing survivors of sexual assault. *Journal of Medicine and Law, 14*, 255–267.

SMITH, M.D. & MORRA, N.N. (1994). Obscene and threatening telephone calls to women: Data from a Canadian National Survey. *Gender & Society, 8*, 584–596.

SMITH, A. (2005). Book review: of restorative justice and family violence. *Violence Against Women, 11*, 724–730.

SNIDER, L. (1998). Feminism, punishment, and the potential of empowerment. In K. Daly & L. Maher (Eds.), *Criminology at the crossroads: Feminist readings in crime and justice* (pp. 246–261). New York, NY: Oxford University Press.

SPOHN, C. & HORNEY, J. (1992). *Rape law reform: A grassroots revolution and its impact.* New York, NY: Plenum.

STRANG, H. (2002). *Repair or revenge: Victims and restorative justice*. Oxford, UK: Clarendon Press.
STRANG, H. & BRAITHWAITE, J. (2002) (Eds.), *Restorative justice and family violence*. Cambridge, UK: Cambridge University Press.
STRANG, H. (2004). Is restorative justice imposing its agenda on victims? In H. Zehr & B. Toews (Eds.), *Critical issues in restorative justice* (pp. 95–106). Monsey, NY: Criminal Justice Press and Cullompton, Devon, UK: William Publishing.
TJADEN, P. & THOENNES, N. (1998). Prevalence, incidence, and consequences of violence against women: Findings from the national violence against women survey. Research in brief (NCJ-172837). Washington, D.C.: Department of Justice.
US DEPARTMENT OF JUSTICE, BUREAU OF JUSTICE STATISTICS (1992). *State and local police departments, 1990*. Washington, DC: Department of Justice.
VAN NESS, D. (2003). Proposed basic principles on the use of restorative justice: Recognizing the aims and limits of restorative justice (pp.157–176). In Von Hirsch, A., Roberts, J.V., Bottoms, A., Roach, K. & Schiff, M. (Eds), *Restorative justice and criminal justice: competing or reconcilable paradigms?* Oxford and Portland, OR: Hart Publishing.
WALBY, S. & MAYBELL, A. (2001). New survey methodologies in researching violence against women. *British Journal of Criminology*, 41, 502–522.
WATERS, H., HYDER, A., RAJKOTIA, Y., BASU, S., REHWINKEL, J.A., BUTCHART, A. (2004). *The economic dimensions of interpersonal violence*. Geneva: World Health Organization.
WEISZ, A.N. (1999). Legal advocacy for domestic violence survivors: The power of an informative relationship. *Families in Society*, 80, 138–147.
WEITEKAMP, E.G.M. (1999). The history of restorative justice. In G. Bazemore & L. Walgrave (Eds.,) *Restorative juvenile justice: Repairing the harm of youth crime* (pp. 75–102). Monsey, NY: Criminal Justice Press/Willow Tree Press.
WEITEKAMP, E.G.M. & KERNER, H.J. (2003). *Restorative justice in context: International practice and directions*. Devon, England: William Publishing.
WENINGER, R.A. (1978). Factors affecting the prosecution of rape: A case study of Travis County, Texas. *Virginia Law Review*, 64, 357–398.
WHATLEY, M.A. (1996). Victim characteristics influencing attributions of responsibility to rape victims: A meta-analysis. *Aggression and Violent Behavior*, 1, 81–95.
WILLIAMS, K. (1981). Few convictions in rape cases: Empirical evidence concerning some alternative explanations. *Journal of Criminal Justice*, 9, 23–36.
YOSHIDA, T. (2003). Confession, apology, repentance and settlement out-of-court in the Japanese criminal justice system—is Japan a model of "restorative justice"? In Weitekamp, E.G.M. & Kerner, H.J. (Eds.), *Restorative Justice in context: International practice and direction* (pp. 173–196). Devon, England: William Publishing.
YOUNG, R. (2002) Testing the limits of restorative justice: the case of corporate victims, in C. Hoyle and R. Young (Eds.), New Visions of Crime Victims. Oxford: Hart.
YUAN, N., KOSS, M., STONE, M. The psychological consequences of sexual trauma. (2006) (pp. 1–10). Accessed September 14, 2006 at www.VAWnet.org.

Violence against Women as a Public Health Issue

JOAN C. CHRISLER AND SHEILA FERGUSON

Connecticut College, New London, Connecticut, USA

> ABSTRACT: Violence can be considered "infectious" in rape-prone cultures that celebrate violence and domination. The number of annual injuries and deaths due to violence against women and girls is high enough to demand the type of active interventions and public policies that have been targeted at infectious diseases by public health agencies. In this article, we review data on the physical and mental health effects that violence has on victims of domestic violence, rape, stalking, and sexual harassment. We also focus on the economic costs to the health care system, business and industry, families, and the broader society that accrue as a result of the widespread violence against women and girls. Victims' suffering can never be accounted for by economic data, but those data may be helpful in pushing governments to allocate funds and agencies to take preventive actions.
>
> KEYWORDS: women; girls; violence; mental health; sexual harassment; rape; economics; domestic violence

The term "public health" probably calls to mind programs aimed at preventing the spread of infectious diseases such as polio, syphilis, or avian flu. However, violence is also "infectious" in a culture that seems to encourage, or at least to tolerate, it. The United States has been classified as a rape-prone culture (Rozee, 1993) that celebrates aggression and domination. Violence is a frequent theme in our films, television shows, video games, comic books, and popular songs. The number of annual injuries and deaths in the United States that are due to criminal violence is high enough to demand the type of active interventions and public policies that traditionally have been targeted at infectious diseases. In fact, in 1985 U.S. Surgeon General C. Everett Koop declared domestic violence the biggest health crisis of the decade. We do not mean to imply that no progress has been made since then, but a lot more needs to be accomplished.

Feminists typically consider violence against women and girls to be an abuse of power in the course of the domination, intimidation, and victimization of

---

Address for correspondence: Dr. Joan C. Chrisler, Department of Psychology, Connecticut College, New London, CT 06320. Voice: 860-439-2336; fax: 860-439-5005.
e-mail: jcchr@conncoll.edu

one person by another, often, but not always, in the context of a relationship. Violence against women by intimate partners includes domestic or courtship violence, stalking, and rape. Violence against women and girls by family members includes child or elder abuse, incest, and incidental injuries in the course of domestic partner violence. Violence against women by coworkers, casual acquaintances, or strangers includes sexual harassment, stalking, rape, and violence in the course of the commission of another crime (e.g., mugging). It would be a mistake to assume that all such violence is committed by men and boys against women and girls. We know, for example, that intimate partner violence is a problem in lesbians' and gay men's relationships (Island, & Letellier, 1991; Renzetti, 1992; Stahly & Lie, 1995), and researchers have begun to document and study instances of violence against men by women (e.g., Anderson, 2005; Brush, 2005; McHugh, 2005). However, because most men are bigger and stronger than most women (hence, able to inflict more serious damage), there appear to be many more instances of violence by men than by women, and more data are available on women's injuries at the hands of men, we focus our attention here on the public health effects of violence against women that was most likely committed by men.

Despite cultural connotations of home as a cozy, safe haven, the home can be a dangerous place. It is the site of more violence against women and girls than any other location. The Australian Public Health Association (1990 as cited in Hegarty, Hindmarsh, & Gilles, 2000) has urged a comprehensive view of domestic violence, which it defines as follows: (1) physical abuse—any action that causes pain and injury; denial of sleep, warmth, or nutrition; sexual assault; violence to property or animals; and murder; (2) verbal abuse—in private or in public, the use of words that are designed to humiliate, degrade, demean, intimidate, or subjugate, including the threat of physical violence; (3) economic abuse—the deprivation of basic necessities, seizure of income or assets, or unreasonable denial of the means necessary for participation in social life; (4) social abuse—usually accomplished through isolation from friends and family members, the control of all social activity, deprivation of liberty, or the deliberate creation of unreasonable dependence. Any given instance of domestic violence can contain a combination of these types of abuse. However, because our main concern here is physical health, we will focus on physical abuse. Keep in mind that all four types of abuse described above produce mental health effects in the victims.

THE COSTS OF VIOLENCE AND ITS AFTERMATH

We begin our discussion of violence as a public health issue with some data from the U.S. Centers for Disease Control and Prevention (CDC; National Center for Injury Prevention and Control 2003) that illustrate starkly the economic costs of violence against women to the victims and to society. These data were collected in 1995, and the costs were calculated and published in 2003. Most of the data we present come directly from the CDC, but some costs we calculated ourselves based on the CDC data. Readers should keep in mind that the data are based on the number of violent incidents reported. Of course, many instances of domestic violence and rape are never reported; thus, the costs are almost certainly higher than the estimates we present.

Why begin with costs? We do this not to reduce women's pain and suffering to dollars and cents, but because (1) the costs demonstrate the impact that violence against women has on society; (2) these costs can be used effectively to shape the attitudes of people who develop public policy and allocate limited funds to projects intended to prevent violence; and (3) costs can also be used to assess the benefit or effectiveness of violence prevention strategies and thus lead to better resource allocation. The data show that health insurance plans do not cover the entire cost of medical and mental health care visits. The fact that victims must pay for part of their treatment adds insult to injury. If we had universal health care in the United States, victims would not have to pay twice (with their finances and their suffering) for a crime they did not commit. Note that productivity costs include lost work time due to injuries, court dates, and psychological sequelae such as anxiety, depression, and posttraumatic stress disorder.

Domestic Violence

The CDC estimates that 4,450,807 women are assaulted each year by their intimate partners. Forty-one percent of those assaults cause observable injuries, and 519,031 of the assaults (28.1% of those injured) require medical care for the victim. The average cost of the medical care per assault is $548, of which the victim herself pays more than one-fourth of the cost. The medical costs include ambulance/paramedic services, emergency room treatment, hospitalization, and visits to outpatient clinics, physicians, dentists, and physical therapists.

The types of injuries that women suffer at the hands of their intimate partners range from minor injuries (e.g., scratches, bruises, welts) to death. Between 1976 and 1996, 30% of femicides in the United States were at the hands of intimate partners, and 41% were carried out by someone else the women knew (Greenfield, Rand, & Craven, 1998). Sixty-six percent of the women killed by their current or former spouse or lover in the year 2000 had suffered from intimate partner violence (IPV) prior to being killed; 50% of them had made visits to emergency rooms as a result of injuries sustained during IPV (Sharp, *et al*. 2001).

Other common injuries that result from IPV include broken bones, broken teeth, burns, bullet wounds, lacerations, knife wounds, and sore muscles. Approximately 67% of women who visit emergency rooms after IPV have symptoms of a head injury; 30% of IPV victims have suffered a loss of consciousness at least once. Between 81% and 94% of women who visit emergency rooms after IPV have facial injuries. Thirty-three percent of orbital fractures, some of which were sight-threatening, are due to IPV. Studies indicate that approximately 68% of victims of domestic violence are strangled at least once; the average is 5.3 times per victim. Strangulation obviously can cause death, but, when it does not, it can lead to problems with swallowing, difficulty speaking, neck pain, dizziness, headache, memory loss, hemiparesis, or paralysis (Wilbur *et al.*, 2001). Strangulation is undoubtedly so common because it is particularly terrifying for the victim.

Pregnancy is a high-risk time for IPV. In a recent British study, the researchers (Richardson *et al.*, 2002) found that pregnancy increased the risk of experiencing violence by a factor of 2.11. In one study of 358 low-income women (O'Campo, Gielen, Faden, & Kass, 1994), 65% reported having experienced either verbal or physical abuse by their male partner or another family member during their pregnancies. Approximately 4–8% of women are physically abused at least once during pregnancy (Gazmararian *et al.*, 2000), and in 5.5–6.6% of all pregnancies there is some trauma to the woman and her fetus (Stewart & Cecutti, 1993). Between 13% and 25% of pregnancy-related deaths are femicides (Dannenberg *et al.*, 1995). The pregnant woman's abdomen is a frequent site of injuries, which are often caused by punching and kicking; the assailants' attempts to damage the fetus are especially frightening to the women. Studies have shown that physical abuse during pregnancy delays prenatal care by an average of 6.5 weeks (Taggert & Mattson, 1996), and can also result in increased risk of miscarriage (Jacoby, Gorenflo, Black, Wunderlich, & Eyler, 1999) and premature labor (Cokkinides, Coker, Sanderson, Addy, & Bethea, 1999), anemia, poor weight gain, vaginal infections, and low birth weight of infants (Murphy, Schei, Myhr, & Bu, 2001). In addition, the women's health behavior often takes a turn for the worse, as they attempt to cope with the IPV and its aftermath with increased use of alcohol, tobacco, and other drugs (Curry, Perrin, & Wall, 1998).

The traumatic nature of some of the injuries as well as the shock, anxiety, and loss of self-confidence that result from violent betrayal by a trusted intimate, means that many victims suffer psychologically as well as physically from incidents of domestic violence. Approximately 26% of victims speak with a psychologist, psychiatrist, or other mental health professional following an assault. Assault victims average 12.9 visits to a mental health professional at an average cost of $78.86 per visit or a total cost of $1,017. The victim herself pays one-third of the cost.

Approximately one-sixth (741,801) of victims of domestic violence lose time from paid work as a result of the assaults. The mean daily earnings lost are $93 or a total (for all victims) of $68,987,493 per day. In addition, 10.3% (458,433) of victims are unable to perform childcare or housework for a time. The mean daily cost to replace the women's work at home is $24 or a total (for all victims) of $11,002,392 per day.

Rape

The CDC estimates that 322,230 women per year are raped by their intimate partners. About 36% of those rapes cause physical injuries, of which 36,161 (31.2% of those injured) require medical care for the victim. The average cost of the medical care per assault is $516, of which the victim herself pays more than one-fourth of the cost. Note that this figure does not include annual incidents of stranger rape. Researchers have estimated that, overall, about 1 in 5 women have been raped (Koss, 1993) and about 25% of rape victims are physically injured seriously enough to require medical attention (Horton, 1992).

Marchbanks, Lui, and Mercy (1990) examined the medical records of rape victims and reported that 82% had black eyes and orbital swelling; 25% had bites, burns, or scalding, and injuries from physical restraints or bindings; 19% had internal injuries and had experienced loss of consciousness; 8% had broken bones or teeth; and 2% had knife or gunshot wounds. Rape victims also frequently experience vaginal injuries and bruises or other external trauma, usually on the mouth, throat, breasts, and thighs (Banks, Ackerman, & Corbett, 1995). Pregnancy, sexually transmitted diseases, and dyspareunia are also common results of rape.

The traumatic nature of rape as well as the fear, anxiety, and victim blame that often accompanies it, means that many victims suffer psychologically as well as physically during and after a rape. Approximately 33% of victims of rape by an intimate partner speak with a psychologist, psychiatrist, or other mental health professional following a rape. Rape victims average 12.4 visits to a mental health professional at an average cost of $78.86 per visit or a total cost of $978. The victim herself pays more than one-third of the cost.

Approximately one-fifth (64,446) of victims of rape by an intimate partner lose time from paid work as a result of the assaults. The mean daily earnings lost are $69 or a total (for all victims) of $4,446,774 per day. In addition, 13.5% (43,501) of those victims are unable to perform childcare or housework for a time. The mean daily cost to replace the women's work at home is $19 or a total (for all victims) of $830,870 per day.

Stalking and Sexual Harassment

Stalking was defined by the National Violence against Women Survey (1996 as cited in Paludi, 2004) as "a course of conduct directed at a specific person that involves repeated visual or physical proximity, nonconsensual communication, or verbal, written, or implied threats, or a combination thereof, that would cause a reasonable person fear." Some stalkers are overtly threatening, but others are not; some stalkers eventually physically assault or even murder their victims, but others do not (Davis & Frieze, 2002). Women are at highest risk of experiencing stalking following divorce, separation, or breaking up with a dating partner if that partner is angry or jealous (Davis & Frieze, 2002; Paludi, 2004). The CDC estimates that as many as 500,000 women are stalked each year by a current or former intimate partner. This number is likely to be a serious underestimate as it does not include women who are stalked by strangers or casual acquaintances. Stalking has only recently been recognized as a separate crime of threat and intimidation and it is difficult to find much information about it. Some data on stalking are likely to have been included in statistics on sexual harassment, which the CDC report does not discuss.

Neither stalking nor sexual harassment typically lead to physical injury, but they do have effects on women's mental health and their productivity. The CDC estimates that 43% of women who are stalked by an intimate speak with a psychologist, psychiatrist, or other mental health professional. Stalking victims average 9.6 visits to a mental health professional at an average cost of $71.87 per visit or a total cost of $690. The victim herself pays nearly one-third of the cost.

Approximately 35% (176,500) of victims of stalking by an intimate partner lose time from paid work. The mean daily earnings lost are $93 or a total (for all victims) of $16,414,500 per day. In addition, 17.5% (87,500) of those victims are unable to perform childcare or housework for a time. The mean daily cost to replace the women's work at home is $24 or a total (for all victims) of $2,100,000 per day. The CDC estimates that as many as 2.9 million work days may be lost per year because stalking victims are afraid that their current or former partners will follow them into the workplace and cause them humiliation or worse.

It is difficult to estimate the amount of sexual harassment that women experience each year. It can be difficult for people to determine when the boundary to sexual harassment has been crossed, and people whose experiences meet the legal definition of quid pro quo or hostile environment sexual harassment are often unwilling to apply the label to their experiences. In addition, there are women who know that they have been sexually harassed, but decide not to file a complaint for fear of losing a job or other benefits (e.g., good recommendations). The incidence of sexual harassment in the workplace is highly variable, but it seems to be greatest in male-dominated occupations. For example, the results of one survey (Yoder, 2001) of women in the military indicate that 76% of the participants had been harassed in the previous year. Surveys of college campuses indicate that 20–40% of women undergraduates have been sexually harassed, and the numbers are higher for graduate students, who are dependent on the good will of a particular faculty member (Paludi, 1996; Sandler & Shoop, 1997).

The anxiety and stress associated with sexual harassment, and the decisions victims must make about how to handle it and whether to report it have both health and productivity consequences. Common psychological effects of sexual harassment include embarrassment, anxiety, depression, fear, self-blame, and lowered self-confidence (Bravo & Cassidy, 1999; Paludi & Barickman, 1998). Physical effects include headaches, eating disorders, sleep disturbances, and lowered immunity (Paludi & Barickman, 1998). Productivity losses occur when victims take days off from work, change jobs or college majors, or drop out of college or graduate school to avoid the harasser (Paludi & Barickman, 1998).

Long-Term Effects of Violence against Women

Physical Effects

Violence against women has long-term as well as immediate health effects. Letourneau, Holmes, and Chasedunn-Roark (1999) found that women who had been victims of physical or sexual abuse were more likely than those who had not to report severe dysmenorrhea, dyspareunia, and one or more sexually transmitted diseases. Victims of violence also commonly report that they experience migraines, infections, gastrointestinal disorders, chronic pain, hypertension, and musculoskeletal problems. Some of these conditions are potentially disabling. Eby, Campbell, Sullivan, and Davidson (1995) found high rates of somatic complaints in their study of women who had experienced physical or sexual abuse within the previous 6 months. More than 50% of their 110 participants reported experiencing the following symptoms, which they believed were related to the abuse: low energy, sleep problems, headaches, muscle tension/soreness, constant fatigue, weight change, back pain, nightmares, dizziness, poor appetite, acid stomach or indigestion, weakness, stomach pain, pounding or racing heart, trembling limbs, severe aches and pains. Physical symptoms such as those described above can persist long after the abuse is over (Mouton, Rovi, Furniss, & Lasser, 1999). The symptoms could be the result of residual effects of injuries sustained during the violence or to stress-induced changes in immune functioning, posttraumatic stress disorder, or an intensified focus on physical sensations as a result of postviolence concerns about bodily integrity (Koss, 1994).

Sexually transmitted diseases and unintended pregnancies can have serious consequences for women's health. In addition to their immediate symptoms, certain STDs can lead to urinary tract infections, pelvic inflammatory disease, cervical cancer, infertility, and even death. Between 40% and 45% of physically assaulted women have also experienced forced intercourse and other risky sexual behavior (Campbell & Soeken, 2001). Furthermore, the inability to plan and space pregnancies negatively impacts women's physical and mental health (Russo, 2004).

Mental Health Effects

The experience of moderate violence is associated with 2.5 times the amount of emotional distress and suicidal thoughts and 3 times the amount of suicide attempts as are found in the general population (Fanslow & Robinson, 2004). Severe violence is associated with 4 times the amount of emotional distress and suicidal thoughts and 8 times the amount of suicide attempts as are found in the general population (Fanslow & Robinson, 2004). Although the psychological effects of violence diminish with time, they can be quite severe and distressing to victims.

Among the problems commonly diagnosed in women who have been victims of violence are anxiety disorders, depression, posttraumatic stress disorder, and antisocial behavior. In addition, women often complain of low self-esteem, body image issues, self-perceived poor health, fear of intimacy, and an inability to trust men (Fanslow & Robinson, 2004). Behavioral and substance abuse problems often develop after an experience of violence, perhaps in an effort to cope with overwhelming anxiety, in an attempt to distance themselves from their damaged bodies, or in reaction to a belief that the victims themselves are now worthless. Higher than average rates of alcohol and drug abuse and eating disorders are often reported among victims as are risky sexual behaviors (West, 2002). Women who have experienced violence may also be more likely than other women to smoke, to have poor nutritional intake, and to not get adequate exercise or sleep (Jenkins, 2002).

Violence also leads to increased use of medication and problems with activities of daily life. Women with chronic physical conditions such as pain or disability also can benefit from counseling or short-term psychotherapy (Kaschak, 2001).

Utilization of Medical Services

Researchers (e.g., Koss, 1994) typically find that victims of violence increase their frequency of health care utilization; the more severe the violence, the more physician visits women make. Koss (1994) found that rape victims, for example, increased their physician visits by 56% from an average of 4.1 visits the year before the rape to an average of 7.3 visits the year after. Victims of moderate levels of domestic violence increase their visits to physicians by a factor of 2. Increased use of medical care services may continue for up to 3 years postvictimization.

It is interesting to note that despite the fact that victims of violence increase their utilization of medical services, they report low rates of utilization of specialty mental health or victim assistance services. The underutilization of such services may occur for several reasons. Medical personnel may not recommend these services to their patients or the patients may prefer to avoid labeling themselves as victims or as in need of psychotherapy. Women victims may not have health insurance or their health insurance policies may not cover these specialized services. Finally, women may prefer to interpret the residual effects of the violence as physical rather than as psychological or psychosomatic sequelae. Talking to a physician may be more familiar and comfortable than talking to a psychotherapist or social worker.

PREVENTION OF VIOLENCE AGAINST WOMEN

Primary Prevention: Risk Reduction

Most primary prevention work consists of educational efforts that seek to inform the general public about violence against women and girls. These efforts define the different types of violence (e.g., date rape, stalking) so that people are able to recognize and label them, to become informed about legal avenues (e.g., restraining orders) and other programs (e.g., battered women's shelters) that women can use to protect themselves, and to provide information about how to get advice and support (e.g., telephone numbers of rape crisis hotlines). These efforts often take the form of public service announcements on radio and television; brochures distributed in libraries, physicians' offices, and community centers; and informational meetings in housing projects, churches, and women's clubs. Other antiviolence efforts have taken the form of lobbying for labels on compact disks and video games to inform parents of the extent of the violent content; ratings of films and television shows serve a similar purpose of restricting the amount of violence children encounter in cultural products.

Most prevention efforts have been targeted at educating women, the potential targets of the violence. However, more recently efforts have targeted men, the potential perpetrators of violence, and children, especially those who have witnessed domestic violence up close. Efforts directed at children are especially important as studies show that children from violent homes are not only damaged themselves by their experiences, but are at increased risk of committing violent acts themselves later in life. Boys who have witnessed their fathers abusing their mothers are 24 times more likely to commit sexual assault and 74 times more likely to commit other violent crimes than are boys who come from nonviolent homes (Jaffe, Wolfe, & Wilson, 1990). Sons frequently try to protect their mothers from violent attacks, often getting hurt themselves in the process. Sixty-three percent of adolescent boys and young men who are in jail for homicide were convicted of killing their mothers' batterers (Stahly, 2004).

More widespread and innovative efforts are needed, especially those that target high-risk groups (e.g., pregnant women, children of abused mothers), people who have already been arrested for or accused of violent acts (e.g., sexual harassment), and young men and boys in general. Some such efforts are described in other articles in this volume. We believe that information about violence should be included in childbirth preparation classes, premarital counseling, student orientation programs on college campuses, and character education units in elementary school curricula. Perhaps Boy Scouts could earn an antiviolence merit badge. We would applaud a movement of Hip-Hop Artists (possible slogan: "Real Men Don't Hit Women") and Athletes (possible slogan: "Aggression belongs on the playing field, not in the home") against Violence. The point is that, in a violent and rape-prone culture, where proviolence messages and images of violence acts are so common as to be desensitizing, antiviolence messages must become much more common before they are even noticed by the people who most need to hear them.

Secondary Prevention: Screening

The American Medical Association recommends both routine (e.g., internists, obstetricians/gynecologists) and opportunistic (e.g., emergency medical personnel) screening for violence. Psychotherapists, dentists, pediatricians, and other health and mental health care workers should also screen patients who are at high risk or present with unusual or suspicious injuries. Screening can be done via questionnaires or by face-to-face interviews, which have been shown to be most effective. Many physicians are uncomfortable about asking patients about violence, even when abuse is suspected, and better training is needed to assist them in this work (Richardson *et al.*, 2002). A study (Fanslow, Norton, & Robinson, 1999) conducted with personnel in an Auckland hospital's emergency room showed clearly how effective training can be—the number of confirmed (or suspected) cases of IPV significantly increased after the training. Such training must include not only how to elicit information about assault and abuse, but what to do if disclosure of violence is successfully elicited. Disclosure of violence to an official can increase a victim's risk of additional abuse and plans must be in place to protect her.

There are many reasons why screening for violence is important. Screening will increase the accuracy of incident rates of violence against women. Researchers (National Center for Injury Prevention and Control, 2003) have estimated, for example, that only about 20% of incidents of IPV are reported; many more are suspected, but not confirmed, and others, of course, go completely undetected. Health-related conditions can become worse (e.g., through repeated injury) if the abuse is not detected, yet abuse can be difficult to predict solely from the type of injuries sustained. Furthermore, violence against women is a drain on health resources, which are increasingly scarce in this economy, as women subjected to IPV return again and again for medical and mental health care.

Often victims of violence against women want to be asked about the origin of their injuries, which they are afraid to disclose, but might disclose during a screening procedure. Many barriers to disclosure have been documented in the literature (e.g., Head & Taft, 1995; Young, 1998), including fear (e.g., victims are often threatened with additional violence against themselves, their children, their pets, or their cherished belongings, if they disclose), denial and disbelief that their partner could be abusive, emotional bonds to their partner, commitment to their marriage, hope that the situation will change, staying in the relationship for the sake of the children, normalizing of (or desensitized to) violence (e.g., the belief that it happens to everyone), embarrassment, social isolation, depression, stress, anxiety, language difficulties, belief that they will not be believed, lack of privacy with the health care provider (e.g., partner insists on accompanying the woman in the examination room), strained relationship with the health care provider, and restricted access to services.

Tertiary Prevention: Coping and Recovery

Tertiary prevention efforts consist of interventions to prevent additional abuse of the victim as well as referral to appropriate medical care, mental health counseling, and other specialized services that will promote her ability to cope with the after-effects of the violence and to heal from her traumatic experiences as well as her injuries. A victim's primary care physician, her psychotherapist, or emergency medical personnel should have information necessary to make referrals to intervention programs and legal services. Calls might need to be placed to the police, a rape crisis counselor, or a battered women's shelter. Immediate interventions could include the arrest of the perpetrator or a shelter stay. Other interventions could include protection orders; advocacy, personal, or vocational counseling; or home visits by police or social workers after an arrest.

Longer-term interventions could include referral to a psychotherapist, a victim's services center, a physical therapist, a support group for victims of violence, children's services, or other specialized services that facilitate coping and recovery. In the case of IPV, the time when a victim leaves her violent partner is often the most dangerous point, and special care must be taken to protect and support the women and her children.

CONCLUSION

Violence against women was a major item on the agenda of the Women's Liberation Movement in the 1970s, and it remains important to feminists today. Thanks to the women's movement many forms of violence (e.g., date rape, sexual harassment) were given names and introduced to the general public as problems, not just of individual women but across society, and feminists have worked hard over the years to create programs and services (e.g., battered women's shelters, rape crisis hotlines) for victims. Few social issues have the power that interpersonal violence has to clarify the point that the personal is political. In fact, most people today accept the feminist notions that rape is a crime of violence and that domestic violence is a form of social control; such acceptance was rare in 1970. Thus, we have come a long way, but there is yet far to go.

A great deal of work needs to be done in all three areas of prevention and a lot more research needs to be done to provide the basis for adequate prevention efforts. There is so much we need to know and the answers to even a few of the questions below could make a big difference in the lives of women and girls. It is beyond the scope of this article to present a complete research agenda, but those who are interested in violence as a public health issue could start with the following:

- How does the experience of violence affect women's health and utilization of health and mental health services throughout their lives?
- How can we ensure that victims of violence will have the ability to access the services they need to help them to heal from their trauma and their injuries?
- How can we reduce the amount and glorification of violence in our culture?
- What are the most effective approaches to use in screening patients for history of violence?
- What are the most effective interventions to protect victims of violence?
- How can the criminal justice system work better to remove perpetrators of violence from society? And how can the system work more effectively to reform people convicted of violent crimes?

REFERENCES

ANDERSON, K.L. 2005. Theorizing gender in intimate partner violence research. Sex Roles 52, 853–865.

BANKS, M.E., R.J. ACKERMAN & C.A. CORBETT. 1995. Feminist neuropsychology: issues for physically challenged women. In Variations on a Theme: Diversity and the Psychology of Women. J.C. Chrisler & A.H. Hemstreet, Eds.: 29–49. State University of New York Press. Albany, NY.

BRAVO, E. & E. CASSIDY. 1999. The 9 to 5 Guide to Combating Sexual Harassment. Milwaukee: 9 to 5 Working Women Education Fund.

BRUSH, L.D. 2005. Philosophical and political issues in research on women's violence and aggression. Sex Roles 52, 867–873.

CAMPBELL, J.C., K. SOEKEN. 1999. Forced sex and intimate partner violence: effects on women's health. Violence Against Woman 5, 1017–1035.

CAMPBELL, J., A.S. JONES, J. DIENEMANN, et al. 2002. Intimate partner violence and physical health consequences. Archives of Internal Medicine 162, 1157–1163.

COKKINIDES, V.E., A.L. COKER, M. SANDERSON, et al.1999. Physical violence during pregnancy: maternal complications and birth outcomes. Obstetrics and Gynecology 93, 661–666.

CURRY, M.A., N. PERRIN & E. WALL. 1998. Effects of abuse on maternal complications and birth weight in adult and adolescent women. Obstetrics and Gynecology *92*, 530–534.

DANNENBERG, A.L., D.M. CARTER, H.W. LAWSON, *et al.*1995. Obstetrics: homicide and other injuries as causes of maternal death in New York City, 1987 through 1991. American Journal of Obstetrics and Gynecology *172*, 1557–1564.

DAVIS, K. & I.H. FRIEZE. 2002. Stalking: what do we know and where do we go? *In* Stalking: Perspectives on Victims and Perpetrators. K. Davis & I.H. Frieze, Eds.: 353–375. Springer. New York, NY.

EBY, K.K., J.C. CAMPBELL, C.M. SULLIVAN & W.S. DAVIDSON. 1995. Health effects of experiences of sexual violence for women with abusive partners. Health Care for Women International *16*, 563–576.

FANSLOW, J.L., R.N. NORTON & E.M. ROBINSON. 1999. One year follow-up of an emergency department protocol for abused women. Australia and New Zealand Journal of Public Health *23*, 418–420.

FANSLOW, J. & E. ROBINSON. 2004. Violence against women in New Zealand: prevalence and health consequences. Journal of the New Zealand Medical Association *117*, (1206):u1173.

GAZZMARARIAN, J.A., R. PETERSEN, A.M. SPITZ, *et al.* 2000. Violence and reproductive health: current knowledge and future research directions. Maternal and Child Health Journal *2*, 79–84.

GREENFIELD, L., M. RAND & D. CRAVEN. 1998. Violence by intimates: Analysis of Crimes by Current or Former Spouses, Boyfriends, and Girlfriends. U.S. Department of Justice. Washington, DC.

HEAD, C. & A. TAFT. 1995. Improving general practitioner management of women experiencing domestic violence: a study of the beliefs and experiences of women victims/survivors and of GP's. Canberra: Australian Department of Health, Housing, and Community Services.

HEGARTY, K., E.D. HINDMARSH & M.T. GILLES. 2000. Domestic violence in Australia: definition, prevalence, and nature of presentation in clinical practice. Medical Journal of Australia *173*, 363–367.

HORTON, J.A. 1992. The Women's Health Data Book: A Profile of Women's Health in the United States. Elsevier. New York, NY.

ISLAND, D. & P. LETELLIER. 1991. Men Who Beat the Men Who Love Them: Battered Gay Men and Domestic Violence. Haworth Press. Binghamton, NY.

JACOBY, M., D. GORENFLO, E. BLACK, *et al.* 1999. Rapid repeat pregnancy and experiences of interpersonal violence among low-income adolescents. American Journal of Preventive Medicine *16*, 318–321.

JAFFE, P.G., D.A. WOLFE & S.K. WILSON. 1990. Children of Battered Women: Issues in Child Development and Intervention Planning. Sage. Newbury Park, CA.

JENKINS, E.J. 2002. Black women and community violence: trauma, grief, and coping. Women & Therapy *25*, 29–44.

KASCHAK, E., Ed.: 2001. Minding the Body: Psychotherapy in Cases of Chronic and Life-Threatening Illness. Haworth Press. Binghamton, NY.

KOSS, M.P. 1993. Detecting the scope of rape: a review of prevalence research methods. Journal of Interpersonal Violence *8*, 198–222.

KOSS, M.P. 1994. The negative impact of crime victimization on women's health and medical use. *In* Reframing Women's Health: Multidisciplinary Research and Practice. A.J. Dan, Ed.: 189–200. Sage. Thousand Oaks, CA.

LETOURNEAU, E.J., M. HOLMES & J. CHASEDUNN-ROARK. 1999. Gynecologic health consequences to victims of interpersonal violence. Women's Health Issues 9, 115–120.

MARCHBANKS, P.A., K.J. LUI & J.A. MERCY. 1990. Risk of injury from resisting rape. American Journal of Epidemiology 132, 540–549.

MCHUGH, M.C. 2005. Understanding gender and intimate partner abuse. Sex Roles 52, 717–724.

MOUTON, C.P., S. ROVI, K. FURNISS & N.L. LASSER. 1999. The associations between health and domestic violence in older women: results of a pilot study. Journal of Women's Health and Gender-based Medicine 10, 861–866.

MURPHY, C.C., B. SCHEI, T.L. MYHR & M.J. DU. 2001. Abuse: a risk factor for low birth weight? Canadian Medical Association Journal 164, 1567–1572.

NATIONAL CENTER FOR INJURY PREVENTION AND CONTROL. 2003. Costs of Intimate Partner Violence Against Women in the United States. Centers for Disease Control and Prevention. Atlanta, GA.

O'CAMPO, P., A.C. GIELEN, R.R. FADEN & N. KASS. 1994. Verbal abuse and physical violence among a cohort of low-income pregnant women. Women's Health Issues 4, 29–37.

PALUDI, M.A., Ed. 1996. Sexual Harassment on College Campuses. State University of New York Press. Albany, NY.

PALUDI, M.A. 2004. Sexual harassment of college students: cultural similarities and differences. In Lectures on the Psychology of Women. J.C. Chrisler, C. Golden, & P.D. Rozee Eds.: 332–355. Third edition. McGraw-Hill. Boston, MA.

PALUDI, M.A. & R.B. BARICKMAN. 1998. Sexual Harassment, Work, and Education: A Resource Manual for Prevention. Second edition. State University of New York Press. Albany, NY.

RENZETTI, C.M. 1992. Violent Betrayal: Partner Abuse in Lesbian Relationships. Sage. Newbury Park, CA.

RICHARDSON, J., J. COID, A. PETRUCKEVITCH, et al.. 2002. Identifying domestic violence: cross-sectional study in primary care. British Medical Journal 324, 274–279.

ROZEE, P. 1993. Forbidden or forgiven: rape in cross-cultural perspective. Psychology of Women Quarterly 17, 499–514.

RUSSO, N.F. 2004. Understanding emotional responses after abortion. In Lectures on the Psychology of Women. J.C. Chrisler, C. Golden, & P.D. Rozee, Eds.: 128–143. Third edition. McGraw-Hill. Boston, MA.

SANDLER, B.R. & R.J. SHOOP, Eds. 1997. Sexual Harassment on Campus: A Guide for Administrators, Faculty, and Students. Allyn & Bacon. Boston, MA.

SHARPS, P.W., J. KOZIOL-MCLAIN, J. CAMPBELL, et al. 2001. Health care providers' missed opportunities for preventing femicide. Preventive Medicine 33, 373–380.

STAHLY, G.B. 2004. Battered women: Why don't they just leave? In Lectures on the Psychology of Women. J.C. Chrisler, C. Golden, P.D. Rozee &, Eds.: 310–330. Third edition McGraw-Hill. Boston, MA.

STAHLY, G.B. & G-Y. LIE. 1995. Women and violence: A comparison of lesbian and heterosexual battering relationships. In Variations on a Theme: Diversity and the Psychology of Women. J.C. Chrisler & A.H. Hemstreet, Eds.: 51–78. State University of New York Press. Albany, NY.

STEWART, D.E. & A. CECUTTI. 1993. Physical abuse during pregnancy. Canadian Medical Association Journal 149, 1257–1263.

TAGGART, L. & S. MATTSON. 1996. Delay in prenatal care as a result of battering in pregnancy: cross-cultural implications. Health Care for Women International *17*, 25–34.

WEST, C.M. 2002. Battered, black, and blue: an overview of violence in the lives of Black women. Women & Therapy *25*, 5–27.

WILBUR, L., M. HIGLEY, J. HATFIELD, *et al.* 2001. Survey results of women who have been strangled while in an abusive relationship. Journal of Emergency Medicine *21*, 297–302.

YODER, J.D. 2001. Military women. *In* Encyclopedia of Women and Gender. J. Worrell, Ed.: 771–782. Academic Press. San Diego, CA.

Young, K. 1998. Against the Odds: How Women Survive Domestic Violence. Canberra: Australian Office of the Status of Women.

Cultural Beliefs and Domestic Violence

MADELINE FERNÁNDEZ

Psychology Department, Pace University, New York, New York, USA

ABSTRACT: The role of cultural beliefs in domestic violence is examined within the context of the identification of more culturally viable options for women who are operating within diverse cultural frameworks and experiencing domestic violence worldwide. Domestic violence advocacy efforts are encouraged to incorporate more culturally informed strategies that complement the worldviews and cultural traditions of women from different backgrounds. The need for a more culturally sensitive definition of domestic violence that is inclusive of a range of domestic violence across cultures and also enhances communication among victims is identified. Points of relevant cultural reference are discussed and a cultural cost-benefit analysis is recommended for culturally relevant domestic violence research and program implementation.

KEYWORDS: domestic violence; women; cultural; implementation

INTRODUCTION

The single most powerful risk marker for becoming a victim of violence is to be a woman (Walker, 1999).

Even with widespread underreporting internationally, the occurrence of violence against women is startling (Sagot, 2005). Estimates of violence against women within the family context are even more difficult to obtain due to conventional perceptions, often held by the women themselves, that violence within the family context (1) is not considered violence and (2) should not be discussed outside of the family (Ellsberg, Herrera, Winkvist, & Kullgren, 1999; Horne, 1999; Kulwicki, 2002; Ofei-Aboagye, 1994; Yoshihama, 2002), let alone reported to external entities. These perceptions reflect beliefs that are embedded within a cultural perspective.

The importance of culture and its influence on how male/female relationships are structured is well established. Cultural influences extend to domestic violence as well, resulting in a wide range of experiences for women. While Walker's quote above might suggest that gender overrides cultural influences

Address for correspondence: Madeline Fernández, Psychology Department, Pace University, 41 Park Row, 13th Floor, New York, NY 10038. Voice: 212-346-1506; fax: 212-346-1618.
e-mail: MFernandez@pace.edu

as a determinant in the occurrence of domestic violence against women, one might argue that culture is equally significant since gender perceptions are culturally embedded. Literature on the cultural context of domestic violence has been limited until recently (Kulwicki, 2002). Examinations of the role that cultural beliefs play in domestic violence have been advocated in attempts to gain greater understanding of women's cultural perceptions of domestic violence and the degree to which their responses to domestic violence are couched in cultural frameworks. In work with immigrant and refugee women, factors such as language, religious beliefs, social networks, and traditional help-seeking behaviors have been identified as influential in how women will respond to domestic violence (Shiu-Thornton, Senturia, & Sullivan, 2005). There is growing recognition that the identification of culturally viable options that may be available to women operating within various cultural frameworks is essential for informing prevention and intervention approaches that are more culturally relevant and effective (Bhuyan & Senturia, 2005).

Examinations of cultural influences on domestic violence are relatively new in the literature (Campbell, 1992). Domestic violence research that has focused on women of color or immigrant and refugee communities has tended to group these into larger categories (Shiu-Thornton *et al.*, 2005), thereby losing the particular details that make them unique (Crichton-Hill, 2001). Research that has focused on specific cultural aspects of domestic violence is emerging (Bhuyan & Senturia, 2005). There has also been some discussion regarding the distinctions between culture on the one hand and political, religious, or societal practices on the other that promote female oppression and condone domestic violence against women. The American Psychological Association's Guidelines on Multicultural Education, Training, Research, Practice, and Organizational Change for Psychologists (2002), define culture

> as the belief systems and value orientations that influence customs, norms, practices, and social institutions, including psychological processes (language, care taking practices, media, educational systems) and organizations (media, educational systems...). Culture has been described as the embodiment of a worldview through learned and transmitted beliefs, values, and practices, including religious and spiritual traditions. It also encompasses a way of living informed by the historical, economic, ecological, and political forces on a group. (http://www.apa.org/pi/multiculturalguidelines/definitions.html).

Implicit in this definition of culture is its inextricability from societal traditions/practices, and economic, legal, and political systems. The social, economic, legal, and political institutional responses that sustain the domestic mistreatment of women in various cultural groups have begun to be identified with the goal of effecting changes that ultimately decrease the incidence of domestic violence against women. While there has been much global advocacy for changes in the economic, legal, and political systems that oppress women, often the assimilation of these changes is met with significant resistance within some communities as they are incompatible with the existing cultural framework. Such organizational changes have not always filtered their way toward implementation at the local level at the point where victims have their first encounter with representatives of these institutions. For example, while laws may be rewritten or introduced to grant protections for victims of domestic violence, the police officers' and judges' responses as well as execution of these new laws may not necessarily reflect the introduced changes (Sagot, 2005). This lack of consistency may reflect the "disconnect" between the changes proposed and the cultural beliefs held by the society in question. The women who are the intended beneficiaries of these institutional changes often are re-victimized when they attempt to seek the protections and sanctions promised. What should be inferred is not that advocacy efforts be abandoned, but rather that these efforts be better informed with regard to the cultural contexts they wish to change and incorporate strategies at all levels that complement the worldview of the communities that are to be helped by the changes introduced. A culturally informed perspective implies that the more the proposed changes are introduced in a manner that is sensitive to the cultural beliefs held by a particular group, the more viable these changes may be perceived by the group in question. By exploring the system of shared beliefs that women from a particular society use to cope with their world in a manner that reflects a true multicultural approach, adequate support may then be provided to help women face the challenges of domestic violence within their particular cultural framework. Such an approach should result in expediting more effective societal grounding of changes in the group's perceptions of domestic violence against women, resulting in shifts in the cultural norms toward reflecting increased support of the female victims.

DEFINITION

A necessary starting point in understanding the cultural context of domestic violence across cultures requires a clear definition of what is meant and understood when speaking of domestic violence. Even a scant review of the domestic violence literature reveals a wide range of meanings and definitions of domestic violence. The problematic issues related to the identification and definition of domestic violence have been recognized (Sullivan, Bhuyan, Senturia, Shiu-Thornton, & Ciske, 2005; Walker, 1999). There is significant discrepancy among different cultures' definitions of what constitutes domestic violence (Sokoloff & Dupont, 2005). The collective understanding of the behaviors that are associated with domestic violence and the driving forces underlying those behaviors reflect considerable variation across cultures (Malley-Morrison, 2004). From a cultural perspective, the "who," "what," and "how" of domestic violence require clear identification. Otherwise, the risk of merging related but distinct groups will persist, diminishing the potential for identification of true cultural differences and similarities among female victims of domestic violence.

Domestic violence as a term is not easily translatable and the vocabulary to describe domestic violence does not exist in some cultures and/or languages. "What" is meant by domestic violence remains ambiguous at times to the very people for whom it matters most. Some investigators have distinguished wife beating from wife battering (Brown, 1992), a distinction that may be lost on the victims of either. Which words are used and how one speaks of domestic violence across cultures are issues that have not been fully examined. Cross-cultural investigations of domestic violence are urged to carefully consider that the language used may be inadequate to fully explore the relevant issues. In Russia, for example, the words for "battering" and "batterer" do not exist and domestic violence is referred to as "home violence"; a term not understood by all (Horne, 1999). In South Africa, the term "woman abuse" appears to be the preferred term used to identify domestic violence (Boonzaier & De la Rey, 2003). Ethiopian women report that there is no shared community understanding of domestic violence despite its common occurrence (Sullivan, Senturia, Negash, Shiu-Thornton, & Giday, 2005). In Ghana, domestic violence has been interpreted to refer to the beating of children. Only recently has it become socially acceptable to speak about wife beating and often this is associated with disciplining. For the "discipline" of a woman to be perceived as abusive, the beating must exceed the norm (Ofei-Aboagye, 1994). In Chile, domestic violence is referred to as "la violencia privada" /the private violence (McWhirter, 1999). The "who" in domestic violence may vary depending on the cultural reference point. "The private violence" in Chile isirected primarily toward women and children (McWhirter, 1999). Whereas in Japan, up until recently, domestic violence typically referred to filial violence: children's physical/emotional reactions to family members (Kozu, 1999). In Japan, it could be the mother-in-law's treatment of the daughter-in-law or vice versa that constitutes domestic violence (Kozu, 1999). Similarly, the "how" of domestic violence varies across culture Many investigations of domestic violence identify physical assault as the primary marker. Others in the domestic violence field have called for a much broader definition that incorporates all behavior patterns whose aim is to threaten, isolate, or exploit. Some Japanese women, for example, have reported that they experience the act of overturning a dining table or being doused with liquid, which are culturally specific forms of abuse, as more severe than physical assault (Sokoloff & Dupont, 2005).

From a cultural perspective then, it would seem crucial to develop a definition of domestic violence against women that (*a*) allows for the inclusion of all potential female victims—"who," (*b*) specifies a broad set of behavior patterns that are sensitive to cultural variation—"how," and (*c*) is described in language that can be easily understood by a specific culture—"what." An additional fourth layer, the "why" of the domestic violence act, also requires furth er probing, particularly as it is perceived by the female victims within their particular cultural frame of reference. Investigators may overlook or presume a false understanding of what the domestic violence means to the women experiencing it. Women's difficulty with extricating their beliefs from the cultural justifications for domestic violence may hinder their capacity to take advantage of the institutional changes sought and introduced by their advocate This may mean that investigators in the field will need to discard the convenience of generic or simple translations of the term "domestic violence." Instead, the use of terms that are more meaningful and relevant in a specific culture may facilitate the gathering of information that will ultimately lead to better research and practice. In some U.S. communities where multicultural investigations of domestic violence are emerging, workers report their avoidance of the term domestic violence in their attempts to open up communication. Some focus on speaking about the patterns of hitting and controlling behaviors, while others choose to discuss the healing aspects (Sullivan, Bhuyan, et al., 2005). Many propose that any definition of domestic violence against women includes not just physical, but verbal, psychological, emotional, economic, and sexual patterns of behaviors whose aim is to control, threaten, isolate, and/or exploit women. Such a broad definition of domestic violence against women would then seemingly incorporate the various forms of oppression and violation that women experience within a sociocultural context. It is evident that even such a broad definition would need to be further operationally defined for specific cultures. This might allow for the inclusion of particular nuances that exist in different cultures' manifestation of domestic violence against women and to assure that these are accurately incorporated in examinations of domestic violence against women across a range of societies.

RELEVANT CULTURAL FRAMEWORKS

From a culturally sensitive framework, the development of effective interventions aimed at decreasing domestic violence against women requires an examination of a cultural group's beliefs/attitudes to identify points of relevant reference. The beliefs held by a society support the customs and practices of the group. The challenge of how to free women from abuse who may not necessarily perceive themselves as being abused (Ofei-Aboagye, 1994) is an intricate one. A woman's response to domestic violence is linked to her self-concept, her beliefs about gender roles/identities, and her beliefs about marriage/family life (Boonzaier & De la Rey, 2003). Efforts to change traditions that support domestic violence against women require that they be guided by knowledge of the cultural beliefs that sustain the practices in question. In determining which beliefs should be addressed, some areas that relate directly to domestic violence against women have been identified (Boonzaier & De la Rey, 2003; Campbell, 1992) and will be briefly addressed.

Worldview

Endeavors that seek to examine domestic violence from a cultural perspective require the identification and understanding of the culture's worldview. Typically, these refer to consideration of the individualistic and collectivist perspectives. The individualistic worldview, characteristic of Western societies, encourages individuals to develop an independent self. Social behavior in these cultures is predicted from an individual's own attitudes and values. In contrast, in the collectivist worldview, typically associated with Eastern societies, social behavior is predicted from the group social norms, perceived duties, and obligations. From the collectivist viewpoint, relationships are of extreme importance even when the costs of these exceed the benefits. Domestic violence investigations as well as interventions would most likely be prone to yield significantly different information and outcomes in cultures that adhere to one or the other of these worldviews. While worldview alone is not a determining factor in the occurrence of domestic violence, a woman's worldview is likely to have a fundamental effect on how she perceives the domestic violence, the likelihood that she will share details of her experience, and whether she will seek assistance and what type of assistance she will be prone to accept. Intervention approaches that have been derived from an individualistic perspective are likely to be met with increased resistance, and perhaps even ignored, when introduced to groups that adhere to a collectivist viewpoint. The literature on domestic violence against women has placed a good deal of focus on the development of programs that support women's efforts to leave domestic violence situations. However, inherent in some of these programs may be faulty assumptions about the women's attitudes about independence, family ties, and their perspective with regard to the domestic violence. Women from Asian cultures are reared in a belief system that stresses the greater need of the family over the needs of an individual member (Rydstrom, 2003; Yoshihama, 2002). In many Latin-American cultures, Marianismo, which originates from the Catholic worship of the Virgin Mary, is the underlying belief held. Women are expected to bear a great deal of suffering without protest for the sake of the family (Kasturirangan & Williams, 2003). Russian women also report pressure to keep the family together (Crandall, Senturia, Sullivan, & Shiu-Thornton, 2005). While one would safely assume that all victims would choose for the violence to cease, not all may be willing or able to strip themselves of the cultural ties that bind them and provide them with a sense of meaning and identity—the price that leaving may entail. Culturally informed domestic violence strategies and interventions call for a sensitive assessment, development and delivery of services that will be experienced as beneficial and viable by the female victims; that will support and strengthen as many of the aspects of themselves, which they value. A cultural cost-benefit analysis is advocated as an integral component in the development of domestic violence research and interventions.

Societal Structure

The structural frameworks that organize societies also require consideration in the cultural tapestry of domestic violence. In patrilineal societies, the male relatives are morally, legally, and economically responsible for women. In some societies, the assault, control, or killing of wives by the husband as well as any male member of the patriline is sanctioned. (Kulwicki, 2002). In patriarchical societies, the male is the acknowledged authority. The abuse of wives by their husbands is often considered a means of control. In some cultures, patriarchal conceptions provide men with a sense of ownership over women (Sagot, 2005). In contrast, matrilineal societies have been identified in which the incidence of domestic violence is nearly absent (McCloskey, 1998; Rivers, 2005; Sudha, 2004.)

Traditional patriarchal customs have been challenged as not having a place in cultural frameworks (Almeida & Dolan-Delvecchio 1999). However, their existence, regardless of whether they are considered cultural or not, requires that they be addressed on some level with the aim of, at a minimum, acknowledging that women experiencing domestic violence in these societies are extremely vulnerable. Domestic violence investigators and advocates in these societies have a responsibility to incorporate safeguards for the victims before initiating investigations and program implementation.

Aspects of Womanhood

The more autonomy that is supported for women within their cultural attitudes, the more their economic role is strengthened. With increased economic strength women may be viewed as less viable targets of domestic violence. Inherent in the beliefs of other cultural groups is the notion that women are in a subordinate position relative to their male counterparts. In the Arab culture, women are believed to belong to their agnatic group and men are responsible for the women. Once married, Japanese women are considered the bride of their husband's family. Many Latin American women are accustomed to allow others to make decisions for them. Domestic violence for the purpose of punishment or "correction" is widely accepted (Ellsberg *et al.*, 1999). Obedience to husbands and in-laws is an expectation of Vietnamese wives. They are held responsible for maintaining domestic harmony, often at all cost (Rydstrom, 2003). In Ghana, a traditional marriage is not a voluntary union and money is exchanged for the bride. In many respects, she is perceived as "owned" by her husband (Ofei-Aboagye, 1994). In the Russian culture, there has been a history of institutional oppression of women; the folklore and religious literature depict women as sinful. Men are entitled to control and dominate the family by any means. The physical disciplining of wives has been considered the husbands' responsibility in many cultures (Crandall *et al.*, 2005; Horne,

1999). These cultural beliefs have direct implications for women's sense of autonomy, how they are perceived within their communities, their own self-concept, and their ability to assume an independent economic role within their culture. An important distinction should also be made between women who are economically active but not self-sufficient in a community (Ofei-Aboagye, 1994).

Role of Men to Men and Women to Women

Relationships between same-gendered individuals are also culturally driven. While there is much documentation in the domestic violence literature regarding the range of cultural attitudes and beliefs related to the relationships between males and females, there is significantly less attention directed to the attitudes/beliefs on how women relate with each other and how men's relationships with other males are perceived. Societal definitions of masculinity prescribe a set of behaviors for men in relating to other men that often place them in opposition to each other (Pleck, 1981; Roberts, 1994). Masculinity in many cultures is associated with power and domination. Given the competitive quality of the Euro-American male role model, it has been proposed that this may lead to a psychological void that alienates men and inhibits their ability to develop significant human affiliation, such as family/marital (Roberts, 1994). Others theorize that male-female battering is an outcome of the disruption in male-male relatedness borne out of the disappointments of traditional male socialization and gender role training (Jennings & Murphy, 2000). In cultures where the coalition of women is supported and there is a diminished expectation for males to establish their positions with their male peers, a reduction in the male/female aggression patterns has been noted (Campbell, 1992). Domestic violence interventions may be informed by the examination of the coalitions that exist for women in particular cultures, or lack thereof, and perhaps developing consolidated efforts to develop and strengthen these.

Isolation of Wives/Sanctions and Sanctuary

The proximity of a woman's family can serve as a protective variable with regard to domestic violence. In cultures that require women to leave their families of origin, the women are often left with little or no support group. It can be anticipated that women who are culturally expected to move in with their husband's family or considered to belong to their agnatic group, are potentially to be in very vulnerable positions. Culturally sanctioned isolation of women results in the reduction of their social supports and inhibits women's access to resources that might ultimately enable them to escape from the domestic violence.

The degree to which a society responds to domestic violence by providing women the immediate availability of safety without the threat of losing their children along with prolonged support lessens the propensity of domestic violence against women. In addition to the formal, law enforcement sanctions, informal sanctions at the spiritual, community, and familial levels have been identified as perhaps even more effective in preventing domestic violence against women (Campbell, 1992; Rivers, 2005; Sullivan, Bhuyan, *et al.*, 2005). It is within the informal sanctions that cultural beliefs generally have the strongest foothold. In some societies, domestic violence has been handled by the male members of the women's family and the perpetrator is ostracized (Kulwicki, 2002; Rivers, 2005). Religious institutions also have an important role in their endorsement of women's safety (Sagot, 2005).

SUMMARY

This examination of the role that specific cultural beliefs play in domestic violence against women reveals that these should be considered crucial in the implementation of strategies that aim to decrease the incidence of domestic violence, improve societal responses, and address variables that affect victims' decisions to seek help (Kasturirangan & Williams, 2003). A cultural approach to domestic violence requires more than providing services in a designated language. Such an approach underscores the importance of understanding what the domestic violence as well as proposed interventions mean to those experiencing it. Necessary steps toward culturally relevant domestic violence investigations require the unveiling of the secrecy of domestic violence (Shiu-Thornton *et al.*, 2005) across cultures and shifting it to a matter of universal public awareness. Also required is the use of culturally sensitive terminology that is inclusive, broad in its incorporation of domestic violence manifestations, and culturally meaningful in its embodiment of an understanding of what is culturally experienced by women. The incorporation of Western beliefs into the cultures of all women experiencing domestic violence is not a welcomed or realistic solution. Rather, reliance on some cultural traditions and beliefs in the development of domestic violence prevention and intervention strategies should lead to more suitable, easily accepted, and relevant approaches. A cultural cost-benefit analysis is advocated as an integral component to ensure that the cultural aspects valued by women are supported and strengthened whenever possible. Domestic violence investigations and programs should aim to be responsive to the expectations of the women themselves. The options offered to women experiencing domestic violence should be perceived as improving their plight and not further unraveling their social and cultural fabric (Ofei-Aboagye, 1994; Yoshioka & Choi, 2005). Consideration might be given to the replacement/substitution of those cultural aspects that the women risk losing when seeking to escape domestic violence.

The empowerment of women experiencing domestic violence can be achieved through the approaches used in domestic violence research. Partnering member participation at all stages of research and program implementation (Sullivan, Bhuyan, *et al*., 2005) has been demonstrated as an effective strategy. Changing cultural traditions and societal structures that undermine aspects of womanhood and support the domestic violence of women can be advocated via formal sanctions at the institutional levels, but should also be approached at the local level through support of cultural traditions that bolster women's roles, increase their self awareness (Shiu-Thornton *et al*., 2005) their self-sufficiency, and foster female coalitions.

REFERENCES

ALMEIDA, R.V. & K. DOLAN-DELVECCHIO. 1999. Addressing culture in batterers intervention: the Asian Indian community as an illustrative example. Violence Against Women *5*, 654–683.

AMERICAN PSYCHOLOGICAL ASSOCIATION. 2002. Guidelines on multicultural education, training, research, practice, and organizational change for psychologists. Washington, DC: http://www.apa.org/pi/multiculturalguidelines/homepage.html.

BHUYAN, R. & K. SENTURIA. 2005. Understanding domestic violence resource utilization and survivor solutions among immigrant and refugee women: introduction to the special issue. Journal of Interpersonal Violence *20*, 895–901.

BOONZAIER, F. & C. DE LA REY. 2003. "He's a man and I'm a woman": cultural constructions of masculinity and femininity in South African women's narratives of violence. Violence Against Women *9*, 1003–1029.

BROWN, J.K. 1992. Introduction: definition, assumptions, themes, and issues. *In*: Sanctions and Sanctuary: Cultural Perspectives on the Beating of Wives. D.A. Counts, J.K. Brown & J.C. Campbell, Eds.: 1–18. Westview Press. Boulder, CO.

CAMPBELL, J.C. 1992. Wife-Battering: Cultural Contexts versus Western Social Sciences. *In* Sanctions and Sanctuary: Cultural Perspectives on the Beating of Wives. D.A. Counts, J.K. Brown & J.C. Campbell, Eds.: 229–250. Westview Press. Boulder, CO.

CRANDALL, M., K. SENTURIA, M. SULLIVAN & S. SHIU-THORNTON. 2005. "No way out": Russian-speaking women's experiences with domestic violence. Journal of Interpersonal Violence *20*, 941–958.

CRICHTON-HILL, Y. 2001. Challenging ethnocentric explanations of domestic violence: let us decide, then value our decisions—A Samoan response. Trauma Violence and Abuse *2*, 203–214.

ELLSBERG, M., T. CALDERA, HERRERA, *et al.* 1999. Domestic violence and emotional distress among Nicaraguan women: results form a population-based study. American Psychologist *54*, 30–36.

HORNE, S. 1999. Domestic violence in Russia. American Psychologist *54*, 55–61.

JENNINGS, J.L. & C.M. MURPHY. 2000. Male-male dimensions of male-female battering: a new look at domestic violence. Psychology of Men and Masculinity *1*, 21–29.

KASTURIRANGAN, A. & E.N. WILLIAMS. 2003. Counseling Latina battered women: a qualitative study of the Latina perspective. Journal of Multicultural Counseling and Development *31*, 162–178.

Kozu, J. 1999. Domestic violence in Japan. American Psychologist *54*, 50–54.

Kulwicki, A.D. 2002. The practice of honor crimes: a glimpse of domestic violence in the Arab world. Issues of Mental Health Nursing *23*, 77–87.

Malley-Morrison, K. Ed. 2004. International Perspectives on Family Violence and Abuse. Lawrence Erlbaum Associates. Mahwah, NJ.

McCloskey, J. 1998. Three generations of Navajo women: negotiating life course strategies in the eastern Navajo agency. American Indian Culture and Research Journal *22*, 103–129.

McWhirter, P.T. 1999. La violencia privada: Domestic violence in Chile. American Psychologist *54*, 37–40.

Ofei-Aboagye, R.O. 1994. Altering the strands of the fabric: a preliminary look at domestic violence in Ghana. Signs: Journal of Women in Culture and Society *19*, 924–936.

Pleck, J. 1981. The Myth of Masculinity. MIT Press. Cambridge, MA.

Rivers, M.J. 2005. Navajo women and abuse: the context for their troubled relationships. Journal of Family Violence *20*, 83–89.

Roberts, G.W. 1994. Brother to brother: African American modes of relating among men. Journal of Black Studies *24*, 379–390.

Rydstrom, H. 2003. Encountering "Hot" anger: domestic violence in contemporary Vietnam. Violence Against Women *9*, 676–697.

Sagot, M. 2005. The critical path of women affected by family violence in Latin America. Violence Against Women *11*, 1292–1318.

Shiu-Thornton, S., K. Senturia & M. Sullivan. 2005. "Like a bird in a cage": Vietnamese women survivors talk about domestic violence. Journal of Interpersonal Violence *20*, 959–976.

Sokoloff, N.J. & I. Dupont. 2005. Domestic violence at the intersections of race, class, and gender. Violence Against Women *11*, 38–64.

Sudha, S. 2004. Women at the center: life in a modern matriarchy. Journal of Marriage and Family *66*, 1339–1350.

Sullivan, M., R. Bhuyan, K. Senturia, *et al.* 2005. Participatory action research in practice: a case study addressing domestic violence in nine cultural communities. Journal of Interpersonal Violence *20*, 977–995.

Sullivan, M., K. Senturia, T. Negash, *et al.* 2005. "For us it is like living in the dark": Ethiopian women's experiences with domestic violence. Journal of Interpersonal Violence *20*, 922–940.

Walker, L.E. 1999. Psychology and domestic violence around the world. American Psychologist *54*, 21–29.

Yoshihama, M. 2002. Breaking the web of abuse and silence: voices of battered women in Japan. Social Work *47*, 389–400.

Yoshioka, M.R. & D.Y. Choi. 2005. Culture and interpersonal violence research: paradigm shift to create a full continuum of domestic violence services. Journal of Interpersonal Violence *20*, 513–519.

Violence against Women in Mexico

Conceptualization and Program Application

SUSAN PICK,[a,b,c] CARMEN CONTRERAS,[b] AND ALICIA BARKER-AGUILAR[b]

[a]*Universidad Nacional Autónoma de México (UNAM), Mexico City, Mexico*

[b]*Instituto Mexicano de Investigación de Familia y Población (IMIFAP), Mexico City, Mexico*

[c]*Written during a fellowship at the Center for Population and Development, Harvard University, Cambridge, MA*

> ABSTRACT: Violence against women has been a problem in human cultures for centuries. This is still the case both in developed and in developing countries, but it is in developing countries where the problem is aggravated as the result of cultural norms that are tolerant of men exerting power over women and girls as a commonly accepted practice. This power is often put into practice through physical and psychological acts of violence. In Mexico, as in many other countries, there is a legal framework that protects women from such acts, yet in the case of Mexico it has not yet been translated into actual improvements in their lives. We present an overview of advances in legal remedies regarding violence towards females internationally and in Mexico. The fact that these advances *per se* do not lead to changes in social norms that tolerate violence against females is emphasized. Also presented is the experience of the Mexican Institute for Research on Family and Population (IMIFAP) with the design and implementation of programs that promote protective factors and changes in behaviors in such a way that violence is effectively prevented. These programs focus on the development of psychosocial skills and knowledge through participatory workshops that promote self reflection, and they are developed and evaluated before being then applied on a large scale in poverty-stricken communities. These workshops lead to more egalitarian relationships between genders. IMIFAP´s programs address not only violence but also other areas are integrated such that the enablement of psychosocial skills is applied in the broader sociocultural context, leading to healthier and economically more productive lives. These programs are derived from the *Framework for Enabling Agentic Empowerment* (FENAE), which enables choice and the development of agentic empowerment through integrating skills, knowledge, and the context in which people live.

Address for correspondence: Susan Pick, IMIFAP, Malaga Norte 25, Mexico City, Mexico 03929. e-mail: pick@imifap.org.mx

KEYWORDS: Mexico; violence; women; gender; cultural norms; agency; empowerment

INTRODUCTION

Violence against women and girls is an ongoing problem that has remained largely unresolved for centuries. Violence is generally enmeshed within a social and cultural context that make women particularly vulnerable to it. This violence is found in both rich and poor countries alike. Although women in the poorest of nations are more inclined to believe men are justified in beating their wives, it has been found that across all settings, in developed and developing countries, women who are abused tend to hold more normative beliefs that justify violence against women (WHO, 2005). In spite of reforms that have been made on the judicial level, many of these advances have yet to be translated into a real change in the lives of women, especially in rural areas where violence against women is generally more prevalent (WHO, 2005). Despite widespread activism and significant progress made on the international level, domestic violence continues to affect the lives of persons in millions of households.

Studies show that, in countries all over the world, anywhere between 20% and 50% of women have been victims of violence (UNICEF, 2004). The Mexican Institute for the Research of Family and Population (IMIFAP) recognizes the critical progress that has been made, especially in terms of international declarations on the position of women and against violence. Moving beyond this, IMIFAP strives to reduce violence against women and girls through training programs building skills and knowledge, and through combating cultural norms and myths that generate, or at least condone, violence against women. IMIFAP's approach targets both the individual level and the level of community context. It promotes new forms of coexistence and conflict resolution between men and women by enabling each to recognize the other's rights as individuals. The objective is to change attitudes, norms, and behaviors to achieve the common goals of improving the way men and women interact with each other.

First, this chapter will briefly introduce the judicial framework defining and condemning violence against women, both internationally and in Mexico. We will highlight the fact that societal change such as legislative progress is not always translated into real changes in the lives of women and will refer to the primordial role cultural norms play in violence against women. In the second part of the article, we describe the approach that IMIFAP follows in programs promoting behavioral change. We refer to a program aimed at changing community responses to wife abuse (Fawcett *et al.*, 1999), and we show how it reflects the conceptualization and implementation strategy that IMIFAP follows. A brief summary of the *Framework for Enabling Agentic Empowerment* (FENAE) will be presented as a possible approach to promoting behavioral changes regarding violence. *FENAE* emphasizes the use of knowledge and skills' training in small, highly participatory, self-reflective workshops facilitating new behaviors. Newly acquired behaviors in turn promote feelings of agency in individuals, and the accumulation of persons who have acquired these new behaviors ultimately leads to the development of a more supportive context.

JUDICIAL REGULATIONS AND THE CURRENT SITUATION IN MEXICO

In the past 15 years major progress has been made internationally with respect to violence against women. In 1993 the General Assembly of the United Nations adopted The Declaration on the Elimination of Violence against Women, of which Mexico was a signatory. This represents the first time that violence was defined as gender-based in an international agreement of this type. In this declaration violence against women includes the following:

1. Physical, sexual, and psychological violence occurring within the family.
2. Dowry-related violence, marital rape, female genital mutilation, and other traditional practices harmful to women.
3. Non-spousal violence and violence related to exploitation.
4. Physical, sexual, and psychological violence occurring within the general community, including rape, sexual abuse, sexual harassment, and intimidation at work, in educational institutions and elsewhere, trafficking women, and forced prostitution.
5. Physical, sexual, and psychological violence perpetrated or condoned by the state, wherever it occurs.

Shortly afterward, in 1994, the Organization of American States approved the Inter-American Convention on the Prevention, Punishment, and Eradication of Violence against Women (Belém Do Pará Convention). In 2000 in the Millenium Declaration, the member states of the General Assembly of the UN vowed to "combat all forms of violence against women and to implement the Convention on the Elimination of All Forms of Discrimination against Women". In the same year, the UN published the report *Women 2000: Gender Equality, Development and Peace for the 21st Century* to raise awareness about violence against women as well as to exhort member states to take responsibility and to actively pursue the eradication of violence against women within their borders. These are just a handful of important examples of the worldwide initiative to put a stop to violence against women.

Despite these efforts on the part of the international community, the problem continues to exist worldwide. In Latin America alone, more than one in every four women has been a victim of physical violence in the home (Saucedo *et al.*, 2002). According to a 2003 survey conducted in Mexico by the National

System of Statistics and Geographic Information (INEGI), 47% of Mexican women over the age of 15 years who live with a partner suffer from some form of domestic violence. INEGI also reports that 4 out of 100 victims of violence in Mexico are men, while the remaining 96 are women (INEGI, 2003). Data from the Secretary of Social Development indicates that 66% of women's deaths in urban areas occur due to violence in their own homes (SEDESOL, 2003). Nationally, there are on average 14 deaths a day of women caused by violent acts. In the majority of domestic violence cases, the main aggressor is male and INEGI reports that 8 out of 10 women who fall victim to domestic violence suffer the most dangerous assaults from husbands or boyfriends.

Maltreatment of women takes many forms, often occurring simultaneously. Most frequent is emotional abuse (98.4% of all cases), followed by intimidation (16%), physical aggression (15%), and sexual abuse (14%), according to the National Survey of Domestic Violence (1999) cited by National Institute for Women (INMUJERES). Furthermore, 85% of households that reported having a man as its head have experienced some form of violence at least once (INMUJERES, 2002a). The households that had a woman as head of household reported violence in 15% of the cases. In Mexico City, 90% of reported sexual crimes against women, 20% of these are against girls under 12 years old, according to the District Attorney of Mexico City (Álvarez de Lara, 2003). A diagnosis of the status of human rights in Mexico, conducted by the Office of the United Nations High Commissioner for Human Rights, indicates that there are 10 million women who suffer from violence in Mexico, the medical cost of which is equivalent to 1.5% of GDP, or 1,292,000,000 pesos annually (Álvarez de Lara, 2003). Social inequality is compounded by economic inequality. According to the World Bank, women in the developed world earn 77 cents for each dollar that men earn in an equivalent job, while in Mexico women earn 68 cents to the dollar (United Nations, 2004).

Although the situation for women in Mexico remains dire regarding domestic violence, there have been legal reforms in Mexico that represent real change in the Mexican system. In 1989 the Penal Code of Mexico City (which comprises most of Mexico City with its more than 18 million inhabitants) was reformed so that sexual crimes were recognized as "crimes against integrity and normal psycho-sexual development" and so that sexual violence was recognized as damaging physical and psychological integrity and sexual liberty. This reform modified the concept of rape, once considered only vaginal, to include oral and anal penetration as well as defining sexual harassment and sexual abuse as a crime (González & Maganda, 2000). The reform eliminated the qualifying terms "honest and chaste" as a condition for lodging a claim of assault. Before this, in order to initiate an inquiry into a sexual crime it was necessary to prove the woman's honesty and chastity. A judge or public minister could dismiss a complaint or a case on the grounds that the assaulted woman did not have these characteristics (González & Maganda, 2000). In 1993 Article 20 of the national constitution was reformed to absolve minors of the obligation of confronting their aggressor in the case of rape or kidnapping as well as to guarantee a victim's right to receive medical attention, judicial consultancy, the reparation of damages, and cooperation and collaboration with a public prosecutor (González & Maganda, 2000).

In 1997 the Mexican Congress approved reforms to the Civil and Penal Code in regard to violence within the home. For the first time in Mexico, physical and psychological violence within the family was considered a crime (González & Maganda, 2000). Other progress was made in the procurement and administration of justice, the agents of which are now obliged to take protective measures for victims. Stated violence against one's wife is now considered a cause for divorce as of September 2005 when the Supreme Court recognized the existence of marital rape. Also, when the violence is against minors, parent offenders can lose guardianship of the children.

The General Rule in Mexico (NOM-190-SSA1-1999) for increasing awareness of domestic violence is a group of criteria and procedures obligatory for all public and private health services in the National Health System. It was created in 1999 for the purpose of drawing the attention of the health services in Mexico to domestic violence and to stimulate more thorough inquiries. In addition to these reforms, government agencies have initiated national plans such as the National Program for Equal Opportunity and Non-Discrimination against Women (President of the Republic, 2001), the National Program for a Life without Violence (INMUJERES, 2002a), and the Institutional Table (INMUJERES, 2002b) to coordinate preventive action and attention to domestic violence and violence toward women.

CULTURAL ROOTS OF VIOLENCE

If there are so many international and domestic efforts regarding violence against women, why does the problem persist even in those member states that vow to combat it? If there are judicial reforms and improvements, why have the lives of women not been radically changed? The answer is likely to lie in the power of cultural norms and practices that have placed women in positions of subservience and in the lack of skills and knowledge that might enable women to talk about violence and change social norms (Heise, 1994, 1999; Kelly, 1996). Later we will discuss how training in skills and knowledge can help women to enhance feelings of agentic empowerment (Pick & Ruesga, 2006) so they can better address the problem.

Norms are social "rules" and expectations of behavior that either prescribe a given type of conduct or preclude it (Fishbein & Ajzen, 1985). Norms embody values, social practices, and gender roles. In many societies, these norms create sexist attitudes and give rise to inequality between men and women. The inequitable organization of society and family is one of the fundamental factors in the high domestic violence worldwide. Another factor is the upbringing of men in such contexts, resulting in their desire to assert power over women at the societal level as well as on the family level (Straus, Gelles, & Steinmetz, 1980). The hierarchical structure within the family creates conditions in which the man feels entitled to exercise control over the others by any means necessary, including violence. This masculine role is considered "normal" in society and is a part of his expression of "manhood." Social constructions of masculinity and femininity are prevalent in which the woman is subordinate to the man. Early on, girls begin learning in the home to behave in a manner that gives privileges to men, to deny themselves the exercise of their sexuality for pleasure, and to accept that they are considered inferior and responsible for others, even at their own expense.

The culture of machismo engenders a feeling of entitlement on the part of the male spouse with respect to the power he can exert both explicitly and implicitly regarding, for example, decision-making, household chores, and the frequency of sex. A study conducted in the states of Mexico—Oaxaca and Sonora—found that most women accommodated their husbands' desire to have sex against their will. For example, Hortensia, a mother of 10 from Mexico City said, "When the baby was small, he would bother me and I would say, 'I don't want to get pregnant again.' But one day he hit me really hard because I said no. He hit me with a shoe. It's always been with force, even now, I have to get out, I have to leave" (Ortega, Amuchástegui, & Rivas, 2006).

Tolerance and acceptance of inhumane practices and discrimination against women in a community is often justified by customs and tradition. Belief systems of a society in which a woman's freedoms, especially sexual, must be restrained and subject to regulation, even by the state, contribute to a mentality in which women have little control over what happens in their lives. Women are often denied civil and property rights through discrimination in the law, and this situation is most severe in nondemocratic or barely participatory societies (United Nations, 2004). Not surprisingly, the brunt of the *machista* society disproportionately falls on the poorest women in the most marginalized communities.

Inequality represents an important burden for both genders; the social and gender role expectations for both sexes are unrealistic. Taking it to the extreme, one could say that the males are expected to be strong, responsible decision makers and economic providers who should have as many sexual partners as possible and who should exert the power on the family. Little space is given for expression of emotional concerns or weaknesses. Women, on the other hand, are supposed to be subservient, obey the man, and neither be interested in sexual pleasure nor in making decisions beyond those pertaining to home duties. Regarding the expression of emotional concerns and needs, women are expected to have more freedom than men. It is acceptable for women to cry, to express feelings and weaknesses. It is as if each of the two genders is being taught to speak a different language while being expected to live together in harmony. It is very hard for this to occur successfully given that these differences are based on social norms, not individual needs. Such unrealistic social demands make for quite stressful relationships that can easily lead to violent behaviors.

Inequality can also be seen in discriminatory practices on the part of institutions that impart justice and offer health services, education, recreation, culture, and regulate the labor market and opportunities needed to acquire economic independence. Indeed, one of the primary reasons for failing to leave a violent relationship is financial dependence on the partner. So it is important to not only educate men and women about gender equality and domestic violence, but also seek to provide real options by enabling women to become financially independent through skill training and loans, as has been successfully implemented in some programs.

A CONCEPTUAL FRAMEWORK AND STRATEGY FOR ENHANCING AGENTIC EMPOWERMENT

Over the last 20 years, IMIFAP has addressed the underprivileged position of women in Mexican society, especially in poor urban and rural communities. A series of programs have been developed and implemented, sometimes on a large scale (Pick & Givaudan, 1999, 2001, 2006a; Ruiz & Fawcett, 1999; IMIFAP, 2002). These programs aim at promoting health primarily through training of skills and knowledge to women in interactive and participatory workshops. The underlying rationale for IMIFAP's approach derives from research in social and health psychology, notably the work of Fishbein and Ajzen (1980), who define behavior changes in terms of underlying factors such as attitudes, norms, beliefs, and intentions, and in terms of Bandura's concept of self efficacy as a characteristic of the person (Bandura 1997). For defining the stages of behavior change, it has borrowed from Prochaska, DiClemente & Norcross (1992). Regarding context it refers to the socio-cultural, economic, and cultural circumstances in which people are living (Berry *et al.*, 2002). This literature, combined with extensive experience among populations living in conditions of economic and educational poverty, has shown that lack of knowledge and skills, especially lack of perceived control over one's life in most everyday situations, needs to be addressed. If a person does not have the opportunity to choose her actions, she cannot commit to achieving behavioral change; it simply does not depend on her. If, on the other hand, she has structural, social, and psychological access to change, it is more likely that she can realize change (Pick & Givaudan, 2006a).

FRAMEWORK FOR ENABLING AGENTIC EMPOWERMENT

The approach has been crystallized in a heuristic framework called the *Framework for Enabling Agentic Empowerment* (FENAE) (Pick, Givaudan,

& Poortinga, 2003; Pick, Poortinga, & Givaudan, 2003; Pick & Poortinga, 2005). FENAE emphasizes four notions labeled: (*a*) context, (*b*) person, (*c*) situation, and (*d*) behavior, tha are presented in the following paragraphs.

Context refers to the circumstances that determine a person's way of living. Economic factors are the most basic. Persons in wealthy societies have access to all kinds of resources, not all of which are available in poor societies. Closely associated with economic wealth are formal education, access to health care, legal factors and governance, and the ways these elements interrelate. Furthermore, context includes the socio-cultural norms and values that are shared within a specific community, namely, its values and norms. Context variables can facilitate or constrain an individual's behavior and performance.

The second core notion is that of the *person*, that is, the characteristic traits and functions that distinguish someone from others and provide for individual continuity in behavior across time and situations. Relevant characteristics include stable attitudes (Fishbein & Ajzen, 1985), and socio-cognitive dimensions such as self-efficacy (Bandura, 1997), self-esteem (Baumeister, 1993), self-determination (Deci & Ryan, 2000), self-regulation (Boekaerts, 1999), locus of control (Rotter, 1966), empowerment (Stein, 1997), and autonomy (Assor, Kaplan & Roth, 2002). Conceptually, these dimensions have much in common and we like to use an overarching concept, namely agency, which has the advantage that it is not only used by psychologists (*e.g.*, Kagitcibasi, 2005) but also by economists with an eye for the socio-cultural dimensions of human development (Sen, 1999).

Agency implies that one feels able to carry out behavior of one's choice, monitor one's progress, and have control over the decisions that generally precede a behavior. Human agency is the recognition that people *can* be, and going a step beyond, *must* be agents of their own well-being as well as being empowered to change the context in which they live, that is, make their entitlements a reality. Thus we have come to define agentic empowerment as a central concept (Pick, 2006; Pick & Ruesga, 2006).

Situational demands refer to the particular situations that an individual faces and to which he or she is required to respond. The central focus of programs promoting health and behavior change in populations with low educational levels has to be on concrete situations. Programs have to provide concrete knowledge and skills (or "life skills" as labeled by the World Health Organization in 1999) that enable individuals to engage in what are for them difficult situations in a socially competent manner.

Behavior, or behavior changes, is the fourth and final component in the *FENAE* conceptualization. Such changes do not occur suddenly. Prochaska *et al*. (Prochaska & Di Clemente 1982; Prochaska, Di Clemente & Norcross, 1992) have distinguished four steps: contemplation of change, preparation for action, action, and maintenance of the newly acquired behavior patterns.

Only when behavior change in critical situations has been achieved will individuals begin to acquire a sense of achievement and control that can facilitate further changes in behavior and their environment, and ultimately also lead to a more agentic person. In summary, programs focus on behavior change in concrete situations. As women gain a sense of control or self-efficacy over their lives, they develop a sense of agency. When they apply it to their overall context, we call it empowerment. It lead to changes in the context.

PROGRAMMING STRATEGY

The strategy that IMIFAP applies in program development and implementation amounts to a sequence of four stages: (*a*) need assessment, (*b*) program development, (*c*) program implementation, and (*d*) upscaling (Pick, Poortinga & Givaudan, 2003; Pick & Poortinga, 2005). For each stage, aims have to be formulated, and appropriate methods selected. Moreover, the strategy entails planned activities for advocacy and program evaluation at each stage. To illustrate the strategy, we will make use of a program aimed at changing community responses to wife abuse, the *Iztacalco* project (Fawcett, Heise, Isita & Pick, 1999). The name refers to the neighborhood in Mexico City where this program on violence prevention was implemented for the first time.

The aim of the first stage of program development, *assessment of needs*, is an analysis of the needs and problems facing the target population as seen by different groups of stakeholders including first and foremost the women themselves, but also administrative authorities, health professionals, program sponsors, and the men in the target population. To arrive at an inclusive overview of needs as well as to enhance ownership of the program, focus groups and interviews are conducted. Also, government statistics and other sources of information are consulted. The information collected at this stage should provide the program developers not only with an overview of the needs of the target population, but also with insight into the contextual and individual constraints and opportunities for bringing about change in important behaviors. For the *Iztacalco* project (Fawcett *et al*., 1999), focus groups were conducted to explore norms, attitudes, and beliefs in the community about issues such as origins of violence against women, possible strategies for a woman living with a violent husband or partner, and how others intervene in domestic violence. To encourage participants to go beyond normative responses (e.g., conflicts "should" be resolved in nonviolent ways), a scenario of abuse was presented with various solutions, each of which was discussed by women in pairs before sharing their opinion with the entire group. In-depth interviews with victims of violence were conducted to further clarify and explore findings from the focus groups.

The main goal of the second stage is the *development of program modules*, including exercises, manuals, and so forth, on the basis of the information obtained in the first stage and informed by psychological theory and professional expertise. This stage also includes the development of activities at the level of communities. Examples include radio campaigns, posters, and banners (often used in Mexican elections), buttons with a program logo, and meetings with the men of a community and with health professionals. In the case of the *Iztacalco* project, the program consisted of two parts: (*a*) workshops to increase knowledge (raising consciousness of rights and options) and interaction skills and (*b*) a parallel campaign directed at the community center.

The third stage entails the *implementation of the program* at a local level. The aims are twofold: to have the client group profit from the program and to evaluate the impact of the program. Implementation is also informed by prior experience and expertise, for example, with groups that have a low educational level, workshops were found to work best if they include a variety of exercises meant to enhance specific skills and knowledge. This is in line with a distinction Bruner (1996) drawn between learning in context and learning out of context. In formal school settings, most learning is by verbal instruction and verbal argument outside concrete problem situations. Learning in traditional societies usually takes place more in the immediate situation where the learning is relevant. Learning comes with doing; this has been called "situated learning" (Lave & Wenger, 1990). Group exercises give opportunities for self-reflection and for practicing skills and knowledge in a variety of situations of increasing difficulty in a way that enhances the probability that the newly developed competencies will be applied in a broad range of situations.

In the *Iztacalco* project, twelve workshop sessions were held with women of the community along the lines described. In addition, there was the simultaneous campaign directed at the community. This was carried out by the women themselves and made use of leaflets with messages, posters, buttons, and photo series in the local community center.

The fourth and final stage of the strategy entails the *scaling-up* of programs that have been found to be effective in evaluation studies. The program carried out in the *Iztacalco* community was determined to be successful (Fawcett *et al.*, 1999) and has been applied in several states in Mexico (Fawcett *et al.*, 1999). Important parts of the modules have been included in other IMIFAP programs, which are referred to in the last section of this article.

Beyond the aims and methods to be realized at each of the four stages, the strategy has two further essential components: namely, (1) advocacy and dissemination and (2) evaluation. The activities engaged in for program development and implementation do not involve a group of isolated individuals, but take place in communities and have to be approved by men and civil authorities. Moreover, they have to be funded by private or government sponsors. All these stakeholders have to be informed. Therefore, programs require advocacy and dissemination, particularly at the context level. Positive attitudes of policy makers and community leaders help in gaining permission for carrying out a program, in creating a friendly atmosphere with health workers and teachers, and in procuring financial support. Dissemination, that is, extending public knowledge about interventions and their results, takes place primarily through campaigns in the (local) media, but also includes pamphlets and posters. Both advocacy and dissemination are also needed to gain support for further up-scaling of a program so that it becomes available for large numbers of participants.

Finally, activities at all stages of the program have to be evaluated. For example, in the first stage the target population has to be defined: What is the age range of the women to be invited? Should resources also be spent on women who have not suffered from abuse? During the stage of the construction of program modules, advocacy activities and invitations to participate have to be realized. It has to be evaluated whether all-important stakeholders have been approached (or that perhaps too little or too much effort was spent on this). As part of the stage of implementation, evaluation research has to be planned and carried out that will provide information on the impact of the program. Qualitative measures (such as testimonies by women) as well as quantitative measures (questionnaires, observations on changes in behavior) are part of well-designed evaluation research. Evaluation requires accountability in all phases of a program as well as objective data on key target outcomes that can help to diagnose strong and weak points and ultimate program effectiveness (Shadish, Cook & Leviton, 1991; Wholey, Hatry & Newcomer, 1994).

AN OVERVIEW OF IMIFAP'S PROGRAMS

IMIFAP defines violence toward women as any gender-based act that violates human dignity and causes pain or physical suffering whether it be sexual or psychological such as threats, coercion, or arbitrary deprivation of liberty, in one's public life as well as in private life. IMIFAP's model is preventative. The prevention of violence through IMIFAP's programs is based on changing behaviors and sociocultural norms regarding coexistence and conflict resolution between men and women by recognizing each other's rights as individuals, despite what one may have learned from one's parents or from societal conceptions of gender inequality. IMIFAP prevents violence in which cultural and psychosocial variables play a role through educational and formative programs. The educational models are able to establish measures of control on violent conduct that the individual has assimilated in his home environment.

The objective of IMIFAP's violence prevention programs is to develop skills in men and women to achieve common goals to improve the way they interact with each other. These skills include: communicating assertively, decision-making, defining priorities and future goals, self-knowledge, and learning to participate in taking control over one's own health and decisions as a means of preventing violence. In IMIFAP's workshops, many women were surprised to learn that they have the power to communicate their needs to their husbands. One participant said, "I learned that we as women have rights, to choose what we want, to do it or not, to decide about the number of kids as well as about our sexual relations with our husbands." This type of assertive communication was novel to these women who had rarely voiced their wishes or set boundaries within their marriages. It is clear that the fight against violence must be fought on an individual level as well as on a macro-level of society.

IMIFAP also strives to promote masculine responsibility and equal relationships through comprehensive programs to achieve changes in gender roles. It is critical that men learn to take responsibility for their anger and that they learn to manage their anger. IMIFAP teaches alternative methods of conflict resolution using communication and negotiation instead of violence (Pick & Givaudan, 2006a). It also aims to sensitize and educate health personnel and professionals involved in the caring for victims of domestic violence so that they develop skills, achieve more control over their lives, and enjoy better well-being. IMIFAP has designed numerous programs to address the problem of violence on various levels.

I Want, I Can ... Prevent Violence (for Adolescents)

This program's objective is to prevent dating violence through information and education to know and detect the characteristics of potential or openly violent relationships, and to create alternative ways to build loving and more satisfying relationships. The results include a greater commitment on the part of the youth to attend violence prevention workshops and greater possibilities of identifying potentially violent relationships through detecting precursors of violence such as extreme jealousy and possessiveness (Ruiz & Fawcett, 1999). It was originally called "Faces and Masks of Violence."

I Want, I Can ... Prevent Violence (for Health Personnel)

The goal of this program is to sensitize health personnel to their role regarding domestic violence and to teach them the skills necessary to detect, register, and focus attention on different causes of violence. The results were that health personnel have a better understanding of the economic consequences, the abuser's intentions, types of violence, and ways to detect it, and also have a better understanding of the process to follow after having detected a case of violence. Health personnel also have a good understanding of how to communicate with patients in an environment of trust (Fawcett *et al.*, 1999). It was originally named "The Role of Health Personnel in the Face of Domestic Violence."

I Want, I Can ... Prevent Violence (for Females)

This is a program for women originally titled "Breaking the Chain of Violence." Its objective is to decrease the level of incidence of domestic violence through the implementation of educational preventative programs targeting women, men, adolescents, and representatives of the community. After the educational workshops were implemented, there was a percentage increase from 32% to 36% of women who recognized having suffered violence within a relationship (Fawcett & Isita, 2000).

With an integral approach to violence prevention, IMIFAP has developed programs that strengthen behavioral skills with women, men, and children. These programs have a solid theoretical base, but above all, they have real and applicable qualities that help people understand the origins of behaviors that harm one's health and suggest ways to change this behavior and regain one's own life experiences and context to create options. These programs include:

I Want, I Can Take Care of My Health and Rights (for Females)

This program, originally titled "If I Am OK, So Is My Family," seeks to strengthen skills in rural women that are necessary to make decisions about health and family. These skills allow women to become the main health promoters in their communities. As a result of participating in this program, women have a greater capacity to negotiate with their partners about contraceptives, and women have made the decision to look for alternative forms of educating their children with respect to what they have learned from their families (IMIFAP, 2002).

I Want, I Can . . . Go Into Business

Many of the women who participated in the *I Want, I Can Take Care of My Health and Rights (for Females)* program wanted to complete their empowerment with full economic independence and asked for help in starting their own small businesses. IMIFAP responded to their request by piloting a microfinance training program paired with small loans. IMIFAP enabled poor and rural women to establish 500 sustainable businesses of which a third have paid employees. The results were such that women who received training and loans returned them at 100%. In some cases, their husbands even switched livelihoods to help out with their wives' lucrative businesses (Bernal, Givaudan, Pick & Martínez, 2006).

I Want, I Can . . . Take Care of My Health and Rights (for Males)

The objective of this program, which is in the process of being developed, is that men learn how and where their concept of masculinity has been formed, how this concept influences the exercising of their sexuality, reproduction, and health-related behaviors, how this concept of masculinity affects the relationships with their families and their partners, and how they have learned this in a social context. Men are also victims of the cultural norms and myths that determine what is to be a man and programs for men are a crucial part of the fight against violence against women (Chaylan *et al.*, 2001).

I Want, I Love, I Can (for Children)

The goal of this program is for children to recognize that they have rights, skills, and opportunities to express their emotions, to participate in tasks and games, to decide what they like, to live without violence, and to receive affection and all the basic elements for one's emotional and physical development. After participating in this program, it was easier for boys and girls to play games together and the girls and boys were better at working in groups with each other. This is an example of a program that attempts to instill the concept of gender equality early on, before cultural norms and gender roles entirely mold the children's attitudes toward each other (Pick, Givaudan, Boynton & Martínez, 2006).

IMIFAP's programs offer distinct and complementary alternatives to the public policies implemented in Mexico because they integrate diverse populations of early ages and include different areas that strengthen agentic empowerment, for example through sexual and reproductive health and rights, citizenship, equality, and successful micro-enterprise development (Pick, Givaudan, Troncoso & Tenorla, 1999; Pick, Givaudan, Tenorio & Fernandez, 2000; Pick & Givaudan, 2006b). IMIFAP's preventative focus begins its work on the individual level to identify the problem accurately through participatory diagnosis and to facilitate real change from below. Communication strategies at the contextual level complement IMIFAP's preventive focus through the mass media and through advocacy efforts at different levels in the government.

CONCLUSION

The fight to stop violence against women cannot be restricted to legislative reform. The key to combating violence against women is found in enabling skills and knowledge so that people can become agents of change. In this way there will also be changes in the cultural context that deems abuse of women to be "normal." Men and women need the skills to communicate with one another like equals. Without the skills, it is too easy to regress to violent patterns of conduct. Only in targeting cultural norms through changes in behaviors and through sensitization and awareness training and outreach can we change the socio-cultural context, and it is only through equipping men and women with the proper skills that they will put their knowledge into practice, creating lasting behavioral change.

REFERENCES

ÁLVAREZ DE LARA, R. M. 2003. *La Violencia Familiar: Un Problema Social.* [Domestic Violence: A Social Problem]. Mexico: IIJ/UNAM.
ASSOR, A., H. KAPLAN & G. ROTH. 2002. Choice is good, but relevance is excellent: autonomy-enhancing and suppressing teacher behaviors in predicting student's engagement in school work. British Journal of Educational Psychology 72, 261–278.
BANDURA, A. 1997. Self-Efficacy: the exercise of control. New York: W.H. Freeman.
BERNAL, M., M. GIVAUDAN, S. PICK & R. MARTÍNEZ. 2006. Development and piloting of a small scale business training program in rural Oaxaca. Report presented to W.K. Kellogg Foundation, Río Negro, Brazil.
BERRY, J.W., Y.H. POORTINGA, M.H. SEGALL & P.R. DASEN. 2002. Cross-Cultural Psychology: Research and Applications. (2nd ed.). Cambridge University Press: Cambridge, MA.
BAUMEISTER, R.F. 1993. Self-Esteem: the puzzle of low self-regard. Plenum Press: New York.
BOEKAERTS, M. 1999. Self-regulated learning: where we are today. International Journal of Educational Researc 31, 445–457.
BRUNER, J. 1996. The Culture of Education. Harvard University Press: Cambridge, MA.
CHAYLAN, S., M. GIVAUDAN, S. PICK & T. VENGUER. 2001. HIV/AIDS prevention programme for men in rural Latin America. Report presented to Elton John Foundation and INDESOL, London, England.
DECI, E.L. & R.M. RYAN. 2000. The "what" and "why" of goal pursuits: human needs and the self-determination of behavior. Psychological Inquiry 11, 227–268.
GONZÁLEZ, G. & G. MAGANDA. 2000. El Cuerpo del Delito: derechos humanos de las mujeres en la justicia penal [Body of Crime: human rights of women in Penal justice]. México: Centro de Documentación del Instituto Nacional de las Mujeres.
FAWCETT, G., L. HEISE, L. ISITA & S. PICK. 1999. Changing community responses to wife abuse. A research and demonstration project in Iztacalco, Mexico. American Psychologist 54, 41–49.
FAWCETT, G., T. VENGUER, L. MIRANDA & F. FERNÁNDEZ. 1999. Los Servicios de Salud ante la Violencia Doméstica. Manual para instructores(as). [Health Services in the Domestic Violence. Instructor's Manual]. México: Editorial IDEAME, S.A. de C.V.
FAWCETT, G. & L. ISITA. 2000. Rompamos la Cadena de la Violencia: un taller para mujeres sobre violencia en la relación de parejas. [Breaking the Chain of Violence: a workshop for women on violence in couples]. Mexico: Editorial IDEAME.
FISHBEIN, M. & I. AJZEN. 1980. Understanding Attitudes and Predicting Social Behaviour. New Jersey: Prentice-Hall.
FISHBEIN, M. & I. AJZEN. 1985. Belief, Attitude, Intention and Behavior: an introduction to theory and research. Reading, MA: Addison-Wesley.

GONZÁLEZ, G.E. & G. MAGANDA. 2000. El Cuerpo del Delito: derechos humanos de las mujeres en la Justicia Penal [Body of Crime: human rights of women in penal justice]. UNIFEM.

HEISE, L. *et al.* 1994. Violence against women: a neglected public health issue in less developed countries. Social Science and Medicin 39, 1165–1179.

HEISE, L., M. ELLSBERG & M. GOTTEMOELLER. 1999. Ending violence against women. Baltimore, MD: Johns Hopkins University Press.

IMIFAP. 2002. "If I Am OK, My Family Is Too," Mexico City: Editorial Ideame.

INSTITUTO NACIONAL DE LAS MUJERES. 2002a. Programa Nacional por una Vida sin Violencia, 2002–2006. [National Program for a Life without Violence, 2002–2006]. México: INMUJERES.

INSTITUTO NACIONAL DE LAS MUJERES. 2002b. Mesa Institucional para Coordinar las Acciones de Prevención y Atención de la Violencia Familiar y hacia las mujeres [Institutional Table for Preventitive Action and Awareness of Domestic Violence and Violence towards Women]. México: INMUJERES. Retrieved May 22, 2006 from http://cedoc.inmujeres.gob.mx/documentos_download/100608.pdf

INSTITUTO NACIONAL DE ESTADÍSTICA GEOGRAFÍA E INFORMÁTICA. 2003. Encuesta Nacional Sobre la Dinámica de las Relaciones en los Hogares [National Survey on the Dynamics of Relationships within the Home]. México: INEGI.

KAGITCIBASI, C. 2005. Autonomy and relatedness in cultural context: implications for self and family. Journal of Cross-Cultural Psychology 36, 1–20.

KELLY, L. 1996. Tensions and possibilities enhancing informal responses to domestic violence. *In* Future Interventions with Battered Women and their Families. J.L. Edelson & Z.C. Eiskovitz, Eds.: Thousand Oaks, CA: Sage.

LAVE, J. & E. WENGER. 1990. Situated Learning: legitimate periperal participation. Cambridge University Press: Cambridge, UK.

ORTIZ-ORTEGA, A., A. AMUCHÁSTEGUI & M. RIVAS. 2006. Porque Yo los Traje al Mundo: la negociación de los derechos de las mujeres en México [Because They Were Born From Me: negotiating women's rights in Mexico]. *In* Cómo Negocian las Mujeres sus Derechos en el Mundo: una Intersección entre culturas, políticas y religiones. [Negotiating Reproductive Rights: women's perspectives across countries and cultures]. R.P. Petchesky & K. Judd, Eds.: Mexico: El Colegio de México.

PICK, S. 2001. Educación para la Salud y la Vida Familiar: Desarrollo de un Modelo Dirigido a la Población Mexicana. [Health and family life education: development of a model directed at the Mexican population]. *In* Psicología Social: Investigación y Aplicaciones en México. N. Calleja & P.E. Gómez, Comps.: pp. 229–266. México: Fondo de Cultura Económica.

PICK, S. & M. GIVAUDAN. 1999. Desarrollo de la Psicología en México [Psychosocial Development in Mexico]. *In* Psicología en las Américas. M. Alonso & A. Eagly, Eds.: 195–215. Sociedad Interamericana de Psicología.

PICK, S., M. GIVAUDAN, A. TRONCOSO & A. TENORIO. 1999. Formación Cívica y Ética. 7th and 8th grades. Yo quiero, yo puedo. México: Editorial Limusa, S.A. de C.V., Grupo Noriega Editores (fifth printing, 2003).

PICK, S., M. GIVAUDAN, A. TENORIO & F. FERNÁNDEZ. 2000. Formación Cívica y Ética. 9th grades. Yo quiero, yo puedo. México: Editorial Limusa, S.A. de C.V., Grupo Noriega Editores (Fourth printing, 2003).

PICK, S., M. GIVAUDAN & Y. POORTINGA. 2003. Sexuality and life skills education: multi strategy interventions in Mexico. American Psychologist 58, 230–234.

PICK, S., Y.H. POORTINGA & M. GIVAUDAN. 2003. Integrating program theory and strategy in culture-sensitive health promotion programs. Professional Psychology: research and practice *34*, 422–429.

PICK, S. & Y.H. POORTINGA. 2005. Marco conceptual y estrategia para el diseño e instrumentación de programas para el desarrollo: una visión científica, política y psicosocial. Revista Revista Latinoamericana de Psicología *37*, 445–460.

PICK, S. & M. GIVAUDAN. 2006a. Violencia: Prevención y alternativas de solución. [Violence: prevention and alternative solutions]. México: Editorial IDEAME.

PICK, S. & M. GIVAUDAN. 2006b. Yo quiero, yo puedo [I want, I love, I can]. Preschool through ninth grade. México: Editorial Ideame.

PICK, S., M. GIVAUDAN, M. BOYNTON & R. MARTÍNEZ. 2006. Life skills curriculum as an HIV/STD prevention strategy. Grant Progress Report presented to National Institues of Health, Bethesda, MD.

PICK, S. & C. RUESGA. 2006. Agency and human development: an empirical view. First Catinamerican Conference on the Human Capabilities Perspective, Mexico City, July 2–2006.

PRESIDENCY OF THE REPUBLIC. 2001. Plan Nacional de Desarrollo [National Development Plan]. México, D.F.: Federal Executive Power Retrieved May 22, 2006 from http://bibliotecadigital.conevyt.org.mx/colecciones/conevyt/plandesarrollo.pdf

PROCHASKA, J.O. & C.C. DICLEMENTE. 1982. Transtheoretical therapy: toward a more integrative model of change. Psychotherapy: theory, research and practice *19*, 276–288.

PROCHASKA, J.O., C.C. DICLEMENTE & J.C. NORCROSS. 1992. In search of how people change. American Psychologist *47*, 1102–1114.

ROTTER, J.B. 1966. Generalized expectancies for internal versus external control of reinforcement. Psychological Monographs *33*, 300–303.

RUIZ, M.G. & G. FAWCETT. 1999. Rostros y máscaras de la violencia: un taller sobre amistad y noviazgo para adolescentes. [Faces and Masks of Violence: a workshop on friendship and dating for adolescents]. Mexico: Editorial IDEAME.

SAUCEDO, I., INTER-AMERICAN DEVELOPMENT BANK, EL COLEGIO DE MÉXICO & THE MEXICAN MINISTRY OF HEALTH. 2002. Violencia doméstica: modelo de intervención en Unidades de Salud. Capacitación para atención en unidades de salud a mujeres maltratadas [Domestic Violence: intervention model for health units. Training for Health Units in Caring for Abused Women].

SECRETARÍA DE DESARROLLO SOCIAL. 2003. La Violencia en México. Informe del Programa Hábitat [Violence in Mexico. Program Report, Habitat]. Mexico: SEDESOL.

SEN, A. 1999. Development as Freedom. Anchor Books: New York.

SHADISH, W.R., T.D. COOK & L.D. LEVITON. 1991. Foundations of Program Evaluation: theories of practice. Sage Publications: Newbury Park, CA.

STEIN, J. 1997. Empowerment and Women's Health: Theory, methods and practice. Zed Books: London.

STRAUS, M., R. GELLES, S. STEINMETZ. 1980. Behind Closed Doors: violence in the American Family. Garden City, NY: Doubleday.

UNITED NATIONS SOCIAL AND ECONOMIC COUNCIL. 2004. Integration of the Human Rights of Women and the Gender Perspective, Report of the Secretary-General U.N. ESCOR, 60th Sess., U.N. Doc. E/CN.4/2004/64.

UNITED NATIONS CHILDREN'S FUND. 2004. Violence Against Women and Girls. Florence, Italy: Innocenti Research Centre.

WHOLEY, J.S., H.P. HATRY & K.E. NEWCOMER. 1994. Handbook of Practical Program Evaluation. San Francisco: Jossey-Bass.

WORLD HEALTH ORGANIZATION. 2005. Multi-Country Study on Women's Health and Domestic Violence Against Women: Summary Report of Initial Results on Prevalence, Health Outcomes and Women's Responses. Geneva: World Health Organization.

Domestic Violence in the Chinese and South Asian Immigrant Communities

ELIZABETH MIDLARSKY, ANITHA VENKATARAMANI-KOTHARI, AND MAURA PLANTE

Teachers College, Columbia University, New York, NY, USA

ABSTRACT: Although the Chinese and South Asian immigrant populations are largely silent on this issue, domestic violence is a fact of life in many families. In this article, we discuss cultural factors that may cause and prolong abuse in Asian immigrant homes, and review similarities and differences between the two Asian cultures in this regard. This article also addresses the psychological trauma experienced by abused Asian immigrant women and the coping strategies that they are likely to employ. Culturally sensitive intervention strategies are presented that may be appropriately used in working with Chinese and South Asian immigrant women for whom abuse is a terrifying and demeaning fact of life.

KEYWORDS: domestic violence; Asian immigrants; psychology of violence

DOMESTIC VIOLENCE IN THE CHINESE AND SOUTH ASIAN IMMIGRANT COMMUNITIES

Domestic violence is a pervasive problem among Asians residing in the United States, despite their reputation as a model minority (Bhandari-Preisser, 1999; Dasgupta, 1998; Merchant, 2000). This problem is generally denied by Asian American groups in national surveys (Tjaden & Thoennes, 2000), and according to Bhandari-Preisser (1999), mainstream American society views domestic violence as a "nonissue" for these groups. However, despite widespread denial, domestic violence has been found to be a serious problem (Ayyub, 2000; Raj & Silverman, 2002).

This article is designed to explore the issue of domestic violence and its psychological manifestations among East Asians and South Asians residing in the United States. It reflects the attempt to comprehend why domestic violence occurs, why it is concealed, what it affords to victims psychologically, and what can be done about it. Although Asian Americans are often studied as a single minority because of the many similarities among them, there are significant differences as well. Our discussion here focuses on East Asian people, specifically people originating in China, and on South Asian communities, comprising people originating in India, Pakistan, Bangladesh, and Sri Lanka as well as Nepal, Bhutan, and Sikkim. While most of the factors presented are common for both Chinese and South Asian cultures, differences also exist between the two.

THE IMMIGRANT EXPERIENCE

To better understand the ecological context in which domestic violence occurs, we begin with an overview of Chinese and South Asian immigration to the United States.

Chinese Immigration

Chinese people have immigrated from their homeland to diverse countries over a long period of time. This movement out of China occurred despite the fact that Chinese imperial governments had prohibited overseas travel from the 14th century onward with the penalty for disobedience being death. The wars between China and other nations impoverished many Chinese people, driving them to seek economic opportunity elsewhere.

By the 17th century, approximately 20,000 Chinese were in the Philippines and 10,000 had migrated to Thailand. Between 1840 and 1900 an additional 2.5 million Chinese people migrated to Africa, Australia, Canada, and the United States. During the first mass immigration to the United States from 1849 to 1889, thousands, most from rural areas, came to labor in the American West. During the second wave from 1882 to 1965, merchants, diplomats, students, and their dependents were allowed to enter the United States; however, they were largely confined to Chinatowns. In the third wave from 1965 to the present, the Civil Rights Act of 1964 enabled Chinese people to seek racial equality and to reunite with family members who had been left behind (Ashabranner, 1993; Wu, 1993).

At the current time, there are approximately 2.4 million ethnic Chinese living in the United States; 2.2 million speak Chinese as a first language. Chinese Americans constitute the largest portion of the Asian American population comprising more than 23% of the group. Indeed, new immigrants from China contributed the greatest portion of the 48% spike in the Asian American population between 1990 and 2000 (U.S. Census, 2004). Furthermore, the Chinese American population continues to grow. The vast size of the Chinese American population today is also underestimated in the official census data due to the number of new immigrants who prefer to remain undocumented for legal, financial, and other reasons.

Chinese immigrants to the United States, like most Asian immigrants, had a variety of motives for migrating here. These include the quest for economic and educational opportunity, and the need to flee war or political turmoil. Many reportedly had no intention of remaining in the United States and thus worked to maintain their cultural ties and facility in the Chinese language. As in most immigrant groups, Chinese immigrants experienced great individual, cultural, and family stress in the process of transition and, ultimately, acculturation (Foo, 2002).

South Asian Immigration

South Asian immigrants have been coming to the United States since 1875. The earlier immigrants consisted of a very small group of men, most of whom were uneducated laborers and migrant workers, and who largely settled in California. In 1965 the relaxation in United States immigration laws allowed more highly qualified and professional people to make their way here (Ayyub, 2000). These new immigrants were educated people who were fluent in English and came with the hope of establishing themselves on a permanent basis; by 1990 there were approximately 900,000 South Asians in the United States. In the 1990s the Family Reunification Act permitted immigration by families of those who had migrated at an earlier time. This group has primarily been of the merchant class and has not been very highly educated. As this large and culturally diverse community has grown, it has become easier to maintain cultural and regional practices in a culture wherein the transmission of culture is a central value (Agarwal, 1991).

Thus, the primary immigrants have historically been men, while female immigrants from South Asia entered the country legally dependent on the men as their wives, daughters, and sometimes their mothers and sisters (Dasgupta, 2000). Legal dependency often translates into financial and emotional dependency in South Asian families. Dasgupta (2000) cites the 1990 census that although 59% of South Asian women over 16 years of age worked outside their homes, their average salary per annum was significantly lower than that earned by the male members of the community. Even when the women's earnings are high, however, domestic abuse occurs. In fact, it appears that migration may increase women's vulnerability to abuse. This may be, in part, because the South Asian immigrant families are under great stress. In addition, the women may face barriers—informational, linguistic, and cultural, to obtaining support (Ahmad, Riaz, Barata, & Stewart, 2004).

DOMESTIC VIOLENCE IN ASIAN IMMIGRANT COMMUNITIES

Chinese and South Asian immigrants have thrived in the United States. Under the façade of the "model minority," Asian communities have generally

TABLE 1. Definitions of domestic violence

Abuse types	American	Chinese	South Asian
Physical	Physical assault, beating, kicking, aggravated assault, battery	Hitting, striking, beating, fighting, physical violence	Physical assault, beating, kicking, torture (hot oil burns)
Psychological	Invalidation, emotional abuse	Not generally viewed as abusive	Denial, minimization, emotional abuse
Sexual	Unwelcome touching, forced sex	Only forced sex is viewed as abuse	Not viewed as abusive. All sex in marriage is usually the right of husband (assertion of male privilege)
Verbal	Verbal abuse or berating, private or public	Not generally viewed as abusive	Mostly public derogation is seen as abusive
Control	Physically restrictive control and coercion, financial control, emotional control denial/withdrawal	Not generally viewed as abusive	Coercion, threat, intimidation, economic control, legal control

been successful in concealing physical, sexual, and emotional abuse, which assuredly does exist. One factor responsible for the problem of apparent concealment may be that the communities may have different definitions of abuse. TABLE 1 presents some of the observed differences in the nature of interactions defined as domestic violence. Thus, for example, if a Chinese woman is belittled by her husband, her earnings are taken from her leaving her with no financial resources and she is locked in the home when she is not at work—then her community will not view her husband's behavior as abusive. If a South Asian woman, on the other hand, is verbally abused and belittled in private (but not in public), and is raped by her husband, then these actions by her husband are not considered to be abusive.

Domestic Violence among Chinese Immigrants

Physical abuse in the Chinese immigrant community has been the subject of research for the last decade; yet, prevalence rates vary widely. Yick (2000) and Yoshioka and Choi (2005) speculate that the reason for this variation resides in the difficulty in obtaining a truly representative national sample. While telephone surveys capture older and more affluent segments, the most susceptible groups such as illegal or new immigrants may be missing from studies because of their fear of detection and deportation. Additional challenges to the research include small sample sizes, disparate definitions of domestic violence (as in TABLE 1), and cultural prohibitions against sharing intimate information with people outside the family.

The data that are available provide valuable insights to the problem in this population. Yick (2000) reported that 10% of a Chinese American sample living in Los Angeles experienced abuse in the previous year, while only 18% had experienced physical spousal abuse in their lifetime. Yoshioka, DiNoia, and Ullah (2001) report that according to the Asian Task Force against Domestic Violence, 24% of Chinese Americans surveyed in Boston are physically abused or injured by a partner. Because of the high potential for underreporting personally stigmatizing facts such as abuse, indirect questioning was used. The use of this methodology led to the finding that 25% of people surveyed were aware of family members who were physically abused by their spouses (Yick, 2000).

Consider, for example, the case of Ying, a middle school teacher who was verbally abused, threatened, and demeaned by her husband. Even after she divorced him, he continued to follow her and to threaten her life and the lives of their two children. He moved into the new home that she had purchased and refused to let her leave, except when she had to go to work. Ying told her family about the continuing abuse, but they responded by joining Ying's ex-husband in saying that her marriage was more important than anything, that she had not been "really" abused (see TABLE 1), and that she should take him back. When she continued to refuse her husband, he raped and brutally beat her, and locked her in her home. Ying, alone and despairing, took her own life.

Xu and her husband came to the United States with their two children, and the expectation of making a good life for themselves. Both were trained as physicians, and expected to do well both socially and financially. Xu's husband was unable to get on his feet professionally and after struggling for a long while, took a job as a waiter in a Chinese restaurant. As the children were getting older, he insisted that Xu take a job to help support the family. In contrast to her husband, Xu had been working on obtaining medical credentials from the day that they came to this country. Unable to practice Western medicine here, she became a skilled practitioner of Eastern medicine including acupuncture, while she worked as a waitress. She ultimately went to work in her field and was far more successful financially than her husband. Her husband's physical and verbal abuse increased concomitantly with her success. When she went to a lawyer to discuss divorce, her husband became so enraged that he slashed her and almost killed her. These anecdotes, which are just two examples of the many that abound, indicate that the numbers of abused Chinese women and the suffering by Chinese women are striking enough for this problem to be treated with great seriousness.

Domestic Violence among South Asian Immigrants

Reports by South Asian women's organizations indicate that large numbers of women have been seeking help with domestic violence issues. Dasgupta (2000) cites records for New Jersey-based *Manavi,* a South Asian group founded to end violence against women that provided domestic violence services to 160 individuals between July 1, 1996 and June 30, 1997. A total of 252 individuals were served between July 1997 and June 30 1998, and 258 battered South Asian women received services between July 1, 1998 and June 30, 1999. Dasgupta also cites reports of violence in South Asian community newspapers based in the United States. She asserts that between March 1990 and December 1999, community newspapers reported 43 spousal murders, 4 attempted murders, and 11 suicides after murder had been committed.

In contrast to the availability of systematic data about spousal abuse among Chinese Americans, there have been few studies on domestic violence against women in South Asian communities. The small amount of systematic evidence that is available suggests that domestic violence is indeed a significant problem in the South Asian community. According to Ayyub (2000), surveys of the South Asian immigrant population in 1998 indicated that one in every four South Asian women reported domestic violence in her home. The author makes the important point that if as many as 25% of South Asians have reported abuse despite enormous social pressures to withhold such information, then it is likely that many others are tolerating abuse in silence. A Boston area survey of South Asian immigrant women revealed that physical abuse was experienced by 40.8% of the women (Raj & Silverman, 2002). Dasgupta (2000) quotes a Boston area survey with 160 highly educated middle class South Asian women between the ages of 18 and 62 years. In this sample, nearly 35% reported physical abuse and 19% indicated a history of sexual abuse by their partners. It is important to note that although the prevalence and extent of domestic violence are not firmly established, the conclusion may be drawn that domestic violence in this population is a critical social issue.

Domestic violence can come in many forms and cultural factors may come into play in at least some of these. Consider, for example, the role that is played by the emphasis on beauty. The South Asian immigrant women who only recently followed their husbands to the United States may be confronted by the Western image of physical beauty to which their husbands may have grown accustomed. Dasgupta (2000) cites the example of Poonam, a woman who came to *Manavi* half starved. Her scientist/academician husband had controlled her food intake from the moment she arrived in the United States and insisted that she must remain slim. He made her weigh herself every morning and kept a chart of her weight. Small increases in her weight were punished with forced fasting, public humiliation, silence, and the withholding of affection. He controlled when and how much she ate and made sure she had no money on her person so that she could not buy any food without his knowledge. He also forced her to hasten her "Americanization" by cutting her hair and burning her traditional Indian garments (Dasgupta, 2000).

Financial control is critical in many cases, as it was in Poonam's case. Because the man, as the first to have immigrated, is the sole financial provider, he has power that may frequently be used to the woman's disadvantage. This is reflected in the case of Shahida, whose husband locked her in the home from the day that she arrived in the United States, while he continued his affair with a neighbor. He gave Shahida no money, forbade her from even walking outside, and forced her to sleep on the living room couch. Her status in the family was that of an unpaid servant who was responsible for cooking and cleaning. Isolation and total financial dependency kept Shahida from leaving the marriage; her acceptance of the abuse was also ensured by her lack of knowledge of the English language and mores as well as constant threats of deportation and defamatory remarks to her family in Pakistan (Abraham, 2000).

Abraham (2000) also cites the case of Malti, a woman with a flourishing career, who had lived in the United States alone prior to her marriage. Her physician husband soon brought her under his control by curtailing her activities and controlling the amount of money available to her. He gave her 20 dollars a week for all her expenses, despite the savings that she had brought to the marriage from her previous employment. Her husband and in-laws (with whom the couple lived) threatened physical assault if she questioned their behavior or interference. Malti's cultural disadvantage was that she was already a one-time divorcee and was more highly vulnerable to the threat of defamation. What this anecdote suggests is that cultural constraints may affect not only dependent immigrants, but relatively independent, well-educated women as well. It also highlights the influential issues of divorce and the extended family system.

Another case described by Abraham (2000) denotes the role of law enforcement in such situations. For immigrant women, the fear of reporting abuse can be exacerbated by their lack of knowledge about their rights within the United States combined with the increase of police insensitivity and ignorance toward immigrants. Geeta was severely abused physically and emotionally, and her husband often threatened her with acts of violence such as burning her body with hot oil. She was a physician herself in India and upon her arrival found herself to be completely helpless in a new environment where she knew no one except her abusive husband. On one occasion her screams were heard by neighbors who called the police. However, her husband convinced her that the person at the door was a security guard and that she should not say anything. While the police insisted on talking to her, they failed to notice the fact that she was being instructed in her mother tongue to tell them there was no problem (Abraham, 2000). The law enforcement system might itself be "supersensitive" to cultural issues, sometimes causing more woe to the victims. Dasgupta (2000) cites the example of a New Jersey family court judge who vacated a South Asian woman's temporary restraining order by commenting that her husband's abusive behavior may be "cultural." Furthermore, language barriers, cultural differences, lack of knowledge about their rights, and immigration policies together keep abused South Asian women from seeking help from shelters or other social services.

CULTURE AND FAMILY VIOLENCE

Domestic violence is a problem that affects people regardless of their ethnicity or class. However, several characteristics of the Asian community may *increase* the occurrence and toleration of violence. On the other hand, other cultural factors may actually serve to *lessen* the occurrence and toleration of violence in homes. In this section, we present both types of intrinsic cultural factors.

Cultural Factors That May Increase the Occurrence and Toleration of Violence

Gender Roles

Gender roles fall into a very rigid framework wherein men and women serve strictly outlined functions. While the specific cultural factors defining a woman's role and behavior may differ among Chinese and South Asian immigrants, in both cases the boundaries of a woman's identity are clearly prescribed.

In premodern China, Chinese tradition was primarily founded on Taoism, Buddhism, and Confucianism. While Buddhism and Taoism were guideposts for Chinese spirituality, conduct and morality were guided primarily by tenets of Confucianism. The Confucian doctrine regarding females is found in the "Four Books for Women," in which women are taught that they are inferior to men. A woman must obey a sequence of men in her lifetime: her father in childhood, her husband when married, and her sons when widowed. The married woman became her husband's property, moved into his family home, and was subsumed into his extended family (Tang, Wong & Cheung, 2002). The woman was always to be quiet, polite, and submissive; the diminutive role is seen, for example, in the binding of the woman's feet, which strongly (and painfully) ensured that the woman would have no choice but to stay in the home. It is also seen in the ideographic Chinese script, in which the character for "woman" (Nu) shows a woman bowing. Similarly, the ideograph for "good" (Hao) depicts a woman with a child. The woman was to engage in "womanly work"—cleaning, sewing, cooking—and never to become involved in public affairs. A woman who did not observe the rules of propriety could be taken to court. In particular, a woman's crimes against men (e.g., adultery) were punished much more severely than a man's crimes against a woman. During the Communist era, women were brought into the labor force and each couple was permitted to have no more than one child after 1979. Nevertheless, women were expected to remain subservient—but here the subjugation occurred both in the private and public spheres (Bond, 1996).

The image of femininity among South Asians includes chastity and submissiveness, and the woman's sexuality is to be confined entirely within marriage. The virtuous woman is one who walks slowly, never runs, never laughs out loud, and never takes care of her own needs before those of her family. More often than not, the girl is molded with the sole intention of finding her a suitable husband. The use of her education is first to provide status for her parents and second, the image and material well-being that it brings to her in-laws (Ayyub, 2000). The ideal wife is devoted to her husband, self-sacrificing when necessary, and is dependent upon her husband for material necessities and for social status. Her job is to satisfy her husband's sexual needs without considering her own. The expectations of complete sexual access even lead women to condone forced sex within marriage. Masculinity, on the other hand, is defined by virility, power, and the ability to control women. Forced sexuality is part of the masculine image, especially within marriage (Abraham, 1999). Sons are more highly valued than daughters as sons carry the family name into the future. While money, power, and status have been handed down from father to son for centuries, daughters are seen as a financial burden by their family of origin as they will marry and become members of their husbands' families. Indeed, it is through fulfilling the roles of good wife and mother that a woman can obtain praise and respect, not through self-expression (Goel, 2005).

Family before Self

The family unit plays a role of paramount importance in the life of every Asian immigrant. Greater value is attributed to the family than to the individual, and the individual's behavior is often seen as a reflection of the family's worth in society. Among Chinese people, one is never conceived of as independent or separate from the community. Loss of face is the penalty for deviating from cultural values. The penalties for breaking with the cultural norms include shame and ostracism (Yoshioka & Choi, 2005). Public shame is cast on the individual, the family, the extended family, the community, and even the ancestors (Ho, 1990). So great is this personal cost that people rarely feel justified in stepping outside family boundaries (Yoshioka, DiNoia, & Ullah, 2001). Therefore, when abuse does occur, it is generally treated as a family secret (Yoshioka & Choi, 2005) to spare the whole family public humiliation (Ho, 1990).

These cultural values are reflected in the relatively infrequent reports of domestic violence until the information can no longer be contained. Of Chinese

Americans polled in Los Angeles, 46% believe problems in the family should be taken care of by the family and not by outsiders (Yick & Agbayami-Siewert, 1997). Chinese Americans largely agree that disclosure of abuse issued outside the family is a violation of family privacy and fear bringing shame to the family. Yoshioka and Choi (2005) reported that 18% of Chinese women say an abused wife should not tell anyone. Over two-thirds refuse to consider a shelter as an appropriate way to leave an abusive situation. Furthermore, younger Chinese people were less likely to perceive alternatives like leaving or divorce as viable options.

In the South Asian community, ideas integral to the cultural norms include the superiority of Karma (destiny), fatalism (acceptance of fate), filial piety (complying with familial and social authority to the point of sacrificing one's own desire), collectivism, and the ascendance of kinship over individual existence (Merchant, 2000). The family boundaries are therefore clearly defined and a strict distinction is drawn between insiders and outsiders. Each individual is made aware of the prohibition regarding exposing family information to the outside world (Dasgupta, 2000).

The Model Minority

The American media have often labeled Chinese Americans as a "model minority," devoid of any social problems including domestic violence. The growing South Asian immigrant community also aspires to this appellation. As a consequence, victims of spouse abuse are often encouraged to suppress evidence of violent acts within the home and community (Dasgupta, 1998). The paucity of reliable quantitative data on the incidence of abuse in the community itself speaks volumes about the invisibility surrounding the topic.

The Requirements of Marriage

Marriage brings with it another set of rules for the woman to follow. For Chinese immigrants, cultural values may also lead a woman to protect the sanctity of marriage to maintain peace and harmony, whatever the cost to herself. Central to both Confucian philosophy and Buddhist tenets are harmonious relationships. Peaceful relationships are the key to well-being and a balanced life (Yoshioka & Choi, 2005). When the sanctity of a harmonious relationship is violated, the reaction can be fierce. Yoshioka and Choi found that more than one-third of Chinese Americans justify a husband's beating of his wife when his wife cheats on him, refuses to have sex with him, or makes fun of him at a party. Over one-fifth surveyed feel that some wives provoke beatings from their husbands (Yoshioka & Choi, 2005). Also, Yick and Agbayani-Siewert (1997) found that Chinese Americans attributed wife abuse first to the husband's bad temper and second to the wife's poor communication with her husband. Marriage subjects a woman to another set of expectations, and punishments for the violation of these expectations are not just condoned, they may even be encouraged.

From early childhood, South Asian parents teach their daughter that the greatest harm that she could inflict upon the family would be the shame they would experience if she were to prove a bad wife and her marriage were to fail (Ayyub, 2000). As a result, a woman in a heavily androcentric (male-centered) marriage might accept domination as her destiny instead of leaving the unhealthy situation. A woman whose husband indulges her is seen as lucky, whereas one whose husband mistreats her is advised to accept things as her fate and misfortune (Ayyub, 2000).

The "Joint Family" Setup

Another cultural structure that increases the acceptance of violence, particularly by South Asian women, is the extended family system. Many new South Asian brides live with their in-laws, which may include brothers and sisters-in-law, so that the new wife becomes answerable to many people. The sources of abuse also tend to increase. At times the husband may be a participant or observer of his wife's abuse at the hands of his parents and siblings. In situations of this kind, the woman tends to rest the blame on the in-laws and believes that her husband himself deserves no blame (Dasgupta, 2000). While the extended family system may be less common among Chinese immigrants, the culturally sanctioned view of women as subservient and obedient may be expected to influence Chinese homes where women live with members of their husband's family.

Financial Dependency

If an employed woman is married to a dominating man, she may not have the opportunity to enjoy the independence and identity that she has earned. For example, among South Asians, men usually control the family finances regardless of the woman's working status. Thus, a South Asian woman's financial security becomes entirely dependent upon her spouse (Dasgupta, 2000). Cultural limitations and gender role conditioning combine to lead even highly educated and financially independent women to feel accountable to their spouses and families (Abraham, 2000). A woman who works outside the family is seen as doing this only as an extended fulfillment of her domestic duties, therefore any development of social ties with coworkers and friends is seen as unnecessary (Mazumdar, 1989). Similar patterns of thought may influence Chinese American communities as well.

The Stigma of Divorce

Intervention strategies for domestic violence victims often stem from predominantly Western values of self-empowerment and self-determination. These values conflict with the Chinese values of family first and placing the individual ahead of others (Yoshioka & Choi, 2005). While a non-Asian may regard leaving the abuser as a means to maintaining self-respect, a Chinese immigrant victim may view staying in the home with the family as the means to save face and to maintain self-respect (Yoshioka & Choi, 2005).

Similarly, a South Asian woman's identity is seen as derived primarily from marriage and motherhood. Therefore a woman without a husband is treated as a person who is lacking a major component of herself. Furthermore, a divorced woman and/or single mother is perceived as having failed in the role of wife and mother, regardless of the conduct of her partner (Dasgupta & Warrier, 1996). Divorced women are further viewed as "damaged goods," the divorce is seen stemming from some intrinsic problem or flaw, and the divorced woman's participation in holy events or celebrations (particularly weddings) is discouraged for the fear that she may bring bad luck (Ayyub, 2000). In some cases, divorce is not considered to be a viable option because of the cultural message that the husband is the only source of security (Goel, 2005).

Second Generation Issues

The pressure to keep up the model minority image transcends generational barriers, and affects immigrant parents raising second-generation Asian American children as well. Having themselves been raised under strict scrutiny in their homelands, immigrant parents become overwhelmed by the omnipresent influence of Western music and culture on their children as manifested through the child's or teenager's increased freedom of expression and open sexuality. The 50% divorce rate in the United States becomes a cause for concern for the parents. As a result, educated immigrant parents who themselves may have disapproved of the iron fist in their own youth turn to those same rules in an attempt to re-create their old family system. The application of these rules can lead to a new round of abusive scenarios, many of which may involve forced and even "tricked" marriages for young, second-generation American girls who may have started to express their identity through their extroverted behavior (Ayyub, 2000). While this has particularly been noted in the literature on the South Asian population, such incidents may occur among Chinese immigrants as well.

Invalidating the Experience of Abuse

Given the gender relations and androcentric (male-centered) power distribution that is inherent to traditional Asian cultures, abandonment, financial deprivation, physical, sexual, and emotional violence can leave the victim unsure of the validity of her experiences (Dasgupta, 2000). This issue is exemplified by the family court judge (cited earlier) who dismissed the abuse charge based on the argument that abusive behavior may be culturally sanctioned among South Asians. Dasgupta (2000) also cites some informal cases from her own work where she found that South Asian victims tend to be reluctant to pursue legal remedies for sexual coercion or spousal rape because they have accepted the cultural view that their husbands "own" their bodies. She further emphasizes that most battered South Asian women feel that marriage denies them sexual control, and their husbands are entitled to unlimited access to their bodies and even to beat them if they have failed to perform their duties satisfactorily. Marital rape, Dasgupta (2000) asserts, is an alien concept among South Asian women; they only recognize violence in the form of excessive physical abuse, sexual perversity, and/or sexual torture. Results of a telephone survey by Ahmad, Riaz, Barata, and Stewart (2004) indicated that women who agreed with patriarchal social norms were less likely to view spousal abuse, described in a vignette, as abuse.

Similarly, the majority of Chinese Americans surveyed by Yick & Agbayani-Siewart (1997) disapproved of abuse, but females were found to disapprove more strongly than males. More males than females blame the victim of abuse (Yick & Agbayani-Siewart, 1997). Chinese Americans subscribing to the traditional view of the female as inherently subservient are less likely to see domestic violence as a crime in need of intervention, and these same traditionalists are more likely to believe myths blaming the victim (Yick, 2000). Older Chinese Americans are more likely than are younger Chinese Americans to subscribe to traditional beliefs and are more likely to accept the use of physical force to solve problems (Yick, 2000). Given the invalidating cultural factors, victims and the community at large may respond to abusive scenarios by justifying the abuser's actions. For instance, 25% of a Chinese American sample polled in Los Angeles agreed that victims cause the abuse and 50% agreed that victims could easily leave the abusive partner (Yick & Agbayani-Siewert, 1997).

The Allure of the Green Card

As mentioned earlier, the issues of financial control and immigration status jointly compound the domestic violence problem. As they are frequently the secondary and dependent immigrants, women often feel the need to justify themselves in the eyes of their husbands and to live by their husbands' rules. Threats of deportation and consequent defamation and helplessness can only make women more vulnerable to the control of their husbands.

South Asian girls are often raised to be entirely compliant with their parents' wishes. Their lack of assertiveness and confidence in their ability to survive independently, combined with the stigma associated with failed marriages, can promote the acceptance of any abuse that may be concomitant with their spousal relationship. Living with an abusive man who holds the key to her permanent residence in the United States, and a probable future of happiness once the green card arrives, may appear to be a better alternative than being forced to return home, and to experience scorn and shame. Similar reactions may be found among Chinese immigrants as well.

Lack of Support Systems

An Asian immigrant woman also lacks extended family support in the United States. The family and cultural support systems that she may have had in her home country are often removed with the shift to a new country (Abraham, 2000). In accordance with Shahida's experience, described earlier, some women are forcibly isolated from any family or friends they may have in this country, which may further exacerbate their feelings of despair and helplessness. Living solely in the domain of her abusive husband, the abused woman may have nowhere to go, even if she wants to speak to someone about the problems at home.

Another problem may be the fact that appropriate shelters and social institutions may not be available for Asian women. Dasgupta (2000) cites examples of South Asian clients who were turned away from a homeless shelter because there was no one in the shelter who spoke the woman's language. Once in shelters, women may encounter cultural insensitivity, racism, xenophobia, classism, and ignorance about immigration policies (Dasgupta, 2000).

Relationship to the Legal System

It is extremely unusual for South Asians to seek help from law enforcement agencies, primarily because South Asians view the police and the legal system as oppressive, and involvement with the police as shameful (Dasgupta, 2000). United States immigration law reinforces the dependency of the secondary immigrants (primarily women in the Asian immigrant context). The Marriage Fraud Provision Act of the 1986 Immigration Reform and Control Act (IRCA) imposes a 2-year conditional residency status on the secondary "alien" spouse whose immigration status confirmation depends on proving to the Department of Immigration and Naturalization Services (INS) that the marriage was contracted in good faith. The 1990 and 1994 amendments to this act such as the Battered Spouse Waiver place a modicum of control in the hands of the victims, but the initial power that the policy places in the hands of the primary immigrant, and the complexities of relief procedures, deter already struggling women from seeking these resources (Dasgupta, 2000). In particular, among South Asian immigrants, the 9/11 tragedy and institution of immigration-related laws have also contributed to the heightened fear of law enforcement and legal systems.

Cultural Factors That May Prevent the Occurrence of Domestic Violence

While several cultural factors serve to exacerbate the occurrence and acceptance of violence in Asian immigrant homes, it is important to note some cultural factors that may have protective functions.

Chinese culture largely subscribes to a collectivist view of the world and imparts the idea of the individual as part of the larger whole. One is never conceptualized as independent or separate from the community. A person's self concept and identity are intricately involved with the roles played in the family, community, and the larger collective. Problems are resolved through collaboration to build a better whole rather than confrontation or conflict to defeat another individual (Yoshioka, DiNoia, & Ullah, 2001). An individual's physical, emotional, and social needs are sought and fulfilled through the group rather than independently. Also, in collectivist societies, defying group norms carries a heavy penalty of shame (Yoshioka & Choi, 2005). This factor may serve to deter violence in at least some Chinese immigrant homes in which potential perpetrators are keenly aware of living under the watchful eyes of their neighbors (Yick, 2000). Collectivist societies encourage each member to act as his or her "brother's keeper," watching over each other (Yoshioka & Choi, 2005). In addition to little personal privacy, the severe penalty of public shame may prevent domestic violence, at least in some instances.

A second interpretation proposed by Yick (2000) is the impact of the collectivist worldview of one's identity. By definition, collectivist cultures place the family ahead of individual needs and goals. Therefore, a crime against one's wife may be perceived as a crime against the family and the self.

The research with South Asian immigrants has not proposed any specific cultural factors contributing to lowering the rates of domestic violence in the community. Further research may highlight South Asian cultural factors that serve protective functions within this population as well.

PSYCHOLOGICAL IMPACT OF DOMESTIC VIOLENCE

There is a noticeable paucity of systematic research on the psychological impact of domestic violence among Asian immigrants to the United States. There is a small amount of research in this area among Chinese immigrants, but studies concerning psychological trauma that may result from domestic violence among South Asian immigrants is very scarce. In fact, South Asian organizations such as *Manavi* report that mental health counseling is sought by very few of their battered female clients. These organizations observe that when the abuse stops most clients see education, employment, and the well-being of their children as more important concerns than their own mental health (Bhandari-Preisser, 1999). However, given the nature of the issues at hand, it is expected that victims may incur emotional damage. In this section, we draw upon case studies cited above as well as theory and research derived from earlier studies to present possible psychological sequelae of violence among Asian American women. Survivors of abuse in the Chinese and South Asian communities may differ from one another in important ways, but only further research can help define specific similarities and differences between the two groups.

Loss of Self-Esteem and Identity

The loss of financial control, as exhibited by the cases of Malti and Shahida, are likely to leave the woman feeling helpless and insecure. Since she has to depend on her husband for financial support, the abused woman may feel indebted or obligated to him. Shahida found herself being treated like an unpaid maid and did not speak up when asked to clean her abusive husband's soiled bed. It is almost as though she accepted her role as his servant and stopped expecting any concern for herself. This is a reflection of how the woman may grow to have a distorted view of the self.

Geeta's case is also an example of this sense of helplessness. She was a physician in her home country, but was convinced that the policeman at her door was really a security guard. This shows how exposure to abuse and enforced dependency may cause a woman to question herself and her instincts. As she loses her self-confidence, she becomes increasingly tied to her husband and his judgment. This only places more power in his hands, leading to an exacerbation of her insecurity.

Such insecurity can also shift her locus of evaluation outside herself, as in the case of Poonam, who was put through rigorous diets to stay slim. Poonam viewed herself as unappealing and unattractive because her husband withheld affection when she gained any weight at all. This sort of situation may crush a woman's sense of self-worth, leading her to evaluate herself based on the amount of affection she is receiving from her husband.

Each of these women explained that she tried to entice her husband and win his love, and that it was her own failure to be "enticing enough" that led him to become violent. This subtle justification of the abuse suggests that the victims may view themselves through the lenses provided by their abusers. The mold into which she is forced by her husband may ultimately shape a battered woman's identity. This, combined with the aforementioned cultural factors, makes it all the more difficult for women to leave abusive relationships. They become caught in a vicious cycle in which they become increasingly more insecure, leading to an increase in their spouses' power and which consequently makes them even more vulnerable to abuse. As the circle closes in on her, a battered woman may find herself living in a state of chronic fear (Mehrotra, 1999). This cycle is encompassed by the "Battered Woman Syndrome," which includes learned helplessness and self-destructive coping

Depression, Anxiety, and Posttraumatic Stress Syndrome

Decrements in an individual's self-esteem, combined with joblessness and isolation, can lead to depression and anxiety. Indeed, Chinese women living in a shelter following wife abuse (both verbal and physical) were found to be both depressed and anxious (Tang, 1997). It has also been found that verbal and psychological abuse can cause intense fear, guilt, and damage to self-esteem, all of which can have longer-lasting effects than physical injury (Goldberg & Tomlanovich, 1984; Walker, 1984 as cited in Tang, 1997). Tang (1997) also found that depressive affects were more common among children of abused women than children of women who were not abused. Research with battered South Asian women may reveal similar patterns of mental health.

Another important similarity between the Chinese and South Asian culture is that they tend to downplay psychological problems, not considering them worthy of much attention (Yick & Agbayani-Siewert, 1997). This suppression of emotional problems may actually cause greater problems in the future than if they were dealt with more expeditiously. Studies with non-Asian populations have shown that anger, which is a commonly experienced emotion among abused women, can lead to depression when suppressed (Dutton, 1992; Swan & Snow, 2003).

Somatic Problems

Studies with abused women from Anglo and African American groups have found that these women are likely to have more health concerns than non-battered women. These may include problems with sleep, fatigue, recurring nightmares, headaches, pains in the chest, back, and limbs, disturbing physical sensations, gastrointestinal and respiratory problems, and menstrual difficulties (Sutherland, Sullivan, & Bybee, 2001). It is likely that in some of these cases psychological problems have become somaticized, that is, expressed as physical illnesses, which are far easier and more socially acceptable to address than is the occurrence of abuse. Because prior research has focused on groups that are culturally different from Asians, and in the absence of empirical data, one can only speculate that somatization may be a consequence of abuse.

STRATEGIES FOR RESISTING AND COPING WITH ABUSE

Often an abused woman, lacking appropriate ways to address her problems, may try to justify her husband's actions. Counselors at *Manavi* reported that the most prominent explanation a South Asian client provided for abuse was that her husband might have a lot of frustration and stress in his life that he expresses through his aggression toward her (Mehrotra, 1999). The need for justification may be amplified if the woman feels the need to maintain a good image of their father for her children. A battered woman may endure the abuse and resist seeking help from agencies and shelters if she worries about having her children see their father being led away by police (Bhandari-Preisser, 1999).

Abused women may also employ strategies to resist the violence, protect themselves from more harm, and preserve their sense of self-worth. Mehrotra (1999) cites cases of South Asian battered women who refused to cook, while others seized some degree of control by duplicating the house and car keys without their partner's knowledge. In other examples of resistance, women also kept their important documentation (such as passports and immigration papers) in a secure place or spit into their partner's food before serving it. Although the literature on Chinese victims of domestic violence did not outline specific coping strategies, research may reveal similar patterns among the Chinese population as well.

IMPLICATIONS FOR WORK WITH ASIAN VICTIMS OF DOMESTIC VIOLENCE

Social service agencies and professionals have generally responded inadequately to the needs of Asian American victims. Efforts to help victims of domestic abuse in the Asian population must take into consideration the cultural issues involved for the client, and the perception of abuse and marital problems within her culture. Unless there is knowledge of the language and culture of the abused women, she is unlikely to obtain the help she needs in her quest to gain control over her life.

If a battered woman seeks legal counsel to remove herself from the abusive situation, her advocate and counselor come to play an important role in her life. Whether the issues have to do with the understanding of her rights within the United States or her visa status, her attorney and counselor become responsible for explaining everything to her. However, effective communication and understanding are only possible if her attorney and counselor comprehend the cultural perceptions and sanctions that dominate her life. The woman may not, for example, be able to report her abusive spouse to the police because he holds her immigration papers. Agencies should particularly consider cultural values about the need to tolerate abuse, mores about child-rearing, dating, and marriage, insider and outsider relationships, and appropriate codes for public and private behavior (Dasgupta & Warrier, 1995).

Mainstream professionals may be unaware that in many instances, influential community leaders (such as temple priests or church leaders) reinforce the prohibition against reporting the abuse to anyone outside the family (Ayyub, 2000; Dasgupta, 2000; George & Rahangdale, 1999; Huisman, 1996; Perilla,

1999; 1998; Raj & Silverman, 2002). Agencies must take into account the reasons that the women keep silent. They must also spread awareness of the availability of resources and educate women on their rights. While doing such outreach, educators should use terminology that is accepted within the community and refrain from using words such as "rape" and "batterer," which may shock the client and deter her from seeking help from the outreach worker (Raj & Silverman, 2002).

Many of the individualistic constructs assumed in Western style interventions conflict with Asian values of "family first," and "loss of face." These Asian constructs emphasize secrecy, the need to protect the family, to keep the family intact at all costs, and to avoid even the possibility of public shaming. Models of intervention that are designed to help a woman leave her abuser and thrive independently may not appeal to an abused Asian woman (Yoshioka & Choi, 2005). This mainstream approach assumes the Western value that it is better to live single and divorced than to live in an abusive marriage. Yoshioka and Choi (2005) call for a paradigm shift wherein interventions for Asian American victims will focus on creating a woman who is safe in her own home rather than "free" and "independent." In educating the community and family—as well as the woman—the point must be made that "culture" cannot be used to justify violence, and that only a distorted view of Asian culture can be used to assert that violence toward women is normative. A distinction must be made between culture, "the positive transmission of rituals, celebrations, and stories," and practices such as wife battering (Almeida & Dolan Delvecchio, 1999).

SUGGESTIONS FOR FUTURE RESEARCH WITH ABUSED ASIAN IMMIGRANTS

Lack of generalizability due to very small samples is the key limitation of the available research. The data presented from national surveys usually combine all Asian groups under the heading "Asian Americans." A separate data analysis isolating Chinese Americans and South Asian Americans will have a better chance of identifying the most likely victims, perpetrators, and communities in need of intervention. A meta-analysis of the existing studies may also help to identify the protective and vulnerability factors in each community.

Additionally, some impediments to conducting comparisons among the communities include the lack of consistent definitions of abuse, varied research frameworks and designs, the diversity of the time frames evaluated, the severity or frequency of abuse, and the use of indirect assessments (Xu, Campbell, & Zhu, 2001). Also, researchers are not doing an adequate job of reaching the undocumented recent immigrants from China and South Asia who may require help. This segment of the population has stayed under the radar of the national census. Creative research collection and intervention methods are needed to reach this group.

CONCLUSION

Domestic violence affects people all over the country regardless of race, class, and gender. This article examines the questions of how and why this problem affects immigrants from China and South Asia. It provides a window into cases of abuse in the South Asian population and data from the Chinese population. This article also highlights cultural factors that may encourage and suppress abuse, the possible psychological impact, some methods of resistance and coping, the implications for working with abused Chinese and South Asians, and suggestions for future research with these populations. Although based on a small body of evidence, this article puts forth the seriousness of the problem for those it affects, and emphasizes the need for academic and clinical attention to this population. While it focuses on Chinese and South Asian immigrant women, this article is not an attempt to say that women are the only victims of abuse. Research might reveal woman-to-man abuse and also intragender abuse among homosexual Chinese and South Asian immigrants.

Domestic violence is a complicated issue that is even more complex when recent immigrants of diverse cultures are involved. Indeed, violence in the family is a problem that has the potential to have critical impacts on whole families and communities as well as on the victims of abuse. To combat domestic violence in these immigrant communities, we need to reach the abusers as well as the abused, the community leaders, and both the formal and informal helpers. With increased cultural sensitivity and education, the silence may be broken, and the curative process begun in the Chinese and South Asian communities.

REFERENCES

ABRAHAM, M. 1999. Sexual abuse in South Asian immigrant marriages. Violence Against Women 5, 591–618.

ABRAHAM, M. 2000. Isolation as a form of marital violence: the South Asian immigrant experience. Journal of Social Distress and the Homeless 9, 221–236.

AGARWAL, P. 1991. Passage from India: Post-1965 Immigrants and Their Children. Yuvati. CA

AHMAD, F., S. RIAZ, P. BARATA & D.E. STEWART. 2004. Patriarchal belies and perceptions of abuse among South Asian immigrant women. Violence Against Women 10, 262–282.

ALMEIDA, R.V. & K. DOLAN DELVECCHIO. 1999. Addressing culture in batterers intervention: the Asian Indian community as an illustrative example. Violence Against Women 5, 654–683.

ASHABRANNER, B. 1995. Coming to America. Millbrook Press. Brookfield CT.

AYYUB, R. 2000. Domestic violence in the South Asian Muslim immigrant population in the United States. Journal of Social Distress and the Homeless 9, 237–248.

BHANDARI-PREISSER, A. 1999. Domestic violence in South Asian communities in America: advocacy and intervention. Violence Against Women 5, 684–699.

Bond, M.H. 1996. Chinese values. *In* The Handbook of Chinese Psychology. M. H. Bond, Ed.: Oxford University Press. Hong Kong.

Dasgupta, S.D. & S. Warrier. 1995. Invisible terms. Bloomfield, NJ: Manavi.

Dasgupta, S.D. & S. Warrier. 1996. In the footsteps of "Arundhati:" Asian Indian women's experience of violence in the United States. Violence Against Women *2*, 238–259.

Dasgupta, S.D. 1998. Women's realities. *In* Issues in intimate violence. R.K. Berjen, Ed.: 209–219. Sage. Thousand Oaks, CA.

Dasgupta, S.D. 1998. A patchwork shawl. New Brunswick, NJ: Rutgers University Press.

Dasgupta, S.D. 2000. Charting the course: an overview of domestic violence in the South Asian community in the United States. Journal of Social Distress and the Homeless *9*, 173–185.

Foo, L. 2002. Asian American Women. Ford Foundation. New York.

George, M.S. & L. Rahangdale. 1999. Domestic violence and South Asian women. North Carolina Medical Journal *60*, 157–159.

Goel, R. 2005. Sita's trousseau: restorative justice, domestic violence, and South Asian culture. Violence Against Women *11*, 639–665.

Ho, C.K. 1990. An analysis of domestic violence in Asian American communities. Women and Therapy *9*, 129–150.

Huisman, K. 1996. Wife-battering in Asian-American communities. Violence Against Women *2*, 260–283.

Mazumdar, S. 1989. Racist response to racism—The Aryan myth and South Asians in the United States. South Asia Bulletin *9*, 47–55.

Mehrotra, M. 1999. The social construction of wife abuse: experiences of Asian Indian women in the United States. Violence Against Women *5*, 619–640.

Merchant, M. 2000. A comparative study of agencies assisting domestic violence victims: does the South Asian community have special needs? Journal of Social Distress and the Homeless *9*, 249–259.

Perilla, J.L. 1999. Domestic violence as a human rights issue. Hispanic Journal of Behavioral Science *21*(2), 107–133.

Raj, A. & J. Silverman. 2002. Violence against immigrant women: the roles of culture, context and legal immigrant status on intimate partner violence. Violence Against Women *8*, 367–398.

Sutherland, C.A., C.M. Sullivan & D.I. Bybee. 2001. Effects of intimate partner violence versus poverty on women's health. Violence Against Women *7*, 1122–1143.

Swan, S.C. & D.L. Snow. 2003. Behavioral and psychological differences among abused women who use violence in intimate relationships. Violence Against Women *9*, 75–109.

Tang, C.S. 1997. Psychological impact of wife abuse. Journal of Interpersonal Violence *12*(3), 466–478.

Tang, C.S., D. Wong & F.M. Cheung. 2002. Social construction of women as legitimate victims of violence in Chinese society. Violence Against Women. *8*, 968–996.

Tjaden, P. & N. Thoennes. 2000. Full report of the prevalence, incidence, and consequences of violence against women: findings from the National Violence against Women Survey. National Institute of Justice. Washington, DC. Report NCJ 183781.

United States Census Bureau. 2004. Facts for Asian Pacific American Heritage Month: May 2003. Available http:///www.census.gov.
WALKER, L. 1996. Assessment of abusive spousal relationships. *In* Handbook of Relational Dignosis and Dysfunctional Family Patterns. F. W. Kaslow, Ed.: 338–356. John Wiley & Sons. New York, NY.
WU, D. 1993. Coming to America. Milbrook Press. Brookfield CT.
XU, X., J. CAMPBELL & F. AHU. 2001. Intimate partner violence against Chinese women. Trauma, Violence, and Abuse *2*, 296–315.
YICK, A.G. 2000. Predictors of physical spousal/intimate violence in Chinese American families. Journal of Family Violence *12*, 249–267.
YICK, A.G. & P. AGBAYANI-SIEWERT. 1997. Perceptions of domestic violence in a Chinese American community. Journal of Interpersonal Violence *12*, 832–846.
YOSHIOKA, M.R., J. DINOIA & K. ULLAH. 2001. Attitudes toward marital violence. Violence Against Women *7*, 900–926.
YOSHIOKA, M.R. & D.Y. CHOI. 2005. Culture and interpersonal violence research. Journal of Interpersonal Violence *20*, 513–519.

Domestic Violence in Israel

Changing Attitudes

VARDA MUHLBAUER

School of Management and Business Administration, Netanya Academic College, Netanya 42365, Israel

> ABSTRACT: For many years, knowledge of the prevalence of violence against women in Israel was marginalized in such a way that it never figured in public discourse. Elite groups of academics and feminist activists with a Western background, together with human rights groups, delivered subversive messages that gradually infiltrated into larger circles and ultimately changed public policies. The issue is now central in public affairs. This article discusses the extent of violence against women in Israel and suggests explanations for the shift from denial to greater public awareness.
>
> KEYWORDS: domestic violence; human rights and feminist discourse; social change.

INTRODUCTION

Violence against women is a multi-faceted phenomenon and domestic violence is but one of its many manifestations. Extensive research in many countries (Walker, 1999) has shown that domestic violence cuts across all social and cultural boundaries. This is true, of course, in Israel as well. Yet for a long time the subject was simply not on the public agenda. On the contrary, there was a long-standing denial of the prevalence of home-based crime against women, particularly among the more affluent veteran Jewish population of the country. This article will endeavor to describe the incidence of domestic violence against Jewish women in Israel and to explain the gradual shift in attitudes. No longer sidetracked, domestic violence has now become a mainstream issue at the heart of the public consensus.

Current research on domestic violence is closely connected with social, cultural, and political trends. It is largely assumed that violence against women—either in the public domain or in the family—is a reflection of the contextual

---

Address for correspondence: Varda Muhlbauer, Ph.D., School of Management and Business Administration, Netanya Academic College, Kiryat Yitzhak Rabin, 1 University Street, Netanya 42365, Israel.

e-mail: vardam@netvision.net.il

gender power system prevalent in society. This assumption looks beyond the link between the individual deviant or pathological personality and violent behavior against women, and focuses instead upon the social situation within which the violence takes place. This approach is helpful in explaining the differences reported by Walker (1999) between the industrialized countries of North America and Europe and countries with different social, cultural, legal and political structures. However, in the last 20 years there has been an overall international trend toward a more unified theoretical perspective, leaning heavily on feminist understanding of the social construction and dynamics of power relations, (Osmond & Throne, 1993) and on the emerging ideology of human rights. Renunciation of violence against women as a severe case of human rights abuse appears to be gaining ground, although this cultural manifestation is often more rhetorical than practical.

TRENDS IN PUBLIC AWARENESS OF VIOLENCE AGAINST WOMEN IN ISRAEL

In the early years of the state, that is, the 1950s, the issue of wife abuse was not considered of vital importance. The first time the subject was raised in the Knesset (the Israeli Parliament) was in 1962 (Swirski, 1991). An attempt to bring the issue of wife beating to the attention of the minister of police was dismissed offhandedly as an issue of no particular importance. It was only 14 years later that Member of Knesset (MK) Marsha Freedman, who had immigrated to Israel from the United States and was known for her radical feminist views, succeeded in getting the attention of the Knesset and placing the subject on the parliamentary and public agenda. This time all the women MKs banded together with a number of other MKs and succeeded in referring the motion to a subcommittee on police affairs (Freedman, 1990). It is interesting to note that even then, in the 1970s, domestic violence was still a marginal issue that rarely engaged public attention. Swirski (1991) states that the establishment of shelters for battered women by grassroots feminist groups and the murder of a woman by her husband in one of these shelters were among the focal episodes that triggered somewhat greater interest in the issues of domestic violence. Still, it required a much a broader change in Israeli society for mainstreaming gender violence to the point where it is almost de rigueur to denounce domestic violence.

STATISTICAL FINDINGS RELEVANT TO THE PREVALENCE OF DOMESTIC VIOLENCE IN ISRAEL

When the first government apparatus was established to research the extent of domestic violence in Israel, it soon became clear that there were almost no reliable data to draw from. The parliamentary subcommittee on police affairs, the 1995 Karp Committee (see below), stated: first of all, that there was no systematic accumulation of data on the subject; and second, that neither the police nor the courts had any provisions for dealing with battered women. The subcommittee then appealed to the major women's organizations who were able to estimate that roughly between 5% and 10% of all Israeli women were exposed to violence at home (Swirski, 1991).

A study carried by the Israel Women's Network, shows that around 10% percent of married women from 1996–1997 were exposed to domestic violence. This exceedingly high percentage is supported by other research. In a study done in Tel Aviv (Israel's largest city) by Steiner and Zemach (1999), findings were analyzed separately for the various communities in the city: Arabs, secular Jews and ultra–orthodox Jews. (The diversified nature [or divisions] of Israel's adult population is as follows: 12% Arabs, 6–7% ultra- orthodox Jews, and the remainder [the large majority] secular and traditional Jews.) Findings indicated that about 7% of Jewish families with children reported physical violence against women. Similar figures were reported for the other two sectors. Yet further analysis pointed to three factors that militated against the severe victimization of women by their partners: greater secularity, higher education and employment outside the home. Concurrently, the demographic status of men does not lend itself to the same conclusions. Studies indicate that men from varying backgrounds are similarly prone to revert to physical violence against their spouses (Lev-Ari, 1986; Edleson *et al.*, 1991). Another survey initiated by Women's International Zionist Organization (WIZO) (1999) indicates that although the likelihood of tension is smaller in families where the women work outside the home, both men and women agree that men tend to use force to re–affirm their dominant position in the family and abuse their power to enforce that position. In recent years, the police, too, initiated a follow-up of complaints on domestic violence. From their records one discovers that since the police were instructed to intensify their approach and enforce rigorous measures against violent and dangerous spouses, the number of women applying for police intervention grew conspicuously. Police files show that whereas in 1996 there were 4736 complaints by women in the age group of 18—44 years of domestic violence, the number in the same age group grew to 7865 in 1997. In the following years, the numbers changed only moderately, rising to 8935 in 2000. Yet it is obvious that police figures do not reflect the real proportions of the phenomenon. They are, rather, an indication of some change in social policy in general and police procedures in particular.

A comprehensive survey to uncover the prevalence of domestic violence in Israel was commissioned only in 2001 by the Minisry of Labor and Welfare and was carried out by the Minerva Center of Haifa University.The major findings of the survey, as detailed by the the chief scientist Tzvi Izikovitz in a press release to Israeli papers (Izikovitz, 2002), refer to 13% of women who are exposed to violence. In addition, it indicates that gender violence is more frequent among the non-Jewish sector of the population and more common among low socioeconomic classes that are exposed to rather chronic difficulties.

The overall picture in Israel indicates that findings are similar to those reported in other parts of the world (Bograd, 1988; Walker, 1999). The question, therefore, is what were the social and cultural dynamics in Israel that kept domestic violence hidden from the public eye for so many years and allowed so many to believe that the problem was virtually nonexistent. As is the case with many other similar dilemmas, several explanations can be offered. This article takes its theoretical framework from the findings of the Karp Committee (1995). (Ms. Karp was the vice-deputy to the legal counselor of the Israel Government). The committee was appointed in 1986 to study the issues of violence in the family and come up with recommendations regarding investigation procedures, prosecution, and the overall judicial process. Although the focus of the committee was mainly legal in nature, its perspective was social and its recommendations reflected a breakthrough in locating the issue in the basic tenets of Israeli society. The committee had added value in that it legitimized and centralized interpretations that until then had been voiced only by marginal feminist and human rights activists. The committee suggested that domestic violence in Israeli society could be attributed to a synthesis between religious values such as the preservation of the family as a central institution in Jewish life, issues pertaining to the national ethos vis-a-vis the physical and cultural survival of the Jewish people, and a pro-natal view placing priority on the role of women as mothers.

NATIONAL ETHOS AND GENDER EQUALITY

Until the late 1970s Israel's self-image was that of an egalitarian society. People tended to believe that the young state had succeeded in avoiding many of the pitfalls so prevalent in other countries. The collective consciousness held that women took an active role in life side by side with men and were considered equal partners. Belief in gender–equality was deeply rooted and for a long time evaded any critical scrutiny. Ram (1993) states that the strong bonds between mainstream Israeli sociology and the national social establishment in the early years of the state produced a blind spot to any digression in real life from the grand ethos of Jewish national revival. It was only in the 1970s that critical sociological analysis set out to expose oppressive undercurrents in Israeli society and to propose an alternative understanding of the social and cultural mechanisms at work.

It was around that time that feminist researchers took a fresh look at the roles and status of women in pre-state Israel and found that as early as the 1930s women had abandoned the struggle for an equal position in running the affairs of state (Bernstein, 1992). Other feminist publications (Swirski, 1991) dealt with the marginalization of women, and their interests and perspectives in a society engaged in a continuous struggle for survival. Moreover, there was an overall demand to prioritize a national agenda in which women were expected to assume supportive roles, mainly that of wives and mothers. In this way, women were gradually transformed in the public image from equal partners to mothers and, later, to working mothers (Halpern, Muhlbauer, & Wassertzug, 2002). The large women's organizations such as WIZO and Movement of Working Women and Volunteers (NAAMAT) went along with this new national ethos. They had established a large and supportive network to help women combine their conventional roles of mothers and housewives with their jobs outside the families. Hawkins and Humes (2002) refer to similar trends where women's concerns became coopted by the prevailing political system and received a a low priority.

From today's perspective, it is clear that the ascendancy of nationalism meant the defeat of other competing worldviews. The egalitarian ideology was one of the greatest losers. The reason for this is that gendered societies, often unintentionally, become fertile ground for the evolvement of hostility and occasional violence against women who do not accommodate conventional and traditional sex-roles. Glick and Fiske (2001)[13] in an enlightening article discuss how nations endorsing sexist ideologies, however benevolent in intention and practice, do, in fact, promote hostility and violence toward women as a social category.

THE TRADITIONAL JEWISH VIEW

From the political perspective it is evident that since the independence of the state of Israel, successive governments had made many concessions to the religious parties to ensure their support and collaboration (Yishai, 1985). For this reason, the entire Jewish population in Israel—even secular and Reform Jews—have to live by orthodox rulings in matters pertaining to the family such as marriage and divorce. From the legal perspective, the fact that the Law of Equal Rights for Women (1951) has not acquired the status of constitutional law renders it open to interpretation. This is why the Supreme Court is often called upon to intervene in disputes between competing claims (mainly rabbinical and secular) regarding the principle of gender equality (Raday, 1995).

Jewish tradition is steeped in patriarchal norms. Some traditional sources express views that are offensive, even harmful to women. Researchers of rabbinical law agree that the subject of wife beating—what constitutes wife beating and what the response should be—is controversial (Frieshtik, 1994). Yet the sources are not unified in their position against such a practice. One reason for this is the ancient custom according to which a woman is her husband's chattel. There are, however, alternative positions within Jewish tradition that do not abide by historical strictures and are reinterpreting the laws according to democratic and liberal norms (Jewish Women International, 1996). Still, religious law in Israel often blocks women's escape routes from distressful marriages.

PRO-NATAL POLICY

Israeli society is, at best, caught between two conflicting forces: postmodernism and patriarchal traditionalism. Massive research indicates that in spite of changes in the manner in which Jewish families are constructed, mainly in terms of dual earnings, very insignificant changes regarding the division of labor within the family have ensued. Fogiel–Bijaoui (1999) quotes researchers (Chafetz and Hagan, 1996) who define house chores as a "Gender Factory" in which masculine and feminine stereotypes are established. On the other hand, liberal and democratic thinking has transformed family–life in a way that blurs gender boundaries and constructs the relationship between the partners around a core of mutual expectations for self–fulfillment (Muhlbauer and Zemach, 1991). Many researchers agree, however, that in spite of post–modern trends, conservative familism is still the norm in Israeli society (Lavee and Katz, 2003). Fogiel-Bijaoui (1999) claims that the principal reason for this is that the family is an ideological mechanism and cherished institution in the biological and cultural reproduction of the Jewish national community. All these arguments together serve as a feasible explanation for the reluctance to expose the underlying social forces that maintain and reinforce gender inequality, often leading to abuse and violence in the family. Levesque (2001) argues that families respond to cultural forces in a way that fosters family violence.

> Cultural forces actually define the experience of maltreatment, create climates conducive to maltreatment, provide important buffers against maltreatment, and affect intervention efforts. To a large extent, then, it seems fair to propose that individual acts of violence and individual victimization experiences remain largely culturally determined. (p. 40)

In Israel, whenever shockingly horrible incidents reached the national news, it was referred to as a singular tragedy. There were two common explanations for such incidents. The first was that the women involved were members of an alien subculture (the reference being to members of the Oriental Jewish communities or Israeli Palestinians), not characteristic of the enlightened mainstream of Israeli society, and the incidents could, therefore, be dismissed as rare happenings. The second view, favored by social workers and psychologists, proclaimed that family violence resulted from a pathological interaction between husband and wife. Following this line of thinking, welfare agencies chose not to look beyond the connection between the deviant or pathological personality and violent behavior to power differences between the partners and the contextual cultural and social environment in which they were allowed to breed (Swirski & Safir 1991). In this respect, these explanations are misleading and play a reactionary role in preserving the patriarchal system.

MAINSTREAMING INTEREST IN DOMESTIC VIOLENCE

No one single factor can explain the downfall of any ideological hegemony. In this case, the credit goes partially to feminist grassroot groups active in the 1970s in major population centers and partially to the infiltration of liberal thinking linked to human rights movements. The broad public became aware of the magnitude of the problem only years later. To a certain extent, feminist thinking, particularly militant feminism, was cultivated by Israeli women with American roots or American connections, influenced, as they were, by the spirit of the 1960s. They helped revive the fighting spirit of the women pioneers from the beginning of the century. They challenged the silence surrounding domestic violence and were the first to open up shelters and hot lines for women in distress. The role they assumed resonantes in the discussion of Lazarus-Black and Merry (2003) concerning the importance of the local-global in interface the creation and implementation of social reforms concerning violence against women.

In retrospect, the accomplishments achieved by the small groups of women seem truly amazing. The odds were initially against them. Jewish nationalism was almost omnipresent in the early 1970s and as such hostile to any alternative ideology especially if it contained subversive messages. As a result, they had initially to put up with ignorance and animosity emanating both from the Israeli establishment and the general public.

It is relatively simple, retrospectively, to highlight the dynamics of the changes that were then evolving. The feminist activists, largely academics with high levels of consciousness, were both "insiders" and "outsiders" (to use Levesque's terminology). That is, they were cognizant of both Israeli society and Western, mainly American, thinking, which was open to liberal and progressive ideas. A surge of academic interest in the subject of women in general gave a dignified and respectful aura to the claims of feminist and radical groups. Research and elective courses were initiated by most major academic institutions and generated an atmosphere of avant garde ideas in line with parallel trends in Western societies. Some of the women academics joined forces with feminist activists, thus helping them to penetrate larger circles of the general public and some of the forums of social policy decisionmakers.

Initial cracks in the monolithic perception of Jewish nationalism opened the way to a pluralistic discourse. Marginal groups were given opportunities to voice their narratives. Bonds of silence were loosened. The Zeitgeist was ripe for taking up issues pertaining to domestic violence and subjecting them to public scrutiny. This tendency was supported by the human rights movement, then gaining a strong foothold mainly in the educated secular sectors of the Israeli population. The basic tenets of human rights backed feminist thinking and practice. It was the human rights movement that also helped to politicize feminist visions and policies when two of the major groups joined forces in the 1974 elections. Thus the initially subversive messages delivered by small groups of women gradually succeeded in transforming public views and sentiments and taking the subject of domestic violence out of the closet.

Interestingly enough, the women organizations tied to the establishment quickly followed suit opening centers and shelters, and joining forces with feminist groups on issues pertaining to violence against women. In a way, joining the fight against violence revitalized these organizations. Formerly, they had been part of the backbone of Israel's national establishment and as such could not afford an iconoclastic image. However, the outcry against violence was basically humane and in line with the human rights approach that, at the time, was introduced and willingly accepted.

CONCLUSIONS

Current research on domestic violence, as we have seen, has come to embrace the cultural perspective. It is evident today that, side by side with universally identifiable trends in gender power relations, there are clearly diverse forms and structures among the nations of the world which cast different lights and shadows on the subject. Attitudes toward domestic violence fluctuate along the axes of the relative social and political importance of much larger core issues such as nationalism, familism, religion and egalitarianism. In other words, the subject cannot be dealt with, let alone understood, in complete isolation from the other formative forces that impact any particular society. The cultural forces embedded in any given society often function to maintain a climate that fosters domestic violence.

In the case of Israel, as analyzed in this article, a cluster of political, social, and cultural factors including both religious and national elements, clearly created a dynamic during the first three decades of the new state (founded in 1948), which enabled domestic violence to go unnoticed. Challenging domestic violence would have opened up a much larger debate touching upon social and political mechanisms that were considered the backbone of the society during its formative years. The breakdown of ideological hegemony, the import of feminist ideas and principles, mainly by Israeli women with American roots or American connections, and the fresh ideas and fighting spirit of the human rights movements in Israel were all important factors in the gradual change of heart and evolving readiness to face up to the magnitude of the problem.

In general, prospects for reshaping attitudes are greater when simultaneous changes occur in the social fabric. In the case of Israel, these changes were the weakening of national and religious values together with the emergence of previously marginal alternative concepts outside the formal power structures.

REFERENCES

BERNSTEIN, D.S., Ed. 1992. Pioneers and homemakers: Jewish women pioneers in pre–state Israel. SUNY Press: New York.

BOGRAD, M. 1988. Feminist perspectives on wife abuse: An introduction. *In* Feminist perspectives on wife abuse. K. Yllo & M. Bograd, Eds.: 11–26. Sage: Newbury Park, CA.

CHAFETZ, J.S. & J. HAGAN. 1996. The gender division of labor and family change in industrial societies: A theoretical accounting. Journal of Comparative Family Studies *27*, 187–210.

EDLESON, J.C., E. PELED & Z. EISIKOVITZ. 1991. Israel's response to battered women. Violence Update *11*, 4–5.

FOGIEL-BIJAOUI, S. 1999. Families in Israel: between familism and post–modernism. *In* Sex, gender and politics. D.N. Izraeli, A. Friedman, H. Dahan–kalev, S. Fogiel–Bijaoui, H. Herzog, M. Hasan, & H. Naveh, Eds.: 107–167. Hakibbutz Hameuchad Publishing House: Tel Aviv.

FREEDMAN, M. 1990. Exile in the Promised Land. Tel Aviv: Fireband Books: Ann Arbor, MI.

FRIESHTIK, M. 1994. Physical violence of husbands as a cause for divorce in Jewish Halacha a Rabbinic judgement. Dinay Israel *17*, 93–118.

GLICK, P. & S. FISKE. 2001. An ambivalent alliance: hostile and benevolent sexism as complementary justifications for gender inequality. American Psychologist *56*, 109–118.

HALPERN, E., V. MUHLBAUER & H. WASSERTZUG. 2002. Empowerment through an intergration of employment and family orientation: An Israeli perspective. *In* The spiritual side of psychology at century's end. R. Roth & F. Farley, Eds: 125–133. Pabst Science Publishers: Lengerich Germany.

HAWKINS, D. & M. HUMES. 2002. Human rights and domestic violence. Political Science Quarterly *117*, 231–257. Retrieved 12 November, 2005 from ProQuest Information and Learning Company.

IZIKOVITZ, T. 2002. The extent of violence against women in IsraelM. Retrieved 8 November, 2005 from www.Ynet.co.il/articles.

JEWISH WOMEN INTERNATIONAL. 1996. Resource Guide for rabbis on domestic violence. Jewish Women International, Breirot.Washington, DC.

KARP, J. 1995. Report of the committee on violence among couples headed. *In* Women's status:Law and society. F. Radai, C. Shalev & M. Liban-Kooby, Eds.: 280–306. Schocken Publishing House: Jerusalem.

LAVEE, Y. & R. KATZ. 2003. The family in Israel: Between tradition and modernity. Marriage & Family Review *35*, 193–217.

LAZARUS-BLACK, M. & S.E. MERRY. 2003. The politics of gender violence: Law reform in local and global places. Law and Social Inquiry *28*, 931–939. Retrieved February 2004 from ProQuest Information and Learning Company.

LEV-ARI, R., Ed. 1986. Violence in the family. Tel Aviv: Naamat.

LEVESQUE, R. 2001. Culture and family violence: Fostering change through human rights law. American Psychological Association. Washington, DC.

MUHLBAUER, V. & M. ZEMACH. 1991. Odds or even. Am Oved Publishing House: Tel Aviv.

OSMOND, M.W. & B. THRONE. 1993. Feminist theories: The social construction of gender in families and society. *In* Sourcebook of family theories and methods: A contextual approach. P.G. Boss, W.J. Doherty, R. LaRossa, W.R. Schumm & S.K. Steinmetz, Eds.: 591–623. Plenum Press: New York.

RADAY, F. 1995. On equality. *In* Women's status: law and society. F. Raday, C. Shalev & M. Liban-Kooby, Eds.: 9–63. Shocken Publishing House: Tel Aviv.

RAM, U. 1993. Society and the science of society: Institutional sociology and critical sociology in Israel. *In* Israeli society: Critical perspectives. U. Ram, Ed.: 7–39.: Breirot: Tel Aviv.

STEINER, Y. & M. ZEMACH. 1999. Violence in the family in the city of Tel Aviv-Jaffa. Unpublished report.

SWIRSKI, B. 1991. Jews don't batter their wives : Another myth bites the dust. *In* Calling the equality bluff: Women in Israel. B. Swirski & M.P. Safir, Eds.: 319–327. New York Teachers College Press: New York.

SWIRSKI, B. & M.P. SAFIR, Eds.: 1991. Calling the equality bluff: women in Israel. Teachers College Press: New York.

WALKER, L.E. 1999. Psychololgy and domestic violence around the world. American Psychololgist *54,* 21–29.

YISHAI, Y. 1985. Women and war: The case of Israel. Journal of Social, Political and Economic Studies *10,* 95–214.

Lack of Mutual Respect in Relationship

The Endangered Partner

AMOS A. ALAO

Careers and Counselling Services, University of Botswana, Gaborone, Botswana

ABSTRACT: Violence in a relationship and in a family setting has been an issue of concern to various interest groups and professional organizations. Of particular interest in this article is violence against women in a relationship. While there is an abundance of knowledge on violence against women in general, intimate or partner femicide seems to have received less attention. Unfortunately, the incidence of violence against women, and intimate femicide in particular, has been an issue of concern in the African setting.

This article examines the trends of intimate femicide in an African setting in general, and in Botswana in particular. The increase in intimate femicide is an issue of concern, which calls for collective effort to address. This article also examines trends of femicide in Botswana, and the antecedents and the precipitating factors. Some studies have implicated societal and cultural dynamics as playing significant roles in intimate femicide in the African setting. It is believed that the patriarchal nature of most African settings and the ideology of male supremacy have relegated women to a subordinate role. Consequently, respect for women in any relationship with men is lopsided in favor of men and has led to abuse of women, including intimate femicide. Other militating factors in intimate femicide are examined and the implications for counseling to assist the endangered female partner are discussed.

KEYWORDS: violence; domestic; women; intimate partner; femicide; Africa; Botswana

INTRODUCTION

One of the key points of the manifesto for the 2000 International Year of the Culture of Peace is respect for the life and dignity of each human being without discrimination or prejudice and to practice active non-violence, rejecting all violence in all its forms: physical, sexual, psychological, economical, and social.

Address for correspondence: Amos A. Alao, Careers & Counselling Services, P. Bag 0022, Gaborone, Botswana. Voice: 267-355-2317; fax: 267-395-6958.
  e-mail: alaoaa@mopipi.ub.bw

It is anticipated that this respect for the individual and nonviolence become more imperative when two people have entered into a relationship.

One way to show respect in a relationship is to recognize the individuality of the two people involved in the relationship and according one another the regard expected in the relationship. Conflict, separation, and loss are a common source of crisis in a significant relationship. These situations make one of the partners or in some cases both partners become dysphonic, angry, and agitated.

Partners experiencing difficulties in relationships may decide to take revenge on the partner or engage in deliberate self-destructive behavior out of anger, hopelessness, or a desire to retaliate against the other partner. Relationships carry the risk of not only physical injury but also death, either homicide or suicide. Male violence on females is more common possibly due to masculinity of the male characterized by size and strength; consequently, this article focuses on male to female extreme violence.

Partner violence affects many aspects of a victim's life. Battered women have been found to suffer from depression and anxiety (Saunders, Hamberger & Hovey 1993). Battered women can be conceptualized as being in a relatively constant state of stress. They are always vigilant for the signs of impending attack, constantly engage in violence-avoidant behaviors, and are constantly at risk for further abuse.

Rosenbaum and O'Leary (1981) assert that partner violence is related to relationship distress. Dattilio (1994) noted that violent relationships are in crisis even when no violence is occurring as the victims live in fear and terror and suffer physical and psychological injury.

INTIMATE FEMICIDE

The killing of women by intimate partners (also known as intimate female homicide) is the most extreme form and consequence of violence against women. Globally, gender differences are found in homicide patterns. Men are at greater risk of being killed than women, and this is mainly done by other men. Women, on the other hand, are primarily killed by the opposite gender (Goetting, 1988). The murder of women by an intimate partner accounts for between 40% and 70% of all female homicides (Dahlberg & Krug, 2002).

This form of violence has received very little attention and the few studies that have been conducted have been mainly in developed countries. The only previous study conducted in South Africa was a pilot study in the Gauteng Region by Vetten (1996). Despite its limitations, this research finding has been used extensively in advocacy campaigns.

International studies reveal that intimate femicide is linked to a history of domestic violence with the risk increasing at the threat of separation or actual separation (Wilson & Daly, 1993; Campbell, Webster, Kozoil-Mclain, Block, Campbell, *et al.*, 2003).

While there is a vast body of knowledge on violence against women, intimate femicide, the most severe form of violence, has received little attention. This is alarming because statistics show that when a woman is killed, the perpetrator is often a man who has been intimately involved with her (Campbell, 1992; Crawford & Gartner, 1992; Stout, 1991; Statistics Canada, 1991, 1989; U.S. Department of Justice, 1992).

THEORETICAL FRAMEWORK OF FEMICIDE

According to Russel and Harmes (2001), the concept of femicide specifically designates the killing of females by males (or in some situations by females) because they are female. To a certain extent, this definition challenges the popular conception that the murder of a woman or a girl is a private affair or a pathological aberrance. Furthermore, it highlights the understanding that when men kill women, power dynamics, and specifically the power dynamics underscoring misogyny or sexism, are always implicated. The killing of a woman by her partner is seen as femicide because it has to do with power and control: batterers kill not because they lose control (of themselves, as the "passion" explanation of the murder suggests), but because they want to exert control over their partner. Thus, symptomatically, women are at more risk of being killed just after leaving their partner. This can be seen as an extreme manifestation of particular men's attempts to assert their ownership and control of the sexuality and reproductive capacity of their female partners (Wilson & Daly, 1992).

The Influence of Social Evolution and Intimate Femicide

In her ecological analysis, Stout (1992) examines intimate partner homicide in various states in the United States and notes that intimate femicide tends to decrease under the following conditions:

(1) when the economic situation of women is "average" (neither very favorable nor very unfavorable);
(2) in states that promote gender equality and social justice for women and;
(3) when shelters for abused women exist.

Furthermore, Stout (1992) observes that after a period of substantial expansion in services for abused women, men's risk of being killed by their intimate partners decreased significantly. However, women's risk of being killed did not. Thus, the expansion of services may have resulted in the protection of abusive men from defensive violence by their female partners without succeeding in protecting women from the violence of their male partners (Gartner, Dawson, & Crawford, 2001).

As noted above, the traditional indicators of homicide generally are better predictors of female, rather than male intimate partner homicide. There is only one exception: population density is negatively related to the rate of female intimate homicide, perhaps because the lack of population density provides a greater barrier to assistance and community support that could help abused women before lethal violence occurs (Jensen, 1996).

A Psychodynamic Explanation of Intimate Femicide

To understand the process leading to intimate partner homicide from a psychodynamic angle, one must articulate two broad fields of thinking: the dynamics of violence and the dynamics of object relations.

Freud and Love

In Freud's basically pessimistic view, the existence of violence is hardly exceptional in any kind of interpersonal relationship: "The evidence of psychoanalysis shows that almost every emotional relation between two people which lasts for some time—marriage, friendship, the relations between parents and children—leaves a sediment of feelings of aversion and hostility, which only escapes perception as a result of repression" (Freud, 1921). To explain this ambivalence, Freud, in *Group Psychology and the Psychology of the Ego,* makes reference to the numerous occasions of conflict of interest that arise in intimate relationships. *En passant*, his preoccupation with intimacy is intertwined with thoughts about how small differences lead groups to hostility: one cannot form a group (or a couple) without accepting a limitation of one's narcissism, and if a group or a couple lasts, a tension will always remain between similarities and differences, narcissism and libidinal bonds.

In the same paper, Freud analyzes love as idealization, meaning that a considerable amount of narcissistic libido overflows onto the object until, at last, it takes possession of the entire self-love of the ego: the object has been put in the place of the Ego Ideal, as in hypnosis, and unlike in identification (in which the object is put in the place of the Ego). But this idealization coexists with what he referred to earlier as the universal tendency to debasement in the sphere of love: two currents, affectionate and sensual, have to be united. For instance, some men cannot express sexuality but with a debased object, which means a splitting of the two currents, between mother and whore. Freud however does not provide any examples of women considering men as debased objects. Instead, he argues (somewhat neutrally) that, "there are only very few educated people in whom the two currents of affection and sensuality have become properly fused" (Freud, 1912).

To better understand intimate femicides, a binary model is proposed. Within this model, intimate femicide is understood as having two different origins;

one involves the murder of an oppressed woman who attempted to emancipate herself and the other is an actual or attempted murder/suicide in which a socially inept and dependent man kills his liberated and independent partner. This model thus divides intimate murders into those who attempted or committed suicide immediately after killing their partner and those who did not (Kerry, 1998).

The binary model follows these two groups of men through five stages. *Stage 1*, termed "Pre-Murder," explores how the men define their masculinity, attitudes toward women, and their relationship with female partners. *Stage II*, the "Precipitating Event," highlights what triggered the ensuing murder in the perpetrator's mind. *Stage III*, the "Lethal Act," considers the actual attack and murder. *Stage IV*, the "Post-Murder," explores the time interval immediately following murder. Finally, *Stage V*, "Adjustment to Incarceration," focuses on the man as he serves his sentence and his present views toward the victim and the offence.

To evaluate the binary model and to identify variables that may differentiate between men who kill their female partner and men who do not, Kerry (1998) administered questionnaires to 86 men sentenced for the murder of an intimate partner (Intimate Murders), 151 randomly selected men sentenced for an offense other than the murder of an intimate partner (General Offenders), and 100 randomly selected nonincarcerated men.

No significant differences were observed between Intimate Murderers and General Offenders in the 24-h period before the offense. However, there is intensification in feelings of dysphasia and anger just before, and more so during, the offense that sets the intimate murders apart from other offenses. This finding may explain the intense violence often found in intimate murders.

INTIMATE FEMICIDE IN SOUTH AFRICA

The findings in South Africa were as indicated by Mathews. Abrahams, Martin, Van der Merwe, *et al.* in 2004. The findings were as follows:

- 8.8 per 100,000 women 14 years and older were killed by an intimate partner in 1999;
- The above statistic amounts to 4 women killed per day by an intimate partner; or
- 1 woman killed every 6 hours by an intimate partner; and
- 1 in every 2 women killed by a known perpetrator is killed by an intimate partner.

Some of the recommendations to curtail intimate femicide in general include:

(1) introduction of law of evidence to be reformed to allow previous history of domestic violence to be introduced in court to establish that homicide is the culmination of a pattern of violence;

(2) gun control to be vigorously reinforced; and
(3) efforts to reduce domestic violence to be prioritized.

INTIMATE FEMICIDE IN BOTSWANA

It has been observed lately that Botswana is experiencing an increase in the problem of violence against women (Maundeni, 2001). This wave of intimate femicide is called "passion killing" in Botswana. This passion killing is directed at females, where either a husband or boyfriend decides to kill the female partner.

A report on intimate partner femicide in Botswana was published by Women in Law and Development in Africa (WILDAF, 1995). The report listed names of 46 women killed by their husbands or lovers between 1985 and 1991. From January to October 2005, 69 women were victims of passion killing in Botswana compared to 56 cases reported in 2004.

The wrong impression is given that people kill because they love. The President of Botswana, His Excellency Festus Mogae, has appealed to the nation on national television to stop romanticizing this act of murder labeled "passion killing."

Some of the factors implicated as encouraging intimate femicide are Botswana is the patriarchal nature of the society, which Njoroge (1997) has described as a destructive powerhouse with systemic and normative inequalities as its hallmark.

Consequently, violence directed toward women labeled as passion killing is viewed as a sign of patriarchal crisis, which should be seen as outdated and dangerous (Gabaitse, 2005).

In a study by Moagi-Gulubane (2003) on intimate partner violence among Botswana college students concluded that almost half of the participants reported having been psychologically abusive to their girlfriends. As psychological aggression has been implicated as the precursor of physical assault in intimate relationship (Follinstad, Rutledge, Berg, Hause, & Polek, 1990), it sounds logical to look critically at the persistence of violence in relationship as a possible precursor of "passion killing" in Botswana.

In recognition of the magnitude of intimate femicide referred to as "passion killing " in Botswana, and in fulfillment of its national mandate, the Criminal Justice Consultative Committee (NCJCC) has decided to address the issue of "passion killings" in Botswana. The NCJCC is a forum comprised of law enforcement institutions and is very concerned about the spate and trend of passion killing in the country.

Consequently, in a letter to the Vice-Chancellor at the University of Botswana, the NCJCC requested that the university assist in identifying "a researcher" to research and determine the wider variables causing the problem of the so-called "passion killing" in the country.

The Vice-Chancellor, Professor B.K. Otlhogile, Professor I.N. Mazonde, the Director of the Office of Research and Development (ORD), and Dr. J. Malete, also of ORD at the University of Botswana, in response to the request from NCJCC, established a multidisciplinary research team to undertake the research requested by NCJCC. The team included K. Frimpong, A.A. Alao, R.M. Gabaitse, S. Moagi-Gulubane, T. Maundeni, R. Mokomane, G. Mookodi, and L.B. Tutwane. It is anticipated the study will contribute immensely to understanding the issues relating to intimate femicide in Botswana.

RELATIONSHIP ISSUES AND COUNSELING IMPLICATIONS

While it is not unusual for one to experience difficulties when in a relationship, it is important to seek ways to resolve such difficulties through personal development or counseling. Professional help can make individuals in relationships understand the dynamics of relationships, how to grow in relationships, and how to resolve and adjust to different relationship issues. When help is not sought, difficulties experienced in relationships can become compounded with disastrous consequences, including intimate femicide.

Seeking and receiving help when in a relationship difficulty or crisis can help prevent intimate femicide. Individuals experiencing relationship difficulties or distress need to seek help and should be assisted.

THE ROLE OF RESPECT IN A RELATIONSHIP

For any relationship to succeed, the two partners need to view each other as a person of worth. The male partner especially must like the female partner as she is. Her rights need to be respected. To reduce unnecessary violence in the relationship, the female partner needs to be allowed to possess and express her feelings. Male partners need to accept their female partners for who they are to limit the incidence of violence in the relationship.

Respect in a relationship entails recognizing the separateness of individuals, the right of each person to utilize his or her experience in his or her own way, and to discover his or her own meaning is a priceless possibility in life (Van Pelt, 1980). While it is true that most African societies tend to be patriarchal in nature, it is equally important that acceptance and respect in a relationship can help to improve such relationship and reduce violence if the male partner recognizes:

(1) that there are no perfections in relations;
(2) that both partners in a relationship may have areas of the relationship that need changing; and
(3) that accepting each person totally will reduce potential sources of conflict and violence.

Concerted efforts need to be made, especially by the male partner, to develop acceptance in the relationship.

In developing acceptance, Van Pelt (1980) stressed the need to:

(1) recognize a self-righteous attitude;
(2) allow freedom to express self;
(3) concentrate on good points; and
(4) express acceptance in words.

Ensuring peace in the society must begin with ensuring peace at its lowest level, in relationships between two individuals. If we cannot cultivate cordial relationships at the level of two individuals, it may be difficult to extend cordial relationships to the larger society. Peace in the society must begin with peace in the home and in a relationship. There should be better ways of viewing our differences or resolving our problems in a relationship than resulting to violence or intimate femicide.

REFERENCES

CAMPBELL, J.C. 1992. If I can't have you, no one can; power and control in homicide on female partners. *In* Femicide: The Politics of Woman Killing. J. Radford & D. Russell, Eds.: 1089–1097. Macmillan. Toronto, Ontario.

CAMPBELL, J.C., D. WEBSTER, J. KOZOIL-MCLAIN, C. BLOCK, D. CAMPBELL, *et al*. 2003. Risk factors for femicide in abusive relationships; results from a multi-site case control study. Am. J. Public Health *93*, 1089–1097.

CRAWFORD, M. & R. GARTNER. 1992. Women Killing: Intimate Femicide in Ontario, 1974–1990. Women We Honour Action Committee. Toronto, Ontario.

DAHLBERG, L.L. & E.G. KRUG. 2002. Violence—a global public health problem. *In* World Report on Violence and Health. E.G. Krug, *et al*., Eds.: 3–21. World Health Organization. Geneva.

DATTILIO, F.M. 1994. Cognitive Therapy with Couples: The Initial Phase of Treatment. Professional Resource Press. Saratosa, FL.

FOLLINGSTAD, D., L. RUTLEDGE, B. BERG, E. HAUSE & D. POLEK. 1990. The role of emotional abuse in physical aggressive relationships. J. Fam. Violence *5*, 107–120.

FREUD, S. 1912. On the Universal Tendency to Debasement in the Sphere of Love. Standard Edition XI. Hogarth Press: London. Pp. 179–190.

FREUD, S. 1921. Group psychology and the analysis of the Ego. Standard Edition XVIII. Hogarth Press: London. Pp. 65–143.

GABAITSE, R.M. 2005. Passion Killing at a Cross Road. Paper presented at the Department of Theology and Religious Studies, University of Botswana.

GARTNER, R., M. DAWSON & M. CRAWFORD. 2001. Women killing: intimate femicide in Ontario, 1974–1994. *In* Femicide In Global Perspective. D. Russel & R. Harmes, Eds.:147–165. Columbia University. New York NY.

GOETTING, A. 1988. Patterns of homicide among women. J. Interpers. Violence *3*, 3–19.

JENSEN, V. 1996. Why Women Kill: Homicide And Gender Equality. Lynne Rienner. London.

KERRY, G.P. 1998. Intimate femicide: an analysis of men who kill their partners. Education Wife Assault Newsletter. *Vol. 9*, No. 1, June.
MATHEWS, S., N. ABRAHAMS, L. MARTIN, L. VETTEN, L. VAN DER MERWE & R. JEWKES. 2004. A National Study of Female Homicide in South Africa. MRC Policy Brief. No. 5, June.
MAUNDENI, T. 2001. Gender and HIV/AIDS. Conference Paper presented in Gaborone, Botswana.
MOAGI-GULUBANE, S. 2003. Predictors of dating violence among Botswana college students: a multivariate cross-cultural analysis. Unpublished Doctorial Dissertation, Ball State University, Muncie, IN.
NJOROGE, N. 1997. The missing voice: African women doing theology. J. Theol. South Afr. *99*, 77–83.
ROSENBAUM, A. & K.D. O`LEARY. 1981. Marital violence: characteristics of abusive couples. J. Consult. Clin. Psychol. *49*, 63–71.
Russel, D. & R. Harmes. Eds. 2001. Femicide In Global Perspective. Columbia University. New York, NY.
SAUNDERS, D.G., L.K. HAMBERGER & M. HOVEY. 1993. Indicators of woman abuse based on a chart review at a family practice center. Arch. Fam. Med. *2*, 537–543.
STATISTICS CANADA. 1989. Juristat Service Bulletin, May, *Vol. 9*, No. 1, Minister of Supply and Services, Canada.
STATISTICS CANADA. 1991. Homicide in Canada. Juristat Service Bulletin, *Vol. 12*, No. 18, Minister of Supply and Services, Canada.
STOUT, K. 1991. Intimate femicide: a national demographic overview. J. Interpers. Violence *6*, 476–485.
STOUT, K. 1992. Intimate femicide: an ecological analysis. J. Sociol. Soc. Welf. *19*, 29–50.
U.S. DEPARTMENT OF JUSTICE. 1992. Crime in the U.S. 1991, uniform crime reports. U.S. Government Printing Office. Washington, DC.
VAN PELT, N. 1980. To Have and To Hold: A Guide to Successful Marriage. The Stanborough Press Ltd. Alma Park, England.
VETTEN, L. 1996. Man shoots wife: intimate femicide in Gauteng, South Africa. Crime and Conflict, No. 6, 1–4, Winter
WILSON, M. & M. DALY. 1992. Till death us do part. *In* Femicide: The Politics of Woman Killing. J. Radford & D. Russel, Eds.: 83–93. Twayne/Gale Group. New York, NY.
WILSON, M. & M. DALY. 1993. Spousal homicide risk and estrangement. Violence Vict. *8*, 3–16.
WOMEN IN LAW AND DEVELOPMENT IN AFRICA (WILDAF). 1995. Intimate Femicide in Botswana. In WILDAF Publications. Gaborone, Botswana.

Violence against Pregnant Women in Northwestern Ontario

JOSEPHINE C. H. TAN[a] AND KATHRYN V. GREGOR[b]

[a]*Department of Psychology, Lakehead University, Thunder Bay, Ontario, Canada*
[b]*Integrated Services for Northern Children, Sioux Lookout, Ontario, Canada*

ABSTRACT: Violence against women during pregnancy is a global problem with adverse outcomes for the mothers and their children. This paper provides a discussion of the prevalence rates of pregnancy-related violence, associated factors, and outcomes. Most of the outcome literature focuses on perinatal and postnatal outcomes, but little is known about the longer term psychological outcome of children born to women abused during pregnancy. Moreover, the question as to whether the abuse increases during pregnancy remains unanswered given the equivocal findings in the literature. Findings from a small study conducted with women in the region of northwestern Ontario, Canada, are presented. The pattern of abuse during pregnancy over the three trimesters was examined. The long-term psychological outcomes of the children born to women abused during pregnancy were also investigated by comparing these children to a sex- and age-matched cohort of children born to women who were not abused during pregnancy. Although key confounding variables were controlled in the study, the results still showed that children born to women abused during pregnancy had greater behavioral problems.

KEYWORDS: violence; pregnancy; pattern of abuse; children; psychological outcome.

INTRODUCTION

In 1993 Statistics Canada carried out a national Violence Against Women survey comprising 12,300 women who were age 18 years or older. About half of the respondents indicated that they had experienced some type of physical or sexual violence since the age of 16 years. Among those who had ever been married or lived with a male partner, 29% reported physical or sexual assault at the hands of their partner (Rodgers, 1994). About 21% of those who suffered intimate partner violence noted that the abuse occurred during pregnancy. This translates to about 3% of all respondents in the survey suffering from pregnancy-related violence. Two other Canadian studies with women receiving prenatal health care and/or who were admitted to the hospital for delivery reported higher rates of violence during pregnancy, 6.6% (Stewart & Cecutti, 1993) and 5.7% (Muhajarine & D'Arcy, 1999), respectively.

In the United States, the Center for Disease Control and Prevention's Pregnancy Risk Assessment Monitoring System (PRAMS) 1998 Surveillance Report that was based on thousands of women across 15 participating states reported rates of 2.4%–6.6% for pregnancy-related violence (United States General Accounting Office, 2002). In other U.S. studies, the rates ranged from 0.9%–20.1% with most estimates falling between 3.9% and 8.3% (Cokkinides et al., 1999; Gazmararian et al., 1996).

Recent studies that sampled from various countries in Europe, Asia, Africa, and the Middle East observed a wide range in the rates for pregnancy-related violence. The highest (31.7%) was in Egypt and the lowest (2.5%) was in the United Kingdom (Bacchus, Mezey, & Bewley, 2004; Bacchus, Mezey, Bewley, & Haworth, 2004; Campbell, Garcia-Moreno, & Sharps, 2004; Johnson et al., 2003; Nasir & Hyder, 2003; Yang et al., 2006). In an interview survey with 24,000 women in 10 countries (Bangladesh, Brazil, Ethiopia, Japan, Peru, Namibia, Somoa, Serbia and Montenegro, Thailand, and the United Republic of Tanzania), the World Health Organization (WHO) found a prevalence rate of 4%–12% among ever-pregnant women who reported having been physically abused during at least one pregnancy (Garcia-Moreno et al., 2005).

Variation in the prevalence rates might be explained by sampling and measurement differences relating to the type of sample (e.g., clinic, general community or population-based surveys, currently pregnant women, women on postnatal visits to clinics), age group of the sample, data collection method and testing measures used, definition and type of abuse assessed, time period adopted to measure the abuse (e.g., first trimester, unspecified time during pregnancy, immediate postpartum, last 12 months including the period before the pregnancy, during the last pregnancy), relationship of the perpetrator to the respondent, and recall accuracy. For more information, the reader is directed to Gazmararian et al. (1996), Ballard et al. (1998), and Jasinski (2004) who provided a more detailed exploration of the link between methodological factors and results obtained in the various studies.

Regardless of the methodological variations in the literature, the statistics obtained by different researchers show that pregnancy-related violence exists across the globe. The published figures are probably underestimates because the research almost exclusively focuses on pregnancies that result in live births. Consequently, statistics involving pregnancies that end in fetal and/or maternal deaths are not included.

ASSOCIATED FACTORS

A literature review by Jasinksi (2004) showed that factors associated with pregnancy-related abuse are low socioeconomic status, low levels of social support, first-time parenting, unexpected or unwanted pregnancy, ethnicity, youth, and alcohol use. Alcohol use by the woman may be a means of coping with the partner's abusive behavior (Rodgers, 1994). Other correlates of pregnancy-related abuse include experiencing an increased number of stressful life events, being unmarried, increased parity (Cokkinides & Cokker, 1998), more negative interactions and verbal aggression in the relationship with the intimate partner (Sagrestano et al., 2004), violence prior to the pregnancy (Bacchus et al., 2004; Campbell, Oliver, & Bullock, 1993; Widdinghedin & Janson, 2000), low education in both partners, (Nasir & Hyder, 2003), patriarchal family situation (Yang et al., 2006), and drinking problem in the partner (Muhajarine & D'Arcy, 1999).

IS PREGNANCY A RISK FACTOR FOR INTIMATE PARTNER VIOLENCE?

If pregnancy were a risk factor for intimate partner violence, one would expect the abuse to begin or increase during pregnancy. In the Canadian Violence Against Women national survey, 40% of the women who had experienced marital violence indicated that the abuse began during the pregnancy (Rodgers, 1994). Similarly, the abuse started during pregnancy for 36.8% of the women in the Bacchus, Mezey, Bewley, and Haworth (2004) study. Other studies have found an increase in the intensity and frequency of violence during pregnancy (Burch & Gallup, 2004; Helton & Snodgrass, 1987; Stewart & Cecutti, 1993).

Data from PRAMS showed the opposite trend. The rates of violence were lower during pregnancy (5.3%) than during the 12 months preceding the pregnancy (7.2%), and in 73% of the cases, the violence during the pregnancy was a continuation of the abuse that occurred prior to the pregnancy (Saltzman et al., 2003). Results from the National Survey of Families and Households (Sweet & Bumpass, 1996; Sweet, Bumpass, & Call, 1998) also suggested that pregnant women were not at greater risk for intimate partner violence. Hillard (1985) reported that the majority of the women in her study (41%) reported no change in abuse during pregnancy. About a one-third (36%) reported a decrease and about a one-fifth (21%) reported an increase.

International findings from the WHO survey indicated that most of the women who had been abused during pregnancy had also been abused before the pregnancy. However, this figure varied from 50%–87%, depending on the site of the survey (Garcia-Moreno et al., 2005). A variable percentage

(8%–34%) of the women who experienced abuse both before and during the pregnancy noted that the abuse worsened during the pregnancy.

The inconsistent findings in the literature might be explained by the younger age of the respondents in studies that found increased risk for abuse during pregnancy (Jasinki & Kantor, 2001). The type of abuse under investigation might play a role as well. Studies with Hispanic women showed that emotional abuse increased during pregnancy while physical and sexual abuse decreased (Castro, Peek-Asa, & Ruiz, 2003; Castro, Peek-Asa, Garcia, Ruiz, & Kraus, 2003). Martin *et al.* (2004) compared an "index group" of women who reported having been physically abused during pregnancy with a "comparison group" of women who reported no physical abuse during pregnancy. They found that rates of psychological aggression increased with the onset of pregnancy for both groups of women. The index group showed an increased rate of sexual aggression but no change in rates of physical violence. The women in their study who experienced physical abuse during pregnancy were subjected to high levels of psychological and physical aggression prior to the pregnancy.

There appears to be a strong link between unintended pregnancies and pregnancy-related abuse. Unintended pregnancy includes mistimed pregnancy that would have been welcome at a later time and unwanted pregnancy that would not have been acceptable at any time (Pallitto, Campbell, & O'Campo, 2005). The risk of abuse around the time of pregnancy increased by 2.5 times for unintended pregnancies (Goodwin *et al.*, 2000). Women with unwanted pregnancies were 4.1 times more at risk for physical abuse than their counterparts with wanted pregnancies (Gazmararian *et al.*, 1995). Canadian (Stewart & Cecutti, 1993) and international (Nasir & Hyder, 2003) findings also find a link between unwanted pregnancy and abuse. Finally, self-reports by a sample of 6,632 men in India indicated a link between unwanted pregnancy and pregnancy-related abuse (Martin et al., 1999).

OUTCOMES OF PREGNANCY-RELATED ABUSE

Women who experience abuse during their pregnancy often have delayed entry into prenatal care, low birth weight of the infants, premature labor, fetal trauma (e.g., miscarriage, placental abruptions, fetal injury and death), and health issues for the mother that include smoking, substance use, alcohol use, unhealthy diet, depression, breastfeeding difficulties, kidney infections, poor weight gain, anemia, hemorrhage, labor and delivery complications (Jainski 2004; Petersen *et al.*, 1997; Valdez-Santiago & Sanin-Aguirre, 1996). Janssen *et al.* (2003) also found a correlation between physical abuse during pregnancy and intrauterine growth retardation. A review by Petersen *et al.* (1997) suggested that there was no pregnancy outcome that could be *consistently* associated with abuse during pregnancy. The authors offered a research strategy in which certain variables (physical mechanisms, psychological state, personal disposition, social support and networks, and health behaviors) might serve to elucidate the link between trauma and stress experienced in abuse and the adverse fetal and maternal outcomes that are often reported in the research literature.

One maternal outcome that has not been researched to any significant extent but is serious enough to warrant acknowledgment is homicide. Homicide is the most frequent cause of injury-related death for women who at the time of death were either pregnant or recently pregnant within the last 6 months (Dannenberg *et al.*, 1991; Fildes *et al.*, 1992). McFarlane, Campbell, Sharps, and Watson (2002) found that abuse during pregnancy was a risk factor for subsequent attempted or completed homicide of the woman by the partner. Reviews of death certificates in North Carolina (Parsons & Harper, 1999) and Maryland (Horon & Cheng, 2001) found that 13% and 20%, respectively, of pregnancy-related deaths were due to homicides.

PATTERN OF VIOLENCE

Not many studies have examined the pattern of violence during pregnancy. Slapping, punching, and threats have been found to be the three most frequent forms of violence committed against the women (Bacchus, Mezey, & Bewley, 2004; Johnson *et al.*, 2003). A study conducted in Taiwan found that the most common body sites of physical violence were the face, arm/leg, head, and neck (Berenson, San Miguel, & Wilkinson, 1992; Widdinghedin & Janson, 2000; Yang *et al.*, 2006). However, Stewart and Cecutti (1993) found that the women were hit most frequently in their abdominal area (63.9%) during their pregnancy. This was followed by the buttocks (13.9%), head and neck (11.1%), and the extremities (11.1%). Between one-quarter to one-half of the women in the WHO study who reported violence during pregnancy were kicked or punched in the abdominal area (Garcia-Moreno *et al.*, 2005).

Targeting the abdominal area might reflect a resentment of the partner toward the pregnancy, especially if the pregnancy was unintended. Issues relating to jealousy, insecurity, and possessiveness on the part of the partner have been identified by the women abused during pregnancy (Bacchus, Mezey, & Bewley, 2006; Campbell *et al.*, 1993). Some of the women noted that their partners had paternity doubts. Other women described their partners' resentment over the women's increased attention to the pregnancy, the decreased emotional and physical availability of the women to the partners, lack of support from the partners, and financial worries associated with the care of the new baby. Other women noted that it was "business as usual" in that the abuse during pregnancy was a continuation of the abuse they experienced before the pregnancy (Campbell *et al.*, 1993).

CURRENT STUDY

A review of the literature establishes that abuse during pregnancy occurs widely in all countries and that it is linked strongly to unintended pregnancy. Although there is no conclusive evidence that physical abuse increases during pregnancy, it is not clear whether the pattern of abuse such as the type of abuse and sites of abuse on the body varies as the pregnancy progresses with an accompanying development in the abdominal area. Furthermore, the literature points to adverse fetal and maternal outcomes during the immediate postpregnancy period. The longer term outcomes on the children have not been studied.

This paper presents the findings of a small study conducted in northwestern Ontario involving women who had been physically or sexually abused during pregnancy ("Index Mothers") and their children ("Index Children") who were between the ages of 3 and 17 years. Women from the same geographical region who were not abused during pregnancy ("Comparison Mothers") and their children ("Comparison Children") who were age and sex matched with the Index Children served as control groups.

One of the objectives of this study was to investigate the abuse experiences of the Index Mothers over the trimesters of their pregnancy. A second objective was to compare the Index Children with their sex- and age-matched Comparison counterpart on their postnatal health, developmental patterns, and current psychological functioning. To minimize the effects of confounding variables, the following restrictions were placed:

1. None of the mothers of the Index Children were currently in an abusive relationship.
2. None of the mothers of the Index Children used tobacco, alcohol, or illicit drugs regularly during their pregnancy (defined as once a week or more frequently). This helped to control for the effects of pharmacological confounds during fetal development (Chen *et al.*, 2003; Johnson *et al.*, 2001).
3. The mothers of the Index Children left their abusive relationships either prior to or within 3 years after the children were born. Children older than 3 years may be cognitively developed and aware enough of the abuse in the home for the milieu to affect their psychological functioning and development, and to influence their behavior through modeling. Younger children might arguably be affected to a lesser extent than older children.

TABLE 1. Demographic characteristics of the mothers and children

	Mothers	
Characteristics	Index Group	Comparison Group
Marital status		
Single, never married	5(33.30%)	6(11.80%)
Married	4(26.70%)	34(66.70%)
Common-law	3(20.00%)	4(7.80%)
Separated	1(6.70%)	4(7.80%)
Divorced	1(6.70%)	2(3.90%)
Widowed	0(0.00%)	1(2.00%)
Ethnicity		
Aboriginal	4(40.00%)	10(19.60%)
Caucasian	8(53.30%)	39(76.50%)
Asian	0(0.00%)	1(2.00%)
African Canadian	0(0.00%)	1(2.00%)

	Children	
Characteristics	Index Group	Comparison Group
Ethnicity		
Aboriginal	5(45.50%)	2(18.20%)
Caucasian	6(54.50%)	7(63.60%)
Asian	0(0.00%)	1(9.10%)
African Canadian	0(0.00%)	1(9.10%)

4. The children in both Index and Comparison groups had no history of physical or sexual abuse or of witnessing intimate partner violence, were delivered through a normal birth process defined as vaginal delivery with no birth complications, and had no history of major illnesses or medical trauma that could have had an effect on their current psychological or behavioral functioning.

PARTICIPANTS

Mothers

A total of 68 women participated in the study. Of these, 15 (22.06%) had been abused during pregnancy. A total of 3 of these women indicated that they were abused in 2 pregnancies. This resulted in 15 mothers who had been abused reporting on 18 pregnancies in total. The women who had been abused (Index Mothers, age $M = 33.62$, $SD = 8.00$) and those who had not been (Comparison Mothers, age $M = 35.54$, $SD = 7.97$) did not differ significantly from each other on age. As shown in TABLE 1, most of the Index Mothers were single (33.30%) while most of the Comparison Mothers were married (66.70%). A little over one-half of the Index Mothers (53.3%) and three-quarters (76.5%) of the Comparison Mothers were Caucasian (see TABLE 1). There were proportionately more Aboriginal women among the Index Mothers (40.00%) than among the Comparison Mothers (19.60%).

Children

Information on 18 children born to Index Mothers was received. However, the data on 7 children were excluded from analyses because of one or more of the following reasons: (*a*) 3 of the children had been physically abused by their fathers; (*b*) the age limit (17 years) for inclusion in the study was surpassed in one case; (*c*) one child was older than 3 years when the abusive relationship ended; and (*d*) 5 of the children had witnessed violence against their mothers. Consequently, the remaining 11 children (age $M = 9.73$ years, SD $=$ 4.28 years) who met the research criteria were categorized into the Index Children group. Information on 79 children born to Comparison Mothers was received. A total of 11 of these children were age and sex matched to the 11 Index Children and comprised the Comparison Children group (age $M =$ 9.83 years, SD $= 4.17$ years). There were 5 female and 6 male children in each group. The 22 children in both groups ranged from 3.33 years to 16.58 years in age ($M = 9.78$ years, SD $= 4.13$ years) and were unrelated to each other. On the average, each matched pair differed in age by 2.73 months. TABLE 1 shows the ethnic status of the children. About 45.50% of the Index Children were Aboriginal and the rest were Caucasian. Among the Comparison Children, 18.20% were Aboriginal, 63.60% were Caucasian, and the remaining children were Asian (9.10%) and African Canadian (9.10%).

METHOD

Recruitment was carried out via radio and newspaper advertisements. Posters were also sent to various women's groups, sexual assault centers, emergency shelters, transition shelters for assaulted women and children, hospitals, clinics, pediatricians, obstetricians, gynecologists, and university settings located within the communities in the region of northwestern Ontario. Women who were interested in participating contacted the researchers through a toll-free number set up specifically for the study. The research was presented as a project that looked at the psychological functioning and health history of children born to women who either had or had not been physically or sexually abused during pregnancy, and to understand the experiences of mothers who were abused during their pregnancy. Anonymity was assured through coding of responses via a numerical tracking system rather than by names. The project received ethics approval from the Lakehead University Research Ethics Board. Women who remained interested in participating were sent a research questionnaire containing a consent form, the measures, an informational list of community agencies and services for abused women and their children, and a stamped self-addressed envelope to return their responses. Women who had more than one child completed one questionnaire for each pregnancy and child. Upon receipt of completed questionnaires, a numerical code was assigned to each respondent to protect their anonymity. A summary of the results without any identifying information was sent to participants who requested feedback.

MEASURES

The research questionnaire contained several sections. Questions in Section A were designed to collect demographic information (marital status, age, ethnicity) about the mothers and their children, and to ascertain whether the mothers and children met the research criteria for the project.

Section B contained detailed questions on the child's development history. Information regarding the pregnancy, birth, medical history, early development, present health status, and school history of the child was collected. Some of the questions (pregnancy, birth, and medical history) served as checks against the research criteria. The remaining questions focused on the child's abilities and challenges, and the age at which the child met the various developmental milestones.

Section C collected information about the type and frequency of assault experienced by the Index Mothers during each trimester of their pregnancy. The items in this section were based on a variation of the Abuse Assessment Screen (McFarlane, Parker, & Soeken, 1996). Physical abuse items included pushing/shoving/grabbing, slapping, hitting with a fist, kicking, biting, hitting or attempting to hit with an object, beaten up, used a weapon, and choking. Sexual abuse items included forced sexual acts, pain during forced sexual acts, and injury during forced sexual acts.

Section D assessed the frequency of attacks during each trimester of the pregnancy that were made on different sites of the body: Upper Torso Area (chest, breasts, stomach, shoulders), Lower Torso Area (pelvic area, buttocks, anus, vagina), Head Area (face, eyes, mouth, hair, nose, neck, ears, skull), Upper Limb Area (arms, hands, wrists, fingers), and Lower Limb Area (thighs, knees, ankles, feet, toes, calves).

Section E consisted of the 80-item Conners' (1997) Parent Rating Scale—Revised: Long Form (CPRS-R:L) to collect the mothers' reports on their children's current behavior. Each item is associated with a 4-point Likert response scale ranging from 0 (not true at all: never or seldom) to 3 (very much true: very often, very frequent). The CPRS-R:L has 10 subscales, namely Oppositional, Hyperactivity, Perfectionism, Psychosomatic, Attention Deficit Hyperactivity Disorder, Cognitive Problems, Social Problems, Anxious-Shy, Restless-Impulsive, and Emotional Lability. It also yields two indicators that show

TABLE 2. Mean frequency of abuse pattern within each trimester

	Type of abuse		
Abuse Pattern	Trimester 1	Trimester 2	Trimester 3
Physical abuse			
M	17.32	10.04	5.88
SD	19.92	11.32	9.38
Sexual abuse			
M	1.00	4.17	5.83
SD	1.61	12.29	18.04

	Sites of body		
Abuse Pattern	Trimester 1	Trimester 2	Trimester 3
Upper torso area			
M	5.75	4.50	2.73
SD	7.85	5.60	3.90
Lower torso area			
M	2.08	3.08	2.67
SD	3.58	6.59	7.08
Head area			
M	11.86	8.36	3.82
SD	18.76	11.03	5.23
Upper limb area			
M	6.55	8.00	4.82
SD	7.57	15.89	8.99
Lower limb area			
M	2.36	2.26	.93
SD	5.34	3.65	1.69

NOTE: The table above does not include nonnumerical responses such as "repeatedly" to questions about the frequency of the type and site of abuse within each trimester.

the presence of DSM-IV symptoms of Inattentiveness and of Hyperactive-Impulsive difficulties. Summary subscale scores were converted into T-scores with particular interest in T-scores that exceeded 70 because they fall within the "Markedly Atypical (Indicates Significant Problems)" range (Conners, 1997, p. 4). The CPRS-R:L has been shown to have generally good internal consistency, test-retest reliability, and discriminant validity (Conners, 1997).

RESULTS

Abuse history of the Index Mothers

Within each trimester, the frequency of all physical abuse occurrences was added to derive a physical abuse composite score. Similarly, a sexual abuse composite score was calculated for each trimester. When the composite scores were compared across the trimesters, it was observed that there was a pattern

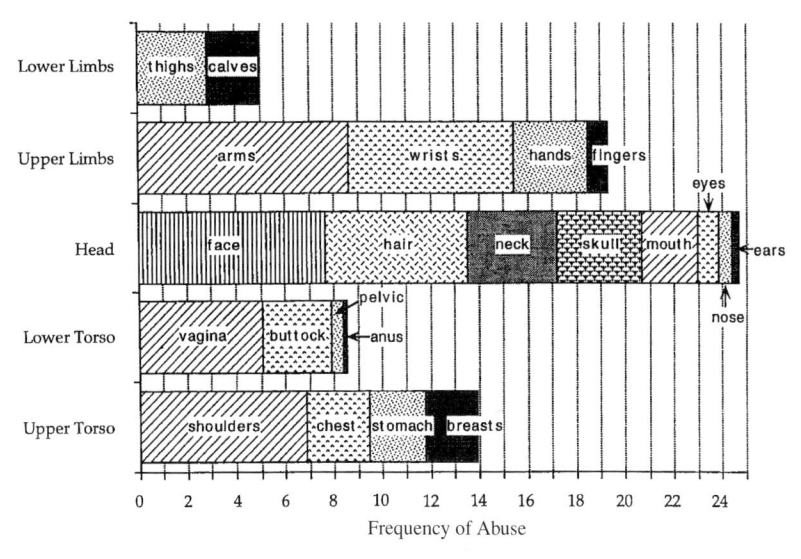

FIGURE 1. Frequency of abuse on different parts of the body throughout the entire pregnancy. The statistics do not include nonnumerical responses such as "repeatedly" to questions about the frequency that different body areas were hit during pregnancy.

of physical abuse decreasing and sexual abuse increasing throughout the pregnancy (see TABLE 2). However, when separate repeated measures ANOVAs with trimester as the independent variable were conducted on the physical abuse composite score and on the sexual abuse composite score, no statistically significant trend across the trimesters was found for either composite score.

Across the entire pregnancy, the most common type of abuse was forced sexual activity ($M = 14.85$, $SD = 61.95$) followed by suffering pain during forced sexual activity ($M = 13.73$, $SD = 57.66$), pushing/shoving/grabbing ($M = 12.64$, $SD = 50.63$), slapping ($M = 10.41$, $SD = 49.01$), being hit or attempted hit with an object ($M = 10.16$, $SD = 49.03$), and hit with a fist ($M = 10.03$, $SD = 49.01$). The remaining types of abuse were experienced at a similar level of frequency of between 6.50 and 8.00 episodes.

Sites of Abuse on the Body

For each trimester, the number of times that each general area of the body was hit was calculated (see TABLE 2). With the exception of the Head Area, all general areas of the body were abused less frequently as the pregnancy progressed. A specific examination of the data for the stomach area showed no change in abuse toward that area from trimester 1 to 3. Statistical testing carried out via repeated measures ANOVA with trimester as the independent variable, which was conducted separately on each general area of the body yielded no

TABLE 3. Mean T-score on the Conners' scales (number of children scoring $T > 70$)

Conners' Scales	Index Children	Comparison Children
Oppositional*	58.64(2)	45.64(0)
Hyperactivity*	65.82(4)	49.64(0)
Attention deficit disorder**	61.18(3)	49.18(0)
Anxious-Shy	65.09(4)	52.55(1)
Perfectionism	50.36(0)	46.91(0)
Psychosomatic	59.73(3)	48.36(0)
Social problems*	63.36(3)	47.09(0)
Cognitive problems	59.36(3)	50.00(0)
Restless-Impulsive	62.91(3)	51.18(1)
Emotional lability	56.55(3)	44.82(0)
DSM inattentive**	60.64(3)	47.73(0)
DSM Hyperactive-Impulsive*	65.27(3)	50.00(0)

*Group differences on T-score significant at $P < 0.01$.
**Group differences on T-score significant at $P < 0.05$.

significant findings. Across the entire pregnancy, the head, upper limb and upper torso areas were hit more frequently than the lower limb or lower torso areas (see FIG. 1 for frequency of abuse to specific parts that comprise the general areas of the body).

Children's Developmental and Health History

Chi-square tests revealed that there was no significant relationship between the status of the children (Index, Comparison) with the following indicators: pregnancy was planned, difficulties during pregnancy, present allergies, current eye and ear problems, and physical or developmental disabilities. The t-tests also revealed no significant difference between the Index and Comparison Children on the duration of pregnancy, duration of labor, birth weight, and age at which they reached the various developmental milestones that included sat alone, crawled, walked, said single words, combined 2-3 words, said simple sentences, day bladder trained, night bladder trained, commencement of bowel training, and completion of bowel training.

Children's Psychological, Cognitive and Social Functioning on the CPRS-R:L

A MANOVA on two externalizing scales, Oppositional and Hyperactivity, revealed a significant effect, $F(2, 19) = 5.82$, $P < 0.01$. Univariate F-tests using the Bonferronni-split approach to keep the overall Type I error rate at 0.05 showed that the Index and Comparison Children differed on Oppositional (F[1, 20] = 8.48, $P < 0.01$) and Hyperactivity (F[1, 20] = 11.50, $P < 0.01$), with Index Children scoring higher on both scales (see TABLE 3).

Significant findings with a MANOVA on DSM Inattentive and DSM Hyperactive-Impulsive scales were obtained, $F(2, 19) = 5.63$, $P < 0.05$. The two groups of children differed from each other on the DSM Inattentive, $F(1, 20) = 6.29$, $P < 0.05$, and the DSM Hyperactive-Impulsive scales, $F(2, 19) = 9.79$, $P < 0.001$. The Index Children scored higher on both scales than the Comparison Children (see TABLE 3).

Multivariate analyses on the three internalizing scales of Anxious-Shy, Perfectionism, and Psychosomatic did not yield any significant findings. Similarly, no significant results were obtained with a MANOVA on the Restless-Impulsive and Emotional Lability scales.

Separate t-tests were performed on the remaining Conners' scales. Significant differences were found for Attention Deficit Hyperactivity Disorder ($t[1, 20] = 2.13$, $P < 0.05$) and Social Problems ($t[1, 20] = 3.67$, $P < 0.05$), with Index Children scoring higher on both (see TABLE 3). No significant difference was found for Cognitive Problems.

The number of children in both groups who had a T-score of greater than 70 on any of the Conners' scales were calculated. In every instance with the exception of Perfectionism, there were more Index Children than Comparison Children (see TABLE 3) who scored more than 70. In almost all of the scales except for Anxious-Shy and Restless-Impulsive, there were no Comparison Children who scored more than 70.

DISCUSSION

The pattern of abuse over the three trimesters of the pregnancy among 15 mothers revealed a trend toward decreasing physical abuse and increasing sexual abuse as the pregnancy progressed; however, the pattern was determined to be not statistically significant. The most frequent form of abuse that occurred throughout the pregnancy was forced sexual activity. This was followed by pain suffered during forced sexual activity, pushing/shoving/grabbing, slapping, being hit or attempted hit with an object, and being hit with a fist. There was no pattern to the location of the body area that was hit over the three trimesters of the pregnancy in that no general location was more likely to be hit during any specific term of the pregnancy.

Overall, the findings suggest that the risk of abuse does not increase with pregnancy. Neither does pregnancy offer a protection for women because the violence against the women did not cease or decrease significantly as the pregnancy progressed. A surprising finding was that the abdominal area was not a primary target for hitting during the pregnancy. Instead the upper half of the body (head, upper limbs, upper torso) was hit more often than the lower half of the body, which is in keeping with reports from other studies (Widdinghedin & Janson, 2000; Yang *et al.*, 2006). Perhaps there might be a cultural explanation for this. In the WHO study, areas that have a high rate of physical abuse do not necessarily show a correspondingly high rate of abuse during pregnancy, suggesting that in some places violence against pregnant women might be less acceptable even if violence against women is prevalent (Garcia-Moreno et al., 2005). Given that a high percentage of the Index Mothers in this study were Aboriginal, it is possible that some cultural factors might have been in effect here that ameliorated the risk of injury to the vulnerable abdominal area of these women during pregnancy.

The Index Children (those born to the abused mothers) did not differ from their Comparison counterparts (children born to nonabused mothers) in their developmental and physical health history. This is not totally unexpected given that the mothers in both groups did not use tobacco, alcohol, or illicit drugs regularly. This possibly preempted adverse effects from substance use on fetal development during the pregnancy. The results might have turned out differently had substance use not been controlled for in the study. Use of cigarettes, alcohol, and illicit drugs during pregnancy have been found to be associated with adverse birth outcomes (Bohn & Holz, 1996; Bullock & McFarlane, 1989; Zuckerman, 1988).

The differences between the Index Children and Comparison Children were found in externalizing behaviors such as oppositional, hyperactivity, attention deficit, hyperactive-impulsive, and social problems. The Index Children also had a higher risk of scoring within the "markedly atypical" range (T-scores > 70 on the CPRS-R:L) on internalizing behaviors, with the exception of perfectionism. These differences were evident even though several confounding influences (maternal substance use, witnessing the abuse, medical history of trauma, child abuse) had been controlled for in the study. The question here is what other factors that are associated with abuse during pregnancy might have contributed to the behavioral differences found between the two groups of children?

Intimate partner violence might not have a direct association with a child's health or behavior but its impact might be conveyed through caregiver and family functioning that have a more direct link with the child's health and behavior (English, Marshall, & Stewart, 2003). Women who are abused are at greater risk for poor physical health and psychological distress (Cascardi, Langhinrichsen, & Vivian, 1992; Golding, 1999; Stewart & Cecutti, 1993; Weinbaum et al., 2001). Maternal mental distress adversely affects parenting practices (Leiferman et al., 2005), that in turn are related to externalizing behaviors in children (Levendosky et al., 2003). Even at a very young age, children born to women who had been abused during pregnancy might have experienced poor maternal attachment. Intimate partner violence is linked to poorer maternal attachment even at 6-months postpartum, which could have made it difficult for the mothers to respond adequately to the needs of the infants (Quinlivan & Evans, 2005).

Even if the children themselves did not witness the intimate partner violence or were not targets of the abuse, they could have been affected during their fetal development stage. The fetus of a depressed woman shows less body movement, more sleep time (Chung et al., 2001), and reduced heart rate response than the fetus of a nondepressed woman (Allister et al., 2001). Women who are abused during pregnancy are also slower to enter into prenatal care (Huth-Bocks, Levendosky, & Bogat, 2002), which could potentially risk fetal health.

Research has shown that abused mothers often live under disadvantaged socioeconomic conditions. They have less education, live in crowded dwellings, and are in financial difficulties (Gazmararian et al., 1995; Goodwin et al., 2000; Yang et al., 2006). Socioeconomic deprivation could impact children directly or indirectly through various means such as physical and mental health of the child and family members, family structure, diet, housing problems, and social exclusion (Roberts, 1997).

Another factor that might contribute to the differences in child behaviors found in the present study is the quality of the current home environment. Although the Index Mothers indicated that they were not in a violent relationship, they and their children could have been living in an emotionally tense milieu. Exposure to emotional abuse in children is associated with difficulties in coping with stressful situations and problem solving, behavioural extremes (Shields, Cicchetti, & Ryan, 1994) and delinquent behaviors (Widom & White, 1997).

The findings of the present study, albeit interesting, need to be considered within the context of its particular limitations that make it difficult to generalize to the larger population. The sample sizes for the mothers and children were small, which reduce the power of statistical tests. The communities that the study recruited have small populations, and were nonurban and relatively isolated; hence the applicability of the findings to bigger urban areas is unknown. Given that the study sampled the general population and not a clinical population (e.g., women attending prenatal clinics), it is highly probable that many women who experienced abuse during pregnancy did not participate in the research project and their experiences are therefore not reflected in this study. As well, the study used a retrospective design that is vulnerable to recall bias, particularly with respect to the details of the abuse experience over the trimesters of a pregnancy relating to an older child. Information that could have helped to elucidate some of the findings was not collected. The study controlled only for physical violence in the current environment but not psychological abuse. It would have been helpful to assess maternal and paternal (in cases where the mothers were with a male partner) psychological functioning and the health of the home environment that might have contributed to the findings. It is also important to remember that the Index Mothers had left their abusive partners and were either living alone or were in a relationship with another man. The attachment between the children and the men living with their mothers and who are not their biological fathers might in itself bring its own set of problems for the mothers and their children.

In conclusion, the present study attempted to investigate the link between pregnancy-related violence and the long-term psychological outcomes for the children. Even though several confounding variables were controlled for in the research design, the findings still reveal that children born to women abused during pregnancy have difficulties, particularly in the area of externalizing behaviors. External factors such as health of the home environment, psychological status of the caregivers in the home and their parenting abilities, and socioeconomic conditions might help to illuminate the findings and might warrant further research attention.

ACKNOWLEDGMENT

This project was funded by a wife assault and sexual assault prevention initiatives grant from the Ministry of Northern Development and Mines awarded to the first author. Sincere thanks are extended to Tanya Spencer and Jennifer Nachshen for their data entry assistance, and to Michael Wesner for his assistance with the graphics.

REFERENCES

ALLISTER, L., B.M. LESTER, S. CARR & J. LIU. 2001. The effects of maternal depression on fetal heart rate response to vibroacoustic stimulation. Developmental Neuropsychology 20, 639–651.

BACCHUS, L., G. MEZEY & S. BEWLEY. 2004. Domestic violence: prevalence in pregnant women and associations with physical and psychological health. European Journal of Obstetrics, Gynecology and Reproductive Biology 113, 6–11.

BACCHUS, L., G. MEZEY & S. BEWLEY. 2006. A qualitative exploration of the nature of domestic violence in pregnancy. Violence Against Women 12, 588–604.

BACCHUS, L., G. MEZEY, S. BEWLEY & A. HAWORTH. 2004. Prevalence of domestic violence in pregnancy when midwives routinely enquire. BJOG: An International Study of Obstetrics and Gynaecology 111, 441–445.

BALLARD, T.J., L.E. SALTZMAN, J.A. GAZMARARIAN, et al. 1998. Violence during pregnancy: measurement issues. American Journal of Public Health 88, 274–276.

BERENSON, A.B., V.V. SAN MIGUEL & G.S. WILKINSON. 1992. Prevalence of physical and sexual assault in pregnant adolescents. Journal of Adolescent Health 13, 466–469.

BOHN, D.K. & K.A. HOLZ. 1996. Health effects of childhood sexual abuse, domestic battering, and rape. Journal of Nurse Midwifery 41, 442–456.

BURCH, R.L. & G.G. GALLUP Jr. 2004. Pregnancy as a stimulus for domestic violence. Journal of Family Violence 19, 243–247.

BULLOCK, L. & J. MCFARLANE. 1989. The birthweight/battering connection. American Journal of Nursing 89, 1153–1155.

CAMPBELL, J., C. GARCIA-MORENO & P. SHARPS. 2004. Abuse during pregnancy in industrialized and developing countries. Violence Against Women 10, 770–789.

CAMPBELL, J.C., C. OLIVER & L. BULLOCK. 1993. Why battering during pregnancy? AWHONN's Clinical Issues in Perinatal and Women's Health Nursing *4,* 343–349.

CASCARDI, M., J. LANGHINRICHSEN & D. VIVIAN. 1992. Marital aggression: impact, injury, and health correlates for husbands and wives. Archives of Internal Medicine *152,* 1178–1184.

CASTRO, R., C. PEEK-ASA & A. RUIZ. 2003. Violence against women in Mexico: a study of abuse before and during pregnancy. American Journal of Public Health *93,* 1110–1116.

CASTRO, R., C. PEEK-ASA, L. GARCIA, *et al.* 2003. Risks for abuse against pregnant Hispanic women: Morelos, Mexico and Los Angeles County, California. American Journal of Preventive Medicine *25,* 325–332.

CHEN, W.J.A., S.E. MAIER, S. PARNELL & J.R. WEST. 2003. Alcohol and the developing brain: neuroanatomical studies. Alcohol Research and Health *27,* 174–180.

CHUNG, T.K.H., T.K. LAU, A.S. YIP, *et al.* 2001. Antepartum depressive symptomatology is associated with adverse obstetric and neonatal outcomes. Psychosomatic Medicine *63,* 830–834. f

COKKINIDES, V.E. & A.L. COKER. 1998. Experiencing physical violence during pregnancy: prevalence and correlates. Family and Community Health *20,* 19–38.

COKKINIDES, V.E., A.L. COKER, M. SANDERSON, *et al.* 1999. Physical violence during pregnancy: maternal complications and birth outcomes. Obstetrics and Gynecology *93,* 661–666.

CONNERS, C.K. 1997. Conners' Parent Rating Scale—Revised: long version. Multi-Health Systems Inc. Toronto, Ontario.

DANNENBERG, A., D. CARTER, H. LAWSON, *et al.* 1991. Homicide and other injuries as causes of maternal death in New York City, 1987 through 1991. American Journal of Obstetrics and Gynecology *172,* 1557–1564.

ENGLISH, D.J., D.B. MARSHALL & A.J. STEWART. 2003. Effects of family violence on child behaviour and health during early childhood. Journal of Family Violence *18,* 43–57.

FILDES, J., L. REED, N. JONES, *et al.* 1992. Trauma: the leading cause of maternal death. The Journal of Trauma *32,* 643–645.

GARCIA-MORENO, C., H.A.F.M. JANSEN, M. ELLSBERG, *et al.* 2005. WHO Multi-Country Study on Women's Health and Domestic Violence Against Women. World Health Organization.Geneva, Switzerland.

GAZMARARIAN, J.A., M.M. ADAMS, L.E. SALTZMAN, *et al.* the PRAMS Working Group. 1995. The relationship between pregnancy intendedness and physical violence in mothers of newborns. Obstetrics and Gynecology *85,* 1031–1038.

GAZMARARIAN, J.A., S. LAZORICK, A.M. SPITZ, *et al.* 1996. Prevalence of violence against pregnant women. Journal of American Medical Association *275,* 1915–1920.

GOLDING, J.M. 1999. Intimate partner violence as a risk factor for mental disorders: a meta-analysis. Journal of Family Violence *14,* 99–132.

GOODWIN, M.M., J.A. GAZMARARIAN, C.H. JOHNSON, *et al.* PRAMS Working Group. 2000. Pregnancy intendedness and physical abuse around the time of pregnancy: findings from the Pregnancy Risk Assessment Monitoring System, 1996–1997. Maternal and Child Health Journal *4,* 85–92.

HELTON, A.S. & F.G. SNODGRASS. 1987. Battering during pregnancy: intervention strategies. Birth *14,* 142–147.
HILLARD, P.J.A. 1985. Physical abuse during pregnancy. Obstetrics and Gynecology *66,* 185–190.
HORON, I.L. & D. CHENG. 2001. Enhanced surveillance for pregnancy associated mortality in Maryland, 1993–1998. Journal of American Medical Association *285,* 1455–1459.
HUTH-BOCKS, A.C., A.A. LEVENDOSKY & G.A. BOGAT. 2002. The effects of domestic violence during pregnancy on maternal and infant health. Violence and Victims *17,* 169–185.
JANSSEN, P.A., V. HOLT, N.K. SUGG, *et al*. 2003. Intimate partner violence and adverse pregnancy outcomes: a population-based study. American Journal of Obstetrics and Gynecology *188,* 1341–1347.
JASINSKI, J.L. 2004. Pregnancy and domestic violence. A review of the literature. Trauma, Violence and Abuse *5,* 47–64.
JASINSKI, J.L. & G.K. KANTOR. 2001. Pregnancy, stress, and wife assault: ethnic differences in prevalence, severity, and onset in a national sample. Violence and Victims, *16,* 219–232.
JOHNSON, J.K., F. HAIDER, K. ELLIS, *et al*. 2003. The prevalence of domestic violence in pregnant women. BJOG: An International Study of Obstetrics and Gynaecology *110,* 272–275.
JOHNSON, C.H., J.R. VICARY, L. CARRIE & D.A. CORNEAL. 2001. Moderate alcohol and tobacco use during pregnancy and child behavior outcomes. Journal of Primary Prevention *21,* 367–379.
LEIFERMAN, J.A., T.H. OLLENDICK, D. KUNKEL & I.C. CHRISTIE. 2005. Mothers' mental distress and parenting practices with infants and toddlers. Archives of Women's Mental Health *8,* 243–247.
LEVENDOSKY, A.A., A.C. HUTH-BOCKS, D.L. SHAPIRO & M.A. SEMEL. 2003. The impact of domestic violence on the maternal-child relationship and preschool-age children's functioning. . Journal of Family Psychology *17,* 275–287.
MARTIN, S.L., A. HARRIS-BRITT, Y. LI, *et al*. 2004. Changes in intimate partner violence during pregnancy. Journal of Family Violence *19,* 201–210.
MARTIN, S.L., B. KILGALLEN, A.O. TSUI, *et al*. 1999. Sexual behaviors and reproductive health outcomes: associations with wife abuse in India. Journal of the American Medical Association *282,* 1967–1972.
MCFARLANE, J., B. PARKER & K. SOEKEN. 1996. Abuse during pregnancy: associations with maternal health and infant birth weight. Nursing Research *45,* 37–42.
MCFARLANE, J., J.C. CAMPBELL, P. SHARPS & K. WATSON. 2002. Abuse during pregnancy and femicide: urgent implications for women's health. Obstetrics and Gynecology *100,* 27–36.
MUHAJARINE, N. & C. D'ARCY. 1999. Physical abuse during pregnancy: prevalence and risk factors. Canadian Medical Association Journal *160,* 1007–1011.
NASIR, K. & A.A. HYDER. 2003. Violence against pregnant women in developing countries. European Journal of Public Health *13,* 105–107.
PALLITTO, C.C., J.C. CAMPBELL & P. O'CAMPO. 2005. Is intimate partner violence associated with unintended pregnancy? A review of the literature. Trauma Violence and Abuse *6,* 217–235.
PARSONS, L.H. & M.A. HARPER. 1999. Violent maternal deaths in North Carolina. Obstetrics and Gynecology *94,* 990–993.

PETERSEN, R., J.A. GAZMARARIAN, A.M. SPITZ, et al. 1997. Violence and adverse pregnancy outcomes: a review of the literature and directions for further research. American Journal of Preventive Medicine. *13*, 366–373.

QUINLIVAN, J.A. & S.F. EVANS. 2005. Impact of domestic violence and drug abuse in pregnancy on maternal attachment and infant temperament in teenage mothers in the setting of best clinical practice. Archives of Women Mental Health *8*, 191–199.

ROBERTS, H. 1997. Socioeconomic determinants of health: children, inequalities, and health. British Medical Journal, *314*, 1122.

RODGERS, K. 1994. Wife assault: the findings of a national survey. Juristat Service Bulletin Canadian Centre for Justice Statistics, *14*(Catalogue 85-002). Statistics Canada. Ottawa, Ontario.

SAGRESTANO, L.M., D. CARROLL, A.C. RODRIGUEZ & B. NUWAYHID. 2004. Demographic, psychological, and relationship factors in domestic violence during pregnancy in a sample of low-income women of color. Psychology of Women Quarterly *28*, 309–322.

SALTZMAN, L.E., C.H. JOHNSON, B.C. GILBERT & M.M. GOODWIN. 2003. Physical abuse around the time of pregnancy: an examination of prevalence and risk factors in 16 states. Maternal and Child Health Journal *7*, 31–43.

SHIELDS, A., D. CICCHETTI & R. RYAN. 1994. The development of emotional and behavioral self-regulation and social competence among maltreated school-age children. Development and Psychopathology *6*, 57–75.

STEWART, D.E. & A. CECUTTI. 1993. Physical abuse in pregnancy. Canadian Medical Association Journal *149*, 1257–1263.

SWEET, J.L. & L.L. BUMPASS. 1996. The National Survey of Families and Households—Waves 1 & 2: data description and documentation. University of Wisconsin. Madison, WI.

SWEET, J.L., L.L. BUMPASS & V. CALL. 1998. The design and content of the National Survey of Families and Households (NSHF Working Paper No. 1). University of Wisconsin, Center for Demography and Ecology. Madison, WI.

UNITED STATES GENERAL ACCOUNTING OFFICE. 2002. Violence Against Women. Report to the Honorable Eleanor Holmes Norton, House of Representatives (GAO-02-530). U.S. General Accounting OfficeWashington, DC.

VALDEZ-SANTIAGO, R. & L.H. SANIN-AGUIRRE. 1996. Domestic violence during pregnancy and its relationship with birth weight. Salud Publication Mexico *38*, 352–362.

WEINBAUM, Z., T.L. STRATTON, G. CHAVEZ, et al. 2001. Female victims of intimate partner physical domestic violence (IPP-DV), California 1998. American Journal of Preventive Medicine *21*, 313–319.

WIDDINGHEDIN, L. & P.O. JANSON. 2000. Domestic violence during pregnancy. Acta Obstetrica et Gynecologica Scandinavica *79*, 625–630.

WIDOM, C.S. & H.R. WHITE. 1997. Problem behaviours in abused and neglected children grown up: prevalence and co-occurrence of substance abuse, crime and violence. Criminal Behaviour and Mental Health *7*, 287–310.

YANG, M.S., M.J. YANG, F.H. CHOU, et al. 2006. Physical abuse against pregnant aborigines in Taiwan: prevalence and risk factors. International Journal of Nursing Studies *43*, 21–27.

ZUCKERMAN, B. 1988. Marijuana and cigarette smoking during pregnancy: neonatal effects. *In* Drugs, Alcohol, Pregnancy and Parenting. I.J. Chasnoff, Ed.: 73–88. Kluwer Academic Press. Hingham, MA.

An Exploration of Female Genital Mutilation

ERIKA M. BARON AND FLORENCE L. DENMARK

Psychology Department, Pace University, New York, NY, USA

> ABSTRACT: Female genital mutilation (FGM) is a form of violence against women that has recently been labeled a public health issue. This article will define and describe the procedure as well as discuss its physical and psychological implications. An exploration of the cultural significance of the practice will shed light on its continued existence in underdeveloped and developed nations. In addition, an examination of suggested guidelines for creating and implementing effective interventions will ensue.
>
> KEYWORDS: female genital mutilation; FGM; violence; women; public health; intervention; procedure

INTRODUCTION

Female genital mutilation (FGM) is a deeply rooted historical, cultural, and religious tradition that has been the subject of considerable debate in the 21st century. Human rights groups deem it as an unsafe and unjustifiable practice that violates bodily integrity, and feminists argue that it is an inhumane form of gender-based discrimination that capitalizes on the subjugation of women, yet nations that endorse the practice define it as an integral feature of the culture. This article will consider various perspectives on FGM via an exploration of the procedure and its implications for physical and mental health. Developing an understanding of the practice's cultural significance in light of the sociopolitical climate will be encouraged and issues of cultural relativism will come to the forefront. Furthermore, an investigation of the presence of FGM in industrialized nations will ensue and shed light upon numerous obstacles to elimination. And finally, a discussion will cover the points to consider when planning and implementing effective interventions on a national, state, and local level.

Address for correspondence: Florence L. Denmark, Psychology Department, Pace University, 41 Park Row, New York, NY 10038. Voice: 212-346-1551; fax: 212-346-1618
e-mail: fdenmark@pace.edu

DEFINITION AND DEMOGRAPHICS

The United Nations (UN) World Health Organization (WHO) defines FGM as "the partial or total removal of the female external genitalia or other injury to the female genital organs for cultural and other non-therapeutic reasons" (UNICEF, 2005, p. 1). Additionally, the practice is categorized into four types:

Type 1: Excision of the precipice (the fold of skin surrounding the clitoris), with or without excision of part of the entire clitoris.
Type 2: Excision of the clitoris with partial or total removal of the labia minora (the smaller inner folds of the vulva).
Type 3: Excision of part or all of the external genitalia and stitching or narrowing of the vaginal opening.
Type 4: Unclassified, which includes pricking, piercing, or incising of the clitoris and/or labia; stretching of the clitoris and/or labia; cauterization by burning of the clitoris and surrounding tissue; scraping of tissue surrounding the opening of the vagina (*angurya* cuts) or cutting of the vagina (*gishiri* cuts); introduction of corrosive substances or herbs into the vagina to cause bleeding or to tighten or narrow the vagina; and any other procedure that can be included in the definition of female genital mutilation noted above (p. 1)

The first type is often referred to as Circumcision or Sunna (which is the Arabic word meaning tradition), and the second type is often referred to as Clitoridectomy/Excision. Both Type 1 and Type 2 are cited as the most common forms of FGM, and they account for approximately 80% of the cases worldwide. The third type, termed Infibulation or Pharaonic Circumcision, is the most extreme form that comprises 15% of all cases. However, it should be noted that in several African countries, infibulation is the practice of choice for 80–90% of the procedures (White, 2001).

It is estimated that 100–140 million females have undergone FGM and an additional 3 million girls are projected to be at risk each year (which equates to a staggering 6,000 cases per day) (WHO, 2000). Furthermore, it is suggested that the "secret veil" underneath which FGM occurs probably results in reported rates that do not reflect the enormous number of females who have been victimized (Lax, 2000). Demographical reports cite that FGM remains active on almost all of the world's continents. It is most prevalent in the northeastern corner of Africa (i.e., Egypt, Sudan, Ethiopia, Somalia, Sierra Leone, etc.) and less common, but extant, in Asia, Europe, Australia, North America, and South America. Although FGM is commonly associated with the Islamic faith, it is virtually unknown in Muslim countries that lie outside of Africa (i.e., Iraq, Iran, Saudi Arabia, etc.). It is a custom that is engaged in by numerous religious followers including Christians, Ethiopian Jews, animists, and nonbelievers (Abusharaf, 1998). Just as diffuse is the age at which females are circumcised. Most often, girls undergo the procedure between the ages of 4 and

14 years, however it can also take place during infancy, late adolescence, prior to marriage, or at the time of the first pregnancy (Chalmers & Omer-Hashi, 2000).

THE PROCEDURE

The details of the procedure are dependent on a variety of factors including ethnic background, geographic location, and socioeconomic status (Amnesty International, n.d.). The child possesses minimal prior knowledge about the excision experience due to the clandestine nature of the ritual. In some cases, one is aware of its proximity as villages might plan ceremonies for the previous night or designate specific days of the month on which the procedure must occur. Female circumcision can be "cloaked in festivity" whereby the young girl is treated like royalty, given extravagant gifts, and nourished with the finest foods. In other instances, the child is unaware of what awaits her and is unexpectedly woken in the middle of the night or pulled from her mid-day duties (Abusharaf, 1998).

Mothers, aunts, and/or older sisters who have previously been circumcised transport the female to a secluded area in the home, a special hut, or a designated place by a sacred river or tree. The child may be permitted to see where she is being taken or she may be blindfolded and gagged, left only to hear the voices and the footsteps of those who surround her with song and dance (McCaffrey, 1995). Once they have arrived, she is often immobilized on her back with her legs spread. Untrained midwives, traditional birth attendants, or elderly women carry out the "surgical" procedure; they might use unsterilized razor blades, scalpels, scissors, knives, broken glass, sharp rocks, tin lids, or even their own teeth to remove the flesh. In most instances, there is no use of anesthesia, antiseptics, or analgesics, and the female must struggle through an undetermined length of excruciating pain (as it is critical that the circumcision be performed to perfection). In the case of infibulation, the raw edges of the labia majora are sewn together using catgut or thorns, and a small sliver of wood or straw is inserted into the vagina to leave an opening for the passage of urine and menstrual flow (Whitehorn, Ayonrinde, & Maingay, 2002). Post procedure, a mixture of herbs, milk, eggs, ashes, or cow dung is applied to the wound to facilitate the healing process. Sometimes a girl's legs are bound together for 40 days and she is brought to a secluded recovery area where she is afforded minimal contact with the outside world.

To truly grasp the experience of genital mutilation, we have provided a lengthy excerpt written by a Somali woman who underwent the procedure at the age of 5:

> The night before my circumcision, the family made a special fuss over me and I got extra food at dinner. Mama told me not to drink too much water or milk. I lay awake with excitement, until suddenly she was standing over me,

motioning. The sky was still dark. I grabbed my little blanket and sleepily stumbled along after her.

We walked out into the brush. 'We'll wait here,' Mama said, and we sat on the cold ground. The day was growing lighter; soon I heard the click-click of the gypsy woman's sandals. Then, without my seeing her approach, she was right beside me.

'Sit over there.' She motioned toward a flat rock. There was no conversation. She was strictly business.

Mama positioned me on the rock. She sat behind me and pulled my head against her chest, her legs straddling my body. I circled my arms around her thighs. She placed a piece of root from an old tree between my teeth. 'Bite on this.'

Mama leaned over and whispered, 'Try to be a good girl, baby. Be brave for Mama, and it'll go fast.'

I peered between my legs and saw the gypsy. The old woman looked at me sternly, a dead look in her eyes, then foraged through an old carpet-bag. She reached inside with her long fingers and fished out a broken razor blade. I saw dried blood on the jagged edge. She spit on it and wiped it on her dress. While she was scrubbing, my world went dark as Mama tied a blindfold over my eyes.

The next thing I felt was my flesh being cut away. I heard the blade sawing back and forth through my skin. The feeling was indescribable. I didn't move, telling myself the more I did, the longer the torture would take. Unfortunately, my legs began to quiver and shake uncontrollably of their own accord, and I prayed, Please, God, let it be over quickly. Soon it was, because I passed out.

When I woke up, my blindfold was off and I saw the gypsy woman had piled a stack of thorns from an acacia tree next to her. She used these to puncture holes in my skin, then poked a strong white thread through the holes to sew me up. My legs were completely numb, but the pain between them was so intense that I wished I would die.

My memory ends at that instant, until I opened my eyes and the woman was gone. My legs had been tied together with strips of cloth binding me from my ankles to my hips so I couldn't move. I turned my head toward the rock; it was drenched with blood as if an animal had been slaughtered there. Pieces of my flesh lay on top, drying in the sun.

Waves of heat beat down on my face, until my mother and older sister, Aman, dragged me into the shade of a bush while they finished making a shelter for me. This was the tradition; a little hut was prepared under a tree, where I would rest and recuperate alone for the next few weeks (Dirie, 1999, pp. 1–2).

At present, Waris Dirie resides in New York and works closely with the UN campaigning against FGM.

PHYSICAL AND PSYCHOLOGICAL IMPLICATIONS

The painful and debilitating physical consequences of this life-altering procedure are dependent upon environmental and biological elements such as the unhygienic conditions, the skill of the practitioner, the resistance of the child, and the body's susceptibility to infection. The immediate and long-term risks are innumerable and often have detrimental effects on general, sexual, and reproductive health. In addition, the subsequent psychological stress can influence a woman for her entire life.

General Physical Consequences

During the proximal aftermath of the procedure, excessive bleeding due to damaged veins is certain and hemorrhaging from dissection of the clitoral artery can result in bodily shock, loss of consciousness, or sudden death. The use of unwashed surgical tools as well as the traditional healing pastes can cause infections such as tetanus, septicemia, and gangrene (White, 2001). In addition, struggles of the child or careless performance on the part of the circumciser can cause injury to adjacent tissue, the urethra, or the rectum (Chalmers & Omer-Hashi, 2000).

Long-term effects are equally nocuous, particularly with infibulated women. The leg-binding process after the mutilation disallows fluid drainage, thus exacerbating the wound and increasing the likelihood of infection in the uterus, fallopian tubes, and ovaries. Chronic kidney and urinary tract infections are a byproduct of these internal disturbances and often lead to severe back pain and cramping (White, 2001). An excess of enlarged, raised, and irregularly shaped scar tissue can produce not only dermoid cysts the size of oranges, but also can cause excessive urine and menstrual buildup that is unbearably painful. Interestingly enough, this occurrence often results in a swollen stomach that can be misinterpreted as premarital pregnancy, a stigma that merits communal ostracism and/or family disownment. Cardenas (1999) shares a harrowing encounter between a physician and a circumcised woman.

> A doctor in Djibouti described the incident of a young girl brought to him with severe abdominal pain who had failed to menstruate for months and had a severely swollen abdomen. However, she was not pregnant. Upon opening the scarred tissue of her infibulated vulva, he discovered the problem was that the hole left from her Infibulation was too small to let out the 3.4 liters of foul-smelling blood she had retained inside her (p. 296).

Not often cited in the literature is an increased risk of blood-born sexually transmitted diseases such as HIV and hepatitis due to laceration during vaginal intercourse, engagement in anal intercourse (because the vaginal opening is too small), and the use of contaminated surgical tools (Amnesty International, n.d.).

Sexual Consequences

Complications arise on a woman's wedding night when marriage is consummated via sexual intercourse. Penetration can be arduous and painful, taking weeks or months to naturally enlarge the narrow vaginal entrance. Coital difficulty can be so intense that a woman must succumb to deinfibulation (splitting the bridge of the skin that covers the vulva). In a study by Dirie and Lindmark (1992), 87% of Somali participants were administered this procedure without the use of instruments, while 23% were deinfibulated by midwives, husbands, or close relatives of the husband with knives, razors, and scissors. Even more invasive is the following procedure that was documented by a traveler on her trip to Africa.

> One of the women...visits the bridegroom immediately before the marriage in order to obtain exact measurements of his member. She then makes to measurement a sort of phallus of clay or wood and by its aid incises the scar for a certain distance and leaves the instrument, wrapped around with a rag, in the wound in order to keep the edges from adhering again (French, 1992, p. 110).

Reduced sexual sensitivity and persistent psychosexual dysfunction was documented in an investigation of 250 women from Ismailia, Egypt. El-Defrawi, Lotfy, Dandash, Refaat, & Eyada (2001) administered an Arabic version of the Sexual Behavior Assessment Schedule-Adult (SEBAS-A) and found that circumcised women were more likely than uncircumcised women to report statistically significant difficulties including less sexual activity, less enjoyment of sex, less frequency of orgasm, and more gynecological problems.

Pregnancy and Childbirth Consequences

Genital mutilation can make pregnancy and childbirth a harmful and fatal ordeal for the mother and the unborn child. Miscarriages occur due to upper genital tract infections and urine seeping into the female organs; in such cases, the fetus may be unable to exit the uterus (White, 2001). At the time of delivery, it is critical that qualified personnel are present to deinfibulate the vaginal area. This procedure will facilitate an unobstructed birth and allow for the use of modern technology to monitor the health of the fetus and mother. In cases where the circumcision has not been reopened, mothers suffer from prolonged labor, perennial tears, and they frequently give birth to brain dead or damaged infants. In addition, the formidable mortality rate for infibulated women is 20% due to the increased chance of massive blood loss (Lax, 2000).

The husband and wife often demand reclosing of the vaginal opening after childbirth is complete. This procedure attracts the same host of short-term and long-term health risks as the original genital mutilation. Gray (1998) interviewed several Sudanese women who claimed that "buttoning up" after giving birth was necessary to "be like a virgin again." One such woman was reinfibulated 11 times and jokingly said that a cesarean operation was a blessing in disguise.

Psychological Consequences

The literature's focus on the extreme physical complications often distracts from a discussion of the intense emotional effects of undergoing the procedure and coping with the lifelong obstacles. Anecdotal evidence reveals mental health problems that run the gamut from irritability, frigidity, and anxiety to depression, posttraumatic stress disorder, and psychosis (White, 2001). Females who feel as though their family members have betrayed them experience humility and lack of trust. Lax (2000) comments on those who are psychologically maimed beyond repair and says that "a sense that the self and its integrity has been destroyed pervades the psyche of the mutilated woman and may lead to suicide."

In an attempt to empirically validate the psychological impact of FGM, Osinowo and Taiwo (2003) evaluated the self-esteem and marital stability of 99 circumcised and uncircumcised women. Researchers administered the Self-Esteem Scale (SES) that evaluated confidence, worth, adequacy, competency, and acceptability as well as the Marital Instability Scale (MIS) that assessed current relational functioning and satisfaction. Results indicated that circumcised women expressed significantly lower levels of self-esteem and higher levels of marital instability as compared to uncircumcised women.

Psychological implications such as low self-esteem and marital instability are often the result of problematic sexual functioning and physical intimacy. The emotional pain that ensues is often undisclosed and can lead to marital discord or dissolution. Gray (1998) reveals two instances that ended in divorce, one in which the woman was unable to have intercourse with her husband due to a narrow vaginal path and another in which the woman decided against reinfibulation after giving birth and did not have a vaginal path that was narrow enough. The woman's subsequent experience of trauma and despair is truly unimaginable.

Anthropologists who inform intervention efforts point out that refusing to have the procedure might be more psychologically harmful than submitting. Women who are uncircumcised (and of age) are often viewed with contempt and disgust. Such a decision would result in communal teasing and isolation, an inability to marry, and shame and dishonor to the family. Abusharaf (1998) comments on the experience of an uncircumcised woman in Uganda.

> [She who is uncircumcised and] marries into the community is always lowest in the pecking order of village woman, and is not allowed to perform the public duties of a wife, such as serving elders. Uncut women are called girls, whatever their age, and they are forbidden to speak at community gatherings (p. 25).

SIGNIFICANCE OF FGM

Although many human rights activists would insist that there is no reasonable justification for genital mutilation, practicing community members share what they perceive as solid and rational explanations for its continuation. "Tradition" is the most commonly cited reason, and this elusive concept can be further divided into sociological, sexual, aesthetic, health, and religious factors (Chugulu & Dixey, 2000). An examination of the sociopolitical and historical context in practicing nations is essential to promote a greater understanding of the native lens through which FGM is viewed.

The societal framework in countries that practice FGM is built upon an overwhelming patriarchal influence and consequent segregation of the sexes. This deeply entrenched cultural pattern is molded early in life as girls are socialized to subordinate to boys in the family setting. Furthermore, "all issues and traditions are viewed and created from the point of the man. Segregation with its various degrees of seclusion and exclusion is the method through which women are kept under men's control and in their secondary place" (Gray, 1998). The following is an exploration of the five most commonly cited explanations for the perpetuation of FGM, all of which are inextricably tied to the distinct ideological structure of practicing communities.

Sociological Reasons

The desire to develop a cultural identity and the pressure to maintain social approval are core components of a female's decision to undergo FGM. The procedure is often termed "a rite of passage" that initiates girls into womanhood and promotes the integration of her rightful place in society (Omer-Hashi & Entwistle, 1995). Females state that the procedure affords them status, is a testament to their bravery, and illustrates their future ability to endure the pain of childbirth. In addition, entering into a marital union is viewed as a woman's primary life objective. "To get married and have children is a survival strategy in a society plagued by poverty, disease, and illiteracy. The socioeconomic dependence on men colors their attitude toward circumcision" (Abusharaf, 1998). The ability to marry is predicated upon a woman's circumcision and this makes the procedure an imperative.

Sexual Reasons

Family honor is of utmost importance in communities where FGM is practiced, and this virtue is highly dependent upon the chaste and modesty of females. According to anecdotal testimony, men and women believe that partial or full removal of the female organ is necessary to significantly reduce a female adolescent's sexual urges (Chugulu & Dixey, 2000). The custom creates and sustains the image of a woman as docile, asexual, obedient, and fertile. If the vaginal area is left untouched, it is believed that women will act wildly and crave men. Undergoing FGM is viewed as "the primary means for bringing the female body into line with what the culture considers to be appropriate sexuality" (Lax, 2000).

Once a woman enters into the covenant of marriage, female circumcision is necessary to ensure faithfulness and sexual temperance. Husbands fear that if uncircumcised, their wives will aggressively demand sex from them. In addition, the narrowing of the vaginal opening achieves the purpose of increasing the male's sexual pleasure during intercourse. According to the personal account of a Sudanese woman, "sex is a man's affair and [a woman] is only a means to approach it" (Gray, 1998).

Modesty and sexual devotion are also critical to patrilineal purity and lineage continuity. It is believed that undergoing female circumcision "guarantees" premarital virginity and postmarital monogamy, and it has been described as "the only means to secure legitimacy for the patriarchy" (Gray, 1998). The inferior status of the female in practicing societies is indisputable and the power differential between genders is only strengthened by the seemingly mandatory custom of FGM.

Aesthetic Reasons

FGM is often seen as a means of removing a woman's masculine qualities as the clitoris is viewed (from the male perspective) as "an unwelcome vestige of the male organ." The unmodified genitalia are described as ugly, dirty, unrefined, and nonhuman, and circumcision is seen as a vehicle that enhances feminine beauty. Women are often told that if the clitoris is left untouched, it will grow down to the ground and drag (Burstyn, 1995). Ridding themselves of a piece of flesh that is perceived as a physical deformity appears to be a preferable alternative to social castigation and bodily displeasure.

Health Reasons

It is believed that FGM is a necessary procedure to allow for a woman to fulfill her designated role as a docile sexual partner and a child bearer to her husband. Less extreme are the beliefs that the circumcision aids menstruation, fertility, and childbirth. More extreme are the perceptions that it prevents vaginal cancer, masturbation, and lesbianism (Omer-Hashi & Entwistle, 1995). Most extraordinary is the belief that the clitoris secretes a poisonous substance that will make a man impotent, kill him during penile contact, and cause infantile death during childbirth (Burstyn, 1995). All of these supposed health benefits of the operation are medically erroneous and leave no room for debate.

Religious Reasons

Muslims who practice FGM explain that its observance is a religious requirement that is delineated by the Koran and the Sunnah (a religious text composed of the words and actions of Prophet Mohammed). Muslim proponents of FGM often quote a vague statement in the Sunnah that makes reference to a woman removing a smaller amount of her genitalia than she originally intended (White, 2001). There is strong debate among Muslims as to whether FGM is a social or religious custom; however, Islamic scholars and historians provide evidence against the latter.

They often cite the fact that religious followers of Christianity, Judaism, and Animism practice FGM, and that it is rare or nonexistent in most other Muslim countries. They also point to several passages in the Koran that, they reason, oppose FGM. The text states that God created the clitoris for the sole purpose of generating pleasure, and scholars argue that because God created it, He must want it to exist (therefore it should not be removed). In addition, the Koran encourages the notion that a husband and wife should pleasure each other during sexual intercourse, and scholars claim that mutilating the genitalia reduces or eliminates a woman's pleasure. Lastly, the Koran says that Satan will try to trick humans into body modification, and this statement is often interpreted as forbidding altering the body as God created it (Religious Tolerance, n.d.). Despite tenuous support for the idea that FGM is a religious obligation, the issuances of fatwas (religious opinions) that support its continuance create confusion among Muslims as to the religion's direct stance on the issue (Cardenas, 1999).

ISSUES OF CULTURAL RELATIVISM

In recent years, the friction between supporters and critics has increased in intensity, and cultural relativists continue to emphasize the fact that a human rights violation in one culture may be viewed as morally and socially just in another. One must begin by acknowledging the historical significance of the custom as well as its value in maintaining the social structure of various communities. Those who claim that eliminating FGM will liberate individuals from an oppressive existence fail to take into account the unwavering support it receives from practicing females. The United Nation's Children's Fund (UNICEF) recently conducted an extensive project exploring prevalence rates, demographics, and attitudinal components of FGM. A statistical analysis revealed that as many as 80% of African females (15–49 years) support the continuance of FGM (UNICEF, 2005). For some women, FGM is not viewed as a human rights issue, but an "act of love" that glorifies the woman and makes her body more beautiful (Omer-Hashi & Entwistle, 1995). Empirical investigations that make use of the narrative interview cite that a high percentage of women are excited in anticipation of the procedure and are proud of the circumcision years later (Chalmers & Omer-Hashi, 2000). The fact that the majority of the practicing population condones the custom elucidates the complexity of the issue.

Several lawmakers have argued that legislation banning FGM violates one's internal and external freedoms, including the right to endorse and make decisions based upon religious or cultural belief systems (Tahzib-Lie, 2000). Richard Shweder (2000) entertains an interesting perspective on FGM, stating that it is a weak example of gender inequality. He points out that most practicing cultures also expect male members to undergo a communal initiation involving genital alteration. Moreover, he explains that FGM is not a practice whereby dominant men target and torture vulnerable women. Conversely, it is the women of society who perform the ritual and articulate its importance to younger generations. Lastly, he cites the lack of empirically sound investigations on the short-term and long-term medical side effects of the operation. Referring to the documented health risks, he says,

> These lists read like warning pamphlets that accompany many prescription drugs, which enumerate every claimed negative side effect of the medicine that has ever been reported (no matter how infrequently). They are very scary to read, and they are very misleading (p. 223).

Anthropologists, in the least, urge nonpracticing nations to surrender their ethnocentric definitions of "normal" and "beautiful" and judge others based on pertinent cultural standards. They highlight the fact that Western nations are equally as influenced by traditional gender roles, citing the drastic increase in extreme dieting and cosmetic surgery (Abusharaf, 1998).

Ultimately, notions of cultural pluralism and relativism are not in place to condone FGM, but to minimize cultural superiority and encourage a broadened understanding of the practice's sociopolitical significance. Acknowledging the practice's cultural rationale will become increasingly important as industrialized nations are confronted with the problem of FGM crossing its borders.

FGM IN DEVELOPED NATIONS

As the immigrant population continues to increase and diversify, developed nations are beginning to see more cases of FGM. Documentation of its prevalence is extremely difficult due to the secrecy with which it is practiced, however, it has been most frequently reported in Europe and North America (Amnesty International, n.d.). The Center for Disease Control estimates 168,000 women and girls (at a minimum) are at risk for genital mutilation in the United States, and that each year 7,000 or more women emigrate from countries in which almost all females are circumcised (Burstyn, 1995). Furthermore, 45% of these women live in metropolitan areas including New York City, Washington, D.C., Los Angeles, Houston, Chicago, and Philadelphia (Jones, Smith, Kieki, & Wileox 1997).

The uncertainty of arriving in a society that is built upon an unfamiliar value system creates psychological stress and emphasizes the need to preserve traditional customs within the confines of close-knit communities comprised of ethnically similar individuals. The acculturation process can seem daunting as they are exposed to Western routines that directly contradict their moral code. "The community here sees explicit sex on television, they hear a lot of alien things, and so it becomes more urgent for mothers to do this to their daughters so the girls don't fall into loose groups" (Burstyn, 1995). Practices such as FGM are purposefully engaged in to prevent complete assimilation and act as a comforting tie-to-homeland traditions.

The practice of FGM in developed countries has posed a serious challenge for the medical community. Specifically, obstetricians are confronted by circumcised women and must determine the safest and most efficient way of monitoring pregnancy given the constraints. Chalmers and Omer-Hashi (2000) conducted an extensive study evaluating the birth experiences of 432 Somali women who had undergone FGM. Most women (74.7%) reported a fear of seeking medical care and, on average, the first prenatal visit to a physician's office took place at 20.1 gestational weeks. Moreover, cesarean section was desired by less than 1% of participants but experienced by more than 50%. Most disturbing is the finding that 87.5% of the women reported receiving hurtful comments by their physicians, witnessing verbal and nonverbal expressions of surprise, being regarded with disgust, being asked for permission to call a colleague, and having no respect shown for their cultural preferences. Unfortunately, physicians often remain silent upon witnessing circumcised genitalia either in an attempt to be culturally sensitive or as a response to shock. Eke and Nkanginieme (1999) argue that "shying away from the issue for the sake of political correctness is morally unacceptable, as the fear of being culturally out of one's depth may cause neglect of the medical and psychological needs of circumcised women."

Another ethical dilemma arises as women request reinfibulation after giving birth. In the past, physicians have resewn the genitals in an attempt to be culturally appropriate. McCaffrey (1995) has conversed with some women who have become angry upon finding out that their genitals have been resutured despite no prior discussions with the doctor. Most recently, various medical communities have issued guidelines stating that no woman should be recircumcised after birth.

INTERVENTIONS

Legislation

The global diffusion of FGM has recently compelled the UN to label the practice as a public health issue that warrants serious attention. International efforts to eliminate FGM began in 1979 when WHO declared it as a human rights violation (Abusharaf, 1998). Since then, governmental organizations including the Convention on the Elimination of All Forms of Discrimination Against Women (CEDAW), the Convention on the Rights of the Child (CRC), and the Vienna Declaration and Programme of Action (VDPA) have published statements against the practice (Cardenas, 1999). To combat the domestic occurrences of FGM, the U.S. Congress passed the Female Genital Mutilation Act of 1996 making it a federal crime to perform FGM on girls under 18 years of age. This act also requires that the Department of Health and Human Services compile data on the number of females who have undergone FGM and educate the health care community on its adverse effects (Williams, Aeopta, & McPherson 1999).

Sociologists and lawmakers argue that that formal legislation banning FGM might force the practice to become even more secretive. For example, parents might be reluctant to seek medical care for their children for fear of getting arrested. Cardenas (1999) elucidates the difficulty with relying on governmental sanctions in nations where the prevalence of FGM is extremely high. She explains, "criminal sanctions might not work if the majority of the society is convinced that female circumcision serves the common good, because criminal sanctions are only effective once a substantial body of public opinion has been raised against the practice." These issues demonstrate the need for legislative efforts in addition to a grassroots approach that targets the practice at a communal level.

Guidelines for Taking Action

An understanding of the rationale behind the practice of FGM, domestically and internationally, is critical prior to policy implementation that attempts to eliminate its occurrence. Such knowledge will only help to create multifaceted, effective interventions (Hayford, 2005). The WHO framework for action delineates an all-encompassing intervention that begins with encouraging nations to adopt and enact a clear policy on FGM. After legislation is in place, countries should establish nongovernmental organizations, social agencies, and advocate groups that work to educate individuals about FGM. The focus should be on informing all community members including religious leaders, traditional healers, birth attendants, men, women, boys, and girls about health risks and alternative options (UNICEF, n.d.). Despite common conceptions that changing male attitudes in a patriarchal society will facilitate eradication, interventions should concentrate on the women who are responsible for the intergenerational transmission of the practice. "Immediate accountability lies with the generation that abuses the next generation" and it is important to gradually enable the younger generations to resist the pressure of practicing FGM (Joseph, 1996).

Interventionists are urged to clarify that eradication efforts are not an attempt to "westernize" nations, but have the purpose of protecting women and children from a physically and mentally destructive practice (Williams *et al.*, 1999). Ideally, community members should implement the programs as they might appear to be less imperialistic. Equally as important is developing rehabilitation centers for women who have suffered from FGM. Such places are safe havens where families can come to receive continuous medical and psychological treatment (UNICEF, n.d.).

International Programs

Humanitarians argue that, "... opposition to female circumcision has become so politically correct" and this has clouded the vision of policy makers and social agencies (Shweder, 2000). Many reformists urge nations to set small goals such as eliminating the most hazardous forms of FGM and making the existing types surgically safe rather than attempting to incite an overhaul of a culture's value system and societal framework. Cardenas (1999) sees condoning any form of the practice as problematic and posits that allowing doctors to perform circumcisions will imply that FGM is safe and destroys attempts to completely eliminate the cultural practice.

Chelala (1998) has reported on an alternative way to stop FGM that is practiced in several Kenyan communities. "Circumcision Through Words" is a week-long program that entails counseling, training, education, and rituals that involve the entire family. More specifically, the girls are secluded and taught basic anatomy and physiology, sexual and reproductive health, hygiene, development of self-esteem, and resistance to peer pressure. The final day of the program is a celebration where women receive special gifts as well as a certificate formalizing the completion. Thus far, 300 women have experienced this alternative rite of passage and it continues to be promoted in other practicing nations.

It is also extremely important to acknowledge barriers to elimination and utilize them to inform the development of future intervention strategies. One should consider the fact that FGM is not necessarily a primary public health issue in places such Northeastern Africa. Situations such as the AIDS pandemic, ongoing civil wars, and the lack of food and water are of greater concern and merit immediate attention (Gray, 1998). Moreover, eradiation of FGM requires the involvement of numerous family members that need to be convinced. There have been several reported instances of a wife secretively whisking her daughter off to be circumcised despite the husband's adamant opposition (Joseph, 1996). The practice of FGM also serves as an economic benefit for the circumcisers as well as the father's of the young women who subsequently "marry off" their daughters in exchange for dowry. Providing incentive such as monetary compensation for promoting less invasive traditional practices is suggested (Chugulu & Dixey, 2000).

Programs in Developed Nations

The programs in developed nations also focus on intervening at the community level; however, extreme difficulty with determining the demographical sketch of FGM (i.e., location, frequency, etc.) has hampered preventative efforts. Various countries begin the intervention process by educating immigrants prior to, or at the time of, their arrival. For example, the U.S. Immigration and Naturalization Service provides information on the health risks and legal consequences of FGM to all aliens who are issued immigrant or nonimmigrant visas (White, 2001). As eradication efforts succeed in Third World countries, the number of individuals who flee their homeland to avoid FGM might increase. As a result, it will be important that surrounding countries willingly grant refugee and asylum status to these immigrants (Bosch, 2001).

The lack of knowledge in the medical community about caring for individuals who have undergone FGM suggests that training for doctors and nurses is crucial. One possibility is to facilitate exchange programs whereby doctors from industrialized nations learn from their African counterparts by providing medical services in practicing nations (Abusharaf, 1998). In the least, specialized care for individuals who have undergone FGM should be readily available and marketed. In addition, the mental health field should prepare to deliver individual, couples, and family therapy to those who have left their country of origin. Psychologists must learn the optimal way to provide effective treatment in a culturally sensitive manner (Omer-Hashi & Entwistle, 1995).

CONCLUSION

After decades of debate regarding FGM, there is agreement among human rights activists, scholars, medical practitioners, and policy makers that the custom must be eradicated. It is an invasive and brutal practice that affects women around the globe, often marring the physical body and psyche for a lifetime. Even more problematic is the fact that FGM is an institutionalized form of violence against women that is accepted by the government and seen by the community as a cultural obligation (Denmark, Rabinowitz & Sechzer 2005).

Addressing FGM as an international and domestic public health issue is a challenging task, and cooperation among governments, social agencies, and community members is of primary importance. Effectiveness is predicated on a deep awareness of the sociocultural dynamics within practicing groups that will inform the educational component of eradication programs. Thus far, educational programs that highlight the health risks associated with FGM seem to have the most influential effect on prevalence rates (Chugulu & Dixey, 2000). There is a common finding that educated women are less likely to circumcise their daughters and conclusions such as this highlight the need for continued exploration of preventative factors.

Deepening the research on sociocultural variables in practicing communities as well as intervention effectiveness is imperative, as empirically supported findings will serve to aid program design and strengthen the communal response. Topics of interest include the behavioral determinants of FGM such as male beliefs, children's conceptions, and social pressures to conform. In addition, reporting on prevalence rates and attitude changes after program implementation will be essential (Leye, 2001). It is important for interventionists to remember that the elimination of a cultural practice with a history that spans more than 5,000 years will require a lengthy commitment. The UN remains hopeful that carefully constructed interventions will effectively reduce this destructive form of gender abuse that violates and exploits women worldwide.

REFERENCES

AMNESTY INTERNATIONAL. N.D. Female Genital Mutilation: A Human Right's Information Pack. Available at http://www.amnesty.org/ailib/intcam/femgen/fgm1.htm. Accessed June 10, 2006.

ABHUSARAF, R.M. 1998. Unmasking tradition. Sciences *25*, 22–27.

BOSCH, X. 2001. Female genital mutilation in developed countries. The Lancet *358*, 1177.

BURSTYN, L. 1995. Female circumcision comes to America. Atl. Mon. *17*, 28–35.

CARDENAS, A. 1999. Female circumcision: the road to change. Syracuse J. Int. Law Commer. *26*, 291–313.

CHALMERS, B. & K.O. OMER-HASHI. 2000. 432 Somali women's birth experiences in Canada after earlier female genital mutilation. Birth *27*, 227–234.

CHELALA, C. 1998. An alternative way to stop female genital mutilation. The Lancet *352*, 126.

CHUGULU, J. & R. DIXEY. 2000. Female genital mutilation in Moshi rural district, Tanzania. Int. Q. Community Health Educ. *19*, 103–118.

DENMARK, F.L., V.C. RABINOWITZ & J.A. SECHZER. (Eds.) 2005. Engendering Psychology: Women and Gender Revised. Pearson Education, Inc. New York, NY.

DIRIE, W. 1999. The Waris Dirie Story. Available at http://www.fgmnetwork.org/articles/Waris.html. Accessed June 10, 2006.

DIRIE, W. & G. LINDMARK. 1992. The risk of medical complications after female circumcision. East Afr. Med. J. *69*, 479–482.

EKE, N. & K.E. NKANGINIEME. 1999. Female genital mutilation: a global bug that should not cross the millennium bridge. World J. Surg. *23*, 1082–1086.

EL-DEFRAWI, M.H., G. LOTFY, K.F. DANDASH, A.H. REFAAT & M. EYADA. 2001. Female genital mutilation and its psychosexual impact. J. Sex Marital Ther. *27*, 465–473.

FRENCH, M. 1992. The War Against Women. Summit Books. New York, NY.

GRAY, C.S. 1998. A case history based assessment of female genital mutilation in Sudan. Eval. Program. Plann. *21*, 429–436.

HAYFORD, S.R. 2005. Conformity and change: community effects on female genital cutting in Kenya. J. Health Soc. Behav. *46*, 121–140.

JONES, W.K., J. SMITH, B. KIEKI & L. WILCOX. 1997. Female genital mutilation: who is at risk in the U.S. Public Health Rep. *112*, 369–377.

JOSEPH, C. 1996. Compassionate accountability: an embodied consideration of female genital mutilation. J. Psychohist. *25*, 2–17.

LAX, R.F. 2000. Socially sanctioned violence against women: female genital mutilation in its most brutal form. Clin. Soc. Work J. *28*, 403–413.

LEYE, E. 2001. The struggle against female genital mutilation/female circumcision: the European experience. *In* Understanding Circumcision: A Multi-Disciplinary Approach To A Multi-Dimensional Problem. G.C. Denniston, F.M. Hodges & M.F. Milos, Eds.:113–128. Kluwer Academic/Plenum Publishers. New York, NY.

MCCAFFREY, M. 1995. Female genital mutilation: consequences for reproductive sexual health. Sex. Marital Ther. *10*, 189–200.

OMER-HASHI, K.H. & M. ENTWISTLE. 1995. Female genital mutilation: cultural and health issues and their implications for sexuality counseling in Canada. Can. J. Hum. Sex. *4*, 137–147.

OSINOWO, H.O. & A.O. TAIWO. 2003. Impact of female genital mutilation on sexual functioning, self-esteem, and marital instability of women in Ajegunle. Ife Psychologia *11*, 123–130.

RELIGIOUS TOLERANCE. N.D. Female Genital Mutilation. Available at http://www.religioustolerance.org/fem˙circ.htm. Accessed June 10, 2006.

SHWEDER, R.A. 2000. What about "female genital mutilation"? and why understanding culture matters in the first place. Daedalus *129*, 209–232.

TAHZIB-LIE, B. 2000. Applying a gender perspective in the area of the right to freedom of religion or belief. Birgh. Young Univ. Law Rev. *3*, 967–987.

THE UNITED NATIONS CHILDREN'S FUND (UNICEF). 2005. Female genital mutilation/cutting: a statistical exploration. UNICEF. New York. NY.

THE UNITED NATIONS CHILDREN'S FUND (UNICEF). N.D. Child Protection: Female Genital Mutilation. Available at http://www.unicef.org/protection/index˙genitalmutilation.html. Accessed June 10, 2006.

WHITE, A.E. 2001. Female genital mutilation in America: the federal dilemma. Tex. J. Women Law *10*, 129–208.

WHITEHORN, J., O. AYONRINDE & S. MAINGAY. 2002. Female genital mutilation: cultural and psychological implications. Sex. Relationship Ther. *17*, 161–170.

WILLIAMS, D.P., W. ACOSTA & H.A. MCPHERSON. 1999. Female genital mutilation in the United States: implications for women's health. Am. J. Health Stud. *15*, 47–52.

WORD HEALTH ORGANIZATION (WHO). 2000. Fact Sheet 241: Female Genital Mutilation. Available at http://www.who.int/mediacentre.factsheets.fs241.en/. Accessed June 10, 2006.

International Sexual Harassment

JANET SIGAL

Psychology Department, Fairleigh Dickinson University, Teaneck, New Jersey 07666

ABSTRACT: This paper on international sexual harassment begins with a presentation of the definitions, models, and consequences of sexual harassment. Following this discussion, a description is given of a nine-country research program that examined reactions to academic sexual harassment. A brief review of incidence studies and international laws related to sexual harassment are also included.

KEYWORDS: sexual harassment; cross-cultural; international laws

INTRODUCTION

Fitzgerald (1993), in a landmark article, stated that approximately 50% of all women in the United States at some time would experience a type of sexual harassment, either in the workplace or in academic environments. In her article, Fitzgerald identified sexual harassment as the most frequent form of "sexual victimization" and as a category of violence against women. Sexual harassment also was described as a form of social control exerted by men to "keep women in their place."

Similarly, in an international context, the Fourth World Conference on Women (FWCW) Beijing Declaration (UN documents, 2004) included sexual harassment in its category of "physical, sexual, and psychological" violence against women.

Sexual harassment has been framed as an issue interfering with human rights in that victims experience extremely stressful and damaging physical and psychological effects, which prevent these individuals from achieving their rightful place in employment and educational settings.

In this chapter, I will discuss international sexual harassment. After presenting definitions, models, and consequences of sexual harassment in general, I will describe a research program that examined cross-cultural perceptions of academic sexual harassment. It is important to explore cultural differences in perceptions because public attitudes influence whether or not legislation

Address for correspondence: Janet Sigal, Ph.D., Psychology Department, Fairleigh Dickinson University, Teaneck, New Jersey 07666. Voice: 201-692-2314; fax: 201-692-2304.
e-mail: Janet2822@aol.com

against sexual harassment is developed and implemented (Sigal & Jacobsen, 1999). Following the description of the program, a brief survey of incidence studies related to sexual harassment and a consideration of international laws will be presented.

DEFINITIONS OF SEXUAL HARASSMENT

The U.S. Equal Employment Opportunity Commission (EEOC, 2005) identified sexual harassment as a violation of Title VII of the Civil Rights Act of 1964 in that it is a form of sexual discrimination. The formal EEOC definition is as follows:

> "Unwelcome sexual advances, requests for sexual favors, and other verbal or physical conduct of a sexual nature constitute sexual harassment when this conduct explicitly or implicitly affects an individual's employment, unreasonably interferes with an individual's work performance, or creates an intimidating, hostile, or offensive work environment" (p. 1).

In effect, the EEOC definition, first promulgated in 1980, categorized two forms of sexual harassment: *quid pro quo*, which basically includes "sex for favors" and a hostile or intimidating work or educational environment. In the most recent classification, the definition included the concept that the attention must be unwelcome, the gender of the victim can be female or male, the harasser can be either a supervisor (employer) or a peer, and the harassment does not have to include the firing of an employee to be actionable. The EEOC guidelines also apply to an educational setting where the harasser can be either a professor or a fellow student.

In recent years, psychologists have investigated authority and peer sexual harassment both in employment and academic settings including universities and high schools. Male to male harassment also has been examined, although the majority of sexual harassment victims are women (Stockdale, Visio, & Batra, 1999).

In 1995, Gelfand, Fitzgerald, and Drasgow identified three categories of sexual harassment: (i) "Gender harassment" includes hostile attitudes and put-downs of women such as insulting sexist jokes or comments, obscene or pornographic materials displayed in the workplace, and other acts designed to make women uncomfortable. (ii) "Unwanted sexual attention" is a category related to behaviors such as pressuring for dates and sexually related comments about appearance but there are no consequences of failure to comply. (iii) "Sexual coercion" is associated with both sexual bribery (sex for favors) and sexual intimidation (threats if the victim does not comply with the demands for sexual favors). Gender harassment and unwanted sexual attention categories are related to the hostile work or educational environment specified in the EEOC definition, and sexual coercion is characterized by *quid pro quo*.

In 1999, Fitzgerald *et al.* expanded the category of gender harassment to include both "sexist hostility," a term related to discrimination based on gender, and "sexual hostility," which is illustrated by persistent telling of sexually related jokes designed to make victims uncomfortable.

Although these distinctions have achieved general acceptance by sexual harassment researchers, Pryor *et al.* (1997) suggested that even definitions of sexual harassment are affected by cultural differences. In this study, the experimenters sampled college students in Australia, Brazil, Germany, and the United States. In the three westernized countries, students generally held negative attitudes toward sexual harassment and characterized the behavior as definitely unwelcome. In contrast, Brazilian students expressed less negative attitudes and tended to view sexually harassing behavior as "less of an abuse of power, less related to gender discrimination, and more likely to be a relatively harmless sexual behavior than did U.S. students" (p. 526). To interpret these cultural differences, Pryor *et al.* referred to DeSouza and Hutz (1996) who postulated that Brazil was a more "eroticized" society than the United States, and that sexual behavior was expected and seen as normal rather than unwelcome in Brazil.

Therefore, although the unwelcome nature of sexually harassing behavior is an integral part of the term, according to the standard definition established by the EEOC, it is apparent that the the same behaviors may be viewed in very different ways in various countries and cultures.

MODELS OF SEXUAL HARASSMENT

Sex Role Spillover Model

This model, which was developed by Gutek (1985) suggested that traditional sex role expectations would carry over into the workplace, particularly when women are employed in male-dominated settings. The sex role stereotype most relevant to sexual harassment would be seeing women as sex objects. In addition, "sexualization of the workplace" (Stockdale, Visio, & Batra, 1999, p. 62) increases the probability that women will be sexually harassed.

Sociocultural or Power Model

Tangri and Hayes (1997) describe the connection between sexual harassment in employment settings (and by extension in academic settings), and power in terms of translating power relationships existing in the world and replicating these relationships in the workplace. This theory suggests that men occupy power positions in the home, in government, and generally in the world (particularly in patriarchal cultures, a concept which will be addressed subsequently in this chapter) and therefore, this power differential will be reproduced in the workplace. This approach is consistent with the concept that sexual harassment is a form of social control, subordinating women in the workplace and in the world in general.

Integrative Organizational Model

Fitzgerald and her colleagues developed a theory of sexual harassment that currently appears to be the most relevant and empirically supported model (e.g., Fitzgerald *et al*., 1997). This model identifies two crucial factors which contribute to the expression of sexual harassment in the workplace: "organizational climate" and "job gender context." Organizational climate refers to workplaces where there is support for sexual harassment or at least where individuals are not punished for sexually harassing behaviors and victims are discouraged from reporting this type of behavior. Under these conditions, sexual harassment is likely to occur. In addition, job gender context once again refers to the nontraditional workplaces in which women are outnumbered by men and are employed in jobs which do not fit with traditional gender-role stereotypes. The model predicts that sexual harassment will be prevalent in these types of workplaces. For example, Fitzgerald, Magley, Drasgow, and Waldo (1999) found that 78% of women respondents in the military, a traditionally male-dominated profession, had experienced sexually related harassment in the previous year.

This model further proposes that sexual harassment experiences can lead to negative consequences including adverse psychological and physical effects as well as job-related reactions (e.g., dissatisfaction, increased absences from work).

The integrative model has received cross-cultural support but Cortina, Fitzgerald, and Drasgow (2002) suggested that cultural factors must inform any attempt to apply theoretical models to non-European-American samples.

OUTCOMES OR CONSEQUENCES TO SEXUAL HARASSMENT VICTIMS

Although general negative consequences to victims were predicted by the integrative model described above, empirical studies have examined specific possible adverse reactions and effects of being a sexual harassment victim. Stockdale (1998) surveyed a large sample of federal employees and found that those workers who had experienced a higher frequency of harassment reported more negative feelings about work and were more likely to quit than other individuals. The authors also found that when employees directly confronted the harasser, their outcomes were more negative than those who used passive coping approaches. Munson, Hulin, and Drasgow (2000) also found support for the integrative model's predictions of adverse consequences of sexual harassment in a longitudinal study of university employees, even though the majority of respondents had experienced only gender harassment. In a culturally significant study referred to earlier, Cortina, Fitzgerald, and Drasgow (2002) found that "more severe harassment phenomenology was associated with lowered satisfaction with work, co-workers, and supervisors as well as increased depressive, anxious, and somatic symptoms" for their Latina respondents (p. 306).

CROSS-CULTURAL STUDY ON PERCEPTIONS OF ACADEMIC SEXUAL HARASSMENT

In this section, I will focus on our cross-cultural nine-country study of reactions to and perceptions of academic sexual harassment (Sigal *et al*, 2005). I will begin with a description of situations in England, which led me to understand that attitudes toward and perceptions of sexual harassment in that country differed considerably from American attitudes. Following a discussion of the basic study and the results, I will present a brief consideration of cross-cultural sexual harassment incidence rates and international laws against sexual harassment.

I began our nine-country study in collaboration with a colleague in England in 1994. While we constructed a scenario of academic sexual harassment, I became aware of the differential attitudes toward sexual harassment of Americans and people from England as a result of several incidents. For example, I contacted an organization in London called Women Against Sexual Harassment (WASH). At that time, it was the primary organization that provided information and assistance to sexual harassment victims in England. WASH was staffed almost entirely by volunteers. After setting up an appointment and inquiring about directions to the agency, the director asked if I wanted the letterhead removed when she faxed me the directions. She indicated that most of the women who contacted her asked for an anonymous directions sheet because they feared retaliation if individuals in their company discovered that they were consulting with WASH. When I arrived at the building the organization was not listed on the directory because the director feared retaliation by the public.

Another incident occurred when I heard from an English university researcher. She replied to my invitation to participate in the study, indicating that she was very interested but that she was afraid to join our cross-cultural research team because she might be attacked on campus.

At the university where I began my collaboration, several incidents strengthened my suspicion that attitudes toward sexual harassment in England were very different from those in America. At that time, sexual harassment was and still is a significant problem in the United States, but following the Anita Hill/Clarence Thomas Senate Confirmation Hearings in 1991, there was considerable attention in the press and among the public focused on the issue. In general, American press coverage reflected negative attitudes toward sexual harassers. Contrary to the generally negative views characterizing these attitudes in the American press, the national press in England appeared to reflect quite a different view toward sexual harassers. At the time of my visit to the university where I was collaborating with my English colleague, a male professor had been "sacked" by a university tribunal after accusations that related to his unwanted sexual attentions toward a female student. A national newspaper reported on an interview with the dismissed professor and also printed an editorial based on the case entitled: "Dons will be Juans." The professor was accused of pursuing a female student who repeatedly told him that his advances were unwelcome. Even though his wife complained when he told her of his pursuit of the student, he claimed that it was justified because his marriage was boring and he wanted some excitement in his life. In the editorial, the newspaper stated that the professor was only behaving naturally and taking advantage of the "perks of being a professor" by seducing his female students. The editorial implied that if it were not for admiring female students, there would be no one to listen to "professors' fusty old opinions and theories." The newspaper also argued that English universities did not want to emulate American universities with "sexual harassment officers" interfering with "normal academic" interactions.

These cross-cultural differences in attitudes became particularly clear when I gave a presentation on sexual harassment to the university community. I was informed by my colleagues that I was treated courteously because I was an American researcher. If I had been from the United Kingdom, these colleagues stated, the audience would have thrown rotten tomatoes and eggs at the speaker!

Design and Materials of the Cross-Cultural Study

We developed a two-part study on perceptions of academic sexual harassment. College students first read a scenario in which a male professor was accused of sexually harassing a female student. The harassment described was in the form of unwanted sexual attention: persistent requests for dates, unwanted nonsexual touching, and sexually related remarks about the student's appearance. There was testimony from the student clearly indicating that the attention was unwanted. In response, the accused professor denied the sexual harassment charge and protested that he only wanted to date the student becaue they were both single. Students were told that the victim was bringing charges against the professor before a University Hearings Committee. Participants were asked to imagine that they were members of this committee.

Following the scenario, participants answered questions related to whether or not the professor was guilty of sexual harassment and what punishment should be administered to the professor if he were judged to be guilty. Responsibility measures also were administered. In addition, students completed the Tolerance for Sexual Harassment Inventory [(TSHI); Lott, Reilly & Howard, 1982] measuring general attitudes toward sexual harassment.

We are fortunate to have considerable international diversity in our masters and doctoral student programs, and several students in the programs recruited student participants from their native countries. In addition, I established some connections with international colleagues who participated on our cross-cultural research team. As a result, we were able to compare the attitudes and perceptions of more than 700 college student participants from the following countries:

1. United States
2. Canada
3. Ecuador
4. Germany
5. the Netherlands
6. Pakistan
7. the Philippines
8. Taiwan
9. Turkey

The same scenario was administered in all countries but researchers in each country reviewed the scenario for cultural appropriateness. Few alterations other than name changes were required in most countries with the exception of Pakistan. In this sample, we had to describe the female victim as being engaged rather than dating someone, because any woman who is dating in Pakistan is considered a "loose woman." In addition, we had to eliminate the section describing the professor touching the victim in a nonsexual way, because any touching between unrelated men and women is forbidden in Pakistan.

The materials were translated in the Netherlands, Taiwan, and Turkey, and administered in English in the other countries. Recruitment details varied from country to country. In the United States, all of our samples were recruited from an Introductory Psychology Research Participant Pool. In the Netherlands, Taiwan, and Turkey, students were recruited from classes. In the other countries, researchers approached student participants on campus. The most unusual recruitment approach was adopted by one of our researchers from Pakistan who obtained some of her volunteer college students during a long flight from Pakistan to the United States.

RESULTS OF OUR CROSS-CULTURAL STUDY

We used the framework of individualist versus collectivist cultures to organize and interpret some of our findings. This cultural distinction was developed originally by Hofstede (1980). Although the concept is more complex than originally thought, and various subcultures, particularly in a country as populous as the United States, may consist of both individualist and collectivist citizens, the classification still has heuristic value. According to this conceptualization, people in individualist cultures such as the United States generally tend to be focused on the individual and the rights of the individual rather than being concerned with the welfare of the group or the community. On the other hand, in collectivist cultures, the emphasis is on belonging to the family, larger groups, the culture, and the country rather than on the rights and accomplishments of the individual.

Based on Hofstede's rankings, we classified the following countries as more individualistic:

(1) United States
(2) Canada
(3) Germany
(4) The Netherlands

The following countries were classified as more collectivistic:

(1) Turkey
(2) The Philippines
(3) Taiwan
(4) Pakistan
(5) Ecuador

As we predicted, students from individualist cultures were more convinced of the professor's guilt and assigned more responsibility to the accused harasser than individuals from collectivist cultures. Individual country participants also exhibited more negative attitudes toward sexual harassment in general than collectivist participants. These results are consistent with the conceptualization of individualist country citizens as being more concerned with individual rights than collectivist country participants. In this case, sexual harassment can be viewed as an infringement on these rights, which would be of more concern to individualist country participants than to collectivist culture participants for whom harmony in society is most important.

The pattern of selected punishment options for the accused harasser was less clear-cut. Including penalty options as a measure has produced interesting results in past studies. For example, DeSouza, Pryor, and Hutz (1998) found that American participants (individualistic culture) advocated more severe penalties for an accused academic sexual harasser than Brazilian (collectivistic culture) respondents. Similarly, we had hypothesized that participants from individualistic countries would select more severe penalties than those from collectivistic countries, but our initial analysis suggested the opposite results. Further analyses revealed that three countries contradicted the expected pattern of penalty selections. Participants from both Germany and the Netherlands selected more lenient punishment, and Taiwanese participants selected more severe punishment than would be predicted from the nature of the cultures in each of these countries. A variety of explanations were offered for these surprising results. We suggested that because German respondents were concerned with the rights of individuals, they might be reluctant to impose severe penalties, which would certainly affect the accused professor extensively. More persuasively, for respondents from the Netherlands, we proposed that there have been indications in previous research that these individuals prefer a more rehabilitative rather than a retaliatory approach to punishment, (e.g., Marlatt & Tapert, 1993) which may extend to judgments about our scenario. On the other hand, although Taiwan is basically characterized as a collectivist society, the large number of offenses which can result in the death penalty in that country suggests a retributive form of justice.

In terms of the preference for more lenient penalties by respondents from the Philippines, Pakistan and Turkey, we offered several interpretations for these results. One major explanation focuses on the patriarchal nature of the culture, and the traditional gender-role attitudes that exist, particularly in Pakistan and Turkey. In patriarchal cultures, the male role is dominant and the woman often is totally restricted to a domestic role primarily in the home. In extreme patriarchal societies, such as has been the case in Saudi Arabia, women are not permitted to leave the home without being accompanied by a male relative. Even in relatively modern cities in Pakistan such as Karachi, a woman may only walk alone and in Western dress in certain areas of the city without being censured and accosted for not being traditionally veiled and cloaked. In this type of culture, individuals may be protective of the "patriarch" and therefore may refuse to assign severe penalties, particularly for this type of sexual harassment. Once again, traditional gender roles also reinforce the relative power roles of men and women in society, thus leading to potential leniency toward men who engage in behavior that might be punished in other societies.

An alternative interpretation relates to the nature of a collectivist society. In the Philippines, for example, individuals may refuse to punish an accused professor because it would interfere with the harmony at the university. Again, protecting the reputation of the group or the organization is paramount. Finally, Ecuadorian respondents may have selected the more lenient punishment options because in Latin America, as discussed earlier, sexual harassment is viewed as more "normal" and less negatively than in other countries. In fact, one of our respondents from Ecuador classified the alleged sexual harassment victim as crazy for even reporting the professor's behavior to the committee and suggested that she be institutionalized.

Finally, our other major finding was that women judged the accused professor to be guilty more often and selected more severe punishment for the harasser than men. This reaction is consistent with the results of other studies (e.g., DeSouza, Pryor, & Hutz, 1998). Women have been victims of sexual harassment more often and would be expected to identify more with a female sexual harassment victim than men.

INCIDENCE OF SEXUAL HARASSMENT CROSS-CULTURALLY

It is almost impossible to obtain accurate figures on the incidence of sexual harassment in nations around the world, particularly in cultures where the topic is not publicly discussed. As a result, it is difficult to compare incidence figures in various countries, especially when victims are discouraged from reporting. In addition, methodological issues complicate the picture, including the use of nonstandardized measures of sexual harassment experiences, the difficulties associated with the recruitment of respondents, which brings into question the representative nature of the samples, and the conditions and procedures of administration in different studies (Sigal & Jacobsen, 1999).

In general, incidence rates in individualistic countries such as Canada and Western Europe are comparable to rates in the United States, although estimates can range from very low rates to more than 90% (Timmerman & Bajema, 1999). A further report by the International Labour Organization (ILO, 2003) revealed that 2% or 3 million employees in European Union (EU) countries had experienced sexual harassment with female workers experiencing higher rates than male employees. The report suggested that these figures vary considerably from country to country and probably do so because of differential rates of reporting rather than varying rates of sexual harassment.

Data from Asian countries suggest somewhat higher rates of sexual harassment. For example, a 2001 survey in Japan indicated that approximately 75% of all respondents had experienced sexual harassment at least once (Killion, 2004). This figure was consistent with the results from a study in Korea also reported in the International Labour Organization's paper. Recently, Killion (2004) suggested that sexual harassment of women is not even thought to be a social problem in Mainland China because economic issues and progress always are considered to be more important than any human rights issue. Killion asserted that in China, laws are not being developed and international standards of safeguards against sexual harassment are not implemented, leaving women without any official options to combat sexual harassment in the workplace.

Although DeSouza, Pryor, and Hutz (1998) suggested that Americans and Brazilian college students may experience similar rates of sexual harassment, Barak (1997) indicated that the picture may be more complex in terms of the type of harassment that may victimize individuals in Brazil.

In the Middle East, Turkey is described as a society in which harassment might be extensive on account of its patriarchal nature (Wasti *et al.*, 2000).

It is extremely difficult to obtain figures on sexual harassment in other patriarchal cultures such as Pakistan (Kamal & Tariq, 1997). However, Barak (1997) speculated that in India, a country in the same regional area, sexual harassment may be very prevalent.

Little research has been conducted in Africa related to the incidence of sexual harassment at the university level. However, one recent study by Simelane (2001) conducted under the auspices of the Forum for African Women Educationalists (FAWE) suggested that "all forms of sexual harassment were reported to be prevalent on the campus" at a major South African University (p. 3).

INTERNATIONAL LAWS AGAINST SEXUAL HARASSMENT

In 1992, Husbands indicated that only 9 out of 23 countries that were considered had specific legislation outlawing sexual harassment. By 2000, 31 countries were categorized as having sexual harassment legislation, but these laws varied considerably in terms of type of laws, penalties and enforcement (Sigal, 2004).

Sigal *et al.* (2005) suggested that there were at least three general types of statutes against sexual harassment:

(1) Statutes which permit sexual harassment victims to sue for damages (e.g., in the United , States);
(2) Statutes which identify sexual harassment as a crime (e.g., the Philippines and Taiwan); and
(3) Legislation which allows employees to quit their jobs and gain compensation from their employers (e.g., in Germany).

The EU and the Council of Europe (COE) have developed policies and directives against sexual harassment, which are translated into "legally binding law" in individual countries. Both organizations describe sexual harassment as sex discrimination, which interferes with a person's "right to dignity in the workplace." EU countries which are subjected to these directives include: Austria, Belgium, Cyprus, the Czech Republic, Denmark, Estonia, Finland, France, Germany, Greece, Hungary, Ireland, Italy, Latvia, Lithuania, Luxembourg, Malta, the Netherlands, Poland, Portugal, Slovakia, Slovenia, Spain, Sweden, and the United Kingdom.

The following countries are members of the COE and are required to implement these directives: Albania, Armenia, Azerbaijan, Bosnia and Herzegovina, Bulgaria, Croatia, the Czech Republic, Estonia, Georgia, Hungary, Latvia, Lithuania, Macedonia, Moldova, Poland, Romania, the Russian Federation, Serbia and Montenegro, Slovakia, Slovenia, and the Ukraine.

Since 1995, laws against sexual harassment have been established in Asia, Australia, Bangladesh, Japan, the Philippines, Sri Lanka, and Hong Kong,

China. In India, the Supreme Court identified sexual harassment as a significant social problem and specified steps or guidelines to prevent sexual harassment (ILO, 2001).

Brazil and other Latin American countries have signed the Inter-American Convention to Prevent, Punish and Extinguish Violence Against Women (TrendWatcher, 2001).

CONCLUSIONS

Sexual harassment clearly is acknowledged as a worldwide problem which particularly affects women (although men also can be victims), and interferes with the rights of individuals to enjoy a humane workplace and educational environment. Whether sexual harassment is viewed as a social problem, a form of sex discrimination against women, a type of violence against women, or a crime, it is clear that victims of sexual harassment in the workplace or in educational settings experience significant and devastating psychological and physical consequences. In workplaces and cultures which are supportive of sexual harassers and/or discouraging to women who try to report their harassing experiences, as suggested by the integrative model discussed earlier, the problem will not be eliminated in the near future.

International organizations including the United Nations, the International Labour Organization, the EU, and the Inter-American Conference have urged member nations to take steps to prohibit sexual harassment, particularly in the workplace. However, considerable research remains to be conducted to determine the exact incidence rates of sexual harassment cross-culturally, the influence of public attitudes on the promulgation of laws and punitive action, the effectiveness of legislation and other strategies on eliminating sexual harassment and implementing punishment of harassers, and the development of effective prevention programs to prohibit sexual harassment before it occurs. Sexual harassment is one of the most prevalent forms of violence against women and is symbolic of attempts worldwide to prevent women from achieving occupational success and economic independence.

REFERENCES

BARAK, A. 1997. Cross-cultural perspectives on sexual harassment. *In* Sexual harassment: theory, research and treatment. W. O'Donohue, Ed.: 263–300. Allyn & Bacon. Needham Heights, MA.

CORTINA, L.M., L.F. FITZGERALD & F. DRASGOW. 2002. Contextualizing Latina experiences of sexual harassment: preliminary tests of a structural model. Basic and Applied Social Psychology *24,* 295–311.

DESOUZA, E.R. & C.S. HUTZ. 1996. Reactions to refusals of sexual advances among U.S. and Brazilian men and women. Sex Roles *34,* 549–565.

DeSouza, E.R., J.B. Pryor & C.S. Hutz. 1998. Reactions to sexual harassment charges between North Americans and Brazilians. Sex Roles *39*, 913–928.
Equal Employment Opportunity Commission. March 2, 2005. Sexual harassment. Accessed March 12, 2006 from http://www.eeoc.gov/types/sexual_harasssment.html.
Fitzgerald, L.F. 1993. Sexual harassment: violence against women in the workplace. American Psychologist *48*, 1070–1076.
Fitzgerald, L.F., F. Drasgow, C.L. Hulin, *et al*. 1997. Antecedents and consequences of sexual harassment in organizations: a test of an integrated model. Journal of Applied Psychology *82*, 578–589.
Fitzgerald, L.F. , V.J. Magley, F. Drasgow & C.R. Waldo. 1999. Measuring sexual harassment in the military: The Sexual Experiences Questionnaire (SEQ-DOD). Military Psychology *11*, 243–263.
Fourth World Conference on Women (FWCW) Beijing Declaration November 8, 2004 to December 2, 2004. Violence against women. Accessed March 20, 2006 from http://www.un.org/womenwatch/daw/beijing/platform/declar.htm
Gelfand, M.J., L.F. Fitzgerald & F. Drasgow. 1995. The structure of sexual harassment: a confirmatory analysis across cultures and settings. Journal of Vocational Behavior *47*, 164–177.
Gutek, B.A. 1985. Sex and the workplace: impact of sexual behavior and harassment on women, men and organizations. Jossey-Bass. San Francisco, CA.
Hofstede, G. 1980. Culture's consequences. Sage. Beverly Hills, CA.
Husbands, R. 1992. Sexual harassment law in employment: an international perspective. International Labour Review *131*, 535–559.
International Labour Organization. 2003. The third European survey on working conditions. Accessed July 29, 2003 from http://www. ilo.org/public/english/protection/safework/violence/eusurvey/eusurvey.html
Kamal, A. & N. Tariq. 1997. Sexual harassment experience questionnaire for workplaces of Pakistan: development and validation. Pakistan Journal of Psychological Research *12*, 1–20.
Killion, M.U. 2004. Post-WTO China: quest for human right safeguards in sexual harassment against working women. Tulane Journal of International and Comparative Law *12*, 201–235.
Lott, B., M.E. Reilly & D.R. Howard. 1982. Sexual assault and harassment: a campus community case study. Signs *8*, 296–319.
Marlatt, G.A. & S.F. Tapert. 1993. Harm reduction: reducing the risks of addictive behaviors. *In* Addictive behaviors across the lifespan. J.S. Baer, G.A. Marlatt & R.J. McMahon, Eds.: 243–273. Sage. Newbury Park, CA.
Munson, L.J., C. Hulin & F. Drasgow. 2000. Longitudinal analysis of dispositional influences and sexual harassment: effects on job and psychological outcomes. Personnel Psychology *53*, 21–46.
Pryor, J.B., E.R. DeSouza, J. Fitness, *et al*. 1997. Gender differences in the interpretation of social-sexual behavior: a cross-cultural perspective on sexual harassment. Journal of Cross-Cultural Psychology *28*, 509–534.
Sigal, J. 2004. Sexual harassment. *In* Encyclopedia of applied psychology. C. Spielberger, Ed.: 393–403. Academic Press. San Diego: CA.
Sigal, J, M.S. Gibbs, C. Goodrich, *et al*. 2005. Cross-cultural reactions to academic sexual harassment: effects of individualist vs. collectivist culture and gender of participant. Sex Roles *52*, 201–213.

Sigal, J, & H. Jacobsen. 1999. A cross-cultural exploration of factors affecting reactions to sexual harassment: attitudes and policies. Psychology, Public Policy and Law *5*, 760–785.

Simelane, N.O. February 2001. Sexual harassment: a case study of the University of Natal, South Africa. Paper presented at the 10th General Conference of the Association of African Universities, Nairobi, Kenya.

Stockdale, M.S. 1998. The direct and moderating influences of sexual harassment pervasiveness, coping strategies, and gender on work-related outcomes. Psychology of Women Quarterly *22*, 521–536.

Stockdale, M.S., M. Visio & L. Batra. 1999. The sexual harassment of men: evidence for a broader theory of sexual harassment and sex discrimination. Psychology, Public Policy and Law *5*, 630–664.

Tangri, S.S. & S.M. Hayes. 1997. Theories of sexual harassment. *In* Sexual harassment: theory, research and treatment, W. O'Donohue, Ed.: 112–129. Allyn & Bacon.Needham Heights, MA.

Timmerman, G. & C. Bajema. 1999. Sexual harassment in northwest Europe: a cross-cultural comparison. The European Journal of Women's Studies *6*, 419–439.

Trend Watcher (2001. Global pressure to end gender bias. Accessed March 1, 2002 from http://www.hrinstitute.info/HRI_Scripts/TrendWatcher.asp?Issue=84.

Wasti, S.A., M.E. Bergman, T.M. Glomb & F. Drasgow. 2000. Test of the cross-cultural generalizability of a model of sexual harassment. Journal of Applied Psychology *85*, 766–778.

United Nations Measures to Stop Violence against Women

EVA E. SANDIS

Fordham University, New York City, New York, USA

ABSTRACT: This article consists of a brief overview of the involvement by the United Nations (UN) and nongovernmental organizations (NGOs) in worldwide efforts to expose and prevent violence against women. It begins with a depiction of the types of gender-based violence in contemporary society. Then follows a short history of the institutions and mechanisms created by the UN and civil society to prevent domestic and public violence against women. It concludes with a sketch of ongoing UN/NGO efforts to build on the momentum of the last decade, and suggests the challenges this presents to each and all of us in the new millennium.

KEYWORDS: nongovernmental organizations; NGO; Commission on the Status of Women; CSW

EXTENT AND TYPES OF GENDER-BASED VIOLENCE

Violence against women remains pervasive worldwide. It is the most atrocious manifestation of the systematic discrimination and inequality women continue to face, in law and in their everyday lives, around the world. It occurs in every region, country, and culture, regardless of income, class, race, or ethnicity.

So began United Nations (UN) Secretary General Kofi Annan's 2005 message on the International Day for the Elimination of Violence against Women (UN Dept. of Public Information, 22 November 2005). Gender-based violence is a global phenomenon, which affects millions of women and prevents them from enjoying their human rights. As the Secretary General pointed out, it cuts across class, race, ethnicity, and continent.

There are three areas of UN/NGO concern under which the major types of gender-based violence can be subsumed: the family, the community, and the State. In the family, women are vulnerable to a variety of gender-based types of violence, such as: infanticide, genital mutilation, marriage without the young woman's consent, dowry-related violence, battering, and sexual abuse. In the

Address for correspondence: Eva E. Sandis, 160 West End Ave. (20R), New York, NY 10023-5612
e-mail: sandis@fordham.edu

community, women are vulnerable to sexual harassment at work, commercialized violence, such as prostitution, pornography, and trafficking in women. Migrant women experience additional vulnerabilities as a result of their minority status. Finally, women are vulnerable to violence by the State, whether in custodial institutions or in situations of armed conflict, where rape is being ever more widely used as an instrument of war (UN/DPI, Feb. 1996/a, pp. 2–8). Unfortunately, even a cursory glance at the media provides a trove of examples of continuing gender-based violence today, worldwide, in all three areas of concern.

DEVELOPMENT OF UN MECHANISMS AGAINST GENDER-BASED VIOLENCE

Commission on the Status of Women (CSW)

Women's issues have been a UN concern since its inception. In the mid 1940s, when the human rights machinery of the UN was being shaped, the Economic and Social Council (ECOSOC) established the Commission on the Status of Women (CSW) as a specific body to deal with these women's issues. Currently, it consists of 45 members, elected by ECOSOC on a regional basis to serve for a four-year period (UN/CSW web site). Since its inception in 1946, the activities of the Commission have evolved from defining women's rights to investigating the factors that prevent women from enjoying and exercising them. The CSW examines women's progress toward equality throughout the world, prepares recommendations on promoting women's rights in political, economic, social, and educational fields, and drafts treaties aimed at improving the status of women in law and in practice (UN/DPI, 2000, p. 234).

Convention on the Elimination of All Forms of Discrimination against Women (CEDAW)

The Convention on the Elimination of All Forms of Discrimination against Women—often described as the international bill of rights for women—was adopted by the UN General Assembly (UNGA) in 1979. The drafting, by CSW, began in 1974, its task encouraged by support from the World Conference of the International Women's Year in 1975. Currently, there are 176 State Parties to the Convention. The USA signed on to CEDAW in July 1980, but it has not yet ratified the Convention and is therefore not legally bound by it (Multilateral Treaty Framework, 2004, pp. 23, 26).

The 16 substantive provisions of the Convention define discrimination, and spell out the appropriate measures, which States obligate themselves to carry out as Parties to CEDAW. They include measures to modify discriminatory social and cultural patterns hurtful to women's equality; to suppress the exploitation of women, including their trafficking; to eliminate discrimination against women in political and public life at the national and international level and in nationality laws; and to ensure women's equality in education, employment, social security, and health care.

It has been observed that CEDAW is the only human rights treaty to affirm the reproductive rights of women (Multilateral Treaty Framework, 2004, p.23). The relevant articles are 12–1 and 16–1e (Human Rights Fact Sheet 22, Annex 1). The Convention also established a CEDAW Committee of 23 experts to monitor the implementation of the Convention.

While the issue of gender-based violence is not specifically addressed in CEDAW, it is fundamental to its basic provisions, as the CEDAW Committee, at its 11th session affirmed, when it formally extended the general prohibition on gender-based discrimination to include gender-based violence, defining it as

> Violence that is directed at a woman because she is a woman or that affects women disproportionately. It includes acts that inflict physical, mental or sexual harm or suffering, threats of such acts, coercion, and other deprivations of liberty... (Human Rights Fact Sheet 22, 30–31)

United Nations Decade for Women (1976–1985)

A major development in consciousness raising on women's issues was the UN Decade for Women, which spanned three worldwide conferences: the first, already alluded to, in Mexico, in 1975; the second in Copenhagen, in 1980; and the third in Nairobi, in 1985. The document emanating from Nairobi, entitled *Strategies for the Advancement of Women to the Year 2000*, identified discrimination and violence against women as major obstacles to the achievement of the three objectives of the UN Women's Decade: equality, development, and peace. The Report noted with special concern the increase in gender-based violence against particularly vulnerable categories of women, such as victims of abuse (288), trafficked women (290), and migrant women (300). It called for legal measures to prevent gender-based discrimination and violence, and national machinery to deal with them (Report ... Nairobi, 1985).

Declaration on the Elimination of Violence against Women

These demands for progress on measures to eliminate gender-based violence bore fruit at the World Conference on Human Rights held in Vienna, Austria in 1993. One outcome of this Conference was the appointment of a Special UN Rapporteur on violence against women. The objective was to have this person serve as ombudsman, looking into causes of violence against women and recommending ways to eliminate them (UN/DPI, Jan.1995, p. 2). A second outcome was the adoption, by the GA in December 1993, of the Declaration on the Elimination of Violence against Women. In the Preamble, the GA expresses the hope that adoption of this Resolution will strengthen the process, set in motion by CEDAW, of implementing measures to end gender-based violence. The Declaration then proceeds to define what constitutes an act of violence against women, namely,

> any act of gender-based violence that results in, or is likely to result in, physical, sexual, or psychological harm or suffering to women—including threats of such acts, coercion, or arbitrary deprivation of liberty, whether occurring in public or in private life. (UNGA Declaration, 1993)

Next, three types of gender-based violence, which the Resolution "encompasses, but is not limited to" are spelled out: violence in the family; violence in the general community; and violence perpetrated or condoned by the State. Finally, the Resolution calls on States to take specific measures to eliminate all forms of violence against women, and on the international community to support these actions (UNGA Declaration, 1993).

Fourth World Conference on Women: Beijing (1995)

At the Fourth World Conference on Women in Beijing in September 1995, representatives from 189 countries unanimously adopted the Beijing Declaration and Platform for Action. The Platform identified 12 critical areas of concern considered to be the main obstacles to women's advancement. Two of these dealt with gender-based violence: violence against women and women and armed conflict. (UN/DPI, Feb. 1996b)

On these women's issues, the Platform's recommendations included actions to: adopt and implement legislation to end violence against women; work actively to ratify and implement all international agreements related to violence against women, including the UN Convention on the Elimination of All Forms of Discrimination against Women; adopt new laws and enforce existing ones to punish members of security forces and police and any other State agents for acts of violence against women; set up shelters, provide legal aid and other services for girls and women at risk, and provide counseling and rehabilitation for perpetrators of violence against women. Further, the Platform called for actions to step up national and international cooperation to dismantle networks engaged in trafficking in women; and to recognize the need to protect women living in situations of armed and other conflict or under foreign occupation, or who have become refugees or displaced (UN/Beijing, 2001, pp. 73–93).

United Nations High Commissioner for Refugees (UNHCR): Guidelines

Only a few months earlier, on International Women's Day, March 1995, the Geneva office of The United Nations High Commissioner for Refugees released a 73-page document entitled *Sexual Violence against Refugees: Guidelines on Prevention and Response* (UNHCR, 1995). Written for nonspecialists, it addresses the physical, psychological, and social effects of sexual violence within refugee communities. UNHCR field workers provided the core of the information for the recommendations in these Guidelines (UN-HCR, 1995). Since then, the Guidelines continue to be reassessed and revised to maximize the protection of refugees and internally displaced persons, with particular focus on preventing gender-based violence (Women's Commission for Refugee Women and Children, 2002).

Division for the Advancement of Women (DAW): Violence against Women Migrant Workers

In 1996, the United Nations Division for the Advancement of Women held an Expert Group Meeting in Manila on Violence against Women Migrant Workers (UN/DAW, 1996). Key issues considered at the meeting included: the dynamics of violence against women migrant workers; abuses faced by these women; and policies and mechanisms to address violence against women migrant workers. The meeting *Report* included a series of recommendations about needed actions to end violence against women migrant workers, for example, holding concerned States accountable, in accordance with the "due diligence principle," for their inaction on issues of violence against migrant women workers (UN/DAW, 1996, p. 21).

United Nations Development Fund For Women (UNIFEM) Campaigns against Gender Violence

On November 3, 1999, the GA passed a Resolution that officially designates November 25 as International Day for the Elimination of Violence against Women. The Resolution was an initiative of the United Nations Development Fund for Women (UNIFEM), created, at the behest of the UNGA, in 1976 to support the UN Decade for Women. Since then, the organization has worked tirelessly to advance women's human rights and foster their empowerment. It has focused its activities on four strategic areas: ending violence against women; reducing feminized poverty; reversing the spread of HIV-AIDS among women and girls; and achieving equality in democratic governance (UNIFEM About Us, 2005).

According to its mission statement, UNIFEM promotes the principle that the protection of women's human rights is fundamental to ensuring women's self-realization and full participation in society. Its activities include systemwide coordination on women's rights issues within the UN; promoting the full implementation of the measures set out in the Beijing Platform for Action; and developing a holistic and multidisciplinary approach to the task of combating violence against women.

UNIFEM has worked on several fronts to end the cycle of violence against women. Its strategies have included: establishing legal frameworks to combat violence against women; supporting research and collection of data on gender violence; supporting violence prevention initiatives from the local to the international level, including in conflict and postconflict situations; and supporting anti-violence initiatives of women's organizations. Furthermore, UNIFEM administers the Trust Fund to End Violence against Women, which offers grants to innovative projects to prevent violence that are run by community, national, and regional organizations (UNIFEM at a Glance: Ending Violence against Women).

UNIFEM has been an active participant in the annual commemoration of the International Day for the Elimination of Violence against Women since its inception, upon adoption of Resolution 54/134 by the UNGA in December 1999. Linked to the commemoration has been the annual international campaign of 16 Days of Activism against Gender Violence, which ends on the commemoration of International Human Rights Day, symbolically linking the two issues (UNIFEM Not a Minute More, 2005).

Beijing +5 (June 2000)

As the UN and NGOs entered the new millennium, the challenges to eliminate gender-based violence continued. The Special Session of the UNGA on Beijing plus 5—"Women 2000: Gender Equality, Development and Peace for the 21st Century," was held at UN Headquarters in New York from June 5 to 9, 2000. The Special Session undertook a comprehensive review and appraisal of progress made in the implementation of the Platform for Action produced at the Fourth World Conference for Women in Beijing in 1995. Before concluding, the GA adopted an Outcome Document, which enumerated further actions and initiatives to implement the Beijing Platform for Action (Beijing+5 Outcome Document, June 2000, pp.189–204, 213–221). The Outcome Document also referred to several areas of concern that had gained momentum since 1995. Prominent among these were the increase in gender-based violence, especially with respect to HIV-AIDS, trafficking of women and girls, and the marginalization of women in peace processes.

Having noted the slow and uneven pace in implementing the strategic objectives spelled out in Beijing five years earlier, participants at the Special Session called for the creation of measurable goals, time-bound targets, and effective monitoring to spur progress. These proposals were partially, but not fully, accepted due to the reluctance of some States to be monitored in these areas (Center for Women's Global Leadership, 24 Aug. 2001, p. 46).

Resolution 1325 (October 2000)

During the 2000–2001 sessions of the UN, the most historic event in support of women as peace builders and their protection against gender-based violence was the adoption of Resolution 1325 by the Security Council (SC) on October 31, 2000. Recalling the commitments of the Beijing Platform for Action, as well as those contained in the Beijing+5 Outcome Document, Resolution 1325 stresses the importance of women worldwide in peace building and conflict resolution, and the need to protect women and girls against violence, particularly in conflict situations. It includes specifically, calls for: an increase in the participation of women at decision-making levels in conflict resolution and peace processes; special measures to protect women and girls from gender-based violence, particularly rape and other forms of sexual abuse, and all other forms of violence in situations of armed conflict; and the responsibility of States to prosecute those responsible for genocide and war crimes, including those relating to sexual and other violence against women and girls (UN/SC, 31 Oct. 2000). NGOs hailed the Resolution's unanimous adoption by the SC as a "historic victory for women," publishing and circulating its contents to further its implementation (Hague Appeal for Peace, no date). Since then, there have been various follow-up studies and recommendations, notably the Independent Experts' Assessment on the Impact of Armed Conflict on Women (Rehn & Sirleaf, 2002).

At the UN, too, the wheels of progress grind slowly. Only a few months after the passage of the SC Resolution, a Council list of 25 candidates for judgeships on the International Criminal Tribunal for the former Yugoslavia contained the name of only one woman (UN/SC, 8 Feb. 2001). The vociferous consternation of a host of women's NGO representatives was relayed to Secretary General Annan in a letter from Angela E. V. King, UN Assistant Secretary General and Special Adviser on Gender Issues and Advancement of Women (King, Feb. 2000).

On a positive note, however, the conviction in February 2001 of three Bosnian Serbs for rape and sexual violence by the UN war crimes tribunal (read by Judge Florence Mumba of Zambia), historically defined rape for the first time as a crime against humanity (not just as torture). According to a *New York Times* editorial of February 24, this landmark ruling "shows the progress that women's issues have made in international justice," which used to consider mass rapes as natural occurrences of war (p. A-12).

The International Criminal Court (ICC)

The Rome Statute of the International Criminal Court, adopted on 17 July 1998, entered into force on July 1, 2002. As of 29 December 2005, there were 100 State Parties to the Statute (Rome Statute, Ratification Status). It is a permanent institution (unlike *ad hoc* tribunals), which acts on the principle of complementarity to national courts. Its function is to try individuals for the most serious crimes of international concern, including genocide, crimes against humanity, and war crimes.

Its establishment marks a new era of international justice and accountability for women (Rehn & Sirleaf, p. 94). The Statute encompasses forms of sexual violence, "including rape, sexual slavery, enforced prostitution, forced pregnancy and enforced sterilization" in the definition of crimes against humanity and war crimes. Persecution (with gender as a basis for persecution), and the crime of enslavement, including the trafficking of women and children, are also listed as crimes against humanity. Furthermore, rape and sexual violence can constitute acts of genocide. Women who testify are guaranteed witness protection, and the Court will establish reparations through compensation, restitution, and rehabilitation. Also, the ICC is creating a Trust Fund for victims (Rehn & Sirleaf, p. 64).

The Court's gender mainstreaming extends to the judges elected to serve on it. Of the 18 judges that were elected, 7 are women, and 2 of these now serve as the first and second Vice Presidents of the Court (International Criminal Court: *Historical Introduction*).

CURRENT UN EFFORTS TO STOP GENDER-BASED VIOLENCE

To gauge prevailing concerns of the UN with respect to the elimination of violence against women, this section focuses on the current activities of the General Assembly's Third Committee, on Social, Humanitarian, and Cultural Affairs. This Committee considers the broad issue of violence against women on a yearly basis, both under the rubric of the Advancement of Women and that of Human Rights Questions. Under the first rubric, its concern is with the situations of violence facing women and their elimination/prevention. In this context, the focus of the current, 60th Session, was on the ongoing study on violence against women, and the Secretary General's interim report regarding the study.

The Third Committee also focuses, on a rotating, biennial basis, on specific types of gender-based violence, such as trafficking in women, crimes against women committed in the name of honor, and domestic violence. The focus during the 60th Session was on violence against women migrant workers. Further, under the rubric of Human Rights Questions, the Third Committee hears from the Special Rapporteurs of the Human Rights Commission about what has transpired in their particular domains. These include violence against women, the human rights of migrants, and trafficking in persons.

Upon completing deliberation on the agenda items before it, the Third Committee forwards the draft texts it has adopted, in the course of its work to the GA for its consideration. The draft Resolutions, which the Committee sent to the GA before adjourning its latest, 60th Session, included one supporting the secretary general's study on violence against women, and another calling for the elimination of violence against migrant women workers. The GA adopted both these Resolutions before its December 2005 adjournment.

Study on Violence against Women Report of the Secretary General

The interim Report of the secretary general on violence against women (A/60/211) is in response to Resolution 58/185 of the GA (UN/SG, 10 Aug. 2005).

It requested him to conduct an in-depth study on all forms of violence against women, as identified in the Beijing Declaration and Platform for Action, disaggregated by type of violence. The GA asked that the study be conducted in close cooperation with all relevant UN entities, with the Special Rapporteur on violence against women, its causes and consequences, and with the collaboration of NGOs. The Resolution specifically calls for the inclusion, in the secretary general's study and in his Report to the GA, of action-oriented recommendations for consideration by States, encompassing effective preventive and remedial measures.

As the director of the Division for the Advancement of Women (DAW) of the Department of Economic and Social Affairs (DESA) Carolyn Hannan noted in introducing the Secretary General's Report on violence against women to the Third Committee on October 11, 2005, the document is an interim report, which highlights the context, goals, and scope of the study and gives an overview of ongoing and planned preparatory activities. The study itself will be submitted to the GA at its next, 61st, session, in 2006 (Hannan, 2005).

A look at the goals and scope of the study indicates the concerns motivating the project, namely: to highlight the global persistence of gender-based violence; to strengthen political commitments to prevent and eliminate such violence; and to identify ways for better and more sustained and effective implementation of government commitments to combat it, and increase accountability. In addition, it is expected that the study will enhance knowledge and expose data gaps regarding gender-based violence, identify good practices, and include action-oriented recommendations (UN/DAW 2005). The proposed chapters of the outlined study annexed to the secretary general's Report take up each of these issues (UN/ SG, 10 Aug. 2005).

On October 21, 2005, the Third Committee adopted a draft Resolution in support of the secretary general's in-depth study on all forms of violence against women. France's representative, its main sponsor, expressed hope that it would be a guiding light to Member States to change the mind-set of future generations to end violence against women (UN/DPI, 21 October 2005).

Violence against Women Migrant Workers Report of the Secretary General

The biennial Report of the Secretary General (A/60/137/Corr.1) on *Violence against women migrant workers* provides information on the legal and policy measures adopted by member States, as well as activities undertaken by entities of the UN system and other organizations to address violence against women migrant workers. In her introductory statement before the Third Committee (UN/SG, 13 Sept. 2005), Hannan noted that despite measures taken, the report shows that violence against women migrant workers remains an issue of concern (Hannan, 2005). As the Report notes in its conclusions and recommendations, "no specific legislation on violence against migrant women workers was adopted by Member States in the period under review" (69); further, "no information was provided ... on trends in violence against women migrant workers, or on surveys that might have been conducted on this issue" (70) (UN/S-G, 13 Sept. 2005).

Among its Recommendations, the Report emphasizes the need to continuously monitor measures to combat violence against women migrant workers (75); to improve access to legal channels for migration so as to reduce the vulnerability of women seeking to migrate to exploitation and trafficking (76); and to encourage governments to ratify international instruments, which address migration issues, particularly the International Convention on the Protection of the Rights of All Migrants and Members of Their Families, the United Nations Convention against Transnational Organized Crime and its two Protocols, and all relevant International Labor Organization (ILO) conventions. Furthermore, the Special Rapporteurs of the Commission on the human rights of migrants, on violence against women, its causes and consequences, and on trafficking in persons, especially women and children, should be invited to pay particular attention to the situation of women migrant workers (78) (UN S-G, 13 Sept. 2005).

On November 15, 2005, the Third Committee adopted a draft Resolution on eliminating violence against women migrant workers. Noting the recommendations in the secretary general's report on violence against women migrant workers, the Resolution calls on governments, particularly those of the countries of origin and of destination, to put in place penal and criminal sanctions to punish perpetrators of violence against women migrant workers. It also urges States to encourage NGOs in assisting and protecting victims of violence, and to cooperate fully with the Special Rapporteurs of the Commission on Human Rights (UN/DPI, 16 December 2005).

Special Rapporteur on Violence against Women, Its Causes and Consequences

Every year, the Special Rapporteurs of the Commission on Human Rights report to the GA their concerns and activities in the course of carrying out their mandates. They also present their findings regularly to the Commission on Human Rights in Geneva, and to the Third Committee of the General Assembly at UN Headquarters in New York. Their activities are also incorporated in the secretary general's Reports to the General Assembly, as, for example, that on his ongoing study of violence against women.

There, the secretary general noted the suggestion of the Special Rapporteur on violence against women, its causes and consequences, Yakin Ertuerk, that the boundaries of existing categories of gender-based violence needed to be broadened to encompass the transnational arena forged by globalization (UN/SG A/60/211, 21, 10 August 2005). In that expanding transnational arena, according to the Special Rapporteur, local and traditional forms of violence against women, such as honor crimes, have become globalized, and new forms of violence, such as trafficking for purposes of sexual and economic exploitation, have emerged (ECOSOC/Commission on Human Rights, 26 December 2003).

The most recent focus of the Special Rapporteur on violence against women has been on the intersection of violence against women and HIV-AIDS, considering violence both as a cause and consequence of HIV (UN/OHCHR, 6 April 2005). Ms Ertuerk's latest Report includes recommendations for an effective and integrated response to HIV-AIDS, first and foremost the elimination of violence against women through such means as full compliance by States with the requirements of the Declaration on the Elimination of Violence against Women; adoption of domestic violence laws; criminalization of marital rape; conducting gender sensitivity campaigns; and adopting gender analysis in overall policy making (ECOSOC/ Commission on Human Rights, 17 January 2005).

IN CONCLUSION: CHALLENGES AND CHOICES

As this brief sketch of UN activities indicates, there has been an ever mounting effort to end global gender-based violence through the creation and use of a variety of UN mechanisms: Declarations and legally binding Conventions; Global Conferences and Plans of Action; Expert Group Meetings, NGO Task Forces and UN Commissions; NGO Briefings and International Days; Press Releases and Internet Communications; Trust Funds; and the newly established International Criminal Court.

Nevertheless, at the onset of the new millennium, gender-based domestic and public violence is still very much in evidence worldwide. A quarter of all women still are raped during their lifetime. Depending on the country, 25% to 75% of women are regularly beaten at home. More than 120 million women have undergone female genital mutilation. Rape, sexual slavery, and forced pregnancy have devastated women and girls in conflict-torn societies around the globe, including Rwanda, Cambodia, Peru, and the former Yugoslavia (UNIFEM, 5 November 1999).

Assessing women's advances in her introductory remarks to the 60th session of the Third Committee, Assistant Secretary General Rachel Mayanja, Special Adviser on Gender Issues and Advancement of Women, stated that "we have made progress" but "many challenges remain," including violence against women, a challenge that requires immediate attention. The problem of gender-based violence is "increasingly becoming one of the highest priorities of intergovernmental bodies, UN entities, Governments, and civil society," according to Mayanja, but the continued support of the international community is needed to meet these challenges (Mayanja, 11 October 2005).

For nongovernmental organizations, on whose resources and partnership governments count, this is a significant opportunity to convince States to embrace their advocacy goals. The priorities with respect to eliminating violence against women are clear: (1) creation and implementation, at the national level, of legal instruments and policies to end/prevent gender-based violence; (2) creation and implementation, at the national level, of governance practices to end/prevent gender-based violence; and (3) regional cooperation among States to prevent the spread of local harmful practices to the transnational arena, or the creation of new forms of gender-based violence within the transnational arena. With international political will and coordinated pursuit of such an agenda, hopefully the challenge of gender based-violence will be met.

REFERENCES

BEIJING+5 OUTCOME DOCUMENT. (www.un.org/womenwatch/daw/followup/ress233e.pdf)

CENTER FOR WOMEN'S GLOBAL LEADERSHIP. (Aug. 24, 2001). *Holding on to the promise: women's human rights and the Beijing +5 review.* (www.cwgl.rutgers.edu/publications.htm)

ECONOMIC AND SOCIAL COUNCIL. 2003. Commission on Human Rights, integration of the human rights of women and the gender perspective: violence against women. *Towards an effective implementation of international norms to end violence against women. Report of the Special Rapporteur on violence against women, its causes and consequences, Yakin Ertuerk* (E/CN.4/2004/66) 26 December.

ECONOMIC AND SOCIAL COUNCIL, COMMISSION ON HUMAN RIGHTS. 2005. Integration of the human rights of women and the gender perspective: violence against women. *Intersection of violence against women and HIV/Aids. Report of the Special Rapporteur on violence against women, its causes and consequences, Yakin Ertuerk* (E/CN.4/2005/72) 17 January.

HAGUE APPEAL FOR PEACE. (no date) *Women count at last.* c/o IALANA, Anna Paulownastraat 103, 2518 BC The Hague, The Netherlands.

HANNAN, C. 2005. *Introductory statement* Item 64: Advancement of Women, 60th session of the General Assembly, Third Committee, 11 October, NY: United Nations.

HUMAN RIGHTS FACT SHEET 22. 1994. *Discrimination against women: the convention and the committee.* Centre for Human Rights, United Nations Office, Geneva, November.

INTERNATIONAL CRIMINAL COURT. *Historical introduction. elections.* (www.icc-cpi.int/about/ataglance/history.html)

KING, A. (Feb. 2001). *Call to implement the principle of equal representation of women and men judges on the International Criminal Tribunal for the Former Yugoslavia.*

Letter to the Secretary-General Kofi Annan, United Nations Security Council. SC/7010, 8 Feb. 2001.

Mayanja, Rachel. 2005. *Introductory statement*, Item 64, Advancement of Women, Sixtieth Session of the General Assembly, Third Committee, 11 October. NY: United Nations.

MULTILATERAL TREATY FRAMEWORK: AN INVITATION TO UNIVERSAL PARTICIPATION. 2004. *Focus 2004: treaties on the protection of civilians*. United Nations. 21–24 September. NY: United Nations.

NEW YORK TIMES (Feb. 24, 2001). *A landmark ruling on rape*, A12.

REHN, E. & E. J. SIRLEAF (October 31, 2002). *Women, war and peace*. NY: UNIFEM.

Report of the World Conference to Review and Appraise the Achievements of the United Nations Decade for Women: Equality, Development and Peace. Nairobi, 15-26 July 1985. (A/CONF.116/28/Rev.1) NY: United Nations. 1986.

ROME STATUTE OF THE INTERNATIONAL CRIMINAL COURT: RATIFICATION STATUS. (www.un.org/law/icc with link to: http://untreaty.un.org/)

UNITED NATIONS 2001. *Beijing declaration and platform for action, with the Beijing+5 political declaration and outcome document,*. NY: UN/DPI.

UNITED NATIONS COMMISSION ON THE STATUS OF WOMEN. (www.un.org/womenwatch/daw/csw.htm)

UNITED NATIONS, DEPARTMENT OF PUBLIC INFORMATION. January 1995. *Focus on women: violence against women*. NY: UN/DPI.

UNITED NATIONS, DEPARTMENT OF PUBLIC INFORMATION. February 1996a. *Human rights: women and violence*. UN Backgrounder. NY: United Nations.

UNITED NATIONS, DEPARTMENT OF PUBLIC INFORMATION February 1996b. *Platform for action and the Beijing declaration*. Fourth world conference on women, Beijing, China. NY: UN/DPI.

UNITED NATIONS, DEPARTMENT OF PUBLIC INFORMATION. 2000. *Basic Facts about the United Nations*. NY: United Nations.

UNITED NATIONS, DEPARTMENT OF PUBLIC INFORMATION. 2005. *Third Committee approves six draft resolutions on disabled persons, ageing, violence against women, crime prevention, drug control*. Press Release, GA/SHC/3827 (21 October); (www.un.org/News/Press/docs/2005/gashc3827.doc.htm)

UNITED NATIONS, DEPARTMENT OF PUBLIC INFORMATION 2005. *Secretary-General, in message on International Day, says violence against women atrocious manifestation of continued systematic discrimination, inequality*. Press release SG/SM/10225 OBV/527 WOM/1524 (22 November); (www.un.org/News/Press/docs/2005/sgsm10225.doc.htm)

UNITED NATIONS, DEPARTMENT OF PUBLIC INFORMATION, 2005. *General Assembly addresses human rights situations in five countries as it adopts60 draft texts recommended by its Third Committee*. Press Release. GA/10437 (16 December); (www.un.org/News/Press/docs/2005/ga10437.doc.htm)

UNITED NATIONS DEVELOPMENT FUND FOR WOMEN. UNIFEM *About Us* (www.unifem.org/about)

UNITED NATIONS DEVELOPMENT FUND FOR WOMEN, 1999. *UN designates day for eliminating violence against women*. Press Advisory. 5 November; (www.unifem.org/news_events/story_detail.php?StoryID=25)

UNITED NATIONS DEVELOPMENT FUND FOR WOMEN. UNIFEM *at a Glance: Ending Violence Against Women* (www.unifem.org/about/fact_sheets.php?StoryID=278)

UNITED NATIONS DEVELOPMENT FUND FOR WOMEN. 2005. UNIFEM *Not a minute more*. (www.unifem.org/campaigns/november25)

United Nations, Division for the Advancement of Women (DAW). June 13, 1996. *Report. Expert group meeting on violence against women migrant workers*, Manila, Philippines, May 1996. NY: VAWMW/1996/1.

United Nations, Division for the Advancement of Women. 2005. *Secretary-General's study on violence against women*. (www.un.org/womenwatch/daw/vaw/index.htm)

United Nations General Assembly. 1993. *Declaration on the Elimination of Violence against Women*. General Assembly resolution 48/104 of 20 December. (www.unhchr.ch/Huridocda/Huridoca.nsf)

United Nations High Commissioner for Refugees. 1995. *Sexual violence against refugees: Guidelines on prevention and response*. Geneva: UNHCR.

United Nations Secretary General. 10 August 2005. *Violence against women: report of the Secretary-General* (A/60/211) NY: UN.

United Nations Secretary-General. 13 September 2005. *Violence against women migrant workers: Report of the Secretary-General* (A/60/137/Corr.1) NY: UN.

United Nations Security Council (SC). 31 Oct. 2000. *Security Council unanimously adopting resolution 1325 (2000), calls for broad participation of women in peace-building, post-conflict reconstruction*. Press Release: SC/6942.

United Nations Security Council. 8 February 2001. Security Council sends Nominations for Former Yugoslavia Tribunal Judges to General Assembly. 4274th Meeting, SC/7010, 8 February 2001.

Women's Commission for Refugee Women and Children May 2002. *UNHCR Policy on refugee women and guidelines on their protection: an assessment of ten years of implementation*. NY: WCRWC.

Summary and Conclusion

FLORENCE L. DENMARK,[a] HERBERT H. KRAUSS,[a] ESTHER HALPERN,[b] AND JERI A. SECHZER[a]

[a]Pace University, New York, New York 10038, USA

[b]Tel Aviv University, Tel Aviv, Israel

This *Annals* had articles written by various experts on different facets of violence—sexual violence, female genital mutilation, cyberviolence, cultural beliefs and domestic violence, international sexual harassment—just to name a few of the topics covered. It was remarkable how much information there was to share and the high degree of competence that many colleagues have to write with authority on this issue. It was a testament also to how much research and scholarship have emerged in this area.

As these articles have shown, violence is a global problem affecting women and girls everywhere. Women still remain the primary victims of violence, and are more subject than are men to physical, sexual, and psychological abuse at home, in their communities, and in the workplace (Hays & Farhar, 2000). Girls, specifically, are subject to such discriminatory practices as female genital mutilation, son preference, diminished educational opportunities and job training, kidnapping, sexual exploitation, and so on. (Hays & Farhar, 2000). The United Nations has identified gender-based violence against women as a global health and economic development issue (United Nations Population Fund, 2000). This problem cannot be viewed in simplistic terms but rather must be conceptualized within a broader, social framework. Individual acts of violence are inexcusable and should not be tolerated. However, each one is but a reflection of a larger, systemic issue, which is confronting our society. Each is a result of a complex network of interrelated factors operating at both personal and social levels. Therefore, the next challenge is to produce a general, more encompassing construction through which to analyze violence.

There has been an evolution in the way in which we, as psychologists, have looked at violence. Contemporary theories now do not blame the victim, as was the case in early research on the violence against women. Previously, violence against women was viewed as a consequence of something that was the woman's fault. It occurred because women were doing something wrong. They were often blamed for not leaving the violent environment, in the case of domestic violence, for example. Violent acts were also seen as isolated and unrelated incidents when they occurred. Rape, for instance, was seen as a sexual act and not a manifestation of aggression, coercion, and power. There was little

SUMMARY AND CONCLUSION

or no mention of violence as a socially prescribed act used to keep women in their place (Denmark & Fernandez, 1985). Violent acts were not viewed as symptomatic of larger societal and gender-based expectations, pressures, and inequality, but were rather seen as random. In other words, violence had been viewed as a problem independent of overarching gender frameworks. Then, increasingly more attention began to be given to the psychological effects of this violence on women and the social and environmental reasons, which made it very difficult for women to just simply leave their abusers and reasons why violence against women occurs so frequently. More attention has also been paid to the characteristics of our society, e.g., its admiration of aggression that makes such violence more likely. Consequently, there has been a much-deserved increase in the amount of literature about and research conducted on domestic violence and all other types of violence.

However, we are now at another crossroads. The conceptualizations that we as psychologists use to analyze and explain violence could and should include not only victims' perceptions and experiences but also the behavior and motivation of perpetrators. Since violence against women is most frequently perpetrated by men, careful analysis of both sides of this problem will prove fruitful in gaining a more thorough perspective of the nature of the violence and how it is embedded in gender-biased systems. This is a prime example of how using a gender perspective in research can help to more fully conceptualize certain phenomena. New theories and explanations, which include more non-biased information, must be developed. For instance, initial research on battered women used "masochism" as a theory to explain why battered women remained in these situations. Until these women's experiences were reexamined within other theoretical frameworks, there was little advance in our understanding of when and why battered women stay or leave abusive relationships (Denmark, Russo, Frieze & Sechzer, 1988), or what factors help or hinder this process. Here we see the importance of constantly generating new theories and explanations for certain phenomena and the benefit of constantly challenging the current theoretical perspective.

Our investigations of violence against women must not be limited exclusively to that between women and men, but also should encompass violence between gay and lesbian couples and situations where men are the victims as well. Many times, victims in these relationships have even less access to supportive services than do women experiencing violence. Most of what is written about violence and gay couples is about violence arising out of homophobia, or violence within the boundaries of a troubled relationship.

From the data presented in this *Annals*, a number of conclusions can be drawn and recommendations made. Violence and exploitation against women and girls must be addressed on multiple levels, including the home, the community, and society. We should work within all of these domains to establish clear strategies for addressing violent behaviors.

REFERENCES

DENMARK, F.L. & FERNANDEZ, L.C. (1985). Integrating information about the psychology of women into social psychology. In F.L. Denmark (Ed.), *Social/ecological psychology and the psychology of women, selected/revised papers. XXIII International Congress of Psychology*, Amsterdam: North Holland. *Vol. 7*. 355–367.

DENMARK, F., RUSSO, N.F., FRIEZE, I.H., SECHZER, J.A. (1988). Guidelines for avoiding sexism in psychological research: A report of the Ad Hoc Committee on nonsexist research. *American Psychologist, 43*, 582–585.

HAYS I.D., & FARHAR, B.C. (2000). *The role of science and technology in the advancement of women worldwide in relation to critical concerns in the Platform for Action of the Fourth World Conference on Women held in 1995 in Beijing, China.* NREL/TP-820-28944, Golden, CO: National Renewable Energy Laboratory.

UNITED NATIONAL POPULATION FUND (UNFPA). (2000). *The state of the world population 2000.* Retrieved June 25, 2006 from http://www.afrol.com.

Epilogue

VITA C. RABINOWITZ

Department of Psychology, Hunter College, New York, New York 10021, USA

In this volume, we propose an ecological approach to the abuse and exploitation of women and girls that considers distal and proximate causes of oppression, and locates the root cause of their oppression in their relative lack of power in virtually all societies. As we have seen, gender inequality affects experiences and interactions at multiple levels and creates contexts conducive to the further devaluation and abuse of women. As a result, the reality, even the potentiality, of violence and exploitation define and limit women and girls in sexual and gender-specific ways, profoundly affecting their life outcomes and sense of possibility.

Increasingly, international human rights law and the global discourse on human rights have proved useful in addressing issues relating to the subjugation of women. In recent decades, using a human rights framework, women's rights advocates have made enormous strides on issues of rape, sexual assault, and sexual abuse, both in the United States and abroad. Sexual crimes are now more powerfully defined and proscribed in state, federal, and international law. Practices like female genital mutilation are increasingly proscribed and decried. But throughout the world there remains a chasm between discourse and policy on the one hand, and practice on the other. Gender inequality is deeply grounded in social and cultural practices, and gendered social roles often have strong family and religious support. Like all powerful groups, men do not generally wish to cede their status and privilege. Time and again, we observe how progress for women can be derailed by forces as varied as war, governmental instability, economic reverses, and rises in religious fundamentalism.

Women have made considerable educational and economic strides over the past few decades that would appear to increase their power within and beyond their families and reduce their vulnerability to violence. In the developed world, women are going to college at rates that are rivaling and surpassing men. With the rise in the use of reproductive technologies that enable some women to limit the size of their families, more women worldwide are working outside the home than ever before, and they are earning more money than ever

---

Address for correspondence: Vita C. Rabinowitz, Department of Psychology, Hunter College, Room 611N, 507 (A) TH, 695 Park Avenue, New York, NY 10021. Voice: 212-772-5552.
e-mail: vita.rabinowitz@hunter.cuny.edu

before. Education and economic empowerment are among the most powerful tools we have in combating inequality. But educational and economic gains are far more prevalent in developed societies, and they vary greatly even there. Beyond this, there is little evidence that increased educational and economic power has changed the division of household labor or child care that greatly disadvantages women. Moreover, the glass ceiling that keeps women from rising to the top of many of the most prestigious professions stubbornly remains in place. Many highly educated, economically privileged women still depend on men for their status and lifestyle, with some of them "opting out" of the workforce entirely to rear families. Critically, it remains to be seen how women's increased educational and economic power will interact with gender inequality to affect violence against and exploitation of women.

Today, we grapple with the globalization of the world's economy and media, great advances in technology of all kinds, massive migrations of peoples due to war, famine, and economic privation, and the explosive growth of cities throughout the developed and underdeveloped worlds. Some of these forces have great potential for good, but they all greatly destabilize the world that we once knew. And they challenge women and families as never before. Let us consider one of these, the urbanization of the world, as an example.

Right now, more than half of the world's population lives in cities, and by the year 2030, it is estimated that more than three-quarters of all people will live in urban areas. And projections are that by the year 2030, all of the world's largest cities will be in Africa, Asia, and Latin America (Galea, Freudenberg & Vlahov, 2006). Research in public health suggests that the urban environment affects every aspect of social life from whether and where people work, the number and nature of their sexual experiences, their family arrangements, their social networks, and their financial supports, to the dangers they encounter on the street. Increasingly, there is evidence that urban living also affects every aspect of mental and physical health. Cities, for all their social, educational, and economic advantages, are more violent and stressful than other settings. National surveys of both adolescents and adults have found higher rates of sexual assault, physical assault, physically abusive punishment, and witnessing of violent events in urban than rural settings, and more violence generally in urban areas than suburban ones (Freudenberg, Galea & Vlahov, 2006). Moreover, there is evidence that city living is experienced as more stressful and traumatic for women and girls than for men and boys (Ruggiero, Van Wynseberghe, Stevens & Kilpatrick, 2006). We have little evidence about what aspects of city living—population density, diversity, complexity, economic and social inequality, social disorganization and social strain, epidemics of disease and substance abuse, poverty and its concomitants—are responsible for poorer mental and physical health outcomes. Importantly, we do not now know how cities in the developing world pose different challenges for women, men, and families than cities in the developed world. Research is also needed on how living in cities might benefit women. We know, for example, that people in cities are often at the forefront of social change, and that crucial aspects of the women's movement, including the sexual liberation of women in the 1970s, took hold in some of the world's great cities. In any case, there can be little doubt that rapid urbanization is a global phenomenon of immense social and psychological significance, and that the relationship of urban living to gender and violence demands further study.

Research agendas of the future must consider the unintended consequences of even the most seemingly benign or beneficial of trends. Advances in reproductive and communication technologies, for example, seem like unquestioned successes, but their effects on the lives of women have been, to date, uneven. Some advances in reproductive technologies have allowed women with access to them the opportunity to make crucial choices about their families and have contributed to dramatic decreases in family size throughout the developed world. But new imaging techniques have also greatly facilitated selective abortion for purposes of ensuring the birth of male babies. The sex ratios of boys and girls at birth are now so highly skewed in favor of boys in some countries that significant social dislocations may result. As Wendy Chavkin has cautioned, "New reproductive technologies in settings of profound gender inequality are not necessarily liberating for women..." (Chavkin, 2006, p. 285). Advances in communications technologies have vastly improved women's access to information and support and increased their employment options, but, as we have seen in this volume, they have also spawned whole industries based on the devaluation and subjugation of women.

As this volume attests, an ecological approach to the study of gender and violence requires an overarching conceptual framework that includes major global and national social, economic, and political forces; social class, community and subcultural conditions; contextual, situational, and interactional factors; and individual or psychological processes. It requires a grasp of the nature and scope of gendered violence and exploitation ranging from rape, physical assault, partner abuse, and sexual harassment to prostitution, violent pornography, female genital mutilation, and female infanticide. It requires a deep appreciation of the value of considering and synthesizing findings across disciplines, such as psychology, economics, history, sociology, political science, public health, medicine, and the law, and a willingness to join forces with scholars across disciplines to design fresh theoretical models and craft new methodologies. It requires an understanding that the journey to gender equality is multifaceted and never-ending, and will vary greatly with the differing characteristics of people, situations, and societies. It requires sensitivity to the clash between the universal imperatives of human rights and the values of local cultures. It requires attention to the opportunities and challenges afforded by trends as international and massive as globalization of the world's economy to those as local and particular as teenage status games. Clearly, an ecological approach is not at all simple, but it is our best hope of achieving our ultimate goal: to illuminate and eliminate all gender-based oppression and abuse. If this volume helps readers grasp the magnitude, complexity, and value of our objective, then we will have succeeded.

REFERENCES

CHAVKIN, W. 2006. Conclusion. *In* W. Chavkin & E. Chesler's *Where human rights begin: health, sexuality, and women in the new millennium* (pp. 270–290). New Brunswick: Rutgers University Press.

FREUDENBERG, N., S. GALEA & D. VLAHOV. 2006. Changing living conditions; changing health. *In* N. Freudenberg, S. Galea & D. Vlahov's *Cities and the health of the public* (pp. 19–45). Nashville: Vanderbilt University Press.

GALEA, S., N. FREUDENBERG & D. VLAHOV. 2006. A framework for the study of urban health. *In* N. Freudenberg, S. Galea & D. Vlahov's *Cities and the health of the public* (pp. 3–18). Nashville: Vanderbilt University Press.

RUGGIERO, K. J., A. VAN WYNSEBERGHE, T. STEVENS & D. G. KILPATRICK. 2006. Traumatic stressors in urban settings; consequences and implications. *In* N. Freudenberg, S. Galea, & D. Vlahov's *Cities and the health of the public* (pp. 225–246). Nashville: Vanderbilt University Press.

Index of Contributors

Alao, A.A., 311–319

Barker-Aguilar, A., 261–278
Baron, E.M., 339–355
Bratt, E., 56–73

Cherneski, L., 35–46
Chisholm, J.F., 74–89
Chrisler, J.C., 235–249
Contreras, C., 261–278
Curtain, S., 56–73

Denmark, F.L., 1–3, 339–355, 384–386
Desouza, E., 103–120
Dicker, K.A., 103–120

Ferguson, S., 235–249
Fernández, M., 250–260
Flores, R.L., 47–55
Freidin, E., 56–73
Frieze, I.H., 121–141

Gerber, G.L., 35–46
Gilroy, J., 56–73
Godfrey, C., 56–73
Gregor, K.V., 320–338
Guttman, M., 90–102

Halpern, E., 1–3, 384–386

Kaplan, R., 56–73
Knibb, K., 56–73
Koss, M.P., 206–234
Krauss, B.J., 56–73
Krauss, H.H., 1–3, 4–21, 22–34, 384–386

McGinniss, S., 56–73

McHugh, M.C., 121–141
Midlarsky, E., 279–300
Minian, N., 56–73
Mowder, B., 90–102
Muhlbauer, V., 301–310

Nadien, M.B., 158–169
Nwakeze, P., 56–73
Nydegger, L., 103–120
Nydegger, R., 103–120

O'Day, J., 56–73

Paludi, M., 103–120
Pick, S., 261–278
Pirlott, A., 178–205
Plante, M., 279–300

Rabinowitz, V.C., 387–390
Rente, K., 56–73
Rice, J.K., xi–xv
Rosen, D.B., 170–177
Russo, N.F., 178–205

Sandis, E.E., 370–383
Saxena, G., 56–73
Sechzer, J.A., 1–3, 384–386
Sigal, J., 356–369

Tan, J.C.H., 320–338

Venkataramani-Kothari, A., 279–300

Walker, L.E.A., 142–157
Welch, C., 56–73

Yasik, A., 90–102

DATE DUE